James Clarence Mangan: A Biography

IN THIS SERIES

James Clarence Mangan: A Biography by Ellen Shannon-Mangan

The Collected Poems of James Clarence Mangan

The Collected Prose of James Clarence

James Clarence Mangan: A Bibliography by Jacques Chuto

JAMES CLARENCE MANGAN

A Biography

ELLEN SHANNON-MANGAN

IRISH ACADEMIC PRESS

This book was set in
11 on 12.5 point Ehrhardt for
IRISH ACADEMIC PRESS
Kill Lane, Blackrock, Co. Dublin, Ireland
and in North America for
IRISH ACADEMIC PRESS
c/o ISBS, 5804 NE Hassalo Street, Portland, OR 97213.

A catalogue record for this title
is available from the British Library.

ISBN 0-7165-2558-5
Set ISBN 0-7165-2556-9

This book was printed on acid-free paper.

The silhouette of Mangan on the title page
and blocked on the case of the book
dates from 1822.

ACKNOWLEDGMENT

The publishers wish to acknowledge the financial assistance
of the Arts Council/An Chomhairle Ealaíon, Dublin.

Printed in Ireland
by Colour Books Ltd, Dublin.

To the memory of

THOMAS AUGUSTINE MARTIN

1935–1995

the General Editor of this series

Contents

List of Illustrations

CREDITS

Luke Golobitsh 2, 3, 7, 8, 9, 10, 14, 15, 18, 21, 23, 24, 27, 28, 29; R.O.V. Lloyd 6; National Gallery of Ireland 11, 12, 16, 17, 20, 25, 30, 31, 32, 33; National Library of Ireland 1, 5, 13, 19, 26; Royal Irish Academy *frontispiece*, 4.

Preface

Almost a century has passed since D. J. O'Donoghue published *The Life and Writings of James Clarence Mangan*, and during that time it has served as the standard biography of the poet. All subsequent memoirs (there have not been many) have been based upon it. Invaluable as it has thus proved, the limitations O'Donoghue had to contend with, and the time that has passed since he wrote, certainly make a reappraisal of Mangan appropriate. Although O'Donoghue's insights were keen and his use of anecdotal records discriminating, he placed restrictions upon himself which were typical of Victorian biographers. Moreover, his access to primary materials was somewhat paradoxically limited by both the proximity and the remoteness of the poet's time. It has only been in the years since O'Donoghue was putting the *Life* together that files of several rare newspapers and magazines to which the poet contributed, assorted letters written by, to, or about him, and a number of pertinent manuscripts have made their way out of private hands and into libraries where they are now available.

Even if no fuller information or startling new evidence as to the mystery of Mangan had been forthcoming, the passage of one hundred years, especially years of such enormous changes in taste and massive social upheavals, is sufficient to render a new biography timely. Indeed, Mangan may even be seen as such a curiously psychological writer as to have need of an age like our own for a reinvestigation of his life.

The present biography has been a long time in the making. Although I am indebted to the helpfulness and generosity of more individuals and institutions than I can possibly enumerate, I cannot let this volume see the light without a few very special mentions. I think first of my husband Richard who did not live to see the work completed and of my children, Amy, Kathleen, and Michael, who gave their love, loyalty—and patience—along with much lively interest in my research and writing. Although the process was well along when they became my daughter-in-law and son-in-law, this list also now happily includes Elaine and Johnny.

I have been privileged during these years to have had the friendship and assistance of a number of wonderful people: Cyrus Day, Criona Gray, David and R.O.V. Lloyd, Sr Petra Mangan, León O'Broin, Oliver Snoddy, Fr Sean Swayne, Thomas Wall—I had better stop lest anyone suppose I mean to give a complete list. I don't—I couldn't. Very great thanks go to the many people who are not named here but who added a little or a lot to the effort. I am especially fortunate in having numerous friends in my hometown of Astoria, Oregon, as well as my cousin Charlotte, who contributed in very special, personal ways to this work, and who stayed interested in the process as the years passed, cheered my victories, sympathised with my disappointments, and made it possible for me to be away from home for long periods of time without suffering too much anxiety. To them go much gratitude and enduring affection.

Over the years, fellow editors on the Mangan publication project have become my close friends, and each has made a unique and valuable contribution to my work. Professor Augustine Martin's direction as supervisor and general editor has been unfailingly enthusiastic and effective. The good fellowship and special assistance given by Peter MacMahon and Peter Van de Kamp have been of immense worth to me. But it is with Rudi Holzapfel and Jacques Chuto, whose pioneering work on James Clarence Mangan began many years before my own, that I have most enjoyed the special pleasure of a shared admiration for the poet who has for so long been the focus of our best attention.

It would be impossible adequately to express the gratitude I owe the courteous and sometimes brilliant assistance provided me by the staff of each library in which valuable Mangan deposits are located: The National Library of Ireland, the Royal Irish Academy Library, University College Dublin Archives, Dublin Public Library (the Gilbert Collection), and the British Library; or of American libraries through which I was able to secure materials over very long distances: Clatsop Community College Library, Multnomah (Portland, Oregon) County Public Library, University of Oregon Library, and Pacific University Library.

I do not think there is anything in the following text which requires advance explication, though it may be useful to the reader to know that when Mangan's *Autobiography* is quoted, the number in the parenthesis which follows refers to the page in that book on which the quotation is to be found. This is a straight-forward biography with a traditional chronological structure, the form which seems most appropriate for a book in the rather remarkable position of being the first biography in one hundred years of such an important figure. I have thus avoided confronting the revisionist questions currently being asked about the art and purpose of biography, leaving that interesting subject to be explored by Mangan scholars who must surely follow in the twenty-first century.

Chronology

1798	Catherine Smith and James Mangan marry in Dublin
1799	First son baptised William
1803	Second son baptised James [the poet]
1804	Third son baptised John; a daughter born sometime during this period
1806	"James Mangan" senior appears in Directory at No. 3 Fishamble Street
1808	Fourth son baptised William indicates death of first child; poet's first childhood memory: "the walk in the rain"
1808–16	Partial blindness results from walk in the rain
1810	Enters Saul's Court Jesuit school; after this year, Mangan senior's name out of Directory
1813	SS Michael and John, new church, opens; Mangan serves there as altar boy
1813–17	Family calls young James "mad" due to his eccentricities
1814	Transfers to Michael Courtney's Derby Square Academy
1816	Transfers to Arran Quay school kept by the Rev. Doyle
1817	Mangans move to Chancery Lane "hovel"; young James transfers to school in Chancery Lane; first "puzzle poems" accepted by Jones's *Diaries*
1818	First verses in *Grant's* and *New Ladies'* almanacs Taken from school and apprenticed to Kenrick scriveners, No. 6 York Street; begins to support family; blindness disappears
1818–21	Lives with family in Chancery Lane
1818–26	Contributes thirty-nine poems to almanacs; some or all of another dozen signed "James Tynan" may be Mangan's
1820	Illness and hospitalization lead to severe emotional disturbance, onset of hypochondriasis
1821	Has allowed quota of verses in almanacs for the first time—three in each; moves away from the family, addresses poems from work address
1822	Silhouette made, the sole portrait of Mangan during his lifetime
1823	First uses a pseudonym: "Peter Puff *Secundus*" in honour of friend James Tighe who uses "Peter Puff"
1825	First nationalist poem published in *New Ladies'*; later appears as "To My Native Land"
1825-26	Apprenticeship ends; ill health persists

	Resumes work, accepts position in office of Matthew Frank, No. 28 Merrion Square North; remains there until 1829
1826–31	Poet's "dark period"; publishes only eight poems besides those in 1826 almanacs
1828–30	A few *Morning Register* poems may be by Mangan O'Connell wins County Clare election; his paper, the *Pilot*, begins publication
1829	First use of a three-initial signature: "I.X.M." in the *Friend* Seriously ill, is "removed for a season" from work; brother John takes his place Meets family of William Hayes, forms close friendship with his young sister, Catherine Falls disastrously in love with so-far unidentified young woman he first calls "Frances"; possibly lasts until 1831
1829–30	December–February: five new poems printed in the *Friend* including his first translation from German, "Two Sorts of Human Glory" Takes job in office of Thomas Leland, No. 6 Fitzwilliam Square; remains there till (perhaps) 1838
1830	Political Tract Society, soon to be Comet Club, founded in Dublin
1831	1 January: Mangan's name appears among law clerks calling for a meeting to consider petitioning Parliament for Repeal of the Union 20 January: *Morning Register* announces Comet Club's publication of *Parson's Horn-Book*, a satire on established church and Government February: *Valentine Post Bag*, second satire by Club, appears 1 May: *The Comet*, the Club's newspaper, begins publication June: Mangan meets the man (unidentified) who introduces him to his "career", presumably that in journalism through the Comet Club Summer: *Horn-Book* Part II contains "Young Parson's Dream" by Mangan Late in year: Comet Club splits; Mangan goes with John Sheehan faction 4 December: first known appearance in print of initials "J.C.M." showing Mangan has chosen middle name
1831-32	Exceptionally bitter winter
1832	Spring: cholera epidemic begins; lasts until autumn James Price and Joseph LeStrange ("J.P." and "Brasspen") join *Comet*

	Editors Sheehan and Browne are charged with libel 3 June: Mangan's work begins to appear in *Comet* September: *Dublin Penny Journal* begins publication and Mangan becomes a contributor disguised as "An Italian Gentleman" Writes long (5000 words) letter to "My dear Tynan" but it is never posted and may even be a "literary exercise" October: Catherine Hayes dies; Mangan devastated by loss December: gives John O'Donovan copy of "The Dying Enthusiast to His Friend" First uses "Clarence" as signature
1833	Spring: Sheehan and Browne begin doing prison time April: signs "Clarence" for the first time in *Dublin Penny Journal*; first expresses interest in learning Gaelic and meets Gaelic scholar Owen Connellan Summer: *DPJ* taken over by Philip Dixon Hardy; Mangan ceases to contribute *Dublin Satirist* begins publication and Mangan soon becomes contributor 4 August: Mangan's last poem in *Comet*
1833–34	Contributes forty-one pieces of prose and poetry to *Satirist*; may have been paid
1834	May: *Dublin University Magazine* accepts three Mangan poems for publication June: first poem, "The Pilgrim", in *DUM* Spring: meets Stackpoole family; later proposes to Margaret, one of fifteen-year old twins, who turns him down Summer: publishes first long poem, "The Lay of the Bell", in *Irish Monthly Magazine of Politics and Literature*
1835	January: Begins series "Anthologia Germanica" in *DUM*; will run for twenty-two chapters Perhaps in love with young woman living in Cook Street 11 February: Phrenological study done of Mangan's head 5 May: John Mangan, the poet's brother, dies
1836	Meets Charles Gavan Duffy in office of *Morning Register* where young Duffy is employed August: first uses pseudonym "Johann Theodore Drechsler" in *DUM*
1837	Early in year introduces Duffy to Stackpooles and relates story of Margaret's rejection of his marriage proposal Autumn: becomes restless, dissatisfied with German poetry; writes "My Adieu to the Muse"

September: first chapter of new series "Literae Orientales" in *DUM*
Late in year O'Donovan hires Mangan to make the printer's copy of his now completed English translation of *Annals of the Kingdom of Ireland by the Four Masters*

1838 January: exceptionally cold and snowy all over Ireland
Only extant series of Mangan's letters shows him at work on *Annals*
March: leaves scrivenery job, presumably the one in Fitzwilliam Square; probably begins work at Ordnance Survey Office under George Petrie, although this does not become final until late summer
May: Duffy founds short-lived Press Association and proposes Mangan for membership
28 June: Coronation of Queen Victoria
July–September: unusually productive period in which Mangan publishes three anthologies for total of 86 poems
O'Donovan first uses "poor Mangan" epithet indicating poet's health is not good, a condition which continues into 1839
October: writes to James Tighe: "Literature in any shape is [for me] the most unfit of all occupations." Mangan in Ordnance Survey employ, but gives Petrie cause for anxiety
October–December: desiring to change career direction, produces two short stories for *DUM*
Fr Theobald Mathew and Cork Quakers begin temperance campaign; will eventually enroll 5,000,000 Irish

1839 January–February: severe winter storms, one a hurricane, cause 1839 to become known as "year of the big wind"
Mangan's illness drags on; "anti-poetical attitude" persists; publishes nothing between July and December
March: publication of Mangan's prose article "A Sixty-Drop Dose of Laudanum" in *DUM*
Begins to write with conviction about the reality of the world of the supernatural; reads Swedenborg
April: Duffy moves to Belfast to become editor of *Vindicator*
November: Duffy returns to Dublin to keep Michaelmas Term at Kings Inns, is told Mangan has become an opium eater; Mangan denies it, Duffy believes him
December: after having averaged almost 100 pages per year in *DUM* from 1835–39, Mangan's total now declines to average only thirty-one pages annually through 1844;

announces via *DUM* article that he has recovered from his attack of "intellectual hypochondriacism"

1840 January: John O'Donovan marries
March: Lieutenant Larcom of Ordnance Survey marries
Fr Mathew expands temperance crusade to Dublin; Mangan declines to take abstinence pledge
April: Daniel O'Connell returns to Ireland from Parliamentary efforts in London
Spring: Mangan first contributes prose to *Vindicator*; four chapters appear in May, July, and August
June: signs pseudonym "Selber", Himself, to "Twenty Golden Years Ago" in *DUM*
July: *Irish Penny Journal* begins publication
29 August: Mangan's first translation from Irish, "The Woman of Three Cows", appears in *IPJ*

1841 Continues work at Ordnance Survey; Petrie's office threatened with withdrawal of funds
December: O.S. must close at end of year; Petrie secures work for Mangan as cataloguing clerk in Trinity College Library, courtesy of Dr Todd

1842 January: "Chapters on Ghostcraft" appears in *DUM*
17 January: takes oath to have name placed on Readers Register in Trinity College Library
14 February: begins work as cataloguing Library Clerk; will have full-time employment in 1842, 1843, and most of 1844, then only half-time through 1846
Reclusiveness increases with solitariness of work
15 October: first number of *Nation* appears; Duffy, John Dillon, and Thomas Davis editors; Mangan's name on Prospectus, and his poem "Our First Number" in this issue, but very little more for over three years

1843 Mangan publishes only one chapter of "Anthologia Germanica" in *DUM* (January); three poems are reprinted in *Nation*
26 September: James Mangan senior dies
October: Daniel O'Connell cancels at last minute what had been planned as greatest Monster Meeting so far; Duffy, with O'Connell and others, imprisoned for sedition

1844 Mangan has few friends now available to him
Works with Owen Connellan on "Englishing" his *Annals of the Kingdom of Ireland*
Meets Edward Walsh, who has moved to Dublin

	Late in year or early in 1845 meets John O'Daly who will be his friend and publisher of *Poets and Poetry of Munster* November: "A Lane for Freedom" carries Mangan's signature "J.C.M." in *Nation* for first time 14 December: letter to Duffy reveals Mangan is caring for his ill mother; plan for his contributions to *Nation* is discussed
1845	Unemployed last quarter of 1844 and first quarter of 1845; thereafter returns to half-time work in Trinity College Library Duffy and Davis begin scouting possibilities for issuing a collection of Mangan's "Anthologia Germanica" poems Midsummer: *German Anthology* published in two volumes June–July: unusually warm weather throughout Ireland Summer: Mangan meets the Rev. Charles P. Meehan, curate of SS Michael and John; he will become a close friend and benefactor Arranges to publish in new *Irish Monthly Magazine*; first contribution will appear in October Produces a "normal" amount of work for first time in five years September: lethal potato blight appears in Irish fields, will destroy almost all this year's crop; the start of the Famine 16 September: Thomas Davis dies; much of the hopefulness of Young Ireland is lost October: Duffy recruits John Mitchel who moves to Dublin to assist him on *Nation*; soon he and Mangan meet
1845–46	Duffy reorganizes the leadership and operation of Young Ireland and the *Nation*
1846	January: last chapter of Mangan's "Literae Orientales" appears in *DUM* February: "The Warning Voice" appears, Mangan's first nationalist poem for *Nation* March–April: Mangan's short, hot series of "hate poems" appears in *Nation*, now temporarily headed by Mitchel Mangan declares he is ready "to devote [himself] almost exclusively to the interests of [his] country" 16 May: begins series of powerful translations from Irish with "The Dream of John MacDonell" in *Nation* 30 May: "Dark Rosaleen" published in *Nation* Over next six months, Mangan reaches crest of poetic achievement

June: closes *DUM* "Anthologia Germanica" series with twenty-second chapter
July: Young Ireland faction separates from body of Repeal Association
6 August: Catherine Smith Mangan, the poet's mother, dies
Autumn: Wm. Smith O'Brien and Duffy put together idea for new organization, the Irish Confederation
December: mistakenly, O'Donovan tells James Hardiman: "The Poor poet, Mangan, is just dead!"

1847 13 January: Irish Confederation holds first meeting
Duffy rejects Mangan's application for membership in Irish Confederation
February: *James Duffy's Irish Catholic Magazine* begins publication; Mangan will have thirteen poems in its pages over 1½ years
Mangan abandons use of pseudonyms, increasingly signs work "James Clarence Mangan"
First installment of "Anthologia Hibernica" appears in *DUM*
April: famine intensifies, soup kitchens active in Dublin
15 May: Daniel O'Connell dies in Genoa, Italy
June: Mangan sends Duffy a document declaring his intention to dedicate himself "soberly and absolutely" to Irish cause; Duffy refuses to make the declaration public
July: Mangan loses family home, becomes a "wanderer"; visits mother's family farm near Kiltale and withdraws from alcohol
August: O'Connell's funeral
October: Mangan in much better health, renews vow of abstinence
Mitchel proffers resignation to Council of Irish Confederation; refused
December: Mangan begins drinking again

1848 January: Mitchel and Duffy split openly; Mitchel plans alternative newspaper
Mangan in deteriorating health, senses his life is past; asks for help from philanthropist James Haughton
Mitchel urges guerilla warfare against British in Ireland; faced with disapproval, withdraws from Council of Irish Confederation
February: first number of Mitchel's *United Irishman* appears
Mangan casts in lot with Mitchel, leaves Duffy and *Nation*

February Revolution in France brings Mitchel and Duffy back together in common cause of Irish revolt
March: Mangan's name appears for first time on masthead of *Duffy's Irish Catholic Magazine*
March–April: Old and Young Ireland try—unsuccessfully—to reconcile
25 March: Mitchel publishes Mangan's letter paralleling in content the Declaration Duffy had rejected
April: Mangan beseeches John Anster for help in finding work for brother William who apparently lives with him
May, early: Mangan enters St Vincent's Hospital
Mitchel and Devin Reilly withdraw from Irish Confederation
13 May: Mitchel arrested, tried, convicted, and sent into exile, all within two weeks
United Irishman suppressed, briefly replaced by *Tribune*, to which Mangan contributes one poem, and *Felon*
May–June: Mangan leaves St Vincent's Hospital, but a fall puts him into Richmond Surgical Hospital
June: Mangan returns to Fishamble Street locale
9 July: Duffy and others arrested for plotting insurrection
Tribune and *Felon* suppressed
29 July: insurrection has single military expression at Ballingarry, County Tipperary, followed by arrest of Mangan's friends with the exception of Joseph Brenan
Autumn: Mangan writes his short autobiography at Fr Meehan's request and his autobiographical poem "The Nameless One"
Joseph Brenan arrested

1849 January: *Irishman* newspaper begins publication; Brenan will be editor when he is released in March
13 January: Mangan's first contribution, "Look Forward!" appears in *Irishman*; before his death, he will have twenty-four items, both prose and poetry, in this newspaper
March: Brenan released from prison and takes over at *Irishman*
March–April: Mangan works with John O'Daly on *Poets and Poetry of Munster* and *The Tribes of Ireland*
April: Duffy released from prison, makes no contact with Mangan
May: Mangan's last contribution, "Gasparó Bandollo", in *DUM;* "impersonal autobiography" written

Mangan contracts cholera, recovers, leaves cholera shed
13 June: Mangan found close to death, is admitted to the Meath Hospital
20 June: Mangan dies
23 June: Burial in family plot in Glasnevin Cemetery; funeral attended by no more than five mourners

One Whose Veins Ran Lightning

[1]

Who would the poet understand
Must enter first the poet's land.
Goethe

When darkness falls over Dublin and amber street lights draw deep shadows from the old red brick buildings along the River Liffey, it does not take too vivid an imagination to conjure up a picture of the Liberties when the poet James Clarence Mangan was the area's most remarkable denizen, some 150 years ago. South of the river, at No. 3 Fishamble Street, he was born on 1 May 1803, and a few blocks away in Bride Street he was found dying in 1849. He rarely left the city. Of almost a thousand poems upon which his reputation rests, not one was first published outside his homeland. He was completely a city child and an urban poet, an aberration among Romantic authors. He was so much a part and product of Dublin that he journeyed even to the farm near Kiltale, County Meath, where his mother's old home stood, as if he were going to a foreign land. Yet he knew only geographical limitations. In the world of his imagination and his poetry, he traveled the earth and beyond.

James Clarence Mangan's intimate Dublin, the region he knew best, was roughly trapezoidal, bounded by Abbey Street to the north, Peter Street and York Street to the south, Merrion Square and Fitzwilliam Square to the east, and Werburgh or Bride Street, a continuation of Fishamble Street, to the west. For him, its center was Fishamble Street. A tintype of the room in which he was born shows it to have been relatively small and high-ceilinged, with one window.[1] The late Victorian furnishings, a heavy bureau desk, a wash-stand, and dark wooden chairs can only suggest how it may have looked in his own day. The Mangans lived at this address from the time of their marriage late in the eighteenth century until the husband's bad management and restless ambition made a move necessary around 1812.

The poet's parents, Catherine Smith and James Mangan, were married in the old Roman Catholic chapel in Rosemary Lane on 22 April 1798, with the curate Fr William Bergan officiating.[2] Catherine, like her son, was probably fair, with blond hair, blue eyes, and a gentle, quiet nature. Accounts suggest that James may have been the opposite, with a wealth of very dark hair and dark eyes. We know that he was gregarious, and that he felt strong passions; he was a man who could be generous to a fault with his friends, but tyrannical and hot tempered with those closest to him.

History has preserved no record of how or when the two met, or whether or not their match was made for love, but chances are that serious financial considerations were at least somewhat involved on both sides. Catherine had been born in 1771 and James in 1765, so they were not in the first bloom of youthful romanticism. Some years earlier, Catherine's aunt, Mary Smith, had moved to Dublin from the country and had married a man known to record only as "Mr Farrell". Together, they had owned and run a grocery at No. 3 Fishamble Street. It was probably when they got on in years that Catherine moved to Dublin to help them in the store and to learn the ins and outs of shop management. It is even possible that Catherine's grandfather was the James Smith who operated a shop at No. 6 Fishamble Street, according to Dublin directories as early as 1802. The couple had no children. When Farrell died, his widow inherited the property, and when she died, she left it to Catherine. This was a substantial bequest, where the young woman's welfare was concerned. It is also evidence in itself that her brothers, John, Michael, and Patrick, were already doing well on their own. Today, two farmhouses diagonally across the road from each other are still the property of descendants of these Smiths, and of the Madden family, with whom they intermarried in the latter years of the nineteenth century.[3] The room where the poet slept and the hills where he walked when he visited are identified for literary admirers who seek out the place.

When James Mangan senior arrived in Dublin from Shanagolden, County Limerick, he was already a mature man. Very little is known about him, indeed nothing beyond the fact of his birthplace and that he was reputedly a hedge-school teacher. Local village lore directs enquiring visitors up the "old road" to the farmhouse which tradition says is the one Mangan left behind. The house, which has had additions made over the years, looks out over gently rolling farmland, property which passed into the hands of the Fitzsimmons family some hundred years ago. Present-day Mangans in the area disclaim any relationship to the poet's family.

Fishamble Street runs down to the Liffey and has been variously known through its thousand-year history by names which bear witness to the fact that it was the city's fish market—Vicus Piscariorum, Le Fishemel Street, Fish Street, and Fish Shambles Street. The house identified as No. 3 was a narrow, four-storey red brick structure probably put up by the famed Usher family sometime in the seventeenth century. At any rate, their motto, "Ne Vile Velis", or "Wish Nothing Base", could be read under a second-storey window until remodelling eradicated the words late in the nineteenth century. A photograph from the 1890s shows that the ground floor was still being used for a shop, the name "John Healy, Grocer" appearing over the entrance. But today, at the end of the twentieth century, only a ghost of the original building remains, the address having been lost in the revamping of the street system and the substitution of Lord Edward Street for a portion of old Fishamble Street. The building where the poet was born, after being partially demolished and semi-restored, was occupied by a series of restaurants in the 1970s and 1980s; one owner-manager kept the original Mangan front door in a below-stairs dining room, as if to preserve at least a remnant of an antique, almost forgotten past.

At one period, both house and street formed part of a respectable, bustling neighbourhood, but by the nineteenth century both had declined, and the flourish and elegance were mere memories. Like all streets with long histories, Fishamble Street had seen its share of sordid life. A woman named Darkey Kelly who ran an "infamous establishment" in the street was condemned and publicly burned in St Stephen's Green as late as 1764. Some twenty years earlier, in 1741, Jonathan Swift, himself born in nearby Hoey's Court, had warned his vicars to stop spending their spare time in the Bull's Head tavern, a musical public house, dubbed "the club of Fiddlers in Fishamble Street".

The architectural diversity of the street made it a rich playground for the imagination. The elegant little Music Hall in which the first performance of Handel's "Messiah" was given in April 1741 stood here. By Mangan's time its glamour as the site of ridottos and masquerade balls had faded, but it was still being used as a small theatre which, D.J. O'Donoghue wrote, was renowned for requiring that ladies and gentlemen wear shoes and stockings to be admitted. It was also a meeting place for Catholics protesting against continued English abuses. Among the street's treasures was a building called The Maiden Tower, which stood until at least 1844.[4] It was a brick "labyrinth of rooms, galleries and doors, so intricate that it was almost impossible for any person to discover the mode of descent from the upper storeys. . . ."

The Dublin directories are of little help on the ownership and occupancy of properties at the beginning of the nineteenth century, although a few years later they began to offer information on property evaluations and occupancy, and to provide a cross reference to an extensive list of residents with the occupations of those who dwelt or worked therein. Neither Mary Smith Farrell nor Catherine Smith was listed at No. 3 Fishamble Street, perhaps because the property did not meet the criteria for inclusion, that is, that the merchant or trader who owned it was "free of the six and ten per cent conformable to the late regulations", a formula for determining rates. In 1806, the address appeared with the name of

"James Mangan, grocer". Even so, ownership had not been officially and finally transferred to him, it appears, for his name dropped out after 1811, and the building remained in the possession of the Smith family at least until the middle of the nineteenth century. The designation "grocer" needs a word of explanation. At the time, the term "grocer's shop" might refer not only to a store retailing dry foodstuffs, but also to the sort called a dram-shop, retailing spirits. This is particularly important to know where Mangan was concerned, as his *Autobiography* will show.

From the start, a mystery of sorts resonated through the marriage of James Mangan and Catherine Smith. The event was recorded accurately enough in the register of the Rosemary Lane chapel, but in the wrong section. With a few others it is to be found listed in the one provided for "births".[5] This fact was only unearthed about 1980 by the scholar R.O.V. Lloyd. Until then, the date the Smith family "for some or no reason" gave for the marriage, 1801, had never been challenged. The little information available about the family has come largely from the Smiths, the Mangan relatives in Shanagolden never putting in an appearance after James Mangan's removal to Dublin. And as we will see, the Smiths were not always accurate in their facts. Whether from forgetfulness or carelessness or the desire to give the past the shape they wanted it to have, they misrepresented certain crucial elements in the poet's story. This was the first.

As for the poet himself, his fragmentary autobiographies are rich in tortuous efforts to explain how the situation in his family, especially his father's violence and his mother's passivity, affected his childhood. Unfortunately, however, he did not give specific facts about their lives or say anything about his grandparents or his background. His friends, who might have been expected to have met his parents and to have had some insight into the life of the Mangans, have contributed nothing. A tendency in the last century to consider only the public life of a public figure as fit material for any sort of biographical commentary militated against it; thus, wives, children, and personal relationships are often not even named or noticed. Moreover, his self-effacement was perhaps so convincing that his friends accepted, as John Mitchel wrote, that no one would ever have a shred of interest in learning about James Clarence Mangan's personal life. Yet the *terra incognita* of the Mangan household held the secrets of much of the poet's emotional distress, and a certain amount of speculation is justified.

On 22 February 1799, exactly ten months to the day after they were married, Catherine and James took their first child, a son, to be baptised in the Rosemary Lane chapel. A run-down little building, having been an old storehouse when it was adapted as a place for Catholic worship some hundred years previously during the Penal Laws, it would soon be replaced by the fine, if somewhat ponderous, granite edifice of SS Michael and John on Lower Exchange Street. The name they chose for this firstborn child, "William", was evidently important in the family. If they were following custom, it was the christian name of James Mangan's father, but this has not been verified, as that individual's name has never been discovered. Like the 1798 marriage, this birth was revealed only recently by R.O.V. Lloyd, earlier biographers having repeated the dates and particulars of births given by O'Donoghue in his *Life and Writings of James Clarence Mangan*. As we will see, O'Donoghue, and before him, his sources (John O'Daly and John McCall), had done what they could to secure accurate intelligence about Mangan, but some of their "facts" were simply untrue. The death date of this first child still remains unknown and even the poet did not know—apparently—of his existence.

On 2 May 1803, a second Mangan son was baptised and was given the name "James", almost certainly after his father. Conducting the ceremony was the famous educator, Fr Betagh; the site was the same Rosemary Lane chapel. The writing on the old records is faded and blurred, but sponsors were apparently Patrick Archbald and Mary Lynch. The poet most probably came into the world on an oddly appropriate date, 1 May being one of two days in the old Celtic calendar most fraught with supernatural significance. *Bealtaine* was, in ancient lore, the time of the conjunction of the dualities, when winter gave way to spring, and the spirits of the dead were free to intermingle with the living.

The couple's third son was born in 1804, and on 21 October he was baptised "John". In all probability, he was named after Catherine's father, John Smith. A daughter was also almost certainly born into the family at some time, but her birth was not recorded in the Parish Register, and for this reason doubt has been cast even on her existence. Mangan spoke of his sister more than once, however, and there is no good reason to contradict his testimony.

It seems to me that the family must have prospered during these years, and that James and Catherine Mangan can be envisioned as going about the grocery business and raising the children in an ordinary, traditional manner. We have seen that Mr Mangan's name first appeared with the No. 3 Fishamble Street listing in 1806, and that it would continue there through 1811; whatever happened to cause it to be dropped no doubt had taken place in 1809 or 1810. Although the almanacs are not infallible, for a name thus to disappear implies some alteration in ownership or control over the property in question.

After a lapse of four years, on 20 June 1808, another Mangan baptism was recorded, a rather surprising one, for it was of yet another son christened "William". What could explain such a duplication? The first little William should now have been nine years old, but, clearly, the only possible explanation is that he was no longer living. Moreover, that James and John had both been given names of their own would indicate their older brother was still alive at the time they were born. In short, his death must have occurred between late 1804 and mid-1808.

In spite of the importance of the firstborn son, the fact of this very first William's existence seems to have been blotted from family memory, at least from *public* family memory. Specifically, no mention was made of him by any family member when facts about the poet and his relatives were being sought from them. Over the years, all recollection of him was either lost or suppressed, and Catherine's and James's children came to be identified as four in number—"the first born" James, John, William, and, born sometime but never named or otherwise identified, a daughter.

Mangan was to write a short *Autobiography* in the autumn of 1848 at the request of his friend and benefactor, Fr Charles Meehan, a curate at SS Michael and John.[6] Its literary importance and "symbolic" truths have always been recognized, but fault has been found since the beginning with its facts. Not the least disturbing chapter is the first. Its darkly ominous tone and the gloomy and indeed really bad picture Mangan paints of his family life have been much criticized as "inaccurate" and even "impossible", especially in the last century. The usually perceptive John McCall, for instance, could not believe that Mangan's father had been as abusive as the poet claimed. In its pages, as well as elsewhere, however, Mangan made one point over and over again: from the time he was a little boy until the time he entered adolescence, he was terribly disturbed emotionally. His behaviour was so peculiar and withdrawn that his family thought he was insane.

This condition was surely pathological. In the *Autobiography* he first stated that his dreadful mental state had existed "from my sixth . . . year". A little later in the same piece of writing, he said that he had been disturbed "from my tenth to my fourteenth year". In the manuscript of the *Autobiography*, he identified his age as eleven at the onset of a period when he did nothing "but read, read, read", but he crossed it out. In his so-called "impersonal autobiography" which was written just before his death, almost certainly by someone else but with Mangan's assistance, he recalled that he had been five years old when the incident occurred which precipitated severe physical symptoms of mental or emotional disorder. In this source, and this source only, did he describe the incident:

> A hair-brained [*sic*] girl, who lodged in his father's house, sent him out one day to buy a ballad; he had no covering on his head, and there was a tremendous shower of rain; but she told him that the rain would make him *grow*. He believed her—went out—strayed through many streets, and by-places,

> now abolished—found, at length, his way homeward—and for eight years afterwards—from his fifth to his thirteenth—remained almost totally blind. In the twilight alone could he attempt to open his eyes, and then he—read.[7]

The elements in this little story of death, loss, and abandonment as well as the symbols of rain, labyrinthine streets, a lost way, and blindness suggest that it may have had some connection not only with the death of the first William but also with the birth of the second child of the same name this year—1808.

When the poet attempted to give his age and pin down the dates for his school and apprenticeship, he dropped six years from his true chronological age which may mean that the memory of the first half-dozen years of his life had been "lost" to him. It will probably never be possible to prove that the death of his older brother, perhaps in some tragic fashion, shocked the little five year old James so severely that it resulted in a disturbance of his personality that was to have a serious and life-long effect on him. What is obvious, however, is that the first William's existence was denied in the family and nothing even hints that the poet knew, consciously, about his older brother.

Before asking the obvious question—Is there any evidence of a tragic death of any Mangan child?—Mangan's own assessment of his mental state at this time needs to be heard. In the *Autobiography*, two passages have particular relevance:

> In my boyhood I was haunted by an indescribable feeling of something terrible. It was as though I stood in the vicinity of some tremendous danger, to which my apprehension could give neither form nor outline. What it was I knew not; but it seemed to include many kinds of pain and bitterness—baffled hopes—and memories full of remorse. . . . Such was my condition from my sixth to my sixteenth years. (pp. 9–10)

And a few pages further on:

> . . . I shut myself up in a close room: I isolated myself in such a manner from my own nearest relatives that with one voice they all proclaimed me "mad". Perhaps I was: this much at least is certain, that it was precisely at that period—from my tenth to my fourteenth year—that the seeds of that moral insanity were developed within me which afterwards grew up into a tree of giant altitude. (p. 15)

The diagnosis of "moral insanity" may well leave the modern reader bewildered. But the term, in the poet's day, was a psychological expression; not at all his own invention, but a diagnosis of a particular condition, it was well-established by the 1840s. Apparently originated by Philippe Pinel and amplified by Jean Étienne Esquirol in the early nineteenth century, it was explained by the American psychologist James C. Prichard in *A Treatise on Insanity and Other Disorders Affecting the Mind*. Published in 1837, it was a seminal work, important enough to have had several modern reprintings. Prichard wrote:

> This form of mental derangement has been described as consisting in a morbid perversion of the feelings, affections, and active powers, without any illusion or eroneous [*sic*] conviction impressed upon the understanding: it sometimes co-exists with an apparently unimpaired state of the intellectual faculties.
>
> There are many individuals living at large, and not entirely separated from society, who are affected in a certain degree with this modification of insanity. They are reputed persons of a singular, wayward, and eccentric character. An attentive observer will often recognize something remarkable in their manners and habits, which may lead him to entertain doubts as to their entire sanity; and circumstances are sometimes discovered, on inquiry, which add strength to his suspicion.[8]

Prichard noted, further, that such persons were often found in a family with some history of insanity or "other diseases of the brain". The onset, he observed, might be a severe shock, perhaps the loss of a fortune, or the death of someone dear. Mangan, with his pronounced interest in health and his long history of trying to diagnose his own mental problem, would have had not only access to all this information, but a distinct interest in it. It would seem fair to give him credit for being not far off in his self-diagnosis. And the line between "eccentricity" and "mental disorder" remains almost as hard to determine today as it was in his time.

According to the poet himself, the "blindness" he suffered was partial and selective. Notably, it afflicted him during precisely the same years he became a wide and eclectic reader. Whether we go so far as to believe that it was a dissociative reaction is not as important as to recognize that, for him, it had the effect of "closing his eyes" to what he could not bear to see, just as, I suspect, his reading took him away from the milieu of his family and into another space and time.

To summarize, then, Mangan's story was this: after a peculiarly significant "walk in the rain" began an extended period of impairment of his sight when he read a great deal but did little else with his eyes. During these years, he kept away from his family as much as he could; he was, at the same time, plagued by apparently groundless feelings of dread, danger, despair, and remorse. It is time, now, to ask: What evidence, if any, is there of the tragic death of a child in the Mangan family? Briefly—some evidence, but no proof: John O'Daly, Mangan's publisher and friend who worked with him preparing the *Poets and Poetry of Munster* during the last two years of the poet's life, sent to Kiltale after Mangan's death for biographical information to include in a memoir for that publication. He heard back from the "old folks", specifically Mangan's uncle John, that Catherine and James Mangan had been married "in 1801".[9] Thus that piece of misinformation was read into the record. Whether innocent mistake or intentional misrepresentation, we cannot know. In a later edition of the *Poets and Poetry of Munster*, Fr Meehan stated in his introduction that the poet had been the couple's firstborn. So another error was added to the account. Interestingly, the priest almost certainly learned what he knew from Mangan himself.

John McCall, while preparing his small but useful volume about the poet's life, wrote in the 1880s to Kiltale also requesting information about Mangan. By this time, Catherine's brothers were all dead, but her nephews still lived on the farm. One of them, Patrick Smith, wrote back telling McCall that James and Catherine had "had four children[:] James[,] William[,] the third one [who] died young, and a daughter who also died from the effects of a scald."[10] Here, we might say, was the smoking gun.

We know with a fair amount of certainty that the Mangan sister grew to adulthood and left home, Mangan having pointedly written that their father "led my only sister such a life that she was obliged to leave our house."[11] We also know that John lived until 1835 and was thirty-one years old, hardly "young" by the standards of the time, when he died—not, surely, of a scald, a death usually associated with babies and young children. William, the younger, outlived his brother the poet. But one "William" very definitely did die young—and information about him was suppressed.

If we put all this together and attempt to develop a theory about what really went on in the family, specifically, if some horrendous event may have triggered the child James's descent into a condition his relatives called "madness" and he called "the beginning of moral insanity", we might come up with something like this: The first child, a son, born in 1799 to the Mangans, died early in 1808 from the effects of a scald. Blame for this dreadful accident was laid on the children by their father. Not long after, the birth of another boy took place, and he was given the dead son's name. The shock of the terrible death and of the immediate "replacement" of his older brother so severely affected the sensitive five-year-old James that his psychic defenses against disintegration included "closing his eyes" to what was too awful to see. Guilt added its patina. Mangan's few citations of "golden childhood hours" seem like, and probably were, fantasized recollections of his years before these events. The family dealt with the death in a way that was unhealthy but is not unfamiliar: they withdrew all remembrance of the dead child; they did not speak about him. Under such conditions, the memory may fade over the years, especially the memory of the very young, though of course it is not quite that simple.

That which is suppressed will almost certainly fester until something therapeutic intervenes and brings about revelation and, in the best cases, healing. Nothing so positive happened for the poet. He was destined to struggle his entire life with "unrecovered memories".

I have avoided so far saying anything about what James's feeling may have been for his lost brother William because that subject is, if possible, even less knowable than the objective facts of the situation. Interestingly enough, McCall, or rather an "informant" of his, contributed to this aspect of the story. In the 1880s, describing to McCall the content of the impersonal autobiography which the memoirist apparently had not seen, this individual mixed with it other memories, perhaps other information, or his imagination, and produced a story that was highly romanticized but also thought-provoking. It included the account of the little boy's walk in the rain in search of a ballad, but instead of a "hair-brained girl's" sending him out into the Dublin streets, the walk was inspired by "a little girl of curling sunny locks, a couple of Summers his senior, who was his constant playmate in their innocent outdoor sports, to whom he unburthened his childish secrets, with whom he shared his gooseberries and sugar-plums . . . ."[12]

McCall's friend thought the little boy was then "eight years old or so", though it is fair to guess that the year was " '08", not the child. Important to this speculative construct is the possibility that the reporter was "remembering" a figure that included not only the girl from Mangan's story but also someone's memory of a child the young James had in fact loved and played with, whom he happily took orders from, and who sent him away (really or symbolically?) to search for a song: perhaps his older brother.

[2]

I have an inward feeling that to him I owe all my misfortunes.

Autobiography, p. 14

Despite all efforts to clarify the mysteries in the Mangan family, we are left almost where Mangan found himself: knowing where the answers were to be found, but unable to tap into the "hidden springs" and, so to speak, release them. Not illogically, he limited the scope of his *Autobiography* to this exploration: "My desire is to leave after me a work that may not merely inform but instruct—that may be adapted to all capacities and grades of intellect—", and he mentioned Godwin, Byron, St Augustine, Rousseau, and Charles Lamb as models for autobiography which he did not intend to follow. His should be, instead, a work that "while it seeks to develope [*sic*] for the thinking the more hidden springs of human frailty, shall also operate . . . as a warning to the uneducated votary of Vice. . . ." Consequently, he omitted many of the details of his life which we should very much like to know and sought mainly for the explanation of his weaknesses.

When he came down hard on his father, it was not without having closely examined that individual's effect on his family. That Mangan senior was an abusive father and husband, emotionally and probably physically, is, I believe, unarguable. Early in the second chapter of this short work, the poet wrote:

> Me, my two brothers, and my sister, he treated habitually as a huntsman would treat refractory hounds. It was his boast, uttered in pure glee of heart, that we "would run into a mouse-hole" to shun him. While my mother lived he made her miserable—he led my only sister such a life that she was obliged to leave our house—he kept up a succession of continual hostilities with my brothers—and if he spared me more than others it was perhaps because I displayed a greater contempt of life and everything connected with it than he thought was shown by the other members of his family. (pp. 13–14)

During the poet's childhood, this man towered oppressively over the whole family. Only one quality in his mother's character stood out: her passivity in the face of her husband's demanding and demeaning behaviour. Often it is apparent that the poet's good feelings for the man, such as they were, and an effort to acknowledge the better side of his father, were crowded out by anxiety and fear and then anger and resentment. One minute he might write that his father "was of an ardent and forward-bounding disposition" and "had a princely soul". The next would find him declaring that the man had "no prudence" and destroyed his family through personal extravagance, giving away "the best part of his worldly property—and in the end he even suffered his own judgment and disposition to become the spoil of strangers." Worse, he was not a family man. "He hated the restraints of social life", by which the poet meant the restrictions of normal day-to-day society, "and seemed to think that all feelings with regard to family connections, and the obligations imposed by them, were totally beneath his notice."

Mangan senior was gregarious, according to reports. One of John McCall's sources told the researcher that Mr Mangan gave "sprees and balls" and loved to entertain his friends, sometimes at home, sometimes in rented rooms in a hotel; other times he might rent a jaunting car and take his companions into the Wicklow Mountains for a picnic.[13] If he was a tyrant in his home, he seems to have been a charmer outside it. Significantly, his irresponsible behaviour did not begin until ten years or more after he married. For years, he seems to have managed the grocery shop prudently and successfully. If he had been indulging in foolish and expensive entertaining, his wife's brothers would not have hesitated to intervene, for they were never far away and were good businessmen singularly appreciative of the property bequeathed to their sister. The change in his behaviour thus came about after the birth of the second son William; it was thus more or less concurrrent with the early years of young James' "madness".

In his memoir, the poet declared:

> . . . I, James Mangan, came into the world surrounded, if I may so express myself, by an atmosphere of curses and intemperance, of cruelty, infidelity and blasphemy—and of both secret and open hatred towards the moral government of GOD—such as few infants, on opening their eyes to the first light of day, had ever known before. (p. 14)

It is exaggeration such as that in the last lines which has, unfortunately, prompted many critics to discredit the reliability of the whole *Autobiography*. A more useful approach is to ask what Mangan could have meant by these extreme expressions. One answer is that only in this way could he articulate a sense of the frightening family reality that took shape after the death of the first William and the birth of the second. When he "opened his eyes" to that, he was , indeed, six years old, but he was as if newly born. What he saw when he was thus "awakened" became his earliest memories.[14]

His account went on: "If any one can imagine such an idea as a human boa-constrictor *without his alimentive propensities* he will be able to form some notion of the character of my father. May GOD assoil his great and mistaken soul and grant him eternal peace and forgiveness!" That use of "assoil", meaning "pardon" or "absolve from sin", stands out in this passage, and it has been misread as "assail", which readers might not be shocked to hear Mangan say about his father. Even in the poet's time, "assoil" was an uncommon verb, and there was probably a serious if unintentional pun in his choice of the expression. The comparison to a boa constrictor is also a feature to which otherwise-admirers of Mangan sometimes have objected. But once again, it was a deliberate choice on his part; he was precise in asking readers to think of the snake as exercising simple squeezing power, unrelated to its own needs. This is a rather horrid thought, as it was meant to be. Moreover, it is interesting to know that as a choice of symbol it was also precise, for the boa constrictor, or any such serpent that contracts to kill, is a powerful metaphor for the choking off of life or the pull toward death.[15] The poet finished, "I have an inward feeling that to him I owe all my misfortunes." It may be a harsh evaluation, and, again, it has been challenged; but in arriving at it, he had been as blunt and accurate as possible.

Significantly, three of the four surviving Mangan children are known to have had difficulty in making life adjustments. About the sister who had to leave home, nothing further is heard. The second William seems never to have functioned effectively, although he was trained as a cabinet-maker. And of course the poet struggled to support the rest of them and to achieve success, holding himself together as best he could, but never finding the peace and normalcy for which he longed. Only John appears to have had a decent relationship with their father; after this son died, it is said, Mangan senior erected a tombstone over his grave in Glasnevin Cemetery, but the present marker is of a later date. As far as we know, none of the Mangan children ever married.

Like the majority of their neighbours, the Mangans were Roman Catholic and probably attended Mass faithfully, although the religious atmosphere in their home may have left a good bit to be desired. Mangan spoke of his father as being "deeply religious by nature", but he also averred that due to him there was in their home an atmosphere of "both secret and open hatred towards the moral government of GOD". They would have gone to church in the Rosemary Lane chapel as long as it continued to be used for services, but by the time James was eight or nine, a large new church was being erected in Lower Exchange Street. It was in this church, SS Michael and John, after it opened in 1813 that he served as an altar boy. Fr Meehan recalled that one of Mangan's poems, "The Message to the Iron Foundry", "raised up before him [Mangan] a vision of himself when a little fair-haired, blue-eyed boy, serving at the altar of the *New* Church . . . the recollection of his childhood and innocence made him shed tears. . . ."[16]

[3]

> Demolished in the making of Lord Edward Street [in the 1890s], [Saul's Court] received its name from a wealthy Catholic distiller of the last century. . . . With Saul's Court many eminent persons are connected. One of the interesting points about it is that it was the *locale* of the Gaelic Society of 1800. . . .
>
> D.J. O'Donoghue,
> *The Life and Writings of James Clarence Mangan*

The first school young James Mangan attended was a Jesuit establishment, a Latin school of some distinction founded by Fr John Austin and located in the above described Saul's Court which opened off Fishamble Street, quite near the seven-year-old boy's home. Although under the direction of Fr Betagh, the elderly priest who had baptised James Mangan, the school was now being taught for the most part by a younger pedagogue, Michael Courtney, who had come to the city from Newry. Fr Betagh had gained fame and appreciation for organizing schools in the Liberties, often night schools, for young working lads and men who had no other means to attain an education. These schools were scattered throughout this run-down section of Dublin, in Schoolhouse Lane, Hoey's Court, Smock Alley, Derby Square and Skinner's Row. They were places where "ignorant journeymen, apprentices, and labourers were instructed after their work."[17] Whether or not the Saul's Court school was a cut above these institutions is not altogether clear, but it seems to have been. A couple of years after Mangan began there, that is, in 1812, Courtney moved to the Derby Square school where later he would again be Mangan's teacher; eventually, he went on to found his own school at No. 23 Aungier Street.

Fr Betagh died in 1811 and was succeeded in his work by Fr Michael Blake who had himself been a Saul's Court student at one time. Impressed by young Mangan's abilities, he placed him under the tutelage of Fr Graham, a scholar who had just returned from the Irish College in Salamanca. Reputedly quite a linguist, Fr Graham introduced him to Latin, French, Spanish, and Italian, with all of which Mangan eventually became conversant, if not expert. German, however, the language he mastered most completely and which he most keenly enjoyed, was not part of the curriculum of the schools. As far as can be known, where it was concerned, the poet was entirely self-taught. Mangan scholar Rudolf Patrick Holzapfel has called attention to Mangan's remarkable facility with German and finds it almost impossible to believe that he could have become such an excellent translator, so aware of the subtleties, nuances, and idioms of the language, without having lived in the country for at least several months. This remains an unsolved mystery, for Mangan is thought never to have been out of Ireland, much less to Germany, but this will be touched on further at a more appropriate point in his story.

He was probably a very bright student, but he almost boasted that he could not pay attention to ordinary rote learning, and his friends confirmed that he could not stand any sort of control, scarcely even guidance, when it came to what he was to read or learn. He was undoubtedly precocious, and perhaps difficult, but his Jesuit teachers seem to have done very well by him and to have appreciated his uniqueness. He had only eight years of formal education, during which time he attended at least four schools. After four years in Saul's Court Latin School, he was moved in 1814 to Courtney's academy in Derby Square. From there, probably in 1816 or 1817, he was transferred to a school in Arran Quay, where he seems to have remained briefly before moving again, this time to an academy run by William Browne in Chancery Lane, the street in which his family by then had its residence.

The locales of the four schools which gave him the rudiments, and something more, of a classical education are for the most part so changed that they are unrecognizable, but until recently Derby Square was a different story. A short hallway led from Werburgh Street into the Square, or more accurately, the court. When I visited the spot in the 1980s, and looked through the cracks in an inner door, I could see a courtyard overgrown with weeds and cluttered with rubbish, evidently tossed there by the occupants of the three and four storey tenements that loomed over it. Today, however, all this has given way to urban renewal. Referring to Derby Square in the 1840s, John Mitchel called it "a small square of dismal brick houses", and continued: "Very few of the wealthier and more fashionable inhabitants of Dublin know the existence of this dreary quadrangle." And this is not much changed: "The houses are high and dingy: many of the windows are patched with paper; clothes-lines extend across from window to window, and on the whole the place has an air of having seen better days—better, but never very good."[18]

The square had been built over one of the oldest and most populous areas of the city, a fact brought startlingly to light one day in 1785 when a portion of the paving caved in, disclosing "a cavern forty feet deep containing a great quantity of coffins and bones."[19] It was assumed they belonged to the ancient cemetery of medieval St Martin's Church. This macabre setting for young scholars was brightened by the erection of an amphitheatre at the northwest corner of the Square just two years after the grisly discovery. There, circus performances and displays of horsemanship were carried on for many years. The entrance to the boxes to which crowds of people made their way every evening was through heavy iron gates, and the whole Square was illuminated by "large globe lamps" which were still in place when Mangan attended the Academy and were not taken down until 1820.

The Academy was almost certainly one of Fr Betagh's schools for working men and boys. Mangan's tell-tale use of the word "evening" in his account of his entrance there reveals as much. It was the sole memory of his school days that he recorded:

> It was the first evening of my entrance, in 1820 [he was six years wrong about the date, which was really 1814] when I had completed my eleventh year. Twenty boys were arranged in a class; and to me, as the latest comer, was allotted the lowest place—a place with which I was perfectly contented. (pp. 16–17)

The schoolmaster, he continued, asked for a definition of "parenthesis". Most of the boys who tried to answer failed miserably, only one even trying to respond with a "blundering explanation from the grammar". The young James was then asked, and he responded correctly, "I should suppose a parenthesis to be something included in a sentence—but which might be omitted from the sentence without injury to the meaning of the sentence." He was praised and told to move up to the head of the class. A moment later, however, he returned to his original spot explaining, "'I have not deserved the head-place: give it to this boy'—and I pointed to the lad who had all but succeeded—'he merits it better, because he at least has tried to study his task.'" There is a sort of *noblesse oblige* in this act, and a curious end to the account rightly or wrongly makes it appear to have been the cause of special attention:

> The schoolmaster smiled: he and the usher whispered together; and I was remanded to a seat apart. On the following day no fewer than three Roman Catholic clergymen, who visited the Academy, condescended to enter into conversation with me; and I very well recollect that one of them, after having heard me read "Blair on the Death of Christ" from "Scott's Lessons"—clapped me on the back with the exclamation—"You will be a rattling fellow, my boy—but see and take care of yourself."

He related this story, he said, to "somewhat illustrate the peculiar condition of my moral and intellectual being at this period." The blend of pride, honesty, and, throughout, the aloneness of the child in the little crowd of schoolboys was perhaps what he meant. Before recounting this anecdote he assured his readers that he paid little attention to the "mere technical instruction" that was given in school, but "rather tried to derive information from general study than from dry rules and special statements." Thus another point of the lengthy account may be that all the boys who had been put to the "dry rules" had failed to give the correct answer, while he, who had not the habit of paying attention to such things and hadn't even had a chance to study their text, was the only one able to answer.

Whether the sort of victory he enjoyed that first day at the Derby Square school was at all the thing to win him friends is highly debatable. In fact, there is little to suggest that he made many friends at the schools he attended. McCall identified two boys, the Devoy brothers, who attended the Arran Quay school and introduced him to the fine art of writing "puzzle poems" for the annual almanacs, but with that exception there is no mention anywhere of school chums. He never got on well in groups, but he did try to fit in because he did not like always to be alone. This was true of him as a young man, and presumably it was characteristic of him as a schoolboy, too. He was torn, inevitably, between his need for companionship and a strong tendency to seek solitude. He saw himself not as particularly shy but as alienated and cut off:

> . . . in my earlier years I was passionately fond of declaiming—not for my auditors but for myself. I loved to indulge in solitary rhapsodies—and if intruded on upon those occasions I was made very unhappy. Yet I had none of the ordinary shyness of boyhood. I merely felt or fancied that between me

> and those who approached me no species of sympathy could exist; and I shrank from communion with them as from somewhat alien from my nature. (p. 17)

This sense of alienation was "a morbid product of the pride and presumption which, almost hidden from myself, constituted even from my childhood, governing traits in my character. . . ."

[4]

> My father's circumstances at length grew desperate: within the lapse of a very limited period he had failed in eight successive establishments in different parts of Dublin, until finally nothing remained for him to do but to sit down and fold his arms in despair. Ruin and beggary stared him in the face. . . .
>
> *Autobiography*, p. 17

Whatever the poet's father did to reduce the family to near destitution, the fact was that no later than 1810 or 1811 things were going badly for him. McCall wrote that Mangan senior had "prospered so well . . . that [by 1811–12] he was enabled to retire with a competence from the grocery trade, and the house in Fishamble Street once more passed to the Smith family."[20] Possibly. But he was only forty-five at the time, and he had a wife and four young children to support. It seems just as possible, and more probable, that he showed serious signs of losing his grip on business, and perhaps even of losing the business itself, if he continued as he was; and that he was replaced by Catherine's brothers and paid a "competence" in his (forced) retirement.

For the next half-dozen years, with time on his hands and money in them, he tried various enterprises, spent funds carelessly, and surely exhausted whatever savings he and Catherine may have been able to accumulate. He was trying to make his fortune, it was said, as a speculator in properties while at the same time, it may be, he worked as a vintner. He is known to have bought old houses in the Camden Street area, particularly around the tavern called the Bleeding Horse, as well as in the Kilmainham venue. The scheme was to repair or remodel these places and let them at good rents as tenement residences for the growing population of the city, but it was very easy to lose money at such a game. It was probably also at this period that he tried several other enterprises around the city; his son said it was eight. John O'Daly's Kiltale correspondent, the elderly John Smith, was less than tactful, writing that Mangan "considered himself rather encumbered with the care of shopkeeping, so he invited my brother, Patt (at that time in London) to join him in trade, which my brother accepted." He added that, being of a "restless disposition", the poet's father "removed to another neighbourhood, left his young son, the late

J[ames]. C[larence]. M[angan]., with my brother who reared him and kept him to school untill he was 14 or 15 yrs, chiefly at the Academy of the late Revd . . . Doyle, Arran Quay. . . ."[21] Mangan himself does not mention such an arrangement.

The directories over the years listed several "Mangans" and their trades, and one or more of these may have been James Mangan senior. There appeared in the 1813 book the firm of "Mangan and Langson, winemerchants" in Greek Street. In 1817, a "James Mangan" was listed as a grocer and corn factor at No. 11 East Arran Street, but as this same name was at East Arran Quay in 1820, by which time the Mangans were in Chancery Lane, it is a rather dubious attribution. That the poet is known to have attended the Arran Quay school when he was about fourteen years old does, however, add some credence to the speculation.

In any event, nothing worked for him. The people he associated with apparently used him mercilessly, and his own weaknesses contributed to finish him off. With "his spirit broken", as his son wrote, he gave up the struggle to work and earn. McCall declared "he died of a broken heart" which was very wide of the mark. In actual fact, he lived for another twenty-five years, dying at the ripe old age of seventy-eight in 1843. But as far as is known, he never again lifted his hand to earn a penny for his family. Mangan observed that the accumulation of debts, the hectoring by creditors, and the "disasters of all kinds [that] thickened around him" overwhelmed him. At this time, the boy "sought refuge in books and solitude; and days would pass during which my father seemed neither to know nor care whether I were living or dead." Finally, he wrote, "as a last resource he looked to the wretched members of his family for that help which he should have rather been able to extend to them." (p. 17)

If they had indeed been living north of the River Liffey, it was no later than the autumn of 1817 that the Mangans moved back south to a residence in Chancery Lane. The house they occupied there earned the poet's life-long hatred, his loathing for the "tottering old fragment" permeating the third chapter of his autobiography. He felt nothing but disgust for this "hovel" with its dirty floors and its bug-infested "dens" for rooms. Nevertheless, it was this year, 1817–18, when he attended Browne's school in the Lane, that he came under a very happy influence, that of the master, "himself a leading correspondent to Jones's two popular diaries", who encouraged "his willing pupils in the mystic art" of writing puzzle-poems. When he was fourteen, James Mangan sent his first shy little verses off to *Grant's* and the *New Ladies'* almanacs, and they were accepted and printed in their 1818 issues.

2

Drear Night Hours

[1]

At this time we—that is, my father and mother, my brothers, my sister and myself—tenanted one of the dismallest domiciles perhaps to be met with in the most forlorn recesses of any city in Europe. It consisted of two wretched rooms, or rather holes, at the rear of a tottering old fragment of a house, or, if the reader please, hovel, in Chancery Lane. These dens, one of which was over the other, were mutually connected by means of a steep and almost perpendicular ladder, down which it was my fortune to receive many a tumble from time to time upon the sloppy earthen floor beneath. Door or window there was none to the lower chamber—the place of the latter in particular being supplied, not very elegantly, by a huge chasm in the bare and broken brick wall. In the upper apartment which served as our sleeping-room, the spiders and beetles had established an almost undisputed right of occupancy; while the winds and rains blew in on all sides, and whistled and howled through the winter nights like the voices of unquiet spirits.

Autobiography, p. 19

Today, Chancery Lane is a characterless alley connecting Bride Street and Golden Lane; back walls of commercial buildings hem in its ancient, bent length. In Mangan's time, though, it was another of those streets which had once been quite pleasant but which were rapidly falling into decay. O'Donoghue described the street in the 1890s as containing "houses which though half-ruined" still bore traces of their former importance. It was at least respectable when the Mangans moved there, being the site of the home of the scrivener to whom the boy was apprenticed, of the Gaelic scholar Patrick Lynch, and of the school run by William Browne. When Fr Meehan accused Mangan of exaggeration, the poet agreed that he had "dreamed" it. James Joyce in a youthful essay perceptively recast that admission as "Maybe I dreamed it."[1]

Although he was so sick when he penned it, the *Autobiography* was not the hasty effort of a dying man to put his last sad recollections of his life down on paper. The manuscript reveals the careful hand of the artist at work, here and there containing improvements which are subtle but effective. Within his physical limitations, he lavished literary care on its pages. Where there is no better contradictory evidence, Mangan has to be taken seriously, and his description of Chancery Lane is no exception. That such a house as he described could have existed in this place, at this time, is not to be doubted. Even twenty years prior to the time the Mangans took up residence in the Lane, parish records listed houses there with valuations varying from £2/10 to £26, the range indicating a vast difference in their quality.[2] Not many years after the Mangans moved away, the *Dublin Almanac* for 1836 listed the occupations of residents of the street as provision dealer, shoemaker, slater, midwife, painter, cabinet-maker, and safe-manufacturer to the Bank of Ireland. Some of these are humble to the point of impoverishment. But specific details aside, it was probably the contrast between the house he had grown up in, and this "dismal domicile" that so appalled the boy. This change, combined with his being taken out of school and put to a confining, boring job, would have provided enough trauma for a heartier psyche than the young poet's.

To all intents and purposes, James Mangan's childhood came to an end with this move. Henceforth, the paraphernalia of Dublin would became the psychic furniture of his poetry as well as of his waking life. The architecture that surrounded him, the tall, narrow tenements, the ruins of timbered Elizabethan cage-houses, the ancient towers and walls, and the glorious new Palladian structures were to be for him what flowers, rivers, forests, and hills were for most Romantic poets. As Yeats observed, Mangan did not grow up among green fields and sylvan brooks, nor did he ever really seek them out. He rarely used the imagery of nature or translated a "nature poem". When he employed images of trees, which was infrequently, their trunks and branches were afflicted by blight, or they were distorted or monstrous. In the *Autobiography*, he depicted the "tree of my existence" as "blasted", a "tree of great altitude" which had grown from early-planted "seeds of moral insanity". He sometimes used the tree to symbolize the living human self, or the soul, that is always at risk in this world—frail, ill-equipped for the encounter, and often stunted almost before its growth can begin. In his poem "Life and Its Illusions", two marvelous lines show just this in a cry of compassion for "The soul, the startled soul, upbounding from the mire/Of earthliness and all alive with fears."

Daniel Corkery called fifteen "That very period of life when one's whole being is like a thirsty mouth, hot with desire."[3] At fifteen, a boy is no longer a child, but is not yet quite a man. At fifteen, Aladdin found himself trapped in an underground cavern, the treasure "difficult of attainment" spread at his feet. At fifteen, Edgar A. Poe began to write poetry, and so, too, did James Mangan. Also at fifteen, he was confronted by his father who wanted a volunteer to go to work, and he put it to his son that he ought to speak up: "Could I not even then begin to exert myself for the behoof of my kindred? If my excellent mother thought so, she said nothing, but my father undertook the solution of the question. . . . " The tone of resentment against his father is obvious but it seems resentment mediated by irony that one hears in the poet's comment on his "excellent mother's" silence. Although it is as close as he ever came to saying that his mother backed him up in any way against his father, it is so involuted that it fails to make the point clearly, that she did not think it appropriate for her son to be taken from school and put to work. In any case, that "solution" was found, and he soon was "compelled, for the miserable pittance of a few shillings weekly, to herd with the coarsest of associates and suffer at their hands every sort of rudeness and indignity. . . . " One of the great ironies of the situation was that his parents now became dependent on the problem child, who could have, but did not, run away from what he reluctantly accepted as his duty.

In these passages, Mangan gives a stripped-down picture of his young life, and a brutally honest if highly coloured recollection of how events appeared to him. Reading his words without too much critical dilution, we begin to understand something about those "hidden springs" that were the source of his adult behaviour. The eccentric, disturbed poet, who nonetheless functioned with remarkable proficiency, tenacity, and artistic genius, can only be comprehended if his personal version of his childhood and youth is also comprehended and accepted as *his* experience. From being a proudful, lonely, "blind" child with a blistered psyche seeking the oblivion available in the fantasy-world of books, he now became the overlord of his family, its most essential member. With this alteration, the queer blindness that had sat upon him for so many years disappeared, and he began to live in the "outside" world.

He also began shortly to demonstrate the extremes of the personality traits for which he became well known: enthusiasm and melancholy. A roller-coaster of moods took him from peaks of elation to pits of despair without any identifiable reason for the swift alterations. That these shifts appeared extremely peculiar and made him sometimes seem mad is stressed by his earliest, if biased, biographer, James Price. Whereas previously the boy could withdraw from most contacts by burying himself in his books, his eccentricities visible only to his family, he was now out in the world where he rubbed up against all sorts of people in office, street, and public house. He was denied his accustomed privacy, and the resulting strain on his already fragile personality almost literally tore him apart.

Although Mangan understandably resented it, there was nothing unusual about a fifteen-year-old being put to work. Child labour was the rule, not the exception in his time and for his class, the Reform Act of

1802 having done little more than reduce to twelve the number of hours per day a youngster could legally work. It did not "meddle" at all in limiting the age at which a child could be employed, and in any case, one was no longer thought of as a child at fifteen. The Mangans appear not to have been indifferent to their son's welfare, for they at least selected an occupation that should have been congenial to his temperament, and one at which they believed he could succeed. (Young Charles Dickens, put to work in a shoe-blacking factory, was considerably less fortunate.) Though at first glance it seems odd that they did not place him in the grocery shop with one of his uncles, it had probably become apparent that the sort of work they were engaged in, wholesale and retail grocery and meat dealing, was going to be all wrong for their son.

Scrivenery, by contrast, must have seemed an appropriate choice for such a bookish lad. It was respectable employment as well, being on the fringes of the legal profession. From being a scrivener, one could become a law clerk, and, with the right backing, ambition, and luck, advance even further. There is a story, though it may be apocryphal, that at the end of his apprenticeship, Mangan intended to do just that. William Lecky, in *Green Graves in Ireland*, a book more interesting than reliable, quoted Mangan as telling a friend, "I have done with this weary business, I am going deeper into the law." The friend assumed he would find "some haven of rest [and] . . . a decent living." With his acceptance of a job in a solicitor's office, he put himself in a position to follow that pattern. But a serious illness probably brought on, or at least aggravated, by the shattering conclusion of his first major love affair, may have been what interfered, and he was thereafter locked into employment at the lowly level of scrivener.

Mangan now became a tiny cog in a vast machine of paper production. The number of barristers and solicitors was already formidable in Dublin, and the amount of copying that had to be done for legal transactions of every description was enormous. There were as yet no mechanical means of reproduction—the invention of the typewriter was underway, but no functional instrument had yet been devised. To fill an ever-increasing need, the profession of scrivenery had come into existence many years earlier and continued to grow throughout most of the nineteenth century. It required workers who were able to sit still for long hours and transcribe legal documents in beautifully flowing script which they had had to learn with infinite patience and practice. Employers thus tended to take on young men of Mangan's studious nature. Even so, the job was not right for him, and the fact is that probably nothing would have been. He was emotionally ill-equipped to follow anybody's routine but his own.

One unpleasant aspect of scrivenery was that it was immobilizing and deadening to the active creative spirit, muffling the soul of youth with long hours of tedious copying in badly lighted, poorly ventilated offices. "Scribbling deeds, pleadings, and bills in Chancery", as Mangan's friend John Mitchel put it, was hell on a restless, nervous temperament. It is interesting, therefore, that Mangan became so very good at it. His script was in itself a work of art. His record of employment, too, reflects his proficiency and dutifulness, for he held his first job after his apprenticeship for three years until illness forced him to quit, and his next—and last—job as a scrivenery clerk for another six or seven years. The obvious question is, could he have disliked the work so much and still have been so good at it? Again, he has to be read very carefully, and when his precise statements are examined it is apparent that what he hated was not the actual work, but the conditions in which he had to do it: the hours of sitting still; the bad air and dim light of the office; and the rudeness and crudeness of the men he worked with.

The stereotypical scriveners of literature tend to be passive and silent: Nikolai Gogol's Akakii Akakievich in "The Overcoat", and Herman Melville's "Bartleby the Scrivener". However, even they only seem humble and subdued. For both, their moments of rebellion and self-assertion lead to psychic salvation but physical death. Of himself, Mangan wrote: "Coerced to remain for the most part bound to one spot from early morning till near midnight—tied down to 'the dull drudgery of the desk's dead wood' unceasingly—without sympathy or companionship, my heart felt as if it were gradually growing into the inanimate material I wrote on." And he wrote in one of his autobiographical letters, "They talk of factory slavery!—I solemnly declare to you that the factory would have been a paradise to me, in comparison with my office." It is easy to say that he didn't know what he was talking about, an objection that he anticipated, for he hastened to add that he had read "with great interest" many of the papers and reports on the subject of working conditions in factories.

The romantic view that poets and artists thrive on adversity is countered by most of the facts of the case. A cursory look at the lives of the English Romantic poets, for example, will show that almost all these men either were raised by sympathetic, educated parents, or attended university—or both. Of Mangan, O'Donoghue said that he "knew himself well enough [even as a boy] to know that his was not a nature fitted to battle in a world which he feared." And in her study of the poet, the perceptive if ultra-sensitive Louise Imogen Guiney expressed the wish that his "ludicrous and . . . endearing figure" could have been "but a thought in Fielding's brain, lovingly handled in two volumes octavo, and abstracted from the hard vicissitudes of mortality." Unhappily, it may be this very sympathetic attitude that has been responsible for critics' and biographers' refusal to believe that things could have been so bad for the poet: that his father could have been as abusive as Mangan claimed; that his home life could have been made miserable by the man; that conditions could have been so extremely unpleasant in the Kenrick office; and that in his first full time job, they were even worse.

[2]

St Louis, 19 October 1887

To Mr. David James O'Donoghue—Dear Sir,

> I knew James Mangan for several years very intimately and highly esteemed him for his talents and virtue. My brother the late Archbishop of Baltimore had never any knowledge of him. After my father's death in 1817, his office was continued for some years in which both Mangan and myself were engaged. The office was in York St., never on the Coombe. Your obedient servant,
> Peter Richard Kenrick, Archbishop

"John McCall Manuscript", Dr Thomas Wall Archives, Irish Institute of Pastoral Liturgy, Carlow

We can envision Mangan when he began his apprenticeship in the fall of 1818, a reluctant, slight figure setting out early as a perhaps rainy dawn broke over the city, to trudge from his home in Chancery Lane to the Kenrick office in York Street. Although not a long walk, it must have seemed endless to the erstwhile schoolboy, and it is very doubtful if Peter Richard Kenrick, son of the owner of the business, kept him company. His path led through a maze of narrow by-ways to Aungier Street, not a very stimulating neighbourhood, and thence to York Street where tall, smoke-stained red brick edifices lowered over the narrow confines beneath.

The office to which he was apprenticed was located at No. 6 in this street, not far from St Stephen's Green. It was owned, and had been operated, by one Thomas Kenrick, who with his wife Jane had resided at No. 16 Chancery Lane until his death the previous year. Perhaps the Mangans knew them and made arrangements for James accordingly. Now, the conduct of the business was in the hands of his brother, the Rev. Richard Kenrick, who continued it for a few years for the benefit of the widow and two sons. These boys were about James's age. Francis Patrick, the elder, had already left for seminary by the time Mangan joined the staff, and he would later become Archbishop of Baltimore, Maryland. But Peter Richard was three years younger than Mangan, and he, too, was an apprentice in his father's office.[4] One probably apocryphal story even relates that this boy received his first German lessons from the young poet.[5] If he did, they no doubt stood him in good stead, for the German community in St Louis, Missouri, where he served as Archbishop in a career that spanned fifty years, was both large and an important social force. The short letter that opens this section was written by this Archbishop upon being asked by O'Donoghue for reminiscences of Mangan as a youth. Then over eighty, he was among the few individuals who had known Mangan personally that O'Donoghue was able to get in touch with, for, as he observed sadly, "Nearly all who looked upon him are now dead . . . ."

We have no way of knowing the exact conditions under which the boy worked in this first office—not how big it was, nor how many youths were being trained or employed there, nor what the physical situation of heat, lighting, and so forth may have been. What we do know is that it made a very poor impression on the young poet:

> I was a slave of the most miserable order. Coerced to remain for the most part bound to one spot from early morning till near midnight—tied down to "the dull drudgery of the desk's dead wood" [from Lamb, his footnote explains] unceasingly—without sympathy or companionship, my heart felt as if it were gradually growing into the inanimate material I wrote on. I scarcely seemed like a thing of life; and yet at intervals the spirit within me would struggle to vindicate itself; and the more poetical part of my disposition would seek to burst into imperfect existence. (pp. 19–20)

These first years as a working-man were among the worst and hardest of his life, in large part because he had no comfortable home to which he could return after his long day's labour was over. The third chapter of the *Autobiography* opened with the previously quoted description of the Chancery Lane "hovel", and continued, "It was to this dreary abode, without, I believe, a parallel for desolateness, that I was accustomed to return from my employer's office each night between eleven and twelve through three long years." For the remaining four years of his apprenticeship, he probably lived elsewhere, perhaps with his family who may have moved, or perhaps by himself. He may even have had a bed in a back room at No. 6 York Street, for in the almanacs of 1821 and 1822 he signed himself "James Mangan, No. 6 York Street", and this kind of arrangement was not unusual at the time, especially for clerks who were expected to begin work very early.

Nowhere did he ever mention how much he was paid, either as a trainee or later as a full-fledged scrivener, saying only that at Kenrick's he earned "the miserable pittance of a few shillings weekly." James Price was more forthcoming, stating in his memoir of the poet that he was earning thirty shillings a week when the two of them met in 1831 on the staff of the *Comet*.[6] As an apprentice, he naturally made less than that. He himself said that after he took a full-time job in a solicitor's office he was paid a salary that "was sufficient to elevate us in some degree above the depths of our former poverty." If in fact he was the sole support for his parents, his brothers John and William, a sister, and himself, then his apprentice's salary would have had to stretch much too far, and they would indeed have been living in poverty—"shabby-genteel", perhaps, but no less poverty. There was also, however, whatever Mangan senior received as a "competence"; in addition, unless exasperation overwhelmed their familial impulses, Catherine's brothers must have contributed at least a few pounds annually to the upkeep of the Mangan family.

Coming earliest among those who questioned the veracity of most, if not quite all, of what Mangan had to say about working conditions in this office, was a man who signed himself only "D.C." in a letter he wrote to the newly revived *Nation* in 1849.[7] That newspaper had reprinted Price's columns about Mangan, and "D.C." was challenging the authenticity of what was termed there an "undoubtedly genuine autobiographical confession." Not only did he think the information could not possibly be accurate, he did not think Mangan could be its source: "I have too much respect for the memory of Clarence Mangan, as a literary man, to wish wantonly to cast a slur upon his character; and I wish to state that it is my firm conviction that this '*undoubtedly genuine autobiographical confession*' is a *forgery* upon the man, and I know it to be a *lie* in itself." "D.C.'s" familiarity with the profession of scrivenery has to be taken on faith, but he was so precise in his figures and so intent on defending it that he probably had experienced it first hand.

Many of the facts in "D.C.'s" letter are open to question, and this, combined with his anonymity, makes it a poor source to rely on. However, he did provide the useful piece of information that scriveners worked only about eight months of the year because of the long vacations and recesses the courts took. Assuming that Kenrick's office busied itself only with legal documents and papers, which was not necessarily the case, Mangan may have had more time off than he seems to have remembered. Another piece of his information was that clerks were paid ninepence per hour. Here, though, he failed to take into account that Mangan was only an apprentice, and his pay would have been commensurate with that lowly status. He also apparently did not take into consideration that beginners were expected to work longer hours than regulars, without receiving anything beyond their usual wage. But what worried him most was based on a simple misunderstanding of what he had read. In the autobiographical letter to McGlashan which Price included, as well as in his

Autobiography, Mangan described the blasphemous louts he had to work with on his first job in an *attorney's* office; "D.C.", anxious to defend Kenrick's good name, had misunderstood him to be talking about employees in the office run by the priest: "Is it within the bounds of probability that the disgusting obscenities and horrible blasphemies alluded to would form the current conversation of such men as these?" he asked rhetorically.

Even the most perfect office would probably have seemed dreadful to the young Mangan, as he set out on the long, long work-road, and though he experienced his task and surroundings as being almost grotesquely awful, he may not have been far off the mark. John Mitchel, later his friend and an impassioned Young Ireland leader, had something of the same experiences for a time in his youth when he was hired as a clerk in a bank in Derry. Mitchel was a hard worker, anything but sedentary in his preferences, and he detested this job because it robbed him almost literally of his life:

> I had no idea that clerks were to be employed in the business of the office except during the public hours. I find, however, that they cannot call a single minute of any day their own. In winter, which is their busiest season, they are usually obliged to attend at six in the morning, and work without intermission, except while they take their meals, till twelve at night.[8]

If the poet had more free time than he remembered or mentioned, it isn't too surprising that he forgot about it, given all those days when he was at work for eighteen hours of the twenty-four.

[3]

> Ye bards of Eblana, who wonders devise
> When ye jovially meet o'er a tankard at Bligh's . . . .
>
> [Joseph Manifold Clonaslee],
> Rebus, *Grant's* 1820

Perhaps Mangan knew in advance, and perhaps he only learned after he got to the Kenrick office on that first day, that James Tighe, whose poems in the annual almanacs he had been admiring for years, was employed there. It must have eased his unhappiness somewhat. Tighe had been the subject of the boy's first accepted contribution to *Grant's*, where it appeared this same year as "Rebus No. 12". Experienced puzzle-solvers probably had little difficulty discovering that "James Tighe" was the solution. In this sort of "riddling poem", the lines describe the sometimes scrambled letters in the answer; Mangan thus identified the almanac's regular contributor:

A verb and pronoun, correctly set down,
An article follows in haste;
A digit once more, I pray you explore,
And in the rear let it be placed.
Transpose these with skill, I'm certain you will,
Display a Diarian of fame,
Whose talents so rare, extend o'er the sphere,
Hibernians, exhibit his name.

[This must refer to the verb "jams" and the pronoun "me", coming after the article "a" in "haste", to form "James"]
[a digit = eight = Tighe
[in the rear; a last name]

At twenty-three, Tighe was several years older than Mangan. He was not a Dubliner, but a native of Dove Hill near Carrickmacross in County Monaghan, and he seems to have been a genuinely decent and sensitive human being. He took the newcomer under his wing, and before many months passed, the two were friends as well as companions in their labour and in the pages of "Jones's diaries", that is, *Grant's* and the *New Ladies'* almanacs. Although they were to go their separate ways after the office closed in the mid-1820's, Tighe to become a family man and a writer for another almanac as well as for the temperance movement, they continued something of their friendship until the poet's death. Tighe may have recognized the name of James Mangan, too, when he arrived for work that morning, having seen it not only in *Grant's* (describing himself) but also in the *New Ladies'* for 1818 where the new employee was represented by a charade, a simpler type of puzzle than a rebus, the syllables of the solution being described in their correct order in the poem. "Penitent" was the answer:

My first is of essential use,
To sons of Lady Di ["pen"]
My next a vowel is, I'm sure,
Tis either you or I; [that is, "u" or "i"]
At Donnybrook my last you've seen
On your first entrance there,
A place of merriment, I ween,
Where banished is all care. ["tent", in reference to those which housed exhibits, games, stalls, etc. at the famous fairs held in Donnybrook, a Dublin suburb]
Behold the culprit doomed to die, [the over-all clue begins]
Become my whole at last;
To drink the cup of sorrow dry,
Atonement for crimes past. [Pen-i-Tent]

Mangan would have been a very proud fourteen-year-old to see his name in print for the first time: "James Mangan, Chancery Lane", when the almanacs appeared for sale early in 1818. O'Donoghue, looking back through the scrim of time, regretted that the poet's genius had had no more serious outlet than these almanacs, and he complained that Mangan "rather deliberately cultivated the gift of writing the ephemerides" which the editors wanted. Somewhat begrudgingly, he allowed, though, "not a few nurslings of genius were reared by these caterers for the intellectual gymnasts of those days." McCall, closer to the scene and himself very fond of puzzling compositions, knew that any young poet's chances of breaking into print in Dublin in the early years of the century were pale to the point of disappearance:

> In Mangan's juvenile days there were no magazines nor cheap periodicals of any kind published in this country through the medium of which young aspiring poets could give their varied inspirations to the world. In fact, Jones's two almanacks were the only publications in our metropolis which encouraged such light poetical flights of fancy.[9]

Or, for that matter, *any* flight of fancy. In John Power's list of Irish periodicals one can find only three possibilities: the *Dublin Examiner or Monthly Journal of Science, Literature and Art*, which would have been too weighty for a beginner to approach; the *Anti-Unionist Weekly Magazine* which would merely have been uninterested in such material; and the *Dublin Magazine*—again, too prestigious for the neophyte poet.[10] A handful of newspapers, largely advertisers, occasionally put in a verse or two, but this was the extent of the published media of the day to which he might have sent his first tentative efforts. Competition for acceptance by the almanacs was intense, so he would have been justified in giving himself a pat on the back for his success.

In 1803, *Grant's Almanack* had been just a pocket-sized paperback containing a mere seven pages of mathematical puzzles along with two enigmas, seven rebuses, and one solitary charade.[11] However, Nicholas Grant, originator of the notion of adding puzzles to the usual information on weather, health, and the like, had a creative editor in a man named Mark Morton, and by 1821, *Grant's*, along with the *New Ladies'*, could boast dozens of word puzzles.[12] They were immensely popular. Solvers sent in not just solutions but also contributions they hoped would be accepted for the next annual publication. Before long, competition for space grew so heated that an annual limit had to be set on the number of entries any one author could contribute—one charade, one rebus, and one enigma per year, per almanac, being the rule. Of course there were ways of getting around the restriction, one of the more obvious being the use of a pen-name, and most of the major contributors, including eventually Mangan, used this device shamelessly.

The first poems that a poet writes are always curiosities. Mangan contributed only the "legitimate" number of verses (or fewer) to the almanacs in the first five years of his association with them, and one searches eagerly for something that might be considered significant to him personally, or a foreshadowing of the brilliant performances that lay ahead. For the most part, one searches in vain. Only one poem, the enigma "Who is he? yon huntsman all clad in dark green?" in the 1820 number of *Grant's* was an exception. The subject, the Earl of Kildare, was a compound of the Wandering Jew and the immortal huntsman of European folklore adapted to Irish legend; this poem was Mangan's first mining of the particularly meaningful vein of weird immortality which he would return to time and again throughout his career. "Who is he? yon huntsman all clad in dark green? How wild his appearance! how noble his mien!" the first stanza began, and continued, " . . . woe to that mortal whoever he be,/That looks on the wanderer's face." It was also in its way, a nationalist poem, Mangan's first, if we consider it in that light. The Earl was "Well worthy the title of 'Humane and Great' because "He mourned that his country her wrongs should endure,/In silence, in sorrow, regardless of cure—."

Because the almanacs soon became collectors' items, the only reason most of these first efforts of Mangan's survive is because John McCall conscientiously copied them into notebooks for a massive history of almanacs and their contributors which he worked on for years. Other early poems survive, though, because Mangan himself kept copies of them. In one of the last pieces he wrote for the *Irishman* in 1849, he told his readers about coming across an old trunk that must have been around for many years; in it, he said were several manuscripts of youthful poems. With two exceptions, these half-dozen poems, which bear the notation "written at sixteen" or "written at seventeen", have not been published; they now form part of the Mangan manuscript collection of the National Library of Ireland.[13] More than any of the almanac poems, they reveal the heart and troubled spirit of the boy who wrote them. They also contain embryonic forms of some metrical constructions and rhetorical formulae which would distinguish the adult poet.

"Lines written at 16" Mangan labeled this comment on a kind of life that attracted him, but which he felt was never going to be his:

> What constitutes the worth or woe of lot?
> Hi! had propitious Heaven to me assigned
> A destiny in some romantic cot
> Far from the sickening follies of mankind,
> Willing were I the troubled world should blot
> My name and history from her chequered page,
> And leave me there, forgetting and forgot,
> Till youth brought manhood on, and manhood age
> And age the awful hour we quit this transient stage.

A figure characteristic of Mangan's work was the hovering spectre, sometimes used literally, or as literally as possible, and sometimes metaphorically. In "Lines written at 17", the spectre put in an early appearance, along with a construction the poet liked, the suffix "less" as in "sleepless", "griefless", and "reliefless", which, taken in the aggregate, have the effect of emphasizing the negativity of the thought more than other formulae he might have adopted—"unsleeping", let us say, or "without relief" or "unrelieved".

> Oh! slowly, oh! sleepless his night passes over,
> But with morn is the close of his wretchedness near?
> Ah! no, for the spectres that evermore hover
> Around his low couch still resound in his ear,
> That he never shall know what it is to be griefless,
> That his woe-bringing pilgrimage ne'er shall be o'er
> Till exhausted by agony—wretched, reliefless,
> He sinks to the bed he shall rise from no more.

Another of the poems is an experiment with a type that he never did much with thereafter, the long romantic narrative. The eighty-line "Fragment of a Romance written at 17" is so obviously the work of a very young writer that the age he gives for its composition can be accepted without any hesitancy. The story is set in the period of the Danish attacks on Ireland, and the scene is "Clan Collona's vaulted halls", which are filled with sadness because "Annally's fairest flower lies dying". The pervasive sense of a paralysis of motion and feeling that is the quality of life here is captured in the first few lines and introduces another recurring Manganism, people transformed into statues. Such a static, or frozen, existence found its most flawless expression in his late fine poem "Siberia". It may best be understood metaphorically, as representing a strange numbing of sensation which is a quality of depression, as psychologists now recognize, and which Mangan knew as melancholy. For him, this state alternated with an intense, excitable volatility which produced anxiety, restlessness, or pervasive dissatisfaction. A few lines follow:

> Even beauty looks dejected now:
>   Her dark-blue hath lost its brightness,
>   Her lovely cheek is pale to whiteness,
> And sorrow marks her marble brow.
> They look like moving statues all
> Who tread that spacious vaulted hall. . . .

The third and last section of the fragment introduces Mangan's first use of the rose, in the girl's name "Rosa". It would be excessive, probably, to look upon this juvenile piece as the first of his "rose poems" which are so beautiful and such exemplary specimens of that particular genre. But the fact remains that the rose would always symbolize *woman* for him, as well as beauty, purity, and eventually Ireland, as in "The Hundred-Leafèd Rose", "The Rose", "Carpe Diem", "Spring Roses", "The Time ere the Roses were Blowing", "Time of the Roses", and the matchless "Dark Rosaleen". Written in the margin, and indicated by a drawing of a small pointing hand, we read two very touching lines: "Hushed is the voice of loved and lover./The dance hath ceased, the song is over."

A second "fragment" and the only one of the "written at . . ." poems to have gained any circulation is "Genius:—A Fragment" which he claimed to have written at sixteen but whose manuscript is not among the others. It was printed first in the *Dublin and London Magazine* in March 1826; again in the 23 June 1849 edition of the *Irishman*, the day of the poet's funeral; and for the third significant time, in the *Irish Monthly* for November 1882, as part of his autobiographical fragment. It has always been taken as a serious expression of his feelings, although not everyone has accepted his claim that he wrote it when he was only sixteen years old, suspecting—justifiably—that he wrote it not long before it was published. He would then have been twenty-two and the "six year age error" would explain his faulty calculation. Like the rest of these poems, however, it may have been composed during that first or second year he was at work; like them it contains sentiments that reflect his terrible unhappiness with what destiny was then busily dealing out to him.

By "genius" he did not mean superlative intelligence, as the twentieth century generally has come to use the word, but rather unique and extraordinary mental capacity along some creative or inventive line—a quality that drove its possessor to passionate endeavour. The first few lines, in the first form in which they appeared in print, were these:

> Oh Genius! Genius! what thou hast to endure,
> First from thyself, and finally from those,
> The earth-bound and the blind, who cannot feel
> That there are souls with purposes as pure
> And lofty as the mountain-snows, and zeal
> All quenchless as the Spirit from whence it flows!

When he reworked the poem for his *Autobiography*, he cut out six lines that probably seemed too personal in his adult judgement:

> Some, of a gentler and more sensitive cast,
> Suffering in shrinking silence, worn and bowed
> By the world's weary weight, and broken-hearted;
> Some, not less alien to the myriad crowd,
> And struggling on unshaken till the last
> Throes of life's lingering fever have departed, . . .

"Genius" concluded on a note of unmitigated despair: "Fathomless and fearful yawns the Abyss/Of Darkness" under all those who have inherited the spirit of melancholia; and those who are "most—or least—illumined by the spirit/Of the Eternal Archetype of Truth ":

. . . even as they begin,
They close, the dim night of their tribulation,
Worn by the torture of the untiring breast,
Which, scorning all, and shunned of all, by turns,
Upheld in solitary strength begot
By its own unshared shroudedness of lot,
Through years and years of crushed hopes throbs and burns,
And burns and throbs, and will not be at rest,
Searching a desolate Earth for that it findeth not!

At first glance it seems strange that he mentioned nothing about his successes nor about Tighe in his *Autobiography*, where he wrote that he was "without sympathy or companionship" in the Kenrick office. But again, the charm of that friendship had nothing to do with the "hidden springs" of his misery, and may have receded into obscurity compared with the unhappiness that often filled his soul. Yet there were in fact some happy times. A friend of Tighe's who also became a friend of Mangan's, Laurence Bligh, operated a grocery and "cozy bar parlour" near Ballybough Bridge, where the young men often gathered to drink and to enjoy one another's company. Just a few years after Mangan arrived on the almanac scene, another almanac poet, "Joseph Manifold Clonaslee", wrote about Mangan and Tighe in the verse that opens this section—"ye bards of Eblana" was certainly a far-sighted prophecy of the role Mangan was destined to play in life. Bligh's territory, Ballybough Bridge, was a fairly long walk from York Street, and home, but perhaps all the more welcome for that. It overlooked a swampy piece of land called the North Lotts, infamous for outlawry and highwaymen who head-quartered thereabouts,[14] appealing to a streak of lawlessness which, as we will see, ran like a scarlet thread through Mangan's life.

[4]

My physical and moral torments—my endurances from cold, heat, hunger, and fatigue—and that isolation of mind which was perhaps worse. than all, in the end flung me into a fever, and I was transmitted to an hospital. This incident I should hardly deem

> worthy of chronicling if it had not proved the occasion of introducing into my blood the seeds of a more virulent disease than any I had yet known,—an incurable hypochondriasis.
>
> *Autobiography*, p. 21

Mangan does not say how long he had worked as an apprentice when he fell ill, though it was probably a year-and-a-half or two years. Simple enough in itself, the illness was to have far-reaching consequences which he tried to pin down in the above passage from the *Autobiography.* Quite possibly, no amount of attention that can be given to this episode will ever bring to light its full significance for him, and by that I mean its psychological significance, but it is certain—as he himself wrote—that his gravest *identifiable* emotional difficulty began at this time.

It was probably in the spring or early summer of 1820 when he was seventeen years old that the young man contracted the illness that he referred to only as a "fever". As was customary, he was moved to a fever hospital, almost certainly Hardwicke Fever Hospital in Cork Street, not far from Chancery Lane.[15] This was a large building three stories high, surrounded by three acres of land and distinguished for "possessing good air and abundance of water." It was somewhat optimistically called a "House of Recovery" and did indeed have a western wing for convalescent patients . The Society of Friends had been instrumental in the development of special hospitals for fever patients, and Hardwicke Hospital had been one of their early sponsorships, having been erected in 1804. Fever frequently swept the city during the warmer months, and the hospital would then be crowded. It could accommodate 200 beds in four buildings at the time he entered, a fourth building using a system of large, presumably open, wards having been added to the original plan in 1814. In 1818, a famine had "crowded the hospitals everywhere throughout Ireland" and another sixty beds had been squeezed into the Hardwicke.

Mangan's story, begun at the opening of this section, continued:

> There was a poor child in the convalescent ward of the institution, who was afflicted from head to foot with an actual leprosy; and there being no vacant bed to be had, I was compelled to share that of this miserable being, which, such was my ignorance of the nature of contagion, I did without the slightest suspicion of the inevitable result. But in a few days after my dismissal from the hospital this result but too plainly shewed itself on my person in the form of a malady nearly as hideous and loathsome as that of the wretched boy himself; and though all external traces of it have long since disappeared, its moral effects remain incorporated with my mental constitution to this hour, and will probably continue with me through life. (p. 21)

That he claimed to have had to share a bed with another patient has always worried biographers, who, to put it mildly, have doubted its veracity. Yet bed-sharing in hospitals was a common enough practice at the time. In Dublin, the Meath Hospital, for instance, which had been erected in 1818, was considered a model of its kind partly because its four wards "contain[ed] 40 beds, admitting only one patient each. . . ."[16] Obviously, a modern improvement.

Even though the child was covered from head to foot with "an actual leprosy", evidently a horrible looking rash of some sort, Mangan wrote that he was not particularly disturbed by being put into a bed with him—at least not at first—which in itself would indicate that this sort of sharing of accommodations was something the poor had to take for granted when they entered hospitals. It was only later, when he himself broke out with similarly disfiguring eruptions on his skin, that the young man reacted. As an adult, it seems, he understood contagion well enough to realize that he had either contracted the disease from the child, or perhaps he even understood the possibility that they were both suffering through one of the stages of the same kind of fever. However, at seventeen, he seems not to have understood anything about the pathology of what was going on, and instead interpreted the "hideous and loathsome" affliction in moral terms. Its "hideousness" became part of his "mental constitution", he believed, and marked the beginning of the "chronic hypochondriasis" that did indeed remain with him all his life.

From a present-day point of view, it seems almost unbelievable that the possible sexual content of this hospital episode has never been taken into consideration, but the simple explanation is probably that Mangan's few serious biographers have all been Victorians who felt extreme reticence about invading what they held to be private territory. Yet the profound moral conclusions Mangan drew would indicate that much more had been going on in his psyche than he was conscious of. The visible mark of "inner impurity" that he believed had been put upon him seemed a physical recognition of his "spiritual" or "hidden" guilt. But, we would have to ask, guilt about what? I am very doubtful that Mangan ever had a full sexual experience, but it is improbable that an impressionable boy of seventeen who was mixing daily with older youths and men could be placed in a bed with another boy, even a "child", and not have had some unwanted, perhaps immediately repressed, but none-the-less authentically sexual thoughts or impulses. That these came in the context of sickness and general physical debility was of great importance. In addition, and much more deeply rooted, was the severe sense of "something terrible", of "some tremendous danger" and "memories full of remorse", which had "haunted" him since childhood. The repugnance and disgust which he now felt so immediately and wrote of so feelingly are exactly what might be expected of a sensitive, religious young man already laden with obscure feelings of guilt and over-shadowing anxiety—and now afflicted with a "disgusting" disease which announced his personal corruption to the world.

A good bit has been said about the poet's "purity" of mind and behaviour by Fr Meehan and others, the gist of it being that in spite of drinking too much or mixing with the low-life of Dublin's worst public houses, Mangan always stayed undebauched and as good as a child. Even Mitchel, who wrote with brutal honesty of "one Mangan known to the Muses, the other to the police", never suggested that the poet was corrupt in any way. As for his work, it is sensual, but only ethereally physical, with an insubstantiality about such details that suggests a lack of intimate carnal knowledge—or even interest.

It is possible that what happened during hospitalization had the traumatic effect of linking physical disease with moral corruption in Mangan's mind in so impressive a fashion that the development of normal sexual interest, much less practice, was swiftly and radically inhibited. In effect, as everything he wrote revealed, he remained curiously childlike, or immature, about such subjects all his life. He felt love, and the need to be loved, and he made heroic efforts to normalize his life. He even planned—or hoped—to marry and settle down. However, he was sadly ineffectual and self-defeating in the actions he took to bring about such a conclusion. For the most part, his fondest, even his romantic, affections were centered on very young women, too young to be eligible partners, although he sometimes seems to have misinterpreted such relationships. If there was any sexual aberration on Mangan's part, it would seem to have been that he was asexual, not homosexual, for there is never any indication that his friendships with other men had a sexual content. Among his male friends, of whom he had several over the years who were very close to him, there was also a preponderance of men several years his junior. Often this was mere coincidence, the result of accidental proximity or normal hero-worship on the part of a young man such as Gavan Duffy. But in addition, Mangan's genuine appreciation for the innocence of the young, and love for all that was good and uncorrupted, marked both his life and his work and prompted him to seek out and cultivate such individuals.

[5]

> Hypochondria: Overconcern for health and bodily condition is given the name of hypochondria. The hypochondriac usually seems self-centered and aloof, since his interest centers in his physical condition. . . . Some hypochondriacs are anxious and depressed.

> They frequent clinics and physicians' offices, seeking examinations for suspected cancers and other diseases . . . .
>
> Floyd Leon Ruch, *Psychology and Life*, 1941

"Hypochondriasis" at the end of the twentieth century seems a rather old-fashioned term; over the years it has been trivialized to such an extent that the original, more complex definition has been almost lost. In Mangan's time it was a serious diagnosis, however, for it denoted a "morbid depression", or a settled melancholy, which had no obvious physical cause but several painful effects.[17] Associated with discomfort or disorders of the digestive system, especially in the region of the transverse colon, it was also generally understood to be a disorder of the nervous system, and, interestingly enough, of the skin, where it might erupt in a disfiguring rash. The notion of any identifying localization has been largely dropped today. Gone, too, is the sense that the hypochondriac of Mangan's time might have of being "*morally* diseased"; the victim of a diffuse unhealthiness accompanied by the feeling of having done something that merited the pain or "punishment" one was receiving.

Twentieth century psychiatry has linked hypochondriasis with neurasthenia, another old-fashioned concept, and has placed these two with hysteria and anxiety states in a catch-all category that is neither neurosis nor psychosis, but is still on the pathological scale, as it were. Writing on this subject in the 1950s, Gerard Chrzanowski made a number of helpful observations. He noted, for instance, that hypochondriasis rarely springs full-blown in an otherwise healthy personality, but will only occur where there has been previous psychological damage of some sort, a "premorbid" condition, as he called it.[18] In a modification of Freud, Chrzanowski pointed out that the hypochondriac needed to maintain, and in fact, *could* maintain a "tenuous relatedness to others" through "one marginally structured channel of communication" which would suffice "to prevent a disintegration of the personality". Perhaps in one sense poetry provided such a channel for Mangan, but he also relied heavily, and, it seems, sometimes oppressively, on the one true friend who almost literally became the saving centre of his often tortuous or unhappy existence. The true friend might change, but the principle and the dependence remained the same. In spite of seriously unresolved conflict in the family, his mother, too, was such a "structured channel of communication" for him, as would become apparent when she died, an event which effectively ended life for him as he had always known it.

Finally, the observations by Otto Fenichel in *Psychoanalytic Theory of Neurosis* seem especially pertinent in identifying the level, as it were, of pathology that hypochondria represents. It is, he believed, a "transitional state between reactions of a hysterical character and those of a delusional, clearly psychotic one".[19] Not many would question that Mangan sometimes exhibited neurotic symptoms or reactions typical of hysteria, in the clinical sense of those terms, but psychotic he was not. Reasons for thinking that he may have had psychotic episodes are tenuous and consist largely of the conversations he allegedly conducted with the ghost of his father, his ability to see auras around his acquaintances, his family's witness to his childhood "madness", and an eccentricity that seemed—to some—to go beyond the bounds of what could be called normal. On the other hand, so much of his behaviour was typical of the syndrome of hypochondriasis that his diagnosis seems as if it may have been remarkably accurate. From his preoccupation with health, medicine, and the disease process in general, to his "self-medication" of alcohol and doubtless opium, he was consistently fascinated with such matters. In addition, his life-long eating disorder, which often led him to renounce food as vehemently as any anorexic might, is also characteristic of the classic hypochondriac.

D. J. O'Donoghue called Mangan's account of his hospitalization "a purely imaginary affair". Others have discounted it because the poet spoke of the child's having "an actual leprosy", a usage easily explained by simple reference to metaphor, as it was only another example of Mangan's use of figurative language to communicate feeling.[20] In fact, the passage is dotted with such instances—"flung into a fever", "seeds of a more virulent disease", "malignity of this ghastly complaint", and so on. He himself used the same figure at least one other time in his writing, when he described Bishop Berkeley's cure with tar-water, a medication Mangan also favoured, of "a hideous malady—a 'gangrene in the blood'—a leprosy in fact. . . . " The thought of leprosy, which has long been a metaphorical disease, causes a shudder of loathing even today, and it was this inflection he needed to communicate the effect the experience had on him.

He was physically weakened and totally demoralized when he came out of hospital. His kindred, he mourned, "scarcely seemed to take notice of this new and terrible mark so set on me. Privation and despair had rendered them almost indifferent to everything." Although he gradually recovered, one illness followed another "until all who knew me began to regard me as one appointed to a lingering living martyrdom." The medical advice of a "kind acquaintance" helped him through the worst of this, he wrote, in a slightly more optimistic tone. But then, as if by an association of ideas, he veered off into the autobiography's most peculiar passage of all, one in which he identified his sufferings as punishment for his "rebellious and gloomy spirit": "I scarcely knew what to think of my own condition, though I have since learned to consider it as the mode and instrument which an All-wise Providence made use of to curb the out-breakings of that rebellious and gloomy spirit that smouldered like a volcano within me."

Now moving on from physical into religious or psychological analysis, the poet invoked the most severe sort of Old Testament theology:

> My dominant passion, though I guessed it not, was Pride; and this was to be overcome by pain of every description and the continual sense of self-helplessness. Humiliation was what I required; and that bitterest moral drug was dealt out to me in lavish abundance. Nay, as if Pelion were to be piled on Ossa for the purpose of contributing to my mortification, I was compelled to perform my very penances—those enjoined me by my spiritual director— in darkness and subterranean places, wheresoever I could bury myself from the face of living man. (p. 22)

The passage concluded with a comparison between these "penances" of his youth and those imposed on him later. Nevertheless, the revisions in this sentence show how punctilious he was in treating the *Autobiography* as a piece of literature:

> And they were all merciful dispensations, these, to lift me out of the hell of my own nature, compared with those which the Almighty afterwards adopted for my deliverance.

In the manuscript, "methods" had been written first, then was crossed out and replaced with "dispensations"; and "deliver", his first choice, was crossed out and replaced with "lift".

At just what juncture he began to see every unhappiness, disappointment, failure and sickness as a punishment for his sins, a corrective to "deliver" him from himself, we do not know. He now wrote: "GOD is *the* idea of my mind", continuing that, as Malebranche "saw all things in GOD, so I see GOD in all things." He then began another sentence which he broke off mid-way and crossed out: "The psychological meaning of Malebranche's expression, I may mention, *en passant*, I know (May my knowledge of it not . . .)" and there it ended. What did he decide not to say about his psychological understanding? It will remain forever a mystery.

As a sidelight to the murky affair of haunting guilt and the conviction of personal wickedness, damnation averted only by day-to-day punishments from a merciful God(!), there is the puzzling statement he made about his penances. That they were required of him by his "spiritual director" is straightforward enough, but that he had to seek out dark subterranean places to perform them is mystifying. At the very least, it emphasizes the appalling inadequacy, as far as he was concerned, of the Chancery Lane house. In Fishamble Street, he had had a private place where he could go to read and get away from the other members of his family. However accurate or inaccurate his other details about the rooms they moved into may be, it is certain that space was extremely limited and that they had to live virtually on top of each other. Where, then, could he go to do the penances set him by the priest? One possible place was the cellar of the familiar old Rosemary Lane chapel. Now replaced by SS Michael and John, the building still remained intact and was used for occasional meetings of one sort and another. And it had a cellar where indeed Mangan may even briefly have attended school, for Fr Betagh, when he was an old man, had used the "wretched cellar at night" as the spot "whither young men who had been at work in the daytime came for instruction. . . ."[21] But the geographical location of the "subterranean places, wheresoever I could bury myself from the face of living man" is less important than the psychological location, which was the alienated, despondent depth of his own young heart. At this point, he was, he wrote, "A ruined soul in a wasted frame: the very *ideal* and perfection of moral and physical evil combined in one individual".

3

A Soul Mated with Song

[1]

> It is said that one Winter's evening, while Mangan, Tighe, and other choice wits were seated round a comfortable fire in a certain house in Bride-street, after many literary subjects had been discussed, the conversation naturally turned on the very ineuphonious name of the deceased butcher, and the difficulty of finding words in the English language to rhyme with the same [that is, Johnny Kenchinow]. Then it was that the hitherto retiring Mangan made a small wager, that by the time the company had assembled on the succeeding evening he would have an elegy composed on the defunct victualler, of *twelve* stanzas of *five lines each*, every line of which should rhyme with either "Kenchinow" or his "stall". And he won the wager!
>
> John McCall, *Life of James Clarence Mangan*

York Street extends from St Stephen's Green to Aungier Street, and in the 1820s, both Street and Green were part of what was becoming a handsome, well-developed area, far more attractive than Chancery Lane and its run-down purlieus. The new College of Surgeons stood on the corner of York Street and the Green, and the latter, as if to come up to the standards of the new construction, had been renovated. The old wall that surrounded it had been torn down, and a moat-like ditch had been filled in. Authorities had decided to get rid even of the stand of massive elms which had darkened the walks, and to level and plant the interior acres. In short, the Green was the heart of some serious urban renewal efforts, and gave promise of being what it did indeed become—a lovely city-centre park. Various reputable householders lived in York Street, among them the author and minister, the Rev. Charles Maturin, a man who was already becoming something of a famous eccentric, and an individual who was to exert a powerful influence on the young Mangan.

James had every reason to feel better about addressing his poetry from "No. 6 York Street" rather than from the despised Chancery Lane, and both *Grant's* and *New Ladies'* for 1821 showed this change. In any event, as he remembered it, he had to return to his home in Chancery Lane for only three years—by which he probably had in mind 1818, 1819, and 1820—and thereafter he was free of the noxious place. Only after he escaped from Chancery Lane did he hit his stride in the almanacs, where in 1821 and 1822, he had the allowed quota of verses for the first time. Thus by the age of eighteen, he was achieving a certain amount of independence, and was starting to become known in a small way among the almanac wits.

The "diarians", as they styled themselves, almost made up a miniature subculture in Dublin. Although never formally organized in any sense, they enjoyed a special sort of challenging fellowship as puzzle-writers and puzzle-solvers. Within their ranks, intense and sometimes bitter rivalries could develop, and small cliques often contended with one another for space and dominance. John McCall's planned history of these publications, incomplete at his death, was taken up by Edward Evans who published a condensed and highly useful *Historical and Bibliographical Account of the Almanacks, Directories, etc. Published in Ireland from the Sixteenth Century.* In his foreword to a facsimile reprint issued by Carraig Books in 1976, Dr Thomas Wall described the charm of the almanac milieu:

> Patrick Street in McCall's time was, as it had been for centuries before, the hub of the almanac industry. Indeed, with ballad-mongering, it could almost be said to be the chief industry of that ancient quarter of Dublin and one which brought men of various kinds and crafts into a happy and harmonious collaboration. . . .
>
> The snug of the tavern was the office of the compiler (sometimes styled computer) and his assistants. As men in similar circumstances do cross-words today, publican and teacher and pupil in the early 19th century gave themselves over to rebus, conundrum, charade, riddle and mathematical problem, prognostication and prophecy, in the congenial atmosphere of the tavern. . . .[1]

To Mangan, it was always important to be part of a congenial group of men; perhaps he sat quietly, keeping to the side, but socializing provided a sort of substitute for a family. Hence the scene which opens this chapter, an evening described by John McCall, himself an almost lifelong resident of Patrick Street. These cheery evenings when the poet met together with others over "a tankard at Bligh's" or in the Bride Street home of the Widow MacDonagh must have been times of precious memory.

That particular evening's challenge inspired Enigma No. 4 in the *New Ladies'* almanac for 1822: "To the memory of the late lamented Mr John Kenchinow, Butcher, of Patrick Street." A couple of stanzas will show the poem's pattern, but they hardly do justice to all the rhymes the poet found for "stall"—Saul, Paul, straw'll, sprawl, yawl, Gaul, awl, scrawl, and so on— nor to the tough additional rule, that each second line should end with a word to rhyme with "Kenchinow", yielding such odd but delightful half-rhymes as "drenching now", "pension now", "wench (and now)", and "fence you now".

Come and get the black, the mourning pall,
    The reason I will mention now,
And with it, blockheads, bards, and all,
Assist to cover Dia's hall
    For the loss of Johnny Kenchinow.

And is he gone? cry one and all.
    To keep you in suspension now
Is not my wish—yes, at the call
Of death was lately doomed to fall
    Lamented Johnny Kenchinow.

The six poems that were accepted from Mangan and printed by the almanacs this year were a mixed lot. In *Grant's* appeared the enigma with the solution "A Vampyre" which we will look at shortly. A rebus in this number was our poet's first specifically nationalistic poem, as compared with his first printed poem on an Irish subject, "The Earl of Kildare". He was inspired by his subject, "Robert Emmet", to some fairly strong language for one so young, but it was a time when anti-Union sentiments filled the Dublin air. A charade on a "Gravestone" completed his entries in this almanac. Besides the enigma "John Kenchinow" whose solution was said to be "Fortitude", his candidates which were accepted by the *New Ladies'* were the rebus "Nothing" and the charade "Blunderbuss".

Although Mangan gave an unrelievedly gloomy report about these years, a small amount of sound objective evidence shows that he was also doing a number of perfectly normal, enjoyable things for a nineteen or twenty-year-old. In 1822, an unusual expedition took him to a silhouette artist to have his likeness made. As far as we know, this is the sole portrait of the poet made during his lifetime. It shows his left profile, a delicate, rather aristocratic face, with a slightly sloping forehead and a somewhat aquiline nose. He is fashionably attired, wearing a hat with a moderately tapered crown, a style then popular. An endearing insouciance marks the face, if one can judge that much from a silhouette, and he is obviously very young.[2]

His friendship with Tighe must have been very rewarding. Mangan's earliest extant letter, written to his friend this year, suggested a curious characteristic which would became more pronounced as he aged: a lack of desire to hold on to anything, or to accumulate possessions, as if he were a wanderer in spirit, and had to travel light.[3] Whimsically, he disclaimed wanting to have anything more to do with the letter after it left his hands—"I have a droll peculiarity, which is that I never wish to hear anything further of a letter after it escapes from my hands", as he put it. And, as if feeling the need for some sort of explanation: "This may—that is, must—arise from the consciousness I entertain of the wretched style in which I pen it", an amusing excuse for one scrivener to make to another.

In 1823 Mangan used a pen-name for the first time. Almost all the almanac writers had some name they signed instead of their own, so this was not in itself a major step, though it may have meant more to him than to the general run of contributors. Biographers have perhaps made more of the poet's use of pseudonyms than the practice deserves, tying it closely to his "elusiveness", his fondness for disguise, and even to his wearing of a cloak. None of his early memoirists did so, however, probably because they were well aware that leaving a piece unsigned, labeling it "Anonymous", or even attaching a false *nom-de-plume* to it was then as common as, and maybe more approved than, actually signing one's own name. Some writers used straight-forward names, frequently a variant of their own. Others chose initials or joke names. Tighe, for instance, sometimes signed himself "Peter Puff", and it is clear that when our poet chose his first pseudonym, "Peter Puff *Secundus*", he did so to link himself with his friend.

Masking, of course, had its charms. The poet appreciated the mystery and the pleasure of being able to lurk behind an identity that could, if he chose, be denied; in short, of being "invisible". A false name functioned for him as a "mousehole" into which he could escape, if such a need arose. It will be seen some thirty years in the future, however, that when he developed the strength of his own identity and wanted to speak in his own voice, he dropped this literary affectation entirely. In the meantime, he felt the pull of opposite impulses, of antithetical desires tugging both ways: one for recognition, one for obscurity. His *Autobiography* makes it apparent that he did not altogether approve of such tricks: "I give my Confessions to the world without disguise or palliation. From the first my nature was always averse [to it], even almost to a fault . . . ." Thus he distinguished between his *nature* and his *practice*, for in the "real world" he recognized the need for "mannerisms".

He signed himself "Peter Puff Secundus" three times in 1823 and twice in 1826, the last year the almanacs appeared. In between, his verses were signed with a variety of pen-names—"M.E.", "P.V. McGuffin", "An Idler", "xxx-xxxx", and "xx-xx". Besides these, he used his own "James Mangan" some twenty-two times in all, although more rarely after he began the use of pseudonyms. As we will see, it did not show up at all in 1826, although at least twice in every other year in which he contributed verses to *Grant's* and *New Ladies'*. As far as can be told, no particular principle of choice dictated whether he put his own name or one of the other signatures to a contribution.

One possible pseudonym of Mangan's has aroused considerable debate over the years. From 1821 through 1826, a dozen poems in the almanacs were signed "James Tynan", and John McCall, after a lot of soul-searching, and the discovery of one piece of hard evidence in Mangan's republication of a "Tynan" verse as his own, decided to ascribe all of them to Mangan.[4] This, however, was probably going too far, since there is evidence, also, that James Tynan was a genuine person. The better possibility is that he was a friend of Tighe's and Mangan's and that the three of them sometimes collaborated on composing the riddling poems that they all loved. This sort of co-operation was common. Tighe himself in his older years confessed to McCall that some of the verses that carried his name were actually Mangan's; unfortunately, McCall did not record which ones.[5] Some of the Tynan poems would have been a credit to any young poet; others are well below Mangan's usual standard, so no conclusion can be drawn from the exhibits themselves. It would certainly be a strange thing if Mangan had used "James Tynan" as his earliest pen-name, rather than the fond "Peter Puff Secundus". Further, there was no reason for any solver not to use his or her own name, yet "James Tynan" appeared in the almanacs twice before our poet employed his first pseudonym, on one of these occasions as a solver of a puzzle from the previous year, 1819.[6]

And finally, there is the fact of a long letter Mangan addressed to "My dear Tynan" which is still extant in the National Library collection.[7] While it has been suggested somewhat halfheartedly that this could have been a literary exercise—it is, after all, almost 5,000 words long—it would appear to be authentic. Written in 1832 or 1833, many years after the demise of the almanacs, it was plainly meant to be sent to someone, for a space was left for the address. It was not filled out. Mangan apologized in the letter for having lost Tynan's address once already, and apparently he did so again.[8]

The best of the Tynan poems, "The Howl Clew Man", was a rebus in blank verse, a form so unusual for Mangan that it raises the immediate question as to whether this could possibly be his work. It was a mock elegy for another picturesque street character, in this case a seller of old clothes. Characteristics which we recognize as Manganesque also appear, however: lists, repetitions, assonance, double or triple-syllable line-end words, and throughout an amused tone of ironic appreciation. After describing the man's dress—brown boots that rose high above his knees, a torn coat, a long and "vast cravat"—the poet continued:

> Oh! 'Twas a soothing and most musical sound!
> Delectable, delightful, and delicious,
> Greatly transcending, in my humble judgment,
> Flute, fiddle, dulcimer, triangle, hautboy,
> Trump, trumpet, huge bassoon, or hurdy-gurdy;
> To listen to the heavy, measured tramp
> Of his enormous boots against the pavement,

Each day, and day by day he wended forth,
To prosecute the business of his calling,
Which for the most part, lay in crying: "Howl Clew!"
His tones!—Oh! They were sonorous to the last
And poured forth with a grand and flowing fulness;
The passengers around him stopped entranced,
And waggoners, and persons who sold fish,
And men who carried sacks of cabbages,
And other men who followed after wheelbarrows,
And many more who had nought to do, but were
Peripathetically [*sic*] recreating
Themselves, and staring upon all they saw,
Paused, and amazed, said: "This is truly wonderful!"[9]

Give and take was the rule for almanac writers. In 1822, Tighe had words of praise for Mangan in the *New Ladies'*. As he had not yet had a chance to read much of Mangan in any publication, he must have become familiar with his work through sharing between themselves. Tighe admonished his readers to "see what breathes thro' Mangan's song . . .

That modest song of minstrel fire;
And wond'ring ask how one so young,
Can wake such music from the lyre."[10]

Mangan, who must have been pleased, had to pretend that he was not, and in the next year's edition responded in a riddle whose solution was "Flattery":

Then see what kind of honey, Tighe,
Makes use of in regaling some sculls,
And wond'ring ask the question, why
Are some so prone in quizzing numsculls.[11]

In this year, 1823, he lavished a great deal of attention on Tighe, in fact. He wrote all four of his puzzles in the *New Ladies'* either to, or about, his friend. Two in *Grant's* were signed "Peter Puff Secundus, Mud Island", and one added "near the Bog". Apparently the place had caught the imaginations of the poet-scriveners. It certainly suggested a much more exciting life than they were leading. Years later, Weston St John Joyce wrote about it:

> Westward of the North Strand, between Nottingham Street and Newcomen Bridge, and extending as far as Ballybough Road, was a locality of evil repute in former times, known as Mud Island, inhabited by a gang of smugglers, highwaymen, and desperadoes of every description, and ruled by a hereditary robber chief rejoicing in the title of "King of Mud Island". For about 200 years down to the middle of the last century, [i.e., about 1850] this den of robbers was a plague spot in the district, enjoying an extraordinary immunity

> from molestation in consequence of what had at length come to be regarded as a sort of prescriptive right and sanctuary attaching to the locality.[12]

A touch of (innocent) larceny was not foreign to either Mangan or Tighe in these years, as they flaunted their poetic skills to take over the almanacs and monopolize all the space they could with pseudonyms, which surely fooled no one, as well as in a few instances with their own names. It was common knowledge that Tighe had worked himself into a position of influence where he could exert virtually single-handed control over the puzzle departments of both annuals, deciding whose contributions were to be published and whose were not. He and Mangan had now replaced the two old hands, James Martin and William Moyle, who had long been the "ruling clique". In 1825, Moyle groused to Martin:

> Sweet Bard, if I dare raise my head,
> From these two Puffs and mighty Ned,
> I'd freely give your merit praise,
> For really, Sir, your candid lays,
> Are fraught with sense and poetry—
> . . . But Sir, this year, it is well known,
> The Diaries are all their own.
> They write so sweet so smooth so strong,
> Each piece at least two pages long . . .

Needless to say, "Ned", or "Ned Numberless", was yet another pen-name used by Tighe and perhaps once or twice by Mangan. Although McCall at first felt sure that Mangan had masqueraded under this *nom-de-plume*, he eventually changed his mind. Still, some lines certainly look like his, lines such as ". . . had I skill in necromantic plans, as/Famed sages have, I'd laugh at human study,—/The mystic stream should flow, deep, dark, and muddy."

[2]

> From my eleventh to my fifteenth year, I read, read, read incessantly . . .
>
> Royal Irish Academy, MS 24/F/20, "Autobiography"

Mangan had always been a great reader. He retreated to whatever privacy he could find and there, as he says, he "read, read, read".[13] Allusions to authors and books abound in his work, some names over and over again.[14] Father Meehan was to provide a valuable listing, also, of his esoteric reading as an adult.[15] Yet getting hold of books could not always have been easy for him. No free lending libraries existed in Dublin when he was a young child, so he must have borrowed, and perhaps his family owned a certain number of volumes, such as the *Arabian Nights* which he specifically mentions having read as a boy. As a young man he was evidently a member of the Dublin Library in D'Olier Street, one division of which was a popular lending library with a £1 membership or subscription fee, but it was not of course available to him when he was growing up. Its 1823 catalogue included many volumes that were high on his list of favourites, among them Goethe's *The Sorrows of Werther, Wieland: an American Tale* and *Carwin and Other American Tales* (both by Charles Brockden Brown), *Gil Blas*, Pascal's *Pensées*, and *German Popular Stories.*[16]

Two books in particular were among those he read earliest and drew upon most: the *Arabian Nights* and *St Leon: a Tale of the Sixteenth Century* by William Godwin. A third, *Northern Irish Tales* by the now unremembered John Gamble, was published only in 1818, but Mangan described himself as enjoying it "a la Werther in my teens". Apparently, Gamble was rather unnoted even in his own time, for Mangan asked Charles Gavan Duffy, himself a northerner, if he had ever heard of him and wholeheartedly recommended Gamble's volumes for reissuing, perhaps in the "Library of Ireland" series. Duffy had more serious concerns on his mind than resurrecting an obscure novelist, and the suggestion was never acted on.

Of all the books Mangan alluded to in his writings, none was a richer source of inspiration for him than the *Arabian Nights*. The fantastic, magical, exotic settings and esoteric lore gave him just what he required for powerful metaphors, and fascinated the dreamer in him. "Like Sindbad in the Valley of Diamonds, the lower the gulf he descends into, the wealthier he becomes", he would write. And he was to use as an analogy for his own plight "an abyss, a pitfall, a maze, a labyrinth, the chance of extrication from which appears as remote as that of deliverance from the Living Charnel appeared to Sindbad the Sailor." Three of the notes in his most personal prose essay, "A Sixty-Drop Dose of Laudanum", have Aladdin as a point of departure for musings about the Illuminati, impatience, and love at first sight. Aladdin also figures impressively in the *Autobiography*: "Like Aladdin in the Enchanted Subterranean Garden, we are permitted to heap together and gather up as much hard bright gold and diamonds as we will—but we are forever therefore entombed from the fresh natural green pastures and healthful daylight." For him, the "hard bright gold and diamonds" stood for knowledge, and this passage is preceded by the judgement, "we purchase Knowledge at the price of Innocence."

The notion of the human turned into stone appalled yet at the same time intrigued Mangan. The Young King of the Black Isles in the story of the Fisherman and the Genie was a peculiarly appealing "statue", having been turned into marble (only) from the waist down. The wicked magician Maugraby, "The celebrated oriental necromancer, whose dreaded name the romances of my childhood had rendered familiar to me", figured prominently in his satiric story "An Extraordinary Adventure in the Shades", first published in the *Comet* in 1833, and in "The Thirty Flasks", which appeared in the *Dublin University Magazine* in 1838. Maugraby's power and lack of moral scruples made him a sort of wicked alter ego for Mangan, who often half-whimsically wished to be a magician. In short, the *Arabian Nights* early peopled his imagination with characters of immense psychological authority and introduced him to the lure and lore of the East.

Godwin's tale of *St Leon*, the French aristocrat, engaged Mangan's attention with its use of the magical extension of life as a major theme and its depiction of dungeon terrors. *St Leon* was written as an autobiographical confession of individual downfall; the emphasis Godwin put on the ravages of gambling and restless dissatisfaction played a part in making the novel one of our poet's most frequent sources of allusion. Indeed, this and other personal references to gambling raise a serious question as to whether or not Mangan himself may have had a problem with this "sport". If he did, it would go a long way towards explaining why he always seems to have been short of money, even when his style of living was penurious and his income respectable.

The story recounts that St Leon, growing restless in his country home, journeys to Paris and seeks excitement in the capital's brilliant society and at its gambling tables. With his fortune lost and his health damaged, he eventually has to go home, where he is visited by a sinister but intriguing old man with whom he strikes the bargain which sets the events of the main plot in motion. St Leon has to listen to the old man's two fantastic secrets, an ominous shifting of the burden of knowledge from the old to the young, which allows the aged character to die. In exchange, the young aristocrat receives an endless fortune and remarkable powers, but of course, he can not tell anyone the secrets until he himself wishes to leave this life. Needless to say, readers are never told what the secrets are, but only that they contain forbidden knowledge which amounts to nothing less than the magical *elixir vitae* or philosopher's stone.

From first to last, St Leon, to his credit, wishes to put his powers to good moral use, yet because of his strange ways, he is frequently accused of having committed some crime, and he spends considerable time in dungeons, the most notable being that of the evil Bethlem Gabor. Ultimately, St Leon is rescued by his son who berates his father for spoiling the lives of all his family, another element with a personal appeal for Mangan. *St Leon* resembles *Faust*, but as the book was published in 1799, thus pre-dating Goethe's great work by several years, the "influence", if any there were, must have been in the other direction. The novel was honoured in its own time for the author's portrayal of the lovely Marguerite. This character, and the theme of the hero's compassionate efforts to salvage a destroyed village in Hungary, "to pour the entire stream of my riches like a mighty river, to fertilize these wasted plains, and revive their fainting inhabitants", sound familiar from Goethe's masterpiece.

The tales in Gamble's work, Mangan explained to Duffy, were "domestic and exceedingly melancholy", which tells us something of his youthful taste in light reading. He was surely most impressed with the one titled "Stanley" about a boy whose plight resembled his own. The young hero is fifteen years old when the story opens; like the poet, he has had a grocer father who neglected him and his family, drank too much, entertained too lavishly, and charmed everyone except his closest relatives whom he generally ignored. After his death, it is discovered that he has made no provision for his son's education or support, so the boy is thrown onto his own resources, a real bed of thorns. The next two-hundred pages document his downward course and inevitably tragic death. The philosophy was simple, but chilling: "We are but of yesterday, and know nothing . . . our days upon earth are but a shadow." It is easy to see why this one of the three stories would have stuck in Mangan's memory, though what charm he could have found in the other two, "Nelson" and "Leslie", it is hard at this distance to understand. For him to empathize with Stanley was perfectly natural, especially as Gamble concluded that the boy "had talents and endowments which, wisely directed, might have given him the happiness he sought . . . but never found . . ." which already both anticipated and echoed Mangan's life.

As he grew older, there were other books which "spoke to" him, or influenced him, or to which he looked for analogies to his own situation. In the early 1820s, he was particularly impressed by three books that we know of, references to their situations or characters showing up time and again in his writings. These were the Irish author and clergyman Charles Maturin's *Melmoth the Wanderer*, Adelbert von Chamisso's *Peter Schlemihl, or, the Man Without a Shadow*, and Thomas De Quincey's *Confessions of an English Opium Eater.* A fourth story, that of the Wandering Jew, he probably also knew early in his life.

Melmoth, which had been published in 1820, provided him with analogies for his own plight and gave him copious draughts of unrestrained violence, blood, revenge, and horror—the whole Gothic experience. Like Faust's, Melmoth's story is that of a malcontent who bargains away his soul for a long period of extended life during which he not only will not, but cannot, die. Like St Leon, he must redeem his bargain by passing along his dreadful secret to some tormented or desperate soul willing to do almost anything for the "gift" of wealth, power, and seeming-endless life. The Rev. Maturin probably was tolerated by the authorities of the Established Church as author of such a book because Catholics, especially Jesuits, were the villains. Nevertheless, he was in bad repute regularly with the Church of Ireland, and his position was often in jeopardy. While *Melmoth* was his most sensational, and most popular, tome, five other novels, among them *The Albigenses* and *Pour et Contre* which Mangan also alluded to, were not far behind it.

For his eponymous character, the malevolent Melmoth, all was doom and cynical spite. The world in which he dwelt, and to which he brought horror wherever he went, was an unregenerate world in which even love had lost its power, and emotional and spiritual healing were beyond the reach of poor humankind. Not only the general imagery, but whole passages of Maturin's shock-value prose lingered with the sensitive Mangan long after he finished reading the novel, as we will see a little farther on in his story.

Peter Schlemihl, or, the Man Without a Shadow may also very well have come into Mangan's hands at this point, for the slim volume by Adelbert von Chamisso, a German poet, was translated into English and printed in London in 1824. It was the only book referred to in the impersonal autobiography, for the amusing reason that it was, he claimed, the only example of German humour he could think of. Mangan keenly appreciated the comic, in reading and in life, though when he encountered it, it might only remind him that its reverse side was sorrow—just as the most heart-breaking tragedy could call up inappropriate mirth, and life itself be a "drama that . . . strangely united the two extremes of broad farce and thrilling tragedy . . . wherein mankind played at once the parts of actors and spectators." (p. 28)

Although Chamisso treated his subject humorously , there was nothing really funny about not having a shadow, for its absence—like the absence of one's reflection in a mirror—meant that the soul had been lost. And Peter had not only lost his soul—he had sold it, another instance of the fictional use of the theme of trafficking with the Devil. Through his bargain with a mysterious man dressed in gray, Peter surrenders his shadow and acquires wealth and power, but thereafter he is so peculiar that no one will associate with him for long. He is shunned by some people and scorned by others, and even a vagabond reminds him, "Respectable people are accustomed to carry their shadows with them when they go into the sun." Even moonlight creates shadows, he discovers to his sorrow. After falling in love, he wishes to be normal again, fearing the effect his condition will have on his innocent sweetheart, Mina. It is then that the man in gray, having identified himself as "a poor devil", makes the ultimate satanic offer: Peter can keep his wealth and get his shadow back, too, if he will but sign in blood a note "delivering his soul to the bearer". To his credit, Peter refuses. Having lost everything, he wanders the earth, not entirely miserable, but never truly happy. As the book ends, he addresses this advice to the storyteller: "While you live among mankind, learn above all things first to reverence your shadow . . . and then your money." This last phrase may come as a surprise to the reader, but Peter's priorities had been skewed; "reverencing" money more than his soul had destroyed him, but money was not unimportant. His new and chastening knowledge was that if he hadn't carelessly spent all of his, he wouldn't have been tempted in the first place.

Certainly, the need for money is a constant theme in the Irish poet's work. Although he always treated the lack of money with a certain disdain, he was aware that it was a very dark element in the lives of many people, including himself. Below the genteel surface of his life and writings lay plenty of thoughts about such money-related subjects as gambling, thievery, murder, exploitation, and demonic bargains.

Also during the early 1820s, in all likelihood, Mangan first came across De Quincey's *Confessions of an English Opium Eater* which had made such a splash in England three or four years earlier. Whether De Quincey had much influence on the Irish poet is a subject that must be deferred to a somewhat later point in his story. However, Mangan alluded to the author only a few times, once as a man who could understand dreams exceptionally well and again as one knowledgeable about the effects of opium. De Quincey's drug experiences, sensational as they were, do not seem to have particularly interested Mangan or inspired him to try the drug or its tincture, laudanum. In the course of his life he admittedly used laudanum as a medicine, as did almost everyone else, but there is no reason to doubt his denial that he was an opium eater. That label carried a strong implication of hedonistic self-indulgence, and he rejected it vehemently when Gavan Duffy challenged him with the rumour that he had heard he had taken to the drug. It is, however, quite possible that through extended use in the course of a severe and long-drawn-out but unspecified illness in 1838–39, he developed a dependence on laudanum. It is important that within his circle of acquaintances and friends, the use of alcohol, but not opium, was accepted. To drink was a man's prerogative; to use opium or laudanum, except medicinally, was considered dangerous, ill-advised and rather contemptible.

No one book about the ancient legendary figure of the Wandering Jew can be identified as the source from which Mangan first learned the story, although Fr Meehan wrote, "Mathew Paris' 'Historia Anglorum' written in 1248–9 . . . proved to him a source of real delight; for it was from the Benedictine's pages he first learnt the weird story of the 'Everlasting Jew'." Mangan was almost certainly familiar with it before he would have had access to the *Historia Anglorum*, or to be more exact, Roger de Wendover's *Flowers of History.*[17] A German version, which George Anderson has maintained "underlies nearly all" the seventeenth and eighteenth century versions, including the English, appeared in 1602.[18] It recounted the now classic story of Ahasuerus who angrily taunted Jesus on the Via Dolorosa, ordering him to move on more quickly. Jesus's response was, "I will stand here and rest, but you must walk!" In a slightly different version, his reply was, "I am going, but thou shalt tarry till I come again." The Wandering Jew thus became a magical figure who comes and goes, who ages and then sleeps and wakes up young again. There were "sightings" in Europe until late in the eighteenth century when the Age of Reason apparently put him permanently to rest although literary interest persisted. The qualities of exile, wandering, homelessness and perpetual remorse along with The Wanderer's intriguing knowledge of places over hundreds of years fascinated the Irish poet.

Mangan first translated "Der ewige Jude" by Christian Friedrich Schubart in irregular blank verse—unusual for him—for the *Dublin University Magazine* in December 1837. A dozen years later he translated Friedrich von Schlegel's "Die Warnung" whose story differed somewhat and which, he said, "we believe is the popular one". Fr Meehan observed that Mangan never got around to writing the long original poem he intended to write on the theme, "with characteristic inconstancy, abandoning his design". Nevertheless, considering all the poet did accomplish, this seems a rather harsh judgement. Especially is this true when his long poem "Khidder" is borne in mind. Although ostensibly a translation from Rückert, it is to all intents and purposes Mangan's poem, and the subject is the "wandering" Elias the Prophet, who, like the Wandering Jew, is "ever young" and ever journeying. "Khidder" made its appearance in August 1845 and will be looked at in due time.

One common thread that runs through much of this reading is the "outsider-ness" or even the outlawry of the characters. To a man, they extended the boundaries of their behaviour far beyond the ordinary. The common, the ordinary, the mundane—these young Mangan found repellent; in St Leon, Byron's Manfred, Faust, Ahasuerus, Sindbad, Melmoth, Peter—even, in a sense, in poor Stanley—he lived vicariously, experiencing their misadventures and victories, and reading hard moral lessons in their ultimate defeats. And they were all defeated in one way or another. At the end of their exciting lives, only emptiness or damnation awaited them.

His taste was eclectic and his memory retentive although, it must be said, not always accurately so. It pleased Fr Meehan to point out in his introduction to the *German Anthology* some of the esoteric books that attracted Mangan and which "in all likelihood, have seldom been taken down [from their shelves] since", books such as Zedler's *Universal Lexicon*, Ugolino's *Thesaurus Antiquitatem Sacrorum*, and Calmet's *Dissertatio in Musicam Veterum Hebraeorum*. Mangan evidently had some interest in music theory (prompted by Byron's *Hebrew Meolodies*?)and, according to the musician and historian W.H. Grattan Flood, "was not only a theorist in the matter of music, but had a very decent and tolerable knowledge of music itself."[19] Both the sounds of words and the sounds of music enthralled him; his sensitivity to musical variation and organization may explain the shape of many of his own compositions.

[3]

> Turning now to the *New Ladies' Almanac* for 1825 he has Charade 1 on the word "Knowledge"; Enigma 17, mournfully inscribed to his dear Mother Ireland, in a patriotic vein; and Rebus 8, addressed to some particular Catherine . . . in it he mercilessly and unfeelingly compares a woman's tongue to the solution, "Perpetual Motion".
>
> John McCall, *Life of James Clarence Mangan*

Mangan's almanac poems grew longer and more mature as the years progressed, just as we would expect, and characteristics that came to be his hallmarks began to make their appearance. There was his strong preference for aural and tactile, as distinguished from visual imagery, for example, and a tendency to avoid lush metaphors and similes in favour of more concrete and direct speech. We also begin to get the odd impression that his poems sometimes have a life of their own, barely restrained by the poet. Such poetry can make uneasy going for readers who want art to function as a bulwark against chaos; for a poem to show it is under the tight control of the presumptive artist-in-charge. But Mangan was in fact already a consummate poet, although he himself was not yet aware of just how good he was. In all honesty, he confessed, he wanted to astound people more than to edify them, and a reader's temporary anxiety that meter or rhyme had broken loose was a deliberate sleight-of-hand of a word-magician creating a special effect with his own version of top hats and rabbits.

Frequently, one of his long poems will have a shape so elaborate it is not immediately apparent to the reader, a good example being an enigma from *Grant's* 1825 issue, beginning "I write upon a bland and breathless night". Consisting of eleven stanzas of eight lines each, and utilizing the

Byronic stanza as we know it in the (by then notorious) poem *Childe Harold's Pilgrimage*, it possesses a complex circular structure that is not at all obvious at a first reading. The first stanza sets the tone, placing, as it were, the whole composition under the dreamy, feminine sign of the moon. Its "dream and doubt and speculate" lead the poet on to what appear to be meandering thoughts about his preference for speculation over certainty, then into a rather rambling consideration of the sort of poem he is now writing; a riddle, a "toy", he calls it, which prompts regrets about his deplorable writing habits. These include a lack of concentration and a tendency to chatter on too long about "facts and fables" which are so much less desirable than "speculation". The first and second sets of four stanzas each follow this same pattern, with the poet deciding he should not mull over the details of his personal life but instead, turn outward to poetry rather than inward to "History/A theme whose thoughts, tepid and trite, are clad/With a sufficiency of cloud and mystery."

A stanza about temperament which is "not made up of milk and water" bridges the two sets. The final two stanzas provide the clues that produce the ironic answer to the enigma which is "The End of the Enigma", thus underscoring the circularity of the poem's structure. The first stanza, the bridge stanza, and the first stanza of the second set are given below:

I write upon a bland and breathless night,
    The nine-and-twentieth of the month of June;
Pausing anon to gaze upon the bright
    Yet melancholy mildness of the Moon;
There is something in that Wanderer's light,
    That always puts me in, or out of tune;
And as my imagination I don't check of late,
She is apt to make me dream and doubt and speculate.

Temper is not made up of milk and water,
    At whiles we are o'erbearing and obstreperous;
Philosophy will sometimes go for nought, or
    How else should everything combine to pepper us?
The soul! exists the man who has not thought her
    A very fount of love! Alas! years leap o'er us,
And truckling, as it must be to society,
We undergo of changes a variety!

Alas! years roll, I've said, or say, and none
    Can feel the fact more forcibly than I;
My childhood, boyhood, whither have ye gone?
    Whither! the echoe of the soul will sigh!
Oh! heaven and earth!—but hold—no more—I have done—

I find I am writing sentimentally;
And I have lately joined a host of railers,
At slip-shod sentimentalism retailers.[20]

In addition to illustrating Mangan's often complex structuring, this early poem, like others from the period, shows him striking a pose of poetic virtuoso, deliberately sprinkling lines with peculiar rhymes and periods, and performing for an audience that appreciated this sort of thing more than the general public would in later years. In time, he would garner both praise and criticism for "showing off". For the moment, other diarians either loved it, or envied him his skill, or both.

There is no way of knowing how many poems the young man composed during these years, but judging from what he had published, he must have been prolific. The almanacs failed to appear in 1824 due to the illness of the owner, but the 1823 issues printed ten pieces by Mangan, while those for 1825 had eleven, and 1826 another ten. Some of these poems had considerable merit within the limitations of their respective genres. Rudolf Holzapfel compares Mangan's observation of the rules governing composition for the almanacs with the metrical strictness which informs the work of Irish language poets of previous centuries:

> Irish poets of the 15th–18th centuries writing in the Irish language were used to expressing themselves in complex lyric (and thus "puzzling") forms. Rhyme and metre and all other poetic "rules" were strictly adhered to (controlled) and much more complicated than parallel English forms. Interwoven "rhymes" or word sound-similarity were also extremely complex. A feeling of delight was produced in the listener when he realized that the poet was "keeping to the rules" and at the same time poeticizing in a seemingly effortless manner. I find a lot of this in Mangan in what I have called his "lyric straitjacket". And I attribute a lot of the essential "Irishness" in him to his Gaelic background. Here, in the almanacs, he is clearly "bridging the gap" between his genetically Irish and his assumed English self for the first time. That is their importance for *me*. For Mangan, of course, their importance is that they provided him with a platform, even a cozy corner, for his first lyric efforts.[21]

In yet another way the almanac poems are important, and that is in being the only block of original verses ever created by Mangan. Throughout his life, he distributed original work only very sparingly among translations and "variations", so what we are looking at here is unique. In these poems we learn something, if only a very little something, about the poet himself—just enough to make us wish for more. "I write upon a bland and breathless night", for example, reveals an apprehensive Mangan already involved in self-analysis, and with an uneasy insight or a premonition that his preferred occupations of poetry and "speculation" are not going to be good for him in some way. We also see an individual by turns depressed and lethargic or, changing quickly, vibrant with nervous energy, a characteristic that would cause him (and his friends) both irritation and delight.

Another of these poems which reveals something about his emotional and spiritual state appeared in the 1822 issue of *Grant's* almanac as Enigma 2.[22] The solution was "A Vampyre", the manuscript of which, as noted earlier in these pages, is among those poems headed "written at 16" and "written at 17". It was his first venture into the realm of the supernatural, subject matter which intrigued Romantic authors in general, and which he would explore in considerable detail over the years.

He probably adapted the poem's story from a popular eighteenth-century tale of warriors and a stranger who turns out to be a vampire. Beyond the Hungarian legend that may have been his source, however, he added touches of his own and produced a different sort of vampire story: one with no truly innocent victim. The warrior who waits in his tower to be joined by an accomplice is intent upon violently avenging some unrevealed wrong. The vampire, arriving in the accomplice's place, tells him:

> And think thee, warrior, as thou wilt
> Thou canst not gain relief from men[.]
> He, the accomplice of thy guilt[,]
> Lies lifeless in the nearmost glen.

Moreover, the vampire warns the warrior against pursuing his aim, insisting that instead he remain in the tower—"Tomorrow best befits the crime". The two of them, the vampire says, "Have much to say, and more to do", but the night passes without his uncovering what this is. No particular surprise follows the reader's discovery that, "in his tower by morning's light,/A bloodless corpse the warrior lay."

It is tempting to analyze stories like this. The symbolic elements are almost too plain to need mentioning: the warrior, the tower, the dead accomplice, the murderous but meditative vampire. One intriguing addition made by the Irish poet is the warrior's freedom to leave the tower at any time; it is only because he remains there, as the vampire urges, that he dies. That Mangan deliberately articulated parts of his own "myth" in this poem is not likely, but he probably recognized personal correspondences: he himself as warrior, his father as vampire (living off the "blood" of others and not such a far cry from a boa constrictor, either), his home as the lethal place he must leave, and his own "other self" or other member of his family—possibly his older brother?—as the accomplice who has already died or been killed.

[4]

Awake! arise! shake off thy dreams!
    Thou are not what thou wert before:
Of all that splendour, all those beams,
    That once illumed thine aspect o'er,
Shew me a solitary one
Whose early lustre is not quenched and gone.
    New Ladies' Almanack, 1825; Enigma: "Ireland"

One innovative poem can be said to mark the line between the work of Mangan the youth and Mangan the man. Not only was it his first on a serious contemporary subject, but also the first in which he raised his voice in the cause of his homeland. Printed as an enigma in the *New Ladies'* almanac for 1825, and titled "To My Native Land" in the *Comet* in 1832, it was a cry of despair for Ireland. And it was not only a cry of despair for her woes, but it appeared also to be a response to some grave but unspecified national disgrace. The third and final stanzas follow:

When other men in future years,
    In wonder ask, how this could be?
Then answer only by thy tears,
    That ruin fell on thine and thee
Because thyself wouldst have it so—
Because thou welcomedst the blow.

* * * *

And till all earthly power shall wane,
    And Time's grey pillar, groaning, fall;
Thus shall it be, and still in vain
    Thou shalt essay to burst the thrall
Which binds, in fetters forged by fate,
The wreck and ruin of what once was great.[23]

What inspired Mangan to write such a bitter and disillusioned apostrophe to his country just at this time? As far as we know, his friend Tighe was not an especially ardent nationalist, and 1824 was not marked by any very special occasion of infamy in Ireland. The question can be addressed more productively if we look for his inspiration beyond Ireland, to that man who was for him a hero among the poets, George Gordon, Lord Byron. The English poet was, of course, a close friend of Thomas Moore, and he had always supported the cause of Catholic freedom and Irish self determination. Only the previous April he had died in far-off Missolonghi where he had gone to fight for the freedom of Greece.

It may well be that Mangan had recently come across Byron's poem "The Irish Avatar", a satire on those sycophants who had welcomed George IV with such enthusiasm on the occasion of the king's visit to

Ireland in 1821. Byron may be thought a little behind-hand in writing this diatribe three years later in 1824, but his immediate motivation was a slur the English periodical *John Bull* had cast on Moore. Byron sent the poem to his friend in a personal letter within days after those comments appeared. Although "The Irish Avatar" was not to be in general circulation for a number of years, it reached Moore in Paris with Byron's directions to have twenty copies "carefully and privately printed off". That was done, the printer omitting a dozen of the more libellous stanzas in the first and second editions. Then, later the same year, another larger edition was brought out with all the excised verses included. It was this edition which Mangan probably had the opportunity to read, and which inspired him to compose "To My Native Land". A couple of stanzas from "The Irish Avatar" will suffice to illustrate how Byron handled the subject of Irish disgrace:

> Shout, drink, feast, and flatter! Oh! Erin, how low
> Were thou sunk by misfortune and tyranny, till
> Thy welcome of tyrants had plunged thee below
> The depth of thy deep in a deeper gulf still.
>
> Yea, I loved thee and thine, though thou art not my land,
> I have known noble hearts and great souls in thy sons,
> And I wept with the world o'er the patriot band
> Who are gone, but I weep then no longer as once.

One further stanza from Mangan's poem will illustrate its affinity with the English poet's "occasional" piece:

> Weep, weep, degraded one—the deed,
> The desperate deed was all thine own:
> Thou madest more than maniac speed
> To hurl thine honours from their throne.
> Thine honours fell, and when they fell
> The nations rang thy funeral knell.

Mangan looked back on the years of his apprenticeship as part of his long history of suffering. Although we have seen that the picture was not as black as he painted it, it is still wise to honour his impression. He might have been, but he "was not yet trodden under wholly", as he expressed it in his poem "Enthusiasm". We can only hope that, to set over against the depression and discouragement which he must have felt very often during these years, came a dawning realization that he could work really well with words and had a true gift for poetry. As Richard Dowling said in a letter to Charles Gavan Duffy, "The essence of [Mangan's] being was genius. If Mangan wasn't a genius there was no such person as Mangan at all."[24]

Interim

As his apprenticeship drew to a close and another phase of his life opened, James Mangan looked forward to the break in his routine, if not exactly to the change itself. Once he was used to something, any change was difficult and unsettling. Given Hamlet's choice, he would probably have chosen to stay with the familiar evils rather than risk trying to improve matters. But search for a full-time position he must, because although his apprenticeship "terminated . . . so did nothing else in my unhappy position. The burden of an entire family lay on me, and the down-dragging weight on my spirit grew heavier from day to day." (pp. 22–23)

He was now twenty-two years old. When he gazed into a mirror, he surely realized that he was good looking, although his slender, ascetic, nervously high-strung appearance did not appeal to everyone. His large blue eyes had a compelling brilliance, but his only real vanity was his blond hair which curled over his collar and fell somewhat haphazardly over his high forehead. He was always too thin for his slightly below medium height, about 5 ft 6 ins, but he carried himself well. He was never said to slouch, even when he was older and became stooped, and as his gait was described as more gliding than walking even during the last months of his life, he no doubt always moved with a certain grace. Further, for quite some time he dressed rather stylishly, or at least as well as he could manage on his limited income; the leader of the Comet Club, John Sheehan, even mocked him for foppishness. Chances are that the overall effect he achieved was a little strange, but at this stage in his life, he was attempting to make a good appearance and to conduct himself as a hopeful young man should. Alienated though he might feel, he had definitely not rejected the standards of his day.

Every step he took in his search for work, every visit to an office, led him further from the life for which he longed, but go he did, to Merrion Square, Fitzwilliam Square, and St Stephen's Green, where many of the most respectable men of the legal profession had their offices. Occasionally, he found temporary employment: "Thankful was I whenever my father and mother were enabled to reap the fruits of my labor", he wrote rather sententiously. Then, more convincingly, "But my exasperated mind (made half-mad through long disease) would frequently enquire—though I scarcely acknowledged the enquiry to myself—how or why it was that I should be called to sacrifice the Immortal for the Mortal—to give away irrevocably the Promethean fire within me for the cooking of a beefsteak. . . ." Note those two "disclaimers" so carefully spun into the fabric of the sentence: He was hardly responsible for his thoughts because he was "half-mad through long disease." Moreover, he scarcely knew he was entertaining such wickedly unfilial feelings, anyhow. Mangan could barely allow himself to think harsh negative thoughts about those people closest to him, a quality he had in common as we now know with the majority of those who have been abused in childhood.

"De Profundis clamo!" he cried, though no doubt silently, as he wandered through the outlying fields around the city: "Out of the depths I cry to you, O Lord." But at least during this time he began to get the exercise he had neglected for so long. Then in the midst of his recitation of agony in the *Autobiography* appears a flash of insight from beyond the parameters of his inwardly illuminated world: "My narrative scarcely appears at a glance to justify me", he half apologized. Indeed, to many readers it has not, and its accuracy has been seriously questioned, as already noted here. It is useful, therefore, to know that he, too, saw a gap between the cause he identified and the effect he claimed it brought about. That he still believed "the circumstances taken altogether were amply sufficient to warrant" such feelings is a second thought worth accepting.

Fortunately, help was forthcoming at this crucial juncture:

> After a short while matters appeared to brighten with me or rather to assume a less dusky aspect. I was advised by a worthy medical friend of mine, Mr Graham of Thomas St.—a man of considerable knowledge and skill, though but an apothecary—to try what such kinds of exercise as fencing or ball-playing might accomplish for me. (p. 23)

Mr Graham must have been blessed with considerable perception. He understood that as long as the young man's active mind was not really engaged with his activities, he was not going to get any relief from the anxiety of its frantic signallings. He put it rather well: " 'The mind, my dear young friend, . . . is the key to the health—a somewhat rusty key to persons of coarser constitutions—but an oiled key to all of nervous temperaments and susceptible apprehensions.' " Walking helped some people, of course, but for his "dear young friend" he recommended focused exercise—"Try the foil or the racket, and you will be a new being at the end of a fortnight." (p. 24)

Mangan took his advice—where, or how, he does not say. But we can envision him with a partner—one of the great advantages of these sports is that they cannot readily be indulged in alone—and, equipped with foil or racket, perhaps one of the early designs with a short handle and horizontal strings, going about this new venture. He was immensely gratified with the results. In an even shorter time than Mr Graham suggested, a week rather than two weeks, he found himself a new man: "Never, perhaps, was such a change witnessed in the health and spirits of a human being as that which supervened in mine. . . . " The "almost miraculously recuperative power" which he now noted in himself, and in fact did demonstrate throughout his life, is said to be peculiarly typical of hypochondriasis. More simply, he needed attention. When the limited but genuine consideration of his apothecary friend provided it, he recuperated rapidly.

Nothing was or could long remain simple for him, however. His health which now seemed improved soon developed a dark aspect manifested in a careless exhilaration, which, like his unexpected powers to recover from illness, anticipated a life-long problem:

> I arose, as it were, out of myself. I had for a long time subsisted upon nothing but bread and tea, or milk, with my heart only for animal food—"bitter diet",—as Byron remarks—giving the grosser aliments they required to my relatives—but I now felt as though I could feast upon air and thought alone. The great overcurtaining gloom which had become to me a sort of natural atmosphere—a fifth element—still in a degree surrounded me; but my experience of existence at this time was that of a comparative Paradise. (p. 24)

Elation followed depression. Yet the passage seems over-burdened with self-pity: The young poet, giving all the solid food to his family, literally starving himself—again, the "Immortal" being sacrificed for the "Mortal"—is a highly self-conscious pose. And there is also the clear and rather contemptuous suggestion that his relatives, being less elevated than himself, required the "grosser aliments" that he could do without. Yet this sensation of needing very little food was authentic with Mangan, a fearful aberration, really, considering the obvious consequences. It was all too often aggravated by his relative poverty and the "usefulness" of being able to "rise above" a need for food. Indeed, it was to lead him almost to court starvation.

For the time being, though, it is a relief to find him with a "glow of soul" that was "wonderful" compared to his usual condition, and to read that he felt his situation had been altered "from absolute bondage to comparative liberty". And what had become of that "entire family" that was dependent upon him? He does not say. In all likelihood, his brother John, who was also an apprentice scrivener, was now earning about what James had been, and was carrying part of the burden. He probably did not look very hard for work during the summer months; there would not have been much to find then, in any event. Lazy June days had given him time and inspiration to compose "I write upon a bland and breathless night" and the ambling, rambling "An Address Extraordinary". June was one of the two months that held special meaning for him, and over the years it would include several of the major events in the calendar of his life, including even his death. (The other month was March which teased him into punning on "March fourth" and "March forth".)

It was this autumn that he finally saw, or perhaps it would even be true to say encountered, the author and churchman, Charles Maturin. Maturin lived in York Street, and it is a little odd, perhaps, that the young man had not seen him before 1824, the very year Maturin died. Mangan after all had been employed in a building near the minister's home for some six years. Be that as it may, three "sightings" now occurred in short order. Maturin long had been something of an idol or alter ego for the poet: a writer, a genius, an eccentric, a man who behaved in odd ways that attracted attention, some of it favourable, some not. Twenty-five years later, Mangan wrote with great vividness about this character in the first article of his "Sketches and Reminiscences" series that appeared in nine installments in the *Irishman* between March and July 1849.

The first time he saw him was a morning in August or September. On this occasion, Mangan walked to Aungier Street, and in front of St Peter's, the parish church of the largest Church of Ireland parish in the city, saw the curate, the Rev. Maturin, about to enter to conduct a funeral. The young man overcame his qualms about entering the Protestant church and followed Maturin inside, where he found a large, open area with pews and "the front of the gallery . . . pannelled [*sic*] and painted white". From the porch, he approached closer and observed the rites with rapt attention:

> Maturin . . . did not read, simply repeated; but with a grandeur of emphasis and an impressive power of manner that chained me to the spot. His eyes, while he spoke, continually wandered from side to side, and at length rested on me, who reddened up to the roots of my hair at being even noticed by a man that ranked far higher in my estimation than Napoleon Bonaparte.

Whether or not the minister had actually been looking at him, Mangan thought he had. He lingered after the service ended, and, seeing Maturin whisper to the clerk at his side, imagined that he "looked steadfastly at [me] . . . If I had been the master of sceptres—of worlds—I would have given them all that moment to have been put in possession of his remark."

St Peter's Church stood just opposite York Street, where Mangan next saw the clergyman author, this time after a funeral had ended:

> He stalked along York Street with an abstracted, or rather distracted air, the white scarf and hat-band which he had received remaining still wreathed around his beautifully-shaped person, and exhibiting to the gaze of the amused and amazed pedestrians whom he almost literally *encountered* in his path, a boot upon one foot and a shoe on the other. His long, pale, melancholy, Don Quixote, out-of-the-world face would have inclined you to believe that Dante, Bajazet, and the Cid had risen together from their sepulchres, and clubbed their features for the production of an effect. But Maturin's mind was only fractionally pourtrayed, so to speak, in his countenance. The great Irishman, like Hamlet, had that within him which passed show, and escaped

far and away beyond the possibility of expression by the clay lineament. He bore the "thunder-scars" about him, but they were graven, not on his brow, but on his heart.

The third and last time he saw Maturin, on a "balmy autumn evening" not long before his death on 30 October, was the most impressive, and Mangan trailed his quasi-idol through the streets of Dublin:

> He slowly descended the steps of his own house, which, perhaps, some future Transatlantic biographer may thank me for informing him was at No. 42 York Street [O'Donoghue said it was No. 41], and took his way in the direction of Whitefriar Street, into Castle Street, and passed the Royal Exchange into Dame Street, every second person staring at him and the extraordinary double-belted and treble-caped rug of an old garment—neither coat nor cloak—which enveloped his person.

The young man especially observed that Maturin did not take the busiest street to reach his destination, and he concluded from that, that the "over sharp and shrewd" individuals who thought Maturin affected eccentricity to attract notice were mistaken:

> . . . instead of passing along Dame Street, where he would have been 'the observed of all observers', he wended his way along the dark and forlorn locality of Dame Lane, and having reached the end of this not very classical thoroughfare, crossed over to Anglesea Street, where I lost sight of him. Perhaps he went into one of those bibliopolitan establishments wherewith that Paternoster Row of Dublin then abounded. I never saw him afterwards.

The poignant ending is the product of Mangan's later sorrows; no doubt he had heard a great deal of gossip about Maturin's behaviour, and he projected his own feelings onto the eccentric, lonely character with whom he identified:

> An inhabitant of one of the stars dropped on our planet could hardly feel more bewildered than Maturin habitually felt in his consociation with the beings around him. He had no friend, companion, brother: he and the "Lonely Man of Shiraz" might have shaken hands and then—parted. He—in his own dark way—understood many people; but nobody understood him in any way.

And so, the months passed. In the autumn business returned to the offices where he might seek employment, and "a situation was offered me in a solicitor's office, the salary derivable from which, though humble enough, was sufficient to elevate us in some degree above the depths of our former poverty". (p. 25) Some nine months after his apprenticeship had ended, he accepted this full-time job: "not gladly—for a foreboding of what was to come haunted me now with more intense force than ever—but resignedly, and in the full belief that I was merely fulfilling a destiny which I could not oppose, and which I had no right to arraign."

4

Herding with Demons

[1]

> Merrion Square: This spacious and elegant area, which contains about 12 acres of ground, is situated at the south side of the city, and but a few minutes walk from Stephen's Green. . . . The houses on the north side of the square are some of the best built and most convenient in Dublin . . . the basement stories of all, on that side, are of mountain-granite and rusticated; and the three upper stories are of brick; the houses on the others sides are entirely of brick. The north side of this square has been a summer promenade for many years.
>
> G.N. Wright, *An Historical Guide to the City of Dublin*, 1825

Mangan began work in the office of Matthew Frank at No. 28 Merrion Square sometime in the winter of 1825–26. It was probably no better and no worse than dozens of other legal offices: dull, rather badly lighted, and, as far as the law-copyists were concerned, perhaps never really warm enough to be comfortable. Several attorneys and solicitors had their offices in the same building, and the clerks may have met and socialized, but the young poet would have worked in close contact with no more than three or four other men. Joining Mr Frank's staff ended a period he knew could be only "a temporary relief", but which gave him a tantalizing glimpse of what another sort of life might have been like. He hated the office, and the people he had to work with; there, each day had a nightmarish quality that exhausted him emotionally and physically.

He had not been at work long before "all the old maladies under which I had laboured returned with double force." Partly, he thought, this was due to his total lack of exercise. Although the hours were surely long, he did not complain of them, merely referring to work which kept him tied down to a desk "all day", and to his reading, which he very unwisely did half the night. The other half usually found him restless or wakeful. Partly, too, he blamed his condition on the bad air in the office, and in that he was probably not far wrong. The fuel almost inevitably would have been the soft coal that is cheapest and smokiest. When this sort of coal is burned inefficiently, which is almost always the case, its smoke can indeed be virtually poisonous, and "sulphurous exhalations" are nothing to joke about. He realized that the air was toxic, but he hadn't much choice. The atmosphere may even have done exactly what he came to suspect—

induced the hallucinations he described in terms reminiscent of Maturin's *Melmoth*:

> My nervous and hypochondriacal [*sic*] feelings almost verged on insanity. I seemed to myself to be shut up in a cavern with serpents and scorpions and all hideous and monstrous things, which writhed and hissed around me, and discharged their slime and venom over my person. These hallucinations were considerably aided and aggravated by the pestiferous atmosphere of the office, the chimney of which smoked continually, and for some hours before the close of the day emitted a sulphurous exhalation that at times literally caused me to gasp for breath. (p. 26)

It is tempting to think that some of the atrocious behaviour, as Mangan perceived it, of the men he worked with was induced by those same noxious fumes; short temper and aggressiveness can be symptomatic of prolonged exposure to this sort of pollution. Certainly, to him, his office-mates seemed intolerable: "The coarse ribaldry, the vile and vulgar oaths and the brutal indifference to all that is true and good and beautiful in the universe, of my office companions affected me in a manner difficult to conceive." And further:

> The misery of my own mind—my natural tendency to loneliness, poetry, and self-analysis—the disgusting obscenities and horrible blasphemies of those associated with me—the persecutions I was compelled to endure, and which I never avenged but by acts of kindness—(which acts were always taken as evidences of weakness on my part, and only provoked further aggressions)—added to these the close air of the room, and the perpetual smoke from the chimney—all these destroyed my constitution.[1]

Now, without Tighe or any other friend close by to turn to, he may have begun to drink to escape the reality that had overtaken him. The passage above continued, "No! I am wrong—it was not even all these that destroyed me. In seeking to escape from this misery I had laid the foundation of that evil habit which has since proved so ruinous to me. I feel my heart getting sick, and my breath growing faint as I recount these details. . . ."

Perhaps he made little or no effort to keep up old friendships, even his dearest companions now seeming as distant as if they lived on another planet. None of his poems in the 1826 numbers of the almanacs were signed "James Mangan", but four of the seven carried the lonely signature "M.E."—"me". Significantly, too, he adapted his "Peter Puff *Secundus*" pseudonym as if to show the distance which separated himself and Tighe. In 1823, it had been "Peter Puff *Secundus*", "Peter Puff Secundus, Mud Island, near the Bog", and "Peter Puff Secundus, of Mud Island". Now, in the *New Ladies'*, it was "Mr Peter Puff Secundus of Mud Island, on the other side of the Bog, or there-aways". It was to "Nobody" that he addressed Rebus No. 1 in *Grant's* beginning with the evocative lines "How the pure night with her stilly myriads,/Of worlds, bewilders our weak and weary heads!" The elevated tone suddenly vanishes in a warning against trying to solve the riddle: "It is twice as deep, and quarter as clear,/As a barrel of Salt and Soot and Beer". The solution was "Cowards". Charade No. 1 in the same almanac described ephemera under the signature "M.E.":

> A sun ray on the waters of December's
>   Gloom; dew drops quivering on a quivering leaf;
> A fire decayed down to a few dim embers;
>   A good man's anger; a young dandy's grief;
> A charming poem which no [one] remembers
>   To have ever heard of; or a plate of beef,
> Before a hungry man are evanescent
>   Things, and yet what's OUR reign? Their's the present!

Also signed "M.E." was Enigma No. 2 in *Grant's*, a lovely Shelleyan poem celebrating absolute stillness and repose, an atypical creation for Mangan which, though effective, evoked the calm, indeed, of death:

> In the unbeginning first ere earth arose
>   From chaos old,
> Thy lovely empire, Spirit of Repose!
>   Thou didst uphold!
> The splendid firmament is vast to view—
>   Can Fancy roam
> That wilderness of silver and of blue!
>   It is thy home!

Shelleyan in language—but hardly in mood and tone. It is the antithesis of the vibrant "Hymn to Intellectual Beauty", and its death-ideal is the opposite of the bright hope of "Ode to the West Wind".

James Tighe, for his part, worried about Mangan and addressed a poem to him in the last issue of *Grant's*, or rather, he expressed his concerns about his friend and then addressed the last two stanzas to him. Specifying the anxiety he had about what "Jamie" was doing, and about his "what d'ye call it?—fear" and "fine-strung nerves", Tighe revealed a great deal. This poem contains the earliest description of Mangan from anyone but Mangan himself. Tighe chose to cast his poem in the Scots dialect, popular in his day, and Robert Burns's metre, which he had used for others of his almanac poems. Because it carried a manly aura, it was appropriate for the bluff expression of the tenderest feelings. Had he used an Irish form, "Shemmy" would have replaced "Jamie". The final two stanzas of the poem follow; the other verses may be found in Appendix A:

Och! Jamie, shake away the dole
That hath *too long* o'ercast thy soul—
I'll no' commend the reeking bowl,
    Or gillhouse fun;
But just a morn' an' evenin' stroll,
    An' loup an' run.

Farewell my friend, in whom I find
Reflected bright loved Leonard's mind— [a favourite diarian who had recently died]
Leonard, the modest, gentle, kind,
    Whose soul's embrace
Enclosed within its love refined
    The human race.[2]

Here was Mangan, then, as seen by his close friend and sympathetic companion: modest, gentle, kind, affectionate, given to nervousness and melancholy—"the dole"—and haunted by some strange fear. Tighe was anxious that his friend might think of committing suicide or turn to destructive drinking—"the reeking bowl"—for relief. These were no idle fears. Mangan not only began to drink more during this year, he also admitted that while he worked in the Frank office, "nothing but a special Providence could have saved me from suicide."

Although in his poem of farewell to the almanacs he attempted to be humorous and casually signed himself "An Idler", suggesting perhaps that he was unemployed when he wrote it, even here Mangan could not suppress his gloomy thoughts:

I wonder who on earth invented verse;
    I likewise wonder who invented prose—
The last is bad enough, the first is worse,
    But both are bores, as everybody knows.

Twenty-four years later he would write in his autobiography that at this time he had pleasure in nothing and admired nothing, almost the words of this passage:

        Some prize a German
    Tale, in all its mummeried mysticism and plot;
Some sleep, some sweep, and some weep o'er a sermon;
    Some doat upon the drama—some do not;
    Some send all brain-births whatsoever to pot,
Saving the "Daily Press"; some look with loathing
    On the same "Daily Press", being early taught
To view it as mere frivolity and frothing.
    Your favourite, if you please? I relish *nothing—nothing*![3]

He could scarcely believe that through all his suffering, his parents still neglected to take any notice of his misery: "The wretched depression of my spirits could not escape the notice of my mother, but she passed no remark on it, and left me in the evenings altogether to myself and my books", as he put it. Whoever penned the impersonal autobiography said much the same thing—"His father and mother never spoke to him, nor could he exchange ideas with them. . . . He had gold and they had copper." In an autobiographical letter to McGlashan, he wrote:

> My father and mother meant well by me, but they did not understand me. They held me by chains of iron. I dared not move or breathe but by their permission. They seemed to watch my every action, and to wish to dive into my very thoughts, few of which, much as I loved them, and I had a morbid love of them, I ever made them acquainted with. My existence was miserable. I often longed for death.[4]

This passage contains a tantalizing confusion of pronouns. Was it to "parents" or "thoughts" that he meant "them" to refer in the sentence "much as I loved them, and I had a morbid love of them . . ."? A strictly grammatical reading requires that it be to "my thoughts", of course; but the passage is emphatically about "my father and mother". Perhaps on a subconscious level he meant both.

[2]

> We are but shadows! None of all those things,
> Formless and vague, that flit upon the wings
> Of wild Imagination round thy couch,
> When Slumber seals thine eyes, is clothed with such
> An unreality as Human Life, . . .
>
> Mangan, "What is Thy Name, Reality?"

How much he drank alone, or with companions, Mangan himself may scarcely have known. The attitude he now brought with him to a joyless indulgence was, in any case, almost as destructive as the alcohol. That his choice was still usually porter rather than whiskey is quite possible, for he spoke of beginning the use of "spirits" at a somewhat later date, and it was also at this later date—1831 or 1832—he placed the start of his serious dependence on alcohol. He was clearly destroyed, over the years, by drink and its side effects such as not eating, so the question raised obliquely by O'Donoghue is especially startling: Could the man have produced so much poetry that is so remarkable without recourse to stimulants, or, more accurately, depressants? It is dreadful that the question seems to imply an answer in the negative, but the fact is that no other palliative for psychological, or, indeed, physical, pain was available except opium which would almost certainly have deprived him of the companionship of his peers and perhaps left him far more incapacitated. Miserably unhappy at work and at home, drinking to escape the unhappiness, with no social motive left for writing—no friends to urge him on, no space to compete for—Mangan wrote little from 1826 until 1831, six years that are sometimes called his "dark period".

The demise of the two leading almanacs was a blow to all the diarians. About the only Irish periodical which they could hope would publish their poetry was the *Dublin and London Magazine*, somewhat later called *Robins's London and Dublin Magazine*, printed in London for the Irish market. To it, Mangan sent two poems, "Genius: a Fragment" and "What Is Thy Name, Reality?", although a full year elapsed between the publication of the first in March 1826 and the second in 1827. James Tighe also was represented here, the April 1826 number carrying his "The Destruction of Chios 1822". "Genius: A Fragment" was discussed in Chapter 2 as one of the poems Mangan identified as having been written when he was sixteen years old; although that has been doubted, the fact that the original copy is not among the other "written at 16" and "written at 17" manuscripts in the collection of the National Library of Ireland perhaps suggests he removed it for use in a periodical, just as he said. By contrast, the original manuscript, or so it appears, of "What Is Thy Name, Reality?" is to be found there, but lacking any "written at" designation.

Clearly, when they decided to submit some work to the *Dublin and London Magazine*, both men went back through poems they had on hand, rather than write anything new for their first venture outside the almanacs. In his procedure, Mangan struck the bolder note, but we would still wonder why he did not value his years of verse writing experience enough to risk writing something especially for the new venue. Being a cocky "diarian"—ruling the roost with Tighe—had not built his confidence in himself as a poet, it would seem. On the contrary, he had had all too much opportunity and encouragement to assimilate the prevailing "amateur attitude". After all, what other standard had he? How could he know how much better his verses already were than those of other contributors? The admiration he expressed for Tighe's "The Destruction of Chios 1822", a poor poem by any standard, was not unusual. That he wrote "ephemera" too long for his own good was O'Donoghue's contention about Mangan. But that probably did his "Muse" less harm than learning so young to admire too much the ephemera of others. Before he could progress very far as a poet, he had to replace that standard with a higher one, and he would do that through the medium of German poetry.

Lodged in the beautiful lines of the third stanza of "What Is Thy Name,

Reality?" were the questions which now occupied, if they did not quite overwhelm, Mangan:

> . . . the soul
> The startled soul, upbounding from the mire
> Of earthliness, and all alive with fears,
> Unsmothered by the lethargy of years
> Whose dates are blanks, at moments *will* inquire,
> "And whither tends this wasting struggle? Hath
> The living universe no loftier path
> Than that we toil on ever? . . .
> Alas! and must Man barter
> The Eternal for the Perishing—but to be
> The world's applauded and degraded martyr,
> Unsouled, enthralled, and never to be free?"

He was the "martyr" whom the world praises while it cannot see that he has "degraded" himself almost beyond the reach of salvation. It was he himself who felt "unsouled", a powerful and terrifying concept for a man who took so seriously the fate of his soul. Perhaps worst of all, it was he who was trapped, "never to be free". As he wrote here, so he would write twenty years later in the *Autobiography*, where, as we have already seen, he spoke bitterly of having had to surrender "The Immortal for the Mortal", of giving away "irrevocably the Promethean fire within me for the cooking of a beefsteak", and of destroying his soul to "preserve for a few miserable months or years the bodies of others". His sense of martyrdom became more pronounced over the years. It sometimes seems when he employs the expression "Man" or "Mankind" that he has become so identified with suffering humanity that "Mangan" should be read for these terms. Perhaps it helped him endure. The feeling that one is a martyr can lend dignity to a role that might otherwise be unbearably degrading.

Dull resignation now enervated his spirit. Not yet thirty years old, he was already almost without hope that things would ever improve for him; worse, he was at least half-resigned to his fate. Moreover, for the moment, at least, he may have said just about everything he had to say on the bitter subject of life. He has been accused of self-pity, but there was actually a good bit of self-restraint in not going on and on about his life's conditions, in maintaining instead a stoic, or, to be realistic about it, perhaps a sullen, proud silence. To set this poet writing again would require a shift in his viewpoint, a change in his circumstances, or, most desirable of all, an irresistible inspiration. Before too long he would have all three at once and be almost drowning in subject matter. But for the moment, life was stagnant and dreary.

[3]

> I do not know if you are aware that in the old files of Michael Staunton's paper 'The Morning Register' some compositions in verse, evidently by James Clarence Mangan, have been inserted, and I think they have escaped the notice of previous writers of his life. When Mr Broderick, now I believe living in Fishamble Street had a bookseller's shop on Merchant's quay, he had six or seven volumes of the Morning Register running over the years before and after 1830, and I had the opportunity . . . to make the discovery to which I have alluded.
>
> The Rev. John O'Hanlon to John McCall, 27 February 1883

How he managed to drag himself to the job in Merrion Square day after day for the next three years is simply impossible to know. To an extent, he must have grown used to the conditions in the office, which may anyhow have improved, and were not as bad in the spring and autumn months as they had been in the winter when he arrived. Nevertheless, after "What Is Thy Name, Reality?", a great silence descended upon the poet. Nothing of his was published, as far as we know, from March 1827 until almost the end of December 1829.

Furthermore, not a thing is known with certainty about what was going on then in his life. Almost anything is conceivable. Although the tenor, if not the exact words, of his autobiography imply that he was at the Matthew Frank office for the whole time, there is an inconsistency in this. Whereas he spoke always of "three years" of employment there, the actual time from early 1826 until late fall 1829 was closer to four. Thus it is possible that he stopped work several months, or even a year, earlier than has been supposed. It may even have been at this point, if ever, that he made his much-hypothesized trip to Germany, a journey of some months' duration. Rudolf Holzapfel surmises this would have allowed him time and opportunity to become familiar with the flow and feeling of the language.

It is intriguing to note in this regard that the poet's sometime friend Charles Lever traveled through Germany during this same period, in 1828 and 1829, going from village to village, enjoying the food, the wine, and the literature of the country. The journal this young man of twenty-two kept is filled with enthusiastic comments on German poetry and copies of poems by Uhland, Körner, Goethe, and Bürger, among others. He also compiled a list of "German Classic Authors, whose works I have already read", and this added many more names to the list, all popular writers at the time, and all or most of whom Mangan would later translate.[5] We know next to nothing about Mangan's relationship with Lever, save that there was once some degree of friendship which had evidently faded by the time

Lever edited the *Dublin University Magazine* from 1842 until 1845. The most provocative clue that Lever may have encountered his fellow Irishman during these travels is his note made in 1829 in Koblenz, that he was not able to get anything to eat at the inn he was stopping at because the visiting Duke of Clarence had ordered everything for his own party. Is it possible that this was a veiled reference to Mangan, who did indeed, as we will soon see, choose "Clarence" as his name this year? Could Mangan have run into Lever in Germany and both young men been inconvenienced by the real Duke of Clarence? At the very least, was Lever in some way responsible for the birth of Mangan's intense interest in German literature which we hear about for the first time in 1830? These months were obviously important—we just don't know how important or in what way.

Lever edited the *Dublin Literary Gazette and National Magazine* from January 1830 until June 1831. Mangan contributed one poem, "Schiller's Address to His Friends", in September 1830. In October, Lever appended his pen-name "Rosenkranz" to his translation for this publication of the last stanza of Ernst Schulze's "Die bezauberte Rose". Three-and-a-half years later, on 15 February 1834, Mangan had his own close translation, accompanied by the German original, of this same stanza in the *Dublin Satirist* with the title "To A Friend. From Rosenkranz", a sly jibe, it may be, at Lever for having taken personal credit for this verse:

I sang thee this, when, with the Spring's young roses,
    My hopes, too, blossomed in their fairy bower;
But Fortune bars the portal Hope uncloses,
    And, while the sunbeams laugh, the tempests lower!
Long now below the cold green mould reposes,
    She who bestowed on me one blissful hour—
And nought remains with me, from that sweet time,
Except—my love, mine anguish, and my rhyme!

Lever was at one time taken to task for plagiarism, and if Mangan were implying some such thing here, it may account for the end of their friendship.

To conclude this speculation about Mangan and Germany: In October 1841, as Lever was set to take over as editor of the *Dublin University Magazine* to which he had long been contributing and for which Mangan, too, had been writing for seven years, an amusing sketch appeared titled "Our Contributors at the Brunnens", that is, at a certain mineral springs located in Germany. It was based on the whimsy that all the *University Magazine* writers had vanished from the Irish scene and journeyed to that country to take the waters. Both Lever and Mangan were among the contributors "discovered" at a hotel in Wiesbaden. While nothing has been found which even remotely "proves" that Mangan ever went to Germany, each of these minor connections is suggestive in its own way and needs to be taken into account when the troublesome question of his intimate knowledge of German is considered.

If the chance is remote that Mangan traveled outside Ireland during this time, it is only slightly better that he seized the initiative and sent a few new poems to the one newspaper which he might hope would publish them. During its early years, the *Morning Register*, founded in October 1824 to be the mouthpiece of the new Catholic Association, was innovative and hot spirited, and it makes stimulating reading even today. Michael Staunton, its editor, came to be known as "the father of Irish journalism" thanks to his favouring of fresh local news over pre-digested coverage of international events taken from the English press. For years, Mangan's name has been linked to the paper largely because in 1836 he met Gavan Duffy, whose first job in Dublin was on its staff, in the editorial offices. D.J. O'Donoghue's conclusion that the poet contributed to the *Register* in the 1830s was natural enough, but his searches proved fruitless. In fact, the only real clue to the poet's presence in its pages came in a late letter, the one quoted at the opening of this section, from the Rev. John O'Hanlon to John McCall.[6] By the time he received it in 1883, McCall had already produced his memoir of Mangan and was an old man with his life's work about over, which probably explains why he did not follow up the tip which at one time would have delighted him.

Nowadays, a search of the old *Morning Register* files is easier than it would have been in McCall's time.[7] From the period between its foundation and the end of 1832, I culled nine poems which have qualities typical of the poet's work. Of the nine, four were, or purported to be, translations; as there is absolutely no evidence that he was translating by this date, much less sending in his efforts for publication, I have discounted those lyrics. The remaining five are unsigned and evidently original; they are more sentimental and softer than his usual style, but he was young; he was experimenting; and he was as yet uncertain as to just what his true poetic voice—if any—was to be. These five strongly resemble some of the manuscript poems and a few from his mature years in their imagery and fineness of thought. They are, however, unlike Mangan's work in the regularity and triteness of their stanza and rhyme forms, the latter being almost entirely masculine, whereas Mangan was already using feminine and hudibrastic endings with enthusiasm. If they are in fact his, these lyrics show a new effort that is more independent and yet more traditionally Romantic than anything he had previously attempted.

The poems that deserve a mention are: "Evening" (2 August 1828); "Poetical Portrait" (28 February 1829); "The Sun Dial" (28 September

1829); "Beauty Vanished" (9 June 1830); and "Song" (28 September 1830). If "Evening" is Mangan's, it was his only publication during 1828, the first to interrupt that long silence from 1827 almost through 1829. These five poems are to be found in Appendix B.

[4]

O blessed Freedom! Thou art worth
(Such magic to thy wand is given)
All other joys we know on earth,
And all we can conceive in heaven.
Anonymous, "Ode on Emancipation",
Morning Register, 23 April 1829

Mangan has never received sufficient credit for being a convinced nationalist early in his life. The emphasis has been rather unjustly placed on how late he was "politicized", and the result has been a down-grading of his intense youthful commitment to the Irish cause. The fact is that as soon as any movement was afoot to rid his nation of English abuses and abusers, he took part in it; granted, it was sometimes a rather eccentric part, but every patriot contributes in a unique way. Mangan's role was characteristic and consistent. Specifically, when he had a choice, he contributed to nationalist rather than unionist publications. Although he may have been *radicalized* only at a late date, in his own fashion he was *politicized* by 1831, and he was a *cultural nationalist* long before that.

The year 1825 proved to be a disturbed and disturbing twelve months in Ireland, although not quite to the extent some people anticipated. The Catholic Association and its newspaper flourished, and this, with the growing popularity of Daniel O'Connell, contributed substantially to an increasing anxiety among Irish Protestants. This anxiety, never too far beneath the surface, was heightened for some by a bizarre prophecy that had been around for quite some time, but which was supposed to come to pass in 1825. This was "Pastorini's Prophecy", the work of one Charles Walmesley, who used the name "Pastorini". A virulent anti-Protestant, he calculated in *The General History of the Christian Church*, published in 1778, that all the Protestants in Ireland would be wiped out in 1825.[8] His interpretation of the biblical apocalyptic vision in Revelations or The Apocalypse of St John moved inexorably through what he termed "The Ages of the Church" to that conclusion in reasoning that went something like this: ". . . We saw in the first trumpet the Roman Emperors persecuting the Christian religion", and they were punished. In the "second trumpet", the Arians arose and were swiftly punished. In the "third trumpet", the Roman Empire "for its idolatry was destroyed. In the fourth, the Greek separated from Rome and were punished. . . . In the fifth trumpet we see the protestants revolting against the Church; upon whom then must the fifth vial fall?" His eccentric arithmetic told him that periods of three hundred years separated the destructions, and that inasmuch as Luther's work had been done in 1525, the nineteenth century date could be practically guaranteed. Most Irish Catholics and Protestants were uninterested in the prophecy. Nevertheless, there was a strong hint of perhaps related apocalypticism in a good bit of the poetry produced in the national interest, and Mangan's was no exception. Over the years, he would utter time and again the somewhat millenarian belief that God would have to intercede on Ireland's behalf for any cure to be effected.

Meanwhile, towards the mid-1820s, a Protestant minister styling himself "Pastor Fido" responded to Pastorini and published *Pastorini Proves to be a Bad Prophet and a Worse Divine*.[9] Addressing "the Roman Catholics of Ireland", he "proved" Walmesley's figures were wrong, and that, instead, the Pope was the Anti-Christ and would himself be destroyed beginning in 1826. Needless to say, both dates passed without incident.

In the real world things were happening which would have a greater influence on Mangan than did either of the two "pastors". O'Connell's goal for the decade was to achieve Catholic Emancipation, that is, to secure by law the right of Catholics to hold public office and be members of Parliament. This in itself could have mattered to only a few male Catholics who might aspire to such positions, but the phrase "Catholic Emancipation" had great appeal; like "Ourselves Alone!" and "Repeal the Union!", it became fraught with feeling, a rallying cry for thousands or millions of Irish who would enjoy no measurable benefit if it were to be achieved. The point is well made, however, that "forty-shilling freeholders", who had been enfranchised since 1793 but had almost invariably voted for their landlord or their landlord's choice of candidate, there being no secret ballot, with "Catholic Emancipation" would feel considerably freer to vote as they saw fit. This "democratic phenomenon" was far more prophetic of the future than Pastorini.

O'Connell, with justification, took credit for channelling the potential for violence, endemic throughout rural Ireland, into political action although the weapon he always held behind his back was the threat that without him and the Catholic Association, bloodshed would be inevitable. The Liberator ran for election in Clare in 1828, and was victorious. The Catholic Emancipation Act was passed the next year, but in a mean-spirited mood and move, the Government refused to allow him to take his seat in the Commons without traveling "all the way back to Clare to re-submit himself to the electorate. . . .This time he was elected unopposed, and under the Emancipation Act could now take his seat."[10]

In November 1828, the *Morning Register* carried the announcement of the founding of *The Pilot*, a newspaper to be published Monday, Wednesday and Friday evenings. This paper would represent Daniel O'Connell and his policies, and gradually the *Register* was to lose its own keen political edge. In this first notice, though, the *Pilot's* identity seemed anything but settled. It declared that it would not be the tool of power and certainly not "that ignoble thing, a CASTLE PAPER", but neither would it be indiscriminately antagonistic to the Government. So entirely was O'Connell behind the *Pilot*, although he always insisted he did not control it, that Sean O'Faolain actually wrote in his spirited biography of the Liberator, *King of the Beggars*, "The people had no newspapers until O'Connell founded an organ, *The Pilot*, to support him. . . ." This surely would have come as a surprise to the editors and readers of the other papers being published by this time.

Four or five morning papers of some quality were now printed in Dublin. Besides the *Register*, there were the *Freeman's Journal*, *Morning Star*, *Saunders' News-Letter*, and the *Dublin Morning Post*. Evening brought forth the *Dublin Evening Mail*, the *Dublin Evening Post*, the *Patriot*, and the *Correspondent*, though the last two were shrinking rapidly into oblivion. They came and they went; only a very few, such as the *Freeman's Journal* and *Saunders' News-Letter*, showed much staying power. The little *Dublin Morning Star* was a case in point, rising and setting in less than a year. Nevertheless, the situation had improved so much from just ten or fifteen years earlier that any prophet worth his pay could have foretold that there would be a wealth of publications before the half-century mark was reached.

[5]

> My morbid sensibilities thus daily increasing and gaining ground, while my bodily powers declined in the same proportion, the result was just as might have been anticipated. For the second time in my life nature succumbed under the intolerable burden imposed upon her; and an acute attack of illness removed me for a season from the sphere of my irksome and melancholy duties.
>
> *Autobiography*, p. 27

During this "season" of illness, James was replaced in the office by his younger brother John, "a stout and healthy lad of nineteen, . . . and I returned home."

Query: Isn't there something wrong with the age Mangan gave for his brother John at this point late in 1829?

Answer: Yes. The age error by which he "lost" six years off his true age distorted his figures. At twenty-five, John was hardly a "lad".

Query: If James now "returned home", does that mean that he had (again) been living away from his family?

Answer: Probably. Although he had lived with his parents for a period of time toward the beginning of this employment, he very much preferred his privacy, and he was hurt by their lack of concern for the sacrifice he was making for them. John was trained as a scrivener, and William, now twenty-one, was perhaps also working at his craft of cabinet-maker, so the household had enough income to allow James the "luxury" of his own room which in any case would have cost no more than four or five shillings per week.

Query: How long is a "season"?

Answer: Used in a context like Mangan's, almost certainly the few months we would expect it to refer to. Thus, the break in work probably extended from late autumn until almost the end of the winter.

Query: What then?

Answer: The "acute attack" of illness over, he would have had to go back to work, but he could hardly have reassumed his old place in Mr Frank's office. Now established there, John Mangan almost certainly stayed on. Nor is it suggested that James returned. It was now up to him to find a new full time job. Probably he again let a few months pass without looking too hard, perhaps picking up temporary work when he could. In fact, he may have taken only temporary posts until as late as the next autumn.

5

Befooled in Love

[1]

> None but good poems are susceptible of being well translated. For it is in this department of literature as it is in love; the maintenance of fidelity towards the beautiful is always easier than it is to the ordinary.
>
> Mangan, *DUM*, July 1838

During late 1829 and early 1830, several uniquely important things happened in Mangan's life. For the first time, he used his language skills "professionally" and began to tutor a young woman, Catherine Hayes, in, it appears, both German and French. With her he formed a close friendship which was precious to him beyond measure and may have inspired his first contribution of a German translation for publication. Also at this time he settled on a professional literary name, "Clarence", which was to be for him not just a pen-name, but a genuine name of choice. For the rest of his life, he would sign himself with some variant that included it: "James Clarence Mangan", "Clarence Mangan", "Clarence", or "J.C.M." He himself spoke of beginning his "career" in 1831; as we will see shortly, it is not entirely clear what "career" he was referring to, but he probably had in mind writing for the periodical press. And finally, it was also now that he fell—disastrously—in love with a young woman whose name unhappily will probably be forever unknown to us. Earlier, in Chapter 2, I spoke of this as a period when he seems simultaneously to have suffered a serious illness leading to the loss of his job in the office of Mr Frank, and his first love affair; and I suggested it marked the end of any hope he may have had to "move up in the law". In short, it would be hard to overestimate the significance to him of these months.

Rehoboth House, Dolphin's Barn, no longer stands; the accidents of the years took their toll of the huge family dwelling, and a fire in the early 1980s left it with a gutted lower floor and boarded-up windows and doors.[1] It was almost certainly in late 1828 or the early months of 1829 that James Mangan first made the acquaintance of the Hayes family then living there. It must have been too large for them, really, unless there were a number of children besides Mangan's friend, William, and Catherine, his sister. Built in 1798 by a Mr Morton for his large family, the house had two enormous wings to accommodate the parents and their twenty-four children; its name in Hebrew actually means "There is room [for more]".

How Mangan met William Hayes, the brother, is not known, but as he appears to have been a law stationer and scrivener, and was said by his friend John McCall to have been a clerk in a distillery, it was probably through some business contact. The warm hospitality the poet enjoyed through his friendship with them and his frequent visits to their big, comfortable home, meant a great deal to him. Because he played down the appreciation he had for physical "luxuries", it is easy to overlook his genuine fondness for creature comforts. But of even greater importance was his close friendship with Catherine. To the best of our knowledge, she was the first of the admiring, youthful friends who meant so much to him, in part because their purity and innocence took him back to the unsullied naïveté of childhood. Although her age is not known, it has been assumed, probably correctly, that she was no older than sixteen when they met, and thus in a way a child compared to Mangan. It has also been suggested that she was the one love who reputedly broke his heart, but this is no more than a romantic fancy. Looked at closely, the circumstances of that romance and of his affection for Catherine bear little or no resemblance to each other. Even more convincingly, the chronology is all wrong.

James Price, he of the Mangan memoir in the *Evening Packet*, who met the poet in 1831 or early 1832, distinguished sharply between his friend's romantic involvement and his affection for Catherine Hayes. For Mangan, Catherine was the friend in whose "perfect communion of feeling [he] ever looked for, and ever found a perfect sympathy."[2] Price had harsh words, by contrast, for the girl, whoever she was, who "rejected [him] perhaps for one over whom his intellect lifted him . . . loftily. . . ." And he differentiated with helpful precision between the two sorts of grief Mangan suffered. Catherine's brother also dismissed the notion that there was more than friendship between his "little sister Kate" and the poet. William Hayes "never once breathed a single syllable of an existence of the tender passion" between the two, according to his "particular friend", John McCall.[3] As for McCall himself, he was convinced that the whole idea of Mangan's ever being in love with any woman was, if not absurd, at least improbable: "The true hearted Mangan, though at a distance he might doat on some particular beauties, never loved them in that sense of making one his wife."[4]

The only one of Mangan's friends to take exception to the consensus that the poet did not love Catherine as a man loves a woman he wants to marry was Fr Meehan, and his opinion is both interesting and important inasmuch as he must have formed it from what Mangan told him. In a private letter to McCall written in 1887, the priest referred to "Mr Hayes, whose sister Mangan meant to marry. . . ." thus perhaps causing McCall to wonder if he had missed some clue somewhere.[5] In one of his better poems, Gerald Griffin used the expression "just less than a lover and more than a friend" to describe the relationship between himself and Lydia Fisher, a married woman of whom he was extremely fond. Mangan's love for Catherine was probably also that for a "beloved friend", an *amitié amoureuse*.[6]

Taking language lessons, being tutored, was not necessarily a matter of studying grammar and doing exercises, but of reading in the literature of the language and learning to speak a little of the foreign tongue in conversation with the teacher. Mangan was not a tutor of the Chekhovian model, as in *The Cherry Orchard*, living in the household and occupying a sort of anomalous position between servant and family friend. Rather, his role was an informal one, that of a friend who came often to visit and perhaps almost incidentally fell into the habit of helping Catherine with her German. Hayes was "quite indignant" when some "captious critic" argued against Mangan's claim to have been "an adept in the German tongue. . . ." To prove the poet's skill to the doubting Thomas, he showed "several of Mangan's admirers . . . an original German lesson, in the poet's own caligraphy, that he had written out" when he and Catherine were "con amore studying that language in their juvenile days."[7] A manuscript copy of the poet's first published translation, Aloys Blumauer's "The Two Sorts of Human Glory", was assuredly this "German lesson". It still forms part of the National Library of Ireland's collection of Mangan manuscripts.[8] Appearing in the 26 January 1830 number of a periodical called *The Friend* (of which more later) it marks the period at which James and Catherine were enjoying German poetry and one another's company.

Perhaps significantly, it also links his lifelong devotion to German poetry with his deep affection for the girl. He gave the copy to William Hayes two years after Catherine's untimely death in October 1832, and written on the reverse side of the sheet of foolscap we read "Wm. Hayes received this from James Mangan, March 1834"; and in another spot, "Given to Wm. Hayes by James Mangan. 4th March 1834, Dublin"; and again, "Manuscript of James Mangan given me 4th March 1834. Wm. Hayes" The paper is neatly folded, and on the outside it is also Hayes who has inscribed further: "James C. Mangan/German poet r[esident?] Dublin"; "Miss Catherine Hayes/German scholar"; and rather puzzlingly, "Miss Catherine Hayes/German and French/Teacher". The implication of that underscored "Teacher" may be that William's "little sister Kate" was doing as much instructing in French, at least, as was the poet, a possibility which throws a somewhat new light on the relationship.

It was curious of William Hayes to say that Catherine and James were *both* "in their juvenile days" in 1829 or 1830. Catherine may have been, but the poet was twenty-six or twenty-seven years old. The custom of the time did not encourage much attention to age and birthdays, and it would not be surprising if the poet's age were unknown to them; his appearance was youthful, so he was assumed to be young. Another person who knew him as a "student" was James Price who described him when the two met as:

> . . . then a diligent German, French, and Italian student, every unoccupied moment in his office—every hour that ought to have been spent in recreation, being devoted to his darling pursuit of language acquirement. In these he soon gained a facility that was most extraordinary, the intense application of two or three months being sufficient to enable him to translate if not literally, with all the true spirit of his author.[9]

At the same time, the fact that both Hayes and Price committed the error may well suggest that Mangan was even at this early date making what I have been referring to as his "six-year age error". If so, it would add some weight to the notion of his having undergone so severe a trauma when he was five or six years old that when he "came to himself" he had "lost" those early years of his life. Thus, when faced with the question of his age, he may well have thought of himself as being twenty or twenty-one years old at this time, which would be in line with both Price's and Hayes's perception.

Mangan remained friends with William Hayes for some years after Catherine's death, presenting him with another manuscript copy of yet another poem on 4 March 1839, the original "What Is Thy Name, Reality?" or "Life and Its Illusions". Obviously, there was something special about 4 March, but whether it was anything more profound than a shared amusement at the possible pun on "march forth" we have no way of knowing. The two eventually had a falling out. Sometime in the succeeding years, Hayes's friend William F. Gibbons wrote to him regretting the "coolness" that had developed between Hayes and Mangan, observing, "It is to be deplored that too frequently men of gigantic mind [in which category the context makes clear he included the poet] allow themselves to drift as it were insensibly into skepticism on matters of revealed religion. Mangan's belief was . . . that the human mind should be thoroughly unshackled. . . ." He went on, "All else they consider intolerance. Yet must we not deal too harshly with them, for after all they are gentle and noble spirits."[10] Gibbons thus summed up Mangan's position rather well. J. Cashel Hoey wrote similarly that the poet was "a Pagan in the eyes of the world, but Catholic in soul and sentiment."[11]

After his illness, Mangan found that even books, his old stand-by, could not hold his attention, and this particularly distressed him, especially as it seemed to have an almost sinister significance. Nor had he yet regained sufficient energy to exercise much. About all he could do was take long, leisurely walks into the country around Dublin, and of this activity he wrote, "The sight of hills, fields and streams, to which I had been long unaccustomed, produced in me a certain placidity of mind, with which, had I understood my own true interests for time and eternity, I ought to have remained contented." Often, he found himself in the neighbourhood of Harold's Cross and Roundtown, present-day Terenure, strolling along little streams such as the Dodder. Harold's Cross, Nathaniel Burton was to write a score of years later, had "a proximity to Dublin [that] has not yet effaced that rural character so rarely observable in the vicinity of a large city", and Mangan enjoyed it.[12] Its greatest charm, however, no doubt lay in its proximity to Dolphin's Barn and Rehoboth House.

In the first flush of creativity since 1827, at least as far as can be known with any certainty, Mangan had five poems printed in the last month of 1829 and the first two months of 1830. The first two were originals, "True and False Greatness" and "The Desolation of Pompeii", but three were translations from German, his first time to go before the public with his newly developed talent: "The Two Sorts of Human Glory" (Aloys Blumauer), "[Mignon's] Song from Goethe", and "The New Year's Night of an Unhappy Man" ("Jean Paul" Richter). Two appeared in the new Dublin periodical, *The Friend*, which, in spite of its name, had no connection with the Quakers; it was extinguished after only ten issues. The Goethe poem was Mangan's solitary contribution to the praiseworthy but almost equally short-lived *Dublin Monthly Magazine*. Mangan's *entré* into these columns well may have come about through one of his acquaintances, for it is unlikely that he boldly submitted poems on his own.

It is thought-provoking that the original "True and False Greatness" should so closely have resembled the translated "The Two Sorts of Human Glory" in title and subject, and one wonders which came first. In any event, the latter was the primary entry in his long career as German translator. The two stanzas that follow, the first and last, illustrate, besides his poetic skill, what would prove to be a lifelong penchant for organizing his work by the thematic device of polarization—light/dark, good/evil, and, here, public/personal—no doubt because he saw life in those terms:

THE TWO SORTS OF HUMAN GLORY

Twofold is the greatness men inherit;
    Each is beautiful to human eyes;
Both are woven in the loom of merit;
    Yet how different are the threads and dyes!
One is all in glaring light arrayed,
While the other is relieved by shade.

* * * *

Greatness hailed by harp and acclamation!
Boundless art thou as the vault of heaven;
But to gain thine altitude of station
Unto few of mortal mould is given.
Tranquil greatness! at thy shrine I fall,
Thou alone art in the reach of all.[13]

[2]

> . . . he often repeated Shakespeare's "Clarence is come, false, fleeting, perju'ed Clarence", but when reminded that such designation did not appear on the Baptismal Register of Rosemary Lane Chapel, and that his nurse never frightened him in Fishamble Street with the portentous title—Clarenceux—he treated the whole matter as a very pardonable assumption.
>
> Meehan, "Introduction", *Anthologia Germanica*

It was likewise in *The Friend* that he gave his first hint that he was on the way to adopting a name which would become his permanent literary and personal identity. The 22 December 1829 issue carried a brief note to "I.X.M." in its "Notices and Acknowledgements" column: "To 'I.X.M.' we are very much obliged. His 'Didactic' ["True and False Greatness"] will appear in our next." These three initials, Jacques Chuto has established, refer to James Mangan. Similarly addressed notes appeared in the same column on 29 December, 5 and 19 January 1830, and 2 February 1830. Five poems, five notices. Mangan was, indeed, conducting an active correspondence with the new periodical.[14]

But what did he mean those three initials to stand for? The "M" presents no problem: "Mangan" without a doubt. As for the "I", he almost certainly followed the Latin, in which it is identical with "J", and used it for "James". The "X" is not so easy. As a rule, it stands for an unknown quantity, and he may have intended it to have that meaning, either because he hadn't quite decided on a middle name or because he wanted to suggest a mystery such as "I am unknown" or "James the unknown Mangan". Conceivably, it stood for *ex*, and the whole should be read with Roman numerals: "One of a Thousand". It is likewise just possible that he used it to represent the Greek "Chi" which could be stretched to be "C" in English and thus stand for "Clarence".[15]

At what exact point he settled on this name is not known, but in the "Answers to Correspondents" column of the 4 December 1831 *Comet*, a newspaper which as we will soon see played an important role in his life, appeared this note showing that he had done so by the time he sent something in for publication: "J.C.M. is at the translator's: as soon as it can be decyphered, we will answer his letter."[16] He would use other pseudonyms from time to time, but he never seriously deviated from this choice, and "Clarence" appeared constantly with his poems and also sometimes his prose throughout the eighteen years of his professional career.

This name was so important to him that it has from the start seemed absurd that the reason for his choice should not be known, and yet that has always been and to an extent continues to be the case. Fr Meehan was the first to suggest in print that the poet adopted it from Shakespeare's Duke of Clarence in *Richard III* whose "Clarence is come, false, fleeting, perjured Clarence" speech the poet would sometimes recite.[17] D.J. O'Donoghue repeated the opinion and made it firmer, and he has, without exception, been echoed ever since: "There can be no doubt, from his fancy for repeating to his friends the lines from Shakespeare, 'Clarence is come, false, fleeting, perjured Clarence', that the Duke . . . was a fascinating individuality to Mangan, who had no other reason for adopting his title as a *nom de guerre* . . . ."[18]

Now, late in the day though it may be, another very good—in fact, a better—explanation for Mangan's choice has come to light. Although the evidence for it is purely circumstantial, it has more claim to be acknowledged as the main reason than the rather thin one cited heretofore. It requires a little introduction. In 1849, when he was very ill and surely knew he had not much longer to live, Mangan prepared a series of nine biographical memoirs for the *Irishman* newspaper, each of which dealt with an Irish author or scholar who had influenced or helped him in some important way. Five were of men he had known: Petrie, Anster, Todd, O'Donovan and Meehan. The rest, three men and one woman, he had not known: Charles Maturin, Gerald Griffin, William Maginn, and Maria Edgeworth. It is the one woman, Maria Edgeworth, who concerns us here. She had, he wrote in the article which appeared in the issue of 26 May, "peculiarly influenced" his character when he was a young man. He briefly discussed several of her works, but he singled out one novel, *Belinda*, to illustrate this influence, and he focused on its protagonist, Clarence Hervey. Reading the novel, one discovers a startling resemblance between Clarence Hervey and Clarence Mangan. Edgeworth's hero had, in Mangan's description, a "high intellectual, yet impassioned and tender character". In Edgeworth's novel, he was chameleon-like and "seemed to vary in different lights, and according to the different situations, in which he happened to be placed. He could be all things to all men—and to all women." She wrote at some length:

> Clarence Hervey might have been more than a pleasant young man, if he had not been smitten with the desire of being thought superior in everything, and

> of being the most admired person in all companies. He had been early flattered with the idea that he was a man of genius; and he imagined, that, as such, he was entitled to be imprudent, wild, and eccentric. He affected singularity, in order to establish his claims to genius. He had considerable literary talents, by which he was distinguished at Oxford [Poor Mangan! This opportunity was never open to him.]; but he was so dreadfully afraid of passing for a pedant, that when he came into the company of the idle and the ignorant, he pretended to disdain every species of knowledge.

Poignantly applicable to Mangan was the close of this paragraph: "He was not profligate: he had a strange sense of honour, and quick feelings of humanity; but he was so easily excited by his companions, and his companions were now of such a sort, that it was probable he would soon become vicious."[19]

Fr Meehan and O'Donoghue were not wrong, however, in tracing Mangan's "Clarence" to Shakespeare's character. Just as *Belinda* gets underway, Clarence Hervey enters the room and an amusing parody of the pertinent scene from *Richard III* ensues, for it has not been lost on this Clarence, either, that his name was also the Duke's. A female character begins the exchange:

> "What are you dreaming of, Clarence?—Why looks your grace so heavily today?"
> "Oh I have passed a miserable night," replied Clarence, throwing himself into an actor's attitude, and speaking in a fine tone of stage declamation.
> "What was your dream, my lord, I pray you tell me?" said her ladyship in a similar tone. Clarence went on—
> "Oh lord, methought what pain it was to dance!
> "What dreadful noise of fiddles in my ears!
> "What sights of ugly *belles* within my eyes!
> —"Then came wandering by,
> "A shadow like a devil, with red hair,
> "Dizened with flow'rs; and she bawl'd out aloud,
> "Clarence is come, false, fleeting perjur'd Clarence!"[20]

Just at the time that he was selecting his name, Mangan, as we will soon see, was also struggling with what he presented as the one devastating romance of his life. From the hints that he gave, and I think his reference to *Belinda* can be counted as such a one, we are justified in drawing at least one conclusion about the young woman: that she had reddish or auburn hair. Because we know the end of the story, it is easy to see Mangan as a foolish lover, not cut out to be a drawing room hero, a smooth and clever talker like Clarence Hervey; but he himself did not necessarily know that yet, and his friends did not know it, although Price would look back and say derisively that his friend "was not formed to win the love of woman". Before he retreated into great solitariness, he was to encounter many social situations of varying degrees of discomfort, and more than one woman, although perhaps never another "shadow like a devil, with red hair", would cross his troubled path.

It is a coincidence and of quite a different significance that the one woman in this group of nine individuals he chose to pay a last tribute to bore the name of Maria, and that to her he attributed the source of his adopted name—his life, as it were. While his allegiance to his "revealed religion" appears to have waxed and waned—and then waxed again—his devotion to the Virgin Mary, as to God, was unchanging, and it was at least appropriate that Miss Edgeworth bore her name.

[3]

> Out of the depths have I called to you, O Lord;
> Lord, hear my voice; let your ears consider well
> the voice of my supplication.
> If you, Lord, were to note what is done amiss,
> O Lord, who could stand?
>
> Psalm 130

His melancholy and "placidity of mind" did not last long. In their place came the second phase of his recovery, a sort of nervous agitation during which he desired to be "aroused, excited—shocked even. My grand moral malady—for physical ailments I also had, and singular of their kind—was an impatience of life and its commonplace pursuits." (p. 28) Mangan always disliked the ordinary, so this was nothing very different for him. What was different was the definitive intensity of the feeling. He wrote:

> I wanted to penetrate the great enigma of human destiny and my own—to know "the be-all, and the end-all"—the worst that could happen here or hereafter, the final dénouement of a drama that so strangely united the two extremes of broad farce and thrilling tragedy, and wherein mankind played at once the parts of actors and spectators. (p. 28)

The representative poem of this agitated time is "The Desolation of Pompeii" which was printed in *The Friend* of 12 January 1830. It was a natural choice of subject, as he craved the sensational and now read only books that "treated of the wonderful and terrible in art, nature and society"; books that contained "accounts of earthquakes, inundations and tempests, and narratives of 'moving accidents by flood and field'." The recent excavation of Pompeii, which had been buried for seventeen centuries, had already galvanized the nineteenth-century imagination, as people wondered that so splendid a city, in some ways so like their own thriving towns, could in one horrendous hour have been hidden as it seemed forever from the face of the earth. Bulwer-Lytton only a few years later would produce *The Last Days of Pompeii*, the novel which, although now very dated, is still powerful enough to win a few readers in the late twentieth century and to remain the most concentrated evocation ever written of Pompeii under fire.

In one way, however, his work took a somewhat different approach to the subject. He discovered in Pompeii a potent moral lesson and theological warning along with, not unexpectedly, a personal metaphor for his destroyed ("buried" or "inurned") hopes and dreams. Evil, guilt, and crime darken and suffocate the atmosphere of the poem just as smoke and ash did the city. From the perspective of his development as a poet, "The Desolation of Pompeii" is more significant than has been recognized. For the first time, he used a specific ruin to symbolize his own plight and that of mankind generally. The extremely youthful "Genius: A Fragment" and "What Is Thy Name, Reality?" were cries of personal anguish. By contrast, "The Desolation of Pompeii" showed, for all its somewhat grandiose rhetoric, the effective deployment of an external symbol to represent an interior emotional state as well as to pose a serious question about man's existential condition. Two stanzas follow:

THE DESOLATION OF POMPEII

We shrink within ourselves when Night and Storm
Are darkly mustering; for, to every soul
Heaven here foreshadows character and form
Of Nature's death-hour. Doth the thunder roll,
The wild wave boil, the lightning stream or strike,
Flood, fire, and earthquake devastate, in vain?
Or is there not a voice which peals alike
To all from these, conjuring up that train
Of scenes and images that shall be born
In living, naked might upon the Judgment morn?

* * * *

The desolated cities which of yore
Perished by flooding fire and sulphury rain,
Where sleeps the Dead Sea's immemorial shore,
Lie, blasted wrecks, below that mortar plain.
They fell—thou fellest—but, renounced of Earth,
Blotted from being to eternal years,
Their image chills the life-blood—*thine* gives birth,
Even while we shudder, to some human tears.
Hadst thou less guilt? Who knows? The book of time
Bears on each leaf alike the broad red stamp of crime.[21]

"It was some time," Mangan wrote, "before this feeling [of unwholesome excitement] merged altogether into another—the sentiment of religion and its ineffable mysteries." To this almost obsessive phase, he devoted the remainder of Chapter Four of his autobiography, relating the progress of what now appears to be a spiritual odyssey. First came an overwhelming sense of awe at the majesty and mystery of God, then the onset of addiction to "ascetic practices" when he studied "the lives of the saints with the profoundest admiration".

This phase ended in the onset of the frightening doubt that he himself had any "capacity for salvation", that is, that he could be saved, although he did not question "the great truths of faith". With this doubt grew a dread that he had perhaps been "created expressly for unhappiness". Beset by anxiety, he became inordinately assiduous in his attendance at Mass and confession. None of it helped. "Scruples of conscience . . . multiplied upon me in such numbers in the intervals between each of my confessions that my mind became a chaos of horrors, and all the fire of Pandemonium seemed to burn in my brain." (p. 29) Logically enough, he turned for help to "several clergymen", probably priests at SS Michael and John. But their remedies were disappointing. "Most recommended me to mix in cheerful and gay society", he wrote. "One alone, I remember, counselled me to pray. And pray I did, for I had so held myself aloof from the companionship of others that I knew of no society with which I could mix." (p. 29)

[4]

> Distrust nine girls in ten who instead of talking to you on a first introduction listen with apparent deference to all that your foolish tongue utters to them.
>
> Mangan, *A Sixty-Drop Dose of Laudanum*, Drop Twenty-Eight

He continued in this appalling frame of mind for "about a twelvemonth". It was a "deplorable interior state; one which worlds and diadems should not bribe me into experiencing again." What had caused it? As he wrote to his editor McGlashan, "My existence was miserable. I often longed for death. Death, however, came not; but in its place came something worse than Death—Love." [22] Thus the year when he was in love was the worst time of his spiritual suffering. The impersonal autobiography gives more detail:

> From habits of prayer and fasting, and the study of the Lives of the Saints, Mangan was at one period of his mysterious life drawn away, and enticed into the snare of Love and was even within an aim's ace of becoming a Benedict. But certain strange circumstances—the occurrence of which he has described

to me as having been foreshadowed to him in a dream—interposed their ungallant proportions between the lady and him; and so he abode a Maledict, and Hymen despatched Cupid and Plutus to look for somebody else.[23]

The name of the young woman who took his mind off the saints and turned it to herself is unknown—nor do we know what her feelings in the matter may have been, nor even how she came to be acquainted with James Clarence Mangan. Yet there was no more traumatic event in the poet's adult life than this first encounter with Love with a capital "L". In the poems and prose that appear to refer to this experience, she has been called Frances, Laura, Eleanor, and perhaps Caroline. The young William Butler Yeats believed, erroneously, that he had discovered who she was through the aid of Charles Gavan Duffy, and identified her as Margaret Stackpoole.[24] (Yeats was also the source of a wild story, which was told to him, that Mangan, with dagger raised, attacked a man who dared to insult his "Frances".)

Likewise full of error was the most influential of the stories of "Mangan's one love" told by John Mitchel who declared that Mangan had loved a girl, "beautiful, *spirituelle*, and a coquette" but that she "whistled him down the wind".[25] This dramatically narrated account became the basis for all subsequent histories. Mitchel had received most of the information from Duffy who was misled, though probably not intentionally, by Mangan himself; then, according to Duffy, Mitchel went on to embellish the story outrageously.[26] As we shall see later, the poet happily introduced Duffy to the above-mentioned Margaret and her family about 1837. Thereby, not surprisingly, hangs a tale, but not a tale in any way related to this first excruciatingly painful romance about which Mangan appears to have told Duffy nothing at all. The whole episode left our poet feeling soiled and stupid—and badly disillusioned about the most beautiful possibility of life. Not surprisingly, the greatest spiritual anguish he described—and again, we can do no better than to take him at his word about this sort of thing—came *after* his absorption in the lives of the saints, and corresponded with the period during which the young woman gave him, as it seemed to him, "every encouragement", and during which he did indeed feel himself to be in love with her, after which she jilted him and thus left him emotionally damaged.[27]

If we co-ordinate what little is known about the chronology of these months in Mangan's life, we arrive at late 1829 or early 1830 as the most probable time for him to have met the destroyer of his tranquillity, and late summer or autumn of the latter year as the most likely time for the romance to have ended although his anguish and anger continued until 1831 or even 1832. Margaret Stackpoole at this time was a little girl only eleven years old, she and her twin sister Eliza having been born in 1819.

Moreover, the girls' widowed mother, Susanna, probably had not yet moved her family to Dublin from the family enclave near Ennis and thus we can, and indeed have to, rule out the possibility that Margaret was the woman who broke Mangan's heart.[28] Similarly we have already eliminated Catherine Hayes as the possible *femme fatale*, although the poet's friendship with the family and his fond relationship with her made a striking, and perhaps emotionally confusing, counterpoint to the stirring events in his "other" life. The poems of the time may have been inspired by either relationship—all, that is, except the Blumauer translation which belonged specifically to Catherine.

What information we have about the affair is little enough, and there is no identification of the young woman at all, but rather a mixture of Price on Mangan and a little bit of Mangan on Mangan. For his part, Price felt assured that this love affair had ended before he and the poet met, in 1831 or early 1832, and made it especially clear that it was over before Catherine's death in October 1832. It had been "a love fresh, pure, fervent, and beautiful as ever lighted passion's flame in human bosom", he rhapsodized. It had collapsed, however. It had been "sported and trifled with, its jealous agony derided, and its first rapturous declaration chilled by cruel and bitter scorn." Price liked to give his prose a good, high colour, and he was a connoisseur of shattered romances, but he seems to have had authentic early memories of the poet which, because he was an excellent observer, are probably fairly accurate. He also quoted in his memoir several snippets from Mangan's letters which he had obtained from the editor James McGlashan who may have asked Mangan to provide information for a biographical memoir for the poet's *Anthologia Germanica*, published in 1845. However, nothing of the sort appeared in those volumes. In any case, Mangan continued the aforementioned letter:

> . . . I formed an attachment to a young lady who gave me every encouragement for some months, and then appeared to take a great delight in exciting me to jealousy. One evening, I well remember it, she openly slighted me, and shunned me . * * * * I escaped from marriage with this girl, but it was at the expense of my health and peace of mind.[29]

An error of Mangan's memoirists, following John Mitchel, has been to accept his dramatic claim that after this romance Mangan "never loved, and hardly looked upon any woman forever more." This was entirely untrue, as we will see. A lot of years lay between 1831 and Mitchel's first acquaintance with Mangan who even learned a certain amount of caution, it would seem, although what Price had to say about his nature remained no less true:

> He was not formed to win the love of woman. Though never did living man possess a soul more generous or truthful in its impulses, more fond, more trusting—more womanly in its gentleness, Clarence had not "those soft parts of conversation that chamberers have," and acutely and keenly, according to his most sensitive nature, must he have felt this, when rejected perhaps for one over whom his intellect lifted him as loftily as the starry heavens above the dull earth.[30]

Not until a year-and-a-half later did the poet write anything about his disappointment in love, nor would he have been expected to bare even a small part of his soul very readily. There are five poems, however, that are usually taken as expressions of his feelings, from the immediacy of anger and hurt to a sort of generalized malaise and loss of trust. "To xxxxxxx xxxxxxx", in later publications titled either "To Frances" or "To Laura", appeared earliest, in a December 1832 number of the paper for which he was now writing, the anti-tithe *Comet* (about which more in due course). The second and third, in the same publication three months later, either were supposed to be about the ex-sweetheart, "Caroline B.", of his new friend James Price, or were disguised to appear to be about her, for they bore the title "Very Interesting Sonnets: To Caroline". The fourth and fifth were summer poems in 1833, even their titles suggesting that at least a simulacrum of emotional distance had been established between the searing event and the poet. "Broken Hearted Lays: Number One" (there was never a "Number Two") and "Life is the Desert and the Solitude" marked the close of this short series.

It is noteworthy that "To xxxxxxx xxxxxxx" was the first poem Mangan signed "Clarence" as well as his first attempt to write about the violence done his heart. "The charm that gilded life is over;/I live to feel I live in vain"—later he would alter that rather poor opening line to "The life of life is gone and over"—began the first of twelve quatrains. The beginning and the ending verses overflow with tenderness, but the central stanzas are filled with angry pain:

> Oh! cold and cruel she who, while
> She lavishes all wiles to win
> Her lover o'er, can smile and smile,
> Yet be all dark and false within!

A little of the fault seems to be shifted, perhaps unintentionally, to the poet-lover himself:

> Who, when his glances on another
> Too idly and too long have dwelt,
> Can sigh, as though she strove to smother
> The grief her bosom never felt!
> * * * *

Alas! and can this treachery be?
  The worm that winds in slime along
Is less contemptible than she
  Who revels in such heartless wrong!

The "very interesting sonnets" addressed "To Caroline" which the *Comet* printed in February 1833 were a different matter. As I mentioned, they either were written about James Price's one-time girlfriend Caroline or were meant to appear so. Readers of the *Comet* were familiar with Price's flamboyant style and back in the summer of 1832 had read the mildly risque, but amusing, story of his love affair at the age of fifteen with the twenty-year-old "Caroline B." The regular feature in which he narrated all sorts of tales about himself Price called "My Recollections". Although popular, it was also a prime target for parody, and even Mangan, as we will see later on, tried his hand at making fun of his friend's writing. An August number of the *Comet* had carried "My Own Early Love", said by Price to be his account of his first romance. Born in 1813, he was only eighteen when he wrote it, but he adopted an experienced tone, as if what he had to tell had occurred many years in the past. "Caroline was small and lovely with auburn hair and large, soft dark eyes", he wrote. Although she was twenty years old and he was only fifteen (making the year 1828) things seemed to go well with them until one evening when he appeared at her house and found her "on the very sofa where I used to recline with her, leaning on the breast of a stranger." Later, she married the other man, and Price went on to further romantic adventures; but, he swore, he never loved another woman with quite the same "pure unalloyed affection" he had felt for "Caroline B." Mangan began the first of his sonnets "To Caroline":

Have I not called thee angel-like and fair?
    What wouldst thou more? 'Twere perilous to gaze
    Long on those dark bright eyes whose flashing rays
  Fill with a soft and fond, yet proud, despair
  The bosoms of the shrouded few, who share
      Their locked-up thoughts with none . . .

The second poem continued his personal musings but extended the suffering of the poet to describe the worst injury that his sweetheart had done him: stealing from him his dream that mutual love was a genuine possibility, to leave him lost of heart and bereft of hope. It seems entirely possible that, when it came to writing their stories, Price appropriated something from Mangan and Mangan appropriated something from Price. In any case, auburn hair is a constant.

The two further love poems published in the summer of 1833 reflected the receding of the event into a mercifully more distant past. "Broken-

Hearted Lays. Number One" was the first of those poems he has been accused of "spoiling" with an ending inconsistent with the previously established tone. The first thirty-six lines were impassioned and high-flown, and listed a stunning number of profound griefs that marked "one desert epoch in the history of the heart . . ."

> . . . when the upbroken dreams of boyhood's span,
> And when the inanity of all things human,
> And when the dark ingratitude of man,
> And when the hollower perfidy of woman,
> Come down like night upon the feelings, turning
> This rich, bright world, so redolent of bloom,
> Into a lazar-house of tears and mourning—
> Into the semblance of a living tomb!

For Mangan, the sustained expression of absolute despair was exceptional. Perhaps it hurt too much. Or perhaps, as I believe, there was always on the alert in him an ironic counsellor who sharply advised, "Oh, come now, nothing's quite that bad!" O'Donoghue strongly disapproved of the poet's putting a twist on the tail of a poem, and he lopped off the last lines when he included this poem in his centenary collection. They were, however, pure early Mangan as well as being a necessity of the poem's structure and may be read in Chapter 7, "With Genius Wasted". O'Donoghue's "version" ended thus:

> When, yielding to the might she cannot master,
> The soul forsakes her palace halls of youth, . . .
> And brooding in her cold and desolate lair
> Over the phantom-wreck of things that were,
> And asking destiny if nought remain?
> Is answered—bitterness and life-long pain,
> Remembrance, and reflection, and despair,
> And torturing thoughts that will not be forbidden,
> And agonies that cannot all be hidden!

By the time he wrote "Life is the Desert and the Solitude", Mangan was expressing a more general melancholy assessment of life and only hinted at personal griefs that had brought him to such a pass. He loved the month of June, its warmth and its agreeable languor, and the poem opened "It is the joyous time of June", when "All is as gorgeous and as grand/As the creations wherewith teems/The poet's haunted brain amid his noonday dreams." Yet, it was not for him, all this joy and beauty:

> Affliction is my doom and dower;
> And cares, in many a darkening throng,
> Like night-clouds round a ruin, lour
> Over a soul which (never strong
> To stem the tide of ill) will not resist them long.

The last stanza presented a sombre picture indeed. The major difference between the handling of this poem and "Broken-Hearted Lays: Number One" was that he sustained the feeling in "Life is the Desert and the Solitude", building to this final scene which climaxed a strong but not over-stated commitment to his theme:

> Alas! for those who stand alone—
>   The shrouded few who feel and know
> What none beside have felt and known.
>   To all of such a mould below
> Is born an undeparting woe,
>   Beheld by none and shared with none—
> A cankering worm whose work is slow,
>   But gnaws the heart-strings one by one,
>   And drains the bosom's blood till the last drop be gone.

At the end of the discussion of Mangan's (possible) *Morning Register* poems I said that there were two, "Beauty Vanished" and "Song", which belonged to the 1830 period of his life and which would be mentioned at that time. They were, indeed, poems of "melting love". The first appeared in the 9 June number of the paper, the second in that of 29 September. Neither was signed. Perhaps he wrote them, perhaps he didn't. If he did, they are obviously of great importance, being the only expression we have of the poet in love, albeit a love nearing its end. If he didn't, they are at least not very long and will take up little of the reader's time, and both may be found in full in the Appendix.

The most intriguing piece of writing Mangan did that may possibly have been on the subject of his romance was not poetry at all, but prose satire. "My Transformation: A Wonderful Tale" appeared in the autumn of 1833 in the new rival to the *Comet*, a newspaper called the *Dublin Satirist*. In this personal essay Mangan mocked Price's writing style, which had now become something of a joke, by retelling, with wild variations and additions of his own, the previously noted story of "My Own Early Love". It is "My Transformation" which up until now has been taken as wholly or at least as partially autobiographical—as Mangan's personal narrative of his romantic fiasco. O'Donoghue actually believed that "the serious part of the sketch may be thoroughly relied upon" because "Price asserts its truth". But O'Donoghue's trust was ill-placed. He evidently knew about neither Price's "My Own Early Love" nor that by 1833 Price and Mangan were on opposite journalistic sides, with Price being attacked in the *Satirist* as "a silly, sentimental wight", self-preoccupied and vain.[31] Eventually Price would make his peace with the *Satirist* and write a cruel but hilarious spoof about a poet, "Adolphus Softbotham", with a deep thirst and an unrequited love, almost certainly getting back at Mangan.

If not the story, many of the serious feelings expressed in "My Transformation" were no doubt derived authentically from Mangan's experiences.[32] But the date Mangan placed on the start of the love story is a main pointer to its being founded on Price's: "I saw Eleanor Campion for the first time in the autumn of 1828", he wrote, and Price, it will be recalled, placed his "early love" in this same year. Eleanor was "a model of all that is witching and winning in women." So had been "Caroline B." A detail that Mangan added has often been taken as his revelation of the source of several references made later to a "false friend" or to betrayal by a friend: After a while, he confessed, he introduced his lovely Eleanor to his life-long friend, Lionel Delamaine, and to his horror, within a fortnight, Eleanor abandoned her lover for his friend. Again, Price's romance had had a similar dénouement. Mangan describes his pain as a rejected suitor:

> I had drunk deeply of the waters of bitterness, and my every sense was still saturated with the flavour of the accursed wave. There was a down-dragging weight upon my faculties—I felt myself gradually growing into the clay I stood upon and almost sighed for the advent of the night that should see my head pillowed upon the green and quiet mould below me.

We find here one of the earliest published instances of a stylistic (or psychological) idiosyncrasy of the poet, the use of the image of a person's growing into something lifeless, hard, and often cold. He was to employ it in regard to the desk upon which he had to work as a youth, and in his writings numerous allusions are made to warm bodies transformed in whole or in part into statutes of wood or stone. It was an apt metaphor for emotional paralysis or perhaps for death, and it is fair to ask what state of mind would inspire such frequent usage.

Before recovery and his "transformation", Mangan's tale continues, many months of anguish passed during which he became a half-crazed creature stalking the sea-battered cliffs: "His dreams were peopled with the most horrible and hideous and misbegotten *spectra* that ever rioted in the desolated chambers of a madman's brain." He saw almost no one. In the following paragraphs, fact and outrageous fiction inter-mingle:

> Few and rare were the visitors who speckled my solitude. I had voluntarily broken the magnetic bonds which united man with man in socialised being. Whenever I happened to be addressed, either at home or abroad, I generally answered by the briefest of monosyllables in our langauge; sometimes, indeed, merely by a groan, and occasionally by a peculiar howl, half human, half canine, such as may be supposed to proceed from the throat of an individual under the spell of lycanthropy.

The house in which he dwelt after returning to Dublin sounds real enough and most likely was one known to Mangan, if it was not one he actually lived in. It was

> in a remote and isolated quarter of the city. Solitary, silent, and prison-like, it was nevertheless a dwelling I would not have forsaken for the most brilliant pleasure-dome under the Italian heaven. To the rere of the house extended a long and narrow courtyard, partly overgrown with grass and melancholy-looking wild flowers, but flagged at the extremity, and bounded by a colossal wall. Down the entire length of this wall, which was connected with a ruined old building, descended a metal rain-spout; and I derived a diseased gratification in listening in wet weather, to the cold, bleak, heavy plash, plash, plash of the rain, as it fell from this spout to the flag beneath.

One passage near the end of the essay shows his spirits fallen about as low as they could get:

> This human world had died to me; the lights and shadows of life's pictures had long since been blended into one chaos of dense and inextinguishable blackness; the pilgrimage of my blank years pointed across a desart [*sic*] where flower or green thing was forbidden to live; and it mattered not how soon some shifting column of the sands descended and swept me into its bosom. Thereafter darkness would swathe my memory forever; not one poor sigh would be expended for me; no hands would care to gather mine unremembered ashes into the sanctuary of an urn.

Mangan frequently uses a landscape with ruins, a desert landscape as here, or a frozen scene as in the late poem "Siberia" to express an emotional state of paralysis and emptiness terrifying to live through.

Another touch that was characteristic, although no one would insist that its zany details were factual, was the attention he called to the changes in his habits of eating and drinking: instead of his usual pattern, he now ate only one day in seven, he claimed, and he smoked steadily through the other six. As for drinking, he had become a teetotaller, drinking two gallons of water daily to keep his salivary glands from drying up and his body from further withering. Nothing was in its normal state. Whether he stood out "under the starless firmamental cope" longing "personally to track the career of the lightning", or, with a nod to the ridiculous, leapt from his window into the street below while speaking only in the groans and howls of a werewolf, he was utterly changed.

Anyone with an ounce of skepticism should decline to take very much (if any) of this literally. The poet exaggerated for a number of reasons in quite a lot of his prose and poetry: for humour; for emphasis; for the enjoyment of it; and for the attention he received from entertaining and outraging readers in a mild, not very risky way. He would, in fact, become increasingly a man of extremes, and a cause of both anxiety and puzzled fascination to his friends; after all, exaggeration is one thing and being "over the top" is something else altogether. It could be argued, though not proven, that the tendency toward absurd exaggeration was a symptom of a disturbed mental state. For a recent evaluation of Mangan's behaviour, the reader may be interested in consulting Kay Redfield Jamison's study, *Touched With Fire: Manic-Depressive Illness and the Artistic Temperament* (1993), of which a few paragraphs appear in Appendix C.

Interestingly, the steps in the development of the story of "My Transformation" are very similar to the steps in Mangan's autobiographical story of recovery from illness. That is, he shows the lover—himself, in the context of the yarn—first passing from extreme melancholy to an attraction to everything violent in nature. After this change, he relates how he seeks out a spot by the sea in Monkstown, creating an amusing pun, if that is what it should be called, on the religiously zealous phase of his recovery. And, finally, he describes his joy when he finds a miraculous remedy for his "blue devils" (depression here, not hallucinations or *delirium tremens*) in reading the new *Dublin Satirist* and becomes "the laugher of civilized society . . . grinner-general to the public at large". By a similar progression he finally finds relief in mixing with society, as the fourth chapter of the *Autobiography* closes.

Ostensibly, the sketch had been written to illustrate the wonderful change wrought in the almost-destroyed lover by picking up a single copy of the new *Satirist*, thus puffing the newspaper. He had wrapped up that task neatly while making fun of Price and ventilating his own lingering sense of having been wronged in love. If the veracity of details, whether in the *Autobiography*, the impersonal autobiography, or "My Transformation: A Wonderful Tale", must be suspected, all three documents agree in their revelation of a period deeply disturbing to Mangan, and of events terminating in loss of trust, not only in "love" but to some extent in religion—at least as he had known it. The linkage between physical illness and emotional distress merely repeats a pattern established much earlier in his life—not once, but a number of times.

With these last pages, we have moved rather far ahead of the history, but his love story and its aftermath consumed the best part of two or three years. It was not, however, all that was going on in the poet's life at this crucial period, and we will return now to about 1830 and see what else filled his nights and days.

6

Sublime or Vapid

[1]

> Fitzwilliam Square: This beautiful little square is at the south side of the city, not far from [Merrion Sq.]. The interior (which is enclosed by an iron railing, resting on a dwarf wall, and ornamented by lamp-supporters at equal intervals, is laid out in shrubberies and flower-plats, and is below the level of the street, consequently the foot-passenger has a perfect view of the whole garden at one glance. The houses here are not so large as those in Merrion-square, but remarkably well finished, and produce a large rent.
>
> G.N. Wright, *An Historical Guide to the City of Dublin*, 1825

It is unlikely that Mangan stayed unemployed later than the autumn of 1829; all practical considerations are against it. His next job apparently caused him no discomfort, for he made no complaint about the office of the solicitor Thomas Leland at No. 6 Fitzwilliam Square West and remained in that situation at least until the mid-1830s and possibly as late as 1838. While there he earned the salary that "rarely amounted to thirty shillings weekly", but which was nevertheless "still sufficient for his inexpensive and unpretending habits".[1] In any case, he had now finished with the ten or eleven years he designated as the period he worked to support his family.

The square to which he walked each day may have been pleasanter than Merrion Square, as well as smaller and somewhat closer to Charlemont Street where the family was now living. If he went out their front door and turned left along the Grand Canal, a short stroll would take him to his office. Away to the south, over his right shoulder, he would have been able to see the Dublin mountains, which had until recently been in splendid view from the square itself, new construction having only recently blocked that prospect. There was every reason why things should have gone well, and in a sense, they did. The successes he enjoyed, and the friends and acquaintances he made over the next few years, were impressive.

Towards the close of 1830 his life was set to take a new and different turn altogether. The 1 January 1831 number of the *Morning Register* carried the notice: "We, the undersigned, request a Meeting of the Law Clerks of the City of Dublin on Monday, the 3rd of January next . . . to take into consideration the propriety of petitioning both Houses of

Parliament for a Repeal of the Legislative Union between Great Britain and Ireland." Among the dozens of signatories of this notice were James Mangan, John Mangan, and James Tighe, and the obvious conclusion is probably correct, that the names were those of the poet, his brother, and his friend. The 4 January issue of the paper reported the meeting which was attended by some 5,000 men in the Arena on Lower Abbey Street. Tighe was one of several who spoke, his message being the optimistic assessment that "the Orangemen were with them, and should remain with them forever."[2] Apparently Mangan went as an observer, but his presence is highly significant, his first public expression, perhaps, of belief in an Irish political identity. His commitment to the cause of Ireland has so often been underestimated—with the emphasis going instead on his attraction to the romanticism and excitement of republicanism—that it is well to know that virtually from the start he exhibited concern for his country's nationhood.

All across Europe revolutions and rebellions had marked 1830, and, as E.J. Hobsbawm has written, "Even Britain was affected, thanks in part to the threatened eruption of its local volcano Ireland."[3] One of the most obvious colonial abuses by Britain was the tithe, a system of taxation by which Catholics and particularly Catholic peasants had to support the clergy of the Church of Ireland, a Protestant institution. The first organized protests now got underway. In 1830, a group of a dozen men in Dublin founded an organization they called the Political Tract Society for the purpose of publishing tracts and pamphlets opposing the tithe and inciting people to rebel against paying it. Perhaps because the name was so dull and might be taken to refer to Protestant biblical sects, it was soon changed to the "Comet Literary and Patriotic Club", a happy choice possibly inspired by the expected return of Halley's comet in 1834. There is no reliable evidence that the poet was associated with the group at this early stage, although John Sheehan, a main founder, placed Mangan's name among the original twelve members.[4]

At eighteen, Sheehan was the youngest member of the Comet Club, and he seems to have been Mangan's closest associate in the group for the first year. In his article about the enterprise written years later for the *Gentleman's Magazine*, he called the founders a band of "merry youngsters", but in fact they were not all very young by any means. The co-editor, Thomas Browne, was forty, but the eldest was Daniel O'Connell's cousin Dominick Ronayne, who already had twice been a member of Parliament. A rather surprising member, Samuel Lover, was over thirty. Painter, novelist, and member of the Royal Hibernian Academy, he necessarily kept his participation in the Club a dead secret. Also thirty years old were George Dunbar and Norreys Jephson, a former MP from

Mallow. Maurice O'Connell, the Liberator's gifted son, was twenty-nine. Besides Mangan, two other members, the dramatist Sterling Coyne and the bookseller Thomas Kennedy, were twenty-eight. John O'Callaghan, soon-to-be author of *The Green Book*, was twenty-six, while the age of the last of the original members, Robert Knox, has gone unrecorded. In short, they were not just lads out for a lark, nor a rag-tag and bob-tail band of troublemakers, but reputable men with a purpose.

According to Sheehan, the "extremely liberal Protestants" among them were Browne, Lover, Knox, Coyne, and Dunbar. With Sheehan himself, the Catholic members were Mangan, Ronayne, Jephson, O'Connell, Kennedy, and O'Callaghan. Editor Sheehan described the poet's religion at this time as "undemonstrative and doubtful", and he added that Mangan said it "would be the foulest judicial murder . . . to make him drink of the poisoned cup for an over-jealous love or hatred of any of the Churches". Years later, McCall was to take umbrage at these remarks, but knowing what we do about the poet's frustration with the clergy, they probably reflect his sentiments accurately enough.[5] These men, along with James Price and Joseph L'Estrange, who joined the Club early in 1832, were to be Mangan's closest associates for the next two or three years.

The poet's introduction to this group has never been fully explained. W.H. Grattan Flood has opined that he became acquainted with Charles Lever and this "led to an introduction to Lover" and thence to the rest of the Cometeers.[6] At the time, it is true, Lever was in trouble with the proprietors of the *Dublin Literary Gazette* (erstwhile the *National Magazine*), of which he was editor, for accepting a too-approving article on Shelley's poetry, and he may well have been in a mood to associate himself with political radicals.[7] There was a streak of self-protective caution in his make-up, however, and, as far as is known, he steered clear of joining this group or contributing to its publications.

The Comet Club launched itself into the world of political journalism in 1831, not with its newspaper the *Comet*, which would not come on the scene until May, but with a couple of diabolically clever little books filled with raw, satirical fun and some direct attacks on selected targets, much in the eighteenth-century tradition of Jonathan Swift. *The Parson's Horn-Book* and *The Valentine Post Bag* appeared in January and February, the *Horn-Book* being announced enthusiastically in the *Morning Register* of 20 January: "This day is published, price in boards and glazed calico, 5s; in watered silk, gilt and lettered, superfine paper, and Proof Etchings, 7s 6d, to be had at *the Comet Office*, No. 10 D'Olier Street, *The Parson's Horn-Book*!!!" In spite of the high price, it was an almost immediate sell-out. The "Proof Etchings" were by Lover, and they alone made the book a delight. Its 129 pages contained twenty-four items—poems, sketches, prose—targeting the Established Church (with a few blasts at Dissenters and Roman Catholics) and its greed, immorality, and general corruption. Parsons and bishops took a drubbing. From "The Churchman's Alphabet" through "The Parable of the Rich Shepherd" and " 'Simony Hall'; or Strange Doings in Foreign Parts", one sharp blow followed another.[8] The *Valentine Post Bag Containing Letters to Public Characters* was cast in the epistolary form and lent itself to obvious personal attacks on individuals, the rock upon which the Comet Club would eventually split apart. For the time being, however, the technique succeeded, and the first thousand copies were quickly sold at half-a-crown apiece.

Almost every newspaper in Dublin had strong remarks to make about the *Parson's Horn-Book*. "The most biting and caustic satirical Volume against the temporalities of the Established Church, that ever issued from the press" said the *Morning Register*; and the *Pilot*, the mouthpiece of the O'Connell forces, followed suit: "The most important and deadly stab at the incubus of Ireland, the tithe system and religious taxation". On the other side of the issue, the *Evening Packet* did not mince words, finding the publication "stupid" and "blasphemous", while hinting darkly that Browne and Sheehan would live to regret issuing any second volume. And *Saunders' News-Letter* suspected that "there is evidently a conspiracy formed against the Established Church" because "the engravings [are] so fine and the writing so good" that without funding from some wealthy source, the price would have had to be twice as high as was the case.

A third book in this series was planned, the title to be *Robin Hood and Little John; or, Exercises in Archery, by the Marksmen of the Comet Literary Club*. However, it seems to have come to nothing, or perhaps its purpose was fulfilled by the issuance of *The Parson's Horn-Book, Part II*, around mid-summer. Mangan's first appearance in print as a Cometeer came in this book. Sheehan's listing of his name among those of the earliest members of the Comet Literary and Patriotic Club notwithstanding, his introduction to the group probably came about as he described it in the *Autobiography*, a story to be taken up shortly. For the publication he adapted his "New-Year's Night of an Unhappy Man", retitling it "The Young Parson's Dream" and substituting "Bishop" and "Parson" for "old man" and "young man".[9] The success of the second part of the Horn-Book was comparable, if not quite equal, to that of the first part.

The gentlemen of the Comet Club had now conceived of a more ambitious venture—a full-fledged newspaper. Launched in May, the weekly *Comet* would run for a total of 136 issues, and in its pages Mangan would become a professional author, albeit he seems not to have been paid a penny for his work. Not many Irishmen would have argued by the spring of 1831 that tithes were fair or just, and the *Comet's* first rule was: *Attack*.

However, its agenda went well beyond simple opposition, and Mangan probably agreed with its statement of position which echoed some of the things he himself had been saying:

> We hold that every man should enjoy freedom of conscience and liberty to practice and profess any and what faith he pleases, exempt from any religious tax but that which is voluntary. We hold that no man, nor body of men should be encouraged or permitted by the State to exact payment for the support of the teachers of one creed from the professors of another creed. . . . And last, though not least, we hold that the Gospels, not only by precept, but by example, show that pure Christianity is a religion of charity, poverty, meekness and humility; while Bishops and Parsons, by their greediness and rapacity made the Established Church appear to be, as at present constituted and supported, a church of arrogant selfishness, insatiable wealth, unbounded assumption and heartless pride.[10]

The first number of the newspaper appeared on 1 May 1831, which, coincidentally, was Mangan's twenty-eighth birthday. Published for a while from No. 10 D'Olier Street, its office would soon be moved to No. 2 Church Lane, adjacent to the members' favourite watering hole—no doubt a great convenience for all concerned—Henry Howard's Tavern. In fact, a son of the house, Alfred Howard, was apparently the wit who wrote as "Paddy Kelly" and had his own newspaper, *Paddy Kelly's Budget*, a few years later, although Dr Crone in his *Dictionary of Irish Biography* awards that place to Sterling Coyne. The eight pages of the *Comet* began, as was usual, with a first page of commercial announcements and advertisements. Much of what was to be found on the second and third pages could be described as news, or history, seen from the *Comet's* own distinctive angle. The fourth and fifth pages were similar, but here the political nature of the newspaper became more apparent. Bits of politically inspired verse were printed throughout while the "Poet's Corner" always appeared on an inside page. So, too, did the gossip columns such as "The World of Fashion", and the scurrilous articles of often heavy-handed satire that pointed up the multiple failings of the Establishment in its various manifestations. The lack of printer's errors would make it the envy of any paper today. All in all, it aspired to be informative, entertaining, and readable: "Our object is to give to the public the ordinary news of the times in the most condensed form; and Parliamentary Debates so compressed as to exclude the verbiage and vain nothingness of long-winded speakers."

Although the tone of the group and their publication was obvious, it was not immediately apparent how uproarious the din around them was going to become. From the start, though, a dangerous amount of emphasis was placed on personalities, and the attacks in print show just how rarely any of the writers worried about libel. It was not unusual for an insulted "father, brother, or lover, stung by some satirical paragraphs . . . to be seen hurriedly entering the office in Church Lane flourishing . . . his good stout cane or horsewhip about him" to lay into Sheehan or some other Cometeer. Street assaults and duels could also sometimes be traced to *Comet* remarks, and "several delicate points of honour arising out of these political satires, had to be decided by pistols in the Phoenix Park. . . ." Occasionally, at night, "when least expected—for some pretended insult given to the old Alma Mater over the way, a shower of stones from the Trinity College boys would smash every pane of glass in the Comet office windows."[11] Add to this atmosphere of continuous confrontation, the nature of the men themselves—McCall described them as "exquisite, refined, irreligious, riotous, champagne-loving, bullying roysterers"—and it can be seen that Mangan had now got himself into a milieu that was almost bound to be terribly destructive for him. With these men he tried to make common cause—and lived to regret it. "They tried to corrupt him, and failed . . ." he declared in the impersonal autobiography. And "when he attended at their drinking bouts, [he] always sat at the table with a glass of water before him". No doubt, one may be forgiven for observing skeptically, but what beverage besides? He complained bitterly at the way he was treated—"at length [they] laughed him to scorn"—and blamed his efforts to be accepted as one of the "merry youngsters" for the start of his "enslavement" to alcohol.

[2]

> On the south side of the city of Dublin, and about half-way down an avenue which breaks the continuity of that part of the Circular Road extending from Harold's Cross to Dolphin's Barn, stands a house, plain in appearance, and without any peculiarity of external structure to attract the passenger's notice. Adjoining the house is a garden, with a sort of turret-lodge at the extreme end, which looks forth on the high road. The situation is lone and unpicturesque . . . .
>
> *Autobiography*, p. 31

On a sunny day in June 1831, the poet took what would turn out to be a fateful walk, although it began like any other of his customary rambles. According to the fifth chapter of his autobiography, his desultory way led him past Rathfarnham and back toward Roundtown, present-day Terenure. When he grew tired on such excursions, his habit was to rest by a hedge-side or on a field-hillock, and on this particular day, he stretched himself out on a long knoll of grass by the side of a stream, probably the Dodder, and began reading the book he had brought with him, Pascal's

Pensées. No sooner had he got comfortable than he was startled by the approach of a young man whom he had occasionally seen before, "sauntering about this neighbourhood", but whom he had never directly encountered. He does not name this individual but the youth's appearance and behaviour suggest that it could have been young John Sheehan.[12] There is no description of Sheehan at eighteen, when he was busily founding the Comet Club and its newspaper, but he used the pen-name "Philander" and enjoyed the reputation of being quite a sharp-tongued wit and man-about-town. He came from a good family, and his refined breeding and manners often got him out of tight spots that his radical political views got him into. He was said to be about 5'10" tall, and, at forty, well-built, clean-shaven, with a ruddy complexion and twinkling eyes. Wearing a "large shirt collar, black tie or stock, dark claret frock coat" buttoned up, and walking "with a deliberate stride, . . . keeping time with each stride. No stick or umbrella, the hands gloved", he appeared "altogether well made up" and looked like "a well taken care of parish priest".[13] If we imagine him twenty years younger, approaching the carelessly dressed Mangan lounging on the stream-side, his loose blond hair falling across his forehead as he bent over his book, the contrast is striking. Mangan called the young man "fashionably dressed and intelligent looking", and he was obviously not shy, for he did not hesitate to open the conversation with a question: "May I ask the nature of your studies?" Mangan thereupon wordlessly handed him the book to see for himself. When the stranger returned it, also without a word, the poet asked him, "You don't read French?" "Oh yes, I do. Who does not now-a-days?" he responded, telling us a good bit about both of them. He went on, "But that is a very unhealthy work."

Aware that argument "hardly ever converts or convinces", and that "a great gulf" divided the two of them philosophically, Mangan answered "indifferently" that, "Everything in this world is unhealthy". Smiling, the young man demurred. "And yet, you feel pleasure, I am sure, in the contemplation of this beautiful scenery; and you admire the glory of the setting sun." The sanguine response drew a sharp reaction from the poet. "I have pleasure in nothing, and I admire nothing. I hate scenery and suns. I see nothing in Creation but what is fallen and ruined." This was not far from the feeling he had expressed earlier in some of his verses. For all its brevity, it captures the essence of depression, or melancholy, as Mangan would have said. Here spoke the voice of negation, the Spirit of Denial, and hence, in theological terms, of evil. In a commonly accepted understanding, loss of hope signifies loss of faith in God's saving grace. Thus according to his religion, Mangan's dread that he was not "a fit candidate for salvation" was not entirely without foundation.

Silenced momentarily by the sharp retort, "My companion made no immediate remark upon this, but, after a pause, took the book out of my hand, and turning over the leaves, read aloud that passage in which Pascal compares the world to a dungeon, and its inhabitants to condemned criminals, awaiting the hour that shall summon them to execution." (p. 33) He read it, however, not to agree with it, but to take issue with it. "Can you believe, my friend, for short as our acquaintance has been, I venture to call you such—can you believe this to be true?" "Why not? My own experiences, feelings, life, sufferings, all testify to my soul of its truth," the poet declared. "But before I add anything further, will you allow me to ask what religion you profess?" he went on. "A good one, I hope; I have been reared a Catholic Christian," was the young man's prompt answer. Almost with a silent "Ah-ha!" the poet said, "Then you know that it is the belief of the holiest and most learned theologians of your church that the majority of mankind will be irrevocably consigned to eternal misery?" "Really I know no such thing," he protested. But Mangan would not give over: "Have you never read Massillon on 'The Small Number of the Saved'?" he countered.

His new friend did not answer that question, so perhaps he had not, but this didn't stop him from disagreeing: "I take the judgment of no one individual even in my own church as my guide. The goodness, the justice of God. . . ." Mangan interrupted him, cutting short his warm testimony to God's goodness, with: "Stop. What do you. . ." And with that, the sentence, too, was cut short, for the *Autobiography* breaks off at the foot of the last page of the booklet. Probably the poet did not stop thus abruptly, caught half through a sentence and a thought, but went on to complete both in another book or on another sheet of paper. As already noted here, however, no such continuation of his history has been found.

The scenario of the meeting between the poet and the young man often has been construed as fiction, as if Mangan invented the whole thing or at best gave a fanciful approximation of what happened. This seems too harsh a judgement against the account. Not only was he struggling in the *Autobiography* to make some sense of what had gone wrong with his life, and why, but he was not in the mood or even the condition to fabricate tales during his last year of life. His use of pseudonyms, for instance, which had been constant since 1823, ended completely with the 1 January 1848 issue of the *Nation*, and his last fiction was written in 1845. The fragment may appear contrived, but it is far better to take the poet at his word than to construct an alternative account on no basis at all. The conversation, obviously reconstructed, marked a very significant moment for him, and he probably recalled the sequence of the exchange reasonably well.

Once more, a fondness for architectural imagery and no doubt a strong awareness of the "feeling presence" of buildings had influenced the poet. He commenced this fifth chapter, not where the fourth left off, but anteriorly to the above scene, with the description of the house in which he met the individuals who introduced him to his "career". The beginning of that passage furnishes our Chapter-section epigraph and continues: ". . . he who should pause to dwell on it must be actuated by other and deeper and possibly sadder feelings than any that such a scene would be likely to excite in the breast of the poet or the artist." Perhaps, he suggested, "he should be under the influence of such emotions as I recently experienced in passing the spot after an absence of seventeen years." There followed an analogy between those seventeen years, which he further identified as those of his "career", and the ruins of Pompeii, Herculaneum, Palmyra, and other great but long-deserted cities of the ancient world:

> The Pompeii and Herculaneum of my soul have been dug up. . . . The few broken columns and solitary arches which form the present ruins of what was once Palmyra, present not a fainter or more imperfect picture of that great city as it flourished . . . than I, as I am now, of what I was before I entered on the career to which I was introduced by my first acquaintance with that lone house in 1831. (p. 31)

From the first, the assumption has been that this was the Hayes's family home, Rehoboth House, although there was never any reason to connect the Hayes family with Mangan's "career". It remained for Nigel Oxley of Queen's University, Belfast, to look carefully at a map of Dublin as it appeared in the first third of the nineteenth century and, like the little boy peering at the Emperor in his "new clothes", to observe that Mangan's description of the locale and of the house bears no relationship to either the location or the appearance of Rehoboth House.[14] Oxley concluded from the map that the house the poet described must have been on Love Lane, now Donore Avenue, which did and still does intersect the South Circular Road between Harold's Cross and Dolphin's Barn. Moreover, a house that fits the description Mangan gave was Brooklawn House, which, until well into the twentieth century, stood at a point mid-way down Love Lane.[15] It was decidedly large and plain, and it would have "looked forth on the high road", the turnpike shown on the maps of Dublin printed during these years. In 1831, Richard Anderson, identified as a calico printer, lived in Brooklawn House, and his calico works were directly across the Lane from his residence.[16] Nothing at all is known about Anderson or his politics, certainly not whether he had some connection with the Cometeers. But then, neither is anything known about the politics of the Hayes family. What is certain is that during the autumn of this year Mangan began sending poems and perhaps prose of some description to the *Comet*.

From the beginning, Mangan's popularity and reputation with the Cometeers depended on his being an entertaining oddity, and his eccentricity insofar as it was affected and not his natural way of being, probably had its inception within this group. Following the lead of the men around him, he adopted a pose, a persona, that, like theirs, was amusing for himself and others. Such a disguise also helped him confront a world that was far more alien than that of the Hayes family home or his office. "Mannerism is a grand thing", he mocked in one of his personal essays for the *Comet*, "every other thing is jelly and soapsuds. You shall tramp the earth in vain for a more pitiable object than a man of genius, with nothing else to back it with."[17] He knew, if he deplored, the importance of clever role-playing, and he did his best to meet its "requirements".

In spite of being a Cometeer by virtue of his meeting in June and his contribution to the second part of the *Horn-Book*, Mangan saw month after month go by with nothing of his own appearing in the newspaper that the Club now published with glowing success. The previously discussed notice to "J.C.M." in "Answers to Correspondents" in the 4 December 1831 number makes it plain that he had sent at least one piece of writing that he hoped would be printed, and there were probably more. The wording in that note also testifies to what his character in this context was to be: that of a peculiar, eccentric fellow, the editor promising that his letter would be answered "as soon as it can be decyphered. . . ."

The winter of 1831–1832 was unusually severe in Ireland with a lot of snow in the north and extraordinarily low temperatures everywhere. Spring, which should have been so welcome, was marred by a long-dreaded outbreak of Asiatic or "spasmodic cholera"; the disease continued to rage for seven months before being officially declared below epidemic proportions late in October. A total of 41,735 cases were reported in Ireland, of which more than a third of the victims died.[18] Originating in India in the mid-1820s, the epidemic moved slowly across Asia, engulfed Europe, and eventually was carried to America, where it ran itself out in the less densely populated areas of Canada and the United States. John O'Donovan wrote feelingly on 27 April 1832:

> I am greatly alarmed at this malady that rages now in Dublin: the people are dropping on all sides around me, which keeps my mind in constant excitement . . . . I have almost formed a resolution to go to the County of Kilkenny [his home] for a month, while this dreadful malady is raging . . . seven persons have been removed to hospital from Essex Street [where he was living] within these 24 hours, who are all now buried![19]

Still, life went on with amazing normalcy while these terrifying events transpired. Late in 1831, there had been a split in the ranks of the Cometeers, and a large contingent of the original members followed editor

Thomas Browne in his separation from Sheehan, largely, it was said, over a disagreement about Sheehan's inclination to attack people rather than their political positions or the tithe system in general. With Browne, or shortly thereafter, went Ronayne, Jephson, O'Callaghan, Knox, and Coyne, although some of them continued to write occasionally for the *Comet*. With Sheehan remained O'Connell, Dunbar, Kennedy, Lover and Mangan, still a silent partner, as it were.

In the spring of 1832, Joseph L'Estrange, always known in print and among his cronies as "Brasspen", and James Price, signing himself rather unimaginatively "J.P."—but then, he probably wanted to be sure to be identified—became regular contributors. About Price, probably enough has been said. Young, cheeky, out-going, a soon-to-be Trinity College man, he seems almost a direct antithesis of the poet. "Brasspen", described as an "amorous old bachelor", may have been more Mangan's type, and the two were said to be "inseparable" friends. Price left a vivid picture of Mangan as he was at this time. It was customary for Club members to get together for dinner parties and in the course of the festivities to "initiate" new members with a "roast". Price described this scene:

> It is eighteen years since we first met Clarence Mangan, and the circumstances of that meeting are fresh in our memory as the events of yesterday. *Primitive* in appearance, simple in habits, knowing nothing of the world, and not yet under the dominion of that fatal indulgence to which, in after life, he was unfortunately a slave, he was not at home among the wild and reckless beings he then encountered. . . . To "roast" the retiring and half frightened student, the President called on him for a song. He declared his inability to sing, and was pressed the more by his boisterous companions. Nervously anxious to court their good opinion, he then, with the utmost simplicity, said he would attempt a recitation, and actually, in a monotonous tone, went through nearly the whole of *Marino Faliero* before he discovered they were only amusing themselves at his expense.[20]

Marino Faliero, by Byron, is a drama almost the length of *Othello*, and it stretches credulity to accept what Price said. Aside from that, the depiction of the anxious poet rings true, however. Price himself was at the time only eighteen years old while Mangan was twenty-nine, and yet his emphasis was on the poet's youth. This may have been done to appeal to his readers and to make a sharp contrast between the promising youth and the broken and pitiable man he would show them later in these sketches. Or, as suggested earlier here, Mangan may have presented himself as half-a-dozen years younger than he actually was. Be that as it may, Price was authentically moved by the poet; such a description as the following is not marred by the self-righteous tone he took when writing of Mangan's addiction to alcohol or opium:

> He was the least worldly being we ever met. His sensibilities were keen and easily excitable, and his whole organisation, physical and mental, was instinct with genius. A peculiar feature of his character was the intense melancholy that rested on him almost continually like a shadow. No matter how great the festivity—how bright with pleasure the faces surrounding him, a deep gloom would suddenly fall upon Clarence—a gloom that he could not shake off, as if a visible presence from what he called the "lampless spectre-peopled shore of Death" haunted him.[21]

This spring both Sheehan and Browne were charged, and later imprisoned, for publishing one libellous article too many. "A Buckthorn [a pseudonym used by Browne] for the Black Slugs [the parsons or bishops]", which appeared in the *Comet* on 29 April 1832, brought the Government down upon the newspaper. Still, the editors paid what turned out to be a fairly modest price for their "crime". Neither ever fully remitted the entire fine of £100, but each spent some time behind bars. Browne, in Newgate, was considerably less comfortable than Sheehan in Kilmainham, and, when he was released, betook himself to the United States and re-entered his old profession of miller. Newgate's conditions were dismal, its 8ft x 12ft cells holding eight to ten prisoners who until quite recently had had to wear both arm and leg irons. In Kilmainham, Sheehan, because of his family connections, his youth and his rather frail health, found himself the pampered darling of George Dunn, the prison governor. Not only was he "constantly entertained at banquets and dances" as well as being able to attend, incognito, performances at the Theatre Royal, but also he was allowed to entertain quite nicely, and to continue editing and writing for the *Comet*.

Mangan's first piece of writing to appear in the *Comet* was "The Two Flats; or, Our Quackstitution. An Apologue", in its issue of 3 June 1832.[22] A satirical essay, not a poem, it took the British Parliament apart piece by piece and held each bit up to ridicule: "Once upon a time there stood, in a certain part of Kingdom-land, known by the name of Undone Town, a large, dull, old building, called by way of pre-eminence—the House. It was a crazy sort of edifice, and was filled with tenants, many of whom were likewise crazy", it began. He continued with a barrage of puns:

> The House consisted of two parts, the Upper Flat or House of Words, and the Lower Flat or House of Clamours. The Upper Flat was subdivided into several departments. The tenants were named Ducks, Merequizzers, Err-alls, Wise-counts, and Barrens. . . . There were also a . . . Bunch of Bye-shops [also called] the Holygarchy, for their principal occupation was preying.

It was a clever satire, though heavy-handed and decidedly weighted down with puns, a form of humour of which he was always enamoured.

In the summer, a short run of his poems in the *Comet* foreshadowed the scope of the material he would compose and translate during his professional life. Just three weeks after the publication of "The Two Flats", two satirical poems were published. For "Sonnets by an Aristocrat" he adopted the persona of a rather dull-witted member of the English aristocracy and wailed, "I'm drowned in tears; alas those good old blind/ Times have departed, and to-day folk bow/Solely before the majesty of mind. . . ." His poem commencing "Awake! Arise! shake off thy dreams" somehow made it past the *Comet* editor with its pessimism for Ireland intact and appeared as "To My Native Land". Significantly, no doubt, it was his first and last nationalistic poem in this preeminently up-beat newspaper.

August produced the gloomy personal words of "The Dying Enthusiast to his Friend". Price claimed Mangan composed this poem in "one of his melancholy moods, in our presence", and implied that he himself was the "friend" of the title. On the other hand, O'Donoghue was of the opinion that James Tighe was being addressed; as Tighe also wrote for the *Comet* from time to time, it is possible that both men were at the table when Mangan penned it. Nor is the possibility to be ruled out that John O'Donovan was the Friend, as we will soon see. Mangan began:

> Speak no more of life,
>   What can life bestow,
> In this amphitheatre of strife,
>   All times dark with tragedy and woe?
> Knowest thou not how care and pain
> Build their lampless dwelling in the brain,
> Ever, as the stern intrusion
>   Of our teachers,—Time and Truth,
> Turns to gloom the bright illusion,
>   Rainbowed on the soul of youth?
> Could I live to find that this is so?
>   Oh! no! no! [23]

The last of the summer poems was Goethe's "Ballad of the Fisherman", a myth of the "humid woman" or mermaid, who in folk lore and as interpreted in modern psychology may represent the ever-unattainable "perfect woman". The story recounts how a fisherman is lured to his death by her siren-song: "Ah! couldst thou guess the dreamy bliss we feel below the purple sea,/Thou wouldst forsake the earth and all, to dwell beneath with them and me." Psychologically speaking, surrender to the sea may represent surrender to the unconscious, an overwhelming element in which one's ego, or conscious identity, is drowned. Goethe's poem ends: "She sings to him, she speaks to him; alas! he feels that all is o'er,/ She drags him down; his senses swim; the fisherman is seen no more!" Mangan was, or had just been, struggling against this very sensation, having surrendered himself and his deepest and truest feelings to a woman who had scorned both him and them.

All his early contributions to the *Comet*, those from June, July, and August 1832, were signed "J.C.M.", and when he changed this practice in December it was to adopt "Clarence", which he henceforth used with impressive consistency in its pages. At the same time, someone else was submitting pieces signed "C", and one of these in the 12 August *Comet*, "The Betrothed", was attributed to our poet by no less an authority than Fr Meehan. He was almost certainly mistaken in this, however. "The Betrothed" is very poor stuff and probably belonged to the "C" to whom the *Comet's* editor addressed this advice on 11 September:

> C is not felicitous in some of his expressions; in others, the tone and association of epithets, affect so much of the glitter of the imitators and translations of Camoens, etc., that, at best, "The Evergreen" would be considered only an imitation, if not a patchwork of namby-pamby poetry. We would like to get something from C. in a less ambitious style, wherein *matter*, more than *glitter*, should prevail.[24]

It was probably because he was all too well aware of this "C"—which, incidentally, was an initial Mangan never signed, by itself, to any work, just as he never signed himself just "J"—that when he began to send Italian translations to the new *Dublin Penny Journal* in September, he carefully signed them "C., Clarence Street".[25]

It was pretty certainly late this summer that he wrote the long, but not at all rambling, letter to "My dear Tynan" which, as I noted earlier, was never posted, although a blank space was left for an address.[26] It is dated by Mangan's comments on Cobbet, for whose political ideas he had slight regard, and the conclusion that "nobody can be an admirable Creichton [*sic*] AD 1832". This, along with his observation that it was a year-and-a-half earlier that "workmen with no work to do and tradeless tradesmen" had been agitating for Repeal of the Union, by which he no doubt referred to the early months of 1831, when he himself had put his name to such an appeal by the law clerks, places the probable date of writing between June and September 1832.

In it he explored, or explained, his thinking on various subjects, often in witty aphorisms: "There is some truth in the remark of Jefferson that all the feeble-minded and unhealthy are tories by nature, and that all the lion-hearted and healthy are whigs by nature—but I still think that all classes, sick or sound, have a leaning toward aristocracy." And, "when the millennium shall arrive it will be very well for us all. In the meantime let us not wrangle about the wool of a goat." And, "An aristocracy . . . is necessary for the sake of variety: were we all democrats there would be no variety and variety is one of the charms of life." This letter, Jacques Chuto and Rudolf Holzapfel have suggested, may have been a literary exercise written for publication in the *Comet*, using Tynan's name as a handy addressee. Whatever the fact may be, Mangan *sounds* politically serious enough; perhaps that explains why it was not printed. It is not at all clear that he meant the following (and foregoing) remarks on aristocracy as a "bam" or hoax:—

> If I could by any means divest myself of a horrible species of laziness which constantly seizes me whenever I attempt to probe a political question, I should be glad to enter into an analysis of the arguments for and against Republicanism. In the meantime, my dear fellow, I am a despot in soul. . . . Despotism is a poetical government; there is a romance in the very idea. . . .

An amusing rhymed speculation allowed him to indulge his "own proper criminality", and the reader is again reminded that Mangan possessed a streak of out-lawry that nothing ever quite subdued:

> Suppose that on some beautiful evening in the merry month of June next when Ennui and Listlessness are clubbing together to kill me piecemeal, I waylay an old woman on the road to Bray; suppose that I transfer her cash to my pocket. As might be expected a mob is collected; I, looking dejected, am quickly suspected: in short I'm detected; my capture's effected; my prayers are rejected, my pockets inspected, my person protected, and its owner directed to march forward towards Newgate. Then the chaplain corrects me for my want of piety, the hangman projects me from the Drop, to take a "New View of Society", and the surgeon dissects me; all this is matter of notoriety. But will the Court of Rome canonize me? Not for some time, nor through all eternity.

And so life, it seemed, after illness, emotional upheaval, and romantic disaster, would move on again. But just when he must have been feeling that he could take a few deep breaths, a genuine tragedy befell him: his young friend Catherine Hayes died. Quite possibly, she was one of the cholera's last victims. Fr Meehan placed her death in October, the month during which the disease's prevalence fell to a point which justified the authorities' decision to declare the epidemic at an end. Mangan was devastated. No record of her burial has been found, the Glasnevin grave of another "Catherine Hayes" from Portobello probably being that of a relative of the proprietor of the Richmond Hotel on Charlemont Mall. Price declared that the poet's "sorrow was intense. He literally would not be comforted. The gloom of his spirit seemed from this period to become more settled."

Just a few months after her death, his elegy for Catherine appeared in the *Comet* of 10 February 1833. Following are the opening three stanzas and two later stanzas of "Elegiac Verses on the Early Death of a Beloved Friend", the only elegy he ever published for someone he loved:

ELEGIAC VERSES

I stood aloof: I dared not to behold
Thy relics covered over with the mould;
I shed no tear—I uttered not a groan—
But yet I felt heart-broken and alone.

How feel I now? The bitterness of grief
Has passed, for all that is intense is brief.
A softer sadness overshades my mind,
But there thy memory ever lies enshrined.

* * * *

The world is round me now, but sad and single
I stand amid the throng with whom I mingle,
Not one of all of whom can be to me
The bosom treasure I have lost in thee.

Enough:—I go to join the hollow crowd—
Mirth rings among us, and the laugh is loud,
For here society exacts her task,
And each assumes his own peculiar mask.

[3]

> Very pretty, Signor, and worthy of the land of comfits and confections, of gilt-edged looking-glasses and sugared plums. Why, man alive, an Irish girl would knock the blubbering block-head down who would sneak after her with zephyrs and sighs, limpid rivulets, and eyes red and swollen, like a child whipt for not taking its physic . . . .
>
> John O'Donovan, *Dublin Penny Journal*, 15 September 1832

Success bred success where publications in Ireland were concerned. The *Comet's* career inspired a swarm of short-lived but vivacious imitations during 1832 and 1833, some, at least, with ex-*Comet* men as editors: *Jonathan Buckthorn's Comet* (with Thomas Browne at its head), *The Repealer*, *The Tradesman's Journal*, *Paddy Kelly's Budget*, *The True Comet*, *The Salmagundi*, *The True Salmagundi* (with Joseph L'Estrange and James Price as its main-stays), *The Dublin Satirist*, *The Weekly Dublin Satirist* (with Sterling Coyne as an editor), *The Penny Satirist*, and so on. After showing great promise, the sober-sided *National Magazine* failed, but the

Dublin Penny Journal rose phoenix-like from its ashes. Before it fell into the hands of Philip Dixon Hardy, whose bad editorial policies had killed the *National Magazine*, it would break all previous publication records with a weekly total of 40,000 copies sold.

The *DPJ* was a good-looking, serious piece of journalism that at its best managed to be both informative and entertaining. With the dimensions of a modern news magazine such as *Time*, though not having so many pages, the *Dublin Penny Journal* was an illustrated publication of general Irish interest. The front page of Volume I, Number 1, 30 June 1832, carried a woodcut of the Custom House, harbour, and busy river, while the lead article was about the history of the city. Further articles dealt with "The Age of Brass and Agriculture", "A Visit to the Zoological Gardens" (newly opened), and "King O'Toole and St Kevin", along with some Irish poems and a translation from James Hardiman's recently published *Irish Minstrelsy*. By avoiding politics as such, and not taking on such inflammatory issues as the tithe, the *Penny Journal* editors escaped the attention the Government lavished so generously on the *Comet*, which, for its part, went out of its way to be offensive and revelled in attracting trouble: "The *Free Press* is to get a squeeze—the *Waterford Chronicle* has got a squeeze with a vengeance—the *Mail* got a twitch—the *Comet* is in for it—the *Pilot* is in for it—the *Freeman* is doubly in for it."[27]

Mangan and the young antiquary John O'Donovan had certainly met by the summer of 1832 or even, perhaps, while O'Donovan was a lawyer's clerk in the office of James Hardiman, a position he left in 1829 to work with the historical section of the Ordnance Survey. Through his early acquaintance with Thomas Larcom, to whom he gave lessons in the Irish language, O'Donovan had met George Petrie, one of the *Dublin Penny Journal* editors, and eventually worked on the topographical division of the Survey out of Petrie's office in his home at No. 21 Great Charles Street.[28] In August 1832, O'Donovan wrote to Petrie to tell him that he had "made a translation of the poem ascribed to Alfred [*sic*], King of the Northumbrian Britons (Saxons). I intend to get a poetical friend to versify it with a view to get[ting] it published in some periodical."[29] In all likelihood Mangan was the "poetical friend".

The next month would see the beginning of what was to be a friendly, but tart, running argument between them in the *DPJ* over the merits, or otherwise, of Irish poetry. Mangan—if the poetical friend were he—did not accept O'Donovan's invitation to work on the Irish poem. O'Donovan, who did not like to give up on anything, went ahead and put it into blank verse himself and Mangan did not make a rhymed version, to be titled "Prince Aldfrid's Itinerary through Ireland", until 1846.[30] Another blank verse poem in the *Journal*, "The Dream of Macdonnell *Claragh*", by which some critics have dated Mangan's first venture into the translation of Irish poetry at December 1832, also was almost certainly O'Donovan's.[31] He would have given a good bit to have been a poet, but while he could turn out serviceable blank verse, he did not have, as he himself was the first to admit, the poetic touch. He felt he had to apologize whenever he made an effort to write poetry, and he was embarrassed at the thought of what judgement Mangan might pass on his attempts.[32]

Mangan entered the ranks of *Dublin Penny Journal* writers in a persona which may well have been adopted specifically to irritate O'Donovan, that of "an Italian gentleman residing in Liverpool" who informed his readers of the merits of Italian as contrasted to those of Irish poetry. Once that has been said, though, it also needs to be pointed out that the whole exchange between himself and O'Donovan may have been planned in advance to amuse readers and to allow O'Donovan to extol the virtues of Irish poetry without sounding merely didactic. Certainly, he soon knew who his "Italian gentleman" correspondent was, if he hadn't from the start. Their give and take lasted well into the spring with seven contributions appearing from Mangan in this guise. Along with his first on 15 September, a translation, "Timid Love", from Metastasio, came his challenge to *Penny Journal* readers to produce "in all Irish poetry a match" to that little aria. As if sputtering with exasperation, O'Donovan took it upon himself to reply, and in a subsequent issue of the magazine answered with the comment at the head of this chapter, which went on:

> Our friend's challenge will have this effect: instead of setting us a-hunting after prettily turned conceits, expressed in mellifluous syllabics, it will only stimulate our previously formed intention of entering the MINE of ancient Irish literature, and bring out [*sic*] from the obscurity of oblivion those treasures of intellect and genius and antiquarian curiosity which are there to be found. . . .[33]

Inconsequential as the Italian poems may be, they were at least a means of entry for Mangan to the respectable, intellectual purlieus of literary periodicals, a stronghold (of sorts) he had not previously broached. His first disguise there, as "an Italian gentleman" and "C. Clarence Street, Liverpool", misled biographers such as John McCall, who believed for a time that the poet lived in England for almost a year; he was set straight at last by Fr Meehan who presumably had the truth from Mangan himself. These poems also show Mangan had mastered Italian (to some degree). And, perhaps most importantly, they allow him, albeit indirectly, to criticize Irish poetry which, it should be added, he did until the very year of his death.

In December of this year Mangan gave O'Donovan a copy of "The Dying Enthusiast to His Friend", posing the question of whether

O'Donovan himself might have been the "Friend" of the title. Indeed, the fact that Mangan now referred to himself as an "enthusiast"—that he and O'Donovan, as we shall soon see, actually shared the trait—and that his poem "Enthusiasm" went to the *Dublin Penny Journal* the next July suggest this was the case. Be that as it may, his action—or someone's —was almost disastrous for the *DPJ*. O'Donovan, either with or without the poet's approval, sent the poem to George Petrie with this note: "I enclose a poem of the original composition of Mr Mangan. I should be glad, if you think it fit for the Journal, that you would insert it." Clearly, Petrie knew by this time who "Mr Mangan" was, for O'Donovan offered no further explanation.

Petrie did consider the poem "fit for the Journal", and it subsequently appeared on 5 January 1833. Unfortunately, he, or someone, added the note that it was "written for the Dublin Penny Journal", which was not true, for it had been printed in the *Comet* only the preceding August. This contretemps almost involved the *Journal* in what would have been for it yet another legal squabble—which it could ill-afford—because the use without permission of material that had been published previously could be considered stealing if the injured party saw fit to look at it in that light. The editors had only just escaped prosecution on a charge for exactly that offense, having reprinted parts of stories by Carleton and Lover from the defunct *National Magazine*. Caesar Otway, who had moved from the *National Magazine* to the *Dublin Penny Journal*, may have thought he had certain rights in that case, but his perception did not spare the *Journal* some embarrassing moments. The accusation had "hung over us, like the sword of Damocles, threatening to nip asunder the slender thread of our penny existence", as he put it.[34]

To his credit, John Sheehan showed great restraint about Mangan's poem, only pointing out with a nice superiority, that it had "appeared in the *Comet* on 4th August last. We have inquired into this circumstance and find that this poem through a mistake was given to the Editor of the *Dublin Penny Journal* as an original."[35] It was, of course, an original poem, but not "original" to the *Journal*. Curiously, Sheehan seems to have taken it in stride that "his" poet was now also contributing to the new periodical, perhaps because he was not using the "charmed name *Clarence*" as John McCall referred to it.

O'Donovan would prove to be a good friend to Mangan over the years. After the energy of their shared youth had declined, it would be he who would help the poet, though it was always a task made bitter by the realization that someone he loved and deeply admired could not rise above weakness and adversity on his own. If O'Donovan had one character flaw, judging from his writings it would be this intolerance of weakness;

perhaps it was because he himself had conquered physical ailments as a young man and had to fight off so many serious lung infections as an adult that he was harsh in his criticism of others less strong-willed.[36] Without a doubt, some of the anger which is heard beneath the surface of his severe comments about Mangan's latter-day helplessness had its source in his own unremitting need to support his wife and nine children while still trying to find—or beg—a few shillings to keep his friend from starving to death on the wintry streets of Dublin.

The poet and the antiquary had much in common; most important, both were, as noted, enthusiasts. Debased by overuse, this word is no longer the expressive term it was 150 years ago. To appreciate its power in Mangan's time, one needs to know its Greek origin: "The fact of being possessed by a god." The *enthusiast* felt fervently, enjoyed or endured intense emotional responses to almost everything, and discovered delight (or horror) in matters to which the world at large managed to remain reasonably indifferent. Relatively unusual subjects such as phrenology, for instance, and Emanuel Swedenborg's philosophical and religious teachings engaged the rapt (if sometimes scoffing) attention of both Mangan and O'Donovan. In addition, the men shared a similar sense of fun, appreciation of the ludicrous, great contempt for "humbug", and a streak of what both called their "criminality". Already noted in Mangan, this last trait also marked O'Donovan's personality, as when he performed this outrageously unprofessional act while working for the Ordnance Survey in County Galway in September 1838:

> It was in my power here to impose upon future investigators of antiquities by borrowing a chisel from a stone cutter at Tuam, and inscribing SOTER on Cloch-breac ["speckled stone"] in the Roman characters of the time of Patrick. Such things have been done and the Corcagians are now collecting them as monuments of history![37]

Curiously enough, the creative nonsense of both men was intimately linked to their desire to search for—and find!—Ultimate Truth, which O'Donovan described as the goal of all his work. One constant frustration for him was the Irish language itself, for such varied meanings attached to many terms. The first line of a poem which O'Donovan mischievously claimed to have translated from Irish Mangan quoted—gleefully—as being an outburst from Nat Lee, a seventeenth century English dramatist who was famous for rant and bombast and died mad:

> Oh! That my lungs could bleat like buttered peas!
> And by repeated bleating catch the itch
> And grow as mangy as the Irish seas,
> To engender whirlwinds for a scabby witch.
> *Not that* a hard red herring dare presume

To swing a tithe pig in a cat-skin purse
Because of the great hailstones which fell at Rome
By *lessening the fall*, might make it worse.
The reason is plain for Charon's western barge
Running a tilt against the *subjunctive mood*
Beckoned to Beasly wood and gave the charge
To fatten padlocks with *Antarctic food*.[38]

Physically, Mangan was slightly taller than O'Donovan, who hated being only 5ft 4in in height, and who was often, one senses, over-compensating for what he called his "reduced stature".[39] The poet was also three years the elder, for O'Donovan had been born on 25 July 1806. In his 1849 biographical sketch of his friend, Mangan observed, "I was rather a young man when I first met Mr O'Donovan, who was still younger than I". Although O'Donovan knew he had been born in July, he was mistaken in his belief that the year had been 1809. That there was any connection between the men's two age errors is extremely unlikely, although it has been suggested once or twice that Mangan may have copied what he believed was the year of O'Donovan's birth in "choosing" 1809 as his own birth year. O'Donovan was merely ill-informed about his age and was not particularly concerned to get it right, anyway, the entire matter of age, as mentioned earlier in these pages, being of much less interest to people in the nineteenth century (before the introduction of cards to commemorate every special birthday) than in the twentieth.[40]

In his study of O'Donovan for the *Irishman*, Mangan dwelt at considerable length on the first impression the antiquary had made on him, an impression that seems to have been largely negative, although he did his best to tone it down by contrasting it with the agreeable features of his character that he discovered on fuller acquaintance.[41] Thus we learn that during the early months of their friendship, Mangan found O'Donovan "thoughtful, slow, and deeply argumentative", while he himself, by contrast, was not at all inclined to take "the trouble of doubting" anything, and had, as he confessed to having all his life, a "large amount of belief in everybody and all things". In O'Donovan, he saw a man who gave every subject a tough examination, who criticized, investigated, and probed every argument. It was a totally different experience to any Mangan had ever had with any of his other friends, and was apparently his first contact with a really incisive mind. He was not at all sure he liked it. Only slowly did he come to appreciate the warmth and generosity that were integral to O'Donovan's nature, and to love him for his "imaginative mind" and "frankness of soul". He closed his memoir warmly: "Personally, I owe him a debt of gratitude which I can never repay. May he flourish and prosper like a tree in its ripeness, for he is a good man, and a thorough Irishman."

There is a great poignancy in this last wish for his friend, for it stands in sharp, sad contrast to his appraisal of his own condition, that he had sensed from childhood that "the Great Tree of [his] Existence" would eventually be "blasted . . . never more [to] put forth fruit or blossom".

It was a fortunate moment for the *Dublin Penny Journal* when George Petrie became part of the editorial establishment some seven weeks after the start of publication, for his reputation as antiquary, artist, musician, author, and scholar was rapidly growing. Petrie, too, was to be a friend and benefactor of Mangan's over the years, and may even have been the individual who interested the poet in phrenology, for it was one of the curious passions of his life, and his opening *Dublin Penny Journal* article was on its origins. Born in 1790, and thus considerably older than the poet, Petrie was temperamentally calm, compassionate, slow to judge, and thoroughly generous-hearted.

Understandably, Mangan seems never to have felt as close to Petrie as he clearly did to O'Donovan. When he described Petrie in his memoir for the *Irishman*, Mangan was strangely negative— or so it appears when read today—before expressing his endless gratitude for all he had done for him personally.[42] His contrast between how deliberately Petrie made decisions and how he himself arrived at them has sometimes been quoted to support the notion that Mangan was careless and indifferent to rational, orderly thought processes:

> . . . my mode of forming an opinion suiteth myself and scandalizeth nobody. I take a few facts, not caring to be overwhelmed by too many proofs, that they *are* facts; with these I mix up a dash of the marvelous, perhaps an old wife's tale—perhaps a half-remembered dream, or mesmeric experience of my own —and the business is done. My conclusion is reached, and shelved, and must not thence forward be disturbed . . .

That this was all "bam", to use a favourite word of the poet's, should have been apparent to any careful reader from the very next line: "I would as soon think at any time afterwards of questioning its truth, as of doubting the veritable existence of the barber's five brothers in 'The Arabian Nights' or the power of Zeyn Alasnam, King of the Genii." Time for a laugh, not a serious "Hmmmm". In yet another instance, his apparent contrariness in disagreeing with Petrie and siding with his opponents on the Oriental origin of the round towers of Ireland was the whole joke. While the intent of these passages may be misunderstood now, Petrie would have seen them as making fun of their old enemy and antiquarian rival, Sir Thomas Betham, and his method of unraveling the mystery of the round towers and other ancient marvels, as we will find later in this account.

With Genius Wasted

The pace of Mangan's life quickened considerably in the first half of 1833. He now had two quite separate groups of friends, the men of the *Comet* and the men of the *Dublin Penny Journal*, and he was writing for both publications as well as working full-time as a scrivener. With its gossip columns and notes between Cometeers, the *Comet* is a mine of chatty, personal information, and from it can be learned something about the way he spent the seven months, January through July 1833, when he was trying to "measure up" to the emotional superficiality of most *Comet* poetry. We will begin with the preceding December.

23 December 1832: "Philander [John Sheehan] will be at home every evening next week. . . . [He] . . . will feel happy if Tim Rooney, Clarence, Ulna, and Peregrine, will call on him together or separately, according to their views of convenience, as he has something very particular to communicate to them, before 10 o'clock. Wild duck, champagne, and the Club at eleven." This issue contained Clarence's clever "The Assembly"; another example of Mangan's peculiar rhyming skills, it was a relatively tame political satire as well as a comic poem. The fourth stanza exemplifies its best features:

O'Connell is himself an Ass—
    ailer of cant and Whiggery;
Bassegio always was an Ass—
    ured hand at wiggery.
Lord Brougham is now pronounced an Ass—
    stringent piece of judgery;
And Eldon's wig-block is an Ass—
    ylum for all fudgery.

Names everyone knew—behaviour they recognized—and, except for the compliment to O'Connell, laughed at, or hated, or both.[1]

30 December: "Clanricarde, next week. Will our talented friend drop us a line, relative to our pressing invitation to call on us during the holidays . . . ? We anxiously expect a communication to the same effect from Clarence and Ulna."[2]

1833: After having had almost nothing in the *Comet* since August 1832, Mangan's contributions began to appear virtually every week in 1833, and in the issue of 27 January, he was represented by four different items: two poems and two personal essays. During the first half of the year, he may well have been juggling his *Comet* and *Penny Journal* loyalties. The *Journal* had to do without him until April (with one exception), and the *Comet* from April until mid-June. It may not have been absolutely clear to Sheehan that "his" poet was also the Italian "Constant Reader" of the *DPJ*. However, that sort of thing could not be kept dark indefinitely, and by early summer he was, in any case, signing himself "Clarence" in both publications.

6 January: Mangan welcomed the New Year in the *Comet* with "A verye Splendidde and Righte Conceited Dittie of and Concernynge the Newe Yeare" in a style somewhat imitative of "The Ancient Mariner", and affecting a pseudo-medieval diction. It began:

I

The Poet calleth aloude for Punche and Cigars.

From eighteene hundredde thirtie-two
I see we're nowe completelie sundered;—
Cigars and punche! - here's to the newe
Yeare eighteene hundredde
33!

And so on, for twelve stanzas, concluding:

XII

Ande the treasurie of his rhymes being exhaustedde, he manufactureth an appropriate conclusion for his taske.

My rhymes being oute, I'll close the beau—
tifullest ditty, scratching under't
On this fyrste forenoone of the newe
Yeare eighteene hundredde
33!
My title—to be seene and talked of far hence,
The whylke is—
Clarence

If anyone had any doubt that he was going to make his mark as a comic correspondent, he followed this extravaganza during the next three weeks with "Very Original Correspondence", purportedly an exchange of facetious letters between himself and "Philander"; three charades which he culled from his almanac poems; the burlesque short story or personal essay "An Extraordinary Adventure in the Shades"; a punning dialogue titled "Flashes of Lightning"; and a witty poem about the newly founded *Dublin University Magazine*.

13 January: Sometime during the past week, Mangan had sent Sheehan a poem titled "Ode to the starry-eyed Miss E--- of Summerhill and her fascinating sister Anna". Sheehan sent back a vicious rejection letter which the poet must have cringed to read:

> "No, Clarence dear, we will not, cannot, ought not admit your indescribable Ode, half in praise, half in exposure [?] of the beautiful 'starry-eyed Miss E--- of Summerhill and her fascinating sister Anna'. From our infancy, we were a shrewd guesser of guesses, and we'll now bet a pipe of claret that you have been jilted in that quarter, and a tun of claret that you deserved it. . . . You say 'You have wept in silence and in sorrow over the shattered wreck of all your hopes!' Devil a tear ever dropped from your eyes. We know you well. You are a mystifier, *Clarence*—a humbugger of the first water."

That the poem had been written about—and perhaps *to*— the young woman who had broken his heart, seems probable, although why a sister is included is unclear. John Sheehan's rejection came just one month after the *Comet* had printed the thoroughly heart-wrenching poem "To xxxxxxx xxxxxxx" which described a similar state of affairs, so the rejection is somewhat puzzling. No poem of Mangan's published at a later date seems as if it could be this "indescribable Ode". Certainly the introduction here of what may be an authentic initial and name is tantalizing. The reader who knows that the next October will see the publication (in the new *Dublin Satirist*) of "My Transformation: A Wonderful Tale" will be particularly intrigued, as that story would feature a "Miss E", so to speak, in "Miss Eleanor Campion". The etiquette of the day required a young man to speak of an older sister by her last name but allowed a younger sister to be addressed by her first name. At the time, only one surname on Summerhill began with "E" according to the *Dublin Directory*: "Miss A. Exshaw"—the "fascinating sister Anna"? A few years later, this listing had changed to "The Misses Exshaw"; within a decade it was back to "Miss Exshaw". That one Miss Exshaw was Mangan's *inamorata* remains sheer—if justified—speculation.[3]

20 and 27 January: "An Extraordinary Adventure in the Shades" is the hilarious account of the writer's surrealistic progression from sobriety to total drunkenness as he awaits a friend's arrival in the Royal Shades, a favourite public house located at the Arcade, No. 34 College Green. The Royal Shades, its name derived from the fact that any wine or beer vault equipped with a bar underground or in an arcade was referred to as "the shades", advertised that both dinner and breakfast were served, and that there was a also a coffee-room with "wines, ales, whiskeys, brandy, rum, soda water and London Ginger Beer", as well as "A Segar Room open from Seven till Twelve . . . supplied with Segars, Tobacco, Pipes, etc. . . ." It was a fine place to rendezvous.

Curiously enough, "Clarence" begins with a serious paragraph "personal to myself", enunciating for the first time in his writings his haunting perception of "the frozen Present—" a very odd start indeed for a comic yarn. Viewing the beautiful Past as lost, he writes, and the Future as problematic at best, he is a prisoner in this narrowest of the cells of Time. His image of a frozen, paralyzed reality in which he has no choice but to dwell is particularly oppressive. He must "resign the brilliant and burning imagery of the past for the frozen realities of the present and the future". But, perhaps with the need for some transition in mind, he makes a small joke: "*Tout est perdu, mes amis*; and when the case stands thus, the unfortunate victim had much better keep his breath to cool his porridge withal . . . ." That said, he puts all sobriety behind him and begins his dipsomaniacal tale.

Although the narrated events happen on 1 April, biographers from Price to O'Donoghue have taken some of the story's passages as "evidence" of the poet's addictions. In actual fact, the piece was written in a style made popular by Maginn, among others, and that, too, should have been apparent. It literally reels, first slowly, and then, as more and more glasses of port are quaffed, with increasing speed, into total inebriation.

At the centre of the joke is confused identity. The poet awaits his new friend "Brasspen" (Joseph L'Estrange, also of the *Comet*) whom he had arranged to meet in The Shades, not recognizing him as the "gentleman of tall stature" seated nearby. Clarence first mistakes the man for a famous linguist, Dr Bowring, and then for the horrible Oriental magician Maugraby. The details which follow of the onslaught of the hideously enlarging nose of the "damned incubus" Maugraby have been misinterpreted and used, first by Price and then by Fr Meehan and O'Donoghue, as a description of the after-effects of "opium delusion". Yet unless Price had private information from Mangan himself or the poet later admitted something to Fr Meehan, there is no reason to read them as anything other than a fictionalized description of a waking nightmare or—perhaps—hallucination of intoxication. "I foresaw the destiny whereunto I was reserved", he wrote. "I saw the black marble dome, the interminable suites of chambers, the wizard scrolls, the shafts and arrows, and in dim but dreadful perspective, the bloody cage, in which, incarcerated under the figure of a bat, I should be doomed to flap my leathern wings dolefully through the sunless day."

Determined not to surrender without a fight, the narrator manages to move a little, and "nature was for once victor over necromancy". Starting up, shrieking, then rushing forward, he tumbles down "in a state of frenzy" and passes out. The next morning finds the author in bed, his temples throbbing violently, looked after by none other than the well-known Dublin physician Dr Stokes, who, ironically, would also attend Mangan on his death-bed. The piece concluded: "Well, said he [the doctor], I can satisfy you of the individuality of your unknown. He is neither Maugraby nor Bowring, but BRASSPEN, of the *Comet* Club. I saw him there last night myself. *Tout est mystère dans ce monde ci*, thought I, *Je ne sais trop qu'en croire.*"

Even speaking through the mists of fiction, Mangan has to be listened to when he describes the irresistible appeal drink had for him at this time:

> I felt renovated, created anew! I had undergone an apotheosis; I wore the cumbrous habiliments of flesh and blood no longer; the shell, hitherto the circumscriber of my soul, was shivered; I stood out in front of the universe a visible and tangible intellect, and held, with giant grasp, the key that had power to unlock the deep prison which enclosed the secrets of antiquity and futurity!

Of all the allurements of alcohol, this vision of a revelation of Knowledge was surely the most dangerous, the one to which he could not say No. Opening gates which imagination might only lead him to, alcohol seemed to offer an opportunity the enthusiast could not refuse for long. He understood the falsity of this perfectly well, but rejecting it was another matter altogether.

27 January: Heralding the advent of the *Dublin University Magazine*, "Clarence" and "Philander" discoursed on its merits in a column titled "Flashes of Lightning". "Philander" scoffed at the new periodical, to which Clarence responded, "Yet the magazine may be of service to literature":

Philander:	Bah! You have just such *litter-at your* feet in any stable . . . . [But] the poetry of the Mag is rather Miltonic.
Clarence:	Rather Mill-stone-ic, say I. [A favourite Mangan pun.]
Philander:	But the story of Bessy Bell and Mary Grey pierced me to the heart.[4]
Clarence:	That merely proves it to be a bore.

Mangan, who assumed something of the role of devil's advocate, finished up with an oddly prophetic little poem addressed to the new *University Magazine*, "Trin. Col. Dub. Con. Mag. (Unknown Tongues) . . . Translation—Maggy, Laud Her!" He observed that while others, including "Philander", might make fun of the new magazine, he, on the other hand, would not. It may have been known by a few of his readers that "Maigaidh Láidir" is Gaelic for "strong woman", personified in an old song as Big Maggy:

> In recompense of which Mag—
>   If gratitude shall govern
> Thy breast—thou will enrich, Mag,

My purse with many a sovereign,
And tip me notes, my Maga,
From treasury of Trinny
Far beyond the notes of Paga-
nini.

The same issue included one of those poems that Mangan has been castigated for "ruining" by tacking on a comic conclusion, perhaps to make them publishable in the *Comet*. "Verses to a friend, on his playing a particular melody which excited the Author to tears" was written, Price claimed, while the two of them were together one evening, in a brief interval "ere the instant of the necessity for the opium tranquilliser" overtook the poet. Here, the poet actually destroys one bathetic image after another, like so many clay pigeons tossed into the air for the sharpshooter, in a poem which aspires to excessive melancholy rather than to profound seriousness. The first twenty-one lines exhaust the potential for gloom after opening:

Oh! hush such sounds, to me for ever mute
Be those fond, wailing efforts of thy lute;
What, tho' they be the tenderest ones
That ever over feeling stole,
The thrilling sweetness of those tones
Is torture to my gloomy soul.

The note of despair in the three continuous sonnets that complete the poem is countered with a fine touch of the ludicrous. Thus, the question, "Where lives my Paradise?" is answered with a triple Mangan favourite, "evanished": "like a gorgeous dream", "like a meteor beam", and "like the mellow glory/Of Autumn", causing the poet to cry a pool of tears which creates a "watery realm" almost on a par with Alice's down the rabbit hole. The second sonnet grows, we could say, seriously silly, beginning with the two lines that ended the first: "Yet, 'pon my word and honour, 'tis a fine transaction/To sail slick right along the surphiz of the ocean." Surely no one could mistake these fourteen lines for anything but nonsense verse. Moving towards a conclusion, the poet makes this marvelous observation, foreshadowing Lewis Carroll:

But 'tis not thus—it is not day,
I see no glittering sunbeams play
Athwart my solitude; for now
The moon illuminates the brow
Of night, like silver on a pall;
And when the moon at midnight sheds
Benignant lustre on our heads
The sun can never shine at all.

Then surprisingly, after this foolishness, comes an authentic cry:

> My drooping heart can nowhere borrow
> Language to paint its awful sorrow!

Mangan called a halt to the exercise with three rows of nonsense syllables, as from a song—"Tol lolderoll, loll, loll", and so on—and rudely asked readers, "Do you want this Englished now? Then here, you sumph, it is—" followed by the quatrain of which he claimed to be very proud:

> *When men behold old mould rolled cold*
> *Around my mound, all crowned with grass, alas!*
> *Mankind, though blind, will find my mind was kind,*
> *Resigned, refined, but shrined like gas, in glass!*

Topical references are not very frequent in Mangan's writings, but this may have been one of them, for Dublin had just acquired gaslights. More significantly, I suspect that the last two lines really told a lot about the poet and his mental organization. "Kind, resigned, refined"—he was all of those. And it might be well to ponder the implications of feeling that you had a mind "shrined like gas, in glass!"

10 February: There was no editorial joking about the poet's "Elegiac Verses on the Early Death of a Beloved Friend" which appeared in this issue some four months after Catherine Hayes's death, nor was a facetious ending tacked on to make it palatable for *Comet* readers.

17 February: The first chapter of the three-part "A Treatise on a Pair of Tongs", perhaps Mangan's most appreciated piece of prose, appeared in this issue. It was yet another hilarious personal essay with inebriation as the pivot of the plot. As he again addressed himself to Philander, Clarence claimed he drank glass after glass of porter, brandy, and whiskey, and went on to develop a long disquisition on an extraordinarily inconsequential subject: the uniqueness, origin, uses, history, and political implications of a pair of tongs. A short sample in which, again, a nose figures prominently, comes from near the end:

> *Why a man ought not to be tweaked by the nose with a pair of tongs merely on account of his politics.* Listen to me now, readers. If you have invited a gentleman to dinner, it is a piece of suburban vulgarianism to tweak him by the beak with a pair of tongs, merely because his political opinions are not in harmony with yours. Truth compels me to add that it betrays a devilish impertinence in you, and affords a strong proof that neither your morals nor your manners were properly cultivated when you were a gaffer. . . . Your criminality assumes a deeper dye if you have taken no pains to ascertain whether or not his beak had been soaped before he came into the room, for whenever the beak has not been soaped, and that well, the tweaking is an

expressibly painful operation to the tweaked party. In conclusion, I must observe, that I have never seen the act done, that I have never heard that any man did it, and that I do not believe any man capable of doing it; any man, at least, who reflects that the beak is the leading article of a gentleman's countenance.

24 February: From "Answers to Correspondents": "Timothy Tell-truth is a liar of the first water; and is ignorant as he is impudent. If we were near him, we would tweak his nose with *Clarence's Tongs* and send him to the *Tong-a* Islands for attempting to pawn on us, as original, an extract from one of the periodicals." And, to "Clarence" himself: "Clear-hence's strange epistle has nearly put us in an XTC. He is XQZ; being what we call a Quiz-i-call X N-trick."

3 March: From James Price's "World of Fashion" column: "Hear ye—hear ye, good people all! I, J.P., do fling down my glaive, and give mortal defiance to the uncourteous knights, they of the *pestle* and they of the *mortar* who came *en masse* to devour the substance of my esteemed friend, James C. M—n, with all the assurance and appetites of men SELF-INVITED. Any weapon they please may decide it,—pistol, dagger, sword, knife, fork, needle, or minikin pin!!"

17 March: From the editor, in "Answers to Correspondents": "As *Scrutator* appears so anxious to be *au fait* with regard to 'the whereabouts' of our innumerable contributors, we will just enlighten him after a manner—First and foremost, *we* ourselves are eternally 'at home' in our deep dungeon at Kilmainham. . . . As to *Ulna*, he may be viewed at Seemuller's; but the Hole-in-the-Wall is the nook to detect *Tim Rooney* in; *Clarence* has no permanent residence fixed on as yet, and may in the meantime be seen of a hazy morning heavily finding his way out of a watch house with other 'Peep-o'-day boys'. *Brasspen* domiciles in Mountjoy-square. As to the remainder, they are here, there, and all over the globe, 'everywhere by turns, and nowhere long'."

By "permanent residence", Sheehan clearly meant favourite drinking place, not the poet's home. As far as his real residence was concerned, Mangan was probably staying most of the time with his family in Charlemont Street, or possibly, in rooms let temporarily somewhere in the familiar purlieus of Dublin south of the Liffey. As to taverns, he is known to have frequented the Royal Shades, Phoenix, Bleeding Horse, and Star and Garter, although it is unlikely that this list exhausts the public houses he could be found in.

In this same issue of 17 March, Tim Rooney addressed an odd, rambling sort of poem to "Philander", who naturally enough was somewhat out of touch due to his stay in his "deep dungeon at Kilmainham", up-dating him on what his old friends were doing. Mangan was included in a note at the end of the parody of a traditional vision poem. Here, he described Ireland all too vividly as a woman who has been beaten up and abandoned like "a well-squeezed orange, only pulp, and no juice left", and closed, ". . . now I am/Wandering like *Clarence B.A.M.*" Mangan was becoming more "X N-trick", and the *Comet* was encouraging it, capitalizing on his idiosyncrasies, pointing him out as a "character". How did he really feel about it? Perhaps his emotions were mixed. In actual fact, lots of the Cometeers were ribbed in print as much as he at this point, and took it in stride; to them it simply meant they belonged to the inner circle. Mangan doubtless tried to go along with this, but it hardly need be said that it was not his style of humour, and often he must have felt like the odd man out.

In this St Patrick's Day number he had two "Very Elegant Sonnets", of which one commencing "My friend Tom Bentley borrowed from me lately" was his first, but far from his last, poem about money:

> My friend Tom Bentley borrowed from me lately
> A score of yellow shiners. Subsequently
> Meeting the cove, I dunned him rather gently;
> Whereat he drew himself up, and looked stately,
> And said, " 'Pon honour!" that he wondered greatly:
> And so he left me. "Well," exclaimed I mentally,
> I calculate this is not acting straightly—
> "You're what slang-whangers call a scamp, Tom Bentley."
> In sooth, I thought his impudence prodigious,
> And so I told Jack Smith a few days after,
> But Jack burst out into a peal of laughter.
> I stared at him, and asked him what he meant.
> "Why, don't you see," said he, "*he keeps the Lent*!"

24 March: No, Philander assured an interested reader, "Tom Bentley" was not a real person, but "a creature of the poet's imagination". The editor liked to hear from readers, for it meant the paper was generating interest, and so his answer to "Clara", that he would certainly "not insert the following" poem which she had submitted, was immediately followed by her rhyme "To Clarence on His Tongs"—

> Dear Clarence, on a Pair of Tongs
> You've such interminable lungs,
> One would imagine that you wrought
> Your *treatise* with a Pair of Tongues.

This was the hundredth number of the *Comet*, and to honour the occasion Mangan saluted the newspaper and staff with "An Ode to the *Comet*". It was, not to anyone's surprise, a mock-heroic ode. From its beginning, "Come down upon my desk, oh, heavenly muse . . ./Come down, then, to my desk, nor wander from it,/Because this day I sing about the *Comet*", to its conclusion's piping "The *Comet* so blazing, amazing, and clever,/The wonderful, thunderful *Comet* for ever!", he lauded the paper and its editor. Sheehan, he praised, was "none of your mawkish, your half-and-half tub-licking,/Lick-spittle sycophants, wait-a-while boobies,/But a hot out-and-outer, a glorious republican. . . ." Thus for the first time in print, the poet used the phrase which he would sign to some of his most startling pieces, the "out-and-outer".

6 April: A milestone in the *Dublin Penny Journal*: Mangan signed his translation from the German with "Clarence", a name hitherto reserved for the *Comet*. He was thereafter absent from the latter paper for the rest of April, all of May, and half of June. It would be fair to deduce that there was some cause-and-effect in this circumstance and that Sheehan was annoyed with him for sharing his *Comet* signature with another publication.

14 April: Price's poem, "Easter Gifts to My Friends", in a letter to the editor, commenced seriously enough: "They claim the body, but the living mind,/From its free range no power on earth can bind." Thereafter, although the various "gifts" had mostly to do with his friends' drinking habits, he reserved a special one for the poet. To "Clarence", he vowed, he would "give a subject, Phil,/That will be worthy of his giant mind." There was no hint of sarcasm or mockery anywhere in sight.

20 April: Another milestone in the *Dublin Penny Journal*: "A Constant Reader", that is, "an Italian Gentleman", "C. Clarence Street, Liverpool", revealed that he was thinking seriously about Irish literature and complained that Irish was a difficult language to learn, partly because of inconsistent grammar. Perhaps he was doing a little fence-mending with O'Donovan when he wrote:

> I saw, it is two years since, two interlinear translations of St John's Gospel announced in the *Dublin Evening Post*; would your able correspondent O'Donovan inform me which is the better for acquiring a facility in translation?

One of these translations, *The Gospel According to St John, in Irish*, was the work of the Gaelic Scholar Owen Connellan who almost certainly was acquainted with O'Donovan and whom Mangan probably met around this time. Mangan and Connellan became fairly close friends, as we will see, and Connellan sought Mangan's help in correcting the English of his *Annals of the Four Masters.* O'Donovan held Connellan in considerable contempt not only as a Protestant convert, but, much worse, as a very shaky scholar. His *St John* had been sponsored by Lord George Augustus Hill, with a lengthy list of subscribers including William Carleton. In any case, Mangan showed no further interest in studying Irish at this time.

19 May: Price described Mangan in words that bear out the suspicion that the poet had a first-hand knowledge about gambling:

And J.C.M.—, who loves a little loo, [a card game resembling whist]
And plays for pleasure *merely*, not for gain;
But *Par parentheses*—in the name of who,
The devil, or bad taste—or was he sane,
To put on such a bloody queer cravat?—
Oh! what the blazes was his fancy at?[5]

16 June: Mangan's "Broken-Hearted Lays. Number One" appeared; did he have a "Number Two" in mind, or written? If so, it never showed up. This poem, as already noted here, was a work of unsustained, that is, "spoiled" mood. It was the sort of verse usually found acceptable in the *Comet*: the poet was free to say what he wanted so long as he tacked on the last few frivolous lines that reduced it all to a passing fancy. Here, the final eleven lines which O'Donoghue elected to cut out when he included the poem in his centenary edition of Mangan's work did just that:

Oh! in an hour like this, when thousands fix
　In headlong Desperation on selfslaughter,
Sit down, you droning, groaning bore! and mix
　A glorious beaker of red rum-and-water!
Then bid your flunky toss you that aggrea—
ble sparkler called the COMET:—this will be a
Treat of which now you're but a dim idea;
And finally, give Care his flooring blow
　By one large roar of laughter—or guffaw—
　As in the *Freischutz* chorus, Haw! haw! haw!—
L'affaire est faite :—you've bammed and bothered woe¡[6]

The *Comet's* editor was still resoundingly enthusiastic about Clarence and announced to readers of this issue that "Clarence's Io Paean in English Hexameter rhyme, in our next, will astonish the natives."

23 June: "Clarence's unparalleled Hexamiter [*sic*], from an unavoidable mishap, is postponed 'till our next."

30 June: The "Io Paean" turned out to be a revision of one of the poet's rebuses with a new acrostic added. A poetic tour-de-force, it assuredly gave the poet some moments of enjoyment, as his busy, anxious mind took time off to devise this whimsy:

ALL	men declare and swear that if we e'er comp	ARE
PAPERS	with other papers we'll pro- nounce them	HUMBUGS:
MAGAZINES	are ('tis said) but shifts for but- tering b	READ
REVIEWS	however high, will stoopify like Le	THE
AN-	nuals make one vomit; so the only gem's the	COMET!
D	on't talk to me, ye flats! don't dare to tell me	THAT'S
STUFF	*dixi scripsi, et jurabo*: there! That's proof	ENOUGH!

Read down the left hand margin, the acrostic is: "All Papers Magazines Reviews and Stuff"; continuing down the right hand side: "Are Humbugs: Read The Comet! That's Enough!"

7 July: Word play was a fad of the time, and Mangan excelled at it. In this issue, "My Mausoleum" dealt facetiously with a subject he took seriously—his grave. All its lines end in homonyms and puns such as "sent your eye" and "cent-u-ry".

13 July: Almost exactly a year after "The Dying Enthusiast to His Friend" was printed in the *Comet*, another such poem, "Enthusiasm", appeared in the *Dublin Penny Journal*. Both poems are among those originals of his which begin, proceed, and end on a sustained note of high seriousness. The two moods that Mangan most often claimed as his own were "melancholy" and "enthusiasm", yet within a half-dozen years he would write, "The most opaque of all the masques that people assume to conceal their real characters is enthusiasm." This *Penny Journal* poem was short, four stanzas only, of which the first two follow:

Not yet trodden under wholly,
Not yet darkened,
Oh, my spirit's flickering lamp, art thou!
Still, alas! thou wanest—though but slowly;
And I feel as though my heart had hearkened
To the whispers of despondence now.

Yet the world shall not enthral me—
Never! never!
On my briary pathway to the grave
Shapes of pain and peril may appal me,
Agony and ruin may befall me—
Darkness and dismay may lower ever,
But, cold world, I will not die thy slave!

The *Penny Journal* had no objection to serious personal poems. In May he had wisely sent it, not the *Comet*, his beautiful but sombre "The One Mystery" in which he declared "The dead, where are they? In their shrouds—/Man knows no more", and propounded this touching, stoical advice after saying we ask such questions as When, Where, and How in vain:

And all philosophy, all faith,
    All earthly, all celestial lore,
Have but ONE voice, which only saith,
    Endure,—adore!

The duality of Mangan was never more apparent than this year when he was doing his utmost to make common cause with the worldly men of the *Comet* while also endearing himself to the more elevated cultural nationalists of the *Dublin Penny Journal*. Price perhaps had to exaggerate only slightly to create his picture of the poet plunging from a mood of too high elation down into gloom—that, too, was part of his twinned light and dark nature.

21 July: There was nothing about "Life is the Desert and the Solitude" that would make any "carping critic" call it "spoiled". Indeed, O'Donoghue has not been alone in deeming it the finest poem Mangan wrote for the *Comet*. Replete with typically Manganesque imagery of ruins, sleepless strife, the martyred heart, memory's pictures, time-trampled love, and life's "all-troubled river", it is perhaps his most definitive personal poem to date. Interestingly, too, it is yet another of his poems with four plain but unmarked divisions. In the first, he describes that "joyous time of June" which never failed to bewitch him; in the second, he contrasts the glowing external world with his own life, a litany of distress; in the third, he turns from this summation to ask "What slakeless strife is still consuming/This martyred heart from day to day?" And finally, he closes with the grisly image of the "cankering worm" slowly but surely gnawing the heart-strings and draining the "bosom's blood" drop by drop, a memorable metaphor for the subterranean "undeparting woe" which, even in the midst of what passed for happiness, persisted in its debilitating work. The poem begins:

It is the joyous time of June,
    And fresh from Nature's liberal hand
Is richly lavished every boon
    The laughing earth and skies demand:
How shines the variegated land—
    How swell the many sparkling streams!
All is as gorgeous and as grand
    As the creations wherewith teems
    The poet's haunted brain amid his noonday dreams.

But ends:

> Alas! for those who stand alone—
> The shrouded few who feel and know
> What none beside have felt and known;
> To all of such a mould below
> Is born an undeparting woe,
> Beheld by none and shared with none—
> A cankering worm whose work is slow,
> But gnaws the heart-strings one by one,
> And drains the bosom's blood till the last drop be gone.

Mangan may or may not have known that his time with the *Comet* was drawing to a close. It was a period of change, this summer of 1833. There can by no doubt that Sheehan was having a hard time keeping tabs on his writers from his prison cell, no matter how much they joked about the situation. The Reform Bill of 1832 was certain to achieve some of the things that the *Comet* had campaigned for, although not abolition of the tithe system, and, with the first burst of energy spent, the whole enterprise may have become weary at the centre. The last issue of the newspaper would appear in November.

At the same time that the *Comet* was struggling to continue publication, the *Dublin Penny Journal* was being taken over by Philip Dixon Hardy. Mangan's last poem in its pages, a "free translation" of the last stanzas of Schiller's "The Lament of Ceres", appeared there the same week that "Life is the Desert and the Solitude" could be read in the *Comet*. Hardy himself was a sometime-poet, known, as O'Donoghue graciously put it, for his evangelical zeal. The *Journal* survived for one more year under his pious editorship and then ceased publication. Mangan had had sixteen items printed in its pages during its first year, and it had brought him together with some of the finest writers and keenest minds of his day. Several men he met in this context were more consistently, if less hot-headedly, patriotic than John Sheehan and would remain his faithful friends for the rest of his life.

4 August: As we might expect, a minor mystery attended the poet's last contribution to the *Comet*, "The Philosopher and the Child". From one perspective, it is an irregular sonnet of sixteen lines followed by a triple-couplet and a two-quatrain ending in quite a different style. From another, it is a twenty-two line poem with eight lines that end in a slang-song that spoils the unity of the whole by reversing the mood and catapulting it into comedy. A clue to who may have done the "spoiling", if so these final lines are viewed, is contained in a privately held John McCall manuscript on which "added by Sheehan" has been pencilled in beside brackets marking those lines.[7] Mangan, it will have been noted, was not in a particularly facetious mood at this point; in any case, he was not a very likely person to have made fun of youthful innocence. Moreover, though the poet probably would not have quit the *Comet* merely on the strength of the insults which Sheehan hurled at him, he might have done so because the editor tampered with his poem and altered it to serve his own comic purposes. The whole exchange, being the last we will hear from Sheehan in his dealings with our poet, is given:

> Clarence was mad!—drunk, dare we say? when he wrote the following. The five lines at the conclusion marked in *Italics*, are sufficient proof of our assertion.

THE PHILOSOPHER AND THE CHILD

I met a venerable man with looks
    Of grand and meek benignity, he wore
    Deep written on his brow the midnight lore,
Accumulated from the wealth of books.
    Wisdom and mildness from his features beamed,
And by his side there moved a little child
With auburn locks, who pleasantly beguiled
    The listening ear of that old man, who seemed
To be her sire, with playful words which from
    The heart of childhood-innocence' fresh fountain,
Spring brightly bubbling upwards, till they come
    To lose themselves on manhood's desert mountain.
So spake that lovely little child, and as
    I gazed on her, and on that aged man,
    With eye so thoughtful, and with cheek so wan,
I mused on Plato and Pythagoras;
    But most I thought of Socrates, and of
    The guardian angel whose undying love
Never forsook the hoary sage of Greece,
Until she closed his eyes in holy peace,
When tyrants, awed, acknowledged with a sigh
How nobly a Philosopher can die!

    And as these thoughts flashed, flitting through my brain,
I heard that venerable man so mild,
Thus mutter to the sweet and blessed child:
    "Bad luck to dat oul' rap from Mary's lane!
Dat come and axed me for to sky de copper!
    Bad luck to him! de vagabone! to rob,
    And swindle me wid pitch-and-toss, an' fob
De penny dat I wanted for de cropper!"

> Oh Clarence! Clarence! Oh! Oh!! Oh!!! order a jarvey forthwith, and drive off to Sir Arthur Clark's. Odds, shower-baths, and stomach-pumps! You are in a raging fever, man, absolute *delirium tremens*. Make your will, and leave Pelthers Paisley, the Coroner, a lock of your wig, for the trouble he will have on your inquest.[8]

McCall added his own fictional conclusion: "The astonished and outraged James Clarence Mangan . . . turned from the door of the *Comet* Office in Church Lane in disgust. He never condescended to write a single line for the publication any more."

The question remains open as to whether or not Mangan was the author of the final eight lines. We have seen him "spoil" a number of apparently seriously meant poems with a comic twist at the conclusion, and this may have been such another. On the other hand, Sheehan's calling attention to the burlesque street lingo may be thought more likely if he put it in himself. That he was annoyed with his correspondent's tendency to write deeply moving poems was surely a fact of *Comet* life, and Mangan had just got away with "Life is the Desert and the Solitude". But to attribute his departure to a single, no matter how unpleasant, tangle with Sheehan would put emphasis in the wrong place. The fact is, Mangan's friends and future were beckoning from the new *Dublin Satirist*.[9]

8

Roll on, My Song

[1]

On Thursday evening, August the 15th, 1833, as I was seated in my back parlour reading "*Burton's Anatomie of Melancholie*", before a few dying embers, I was startled by the sudden entrance of an old acquaintance, who advanced and, shaking me by the hand, hastily apologized for his refusal to take a denial from my servant, and added that he had news for me of the most cheering character. . . . I gathered the courage for a phrase or two. What mean you? I asked; do you not know that unseen hands have dug my grave, and that I am even now tottering into it?

You are a confoundedly long time tottering into it, he answered, but my business is to establish you stoutly on your pins again. Look here! he continued, taking what appeared to me to be a newspaper from his pocket; look at this! and he held it at arms' length before me. I gazed as if fascinated, and saw at the head the words, "THE DUBLIN SATIRIST". . . .

Mangan, "My Transformation", *Dublin Satirist*, 19 October 1833

The Dublin Satirist or *Weekly Magazine of Fashion and Literature* began publication on 22 June 1833, "Edited by the Buckthorn Club". When you call yourself "a magazine of fashion and literature", your chances of survival in a politically carnivorous world are markedly improved. The proprietors of *The Dublin Satirist*, Sterling Coyne, Robert Knox and John Boulger, being keenly aware of this fact, had chosen their newspaper's name astutely. Besides that, it gave them plenty of leeway to include what they wished and provided an excellent cover for the attacks on governmental abuses that they fully intended—and succeeded in—publishing. Two of the three men we have met before as founders of the Comet Club; Boulger, too, had been writing under the pen-name "Beppo" for some time. Coyne's parents whimsically named him "Sterling", on which he seemed to pass a wry comment by calling himself "Perdu". Knox was "Bertor", an anagram for Robert. The same custom prevailed as on the *Comet*, that is, virtually all contributors wrote under some pseudonym, or sometimes anonymously, a practice that probably has caused literary historians of the nineteenth century more frustration than any other single foible their subjects exhibited.

For some reason, the three founding editors were irate with Sheehan, Price, and L'Estrange, and one main reason for their beginning the *Satirist* was to get back at this trio of writers. So much personal and professional jealousy was involved in publication at this time that perhaps this action was less extreme than it seems today. I noted earlier that these years saw an absolute eruption of short-lived, but racy, periodicals. Noting that Fr Meehan had mentioned Mangan in relation to one of the less prestigious, the *Salmagundi*, McCall made a particular point of stating that "it must be understood that our poet never condescended to write for it, or any other of the other penny publications", a derogatory term not meant to include the *Dublin Penny Journal*. The milieu in which he lived and worked was one of rivalry for popularity by publications major and minor. If he did not contribute to *Paddy Kelly's Budget*, *Salmagundi*, *True Comet*, or others of their merit, or lack thereof, it was surely because he preferred something better or nothing at all.

The Dublin Satirist welcomed Mangan with open arms and was always out-spoken in its appreciation of his work, partly, no doubt, because every mention of "our correspondent 'Clarence' " was a dig at Sheehan. But he was also appreciated as a poet, particularly as a translator of German verse, for the *Satirist* took seriously its identification as a literary publication. We frequently find snippets addressed to him in the "Answers to Correspondents" column. "M's 'Stanzas to My Cigar' next week" may or may not have referred to Mangan's tribute to cigars and smoking in general, "A Song for Cloud-Blowers", which did not make it into the paper until 28 November 1835. But there is no question about "Clarence's 'Pompeii' awaits a favourable moment for insertion." So, too, we read that "Clarence merits our best thanks: he shall figure in the first number of our stamped publication." In fact, his name, or rather, his chosen literary name, became really well known for the first time through exposure in the *Satirist*.

His arrangements must have been more concrete with the *Satirist* than with the *Comet*, for his present editors had a clearer idea what they wanted from him than Sheehan was able to enunciate. He was to be primarily a translator of German verse, and his appearance in the pages of the new publication was to be as close to weekly as possible. His number of contributions, prose and poetry, would total forty-one, largely in 1833 and 1834; during the first year he racked up just over two dozen. Thereafter, the *Satirist* vied with the *Dublin University Magazine* for his contributions, and he became more and more closely identified with the latter, as we will see anon. He may even have been paid something for his *Satirist* translations, although it is unlikely he commanded the going magazine rate of £1 per one-hundred lines. Even if he had been fully remunerated, he would not have earned much because most of his lyrics were only a few stanzas long. Still, it would have supplemented nicely the thirty-shilling weekly stipend at his scrivenery job.

More importantly, this experience showed him for the first time that he might be able to earn his living by his translator's poetic pen. This was a notion which he had not entertained before, as far as can be ascertained, and its introduction must have raised fantastic hopes of freedom. The creation of prose and certainly of original verse was a shaky and often thankless endeavour by comparison. No longer would he have to be tied to a desk, to labour at someone else's order, to to sacrifice the "Promethean fire of genius" to dull routine. What a vista must have opened before him! In fact, the solid apprentice-like stint he did with the *Dublin Satirist* prepared the way for the consistent work he would soon be doing for the *Dublin University Magazine*.

One by one, the *Satirist* translations increased the volume of the poet's so far quite limited canon. Here, he affected no mannerisms because there was no "merry youngster" mask he felt obliged to wear, nor had he any need to cast every thought in the form of an enigma, rebus, or charade as in the almanacs. Thus the early "magazine character" of the "poet-translator" was able to emerge: competent, disciplined, and individualistic.[1] It is as if we were seeing in this incarnation an untormented, undisturbed James Clarence Mangan. Gone was the erratic, eccentric *Comet* persona. Present instead was a professional poet who could be witty or pensive, very much as his muse or his original required.

He had now been studying the German language for perhaps fifteen years, and he had familiarized himself with a fair amount of the history and more recent poetry of his chosen country. Like most largely self-taught individuals, he had serious gaps in his learning that, being Mangan, he would eventually try to fill with scholarly derring-do and a sort of spurious expertise. But for the time being, these gaps did not much matter. He could pick any poem he wanted to translate, include the original alongside it, and not be obliged to say anything learned about it or its author.

To know his reasons for selecting the poems he did would open a fascinating door into his psyche, but informed conjecture, by itself, can often discern a probable link between his life and his choices. Later, when he was translating so many poems from the German, "translating Deutschland out", as he put it with his usual exaggeration, some of his choices may have been dictated by simple convenience or superficial interest. But in 1833 and 1834, we can be sure he was picking poems that had meaning for him. When he had the opportunity not many months later, he saw to it that most of them were reprinted in the more durable *Dublin University Magazine*. These are minor poems, almost exercise-like in their length and simplicity, but they are worthy within their limits, and they speak volumes.

Even the first chapter of his "Anthologia Germanica", the series for which he would become very well known in the *Dublin University Magazine*, contained five of them, and in every instance we can readily guess why he liked the little verse. "The Maiden's Lament" struck the broken-hearted note of the young, innocent girl mourning her dead lover. In "The Dying Father", the father of two sons (one of those persistent motifs for Mangan) left everything he owned to the bright one, Christy, who generously asked what was to become of his brother George. The father responded, "Be sure thy brainless booby of a brother/Will make his way through life by sheer stupidity." (Mangan would use this theme of surviving on one's stupidity, which happened to be rather popular at the time, in a number of poems before he was finished with it. It must have been significant that a few years later he changed "George" to "Will", the name of his feckless brother.) In "The Wee Little Hut" he again eulogized the childlike, emphasized by the miniaturization of everything, even the speaker's beseeching, "Wilt let me share thy hut with thee?" underscoring the innocence of the affection. "The Maid of Orleans" paid homage to young, noble, uncontaminated womanhood. A complete departure was "The Song for Punch Drinkers", one of the earliest, if not the very earliest, of his drinking songs. These first rhapsodic testimonials to ale-house pleasures have a charming guilelessness which would unhappily be overwhelmed later by his guilt, and by Fr Mathew's temperance crusade. Here, the burden of the "Song" was simply that the soul warms man's "cold mortar" the way punch warms his soul.

He had not yet had a chance to muse, in print, on the various theories about translation which were pondered in the early nineteenth century, much as they continue to be in the late twentieth, so we have no way of knowing what his early theorizing may have been. His *Satirist* works, while not slavishly bound to their originals, nevertheless followed close enough to them in form and content to avoid rousing any purists' protests. Later on, one of the distinguishing characteristics of the "Manganesque" was the poet's personalization of his translations, or "transformations"; that is, his radical departure from the original poet's style and even content, to make the poem what he believed it should be, or was *meant* to be. This has drawn the fire of literary critics from his day to our own.

He was assuredly familiar from the start with the general outlines of the opinions of such masters as Dryden, Anster, Voltaire, and Shelley. Dryden's explanation of his approach to the *Aeneid*, that he had tried "to make Virgil speak such English as he would himself have spoken, if he had been born in England and in the present age", was echoed by Mangan in his laudatory comments on John Anster's translation of *Faust*: "It is precisely such a work as Goethe himself, if he had written in English, would have bequeathed us."[2] Since Anster was such an early and impressive model, it is almost certain that Mangan had this dictum in mind as he approached any significant poem. In 1847 he was to assure readers, "I have had in every stanza [of the poem under discussion] the wholesome terror of Voltaire's denunciation before my eyes", and not surprisingly, Voltaire's "denunciation" also supported Mangan's technique: "*Malheur à vous, faiseurs des traductions littérales, qui, traduisant chaque parole, énervez le sense. C'est bien là qu'on peut dire que le lettre tue et que l'esprit vivifie.*"[3] Shelley's comparison between the effort to "transfuse from one language to another the creations of a poet" and the attempt to "discover the formal principle of [a violet's] colour and odour by casting it into a crucible and subjecting it to whatever scientific tests might go on there" would also have been well understood by the Irish poet.[4]

"*Traduttore, traditore*" did not give Mangan sleepless nights. "The translator is a traitor", whether he "turns out a translation that is better or worse than the original", is a tight-lipped truism which, if taken to heart, could cause a potential translator to lay aside his dictionaries forever. John Millington Synge, decidedly in the spirit of Mangan, put these words into the mouth of one of his characters in *The Aran Islands*: "A translation is no translation . . . unless it will give you the music of a poem along with the words of it."[5]

[2]

> We accept with pleasure, the contributions of J.C.M. of which we shall avail ourselves for the ensuing month. *DUM*, May 1834

The *Dublin University Magazine* had been in existence for only a year when the notice of acceptance quoted above went to Mangan via its "Notices to Correspondents" column. In June, "The Pilgrim", translated from Schiller, appeared; "Curiosity" followed in August; and in October he was represented by two poems, "To My Friends" and "The Opening of the New Century". His one-word signature "Clarence" was now on its way into oblivion; although signed to the first two, after 1835 it would be used by itself only one more time. "James Clarence Mangan" and its variants would be preferred where he used a signature, while in the *University Magazine* his work usually would be unsigned.

The *Dublin University Magazine*, or "Maggy", as Mangan and the wags of the *Comet* and *Satirist* had called it, was the product of an intellectual, conservative, elitist group of young gentlemen of Trinity College—according to the first editor, Charles Stuart Stanford, himself and three undergraduates: Isaac Butt, William Archer Butler, and John Francis Waller. Samuel Ferguson may also have been part of the group, although the *Alumni Dublinensis* recorded a later date for his registration in the College.[6] In any event, he had received his Master of Arts degree in 1832, and he became a contributor to the *University Magazine* virtually upon its founding. Stanford gave a distinctly Tory and Protestant stamp to the publication, which Michael Sadleir condemned as "antifeminist", "pompous", and "tiresomely verbose", although it always aimed to set a high literary standard.[7] From the start, Stanford attracted a good calibre of writer. William Carleton's work appeared from December 1833 onward, and Mangan's, at first a little hesitantly, perhaps, but with increasing frequency, from the spring of 1834.

Mangan may have been feeling sufficiently emboldened by his success with the *Dublin Satirist* to send a few poems to the new publication on his own initiative, but chances are, he was encouraged by the senior editors, publishing veterans John Anster and George Petrie, with whom he had been acquainted for a couple of years through the *Dublin Penny Journal*. Along with Caesar Otway, that old enemy of the Cometeers, and James Wills, who had generously given his lengthy poem *The Universe* to Charles Maturin years earlier in that cleric's hour of need,[8] Anster and Petrie contributed expertise and publishing advice to the young founders. In a sense, they no doubt saw the *Dublin University Magazine* as a rebirth of the *Dublin Penny Journal* on which all, with the possible exception of Wills, had worked; in a sense, they were not mistaken. The *University Magazine*, however, was a far more ambitious undertaking. The founders had a dream and £60 in their pockets. They envisioned their brainchild as a high-quality Irish literary periodical modeled on the famous *Blackwood's* and *Fraser's* and forming, with them, an "intellectual triad in the realm".[9] As it turned out, they were not far wrong, for the *Magazine* remained the outstanding Irish literary publication for fifty years and in fact is one of the best such publications ever to have appeared in the English language.

Mangan had a total of eight poems in the magazine during his first year as a contributor, a modest but not inconsiderable triumph. Probably he was on a sort of probation, as some of his past associations, such as with the *Comet*, were dubious. No formal arrangement of any sort was made with him as to how much of his work they would be willing to accept,or how often, until the following year. The first four poems were translations from Schiller. The rest consisted of the famous "Ballad of Leonore" by Gottfried Bürger, a romance by de la Motte Fouqué, a song by Hölty, and a lyric by Heine. These translations all appeared for the first time in the *University Magazine*; he was not yet ready to risk sending them material that had had a first airing elsewhere, although that followed soon enough, because the magazine's expressed policy was rigid on that score.

How did he pick out the poems that he wanted to work on for this new publication? As we saw from his funny little poem to "Maggy", he had high (if not fully recognized) hopes from the start as to what the *Dublin University Magazine* might mean for him—a legitimate, prestigious, and remunerative outlet for his verse. So, many things came into play: his own state of mind, his editors, his audience. "The Pilgrim" was anything but complicated, yet there are a number of elements in it that came to be typical of Mangan. The young "pilgrim" of the title, abandoning a pleasant home, sets forth blithely on his quest in search of a magical palace in the East where "the elect among mortals/May drink of eternity's life-giving chalice." Although he fails to find this idealized spot, his nobility is never in question, for he has, after all, attempted to reach a sacred place, and the age-old search for eternal life is no ignoble one. The final stanza in Mangan's translation is more compelling, more total in its hopelessness, than in Schiller's original:

But woe is me! the billows but bore me
    To the barren and wreck-strewn region I tread:
Dark skies are o'er me, wild wastes are before me,
    And my goal is lost, and my soul is dead.

Contrast this with:

Ach kein Steg will dahin fuhren,
Ach der Himmel über mir
Will die Erde nie beruhren,
Und das Dort ist niemals Hier.

As we will see over the years, when Mangan takes hold of a poem and translates it seriously, he almost always raises its emotional temperature. His vocabulary and his syntax may not be very much at odds with his original's, but taken together, they significantly increase the density of the poem.

Mangan was a trickster from the start, although he began cautiously. Thus the second *Dublin University Magazine* poem, "Curiosity", without saying so, picked up where the first left off. It perhaps even explains why he dropped Schiller's title "Sehnsucht", substituting one of his own. Here, the persona, who might well be the Pilgrim, is stranded in a place very much like the grim "wild wastes" in which the first poem ended. He has, predictably, been "longing" to be rescued, and indeed, an enchanted ship does arrive to bear him to the land with "a sun whose glory ne'er declines". Like many an enchanted ship, it has no one to steer it, but rushes forward on charmed sails, a circumstance that confronts the Youth with two choices, either to give up his dream or to board the vessel:

Thou must believe—thou shalt not falter,
The gods disown the doubter's altar,
Nought but a wonder like to this,
Can waft thee to the land of wonders and of bliss.

The burning, unresolved question that remains at the end of the poem, the subject of the curiosity, is, will he or will he not accept the dangerous invitation?

These poems can be read on two levels. On one, a "life journey" is implied; on another, a more limited "aesthetic journey". Mangan may have identified with the Pilgrim-persona, or he may have seen Schiller's creation as quite distinct from his own too real, unromantic self, slogging along his drab, work-a-day way. Certainly, he seems—at one moment—to be issuing a clarion call to seekers and hopers to follow the mystical lead of their Fancy. At another, he cautiously holds back such recommendation. It would be no small matter to leave solid ground on a rudderless, enchanted ship bound for a land of fantasy.

He was, indeed, of two or perhaps several minds about the Actual and the Ideal and the extent to which one could or should yield "Practicality" to "Imagination". That may seem only a theoretical problem. But in reality, also, he was faced with much the same dilemma: whether to keep on dutifully as an employee at a "9-to-5" job, finding time when he could to live his chosen life, or to throw it all over and go his own way. Ten years later, he looked back to this moment at the beginning of his career and in effect told readers what his own choice had been, that he had come down on the side of Idealism; and that, in spite of everything, he did not regret it. Once again he turned to the *Arabian Nights* for an analogy:

> The fisherman in the Arabian tale fetches up from the sea a bottle, whence ascends a column of smoke, which assumes the form of a "genius", who makes his finder's fortune. The Poet reverses this order of circumstances: *he* begins by setting *his* "genius" to work at once,—revels in visions of wealth and glory on the strength of it,—and ends by witnessing the melancholy metamorphosis of all his fine projects into a—bottle of smoke!
>
> So some people think—or, rather, write. For myself, I disbelieve every word of the statement. The lot of the Poet is, I admit, not the happiest; but it is happier than that of most men. Compare it with the stock-jobber's—or the politician's—oh, Heaven![10]

[3]

And, oh! whene'er you speak of Clarence,
Tell it here, and tell it far hence,
How he sighed until he died,
Consumed by love, unhappy Clarence.
Mangan, "Oh, no one knows . . ."

Anyone attempting to be part of a group of men such as the *Satirist* crew, whose one interest is national politics and whose other is young women, had better try his hand at both. Apparently, Mangan too, was not without this latter, light side to his nature. McCall uncovered evidence, for instance, that a young woman who described herself as a poetess and who signed herself "Francesca" wrote frequently to, and for, the *Comet* and then the *Salmagundi*, and "all the poets . . . fell in love" with her. Although "Brasspen" seems to have been especially smitten "Mangan, John Shean [*sic*], Sterling Coyne" and others also came under her spell.[11] McCall either did not know, or did not choose to reveal, her real name. It is intriguing that Oscar Wilde's mother was Jane "Francesca" Elgee, and that she had the poetic skills and spirit to engage in such a literary frolic; as her date of birth was 1821, she might just possibly have been this flirtatious girl.

As recently as 1994, Jacques Chuto discovered a Mangan poem which must date from this period but which was appearing for the first time in print in the 2 May 1903 issue of the (Dublin) *Saturday Herald*. It was preceded by the comment: "The following poem is from Dr Sigerson's valuable collection of Mangan's MSS, and has never been published. It is scarcely worthy of his name:—". At the centenary of his birth, Mangan had admirers who may have been disappointed not to come across another "Dark Rosaleen", but the poem is amusing and interesting for itself, and it is priceless for its rare illustration of Mangan making fun of his own romantic propensities:

Oh! no one knows how much I sigh,
  What hours I waste in weeping,
How many times I wipe my eye
  When bumpkin souls are sleeping.
As Cupid's shaft has conquered kings,
  I couldn't hope to fly it—
Thine eyes, dear Mary, were the things
  That massacred my quiet.

Oh! my long-lost Mary,
Flower of County Tipperary!
Blighted blossom! in this bosom
Treasured is thy memory, Mary.

High ho! alas! and woe is me!
Ah, dear! alack and well a
Day, why did I meet with thee,
Divinest Isabella?
I loved thee often, loved thee long,
I loved thee best of any,
Until among the dazzling throng
I first laid eyes on Fanny.

Oh, plus belle! resistless Frances,
Thou hast slain me by thy glances,
Coal-black hair and killing air—
My death lies at thy door, oh, Frances!

Now, would to Herrings I had been
Last twelve month at Havanna,
For there I never could have seen
The pink of angels, Anna.
I squeezed her hand—it didn't please—
And I, alas! before a
Week elapsed was on my knees
To lovely Leonora.

But, oh, ye swains, shun Leonora—
Rather, oh, ye swains, implore a
Marble block or ocean rock,
They're not so cold as Leonora.

My heart is now a funeral pile
Of black sepulchral sorrow;
I'll never more be seen to smile,
Or heard to bless the morrow.
I'll die in loneliness and gloom
Before the month is over.
Then, Brasspen, chisel on my tomb
That I, too, was a lover.

And, oh! whene'er you speak of Clarence,
Tell it here, and tell it far hence,
How he sighed until he died,
Consumed by love, unhappy Clarence.[12]

By the spring of 1834, Mangan was in a relatively good frame of mind, and while he was enjoying this unusual respite, he probably met the Dublin family named Stackpoole with whom he would soon become close friends. Living in Lower Mount Street, their entourage consisted of the widow Susan Stackpoole, her two grown sons, John, aged twenty-three, and William, aged twenty-two; and three daughters, Susanna, seventeen, and the twins, Margaret and Eliza, fifteen. The father, Charles, had recently died. He had been a member of the Royal Meath Militia, and, just as importantly, part of the old and well-established Stackpoole clan of near Ennis in the County Clare. One branch of the family appeared in the "Nobility and Gentry" listing in the city directories of the early part of the century, and Charles himself had been listed in Burke's *Irish Family Records* as "of Fitzwilliam Square". The family had converted to the Church of Ireland, and by the nineteenth century some of their number had become fairly prominent churchmen. It may be that Mangan was introduced to John or William by someone in his office, or perhaps by a friend such as William Hayes. He must have made a good impression, for he would scarcely have been so welcome in their home if he hadn't presented a gentlemanly demeanour.

Charles Stackpoole's death had left his widow Susan with a rather large responsibility. After William's birth in Suffolk in 1812, they had at some time returned to Ireland and settled in the family's home in Tullamore, and there Susanna had been born in 1817, the twins in 1819, and the last child, Charles, who died young, in 1821. In 1832, the father's unmarried older brother John died, leaving his property to his namesake nephew. The only further reference to this eldest son is later in Burke's where he is said to be "of Lower Mount Street".[13] Susan Stackpoole's name showed up in a Dublin directory in 1835 with the address of Cottage Terrace, Baggot Street, so they had probably moved to the city in 1833 or 1834. Residing there made it easier for William to enter Trinity College, which he did in 1835, and also brought them nearer Susan's relatives, the Church family of Killeen near Trim in County Meath.

Within a short while the family moved to No. 42 Lower Mount Street, fairly near No. 55 which had been a Stackpoole residence since the early years of the century. If the *Directories* are at all reliable, Mangan must have met the family shortly after they made this move. In fact, he may have been employed to give language lessons to the young ladies who attended Susan Stackpoole's "select school", for it appears that she had been reduced to this expedient of respectable but impoverished gentlewomen. Running such a school was a logical choice, certainly, for she had three daughters who were of an age to assist her.

Easter fell on 30 March in 1834, and Mangan, still with a scrivener's customary holidays, left the city without telling his friend Owen Connellan where he was going. Either the bonds of their friendship were exceptionally strong or Mangan's friends already tended to club together to look after him, for Connellan worriedly wrote O'Donovan that he had not seen "Clarence since I am beginning to think that he has gone into the country to rejoice in the shade or cover himself under some green leaves that are now flourishing spreding [*sic*]." (Connellan's Irish was presumably better than his English; for his soon-to-be-undertaken translation of the *Annals of the Kingdom of Ireland by the Four Masters*, he was to have Mangan's assistance in "Englishing" the sentences.) He continued most significantly, "I am sorry at the same time that I have said so much against his DesDemonas as they are such a source of pleasure to him." Who were "his DesDemonas"?[14] For this question there would seem to be a good answer. According to Duffy, Mangan told him that Margaret Stackpoole listened to him "the way Desdemona listened to the Moor", and that partly for that reason he fell in love with her and proposed marriage. As will soon be clear, this romance was not destined to be, but there is an excellent chance that the fifteen-year-old Stackpoole twins were indeed "his Desdemonas".

Connellan, more worldly-wise than the poet, probably said "so much against" the girls because he, if not Mangan, could see that they were too young for a thirty-one year old man. How touching it is, though, that in regretting what may have been some rather sharp words on the subject, he also made the innocence of the relationship so clear: "They are such a source of pleasure to him." In fact, the question of when a girl ceased to be a child and became an eligible young woman was a delicate one. To some extent, it depended on the individual's maturity, but thirteen or fourteen was almost always deemed too young and sixteen almost always sufficiently grown-up. James Price, faithful to his reputation of bounder, wrote enthusiastically about a girl of fifteen as "a *springer*, a tall novel-reading ready-for-love girl", but his view was not necessarily the prevailing one.[15]

Mangan's poems had so far been relatively short, with the sole exception of a few of the almanac entries for 1826, one of which reached a length of one-hundred lines. In the late summer of 1834, however, this caution ended with Schiller's "The Lay of The Bell", a poem of thirty stanzas and more than 430 lines. Why he did not present it to the *Dublin University Magazine* is one of the mysteries of his career. Instead, it went to the *Irish Monthly Magazine of Politics and Literature* which was described by an editor of the *University Magazine* when they reprinted it—eagerly—only six months later, as a periodical that "never attained to any but a very limited circulation, and was indeed hardly known to the literary world".

"The Lay of The Bell" is a masterful translation. Mangan not only preserved Schiller's rhythms and rhyme schemes, and followed the word and phrase sequences closely, but developed an exciting, readable English poem that is faithful in tenor and pace to the German original. As Jacques Chuto has pointed out, this poem alone negates the opinion of Louise Imogen Guiney and Robert Welch that Mangan was never really a translator in the truest sense of the word.[16] It also confirms his remarkable skill in creating auditory effects, as witness this short section from "The Fire-Bell":

> Now the white air, waxing hotter,
> Glows a furnace—pillars totter—
> Rafters crackle—casements rattle—
> Mothers fly—
> Children cry—
> Under ruins whimper cattle.
>   All is horror, noise, affright!
>   Bright as noontide glares the night!
> Swung from hand to hand with zeal along,
> By the throng,
> Speeds the pail. In bowlike form
>   Sprays the hissing watershower,
> But the madly-howling storm
>   Aids the flames with wrathful power.

Almost certainly Mangan's poem—or, more accurately, Schiller's—was the model for Edgar Allan Poe's popular recitation piece "The Bells", which also had sections for alarm/fire bells, wedding bells, and passing bells, although opening brightly with merry sleigh-bells. This particular influence seems never to have been considered and certainly not in the highly romanticized account of how Poe wrote the poem, published in 1848, which is customarily repeated.[17]

[4]

> *1835*:
> —The steeple of St Werburgh's church taken down.
> —The Dublin Historical Society founded.
> —The steam carriage for the first time driven through several of the leading streets in the city. Shortly afterwards withdrawn.
> —The Royal Mail conveyed to and from Kingstown by the railway for the first time.
> —Halley's comet seen over Dublin in September.
> "Annals of Dublin", *Dublin Almanac and General Register*, 1843

A momentous year for Mangan from one aspect, an emotionally traumatic year from another, 1835 saw the poet settle in as a serious *Dublin University Magazine* writer. It was also this year he had to deal with the death of his brother John, the first death in his family, in all likelihood, that he could remember. In Ireland, there was a lull, a truce, in violent political actions, with O'Connell away in Parliament exerting some beneficent influence for his country's sake and in general trying to bring about changes in a moderate manner. Over the English literary scene, almost a hush had fallen. Coleridge and Lamb had died in 1834, their deaths defining the term of British Romanticism. The earlier echelon including Byron, Keats and Shelley, had died in the 1820s. Wordsworth lived on to become poet laureate, but most of his productive years were behind him. Tennyson and Browning may have been in the wings, but their literary identity had not yet come into being.

Among the Irish poets working alongside Mangan, metaphorically if not actually, most had close associations with England or the continent. Thomas Moore had absented himself from Ireland to live in England where, in Stopford Brooke's phrase, he produced too much "bric-a-brac poetry". Poor J.J. Callanan had died in 1829 in Lisbon, leaving behind that lovely line, "There is a green island in lone Gougaune Barra." Francis Mahoney, "Father Prout", moved to London in 1834 and scattered poetry from there to Rome for the next thirty years, but he would be remembered solely for "The Bells of Shandon". Gerald Griffin and John Banim, too, had sought out the English capital, though both returned to Ireland, more distressed, more inward-looking, and more disillusioned, than when they had gone abroad. In Griffin, melancholy grew progressively deeper, until he made his last visit to London in 1835 and thereafter prepared to enter the Order of the Christian Brothers. Of all these poets, it was he with whom Mangan had the most in common, although the two may never have met. Honourable and dutiful, Griffin had loved the happily married Lydia Fisher since 1830, without the faintest hope of fulfilling his passion, which he always spoke of in platonic terms. To her, and for her, he wrote a few exquisite, and a few excruciatingly banal, love poems. Among the former was "To * * * * " a stanza of which has been mistaken at times for Mangan's work.

In the time of my boyhood I had a strange feeling,
   That I was to die in the noon of my day;
Not quietly into the silent grave stealing,
   But torn, like a blasted oak, sudden away—

Another rumoured romance of Mangan's also (may have) occurred around this time. Two small clues, unfortunately both more interesting than reliable, point to Cook Street as the residence of a young woman whose name was linked with his. The first comes from a story told by a daughter of an O'Neill and had its first airing in 1893 in a yarn titled "Romantic Career of an Irish Princess" by John Petrie O'Byrne in the *Dublin Weekly Freeman*; O'Byrne had found it in a London paper which originally had picked it up from a newspaper in New Orleans.[18] It had, purportedly, been related by one Eva O'Neill Manning on her deathbed in the Louisiana city. It was a daughter of her father's brother, she had revealed, who had been Mangan's early sweetheart. She knew this because she herself, a child in the 1840s, had been well-acquainted with the poet, having often fetched him home from Winetavern Street public houses. Her father, a coffin-maker, Francis O'Neill, had been a close friend of his. She claimed to own a manuscript of "The Nameless One", but what became of it, the article did not say. O'Neills did live in Cook Street, the so-called Street of Coffins, in the 1830s, and the directories listed one of them as a coffin-maker and undertaker, but whether any of the rest of the tale was true is not certain.[19] Presumably, Eva O'Neill did not explain how the romance between Mangan and her cousin ended, although she implied that it was sad.

Another story, different in tone but also linking Mangan with Cook Street, was narrated by James Price in the 21 March 1835 *Weekly Dublin Satirist*. I do not think there can be much doubt that Mangan was the prototype for the poet in Price's "Adolphus Softbotham" narrative. Mangan had almost certainly been poking fun at Price a year-and-a-half earlier in "My Transformation", and now Price, having made up his differences with the *Satirist*, was getting back at his friend. "Adolphus" was described in terms that Mangan almost surely inspired. He was a melancholy genius with a fragile frame, high, pale brow, blue and melancholy eyes, and a nose in which the enthusiasm of his character was centered. His soul was elevated, so he fell in love consumingly, a love which "rendered his heart a perforated pump" and wore him down until "he stood a skeleton umbrella . . . a human conjunction of withered fibers", his body shrunken "to the dimensions of a kidney bean". He was a terrific lyricist, with a heart for love and a stomach for whiskey.

The story Price told about this character's love affair with "Olivia" was brief and tragic and very amusing. Arriving at Adolphus' garret one evening, he found him, along with an "attenuated cat", gazing raptly at a single herring and pondering the bitter truth that "Olivia has not noticed my stanzas and my landlord has noticed me to quit." Olivia, interestingly enough, lived in a house in Cook Street. There, they went; the poet, failing to charm her, was overcome by despair, ran amok, and ended up in the Watch House where Price claimed to have left him. The next morning, however, when he went to his lodgings to find his friend, he was not there, and the landlord suspected him of bolting. Price suspected something worse. The "Puddle-hole", that is, The Poddle, a small Dublin stream, was dragged and there, sure enough, his remains were discovered. "*Love*, unrequited made the suicide", the satirist concluded. "Peace to his ashes. His pipe and poetry still survive in our possession." It was good fun and not too harsh, generally on a par with Mangan's earlier piece.

A concluding note on "Olivia" may possibly be found in the *Weekly*

Dublin Satirist of 4 April. In the catch-all "The Lion's Mouth: The Gleanings of Our Letter-Box" was a four-quatrain verse titled "An Oriental Poem" and signed "Hafiz". The author, perhaps Mangan, declared, "I presume you are lovers of Persian and Arabic poetry; if so, you will not scruple to insert the following; which, I protest to you, upon my honour as a gentleman, and a man of learning, is perfectly original." Its reference to "my olive maid", in combination with the signature, the interest in eastern poetry—Mangan's own was soon to become explicit—and the "learned" footnotes may suggest the hand was Mangan's, but the little poem falls apart so badly after two stanzas, given here, that the probability is not great:

AN ORIENTAL POEM

Fain would I take a soft meander
Along the banks of blue scamander,
Where love made Hero and Leander
Much like a goose, also a gander.

But in the orange bowers of Sabia,
Or in the wilds of spiced Arabia,
From whence to Solomon came Sheba,
I'd like, my olive maid, to leave you . . . .

Having brought up the subject of dubious attribution, it may be a good time to give the reader a glimpse into just how formidable the task is of determining if a poem "could be", "may well be", or "can't possibly be" by Mangan. In the issue of the *Satirist* containing "An Oriental Poem", only the first page (of eight) contains no poetry at all. The "Original Poetry" column has one (probably) authentic signature—Tim Rooney—and two pen-names, "Philomel" and "Alastor". Could Philomel's "The Bee and the Rose" be Mangan's? A lot of thought goes into it, and a decision in the negative is made for reasons too technical to go into here. The next page's "The Lion's Mouth" offers not only "An Oriental Poem", but also two others, one unsigned, the other signed "Nomen". Both are clever in idea and rhyme scheme, but they are reluctantly passed over because they "don't seem right". Nothing definably technical here. "Answers to Correspondents" on the next page has three verses, all signed with pseudonyms that are not Mangan's (although when a poem is a real "suspect", the business of how it is signed carries less weight). The rest of the poems in this number—nine—are either songs to certain airs, the context ruling out the possibility Mangan had a hand in them, or are culled from another publication; one of them is our poet's "Song Exciting to Gladness" from the *Dublin University Magazine.* These poems and dozens like them in the periodicals of the time pose intriguing questions in the process called "attribution". Although Mangan's style is unique, there are still borderline, anonymous, and curiously signed poems to be evaluated.

In January 1835, Mangan introduced his *Dublin University Magazine* readers to the first of what would become his most important series of translations, "The Anthologia Germanica". It would run for twenty-two chapters, twelve years in all, and contain what he himself judged to be the best of his work from the German poets. From these several-hundred poems he made his selection in 1845 of the poems he wanted to include in his *German Anthology*, the only book of his poetry to be published during his lifetime.

From 1835, too, he had at least an informal working arrangement with Isaac Butt who had succeeded Charles Stuart Stanford as editor in the summer of 1834. He would have, as he himself put it, "A field of sixty pages, or thereabouts, [per year] to gambol in. . . ."[20] He met that quota for the first five years with the sort of regularity he had demonstrated on the *Satirist*, usually with four anthologies of one sheet, that is, sixteen pages each, per quarter. It would be difficult to overestimate the professional and, needless to point out, financial importance to him of this agreement. In effect, it was not only a seal of approval placed on past work, but a contract for the future. Although it did not entirely give him *carte blanche*, it certainly offered a great deal of freedom of choice.

For his first chapter of the "Anthologia Germanica" he chose "the lyrical and smaller poems of Schiller". Anyone listening carefully would have heard a forecast of what his practice in translating was going to be in his explanation about a few of these "vagrant reliques": "We have (for no base purposes) disguised them to the best of our poor ability; but we should, after all, be loath to hear that they had forfeited their identity." In those thirty words can be found most if not all of Mangan's Theory of Translation.

In January, February, and April, he busily filled his anthology chapters with previously published poems in errant violation of the *University Magazine's* supposedly inviolable policy of not reprinting anything that had already appeared elsewhere in print. And he got away with it. February's "Lay of the Bell" by Schiller was a lengthy and outstanding work that the editors obviously were happy to use, but they still explained why it was in the magazine when it had appeared less than a year earlier in the now defunct *Irish Monthly Magazine of Politics and Literature*: The obscurity of the *Irish Monthly Magazines*, its disappearance from the scene, the many revisions Mangan had made in the poem, and so on. But the fact was, they seem to have been prepared to let him do about as he pleased, a decision which Anster and Petrie doubtless approved. In April he began submitting original poems, but he was to cautiously put the name of some German poet on most of these, whether of a genuine poet, or one he invented. His distrust of his own works' ability to appeal to anyone continued, little abated by his successes.

At £8 per sheet, his earnings from the anthologies alone in 1835 must have been no less than £32, and a number of individual poems, for which he should have been paid £1 per hundred lines, increased substantially the total he earned by his pen. Add to this sum his salary from the scrivenery job, at which he continued to be employed at 30 shillings weekly if the figure Price named for 1831 still held true, and, though we cannot know how many weeks he worked, it is apparent he made altogether the not inconsiderable sum of £90 or more. His brother John was undoubtedly working, and William, too, in all likelihood had some form of employment, although as a cabinetmaker he could not have received a large wage and always seems to have hovered on the brink of joblessness. In short, the family now enjoyed an adequate income, especially if they all continued to live under one roof.

If so much money were at his disposal, is it likely, though, that the poet stayed in the same house as his father? Perhaps not. Yet the decision to move out would not have been a simple one. The drudgery of taking a trunk with him would not have been especially onerous, since he possessed very few clothes and probably not yet very many books. But where *home* was concerned, Mangan was quite choosy, at least when his circumstances allowed. He enjoyed comfort. All we need do to appreciate its importance to him is remember the hatred he retained for the *discomfort* of the Chancery Lane "hovel". Add to this the severe difficulty he had making changes, even when they might be for the better, and the chance that he remained with his parents and brothers throughout this period is seen to be as great as that he moved away.

[5]

Dear nature, constant in her laws,
    Hath mark'd each mental operation;
Bumps are effects which spring from cause,
    Well known in this most fighting nation!
For no deception here can be,
    Each little hillock hath a tongue,
Uttering words which all agree
    Might save a man or have him hung!
May future times much wisdom cull
From my own head when it's a skull!

Mangan [?], "Verses—Inscribed by a phrenologist on a skull", *DPJ*, 28 July 1832

The actual fact must have been that he had more money in his pocket at this point than at any time in the past, so it is gratifying to discover him spending a few extra shillings on himself, and on something other than the ever-tempting alcohol, in the early spring of the year. On 11 February, he found his way, perhaps with John O'Donovan, to the office of a phrenologist, "Professor" J. Wilson, who had advertised a few days earlier in the *Satirist*:

> *Phrenology*—J. Wilson, Hon. Member Phrenological Society Dublin, having for a short time returned to town, will be happy to afford an opportunity of enjoying the many important benefits of this now well tested science.
>
> Mr Wilson gives, to all who may desire it, a written description of character, showing what they ought particularly to avoid, what studies they may with most success pursue, what line of life they are best fitted for, etc.; for such Portrait of Character, 10s. . . . for a Verbal statement, 2s.
>
> Phrenology, both as to Theory and Practice, taught in Class, One Guinea a Course. 116 Grafton Street, opposite the College.[21]

O'Donovan, who was as perpetually strapped for funds as his friend, probably had what was described as a "sketch of character" which "Professor" Wilson did orally. Years later he recalled that he had been told he had "too much benevolence and wanted combativeness to a fault", an almost ludicrous mistake, considering his well-known temperament. Mangan, on the other hand, must have splurged on the "Portrait of Character", because such an "analysis" survived for at least the next fifty years, being reprinted in Fr Meehan's book of Mangan's verse and prose. Something over 500 words long, it is reproduced in full in Appendix D. The summary paragraph read:

> In conclusion, this is the head of one who is susceptible of strong impressions, great joy or great sorrow, but who would live much more in the past and future than in the present, and would be reckoned somewhat eccentric by the world. The principal ingredients of the character it indicates, are taste, wit, extravagance, vividness of fancy, generosity, and proneness to yield to the solicitations of others.

He found Mangan to be almost everything that tradition and witnesses say he was: capable of warm attachment, inclined to "cherish fanciful notions" of women's dispositions and characters, possessed of the "spirit of poetry", subject to great extremes of mood, interested in (but not especially suited for) philosophical studies, blessed with great compassion particularly for the young and innocent, desirous of the esteem of others but lacking in self-esteem, not inclined to "yield much submission to authority", and gifted with an "exquisite perception of the beauty of figure" of Form and Language along with "a remarkable memory for words". The uncanny accuracy of this reading was marred by one omission.

Nowhere is there any hint that Wilson's subject showed the slightest inclination to melancholy or hypochondriasis. Was that just another flaw in the practitioner's interpretation, similar in origin, we might guess, to the error he made about O'Donovan? Or did Mangan just not show him any of the tell-tale signs of those afflictions? One thing is plain: If the "Professor" had noted the mannerisms and bearing of depression, he would not have ignored them. That they were absent, at least when the poet visited Grafton Street that February day, is in itself a pertinent addition to what we know of his character.

Mangan's belief in phrenology has been taken as evidence of his preoccupation with things strange and marvelous, but in actual fact, it was not necessarily any such thing. Though we know it now as a pseudo-science that somehow inflicted its wild premises on vulnerable individuals, phrenology was a widely accepted if somewhat dubious early experiment in psychology with many learned and reputable adherents. Mangan was so interested in it that he planned at one time to open his own academy of phrenological studies where, like Wilson, he could give instruction "both as to theory and practice". Something interfered and undermined this ambition, it would seem, for Mangan never acted on it.

If he had tried to bring his dream to life, he would have had no shortage of materials to work with. The "phrenological head", with its dotted lines marking off the areas below which the various attributes, skills, and feelings were believed to originate, could be readily purchased, as could a picture of such a head, the phrenological chart providing a cheap substitute for the three-dimensional article itself. Books on the subject were numerous, too. The Dublin Phrenological Society, founded in 1829, was a centre for advocates, sponsoring visits by such famed practitioners as George Coombe, a British phrenologist and author of a 500-page tome on the subject. His visit in 1833 had electrified even skeptics, for he had performed such an amazingly accurate "cranial analysis" of a patient in Richmond Lunatic Asylum that the viability of phrenology was advanced in many people's minds almost beyond doubting. Petrie's lead article in the *Dublin Penny Journal*, it will be recalled, had dealt with phrenological theory, and it was now the *Dublin University Magazine's* turn to ask, "Is it possible to say of a system which enables a mere observer, at a single glance, to form a judgement of character so nearly approaching to correctness, that there is nothing in it?" And the reviewer of *Memoirs of the Life and Philosophy of Spurzheim*, one of phrenology's founders, answered his own question: "We think not."[22]

Although "Professor" Wilson advertised in the *Satirist*, the paper tended to scoff editorially at phrenology. Its editor Coyne aspired to be a dramatist and his first play, a farce, was titled *The Phrenologist*, and was written as a vehicle for his friend and popular comic actor James Browne. Mangan has almost nothing to say about plays, concerts, and so on, but it is unlikely that he missed this performance. It probably had a good bit of the sort of humour typified by the *Satirist's* teasing about the subject, and the mocking of its vocabulary, as in referring to Daniel O'Connell as a man in whom "the organs of self-approbation, blarney, and jaw-waggishness, are all full: philoprorent-tiveness is very large; and cock-of-the-roostativeness uncommonly prominent."[23]

Among Mangan's friends and acquaintances, James Hardiman, antiquary and editor of *Irish Minstrelsy*, possessed the entire six volumes of *Dewhurst on Phrenology*, published in 1831,[24] and both John O'Donovan and James Tighe held the "science" in some respect, although O'Donovan characteristically retained a fair amount of skepticism. Nevertheless, when O'Donovan was doing field work for the Ordnance Survey, he was cajoled by his friend the antiquary Myles O'Reilly into dealing with the delicate problem of getting the purported skull of the bard Carolan back to Dublin for phrenological analysis. It would have to be, O'Donovan protested, wrapped carefully in wool if it were to be sent to the capital from its resting place in a private museum at Castle Caldwell, and he didn't really want to be bothered with it. Besides, "Hardiman states that the old Bard's skull was shot to pieces by an orangeman from the North."[25] Under the mellowing influence of "Holy Eve . . . in a wild country village", he weakened, and even though he had no way of carrying the "supposed skull of Carolan" around with him, wrote a half-serious, half-comic phrenological analysis of the relic for his friend. O'Reilly was not amused. He wrote back in red ink fuming that what O'Donovan had to say about the skull was really "highly consonant" with Carolan's known character. O'Donovan, realizing he had overdone the sarcasm, diplomatically apologized. As for James Tighe's interest in phrenology, it was, like Mangan's own, much less critical. Tighe's "phrenological examination" of the head of an almanac poet named John Forde was recalled years later by the subject's son when asked by D.J. O'Donoghue for reminiscences about Tighe's circle of friends, although he did not recall the findings.[26]

Another surviving fragment of the poet's history that lets us follow him on his reasonably happy way for the first few months of 1835 is a letter he penned to O'Donovan on 10 March. O'Donovan was in and out of Dublin frequently during this period, although he spent the months of good weather mostly at work in the field for the Ordnance Survey as they completed the northern counties. His new residence was No. 1, the corner house, St Stephen's Lane, centrally situated between Upper and Lower Mount Street, and it was this house that Mangan went looking for one night—unsuccessfully, as it turned out. Whenever he failed to keep an engagement, as here, he tended to placate his friends by writing an entertaining apology. That is not to say his explanation was contrived merely to get himself forgiven. He really did experience life as inordinately complex. Simple daily matters could almost overwhelm him, for he lacked the capacity to prioritize. When everything looms as important, the only way to achieve some control may be to take oneself out of the pattern altogether. He did that with alcohol sometimes, and I suspect also by missing, or being late for, appointments, a strategy which could backfire, leaving him in control, it may be, but embarrassed and apologetic:

> My gay fellow,
>
> I set out last night with a lantern in my hand and determination in my heart in search of your invisible castle, but after I had perambulated about 38 or 40 of the by-courts and labyrinthine lanes of Mount Street, the devil of doubt and delusion somewhere and somehow got hold of me, broke my lantern, dissipated all my determination and sent me home again in a quite anti-philosophical frame of mind. All the blame being fairly attributable to him, it would be ridiculous for me to proffer you any apology. Meet me tomorrow evening, I impressively adjure you, at that end of the Arcade which looks out on what they call College Green. Let the time be either 7 p.m. ¼ past 7 p.m. ½ past 7 p.m. ¼ before 8 p.m. or 8 p.m. as may suit your convenience. You will find me whistling either a jig or a dirge, according as I chance to feel merrily or truculently disposed—
>
> Tuesday 10th Yr's in a hurry. JCM[27]

Then, just when everything was going as well for James Clarence Mangan as it had ever gone in his life, another blow fell. His brother John died on 5 May. He was the first Mangan to be buried in the family plot in the newly opened Catholic burial ground, correctly called Prospect, but more usually, Glasnevin Cemetery. Of course, the poet could say nothing directly about his grief in the pages of the *Dublin University Magazine*, but a passage in his October "Anthologia Germanica" certainly referred to this event, as he explained why he had had no German collection in the magazine for the past several months:

> We have not forgotten our German. Months, it is true, have elapsed since we last presented our readers with any of those gems from the rich mines of German poesy wherewith we were wont to deck our pages. Yet our studies have not been discarded, although they have been laid aside. They have been laid aside, not because there was any intermission in the depths of that worship which, in our soul, we pay to the grand, albeit sometimes gloomy spirit that presides over the song and legends of the land of Goethe—but because other, and far less pleasing occupations intervened to disturb the stillness of our devotion, and we have not had a peaceful hour to weave an offering that might be worthy to lay upon the shrine.[28]

Very well. But it seems a cold way to speak about the loss of a brother, and one suspects not so much that unnamed but onerous responsibilities got in the way of feeling for a time, as that such a pose was essential camouflage for grief. Certainly responsibility for the family did devolve at least in part onto the poet. It may be that, deprived of John's earnings, the family had to look around promptly for a less expensive place to live than Charlemont Street. According to the meagre records that have come down to us, they moved to No. 9 Peter Street before the end of 1837, and quite possibly the change was made soon after John's death.

Mangan did not go long without incorporating his loss into his poetry. Over the next few months his work held many oblique expressions of sorrow and tributes to lost love. Two poems that must have been penned shortly after John's death are Mangan's first acknowledged original pieces for the *University Magazine*. They appeared in the June issue. "Sonnet" concluded:

Bird of the poet's paradise! by thee
  Taught where the tides of feeling deepest tremble,
Playful in gloom, like some sequestered sea,
  I too amidst my anguish would dissemble,
And tune misfortune to such melody,
  That my despair thy transports should resemble.

"Stanzas" had untold love as its theme:

So lone a thing it is to love, where love's forbid to grow;
So desolate and dark the secret soul's unspoken woe:
In silence smoulders on the flame, consuming night and day,
Till hope, heart, and the thing it loved, alike have passed away.[29]

Two further original sonnets in September show how capable he was, when he chose, of handling such a restrictive verse form. In "Life" he paid homage to that inscrutable Mystery and begged Time to spare "for their final sphere the Noble and the Fair". These lines set the tone:

O, Life! whose page, a necromantic scroll,
  Is charactered with sentences of terror,
  Which, like the shapes on a magician's mirror,
At once bewilder and appal the soul,
  We blindly roam thy Labyrinth of Error,
And clasp a phantom when we gain thy goal.

The Spirit of Wordless Love, subject of the second sonnet, could as well rule the love of a man for his brother as for his sweetheart. "Love" closed:

We weep not, for the world's bleak breath hath bound
  In triple ice the cisterns of our tears,

But ever-mourning Memory thenceforth rears
Her altars upon desecrated ground,
And always, with a low, despairful sound,
Heavily tolls the bell of all our years.[30]

In his October *University Magazine* anthology Mangan acknowledged, perhaps with a wince, that his work had been the subject of a certain amount of criticism:

> It has been alleged against us that our Anthologies are somewhat deficient in the information which essays purporting to treat of German literature should contain. . . . As translators we are very much at a loss to discover what species of information it is that our censurers or counsellors require of us. Do they wish us to furnish histories of the lives and adventures of every poet we chance to take down from the shelf?. . . Or do they, perhaps, expect that we are to engage in disquisitions upon the genius and character of every individual from whom it may be our good or ill fortune to translate or travestie a stanza?

What he did not say was that some, if not all, of this criticism had appeared in the *Satirist* as far back as April in a review of the third chapter of his German anthology. The reviewer had written that the chapter was interesting but "deficient in the information which a paper on such a subject should afford. We would advise the clever author to indulge his readers with critiques on the distinctive genius of German poetry, rather than on abstract questions of a cloudy philosophy." The problem, of course, was not only Mangan's lack of specific information but also that he had more interest in "abstract questions" than in concrete details about German poetry or poets. It was absolutely essential that he should adopt a high tone in answering, for the fact was, he was writing for an audience almost certainly better educated than himself. He was, in a sense, always under the gun. A great many of his readers came from backgrounds which would have given them access to the language and its literature. The information they gained from travel or tutors might not have been entirely accurate or very deep, but it added a dimension to their knowledge that Mangan's simply did not have.

The best he could do was brazen it out. So he wrote authoritatively that such "histories of the lives and adventures of every poet we chance to take down from the shelf" were not useful, were often left unread, were "scarcely half understood", and often were not true, anyhow. "We believe that the heart and intellect of a poet", he declared, "are ever more easily susceptible of analysis by a simple reference to his works than by the aid of the most elaborate explanatory criticism". These were, he concluded, his "undecorated sentiments", and, "We are vain enough to imagine that, if they were also the sentiments of others, neither the cause of poetry nor that of common sense would be a loser."[31]

Already, although he certainly did not admit as much, he had begun to test his *Dublin University Magazine* readers by deliberately throwing in bits and pieces of information that were not true. The earliest examples of his hazarding such a game came in this same chapter of the "Anthologia Germanica", where five of the dozen poems were not what they claimed to be. Either they were the work of different poets than those whose names appeared on them, or they were Mangan's own. Apparently nobody called him to account. He was surely aware that this practice was not really acceptable, but more and more, he was coming to see everything as possessing a dual and dubious identity, a "face" and a "mask", and the "face" and "mask" as being interchangeable. Thus of German poetry he wrote:

> Wearing the outward mask and semblance of that which it professes to be, it stands exposed, when stripped of those, as a revelation of incongruities and absurdities—a picture, the grouping of which presents us with but a mass of blots and shadows, an anomaly with which the heart cannot sympathise—which the understanding is powerless to grapple with. . . . There is a certain deranged arrangement in it which we long to call chaotic. It is the perfection of magnificent inanity.

With a certain contempt for the true but hidden face as well as for the "face" that is presented to the world, he had nowhere to turn for solidarity or solace. We can, he wrote, reveal our true selves only in the moment of death; meanwhile "each assumes his own peculiar mask."[32]

This December, the *Satirist* carried "Lines to xxxxx", a poem that seems highly personal and yet is different in its import to any other personal poem he ever wrote. It appears to be spoken to a young woman friend, Jane, who has lost someone she loved, though not necessarily a lover. "Weep", he admonishes her, while you can, for, "The snows on the mountain/Will soon be less cold than thy soul." Nothing the young woman has done accounts for this bitter expectation, but, he declares, "chill habitude" over the years inevitably paralyzes feelings. More, perhaps, than any other single affliction, this human vulnerability to becoming deadened, anaesthetized to emotional pain, appalled Mangan. Not being able to feel—like his statues of frequent reference—or being "empty" or "flat" was the nightmare of a true enthusiast. The poem, from its grim opening, "I knew that Disaster/Would shadow thy morning, and must", to its somewhat comforting conclusion that "the heart's recollections/May hallow their shrine to the last!", is a strong statement about the bitter irony of life: pain is bad, but not being able to feel it is worse. Who this young woman was, if indeed he had someone particular in mind, is not known. One thing we do know, though, is that when Mangan used "x's" or asterisks in this manner he characteristically disguised a real person.

Close to half a year would elapse before the next chapter of the "Anthologia Germanica" appeared in March 1836. During this time Mangan published only one poem, a translation, in the *Dublin University Magazine*. In November and December he seems to have cleared out his desk and sent the *Weekly Dublin Satirist* the poems he found there: In addition to the foregoing "Lines to xxxxx", there were "A Song for Cloud Blowers", "Humanum est Errare", and "Versus-Verses", all originals. These mark the end of his association with that publication and just about the end of the *Satirist*. He was also almost finished with submitting old poems for republication. From now on, most of his work would be appearing for the first time, and all of it for the next few years would go to the *Dublin University Magazine*. By having secured a place with that already esteemed periodical, Mangan was drawing away from Price and his other old friends. Many of their names continued to appear in poetry columns, however. Sheehan made good as a journalist in England, as did Coyne, who, after a successful career as a dramatist, became one of the founders (1841) of *Punch*.[33] Price became an editor of the ultra-orange *Evening Packet*. As for "Brasspen", he seems to have dropped from sight; perhaps it was Age which won the "amorous old bachelor" at last.

Young Hopes

[1]

> Mangan [was] pale, slight, shy, reserved and slow of speech. . . . When he emerged into daylight, he was dressed in a blue cloak midsummer or midwinter, and a hat of fantastic shape, under which golden hair, as fine and silky as a woman's, hung in unkempt tangles, and deep blue eyes lighted a face as colourless as parchment. He looked like the spectre of some German romance rather than a living creature.
>
> Charles Gavan Duffy, "Personal Memories", 1908

This, said Duffy, was Mangan's appearance when he and Mangan met in 1836. People took note of the poet's blue broadcloth cloak not because it was unusual but because such a garment was intended for evening wear, and Mangan, as well as wearing it winter and summer, also seems to have worn it night and day. Another friend described him as garbed in a brownish coat and pantaloons that were obviously too large for him, although such trousers, like the cloak, were also in style at the time. Sometimes he wore a soldier's fatigue cap, but his hat, often described as high and peaked, was of a style popular with artists during the earlier years of the century. Thus his costume was not particularly eccentric piece by piece, but put together, the various articles of clothing probably looked very odd indeed. He apparently continued to wear the same thing, year in and year out, so his appearance became increasingly peculiar.

Charles Gavan Duffy, who penned the description at the head of this chapter, had only recently celebrated his twentieth birthday in his home in Monaghan, when, inspired with a burning desire to become a journalist in the city, he moved to Dublin in the spring of 1836. Through a relative who was already a journalist, he had received the promise of an unpaid apprenticeship on Michael Staunton's *Morning Register.* The young man expected a lot from Dublin, not least of all an opportunity to meet William Carleton and Clarence Mangan, "whose writings had mitigated the monotony of life in a country town". And indeed, he met both men, although it was with Mangan he formed the closer friendship, for the two shared spiritual values and a fineness of nature not present in Carleton's make-up. D'Arcy McGee described Duffy as being of middle size and apparently suffering from a "dyspeptic constitution"; his manner "was frank, short and decided. He was always in action, planning, suggesting and negotiating. . . . His mind was fruitful in expedients, stored with examples", and, perhaps more in tune with Mangan's, "poetic in its tone, practical in its operation, comprehensive in its judgments. . . ." McGee paid him a characteristically nineteenth-century compliment declaring, "He was brave, yet gentle, firm though full of feeling, a soldier in resolve, a woman in affection."[1]

Duffy's introduction to journalism included a quick course in the reality of newspaper publication. Here, he discovered that newspapermen were not idealists, "erudite, dedicated men with a sense of mission", but rather, "the gipsies of literature, who lived careless, driftless lives without, public spirit or thought of tomorrow".[2] That Catholics edited Protestant papers, and Protestants edited Catholic papers, and that not one of them wrote what he personally believed, was almost more than he could stomach.

Duffy and Mangan, the one scarcely out of his teens, the other thirty-three years old, met in the office of the *Register*. Imagination readily conjures up the scene: two idealists, the young, dark-haired, somewhat horse-faced country boy introduced to the thin, shy, fair-haired, intense poet. Who, beholding the meeting, could have guessed that the lives of the two men would become so intimately connected, that they would be close friends and compatriots until the death of the one and the soul-destroying imprisonment of the other?

With just one day off a week, Duffy had to make every minute count. On Sunday, he usually explored the city with three close childhood friends of his who were in Dublin at the same time as himself, Matt Trumble, Henry MacManus, and Terence MacManus. For a while, he and Henry also shared lodgings, and together they toured historical, artistic, and architectural scenes and sites. Visits to theatres and public meetings were important, too, although unhappily, both held disappointments. Expecting to be thoroughly amused at the Fishamble Street playhouse where audience participation was the custom, Duffy found "the wit was dreary and scanty". Daniel O'Connell, when he saw him in person, appeared no heroic figure, but a practical man made up of a none-too-inspiring mixture of "humour, fierceness, vulgarity, and a capacity for cold, logical analysis".[3]

Mangan, on the other hand, did not disappoint Duffy. Somewhat apologetically the young man confessed that he had "relished most" the poet's "mad pranks in the *Comet* newspaper" rather than the serious things he had been writing, but it soon became their practice to get together on Saturday evenings, Mangan joining Duffy for "nights of blessed memory". As we have heard before, the poet was skilled at monologue and could recite Shakespeare, Schiller, and Byron, their speeches being "as familiar to him as the alphabet". Duffy's account of his visits to his new friend is eloquent:

> . . . Since that time I have lived with many notable men, but the innocent recreation of those nights, when the young poet poured out the masterpieces of dramatic literature, interspersed with speculations and recollections of his own, are more fresh and vivid in my memory than the talk of statesmen or diplomatists. He had a soft, sympathetic voice, which vibrated with passion, or, in milder moods, quivered with sympathy. I expressed my wonder at his inexhaustible supply of subjects and his perfect memory of them. "Ah," he said, "they are my friends and comrades, my only friends and comrades."[4]

Duffy embroidered his memories, as did so many writers in the nineteenth century (and no doubt do in the twentieth), with verbatim conversation which one knows must be a reconstruction. Thus with Mangan's next words:

> . . . Many a time they have peopled my solitude with engrossing visions, when otherwise I would have been miserable and desolate. Many a hundred times I have declaimed them aloud in my solitary garret for my own enjoyment, till my brain throbbed with ardour or my face was wet with tears.

Mangan treasured Duffy, valuing him as a friend and turning to him for help in later years. Besides becoming his confidant and his editor, Duffy impressed Mangan for better or worse with his first youthful preference for the poet's "facitiae" and jokes, so that for a long time Mangan continued to write that sort of material for the *Nation* although the editor begged him to be more serious. It frustrated Duffy. In due course we will see that only when he himself left town and turned the editorial desk over to John Mitchel, did Mangan change his *modus operandi*. In spite of all Duffy's good offices on his behalf, Mangan might never have written his finest Irish poems, including "Dark Rosaleen", had he never met John Mitchel.

For the most part, 1836 was a tranquil and a pleasantly stimulating year for the poet. His fifth, sixth, seventh, and eighth German anthologies appeared at regular intervals, in March, May, August, and December, and were all very much of a length, ranging between 516 and 614 lines. He started with Goethe and ended with Schiller, both conservative choices, and if, in between, he ventured into the fantastic with a selection from the German "fabulists" and a few pages of prose recounting a wild dream, it was a controlled venturing. In fact, his most intriguing poem to appear this year was the first to be significantly strange or eccentric: "The Four Idiot Brothers" in the August anthology. Something of a harbinger for other off-beat pieces which would follow soon enough, it was also a weird instance of the father-and-son genre poem which, for involved personal reasons, so engaged his imagination. Here, four reprobate brothers, having scorned their good old father's dying advice, end tragically. Did Mangan know by this time that he was one of four, not just three, brothers? We have no way of knowing. A sample of this Gothic gem is worth reading:

And now, dried to skeleton-chips,
    In the Mad-cell sit the Four,
Moveless:—from their blasted lips
    Cometh language never more.
Ghastly, stony, stiff, each brother
Gazes vacant on the other;

Till the midnight-hour be come;
    Bristles then erect their hair,
And their lips, all day so dumb,
    Utter slowly to the air,
"*Dies irae, dies illa,*
Solvet seclum in favilla."[5]

Since adopting "Clarence" for his middle name in 1832, Mangan had been faithfully using it, with variations such as "J.C. Mangan", but this August he sported a new pseudonym, "Johann Theodore Drechsler".[6] Thus he signed "Stanzas to xxxx", the poem "Lines to xxxxx" beginning "I knew that Disaster/Would shadow thy morning and must", which had borne his "Clarence" signature in the *Weekly Dublin Satirist* only the preceding December. Obscuring its earlier publication by changing its title from "Lines" to "Stanzas" and presenting it as a German poem, he evidently intended to guarantee (if such were possible) that *University Magazine* editors and readers would not recognize it. Either his ruse worked or nobody cared. Of course, by this point so many obscure German poets had found their way into his columns that his readers no doubt assumed this was just one more.

"Drechsler" was a whimsical choice, in any case, for in German the word means "turner". Although referring to one who works a lathe, it would be more than a little appropriate to a translator, especially to a poet who had "turned" an original English poem into a German translation. Interestingly, this was his first serious deception in the magazine, the first time he seems to have "practised to deceive". He was to use "Drechsler" only three more times, once in 1837, again in 1838, and finally in the semi-burlesque "Polyglott Anthology" in 1839. One of his characters in that anthology, Tutchemupp, replies to a question from another, Baugtrater, about how Drechsler is getting on: "Every day spoils him more and more. He has been too popular. It is a pity, for his faults are the result of sheer wilfullness." The running joke in this anthology is that the characters almost always say the opposite of what is true, although that "Drechsler" was growing thinner and thinner was surely more fact than fiction.

Also in this rather peculiar August chapter came Mangan's first recorded dream, incorporated into the prose commentary where it more or less fitted the context.[7] There would be a few more dreams reported over the years, but they would be sombre and at least seem authentic, whereas this one was comic and almost certainly an invention of his imagination. But dreamed or invented, its terms deserve noting, if only because their mere existence reveals something about his state of mind at this time.

To start, he claimed this was the only dream he had ever had, and that he was not "excitable even by opium, though we have repeatedly devoured stupendous quantities of that drug—and we now begin to despair of ever becoming a vision-seer." The reader is not expected to take this literally, but it sets the tone. Like some of his best poems, the dream has a four-part structure. Its setting is mysterious "Stamboul", the Turkish name for Constantinople, and the dreamer is gleeful because he knows that here he can "perpetrate any devilment with impunity". Each of the four episodes has its ruling figure. All but one involve an obvious pun. The first thing to catch the dreamer's eye is "a colossal pillar inscribed with sentences from Dutch poets", plainly, a pun on a "column" of print with a German poem— this he immediately causes to vanish. The second figure is a rhinoceros with a man riding on his back. With flawless dream logic, the dreamer inquires of the rhinoceros what he is doing, to which the beast replies that he is "following the horn". With this, Mangan created a remarkable triple pun, the first on the rhinoceros' "following" its own horn, that is, coming bodily "after" it, as a person's body "comes after" the nose; the second on the foxhunting expression "to follow the horn"; the third on the "horn" which, the reader discovers upon turning the page, is the subject of the next poem, his translation of Kerner's "Alphorn".

The dreamer becomes more convulsed with laughter and more criminally inclined as each of these encounters unfolds until the fourth and final one in which he runs into the only real opposition he has faced. In a small shop in a clothing bazaar he sees a juggler's costume and determines not to buy it, but to steal it. The pun involves situational irony in that an alternate meaning of "juggler" is "deceiver", or "imposter", so that in effect a thief prepares to steal the costume of a thief. The shopkeeper, an old Musselman, challenges the dreamer and the two grapple. Just as the dreamer prepares to "pulverize" the old man, his opponent attacks and shouts for help. Again, the dreamer laughs. Protesting that the shopkeeper is nothing but "a make-believe, a bull-beggar, an unreality, a humbug, a nobody", the dreamer wakes himself up.

Without going into dream analysis, which should always be left to experts, a few observations can be made about this sequence. First, each of the "entities" or rather, "non-entities", seems to represent some image of the poet himself. Thus there are the German poet of the pillar, the man on the back of the rhinoceros (with difficulty following his "call"), the Turkish warrior, and the merry thief who is prepared to steal a revealing disguise and to thrash the old man. Second, the narration is charged with somewhat sinister energy and inappropriate humour, and the tone is throughout highly confrontational. Both humour and belligerence were poses Mangan assumed to respond to challenges in his own life. And, finally, the only figure that confronts him also threatens him—the shopkeeper. The only shopkeeper who mattered to the poet was his father.

[2]

> Ah, she has made my life desolate, but I cannot help returning, like the moth to the flame.
>
> Mangan, as quoted by Duffy, in "Personal Memories", 1908

Not long after meeting Gavan Duffy, the poet took him to visit his friends, the Stackpooles. It was probably no earlier than the first months of 1837 that he made this move which, though he could not know it at the time, would prove so important to his own story. Duffy fitted in well with the family, made up, as noted earlier in these pages, of the mother, the twenty year old Susanna, the twins Margaret and Eliza who were now almost eighteen, and William who, at the somewhat advanced age of twenty-five, was a student in Trinity College. Duffy thoroughly appreciated the company of the sisters and visited in their home several times, but always, he pointedly wrote, in Mangan's company.

One moonlit evening just after the two men left the Stackpoole house, Mangan stopped suddenly in the street and faced his friend. Laying his hands on Duffy's shoulders and peering intently into his face, he asked, "Isn't it true that you are becoming attached to Margaret?" Duffy was a little taken aback by this straightforward approach, but he somewhat hesitantly admitted that, Yes, he definitely did find her attractive. With that confession, Mangan went on, as Duffy recollected years later, with an admission of his own:

> I will save you from my fate by telling you a tragic history; when I knew Margaret first, I was greatly attracted by her charming manners and vivid *esprit*. I talked to her of everything I did and thought and hoped, and she listened as willingly, it seemed, as Desdemona to the Moor. I am not a self-confident man—far from it; but when I besought her to be my wife I believed I was not asking in vain. What think you that I heard? That she was already two years a wife and was living under her maiden name till her husband returned from an adventure which he had undertaken to improve their fortune.[8]

After the poet delivered this startling piece of information, it was

Duffy's turn to ask a question of his own: "You cannot think that she deceived you intentionally, since you have not broken with her?" Without saying precisely No, he did not think she had, or Yes, he feared that was the case, Mangan answered ambiguously, in the words of the epigraph, "Ah, she has made my life desolate, but I cannot help returning like the moth to the flame." However Duffy chose to interpret this response, he must thereafter have looked at Margaret with rather different eyes. Obviously it made quite an impression on him; although once again we are reading a conversation which doubtless has been reconstructed, he surely recalled the episode vividly.

The strangest element in the Mangan-Margaret romance is that the interpretation of it, perpetuated for well over one hundred years, has been grounded in ignorance of Margaret's age. Mangan almost certainly did not know that Margaret and Eliza were scarcely fifteen years old when he was enjoying their company back in 1834. Duffy had no way of knowing how old the girls were; if he had known, he would hardly have believed the story that Margaret already had been married for two years when Mangan was first smitten with her. (Nor was he aware, it seems, of his friend's painful romance in 1829 and 1830.) Some ten years later, Duffy told Mangan's story to John Mitchel and John O'Hagan, although as far as he could recall, he did not mention names or relate "the curious nature of the *dénouement*" because for Mangan it was still "too profound and painful a secret". Mitchel had no way of knowing how old Margaret was, either, and it fell to him to be the first to publish "Mangan's romance" from which all other biographers have drawn their information:

> Paradise opened before him: the imaginative and passionate soul of a devoted boy bended in homage before an enchantress. She received it, was pleased with it, even encouraged and stimulated it, by various arts known to that class of persons, until she was fully and proudly conscious of her absolute power over one other noble and gifted nature— . . . then with a cold surprise, as wondering that he could be guilty of such a foolish presumption, she exercised her undoubted prerogative and whistled him down the wind. His air-paradise was suddenly a darkness and a chaos.[9]

Some of this was invention, no doubt, or bits of history picked up from other sources, and Duffy objected to it, especially the claim that Mangan was "a devoted boy" when he had actually been a man at least thirty-three years old. He also charged Mitchel with sheer romaticizing, and called "a mere freak of fancy" the flowery conclusion: "As a beautiful dream she entered into his existence once for all: as a tone of celestial music she pitched the key-note of his song. . . . He never loved, and hardly looked upon, any woman forever more." But Mitchel had struck the right chord to appeal to the popular ear. Little fragments of the poet's first early romance, of his affection for Catherine Hayes, and of a somewhat more adult love for Margaret were thus for decades bound together in a story of "Mangan's romance" that was deeply satisfying, fitting into and filling out the "myth of Mangan".

If the story about Margaret's early marriage was a fiction, which I feel reasonably sure it was, who had made it up? Almost certainly that guilty party was Margaret herself. Looked at objectively, we can see that it is one of the most generous and efficient of fibs. It spared Mangan's feelings, while at the same time it put a very effective stop to any advances he might have wanted to make to the young woman. It spared Margaret's feelings, too, which we can easily believe included sympathy and affection for the poet, and allowed them to continue as friends. It was just "secret" enough that neither Mangan nor Margaret nor Margaret's family would be expected to mention it; thus embarrassing questions were avoided on all sides. And, we might add, it was fun for Margaret, giving her an undoubtedly attractive air of maturity and mystery. Until some record of a (most unlikely) ceremony shows up in Church of Ireland marriage records in Ennis, or elsewhere, Margaret's story of her youthful wedding had best be taken as just that—Margaret's story.[10]

One thing at least is clear in all the accounts: Mangan was a very good friend of the Stackpooles, comfortably visited in their home over a period of some years, and no doubt missed all of them deeply when they moved to Kingstown in 1838 or 1839. By that time William had passed his Trinity College examinations to become a "scholar" which made him eligible to receive "free commons, rooms at reduced rent, reduced fees, a salary of £18.9s.3d per annum and [the] right to wear a velvet cap and graduate's gown."[11] His mother continued to keep her "select school" at their new home in George's Place, at least until William finished his Bachelor's degree in the spring of 1842 and joined her, and probably his sisters. By 1845, he was the principal of the Collegiate Institution attached to the Mariner's Church, and he continued in that capacity for many years, eventually also receiving his LL.D. from Trinity. As for the sisters, Anna, like her older sister Maria, died without marrying, but Eliza married Edward Alexander McEntee in 1844 and Margaret married James Maxwell in 1846. Nothing further is heard of them, but William's marriage to Charlotte Mountjoy in 1849 produced a number of children, among whom was the writer Henry de Vere Stackpoole. Indirectly he is known in our own time as the redoubtable author of some sixty mild-mannered romantic adventure novels, although the only one remembered by name is *The Blue Lagoon*. This story of a young boy and girl shipwrecked on a tropical island was first made into a film starring Jean Simmons in 1948, and again in 1980 starring Brooke Shields. The release of a sequel, *Return to the Blue Lagoon*, in 1991 would seem to confirm that Margaret's nephew had hit upon a perennially attractive theme whose vitality is not yet exhausted.

* * * *

In January 1837, the ninth "Anthologia Germanica" consisting of Part II of Schiller's drama, *Wallenstein's Camp*, appeared in the *Dublin University Magazine*, and it was followed in March by the tenth installment in the series, "Tieck and the Other Song-Singers of Germany". These fifteen poems from a selection of German authors were accompanied with several pages of sizzling commentary. As was often his procedure, Mangan based his anthology on recently published volumes of German verse, and his primary target this month was Ludwig Tieck's *Poems and Songs*. Tieck is rarely anthologized today, but in his own time he had no mean reputation, and Mangan in general sympathized with his themes of longing, wandering, and sadness. But he was in a self-confident and hence—perhaps—assertive mood at this moment, and he chastized the German poet roundly. After calling him "man-milliner to the Muses, poet, metaphysician, dramatist, novelist, moralist, wanderer, weeper and wooer, a gentleman of extensive and varied endowments, [who] is, notwithstanding, in one respect, a sad quack", he attacked the poetry itself: "Such rubbish, such trumpery, such a ferrago of self-condemned senilities, so many mouthy nothings, altogether so much snoring stupidity, so much drowsiness, dreariness, drizzle, froth and fog. . . ."

Readers of the *University Magazine* had apparently readjusted their sights and no longer expected the well-informed, serious biographical and academic information such as he had at first been castigated for not producing, and this chapter provided a lot of good laughs. Indeed, they had come to like him the way he was, and one of the ways he was, according to himself in a number of these articles, was *plural*. His rather idiosyncratic insistence on his plurality began with the authorial "we", which was common enough, but went far beyond that:

> The apex of Tieck's cranium must, we should think, display a mountainous development of the organ of Self-esteem [the vocabulary of phrenological analysis]. It is quite manifest that whatever he chooses to pen becomes in his own conceit inerasable and inestimable. A piece of bizarre barbarianism that Rabelais would have blotted out on a first reading is reckoned as the production of Ludwig Tieck, worthy of being enshrined in gold and amber. With submission, nevertheless, to our esteemed, he here reckons without his host; that is, without his host of readers, and also without us, his knouter, who are a host in ourself.[12]

The most thought-provoking poem of the month's selection was not from Tieck, but—purportedly—from the poet-doctor Justinus Kerner. In actual fact, though, Mangan came close to claiming all or at least a fair portion of it as his own, for, he wrote, making a joke as usual, he had already, "doled out, to the fraction of a pennyweight" the exact amount of praise the author deserved. "But if, as we suspect, he remain still as dissatisfied as ever, we would just request his attention to the following translation, and ask him whether he be not, after all, our debtor to a very serious extent." Adding to the suspicion that "My Adieu to the Muse" is Mangan's own is the fact that Jacques Chuto was unable to find an original for the poem.

It becomes apparent as we watch Mangan's life unfold that he was one of those persons made very nervous by things going "too well". Much as change upset him, he required it when this still more disturbing condition prevailed. He was now just on the verge of growing restlessly impatient with "Germanism", and before long he would be impatient with poetry altogether. "My Adieu to the Muse" reflects this state of mind. It is a rather fine poem. The speaker, nearing death and looking back over his life, meditates that it is tempting to blame someone else for his disappointments, but that he must curb that "ugly impulse" and find the fault in himself:

If I have looked for nobleness and truth,
    In souls where Treachery's brood of scorpions dwelt,
    And felt the awakening shock as few have felt,
And found, alas! no anodyne to soothe,
    I murmur not; to me was overdealt,
No doubt, the strong and wrong romance of Youth.

In the noble conclusion, the poet wishes the world well—"May the green Earth glow in the smile of God!"—and closes:

    And, for myself, all I would care to claim
    Is kindness to my memory—and to those
    Whom I have tried, and trusted to the close,
Would I speak thus: Let Truth but give to Fame
My virtues with my failings; if this be,
Not all may weep but none will blush for me;
And—whatsoever chronicle of Good,
    Attempted or achieved, may stand to speak
    For what I was, when kindred souls shall seek
To unveil a life but darkly understood,—
Men will not, cannot write it on my grave
    That I, like myriads, was a mindless clod,
    And trod with fettered will the course they trod,
Crouched to a world whose habitudes deprave
And sink the loftiest nature to a slave,
    Slunk from my standard and renounced my God.[13]

In September 1837, he began a new project, the exploration of what he called Eastern, and we would call Middle Eastern, poetry. Six chapters of the "Literae Orientales" would appear over the next nine years, anthologies of Persian, Turkish, and Arabic poems. Mangan was such a performer where languages were concerned that some critics have actually credited him with the knowledge of one or more of these tongues. Such was not the case, however, and except for his claim that practically all the poems existed only in obscure manuscripts or unobtainable documents, he really made no mystery of his use of whatever material was accessible.[14] "Here, now, at the outset, we request it to be understood, that we shall avail ourselves of all such sources of information as may be open to us." Further, he was "premising only this, that we shall hold ourselves responsible for all that we may here or hereafter assert, and that our translations shall be our own and our own only."[15]

The opening remarks extended to ten pages. He presented the East as a realm to which all states and conditions of mankind are irresistibly attracted. In short, he himself had become fascinated by the lure of the region, and he knew he was far from being alone. Fascination with Arabia and the eastern Mediterranean was in the air in the nineteenth century, and the Irish enthusiast had only to look as far as Thomas Moore's *Lalla Rookh*, which appeared in 1817, for a home-grown example of the genre of pseudo-oriental writings. The *Rubaiyat of Omar Khayyam* would be published mid-century, and O'Donoghue cautiously suggested that "the supposition that Edward Fitzgerald was acquainted with Mangan's articles when he produced those remarkable quatrains which have captured and enraptured the English critical world is not an extreme one."[16] In a sense, Sir Richard Burton's 1885 *Book of the Thousand Nights and a Night* climaxed this phase of orientalism, for with the invention of the internal combustion engine and the opening of the oil fields of the Middle East, magic gave way to mercantilism and true fascination passed into history.

From children to "the coldest of cosmopolites", Mangan affirmed, all feel drawn to "the land of the sun". For himself, he had first been attracted by the tales of the *Arabian Nights*, and his fancy for a realm exotically perfect had been complicated as he grew older by the longing for a home, for the unattainable Past, or for perfect harmony:

> If the East is already accessible, so may be at last—the reverse who dares prophesy?—"the unreached Paradise of our despair"; and so long as the Wonderful Lamp, the dazzler of our boyhood, can be dreamed of as still lying *perdu* in some corner of the Land of Wonders, so long must we continue captives to the hope that a lovelier light than any now diffused over the dusky pathway of our existence will yet be borne to us across the blue Mediterranean.

He could see the peril implicit in this sort of thinking, and yet . . . "it is on the whole fortunate that Speculation can fall back upon such resources. Slender and shifting though they seem, they serve as barriers against Insanity."[17] Thus in the midst of a not very profound piece of literary musing could the poet insert what was for him a terrifying truth. He never had a great deal to say about insanity, but from his autobiography we know that he lived with the frightening possibility of his own madness from at least the age of ten or twelve, and perhaps much younger. So the observation that a "hopeless" Hope served him as a "barrier against insanity" is extraordinarily disturbing.

Mangan had always been enchanted by things strange and marvelous, but this dip into Eastern poetry was his first thorough-going exploration of the gorgeous and exotic in verse. He closed this chapter of the "Literae Orientales" with the first outstanding specimen of his splendid "rose poems", "The Time of the Roses". The symbolism of the flower was nothing new to him, of course, but it was amplified here by its oriental associations, preparing the way, as it were, for the richly-patterned "Dark Rosaleen". The first, fourth, and eighth stanzas, of eleven, follow:

Morning is blushing; the gay nightingales
Warble their exquisite songs in the vales;
Spring, like a spirit, floats everywhere,
Shaking sweet spice-showers loose from her hair;
Murmurs half-musical sounds from the stream,
Breathes in the valley and shines in the beam.
    In, in at the portals that Youth uncloses,
    It hastes, it wastes, the Time of the Roses!

See the young lilies, their scymitar-petals
Glancing like silver 'mid earthier metals;
Dews of the brightest in life-giving showers
Fall all the night on these luminous flowers.
Each of them sparkles afar like a gem.
Wouldst thou be smiling and happy like them?
    O, follow all counsel that Pleasure proposes;
    It dies, it flies, the Time of the Roses!

Now the air—drunk from the breath of the flowers—
Faints like a bride whom her bliss overpowers;
Such and so rich is the fragrance that fills
Ether and cloud that its essence distils,
As through thin lily-leaves earthward again,
Sprinkling with rose-water garden and plain.
    O! joyously after the Winter closes,
    Returns and burns the Time of the Roses![18]

Perhaps it was part of his desire to become a philosopher—he claimed to want to do that—which led Mangan to become as aphoristic as this anthology shows he had grown. One after the other, "sayings" flow from his pen, the following gleaned from only the first four pages:

—"The great art of securing a triumph in reasoning is to make your conclusions wait upon your facts."
—"It is well to be ingenuous, but better to be ingenious."
—"A principle grounded on a fact is Pelion based upon Ossa."
—"Nationality is not always rationality."
—"No soil not classic is consecrated ground."
—"The mind, to be sure, properly to speak, is without a home on the earth."
—"The mind is a Cain that may build cities, but can abide in none of them."
—"No private principle worth preserving is interfered with by reason of the dominance of a certain great catholic feeling in the human spirit."
—"Imagination feels averse to surrender the paramount jewel in the diadem of its prerogatives—a faith to wit, in the practicability of at some time or another realizing the Unreal."
—"Few ploughmen dazzle us, and no *millionaires*."
—"Power and Beauty best vindicate themselves."
—"He who passes ninety-nine altars without worshipping must perforce kneel before the hundredth."

By December, he was seriously expounding upon the nature of translation. "If translators have declared certain tasks impracticable", he wrote, "the declaration may be a proof of their unwillingness to undertake those tasks. . . ." He continued, "They find it convenient to talk of impracticability whenever it is not practicable for them to conquer their own indolence." They suffered from "want of spirit". Or, it might be, "It is not the way that is wanting; it is the will." He assured the readers of this eighth German anthology, "The statue is in the marble, said Praxiteles to his pupil; the point is to hew it out. The equivalents lie ready for all translators; the business is to look for them in the right places." The doctrine of "equivalency" was a slippery one, allowing for much more variation from straightforward literal translation than many critics thought proper, and he drew down a certain amount of criticism upon his head because he espoused it. But, for him, every poem he worked on was a real challenge, and every success a real victory.

A sort of sea-change was going on in Mangan's thought at this period, a change that would seriously alter his future. It is visible in retrospect, but at the time he probably continued to live his life much as he had for the past year or two. Certainly nothing happened to him as dramatic as the catastrophe that overtook the famous Arcade in College Green on 25 April of this year, when it was completely destroyed by fire. A relatively new building, opened only in 1820 on the site of the old Post Office, the Arcade was a "handsome edifice" which had cost £16,000 to erect. It was a fine shopping center, the lower level containing thirty shops under a roof "supported by a double range of Grecian doric columns", the whole illuminated by lanterns which extended along the length of the building.[19] It was a popular place to stroll and to meet friends. No. 34, the Royal Shades, where the poet had set the scene for an assignation with "Brasspen" in his *Comet* story, went up in flames with the rest. Not many years elapsed before the prime business properties were rebuilt, and in the new configuration a smaller building belonging to the Bank of Ireland occupied the Shades' old address with the Royal Arcade Hotel next door. Thus the old names were not altogether lost. But there was to be no public house and cigar-room to replace the Royal Shades that Mangan's generation had enjoyed, and if what the *Directories* show is an accurate reflection of things as they were, College Green was henceforth without any such social gathering place.

That Pit Abysmal

[1]

> I have acquired the power of walking without stockings and even barefooted, to peel potatoes with my nails and drink whiskey—*poitin*— out of scooped raw potatoe! . . . Mr Larcom is hurrying me very much; otherwise I would attempt to write something about the customs of these primitive people. . . .
>
> John O'Donovan, June 23, 1838
> Royal Irish Academy, MS 12/N/5, "Petrie Papers"

Sometime in late 1837 John O'Donovan paid his friend James Clarence Mangan the considerable compliment of employing him to make the printer's copy of the antiquary's monumental English translation of the *Annals of the Kingdom of Ireland by the Four Masters.*[1] "J. O'D", as he so often signed himself, had begun the endeavour in 1832.[2] He was at last ready to get a fair copy prepared for the printer, George Smith, who, in his turn and to his credit, had undertaken the enormous task of printing the tome. Of the numerous "books" which comprised the *Annals*, Mangan would, in the end, copy out two-thirds and O'Donovan himself one third. For his work, the poet was paid £2 per book, from which it can be gathered that each was assumed to represent eight days' employment at the usual rate of five shillings per day.[3] As he was also still holding, in all likelihood, a regular position in a scrivenery office, he must have put in the extra hours at home, at whatever desk arrangement he could improvise, copying by candlelight or lamplight during many a long winter's evening.

What O'Donovan turned over to his friend was almost certainly his own "Englished" copy of the *Annals*. He gave Mangan three books at a time and Mangan was paid when he delivered the fair copy. That he was a superb scribe has never been questioned, his handwriting, at its best, being a work of art. But his reliability has so often been impugned that O'Donovan's willingness to trust him with the fruit of so many years of toil means that certain conceptions have been patently erroneous and simply have to be revised. His role in the production of the *Annals* only recently came to light in the discovery of three of his letters that rested, unknown and undisturbed, among unsorted miscellaneous dozens, in a strongbox in the Royal Irish Academy Library. Interestingly, they are also the poet's earliest extant letters and the only series that we have. Written to O'Donovan on 20, 26 and 30 January 1838, they show the poet's progress on the copying and give intimate glimpses into his daily life.[4]

It was exceptionally cold in Ireland in January 1838. The second week of the new year saw the onset of many days with frosty, below-freezing mornings. Snow began to fall before noon on the 18th, and by mid-afternoon, over eight inches blanketed the ground. The temperature dropped, and the next morning snow was again drifting down over the white city. Eventually, a "great fall" covered Dublin, followed by such a "severe frost" that parts of the Liffey were completely frozen over.[5] A thin man in a not very heavy coat and a little cloak must have felt severely the bitter cold as he made his way to and from work this Thursday and Friday.

The temperature moderated slightly by Saturday, and it was no doubt in the Dublin Library that he penned the first of these letters. In spite of the extraordinary conditions in the world outside, he had not a word to say about the weather. Perhaps he just was not interested; except for noting the magic of June's mildness and a few allusions to storms, his writing is singularly barren of references to the climate. Or perhaps he feared he might sound as if he were complaining, while O'Donovan, who hated whingeing, must have been considerably less comfortable where he was, working in the country around Birr and Banagher.

Mangan was concerned just now to arrange how he was going to be paid. As usual, he had more debts than cash, and he dreaded the approaching end of the month, when bills fell due. No one likes to ask for money and no one likes to be asked for money—so Mangan would have said. Consequently, he attempted to gift wrap his request in entertaining banter and jokes. The entire central portion of the first letter spilled over with Rabelaisian extravagance:

> My dear O'Donovan,
>
> I beg to salute you solemnly. May your shadow never be less! May you live a thousand years! May you flourish (your quill) as long as sun and moon shall endure, and after that by lamplight, candlelight, gaslight or any other sort of light you fancy!
>
> Will you, can you, dare you or should you send me Six pounds sterling; I think you will, can, dare and should, and also that you may, shall, might, could, would and ought to do so. You, perhaps, may be of a different opinion. If you be, why, all that is to be said in that case is, that you are of one opinion and I of another, . . .
>
> Supposing, then, the case to stand thus, it is manifest to me that your opinion, and not mine, should undergo that alteration. I will not, for the purpose of establishing my position, cite to you the authorities of Zeno, Puffendorf, . . . Aristotle, Leibnitz, Locke, Peter Piper, . . . Dugald Stewart, Godwin, Mendelsohn the tile-counter, . . . Quevedo, Feyjoo, Xo-Ho-Hum, . . . Erasmus, Scaliger, Chronontotonthologos, or any other eminent writer of

> ancient or modern times. I shall merely state that the three books you left me are finished and that I shall have to meet a bill at the end of the month. Verbum sat.

Critics have said, and most readers today will agree, that a lot of Mangan's witty prose is ruined by being forced. The straining to be funny that modern ears hear was probably no issue for O'Donovan, however. He and the poet shared much the same type of humour, and in fact it was a popular sort generally in their day. It is true, though, that he had "dangerous literary heroes". Rabelais, Swift, Smollett, the author (Arbuthnot?) of the satirical tale *Memoirs of Martinus Scriblerus*, and his countryman Maginn wrote in styles marked by outrageous exaggeration and wild extravagance which perhaps did his own style little good.

Once he succeeded, after the long introduction, in asking his friend to send the money now due him, Mangan went on to discuss his own plans:

> As soon as you come up to town I shall leave my present situation (which on many accounts I dislike) and devote myself to the remainder of the Annals exclusively. *This I have settled on*. If you should not come up this side of Summer I will leave it at the end of March. A few weeks will suffice for the completion of the Books,—notes, comparison and all. I expect to accomplish at least 16 pages a day. Nothing will then remain to be done but to have it printed off in the twinkling of a bedpost.
>
> Mr Petrie has told me your address. I hope you and your health are on a good understanding with each other. Take care of yourself. I am getting stout, savage and stupid.
>
> If you think well of sending the £6 up in half notes in two letters, one after the other, do so. You may direct to me either at "*9, Peter St.*" where I stop, or at "*36 Dame St.*" It would very greatly serve me, if you could stand to me on this occasion.

The poet is thought to have left his scrivenery job in Fitzwilliam Square sometime earlier than this year, though how much earlier is not known, and thereafter he may have taken employment with the printers Pettigrew and Oulton at the address in Dame Street. The phraseology suggests that he was not living with his parents at this point, but was temporarily staying at No. 9 Peter Street. From the letter can also be gleaned the information that he was engaged in a not very pleasant but apparently successful struggle to take himself in hand and limit his drinking, and had consequently grown "stout, savage and stupid". O'Donovan did not think highly of teetotalers, and this unattractive image of the abstemious poet, surely an exaggeration or even an invention, catered to this prejudice while at the same time it reassured him that his copier was being businesslike.

Early the next week he received O'Donovan's answer. His quick pleasure at holding in his hands the solution to the pressing problem of bills was dashed by what his friend suggested he needed to do. On 26 January, a Friday during which more snow fell all day and the temperature stayed a cold 35°F, Mangan wrote a shorter and more intimate letter than the first. With frankness he confessed:

> My excellent friend,
>
> I have an insuperable objection to applying to Mr Smith [the printer]. Some time back I happened to meet him and he requested me to let him have such of the volumes as I had copied; of course I promised them in a few days, but weeks elapsed and my promise remained unfulfilled because the books until within the last week remained unfinished. I am now, therefore, I acquaint you candidly, unwilling to appear before him at all, and whether you send me the money or not I will deliver the books into no hands but your own.

His stubborn determination when he took a stand on something was a trait probably well known to his friends. It does not appear to have disturbed O'Donovan any more than did the peculiarly belligerent tone that marks these letters whenever the £6 has to be talked about.

The central paragraph, full of charm and interest, is the last thing we have in writing about Mangan in love:

> With regard to love, London, talent, Briareus and so forth, I shall reserve my remarks on all the topics of your pleasant and quizzical epistle for a future time. In the meanwhile however, I pledge myself and my troth most solemnly to you that I am not in love, that I have not the remotest intention of exporting myself to London, and that I have grown, as I told you in my last letter, quite a steady, staid, sober, sullen, stern, stiff, stupid and savage character.

And then it was back to business. Now he suggested that the antiquary could "lodge the £6 in Birr, if there be a provincial Bank there, and send me a letter of credit for the sum on the Bank of Ireland", with an underscored reminder that he needed the cash "*before the 1st of February*". O'Donovan had also given him his date for returning to Dublin, "about the 10th of next month", which pleased the poet. "Will you be good enough, as soon as you arrive, to send me a note, telling me where you stop, for I don't like intruding unnecessarily on Mr Petrie. . . ." Mangan could be extremely self-focused and at the same time the most considerate of individuals.

The cold eased at last and Dublin became again its familiar misty and relatively mild self. Mangan's anxiety also eased, for his friend sent £4 in half notes. Though the poet cross-wrote[6] at the top of his 30 January letter, "If possible, would you be good enough to write tomorrow (the 31st) so that I may be able to meet the acceptance [the bill] of the next day?", and pointedly mentioned in his first paragraph, "you can send me the other halves as soon as you please", he was no longer primarily concerned with the money. Thus there was time to give attention to what seems, even at this early date, to have been a major preoccupation with details of physical health—in this instance the health of his friend:

> I am very sorry indeed that you should have suffered so much in the way you describe. It looks like acute hepatitis. The nightmare and the depressing dreams would especially favor this supposition. Of course you have had the best advice you could get. But physicians, after all, know little of diseases—they make no allowance for idiosyncrasy, which is the most important thing of all to be considered. I will tell you what—I have derived more benefit, mental and bodily, from early rising, abstinence from intoxicating liquors, and the drinking of tar water than from all the drugs I ever swallowed. I take a pint of tar water every day, half at night and half in the morning; I use cocoa instead of tea or coffee, and I keep regular hours; and the result is that I am growing stronger and less nervous every day, although I take no exercise, think a great deal, write a great deal, read a great deal and now and then (but as rarely as I can) fret a great deal. . . .
>
> Until you can come to town and be situated more to your convenience I would recommend you (always supposing that you live temperately) the use of the flesh-brush, or, if you have no such thing, friction of the abdomen with a coarse towel for a quarter of an hour every morning, taking care to rub yourself circularly from the right side to the left. This mode of treatment for diseased liver, stomach, pylorus, mesentery or hypochondrium has succeeded where medical treatment has failed—and sometimes in the most deplorable and hopeless cases.
>
> Until we meet, Believe me ever
> Your's [*sic*] faithfully—J.C. MANGAN

His fascination with things medical, as he struggled to understand himself both physically and psychologically, was a constant in his life. At about this time the medication called "tar water" became a panacea for him. Not a new remedy by any means, it had been popularized by Bishop George Berkeley some hundred years earlier, especially in *Siris*, an "almost mystical work", dealing with tar-water as "the vital spirit of the world". The idea seems surrealistic, certainly, but suggests why Mangan first became enamoured of the "Western Balm of Gilead". Like all good panaceas, it was cheap and easy to make. Tar steeped in water for a few days produces a light amber-coloured fluid that apparently, if it does one no good, at least does no great harm. After he began work in the Ordnance Survey office, the poet always carried a bottle of it with him and sipped from it regularly. Or at least, he claimed it was tar-water, which he also described as a "jealous medicine" that "knows its own power" and will not allow any intoxicating liquor to be imbibed.[7] If this sounds contrived, that possibility also occurred to his co-workers, and Dr Petrie and young W.F. Wakeman investigated. Stealing upon Mangan one day as he napped at his high deal desk, they discovered that at least on this occasion the bottle contained rum and water.[8]

One of his fellow poets on the *Nation* in the 1840s was John de Jean Frazer, who did not much admire him as a poet, but who seems to have been interested in this remedy. Mangan wrote out the tar-water recipe for him, observing that the dose he had suggested to O'Donovan, half a pint morning and evening, was about right for most complaints, but that one of "a desperate character", such as the "hideous malady—'a gangrene in the blood'—a leprosy in fact" that the Bishop had cured, might require double or triple that amount. Faithful as he remained to tar-water, not a word is said about it in the "impersonal autobiography", although the columns which describe his nervous make-up and something of his final illness would seem to be a a logical place to make some last observations on a favourite medicine. The lack of any such mention is another reason to doubt that Mangan himself penned what is called the tenth in his series of "Sketches of Modern Irish Writers".

Perhaps O'Donovan was back in Dublin, as he intended, by mid-February; perhaps not. During that month even Petrie got fed up with the limited funds available to the Survey staff, the need to stretch too thin the small number of workers they could put in the field, and the poor pay. It was Larcom's challenge to keep him working, and to do so he used the most flagrant manipulation, subtle (and not so subtle) insults included: "I yet believe you would never forgive yourself if you left to become instead a scribbler of articles for Irish Annuals or the Penny Pirate—or to return to your easel. . . . I believe a man must be something of an enthusiast to do anything great for humanity's good—".[9] And he allowed only one loophole, one which by its very nature implied a human "weakness" on Petrie's part: "But I have no family and you have." Petrie stayed.

Matters even improved a little bit. Wakeman, a sixteen-year-old budding artist, was taken on to trace maps at the bottom pay of 1s.6d. per day, and by early April, James Clarence Mangan, too, was either hired or was being considered for employment, having quit his job just as he had told O'Donovan he was going to do. According to O'Donoghue, Mangan's drinking was getting out of control at this time, and the position was found to give him a routine, a place he had to be, and a job he had to do virtually every day. Possibly. But the Survey letters make it eminently clear that another competent scrivener was a necessity if the team were to stand a chance of completing anything close to the work their ambitious plans called for.

The Ordnance Survey's formidable scope, to make a complete survey and valuation of Ireland, was expanded by the imaginative enthusiasm of the men working on it, especially the youthful Lieutenant Thomas Aiskew

Larcom, stationed in Mountjoy House in the Phoenix Park, and Dr George Petrie, whose home at No. 21 Great Charles Street was his staff's headquarters and workshop.[10] O'Donovan had been a member since 1830, tutoring Larcom in the Irish language as noted earlier, even before meeting Petrie, an introduction that came about not long before the latter's founding of the *Dublin Penny Journal* in 1832.

Petrie's working group was made up of roughly two-thirds field men and one-third town men, though a very few, and especially O'Donovan, came and went as required.[11] Although his work in the field was of primary importance, O'Donovan was highly valued by Petrie, who longed to keep the reliable, indefatigable, and spirited "J.O'D." at his side whenever possible. In December 1837, Larcom had cautioned him about this, reminding him that he could not count on having O'Donovan in town "at the utmost more than three or four months in any year . . . for the next 3 or 4 years to come".[12] In 1838, he was certainly away again by May, having spent no more than two or three months in the city.

Whether or not Mangan finished copying the portion of the *Annals* assigned to him it is impossible to say. He certainly planned to do so, in spite of those weeks he had put off getting down to the task. It is not clear, either, whether he was working on the part that was published first, whose books covered the years 1172–1616, or the whole work which included accounts from Irish pre-history. As noted, two-thirds of the printer's copy was in his handwriting, but the sales catalogues that give the description do not say if it was the first or the last third that O'Donovan himself copied.[13] Whatever the case, when Mangan observed that once the work was done, it could be printed off "in the twinkling of a bedpost", he was probably sharing a rueful joke with O'Donovan. Still, neither man could have had any idea that it would take as long as it did—almost ten years elapsed before even the first part was published.

The copy in Mangan's handwriting, as the reader has perhaps surmised, is a missing article, an historical and literary treasure for which the search still goes on. After being auctioned off in three bundles at O'Donovan's estate sale in 1868, and as seventeen nicely bound volumes in Dr R.R. Madden's estate sale twenty years later, the printer's copy was taken to San Francisco by one Edward McGrath "in order that they [the *Annals*' stories] might inspire young Irishmen in that distant clime with a love for the history of the land of their forefathers". It subsequently disappeared, all too probably forever in the San Francisco earthquake and fire of 1906.[14]

Knowing Mangan as we now begin to, and understanding the stress that any change placed on him, we can assume that the good habits he described to O'Donovan in January did not survive the upheaval of his life in March. The first thing heard about him thereafter is in a letter

Larcom wrote to Petrie on 3 April in which he dealt at length with the poet and his work—or lack thereof—on the Ordnance Survey. He was specific and tart but not inflexible. Mangan had obviously been working in Petrie's home headquarters but for how long, and on what basis, is not mentioned:

> Mr Mangin [Larcom always spelled the poet's name this way] [should understand] the hours of attendance at your office are from 9 to 4 and that his services are not sufficiently valuable to compensate [for] the jealousy and confusion which must ultimately be the consequence of anyone being different from the others—but as his health is now delicate I see no objection to his having leave to go away an hour—or two hours earlier—for some definite period—say a month—till his health is re-established.[15]

Larcom's observations on the length of their work day and on Mangan's previous experience are revealing:

> The time from 9 to 4 is not too great for anyone of moderate health[,] strength and industry to devote to duty.
>
> I should have thought Mr Mangin must have been accustomed to much more arduous and continuous study—
>
> Do not let Mr M. suppose his services of any material [illegible, but probably "necessity" or "consequence"] to you.
>
> Perhaps time can be deducted next month—but no one ought to be absent without first your permission—this occurred during your absence.

Larcom failed to deal with an obvious problem—how a person who found himself ill upon rising could readily get word to the office that he was taking the day off, especially someone like Mangan, who lived on the south side of the city. Larcom finished: "If you cannot make Mangin regular you will not get much good out of him—but regularity would probably be [contrary] to himself and his own habits." As far as I have discovered, this is the first direct reference to Mangan's "habits". It is also an unusually blunt reference to his ill health, which may or may not have been a euphemism for the after-effects of drinking too much. There are allusions earlier, but Larcom never minced words, and what we have as a consequence is a straight-forward acknowledgement that the poet had been for some time a very difficult person to rely on for a steady day-in-day-out job. He was getting towards the point, not yet there but drawing closer, when it would be necessary for those who employed him to admire him for his poetry and love him for himself, and to overlook his weaknesses and the bad aspects of his eccentricity.

The next thing we hear of him is in July, in another Larcom letter. Here, Larcom asks, strangely enough, "What about Mangin? did you take him?" What was the story? It would seem that Mangan, having begun work with them, had not continued. When we recall how often he yearned for free time, and now found himself with a chance to stay between jobs for a while, there is every possibility that the temptation to seize a few months of leisure was irresistible. Conversely, ill-health, whatever its cause, may have been the explanation. In any case, it was not until summer that he became a regular full-time employee of the Ordnance Survey.

In September, Larcom enquired of Petrie, "How does Mangin go on? Advancing to general use?" And, he assured O'Donovan, "Mangin is at work for you, and an admirable scribe he is—first rate." On 9 September, to Petrie, O'Donovan wrote one of his wildest letters. Urging Petrie to publish his essays swiftly "before I settle in Connaught" where he planned "to get married to an old woman", he swore to "implore the shades of all the cyclops, Giants and saints of this Island of Saints and Druids" to bewitch Petrie if he didn't do so. Afterwards, sending regards to the kindly Mrs Petrie, his friend's stepmother, he closed: "I am glad to find that you have poor Mangan. I hope his health is good." This is the earliest use I have seen of that epithet "poor Mangan" which would become so common over the years.[16]

From a letter Petrie sent O'Donovan about the middle of the month it is clear that something was decidedly not right with this "first rate scribe". One would suppose he had now been in the office long enough not to require the sort of attention his supervisor had had to give him at first, but we read: "My dear John, you must pardon me for not sooner answering your last letter, as I am not so guilty as you may have supposed, the truth being that my time was so occupied by 'the Bard of Erin' as the people of the Hog-Loft call him, that I could not find leisure to write."[17] Although this is the only reference to Mangan as "the Bard of Erin" that I have ever seen, it is only to him that the remarks could reasonably apply. (Presumably the "Hog-Loft" was the men's familiar name for their chief's back parlour.) Patently, Mangan was unwell, but the nature of the illness remains problematical. "Delicate health", Larcom's phrase, could easily refer to incapacitation caused by drinking too much or by over-using opium, even medicinally. One fact is perfectly certain: from March 1838, through that summer, and autumn, and winter, and even into 1839, Mangan was "not himself". Or at least not the "steady, staid, sober, sullen, stern, stiff, stupid and savage character" he had portrayed himself to be when he wrote to O'Donovan in January.

[2]

We meet with treasures in the cold, hard crock;
  The kernel shoots within the roughest nut;
So no man wholly grows into a rock;
  Even the Young King of the Black Isles was but
Half marble; o'er his breast and brain the block
  Was given no power; his heart remained unshut
Against the influences that soothe or shock.
  Things are the same, saith SAAD, in dome and hut;
We must bewail our nature when we scan it,
But Man, at worst, is made of clay, not granite.
Mangan, "Saying of Saadi", *DUM*, March 1838

In spite of everything, he continued to function extremely well as a poet. This is indeed one of the amazing facts of his character, that he could continue to write under horrendous hardships or illness, sometimes, as here, with a flare and intensity that he simply did not achieve when times were happier. This quality of endurance prompted the author of the impersonal autobiography to write:

> I have never met anybody [else] of such a strongly-marked nervous temperament as Mangan. He is in this respect quite a phenomenon: he is literally all nerves and no muscles. In accordance with such a temperament Providence has endowed him with marvellous tenacity of life. He has survived casualties that would have killed thousands—casualties of all kinds—illnesses, falls, wounds, bruises, wet clothes, no clothes at all, and nights at the round table.[18]

In March 1838 he had produced the second article in his Eastern poetry series, this one dealing with the poetry of Turkey. He included in it a wide range of poems, from his shortest ever, the two-line "I am blinded by thy hair and by my tears together;/The dark night and the rain come down on me together", to one of the most sensual, "To Mihri", with the exquisite refrain, "My starlight, my moonlight, my midnight, my noonlight,/Unveil not, unveil not, or millions must pine." At the end of the chapter there is a suggestion that he was getting fed up with exotic effusions, however, and the following sounds a lot like his testy observations on German poetry when he was getting tired of translating it without any variation:

> Our next article will probably terminate our review of Ottoman Poetry. It will depend upon circumstances whether we shall afterwards enter upon Persian and Arabic. At present we have no great inclination to either. To acknowledge the truth, at the close of our paper, *we dislike Eastern poetry*. Its great pervading character is mysticism—and mysticism and stupidity are synonymous terms in our vocabulary.[19]

A great deal has been said about Mangan as a mysterious, elusive plurality of selves, and it may be too little about his insistence on lucidity and clarity of language. But in this passage he expressed a firm literary conviction on this subject:

> A poet above all men should endeavour to make words the image of things . . . . The shadow on the wall can as easily strike a blow as the poet can produce an impression without lucidness both of conception and language. It is the error of poets that they consider themselves bound to be at all hazards original . . . . They may be assured that every thought worth expressing has already been expressed forty thousand times over. . . . Instead of creating nondescript forms out of no materials they should rather endeavour to mould the existing materials into new and more beautiful forms.[20]

He had made no secret of the fact that he was using the German translations of Hammer-Purgstall ("perhaps the first Orientalist of his era"), and he took this "universal linguist and philologist" to task for some of his translations: "In what corner of M. Von Hammer's brain was his good taste slumbering while his fingers were busy in filling his volumes with such trash as this?" One of Mangan's own freshest translations followed hard on the heels of this rebuke. Two stanzas will illustrate the charm of "Ghazel and Song":

> Summer yet lingers, yet blushes and blesses,
> Dazzling the dells with her sunbeamy tresses:
> Here let us revel, defying excesses,
> SKY-SCALERS—MADCAPS—with WINE-WETTED DRESSES!
>
> * * * *
>
> Man cannot live upon berries and cresses;
> Life's is a banquet luxuriant in messes;
> Deep let us drink while Existence pro-gresses,
> SKY-SCALERS—MADCAPS—with WINE-WETTED DRESSES![21]

Nagging Petrie to keep his men hard at work was Larcom's unpleasant job, and there was a lot of it done in this spring's letters.

> *16 April*: "The danger you have to look in the face is gradual dissemination of historic illustration and interest and scramble at the last moment . . . if I loved you and your work less—I should be less uneasy—that's all—."
>
> *20 April*: "Do not for a moment think I want you to be content with mediocrity or anything less than the utmost *attainable* perfection. We must not faint now—we were far worse off a year ago."
>
> *21 April*: "I need not tell you how gratified I was at what you [told] me last night—nor how inestimably valuable I feel such elaborate research on minute localities like our townlands will be—only we must try to proportion the means to the end—lest by grasping at more than we can manage we run the risk of losing all—."

Mangan's friendship with Duffy also continued to flourish this year. In May the young journalist who was working so hard that he almost permanently wrecked his health, founded a bellwether press association. He intended that it should be composed of men from the staffs of the various periodicals, and as the founder, he proposed his friend Mangan for membership. Duffy had a great admiration for success, and Mangan was enjoying considerable success as a writer and was apt to receive more accolades in the future. Thus when Duffy introduced him as "one of the most accomplished and popular writers for the *University Magazine*", he was not exaggerating. Unhappily, the association appears to have faded and failed after Duffy moved to Belfast. Nothing more is heard of it, and even the record of its founding has now disappeared from the Duffy collection in the Royal Irish Academy Library.[22]

June was high summer in Ireland, and this year, the month seems to have been blessed with many mild days, the temperature sometimes reaching 70°F. On 28 June, young Queen Victoria's coronation was celebrated. Everywhere in the Empire shops and offices closed and employees received that almost unheard of treat, a day off with pay. Larcom proposed to Petrie that, since "all the world will be in the Park", they should "take a prowl" somewhere else. Where Mangan himself prowled this exceptional Thursday, we do not know. Possibly he worked on some of the poetry that filled July's anthology in which he begged Schiller's pardon for having a "muddlement" in his brain caused by the "balmy, sleepy, June afternoon" on which he wrote. The eighteen pages of this anthology were comprised of his favourite German poet's "less translatable poems". In August, sixteen more pages of translations from a mixed collection by Klauer-Klattowski appeared, and in September, another eighteen-page anthology, this time of more Turkish poetry, made this a remarkably productive period.

August's collection is not so random as the fact that over a dozen German poets are sampled might lead one to expect, largely because the selection is top-heavy with verse in praise of wine and beer and the pleasures of drinking. "A Song Concerning Rhenish" opened the anthology—

> This liquor is an exorcist of hippishness and pain,
> And, according to my own idea,
> Is for every affection of the stomach and the brain
> An indubitable panacea.

"A Cosmopolite" followed—

> I travel about for the good of my mouth,
> And to gather effront'ry;
> The world is my inn: when I'm kicked from the South
> I've the North for a country.

Then "Pathetic Hypothetics"—

Were wine all a quiz,
I should wear a long phiz
As I mounted each night to my ninth-story garret.
Though Friendship, the traitress, deceives me,
Though Hope may have long ceased to flatter,
Though Music, sweet infidel, leaves me,
Though Love is my torment—what matter?
I've still such a thing as a rummer of claret,
Claret, claret,
A rummer of claret,
I laugh and grow fat on my buttermilk claret.

And "Love and Wine"—"Without the tender Passion and a pitcherful of wine,/Life were a round of dull employments."[23] It is almost with nostalgia that a reader can watch Mangan's innocent enjoyment before he and everyone else recognized the seriousness of his drinking problem, and before the great temperance crusade of Fr Mathew, already beginning to take form in County Cork, changed drinking alcohol in any form into a problem of national morality.

The symbolism of the rose was precious to Mangan. In his own culture, the flower carried the meaning of purity and beauty, and even more than the lily, was associated with the Virgin Mary. But he would have learned only from his reading that, for the Arabian mystics, the rose was sacred in and of itself as a living, breathing representation of the enigma of God. Their temple was called a *Gulistan*, or Rose Garden. The rose Mangan and the Oriental poets were thinking about was not the tightly-rolled hybrid of today, but a "blowzy, Rubenesque beauty", the Hundred-leafèd Rose, that still flourishes in some country gardens, offering a wide flower-face of fragrant petals, or "leaves", for delectation. Mangan rarely expatiated on the beauty of a poem—that was not his style. In fact, he was much more likely to understate than to exaggerate its merits, letting the reader discover its wonders on his own; but he must have set a personal record for minimizing when he referred to "The Hundred-Leafèd Rose" as an "episodical conceit". Only a few of the 104 lines can be included here, so the reader needs to remember that part of the poem's effectiveness comes from the accumulation of gorgeous images:

Like crispèd gold, laid fold over fold,
Like the sun that at Eventide glows,
Like the furnace-bed of AL-KHALILL [Abraham, the Friend of God]
Is the Hundred-Leafèd Rose.
Her cloak is green, with a gloomy sheen,
Like the garment of beauteous JOSE, [Joseph's coat]

And prisoned round by a sentinelled wall
Is the Hundred-leafèd Rose.
Like ISSA, whose breath first woke from Death [Jesus]
The souls in this world of woes,
She vivifies all the fainting air,
The Hundred-leafèd Rose.[24]

More than many religious poets, Mangan could create an almost breath-taking holiness around such an object. He himself stood in profound awe of the sacred, and it is this emotion of the spirit which he succeeded so well in communicating.

By dramatic contrast, he closed this anthology with an "extraordinary and fantastic" poem titled "Bang u Badeh", or "Opium and Wine", a poetic debate between the two intoxicants. Briefly, the story is that Opium and Wine, with their cohorts, debate their respective merits, with the Poet acting as a sort of referee. "Bang" is identified as "opium", the poet himself correctly suggesting at the start, however, that the drug, "not interdicted by name in the Koran, and probably . . . not known to the Arabians in Mohammed's era", was more likely hashish. "Bang" today is described as a product of the cannabis plant gathered green, then dried, and made into a drink with opium and water or milk added. Opium and hashish, like wine, can be incorporated into candy, and in the poem "Sugar-Candy" and "Cinnamon" are represented as neutral, coming between "the high belligerent powers".

Mangan summarizes most of the poem in prose, reserving poetry for the main speeches and the final debate. Wine's argument after being informed that Bang is never drunk, but wears "a divine and philosophic air", goes thus:

> O, ingrate and driveller! . . . O, viperous drinker of Me, I am astounded at thine unexampled and detestable ingratitude. . . . I weep also for thy bad taste, which afflicts me with intense and particular melancholy: can it be that thou art sunk so low as to acknowledge thyself a *Banghi*? [an opium eater][25]

Wine then praises herself:

I am called WINE, and I stand alone
As the Light of the Soul and the Prop of the Universe,
Bright as the sun, and deep as the sea,
Where is the recreant poet whose puny verse
Dares to prefer another to Me?

If Wine has her troops—Cider, Brandy, Beer and so on—Bang does as well —Habb (a thirty-grain Opium Pill), Esrar (a Persian Opiate), and "an army of opiates, fluid and solid". Bang's chief argument:

Kings and Kalenders combine
    To honour Me, the Pure and Placid,
Knowing that, unlike to WINE,
    My sweetness never turns to acid,
For I am the Seal of Perpetual Grace,
    The Mirror of Truth, the Key to Fame,
And he who would find a resting-place
For his fainting soul in Eternity's race,
    Must fly to Me, as the moth to the flame.

A "wordy skirmish" follows, of which a few exchanges:

Says WINE: I kill in mortals
                The Soul of Grief.
Says BANG: I burst the Portals
                Of Unbelief.
Says WINE: I sparkle gaily
                In darkest night.
Says BANG: All mankind daily
                Confess my might.

Ultimately, the victory is Wine's:

Worsted and howling, BANG slunk away,
And thenceforth never by night or day,
Durst shew himself in his ancient array,
But hid his face with a lilac mask   [lilac coloured opium pills]
        While WINE, as glorious as before,
Shone rosily out in the same bright flask
        That shewed her beauty in times of yore.[26]

Mangan called this a "bizarre poem", probably "an allegory of some kind or other, and Wine and Bang may be meant as personifications of some of the Divine attributes." The mere fact that such a poem appeared in the *Dublin University Magazine* suggests, however, that fairly sophisticated opinion viewed the use of opium with interest, if not necessarily with approval. That Mangan's rather keen interest in the drug sprang from personal experience with it is not clear, but it is extremely unlikely that he or anybody else would have suffered through physical or nervous disturbances without recourse to opium's common tincture, laudanum. Laudanum can, in turn, very easily become a problem itself.

The spate of three lengthy anthologies in a row would seem to confirm that Mangan was not employed on any other job during these months; as we have already heard, work for scriveners was slow during the summer. Some of the poems were very short, but some were quite long, and there were eighty-six in all, a great many of any length for any poet, and especially for one suffering some vague but troublesome ailment, to produce in a three-month period. It is, therefore, particularly impressive that the over-all quality was so high and the variety so great. It was a pouring forth of his inspiration in a rush unmatched in any other period during his career.

[3]

> I find that any attempt even for five minutes together, at an original composition, has no effect except to increase the illness I am labouring under. . . .
> Mangan, in a letter to Tighe

Petrie and O'Donovan, when he was in town, worked in the large front parlour of Petrie's home while Mangan and the other "minor officials" occupied the smaller back room. Among the members of this latter group were Eugene O'Curry and his nephew Anthony O'Curry, the artist G.V. Du Noyer, Patrick O'Keeffe, Thomas O'Connor, and young Wakeman, all of whom belonged to the country staff. On a small slip of paper now tucked into the "Petrie Papers" in the National Library collection Larcom listed the wages of these men. All were pegged to O'Donovan's, and as he was never paid more than ten shillings per day no matter how long or arduous his hours, they received proportionately less. Among them were Patrick O'Keeffe, 6s 6d; Thomas O'Connor, 7s; Eugene O'Curry, 7s; Anthony O'Curry, 4s; and W.F. Wakeman a mere 3s in town, but 6s when he was working and sketching in the field. "James Mangin" was listed as a copier of Latin and English, though we learn from Larcom's and Petrie's correspondence that his Latin skills were very limited. He received 5s per day, the same wage he earned as a scrivener.[27] Their names appeared in O'Donoghue's *Life of Mangan* in a passage the author discreetly closed:

> It is almost certain that Mangan began to drink heavily while here, and that a certain member of the staff, who was a confirmed toper, and whose name may be left in obscurity, seriously injured his chances of ultimate conquest of his tendency to excess in stimulants. Mangan and he foregathered very much, and were constantly tippling.
>
> A favourite evening resort . . . was the Phoenix Tavern, now the Tavistock, in D'Olier Street. Here he could generally be found, seated in the pew-like compartment nearest the door, with his writing materials, or with a book, and imbibing his liquor.[28]

Suspicion of being that "confirmed toper" falls naturally enough on three men whose names also appeared on Larcom's wage list but were omitted by O'Donoghue: J. Sullivan, George Lawler, and a Mr Austin. No finger can be pointed, but as they were the poet's office mates, a fair chance exists that one of them was his unnamed drinking comrade. At the same time, there were two men on the country staff, O'Connor and

O'Keeffe, who drank so heavily and had such irregular habits that they were back in Dublin much more frequently than was desirable, so they, too, must be seen as possibilities. Their valuable skills were all that kept them employed. O'Connor was a hardy country man, O'Keeffe a city youth looked after by a protective mother. It would be hard to say which might be the more likely to have befriended Mangan. Precise identification remains as elusive today as ever, but "someone" at the Ordnance Survey office companioned the poet who found active socializing so uncomfortable but who apparently hated to drink by himself.

It was also this autumn that Larcom first felt the need to recommend that an attendance book be kept at Great Charles Street. He ordered that each of Petrie's men should sign his name to the record each day "with the hour at which he arrives and at which he leaves off work". The arrangements had so far been informal with lots of coming and going, especially as copying often had to be done elsewhere, such as in Marsh's Library or Trinity College Library. Moreover, Larcom did not particularly want to change the *status quo*, for he feared that it would open a door to the principle of making up time missed, "a class of irregularity" to be avoided. Still, some system of keeping tabs on employees seems to have become necessary. No one liked the fiscal side of running the Survey, and Larcom wrote Petrie on 29 September:

> There is no part of my function gives me so much thought and anxious care as the regulation of pay—here are more than 100 persons no two of whom are performing exactly the same work—nor with exactly the same aptitude . . . you who see them all daily can judge of these things better than I.[29]

Petrie did not, of course, see the entire hundred every day, or anything like it. But Larcom's responsibility was onerous, and he thus shifted a little of the burden to the man on the spot. By 3 November, he was able to congratulate Petrie: "I am glad you have adopted a system for entering the time and occupation of the people [at the office]—the objects to be attained are that you should know *every day where every person is* and *what he is doing*."

Mangan missed some time in October. How much is not mentioned, but on the first of November, perhaps enabled by Petrie's new system for signing-in, Larcom observed that the poet had not been on duty every day that he should have been: "I have not stopped any days from Mr Mangin for October—but you should be certain he was at work actually on the 2 days he was not in Charles Street."[30]

Finally this month Mangan felt well enough to answer a letter he had received from James Tighe back in the late summer. Now a temperance writer as well as a bookseller who published his own work, Tighe was never very prosperous. His shop at No. 38 (later No. 175) Great Britain Street was in a not very elevated locale, his immediate neighbours being a rag shop, a straw bonnet maker, grocers, and spirit merchants. Tighe had asked Mangan to write something for one of his publications, and Mangan wrote to apologize for being unable to oblige. This letter Mangan addressed, not from Peter Street, but from No. 5 Richmond Street. Although "South" or "North" was not specified, it may have been the latter, for this locale would have put him a great deal closer to his work. Conversely, Richmond Street South was in the neighbourhood of his father's Camden Street real estate ventures, and No. 5 may have been in one of those buildings. But all this is highly conjectural, and in any event, he seems not to have stayed at the address long.

Although the letter itself has been lost, O'Donoghue intended to include parts or perhaps all of it in his planned revision of Mangan's life and copied out this much:

> My dear friend
>
> I have not forgotten you, but the truth simply is that I am not able to present to you a single contribution. . . . I find that any attempt even for five minutes together, at original composition, has no effect except to increase the illness I am labouring under. . . . I have been obliged even to discontinue writing for the [University] Magazine and, in short, I begin to see that for me literature in any shape is the most unfit of all occupations.
>
> If I can recover my health I shall endeavour to dedicate the very limited powers I possess to something of a more practical and profitable character. Meantime, I know you too well, [to imagine you] to be displeased with me for what I really cannot avoid—my inability to be of the slightest use to you in your undertaking.[31]

He must really have been quite miserable to have thought of giving up literature, especially poetry. Customarily, he had kept doggedly on, but he now reached something of a spiritual and emotional nadir. Its exact cause remains obscure, although one wonders if the summer burst of creativity had simply exhausted every such impulse for a while. He was well into his thirty-sixth year now, also, and thus had passed the half-way point of the time allotted to him according to the biblical "threescore years and ten" of a man's life. He was not the first poet to take note of this crucial moment. Dante had commenced his *Divine Comedy* "Midway this way of life we're bound upon,/I woke to find myself in a dark wood,/Where the right road was wholly lost and gone." Not a very promising outlook. And Byron had grieved the milestone in "On This Day I Complete My Thirty-sixth Year":

> My days are in the yellow leaf;
> The flowers and fruits of love are gone;
> The worm, the canker, and the grief
> Are mine alone.

As he took stock, it must have appeared to Mangan that he had endured too much of "the worm, the canker, and the grief" for the quality and quantity of the rewards he had received. The author of the impersonal autobiography was to declare: "His misfortunes have been very great; and he ascribes them all to his power of writing, facetiously deriving *calamity* from *calamus*, a quill."

W.F. Wakeman, "young Wakeman" who joined the Ordnance Survey staff at about the same time as Mangan, vividly described the poet as he remembered him in one of the earliest of the delineations which show him as quite eccentric, a curious, beguiling, but for some a strangely off-putting figure. Thus, from O'Donoghue's *Life*:

> We were supposed when on home duty to meet daily in the office at 10 a.m. All were usually punctual except Mangan, who, as a rule, was late, would often not appear before eleven or twelve o'clock, and would not infrequently be absent altogether. He had in our room a large unpainted deal desk, about breast high, supported upon four legs, and to match, an equally plain stool or seat, both being his own property, and of his own introduction. Upon this desk, when he worked at all, he would copy documents as required. He had nothing else to do, so that his training as scrivener made the task all the more easy. At times he would be very dull and silent, but occasionally he was apt to make puns and jokes. He generally had some awful story of a super-natural character to tell us as he was sipping his "tar-water". . . . At the time I speak of Mangan could not have numbered more than thirty-five or thirty-six years, yet he was then physically worn out—aged in fact—as far as the body was concerned. His mind, however, still was that of the poet. . . .
>
> He possessed very weak eyes, and used a huge pair of green spectacles; he had narrow shoulders, and was flat-chested, so much so, that for appearance sake the breast of his coat was thickly padded. Of course there was no muscular strength, and his voice was low, sweet, but very tremulous. Few, perhaps, could imagine that so odd a figure might represent a genius, and Mangan himself did not appear to care a fig what people thought of him. . . . His coat was of an indescribable fashion both in cut and colour; it appeared to have been a kind of drab. Out of doors he wore a tight little cloak, and his hat exactly resembled those which broomstick-riding witches are usually represented with. Sometimes, even in the most settled weather, he might be seen parading the streets with a very voluminous umbrella under each arm. The large coloured spectacles, already referred to, had the effect of setting off his singularly wan and wax-like countenance with as much force as might be accomplished by the contrast of colour.[32]

At the risk of some repetition, it is interesting to hear Wakeman as cited by William Stokes in his *Life and Labours in Art and Archaeology of George Petrie*:

> I should like to dwell a moment on the scene of that very happy time when we used to meet in Dr Petrie's back parlour. There was our venerable chief, with

> his ever ready smile and gracious word; then poor Clarence Mangan, with his queer puns and jokes, and odd little cloak and wonderful hat, which exactly resembled the tiles that broomstick-riding witches are usually represented with, his flax-coloured wig, and false teeth, and the inevitable bottle of tar-water, from which he would sip and sip all day, except when asleep, with a plain deal desk for a pillow. . . .[33]

Both O'Donoghue and Stokes, it seems, took the liberty of tempering the wind to the shorn lamb. Wakeman's original account was ruthless by comparison.

> His hair had gone, and given place to a very common-looking flax-coloured wig; his teeth were a false and ill-fitting set, as evidenced by the fact that the wearer was ever fixing them with his fingers lest they should fall from his gums; . . . his coat was thickly padded [to fill out his flat chest and narrow shoulders] . . . his voice was low, sweet, but very tremulous. . . . Such was the appearance of Mangan before his later self-abandonment. It is strange that genius of high order should not unfrequently be found associated with temperament which seems inaccessible to reason, and is ruled only by infatuation.[34]

[4]

> "I am *now The Man in the Cloak*. In other words, I am henceforth a being of mystery—none must see me as I really am."
>
> Balzac, "Melmoth Reconcilié", translated by Mangan

If he could not withdraw entirely from a literary career, Mangan wanted very badly to make some drastic change, and he turned to something that had always held considerable attraction for him and that also promised to be "of a more practical and profitable character"—the writing of prose. So far, the only prose he had written for the *Dublin University Magazine* had been commentary to accompany the translations, but he enjoyed telling stories, the more outlandish the better, and he had a gift for going on both lengthily and cleverly. His last fiction, "Love, Mystery, and Murder. A Tale Foundered [*sic*] on Facts", had appeared four years earlier in the *Weekly Dublin Satirist*. A mildly outrageous, highly episodic send-up of the Gothic tale, it had been complete with violence, glamour, and typical Gothic characters including a Monk and a beautiful heroine named Amelrosa. Now, he turned his hand to fiction again, and this time he would both invent and translate in a procedure something like that he followed in his poetry.

His two stories, in the October, November and December numbers of the *University Magazine*, can both be traced to Balzac. The least derivative, "The Thirty Flasks", appeared in two parts in October and December, while the true if highly adapted translation, "The Man in the Cloak: A Very German Story", was published in November. Although Balzac was not mentioned as the author of either, the former was signed "An Out-and-Outer", Mangan's first use of that pseudonym, and the latter "B.A.M.", that is, "A Hoax". Both stories were what O'Donoghue would have called "extravaganzas" and were frequently farcical.

"The Man in the Cloak: A Very German Story" was a translation of Balzac's sequel to Charles Maturin's *Melmoth the Wanderer*, so there is no mystery about the origin of Mangan's interest. To make it more his own, perhaps, he changed the setting to Germany, introduced a comic phrenologist named Queerkopf, and rechristened the protagonist "Braunbrock", no doubt after the American author Charles Brockden Brown whose novels, especially *Wieland: or the Transformation*, the Irish poet had read with enthusiasm. He also identified himself with "The Man in the Cloak", that is, Melmoth, and from this time, "The Man in the Cloak" became a favourite signature.

The second story, "The Thirty Flasks", had ties to Balzac's "La Peau de Chagrin" or "The Magic Skin", but it is unfair to both authors to link their stories very closely together, for Mangan actually owed only some dozen sentences to the French novelist. What Mangan took from other sources is more striking. The motif of the "displaced effect", used by both Balzac and Mangan, was quite common in European folklore, and nothing suggests that Balzac's tale was Mangan's first encounter with it. But here he employed the popular (and one might say appropriate) "displacement" agent of the magical drink. In Mangan's plot, with each flask of the "Black Elixir" he drinks, the hero loses an inch of his height and some of his good looks to the evil *Arabian Nights* magician Maugraby who also appears here. He receives in exchange great power and wealth. The bargain has a loophole; it can be reversed up to the thirtieth flask, and Mangan (with the aid of a *deus ex machina*) indeed rescues his hero and produces a fairytale happy ending. It was not thus in "La Peau de Chagrin", whose tragic conclusion underscored the ethical and practical dangers of the possession of vast power.

Mangan's other sources must have included a tale or tales in the public domain with perhaps a smattering of Irish folklore such as certain accounts of the origin of the leprechaun. According to one of these, back in the time when the leprechaun people were full-sized and druid people were short, the envious druids cast a spell over the leprechauns, reducing their size and inhibiting their women from giving birth more than once every thirty years. In exchange, though, they received inexhaustible wealth. A variant of this legend has it that the ugly druid dwarf Fernal offered King Brian Boru and his wife the blessing of a son, which they very much wanted, for every inch of the king's height and share of his good looks he was willing to bargain away. In a complicated sequence of events, the king is reduced to a short, ugly creature with twenty-nine sons and is saved from the ultimate thirtieth, and a permanent fate as an ugly dwarf, only by the wisdom and compassion of the wood-nymph Oona. It may be no coincidence that at this time O'Donovan had been in Connaught and had come back bubbling with wild lore which he loved to recount to the Survey's stay-at-home city crew.[35]

Striking a bargain with a demonic force was a favourite theme of Mangan's, as already noted in these pages. In these stories, two young men fall from grace because of bad moral choices. Like himself, the poet might have said, they were unfortunate in being exposed to extremely attractive temptations, and, also like himself, they lacked the strength of will to do what they knew should be done.

How his readers received these tales we can't be sure, but it may be indicative that he had no further stories printed in the pages of the *University Magazine*. Unlikely as it seems from the signatures, both were at one time mistaken for originals written by Mangan himself. Fr Meehan, however, seems to have been aware that they were not the poet's own, or at least he was uncertain, for he left them out of his collection of Mangan's prose in the *Essays in Prose and Verse*.

Spirits Everywhere

[1]

> Experience is a jewel picked up by a wrecked mariner on a desert coast—a picture-frame, purchased at a preposterous cost, when decay has done its duty on your finest Titian—a prosing lecturer who sermonises a sleeping congregation . . . a sentinel who mounts guard over a pillaged house . . . a monitor that, like Friar Bacon's Brazen Head, tells us that *Time is past* . . . or any thing else equally pertinent and impertinent. Why then do we panegyrise it so constantly?
>
> Mangan, *A Sixty-Drop Dose of Laudanum*, Drop Forty-Six

In spite of the congenial atmosphere of the Ordnance Survey office, Mangan did not soon pull out of the neurasthenia that now left him wearied of life. In his own words, he continued in 1839 to endure "anti-poetical modes of thought and tendencies of mind", an unhappy state that soured him on most literary effort. His silence from July to December, between two "Anthologia Germanica" articles on the poetry of F.C. Wetzel, testifies to the fact, confirmed by this late-in-the-year explanation to his readers:

> It so happened that about three months back [written in November, this would date the "attack" to August or September] we had the misfortune to sustain a severe attack of intellectual hypochondriasis, the effect of which was to revolutionise for a season all our literary tastes. . . . Neither physicians nor metaphysicians were able to comprehend, far less to remove, our malady. Whence it originated we ourself can hazard no conjecture; for who shall fathom the abysses of the human mind?[1]

Not only did this illness, whatever it was, leave him wretched, but it must have had a deleterious effect, to put it mildly, on the family budget, only partially off-set by the high level of his productivity from January through July. His three full-length anthologies in January, April and July, and "A Sixty-Drop Dose of Laudanum" (March) would have brought him around £35 for the first seven months of the year. Added to his Survey earnings, there would have been enough to survive on—would have been, that is, had his attendance at No. 21 Great Charles Street been regular. But it was not, evidently, and he was paid a wage for the hours worked, not a salary by the week. Thus his shillings must have been thin on the ground during the last half of 1839.

The January anthology of the German poet C.F. Gellert's tales and fables signalled a return of his poetic Muse from a "holiday" taken in the last quarter of 1838. This cluster of poems was as self-concerned and as filled with irony as anything previously seen from his pen. A book was lying before him, he wrote, "and we hail it as an old friend,—nay as better than a friend, *because* it lies before us, while a friend commonly lies behind our back." Was this a veiled criticism of someone? And his comment on himself—"our originality is too mighty for us and refuses to be burked; we must therefore have *carte blanche* to out-and-out it, *i.e.*, to perform our task in a mode characteristic of Ourself"—was this irony or merely exaggeration? His reference to his translations as "paraphrases" might seem like a slip of the quill, were this not a "fault" to which he had already pled not guilty. The two columns in which he expounded on his stupidity—"sunken, lost, buried, immeasurable toises down in the nethermost depths of the lowest gulf of the last vortex of stupidity"—carry irony as far as it can go, and they force the realization that desperation is the true tone of this anthology in the same sense that it may be heard in Rabelais' most extravagant passages. At the same time, it catered to the taste of the day, adopting, for example, the peculiarly popular mannerism of "stupidity", and carrying it to great length:

> By means of our stupidity we flourish; we prosper; we laugh and grow fat; we are monthly winning greener laurels, and hourly getting on at an ever-accelerated pace, towards the Goal of Fame. Would that all mankind could imitate us!—could be as stupid and triumphant as we! But this may not be; some must be wise and others otherwise; what is one man's meat is another man's poison; that which is bred in the bone will not come out of the flesh; we cannot put old heads on young shoulders; and one man is born with a silver spoon in his mouth, and another with a wooden ladle.[2]

He concluded with a poem of his own masquerading as Gellert's. Written to pun on the saying "the devil's in it", "The Bottle Conjuror" claimed he would show his audience the devil in a bottle, and then, when he faced them from the stage and showed them a bottle of brandy:

> "How!—brandy!" was the cry, "What! is't a hoax?"
> "By no means," quoth the Conjuror. "But list!
>   Here be three pints of brandy!"—"Come! no bam!"—
>   "Now, my good people, I, Von Dunder, am,
> And swear to be, as long as I exist,
> A—" "What? Go on!—" "A staunch tee-to-ta-list;
> And so, you mind, I *cannot* wet my throttle
>   With any of this stuff!"

Whereupon his audience grew "fierce and stormy", protesting he had promised to show them the devil in a bottle. "I am come to that", Von Dunder agreed:

> ". . . and I needn't shrink;
> For when a thirsty dog like me has got
> A bottle full of brandy in his hand
> *The devil's in it* if he cannot drink!"[3]

Sandwiched into the middle of the anthology were the two poignant sonnets "To Caroline"; his nonsense verse ending "and when the Moon at midnight sheds/Her ghastly radiance on our heads/The Sun can never shine at all!"; and the delicate but telling little whimsy, "When men behold old mould rolled cold. . . ." This was the most republishing he had done in quite some time, and an idiosyncratic choice, certainly. All were presented as the work of "the Poet" in the poem that immediately preceded them. The last, an "allusion to his own grave", was even said to have been taken from his (invented) "*Troglodyte Anthology*, Vol. I, Book II, Part III, Chapter IV, Sec. V", and finally, the suggestive "Page 666". Also included here was another version of "The Dying Father", in which, it may be recalled, a generous genius brother received everything from his father on his death bed, the stupid brother, nothing. The name of the genius brother continued to be "Christy", but in this version, the stupid brother's name has been altered from "George" to "Will". That this was not accidental is patent: Ah, yes, Mangan's brother's name was William, one thinks; but it also has to be noted that at this period in his life the poet was deeply concerned about his own ineffectual, weak, "stupid" *will*.

The weather as the new year opened was memorably violent. A hurricane swept through Dublin on 6 January that "for severity [was] unparalleled by any other ever felt in the city",[4] and 1839 came to be known as the Year of the Big Wind. The wind blew hard all night, causing such alarm that "the majority [of the city's residents] quitted their beds and remained all night in indescribable terror." Eighteen were killed. A survey of property damage showed 157 houses partly or completely leveled, 362 partly or completely unroofed, and 1,527 chimneys blown down. The crush of glass underfoot must have been frightening in itself, for 30,358 panes were "*ascertained*", presumably in contrast to "rumoured", to have been shattered. The next month was little better. The day before St Valentine's Day, yet another storm descended on the city with high winds that stripped the roofs off several houses, although this time, mercifully, no one was killed.

For a man who had once expressed total fascination with the wild manifestations of nature, Mangan was strangely silent about all this, although his March contribution to the *University Magazine*, "A Sixty-Drop Dose of Laudanum", might be considered a perfect venue for airing his reactions. This article contained a remarkable assortment of his opinions on various subjects, but weather was not among them. From girls and poets to dreams and death, from two lines to several paragraphs in length, he presented his readers with a highly selective portrait of himself as revealed in his thoughts and attitudes . In spite of the title, he had not a word to say about laudanum in the "Sixty-Drop Dose of Laudanum", but all five headnotes were quotations about the drug. The first explained that the name was derived from *laudare*, to praise. The second, taken from the works of the infamous opium advocate Dr John Brown of Edinburgh, whose patients included both Coleridge and DeQuincey, revealed the reason for the "sixty drop" formulation: "You may exhibit thirty, fifty, eighty, or a hundred drops to produce sleep; everything depends on the temperament; but where your object is to excite and enliven, I recommend you to stop short at SIXTY." Obviously, what Mangan wanted to do was "excite and enliven" his readers. Three further brief observations were given: "A dose to dose Society . . . then it must be uncommon strong, comrade!" from a work called *Adventures of a Half-crown*. Then, "So saying, he shed sixty drops of the liquid in his black flask into a cup, muttering mysterious words all the while", which Mangan attributed to *The Rival Magicians.* And lastly from Byron's *Childe Harold's Pilgrimage*, the shortest selection: "—Count o'er/—threescore!"

Given that his intent was to entertain, and that his form frequently was to be the extended aphorism, it may be surprising that the overall movement of his subject matter is from innocence to experience, from joy to sorrow, from light to dark. And readers were forewarned. Immediately into Drop One, he only slightly misquotes Wordsworth in two lines that chart the course of the next fifty-nine Drops:

> Thus poets in their youth begin in gladness
> Though thereof come in the end despondency and madness.

Lightness and charm characterize the first thirty Drops, though even here, death is not without its day, as in Drop Nine's observation: "The longing which men continually feel for *rest* while engaged in the struggles and stormy turmoils of Life, is an unconscious tending of the heart towards its natural goal, the Grave." Drops Seven and Seventeen on the subject of women are more characteristic: "The idea entertained by all girls under twenty of literary men is, that they are *very clever*. . . . With them the sonnetteer and the epic poet are on a common level as to talent; the sonnetteer, however, is usually the greater pet, as he has more small talk"; and, "There are some few women who will despise you for loving them, but none who will *hate* you without a much better reason." Women's hair and dancing engage his attention, also. In Drop Eleven, after declaring that he "never cared what the colour of a woman's [hair] was", his comments about red-haired women at least seem distinctly personal: "Usually the liveliest of their sex", they are also the most changeable: "There is an absolute passion for coquetry in them: you can no more steady them to one object, *i.e.* yourself, of course, than you can fix a ball of quicksilver." Drop Fourteen somewhat disparages women's dancing, which he claimed never satisfied him: "There always appeared to me some mysterious huggery-muggery about the movements: it was their drapery that danced,—not they."

Some of the Drops are stunning in their frankness, perhaps the first of these, Drop Six, being the most so:

> I should far and away prefer being a great necromancer to being a great writer or even a great fighter. My natural propensities lead me rather to seek out modes of astonishing mankind than of edifying them. Herein I and my propensities are clearly wrong; but somehow I find that almost everything that is natural in me is wrong also.

Drop Twelve is almost a match for this: "The most opaque of all the masques that people assume to conceal their real characters is enthusiasm. In the eyes of women enthusiasm appears so amiable that they believe no impostor *could* counterfeit it: to men it seems so ridiculous that they are satisfied nobody *would*."

Mangan recognized but did not pretend to understand the enormous complexity of the relationship of the real Self to the selves one showed the world. He knew chiefly that when one "layer" of identity had been removed, yet another was to be discovered, and another, and another after that; and that the whole, like a portmanteau word or a compound German noun, was different to the mere sum of its parts. "Within the lowest deep a lower deep" was a favourite quotation of his, and even his fascination with caverns and dungeons would seem to have some bearing on this preoccupation with the nature of the hidden, and hiding, Self. Drop Thirty is perhaps the most impressive on disguises. For many sentences he rhapsodizes about beautiful women and the devotion to beauty one feels in youth, and then, "Well! a few years and all this sensibility passes away. . . . Are we happier for the change? . . . While we can neither adore nor abhor as of yore we are compelled to praise and scold much louder than ever." With what bitterness the next lines were penned, the reader can but surmise: "We care nothing for any thing, yet are forced to seem interested in every thing. One only hour remains to us in which we are privileged to throw off the mask and be ourselves,—and that is our death hour."

Another trait that Mangan presents as amusing, but that seems to have worried him more than he had previously hinted, is the streak of criminality he found in himself. Drop Fifteen commences by observing that if individuals put down their "inmost dispositions" in writing, publishers would get rich on the sales. He continues with the admission that he himself, "with all my sins, [no] wickeder than my neighbours", still has a "continual longing to become a captain of robbers". Why was this? he asks himself. He cares little "about the plunder. It is the idea of exercising influence, of controlling and coercing, that captivates my fancy." It is far removed from the usual image we have of the poet to hear him confess how much he craved the power that life denied him.

Perhaps he felt he had gone too far, for this was the last of the intimate revelations. Other Drops were only marginally personal. Thus Drop Twenty, the longest in the collection, showed him tormented by a dream repeated over and over again without the dreamer's exercising any will, memory, or imagination to bring it about. Here, his interest was, he claimed, more in the mechanics of the process than in the dream itself. As the dreamer, he passed repeatedly through a series of twenty-four rooms, each with some architectural peculiarity: "a pillar perhaps in the centre of it—a strange picture on the wall—a sphynx on a marble table". Sleeping, he was "conscious" of not remembering anything about the chambers; but when he was "compelled to return through the chambers back again", memory revived, "and I recognise at once, *in the correct order of their succession*, the objects I saw as I passed along first."

As he had begun, so he closed, the "Sixty-Drop Dose of Laudanum". The couplet from Wordsworth had promised that a poet ended in "despondency and madness", so the parable of Drop Fifty-Nine is despondent, and Drop Sixty, if not mad, is at least weird and seemingly nonsensical. Drop Fifty-Nine:

> Love, even fortunate love, never leaves the heart as it found it. An angel once dwelled in the palace of Zohir, and his presence was the sun and soul of that edifice. But, after years, there came a devil, stronger than the angel; and the devil drove the angel from the palace and took up his own abode therein. And a woeful day was that for the palace, for the devil brake up the costly furniture and put all things at sixes and sevens, and the mark of his hoof was every where visible on the carpets.

Presumably the "devil" who took up residence in the palace of the heart may be understood as anything or any force that might drive out the "angel" of love and innocence, but the reader is justified in hearing a reference to Mangan's own "devil", a weakness for liquor:

> . . . when some time had passed, he too, went away; and now the palace was left a lonely wreck, for the angel never more would return to a dwelling that had been desecrated by a devil. So it continued to wax older and crazier, till at last one night a high wind came and swept it to the earth where it lay ever after in ruins. Many say, however, that the angel might have remained in it to

> this day had he [from this point to the end, the pronoun seems to refer to Zohir] combated the intruder with might and main in the beginning, but that he chose rather to hold parley with him, and even invited him to come under the roof.

Mangan may have read such a story in the Jewish *midrash*; moreover, the name "Zohir" echoes "Zohar" in the Book of Zohar, or the Book of Splendor, in the Kabbalah. He read so widely in such curious old tomes that it would have been easy for him to have come across such a thing. Certainly Jewish teachings recognise the power of the evil inclination, and the saying "The evil impulse is first like a passer-by, then like a lodger, then like the master of the house" sounds very much like this Drop.[5]

Drop Sixty defies analysis:

> Inscribed in the Chronicle of the Forty-four Mandarins is the record of the confessions of A-HA-HO-HUM, Man of Many Sciences, Son of the Dogstar, and Cousin to the Turkey-cock; and thus it runneth: I, A-HA-HO-HUM, HAVE TRAVERSED THE EARTH, AND THE HEARTS OF MEN HAVE BEEN LAID BARE TO ME; AND LO! MY TESTIMONY CONCERNING ALL THINGS IS THIS:—*No Wall is Dense, and no Well is Deep, where a Will is Daring.*

The parts are not lacking in meaning, but put together, they appear to come to nothing. Mandarins suggest immense age and wisdom, but there are, or were, only twenty-seven, not forty-four, members in the body of Chinese mandarins. Sirius, the Dog-star, was known anciently for its heat and for causing pestilence and fever, while a turkey-cock has long stood for a vain, strutting person. The exclamation "Ah-ha!" followed by the yawn "Ho-Hum" is self-explanatory, leading to the final self-evident or perhaps foolish "wisdom".

Were his readers entertained, "excited and enlived"? Certainly they learned some interesting things about the author—things he was willing to have them know. But he would have only one other piece of separate prose in the *University Magazine*, "Chapters on Ghostcraft", which did not appear until 1842. It would be not only quixotic, but Catholic, and would mark the end of his prose in this periodical, although prose would continue to flow from his pen and to be printed in several other publications.

[2]

It was a vision of the night,
Ten years ago—
A vision of dim FUNERALS, that passed,
In troubled sleep, before my sight,
With dirges and deep wails of woe,
That never died upon the blast!
Mangan, "The Funerals"

The poet's second dream of the year was a nightmare. Although he claimed to have dreamed it in 1839, he did not write about it until ten years later, so his statement about the date has to be taken on trust. Because of the subject matter, "The Funerals", appearing in the 31 March 1849 number of the *Irishman*, has been read as a prophetic representation of the Famine, and for some readers it may have enhanced his reputation as a "seer". Others probably suspected that he gave the early year of origin largely to make it appear he had foreseen the tragic events that in the meantime had overtaken Ireland. If their suspicions were correct, it can be seen from the poem itself that he chose a most ineffective way to achieve his end; while he could readily have called attention to his "prophetic powers", in reality the poem avoided saying anything that might have led to the conclusion that he had foreseen actual events. The opening stanza appears as a headnote for this section. The second stanza pointed up the contrast between his own past and present:

Swiftly—not as with march that marks
The earthly hearse,
Each FUNERAL swept onward to its goal—
But, oh! no horror overdarks
The stanzas of my gloomsome verse,
Like that which then weighed down my soul![6]

That is, the distress of 1849 could not compare with that of 1839—for him, at least. In the third stanza, more than any other, he struggled to articulate the comprehensiveness of his personal horror:

It was as though my life were gone
With what I saw!
Here were the FUNERALS of my thoughts as well!
The dead and I at last were one!
An ecstasy of chilling awe
Mastered my spirit as a spell!

We expect a poet of Mangan's sensitivity to feel intensely the sufferings of his country and to draw both energy and inspiration from the great furnace of its agony, and "The Funerals" has been read in that light. However, the poem is not about that agony. Rather the reverse. In the national disaster he found a representation of his personal dissolution; he did not call up images of personal dissolution to serve as metaphors for the national disaster. In the midst of Ireland's tragedy he is almost breathtakingly self-concerned. The next three stanzas describe the sweep of the Funerals to the West and the South; in noting these geographical references which appear to relate to Ireland, a reader can easily err and overlook the poet's fact that the spread of the Funerals is across the entire *earth*. They cover *all* "the isles and lands". It is the universality of the experience which is so impressive. "The dead and I at last were one" draws together the sum total of the dead, and the living poet, in one vast congregation of non-existence.

Like so many of his best works, "The Funerals" has a four-part structure. In the brief third section, reason returns with the day and judges the visions of the night to have been "illusions", "phantoms", "cheats of the imagination". But the respite is not long. Night returns, the dream returns, and every day and every night thereafter, the sequence is repeated.

In the final two stanzas, he posed unanswerable questions: What was this mystery he saw portrayed? Were the visions "mockeries of a dream"? or "signs of looming wrath"? Once again he had arrived at a moment in the poem which could be used to show that, ten years earlier, he had had a dream that prophesied the onslaught of the Famine. But he let the "opportunity" pass. Instead, he confessed he did not understand what the dream had shown him. Sometimes, it is true, he spoke of himself as a "seer"—the image of the Prophetic Poet is not an unusual one. But not here and not now. The prophetic power of the soul, he declared, had to do with something far out of the ordinary:

> . . . within the soul
> I know there lives
> A deep, a marvellous, a prophetic power,
> Far beyond even its own control—
> And why? Perchance, because it gives
> Dread witness of a JUDGMENT HOUR!

In spite of what has customarily been written about the Famine and "The Funerals", the poem can best be read as having been *prompted* by the Irish condition in 1849, but as being *about* the poet's state of mind in 1839 and his fear of personal apocalypse, or "Judgment Hour".

Not until January 1842 did Mangan write "Chapters on Ghostcraft", but his fascination, and above all, his experience, with the spirit world began considerably before that date. Like most poets of the Romantic era, he had tended to speak of "spirits", and to put more than a little credence in the world of the supernatural. But from about 1839 onward, he went beyond these in references that differed from earlier ones in both tone and content. He became certain somewhere around this time that there were, indeed, not only " spirits everywhere", but that he himself could cross the barrier that separated the worlds of the dead and the living and converse with them. "The dead and I at last were one" really did signalize the end for him of the clear-cut demarcation between the two. When, near the end of his life, he would write, "Dream and waking life have now been blended/Longtime in the caverns of my soul", 1839 may well have been the year from which he dated that "longtime".

The element of supernaturalism is a somewhat awkward one for the biographer who knows before venturing into the territory that skepticism will raise a flaming sword between the material and many readers. Yet without this subject's being included, Mangan's story is incomplete. During this year, and for the next several years, spirits, spectres, phantoms, and ghosts put in frequent if irregular appearances, if the word is not ill-chosen, in his poetry, his prose and, all his volunteered evidence attests, his life as well. Only in "Ghostcraft", however, did he deal with this as being unusual in any way. Even there he theorized that it is not the people who see ghosts who are "credulous", but rather those who argue that no such thing exists. This may not be disconcerting as an intellectual theory, but it is difficult for many people to take the further step and accept that he was matter-of-fact because the experiences were within his own ken. Although his visions seem often to have come to him while he was in a borderline dream state, as described in the quotation at the top of this section, this did not make them any less authentic for him. Obviously, his experiences began well before the death of his father in 1843, but the only ghost that he actually claimed to have seen was that of his deceased parent.

Because most readers probably have some reservations about the genuineness of ghosts, and I join them in this, and perhaps also have some question about the sanity of ghost-seers, where as a general rule we have to part company, it is interesting to know that psychology offers a certain amount of explanation for some of these phenomena. Both Freud and Jung attempted to understand and explain ghosts in terms of the psychological make-up of the ghost-seer. A true ghost, they suggested, may be a manifestation or projection of a "split off complex", that is, of "a cluster of ideas or impulses . . . strongly toned with emotion and wholly or partly repressed". Such a complex is often "in strong conflict with other aspects of [the] personality" and so powerful, and so deeply buried in the unconscious, that it has not been accessible through the usual channel of dreams.[7] Plainly such a psychological explanation does not, nor was it meant to, account for all the ghostly manifestations that flesh has been heir to, and has written about, for hundreds of years. But it may explain the only actual ghost that Mangan claimed to have seen, for it takes little psychologizing to figure out that the poet harboured a severe complex in regard to his father and indeed to the whole family constellation, being unable to harmonize the conflict between his feelings of love and obligation with those of resentment, hatred and fear.

But Mangan's experiences of things beyond the everyday world included much more than his apparently rather limited ghost-seeing. In the past, it will be recalled, his physical illnesses had had well-identified psychological effects. And, it would also seem, vice versa, for his illnesses often appear to have come about as the result of intense psychic punishment. Thus, as early as 1808 there had been the unsatisfactorily accounted for but vividly remembered "walk in the rain" episode that resulted in prolonged "blindness" and the family's labeling the child "mad". A permanent hypochondriasis had followed fever and hospitalization in about 1820. Only a few years later, another illness, though less serious, was still bad enough to put the youthful scrivener out of commission for a long period of recuperation marked by depression, atypical states and behaviours, and scarifying religious doubts. Some similar after-effect from this 1838–9 physical collapse might logically be expected, and his heightened awareness of the spirit-world and what he recognized as communication with the spirits of the dead should probably be linked with the illness that preceded them.

Most people in Mangan's time did not believe in ghosts, spirit communication, and so on, any more than a majority do today. But his friends do seem to have taken his rather startling assertions in stride, accepting his claims at face value. Of course, the men of the Survey were in a sense ghost-haunted themselves, or, as Wakeman expressed it, "Indeed we lived in such an atmosphere of antiquarianism, that a thousand years ago seemed as familiar to us as the time when we first donned breeches."[8] If the "socially acceptable insanity related to ghosts is becoming a collector of antiques", as was only half-jokingly observed by Jungian scholar David Miller,[9] then the men of the topographical department enjoyed a sort of mutual madness, citizens of an alternative world in which they dwelt with phantoms of such long-gone heroes as Con of the Hundred Battles (or Bottles, as Mangan sometimes said) and Niall of the Nine Hostages.

Mangan was less isolated here than in most places he worked, and given the length of time he had been struggling to keep his spectres tamped down, and to understand them when they entered his dreams, it was almost predictable that something should trigger the release. As steam and magma escape through the fumaroles of a volcano, his "phantoms" rose through the psychic fumaroles of this sympathetic environment, and henceforth, the supernatural was to be an acknowledged facet of his existence. Undoubtedly, it added a new dimension of strangeness to the poet, who almost surely was already regarded as quite uniquely "different"; and it distanced him further from most individuals although they might look on him sympathetically and at his poetic and linguistic gifts with something like awe.

Among those manifestations of his contact with the supernatural that Mangan's friends seem to have accepted were his ability to talk with spirits and, like Emanuel Swedenborg, to see "a sphere of light about men's souls". Thomas D'Arcy McGee declared that Mangan had become a "disciple of Swedenborg in religion" and firmly believed "in all the inhabitants of his invisible world".[10] John O'Donovan maintained his skepticism, but it did not dull his curiosity; when he wrote a friend in 1847 that Mangan "insists he visits the other world regularly and converses with spirits there", he did not question the statement—one only senses a certain amazement in his voice.[11]

Another facet of Mangan's preoccupation with the supernatural was his idea of making visits to the other world, a notion which almost certainly grew from his reading of Swedenborg. Not that he derived the concept from the philosopher, but rather that he found in the earlier man's work a validation of something he himself was experiencing. This particular claim had nothing to do with ghosts *per se*, but was another type of paranormal, or at least extra-normal, experience, one that comprised most of the subject matter of Swedenborg's *Heaven and Hell* and in fact of a large portion of his writings. In his memoirs, Gavan Duffy recalled that the poet "had a passionate admiration for Swedenborg, and he finally sent me one of his books ('Heaven and Hell', I think), with a letter exhorting me to study it." Since Duffy could not be quite sure that he was remembering the right one among the many Swedenborg texts, chances are he never got around to reading it, for *Heaven and Hell* is nothing if not memorable. To be accurate, however, much the same thing might be said about *The Spiritual Diary* and *Arcana Coelestia* which were also very popular and were early translated from their original Latin. But *Heaven and Hell* is the only Swedenborg tome specifically named in relation to Mangan.

O'Donovan, too, was reading Swedenborg in 1839. Writing in August from the Aran Islands he related a wild story the islanders told to explain why their roofs were "thatched" in stone: St Kieran, it was said, had done the threshing so well that he powdered all the straw. About this O'Donovan observed, sarcastically, "I do not know of anything ever written to equal this in point of gravity and wisdom but the . . . passage in Baron Swedenborg on the spirits who inhabit the planet Venus." As he was able to quote a considerable portion of the passage, he presumably had his Swedenborg with him. He went further. Of a long poem in Irish and English and especially of a section of it called "Colgan's Notes", he observed, "Let the reader compare it with Baron Swedenborg's account of the spirits of the planet Mercury and he will perhaps come to the conclusion that the prophets of ancient times had visits from angels as well as the modern ones." Various angels and their "days of visiting" are named in this poem, among them Sariel, or Saraqael, the archangel set over spirits, according to Hebrew lore. O'Donovan, commenting on Swedenborg's discourses with generous spirits and angels, closed his notes, "I fear that the good Sariel will never pour any of those benefits on the bare stones of Aran."[12] By contrast, D'Arcy McGee wrote of Mangan in a more critical tone:

> Between Count Emanuel [Swedenborg] and the opium, he is nightly exposed to supernatural visitors, who are sometimes as unwelcome to him, as if they were of the earth, earthy. I remember he complained bitterly of them to a friend, a Catholic clergyman [this would have been Fr Meehan, probably], especially censuring "that miserable old man (his father)" who would not let him sleep o'nights, coming to the side of his bed, and entering into conversation.[13]

How far Mangan went into the study of Swedenborg's works is not known, although he denied being a committed Swedenborgian. The philosopher's disciples had founded the Church of the New Jerusalem, usually called simply the New Church, before the close of the eighteenth century, and by the 1820s it was operative in Dublin, although on a very small scale; records from 1831 show the "Society" then had only twenty-five members.[14] In theory, there was no conflict between belonging to a Christian denomination and being a member of the New Church, but in practice, it is doubtful if a Roman Catholic would have accepted that opinion. This alone would have prevented Mangan from becoming a member of the sect, for in spite of his fascination with mysticism, Oriental religions, Judaism, and assorted varieties of Christianity, staying a Catholic was like staying in Dublin for him, part of his very being. Nevertheless, the influence of Swedenborg's vision of a dual, interacting reality was a potent influence on the Irish poet.

Emanuel Swedenborg was born in Stockholm in 1688, the son of a Lutheran clergyman, and he died in 1772. Until the age of fifty-four, he had lived a genteel, orthodox life as a scientist, contributing in the diverse fields of paleontology, astronomy, physics, and physiology. For years, he earned his livelihood as a mining engineer. His concentration on hidden matter, from the distant stars to the interior of the human body, may have grown from, or perhaps it led to, his break-through into the realm of mysticism. Whatever the cause, between 1742 and 1745, he underwent a stunning spiritual crisis which he termed a "vastation". At this time, "His dreams became carnivalesque and nightmarish, he experienced extremes of mood from ecstasy to depression, his thoughts were fragmented. He experienced waking visions. His body vibrated, and he describes being flung about his rooms . . . by psychical forces."[15] He was thereafter to spend the rest of his life, some thirty years, describing, defining, and writing lengthily about the spiritual universe into which believed he was admitted on regular, extended, but evidently visionary visits.

Swedenborg's writings captured the imaginations of numerous artists and authors over the years. Among the latter were Balzac, William Blake, Baudelaire, William and Henry James, and William Butler Yeats, so Mangan, we might say, was in good company. Among the artists were those of America's Hudson River School and the "visionary painters" of France, including Redon and Bonnard, who "looked for the same luminous transparency in life and nature" as envisioned by the Swedish philosopher.

In "Swedenborg, Mediums, and the Desolate Places" Yeats quoted at some length from a Swedenborg passage which also obviously had struck Mangan. It is an ominous portrait of hateful spirits set on doing harm: "Their faces in general are horrible, and empty of life like corpses, those of some are black, of some fiery like torches, of some hideous with pimples, boils, and ulcers; with many no face appears, but in its place something hairy or bony, and in some one can but see the teeth."[16] A passage from Swedenborg's *The Universal Human* is similar. In it, the spirit of a robber wants to attack him: "Then I was shown what his face was like. He had no face, only something utterly black instead. In it was a mouth, opened threateningly and savagely like a maw, with teeth set in rows . . . all gape and no face."[17]

The imagery of evil held a nightmarish attraction for the essentially moral Mangan, and "facelessness", or a distorted face where a normal human face should be, effectively embodied evil. The descriptions from Swedenborg resemble one Mangan created in his macabre poem "A Tale of a Coffin", written in 1847. It told the story of two brothers—that familiar theme—one of whom, the "sodden sot", died and had to be buried, though the townspeople forbade it. Only his brother cared and watched over the coffin. Suddenly, a dark Form entered the room. "O'er a chasm of face he wore/A large copper mask, whereon was graven/These words: 'Rivetted for ETERNITY'." The listener said in awe, "I too dream, dreams/ Of human faces all black hair." The dark Form moved toward the coffin, lifted it like a feather, and set it down again, after which he wordlessly departed. The watching brother, upon raising the coffin lid, discovered the body had disappeared.[18] That he had no face, or a distorted or hideous face, may have been one nightmare of this poet who donned a mask so agilely; but a worse nightmare would have been that he might never be able to remove that mask, being, instead, doomed to wear it "for ETERNITY".

Not everything Mangan published this spring was dark, however, although the flashes of wit in the "Polyglott Anthology" were brief—a wealth of epigrammatic verse—or perhaps somewhat forced, and the chapter also included the sombre elegy for Catherine Hayes (now revised as from the Irish) and "To Laura". One of the poet's most pun-filled comic pieces appeared here, a mock elegy "on the Death of Tchao King, Fisher and Angler", of which two stanzas follow:

His wife and he were two—a common case—
    And when *gin-seng* had made his utterance thicker,
He'd swear upon his Sole he'd leave the Plaice,
    Unless Perch-ance she sold Her-rings for liquor.

* * * *

But Tchao's no more himself; for t'other day,
    After a dinner of Hashed veal and Pease,
He perished in a storm;—so let us say,
    Pease to his Hashes in the boiling seas!

We know little about Mangan's feelings for his own poems, but he seems to have enjoyed not only his punning effusions but such poems as "The Time of the Barmecides", about which a touching story is related. Mangan, it seems,

> was dining with Father Meehan one night, and there met [Dr Nedley] who had a like invitation. As Fr Meehan was called away on some parochial matter, the doctor, then very young, was left alone with the poet, and had a long talk with him. Mangan had just previously heard him sing "The Time of the Barmecides", to the old air of "Billy Byrne of Ballymanus", and was so charmed with the singing . . . that he promised him an autograph copy of the poem, telling him at the same time that he thought it the best thing he had ever written. This copy Dr Nedley duly received and has religiously preserved.[19]

The poem began:

My eyes are dimmed, my hair is grey,
    I am bowed by the weight of years;
I would I were stretched in my bed of clay,
    With my long-lost youth's compeers!
For back to the Past, though the thought brings woe,
    My memory ever glides—
To a long, long time, long time ago,
    To the time of the Barmecides.[20]

Mangan parodied it in the very next paragraph—again, there was always the wit, "quaint and rich" as Joseph Brenan styled it, ready to assert itself: "Ere my nose was red, or my wig was grey,/Or I sat in the civic chair,/I often left Rome on a soft Spring day/To taste the country air—". He even had the audacity to claim the verse was "from the Italian". The poet's young friend Richard D'Alton Williams also wrote a parody of the poem which must have delighted Mangan. It was titled "The Barmaid's Eyes", and began:

> My eyes are goggled, my whiskers dyed,
>   I am stooped, notwithstanding stays;
> I would I were stretched that stream beside,
>   Where I fished in my zigzag days;
> For, back to that spot—(it costs nothing, you know)—
>   My memory ever flies,
> Where I first saw glow, long, long ago,
>   The light of the barmaid's eyes![21]

Chances are the poet was indebted to his old friend the *Arabian Nights* for the theme. There, he would have read the story of "The Barber's Sixth Brother", and the "Barmecides' Banquet". The man who wryly penned "I sometimes carve but mostly starve" would have been sensitive to such a tale as this: A rich merchant prince of the Barmecide family of Bagdad invited a poor beggar to dinner, apparently for the sole purpose of amusing himself by setting empty plates before him and making him say how much he liked the "food and drink". This being the *Arabian Nights*, the beggar proved too clever for the prince and praised all that he was told he was being served. Finally, he pled that he was much too drunk to enjoy any more "wine", and in the process, knocked the prince down. This gentleman, for so he really was, appreciated that the tables had been turned on him, and fed the poor man royally.

The fifteenth German anthology in July had the poems of F.C. Wetzel as its subject, and Mangan prefaced the selections with a premonitory apology:

> None of them are certainly of a worse order than any we have hitherto published; and some of them may perhaps be of a better. Our own anti-poetical modes of thought and tendencies of mind, indeed, license the likelihood that we see in them blemishes which to those better qualified for understanding them may be invisible.

His "anti-poetical mode of thought" was an ominous sign. The poet closed this chapter with "Farewell to Poetry": "Good Night, Good Night, my Lyre!/A long, a last Good Night!" The silence that followed this installment did indeed last for almost six months. Just what ailed him, and why whatever it was so affected his writing, we cannot be sure, but it may have had some connection with the relatively new and eerie "presences" in his life.

One noticeable effect of these "presences" would be the emphasis in his poetry on the company of spirits, for he had entered that weird state of living with the pervasive consciousness of being in the presence of the supernatural. It is not as pronounced in this particular anthology as it will be later on, but even here we begin to feel the pressure the other-world and its entities (or, as he would have said, its non-entities) exerted on the poet, as if clamouring in spectral silence for attention. From "Live":

> Life now hath colder duties,
> And Man hath sterner toils
> Than freeing spellbound beauties
> Or gathering knightly spoils:
> Dark Earth is disenchanted
> By Want, and Thought, and Pain,
> And nought is phantom haunted
> Except the Poet's brain.[22]

So, too, in the uncanny "The Three Dead Men of Harlkoll". Three evil men who are dead, but do not know they are dead, are enclosed in a cave with the body of the man they have killed. To the Pilgrim who has chanced by they can say only "*We are shadows! We weep not! We breathe not! Away!*" Rather like it, "The Mighty Dead" recounted the German legend of the defeat of the Huns by the risen dead of Wehrstadt: "—suddenly bursting their coffin-bands,/In the graves through the burial grounds—/The Buried, with swords in their fleshless hands,/Rise up from their hillocky mounds!" And here, too, was the "Ghost-conceit" titled "Love in Death", the story of the young lover whose dead beloved comes to him as a phantom and steals away his soul.

* * * *

During this same period, important editorial changes were made at the *Dublin University Magazine*. Isaac Butt, who had been editor for some years, resigned in late 1838, and after a short stint by James Wills in the post, James McGlashan took. He would act as the editor for the next three-and-a-half years until Charles Lever replaced him in March 1842.[23] McGlashan was a shrewd editor, but his stinginess was well known, and he evidently sometimes held back a portion of Mangan's pay because he suspected the poet would spend it on drink. Certainly, the poet's level of contribution underwent a drastic change. From having commanded some one hundred pages annually for the five previous years, 1835–9, Mangan would now enter a period from 1840 until the end of 1844 in which he averaged only thirty-one pages a year: twenty-six pages in 1840, thirty-three in 1841, fifty-five in 1842, thirteen in 1843 (although his father's death this year may explain this drop-off), and twenty-six in 1844. Finally in 1845 under the editorship of John Francis Waller, the magazine would see Mangan's total number of contributions return to something comparable to what it had been earlier.

[3]

> In Belfast, which was pronounced solid for the Union, a weekly Repeal meeting was held as regularly as in the Corn Exchange [in Dublin]. . . . The Orange Press was furious, but no longer contemptuous. . . . "The *Vindicator* (screamed the *Northern Standard*) is to be found in every hamlet; it has become the oracle of the peasantry, and the manual of respectable Romanists."
>
> Duffy, *My Life in Two Hemispheres*

In the spring of 1839 an enormous change over which he had no control whatsoever came about in Mangan's life. Sometime prior to the first of May, Gavan Duffy abandoned Dublin for Belfast, leaving the *Register* and Mangan and their "Saturday nights of blessed memory" behind, to seize an opportunity offered him in the northern city. The Catholics of Belfast had decided that they needed a paper of their own, and eventually, and with the assistance of Daniel O'Connell, they acquired Duffy to be editor of the new Belfast *Vindicator*. Despite overwork and ill health, he had discovered, much to his relief, that he apparently had not inherited a tendency toward consumption, the disease common in his family. Moreover, he now would be able to put behind him the "exhausting slavery of a daily paper". The first number of the twice-weekly *Vindicator* came out on 1 May 1839. Over the next three years, the paper achieved what, given the circumstances in the north, was a high level of success, and Duffy consolidated and expanded his abilities and reputation as its editor.

But his ambitions soared beyond journalism. Although he remained in Belfast, he was determined to become a barrister, and was admitted as a law student at King's Inns in Dublin. The first term that it was necessary for him to keep was Michaelmas, 2–25 November 1839, which may well have been his first visit back to the city after leaving it in the spring. It was almost certainly this fall that he was told, evidently by William Carleton, that James Clarence Mangan had become an opium eater. He immediately challenged his friend, and Mangan vehemently denied the charge, as mentioned earlier here. Duffy, who was to be closely associated with the poet for much of the next decade, declared with equal vehemence that his "denial was so frank and specific that I believed it on the moment", and had never had any occasion to doubt it. "The suspicion arose from the splendour and terror of his visions of the mystical world", he concluded sensibly.[24]

And so, Mangan's months of silence passed. Then, in December, as noted on the first page of this chapter, he cheerfully announced in the pages of the *University Magazine* that he had recovered from his attack of "intellectual hypochondriasis", and named Carleton as being among the friends who had complimented him on getting over the disability that, "while it lasted . . . either paralysed or perverted all our faculties,—converting us, even while we fancied ourself an eagle, by turns into an owl, a raven, and a gander." His recovery he attributed to "gymnastics and toastwater", that is, exercise and his old favourite, tar-water. That Carleton was also the source of the rumour (denied by Mangan) that the poet had at one time been an opium-eater significantly links this 1839 episode with his use of that drug. With a characteristic and wistful pun, he assured Carleton that he would try to act on his injunction "to make the most of the great change that has overtaken us . . . the more especially as any small change that may overtake us stands, we lament to observe, a very slender chance of being made the most of in such hands as ours."[25]

Still, the sigh of relief is almost audible. "Who shall fathom the abysses of the human mind?" he once asked trenchantly. But that this had been the final period in whatever illness he had been suffering for more than a year seems likely. Moreover, this extended illness was probably also the "one occasion" he meant when he acknowledged taking laudanum "as a medicine"—the "occasion" stretched out to many months, it may well be, and the "illness" recurred from time to time throughout the rest of his life.

Without exception, his early biographers, Thomas D'Arcy McGee, James Price, Joseph Brenan, Maurice Leyne, and John Mitchel, believed that Mangan used opium. Fr Meehan denied it at first, but in his later years reversed himself and even claimed that his friend was more addicted to opium than to alcohol, having been advised to use it "on account of his consumptive physical condition".[26] Gavan Duffy, as noted, did not think the poet used the drug. Towards the end of the century, Louise Imogen Guiney and D.J. O'Donoghue argued emphatically that he took opium off and on throughout his life, though their evidence was circumstantial and highly questionable.[27] William Carleton's daughter, Jane, when asked by O'Donoghue, acknowledged that she had "heard him [her father] say too that he [Mangan] was an opium eater but this was a fact that he learnt from others".[28] John McCall, for his part, left the subject discreetly alone. To conclude, that Mangan used laudanum to break the chain of alcohol dependence or as a medication is an entirely feasible idea. But that he used it merely to entertain himself is highly dubious for both personal and cultural reasons.

His sensitive (or morbid) awareness of the presence of "spirits everywhere" would continue to be expressed in all sorts of ways for the next five or six years. To anticipate slightly, the first anthology of 1840 was the fourth "Literae Orientales". In it he described Eastern poetry as "a lawless, unfixable, ghostlike thing, irreducible to rule, unamenable to criticism, and in its constituent elements as little to be trusted for permanence as the colors of the cameleon or the tableaux of the kaleidoscope."[29] And he referred his reader to Goethe's maxim quoted as the epigraph for the first chapter of this biography: "Who would the poet understand/ Must enter first the poet's land." To understand this poet, the reader, it seems, has to take what amounts to a spirit-journey, "entering into" a new and different realm.

In one of the poems, a spirit is summoned "from his far-away wanderings among 'Bagdad's shrines of fretted gold' " to speak in a melancholy voice about a ruined kiosk.[30] Still another spirit, "groaning our sentiments", recited "The Howling Song of Al-Mohara", surely one of Mangan's most macabre efforts and a last flourishing of the inexplicably attractive theme of blood-guilt:

My heart is as a House of Groans
    From dusky eve to dawning grey; . . .
The glazed flesh on my staring bones
    Grows black and blacker with decay; . . .
    Yet am I none whom Death may slay;
I am spared to suffer and to warn;
            Allah, Allah hu!
My lashless eyes are parched to horn
    With weeping for my sin alway;
            Allah, Allah hu!
        For blood, hot blood that no man sees,
            The blood of one I slew
        Burns on my hands—I cry therefore,
        All night long, on my knees,
                Evermore,
            Allah, Allah hu![31]

A couple of poems farther on, in "a voice from the world of spirits" came the poignant "Night is Nearing", followed by three "war songs" which were introduced with the nearly whimsical half-apology ". . . it seems almost a profanity to hope that our readers will sympathise with the spirit of our next extract."

As is invariably the case with Mangan, the main impression is counterbalanced by another; his thesis always has its antithesis. Perhaps feeling that "The Time of the Barmecides" (because it had appeared "some months back . . . in such suspicious company", that is, in the "Polyglott thology", as from "The Arabic of Al Makeenah") deserved another ng, it was reprinted here. And more forthright comedy, too, had its n in the marvelous "Stammering or Tipsy Ghazzel by Foozooli, of mboul"—*Fusuli* was indeed the poet, but Mangan played with his ne as with his poem, of which a few choice lines follow:

I am so – drunk – that I ca – ca – I cannot
Make out – what – the – fun – is – at – all!
Ca – cannot say if – this pla – this pla – planet
Be an – gu – lar – square – or – a ball.
Nin – pom – cooks – nin – com – poops – tell us that – Fancy
And Judg – ment – are "drowned – in the – bowl;"
All round my – turban! – 'tis Necro – ma – mancy
That – gets – the blind side of – the soul![32]

ıe feels he must have been peeking through the eyelet holes of his cloak 1 laughing as he closed this installment by observing, "We really must t, or some screw in our rhythmical machinery will drop out", while still ging "the spirit of enterprise" on lazy translators:

O! when Translation's so feasible,
Where is the scamp would be scheming off?
Bowring, you sponge! have you ceased to be squeezable?
Anster the Bland! what the deuce *are* you dreaming of?

Twenty Golden Years Ago

[1]

> Mrs Petrie, the stepmother of Dr Petrie, took a great liking to Mangan, and often obtained his promise to call and take tea with her, but he occasionally found the attractions of the tavern too powerful. . . . those who were able to secure Mangan's presence of an evening were privileged persons. He preferred to be left alone with his thoughts, with his liquor, and a book.
>
> O'Donoghue, *Life and Writings of James Clarence Mangan*

The new decade that opened in 1840, for most people consider that a new decade begins when the old number is replaced, brought a change to Ireland which was to have incalculable repercussions: the return of Daniel O'Connell from his Parliamentary "adventure" and the founding of a new Repeal Association. The 1830s had not been auspicious for the Liberator. The wonderful psychological victory of Catholic Emancipation had borne only meagre rewards for most Irish, and the promising English Reform Bill of 1832 had reformed very little where they were concerned. It need not be suggested that "the Liberator" should be replaced by "the Placator" to reflect the opinion many had of O'Connell's efforts over the decade, but it was time for the ageing leader to return to work on his home soil, if he was ever going to do so.

Personally, too, the ten years had taken a heavy toll of O'Connell. In 1837, his wife's death had been a stunning blow. In "the wild winter of 1838", a pilgrimage to the Trappist Abbey of Mount Melleray had moved him to formulate "twelve spiritual reforms" he felt he needed to make to prepare himself for death, which he more realistically than fatalistically accepted could not be too far in the future. In 1839, he had suffered a parent's agony as his beloved daughter struggled through a spiritual crisis. And finally, in April 1840, at the age of sixty-five, he came home.

In many ways, Mangan's fortunes would henceforth be linked to O'Connell's. Though the poet seems rarely to have said much on the subject of the national leader, he was prepared to write a massive elegy for the *Nation* when O'Connell died in 1847, and it was probably only the falling-out between the political factions, Young Ireland with Duffy and the newspaper on one side and Old Ireland with its dead chief on the other, that prevented or at least discouraged his doing so. He admonished his editor, "You must throw me two columns of the NATION open" for the poem, but apparently his demand came to nought.[1]

In spite of "spirits everywhere" Mangan entered this decade as healthy and stable as he would ever again be, and in 1840 he managed what would turn out to be a fairly high level of literary productivity. There is about his life, however, an uneasy sense of its being undirected, of his merely moving with the currents and tide of the time. So much had been lost. Gone was "the grand Byronic soul", as he would describe his early temperament in "Twenty Golden Years Ago". Gone, too, was the inflated but stimulating hope "to translate Deutschland out". Gone, in a word, was youth and what he had had of its energetic hope and promise. Although he seems always to have maintained a certain childlikeness, from about this age onward he often impressed people as being older, not younger, than his years. His hair turned prematurely grey or, it was said, white. "Sleep!—no more the dupe of hopes or schemes;/Soon thou sleepest where the thistles blow—" he declared.

Nevertheless, along with supernatural company, the poet also had a rich assortment of living, breathing associates—many acquaintances, a coterie of intimate friends, and of course his ever-present family. His father and mother, now seventy-five and sixty-eight years old respectively, continued to live in apparent comfort at No. 9 Peter Street. They were, in fact, something of a rarity for their time, an elderly couple who had been together for over forty years of married life. In the directories of the day their address is given with the name of Thomas Stewart, probably the owner and landlord to whom they paid their rent. Payment days were quarterly, on the 29th of September, December, March, and June. With his parents almost certainly lived their youngest son William and probably James, at least some of the time. Because of the nature of his autobiographical writings—none of them carrying his story past youth in any detail at all—Mangan's mature feelings for his parents are open to speculation, but probably his not very successful efforts to be objective about his father and to see some of his redeeming qualities originated in these later years.

The poet's closest companions continued to be, as they had been in 1838 and 1839, the men of the Ordnance Survey office. But except for his friendship with O'Donovan, his association with the "confirmed toper", and his going with young Wakeman to take tea with Petrie's stepmother in Dame Street, nothing is known about how much they socialized. Practically speaking, his friendship with O'Donovan underwent a considerable change this year when his friend married Eugene O'Curry's sister Mary Anne Broughton. The wild "plan" he had described to marry a black-haired Connaught beauty had either fallen through or been all "jelly and soapsuds" from the start, for on 18 January, he and Mary Anne were wed in the Pro-Cathedral.[2] They moved in with the O'Currys at No. 32 Bayview Avenue in north Dublin, and O'Donovan's days of trekking the city with bachelor friends came to an end. The married state did not immediately agree with him, however. On 25 February, he wrote an irate letter to Hardiman in Galway complaining sourly that he had been desperately ill for nine days, but was totally neglected by "the literary men, who pretend to be so much my friends". The worst of the lot was Petrie who lived only "a musket shot" away. He longed to get out. "I am like a wild bird caged in a house!"[3] he fumed.

O'Donovan was back on the job, this time in County Tipperary, in October, and thus was away from his wife when their first child, a son, was born on the seventeenth of the month. O'Curry was on hand, though, perhaps again, to Larcom's despair, having found an excellent excuse to avoid country duty, and he wrote on 22 October that "Maryanne and your son and heir, continue to improve in every way that it is natural for them to do: the boy indeed is as pleasing and quiet a lad as any of his age in Dublin."[4] Presumably because the news continued to be good, they decided to wait for his father to return to the city to have the baby christened with the name Edmund. The death of this little boy some two years later almost broke John O'Donovan. His letter about Eddy's suffering and slow death reveals depths of feeling which the antiquarian generally repressed, his more usual response to illness and pain being tough and intolerant, as it appeared to be when Mangan sought out his Bayview Avenue house to beg for help on a bitter cold Christmas Eve several years later. Considering the poet's long friendship with O'Donovan, it is helpful to have this glimpse of the soft and vulnerable side of his nature, and to see that his peremptory reaction to another's distress could be only a mask for heart-wrenching sympathy.

O'Donovan's brother-in-law, Eugene O'Curry, was never a friend of Mangan's in the same sense that O'Donovan was, if, indeed, in any sense at all. He almost certainly lacked the flexibility of temperament that people needed to keep from being irritated with the poet's idiosyncrasies and apparently casual regard for such social niceties as punctuality. But he was a close associate for years in a professional capacity, and he provided—at a price—several of the literal English versions of Irish poems from which the poet did verse translations, the first of which were to appear this year. O'Curry always held a slight grudge against Mangan, because he did not think the poet gave him enough credit for his translations, and to an extent he was probably justified in this. In fact, very little credit is ever given anyone who sets down prose equivalents, but O'Curry was not a man to tolerate neglect just because it was common practice. He wrote to Thomas Davis that:

> Mr Mangan has no knowledge of the Irish language, nor do I think he regrets that either. . . . It was I that translated those poems [Mangan's in Duffy's *Irish Ballad Poetry*] from the originals—that is, I turned the Irish words into English, and Mr Mangan put those English words, beautifully and faithfully, as well as I can judge, into English rhyme.[5]

According to O'Donovan, who himself sometimes barely managed to get along with O'Curry, it would have been hard to satisfy his brother-in-law on this matter: "He is exceedingly jealous-minded and has been offended at all the notices of him. . . . [that is, reviews of papers he had given] His head is very clear; his learning altogether muddy and *fake*", a damning charge to lay against a fellow scholar. Moreover, "he cannot bear to be set right. . . . This is the great *vice* of his mind, and on account of which I have to humour him like a big spoilt child."[6]

Marriage must have seemed pervasive to Mangan these months, as first O'Donovan and then their superior, Larcom, paired off and settled down. To Petrie on 18 March, the latter wrote, "This day will close my career of Bachlorhood [*sic*]. I must dress and be ready."[7] It would not be long, either, before Duffy took the same step. He had already formed a warm friendship with a young Belfast woman, Emily McLoughlin, whom he would marry near the time of his return to Dublin in the late summer of 1842. Thus the poet saw old familiar alliances breaking up and being replaced by new ones from which he would be largely excluded.

For the most part, references to wives or bachelorhood are scarce in the verses of serious nineteenth-century poets, but Mangan included comments in two outstanding original poems. Of the later, "The Wayfaring Tree", more will be said at the appropriate moment in his story. Suffice it to quote, now, these lines that opened the four-stanza composition:

We
Old bachelor bards, having none to mind us,
Are seized at seasons with such a heart-aching
That, leaving home and its wants behind us,
We hie elsewhither, the spirit's car taking
Us east and west, and aloft and nether,
And thus I, also, both night and day faring
From Hartz to Hellas, pass weeks together
(In vision) under mine old Wayfaring
Tree,
My childhood's dearly beloved Wayfaring
Tree![8]

The midnight musings of the earlier of the two poems, "Twenty Golden Years Ago", were printed in the "Second Drift" of his new anthology for the *University Magazine*, "Stray Leaflets from the German

Oak", in June 1840. Attributed to "Selber", "Himself", the poem closed a collection of eight genuine translations from the German, poems rich in folklore and supernatural elements. Paradoxically, it is one of the most down-to-earth poems Mangan ever wrote. The poet-persona, a German, is seated in his garret looking down through rain-streaked windows at the silent, empty streets below. Using the realities of the moment—coffee in his cup, a clock that shows it is half-past twelve, a fire that has to be fed—he compares them to the past, characterized by wine that flowed in taverns, time that flew past in happiness, and the "fire" that he had "when young and bold":

> O, the rain, the weary, dreary rain,
> How it plashes on the window-sill!
> Night, I guess too, must be on the wane,
> Strass and Gass around are grown so still.
> Here I sit, with coffee in my cup—
> Ah! 'twas rarely I beheld it flow
> In the taverns where I loved to sup
> Twenty golden years ago!

Although the theme is common and sad, the tone is not morbid or bitter. It is too universal for that, inviting the reader into the poem's domain of unprotesting acceptance of the way things are. Its homely touch, and easy metrics and rhyme scheme, add to the impression, rare in Mangan, of a plight made more tolerable by being shared. His sense of alienation usually over-powered such fellow-feeling.

> Wifeless, friendless, flagonless, alone,
> Not quite bookless, though, unless I chuse, . . .

he wrote with a gently wry smile, it seems, and even that possibility of choice takes the edge off the totality of misery.

There is, however, a hint of sinfulness, and of personal responsibility for his aloneness: "They who curse me nightly from their graves/Scarce could love me were they living now—"

> But my loneliness hath darker ills—
> Such dun duns as Conscience, Thought and Co.,
> Awful Gorgons! worse than tailors' bills
> Twenty golden years ago!

Why "twenty"? Perhaps because the start of a new decade took him back in memory to other such moments. In 1820, at seventeen, he was still full of hope, ambition, and, as he declared to the world, "genius". In addition, he was undoubtedly familiar with the old Irish saying, "Twenty years a-growing, twenty years in bloom, twenty years a-stooping and twenty years declining". More to the point would be the question, Why "golden"? He certainly had not had much good to say about the period he now eulogized. In fact, a close reading reveals just how little Mangan and his "Selber" character have in common. "Selber" speaks of himself as a dashing young man who "broke all hearts like chinaware" and ran up terrific bills at his tailor's, something it is virtually impossible to imagine Mangan doing.

It is probably not stretching the imagination too much to speculate that "Selber" was his fantasy of himself as the *Dublin University Magazine's* suave, satirical, young poet-translator, master of the cutting criticism and the unique rhyme. "Selber" was in reduced straits, true, down—but not out; able to put life into perspective and to win his readers' (mild) sympathy while he (gently) amused them. And he had a lovely past to remember. If he were Mangan as he never was, he was also Mangan's conception of himself at his most balanced: able to look back with wistfulness but without breast-beating; able to look forward without agonizing:

> Yet may Deutschland's bardlings flourish long!
> Me, I tweak no beak among them;—hawks
> Must not pounce on hawks; besides, in song
> I could once beat all of them by chalks.
> Though you find me, as I near my goal,
> Sentimentalizing like Rousseau,
> O! I had a grand Byronian soul
> Twenty golden years ago!

Mangan was constantly in touch with George Petrie during these months, often working under his roof in Great Charles Street, always under his direction when he reported in and out for copying assignments in one of the libraries. Petrie played the role of benign father, but he was perhaps almost intimidatingly a "do-er", an accomplisher. Mangan was too fair-minded not to be grateful for all the support and assistance he received from him, but it would have been uncharacteristic for him to have assumed a subservient posture on the strength of it. In his 1849 memoir, he warmly praised Petrie's "indulgence towards the errors and shortcomings of others", but he criticized him for not having a sense of humour, a vigorous writing style, or an appreciation of Rabelais' wit. Petrie had, in fact, borne with the poet's lateness, drowsiness, and "tar-water" bottle just as he had borne with O'Keeffe's unpredictability and O'Curry's habit of finding just one more excuse to delay his departure from Dublin. Shortly after the topographical department had to close, Petrie drew tart criticism from "A Protestant Conservative" for having favoured Catholics, nationalists, and personal friends, as well as for giving drawing lessons and discussing religion and politics with his men when they should have been hard at work.

The battle of the rival antiquarians boiled over in 1840, when Sir William Betham withdrew from the Royal Irish Academy to protest what he took to be unfair favouritism shown Petrie in the awarding of prizes and publication. With him in a scholarly huff went Mangan's friend Owen Connellan, who, perhaps largely for the sake of the payment he received and to be on what looked like the side of the more powerful contingent, had been a Betham follower. Connellan won a few little rewards for his loyalty such as being appointed Irish historiographer to George IV and William IV. But he also wrote pitiful, begging letters to his patron, who apparently held him in slight regard. In December he asked for his assistance against "the pretenders", reminding Betham that he, that is, Connellan, had "long since declared in the Royal Irish Academy before Mr Curry in opposition to Petrie" and adding that "they have not since forgotten it to me. . . ."[9] In fact, only the previous year, Connellan had been denied a job on the Ordnance Survey team, although sponsored by Lord George Hill.

In retrospect, the antiquarians' round tower debate has its comic elements. Petrie's well-grounded theory that these remarkable structures were early Christian watch, and perhaps defense towers, has now been acceptably proven, but in the 1830s a number of fantastic and fascinating theories were advanced. The Vallancey-Betham-Connellan school took a mainly inductive approach, adopting an attractive theory based in myth and legend, and then searching for bits and pieces of "evidence" that would bear it out. Among the various notions were that the towers had a pagan origin, perhaps Persian (or Egyptian, Phoenecian, Greek, Chaldean, or at any rate Eastern), and had been used as phallic temples, fire-worshipping temples, temples of Vesta or of magi, or "astronomical gnomons". In 1840, the South Munster Society of Antiquaries came up with the further speculation that they had been sepulchral monuments and also fire temples.[10] In the midst of all this, Petrie was like a man in a swarm of gnats. As for the poet, he seems not to have held against Connellan any of his humbling, indeed humiliating, behaviour. Although the man fitted the description of what Mangan once called a "lick-spittle sycophant", the poet also had a great well of reserve sympathy for anyone who was, like himself, an "uphill struggler", and that, too, described Connellan.

Among Dublin literary men in general, Mangan seems to have made few friends. Of the lesser lights among his acquaintances, almost nothing is known. Of the important names, there are John Anster, Samuel Ferguson, Charles Lever, and William Carleton. Of these, it would appear that only Carleton was a social friend. That Mangan would have been moved by the early death of Griffin on 12 June this year is obvious, for the two had much in common—age, temperament, religion, demanding consciences. But there is only the most minute possibility that Mangan ever met his fellow author. In fact, he so clearly identified those subjects of his 1849 articles whom he had met, distinguishing them from those he specifically had not, such as Maginn, Maturin, and Edgeworth, that he as much as told his readers that he and Griffin were not acquainted. Why he chose to include him in this group of individuals who had influenced him or touched his life remains unknown.

Mangan's admiration for Anster's translation of *Faust* was immense, and Anster, too, admired Mangan's poetry. Not only did he feel genuine compassion for the weaknesses of the man himself, but the two shared a fondness for a punning style of humour. In the last terrible months of his life, when even O'Donovan lost track of him, the poet could only be located "by great exertion through Anster, who is a good and kind friend of his, and who has been advising and assisting him for years unknown to the world."[11] On the other hand, Anster was not always patient with Mangan's drinking. O'Donoghue, collecting anecdotes about Mangan for his *Life*, got in touch with the author J.R. O'Flanagan who told how he, upon asking Anster to introduce him to Mangan, "was steadily refused—'You, he said, would be plagued by repeated requests for money which would go for drink'."[12] But Mangan's observations make it clear that he liked and admired Anster whom he described as "quick-thoughted, shrewd, and deeply penetrating. . . . a happier man than he thinks. . . . He mistakes a certain restlessness which belongs to his character for dissatisfaction; whereas it is as Byron observes 'merely what is called nobility'."

Samuel Ferguson, like Anster, went to Mangan's assistance when he was really in dire straits. A Belfast man, a Protestant, a Trinity graduate, a barrister, and eventually a recipient of Britain's high accolade of knighthood, Ferguson was a devoted Irish unionist. He was also intent on resuscitating ancient Irish poetry, and O'Donoghue was not alone in thinking him "one of the best of Irish poets", perhaps even "the greatest of all". Yeats shared this opinion and included Ferguson in his oft-quoted lines, "Nor may I less be counted one/With Davis, Mangan, Ferguson . . . " from "To Ireland in the Coming Times". In spite of his friendship with many leaders in the Young Ireland movement and with cultural nationalists such as Petrie, Ferguson held himself aloof from active participation on the *Nation*. Duffy's description of him in political action is touching. It is from a time when, as Duffy observed, "many of the gentry began to talk a sort of conditional and speculative nationality", some half-dozen years later than the period we have now reached: "It was pathetic to witness his continual and quite hopeless efforts to inflame their patriotism, like a man labouring to kindle a vesta [a match] by rubbing the end where there was no phosphorus."[13]

With all his personal merit, kindliness, and fair-spiritedness, Ferguson remained a prisoner of a mind-set so deeply inbred that it was literally part of him. His ability to hold mutually exclusive beliefs seems not to have caused him the uneasiness or philosophic neurosis that it usually does, but it is certain that he and Mangan could never have been friends in the true sense of the word.

Charles Lever entered Mangan's life several times at oblique angles, as noted previously. Three years his junior, Lever had led a full and exciting life by the time they met, probably between 1828 and 1830. Having studied at Trinity College, he graduated from Göttingen in medicine. He could have been no older than twenty when he journeyed to Canada and lived four or five years in the backwoods before returning to Ireland to practice in Kilrush. Mangan's first and indeed only allusion to him in print had been made in 1834 in "To a Friend. From Rosenkranz", with the German original supplied, as discussed in Chapter Four. In all probability any friendship that had existed between Lever and Mangan cooled after the latter's lightly veiled accusation of plagiarism against the former. An unusual number of allusions to the wilderness of North America occur in Mangan's work from these years, and his ever-present fascination with medical matters may have found close-at-hand reinforcement in Lever's being a much-travelled physician. But the fact is that no solid evidence of their ever having met can be cited. Suffice it to say that if there had been a friendship between the two men, there must have been a falling away over time.

According to D.J. O'Donoghue, who was also William Carleton's biographer, the novelist was "in some sort a boon companion of [Mangan's], though Mangan had no moral sympathy with his coarser nature, and hardly one single point in common with him." Unfortunately, one thing they did have in common was a fondness for liquor. The same O'Flanagan who had asked Anster for an introduction to the poet was well enough acquainted with Carleton to hear the following story from him.

The poet had "rather to the astonishment of his friends" accepted an invitation "to a social party at the hospitable house of Mrs [Thomas] Hutton of [116] Summerhill." In fact, it is surprising to find Mangan invited to such a gathering, and O'Donoghue suggested that it may have been "for the purposes of curiosity [rather] than from motives of admiration or sympathy" that the invitation was issued. By the time Carleton arrived, Mangan had already disappeared somewhere in the house, nobody knowing just where he had got to. The novelist was sent to find him and bring him in to join the company, his hostess so far having been unable to "induce him to come into the drawingroom". Carleton, evidently all too sure of how to proceed, asked if there was whiskey available and was shown by the butler to the supper-room where a decanter stood on the sideboard. He equipped himself with it and a couple of glasses and went looking for the poet

> whom he eventually found hidden under cloaks, coats and wraps in one of the rooms. "What are you doing there?" queried Carleton. "Seeking an opportunity of escape," faltered the poet: "I had no right to come here—I don't know how I did come." "Well," said the novelist, "come and have a nip of something which will put courage and life in you." He gave Mangan a glassful of whiskey, and took one himself, and after a while the timid poet allowed his captor to introduce him to the hostess and her guests, whom he soon delighted by his brilliant talk, but whom he also gladly left.[14]

Carleton had a growing family at this time, among them his daughter Jane, who would eventually be asked by O'Donoghue about her father's having spread the rumour that Mangan was an opium eater, as already noted here. To O'Donoghue she observed that her father had known Mangan, "but not intimately. I do not think it was easy to get to know Mangan intimately: you could only know the best of him through his works." She herself had seen him only two or three times "when he called upon my father which was generally early in the day." Carleton resented almost personally the smallness of the sums the poet was paid for his translations, but he rather cancelled out this sympathy by agreeing in principle with McGlashan, that "if he threw away his money upon opium and gin, there was little use in giving it to him". Like those others among the poet's acquaintances who had anything to say on the subject, Carleton did not hint that Mangan had a family to support, or that it would have been those individuals who suffered because of his alcohol or drug habits. In fact, it seems improbable that the Mangans were now depending on their son James for their sustenance, although he may have added something to the total household income.

All things considered, the poet would seem to have been well provided with companions at this point. The benison of his position on the Ordnance Survey cannot be overstated. It was, without exaggeration, a lifesaving association. Curiously enough, he never suggested that he wanted the company of fellow authors. But what was lacking, obviously, in 1840, and what he probably did miss, was a single impassioned attachment to one close friend. This may have left him feeling not so much lonely as hollow, beset by what the medical profession term "anomie", an enthusiast without that essential something or someone to be enthusiastic *about*.

[2]

> [The Irish laborer] drank nothing for some 350 days in the year; but once, or maybe oftener in the month, he got roaring drunk. . . . He then forgot all his wrongs. . . . Irish intoxication was the luxury of despair—the saturnalia of slaves. Irish temperance is the first fruit of deep-sown hope, the offering of incipient freedom.
>
> Thomas Davis, "Fr Mathew", *Nation*, 28 January 1843

In 1838 a movement had begun in Ireland which was to have incalculable effects on the lives of millions of Irish men and women, among whom was James Clarence Mangan. The temperance crusade launched at first tentatively by the Quakers of Cork applied early on to Fr Theobald Mathew, a young friar, to be the leader. After much thought and prayer, he decided to "throw all personal considerations aside" and devote his time and energy to the cause of making "our working class sober and self-respecting". These "personal considerations" were no small matter, one of them being that he came from a well-to-do distillery-owning family and might not be deemed the most suitable leader for a temperance campaign. Fr Mathew, however, had already put that concern largely behind him, for he had previously dedicated his life to working among the terribly poor, which with almost predictable frequency meant among people whose lives had been damaged by heavy drinking. Alcohol was consumed at a shocking rate in Ireland at this time, and the Quakers' crusade was not the first effort to try to reduce it. It would, however, be the most successful. From 1839 through 1842, the annual consumption of 900,000 barrels of beer and 11,500,000 gallons of spirits—in which the government included brandy, gin, rum and whiskey—was cut in half.[15]

From the start, as that "statement of purpose" noted above made clear, the target of the operation was "our working class", which meant city labourer, rural peasant, tenant, or small farmer. By implication, then, anyone socially or economically "above" this level was *de facto* if not *de jure* excluded. They were, presumably, well enough off, and well enough bred or educated, to know how to behave and to maintain their poise and "self respect" even when they were intoxicated. Thus a great point is always made of the fact that Mangan remained a "gentleman" even when known to be drinking. When John Mitchel wrote that "There were . . . two Mangans, one well known to the Muses, the other to the police; one soared through the empyrean and sought the stars—the other lay too often in gutters of Peter-street and Bride-street", he was castigated and contradicted.[16] Yet, save for what may have been some exaggeration for the sake of the syntax, Mitchel was probably right. That, however, is a story that belongs to a later year than 1840.

The Apostle of Temperance, as Fr Mathew came to be called, remained in the area around Cork for the first two years of the crusade, partly because the work there was all-consuming. In the first three months, 1,400 people signed the pledge to abstain from alcohol; in six months, that figure had grown to 4,000. In eighteen months, the total had surely reached 1,000,000, since the uncontested total by the summer of 1840 was an almost incredible 5,000,000.

The whole south and west of the country must have seemed, sometimes, to be pouring into County Cork to take the pledge directly from the man who was becoming almost an idol. In December 1839, worn out with months of work in the field, O'Donovan literally ran into the "Mathewites" in Limerick.[17] "I could not get a single room in that city in which to sit quietly, in consequence of the awful number of Matthuites," he declared. "And this annoyed me, who am a being of a very irritable configuration of nerve, and as anti-Matthusian as I am enthusiastically anti-Malthusian." So were others on the Ordnance Survey staff "anti-Matthusian". Petrie loved his porter and O'Curry his whiskey. The "problem drinkers", to use a modern term, were recognized and dealt with, but for the most part the men were of the class in which the ability to use alcohol in moderation (or to drink in excess discreetly) was taken to be a private matter, not anything for general knowledge or "meddling". Duffy felt differently. He met the friar in Belfast and they became fast friends, Duffy sticking by the priest even as the crusade began to decline, as it did shortly after expanding into the rest of Ireland.

The reasons for the over-heated enthusiasm which had marked the crusade during the first couple of years were complex. The times were highly emotionalized around a millennial expectation for 1844. Politically, a general republicanism was gaining strength and would, over the years, expand revolutionary activity almost literally around the world. Fr Mathew was without doubt a highly charismatic individual: energetic, attractive to rich and poor alike, compassionate, and single-mindedly pure of spirit. When less inspired followers stained the radiance, and accusations of profiteering, inciting to mass hysteria, employing charms and magic, and making suspect if not downright heretical claims and statements began to multiply, the crusade leveled out and then waned. Fr Mathew's exertions, however, had succeeded beyond the wildest dreams of the founding Quakers, even reaching to England and America. He was awarded a Civil List pension in 1851 and would have been made a bishop, had his health not failed. He died, back in County Cork, in 1856. With the Famine, teetotalers by the hundreds of thousands broke the pledge they had taken, but total consumption of alcohol remained well below the earlier figure. In 1849, the *University Magazine* praised Fr Mathew as bringing about a "revolution in the drinking habits of the lower classes", while regretting that in many cases it was only "for a season".[18]

Until 1840, the priest did not take the crusade off its home ground. Then, in that year, the strategy changed, and both Belfast and Dublin were visited. In March he arrived in the capital. One of the most important venues was SS Michael and John, Mangan's parish church and the church in which he had served as an altar boy some quarter-century earlier. There, in front of the ponderous granite quay-side facade, the priest spoke for hours, pleading, exhorting, challenging. And as he did so, groups of men and women were led forward by his assistants, and to these thousands he administered the pledge.

At this time, Fr Mathew may still have been using the first of the two pledges employed by the campaign: "I promise to abstain from all intoxicating drink", the participants recited, "except used medicinally and by order of a medical man and to discountenance the cause and practice of intemperance." After the men and women made this declaration, pewter medals especially designed and struck-off for the crusade were distributed. The reuniting of broken families, the tears, the promises of reform, and the renewed hope, all made for highly emotional scenes.

When it became his friends' urgent project to get Mangan to take the pledge is not certain, but without a doubt the date was after 1840, and may even have been as late as 1845 when he and Fr Meehan first became acquainted. In all likelihood Mangan was not very actively practising of his religion at this point. If he had been, he would have met the dynamic Fr Meehan much earlier than he did. The latter, however, wrote that the poet had been present on the occasion of Fr Mathew's Dublin appearance at SS Michael and John—Mangan must have told him this—"but could not be induced to take the pledge, simply because he doubted his ability to keep it". The priest's intention, writing as he was at a much later date, was to show Mangan in the best possible light, and so he added, "Withal, what he had seen of the marvellous revolution wrought by Fr Mathew impressed him beneficially, so much so, that for whole months he would avoid the use of alcohol. . . ."[19] Plainly, some time must have passed between the first impact of Fr Mathew and the last years of Mangan's life for him *to have refused to take the pledge because he doubted his ability to keep it* and also *to have taken it and broken it several times over*.

In actual fact, Mangan's reason for not taking the pledge earlier than he did was almost certainly more complicated than Fr Meehan portrayed it. As noted, the crusade at some point altered the pledge, and the second version was tougher than the first. The loophole of "medical man" and the weakness of "to discountenance" were eliminated, and the wording became: "I promise with the divine assistance to abstain from all intoxicating liquors, and to prevent as much as possible by advice and example intemperance in others." This made even more crucial a question which had been raised earlier as to whether the pledge was merely a "promise" that a person would try to keep, or a much more serious and binding "vow" which would be a sin to break. The difference was hardly a minor one. If it was a promise, breaking it could be forgiven readily. But if it was a vow, many teetotal priests asked, could anyone but the administering priest, that is, Fr Mathew himself, forgive the individual who broke it?

As a result, many priests refused absolution to those who broke their pledge; instead they had to see Fr Mathew and receive forgiveness directly from him.[20] Naturally, Fr Mathew might be many miles away when he was needed and totally beyond the ability of the backslider to get to. On the strength of this distinction and its implications, Frederick Lucas, editor of the influential English Catholic journal the *Tablet*, dissociated himself and the publication from the crusade, although he had previously been a supporter. Mangan, always concerned about the health of his immortal soul, did not choose, at least in the crusade's earlier years when he still felt he had control over his own drinking, to risk putting it in such jeopardy. Thus Fr Mathew came to Dublin, and went, and the crusade rolled on, without enlisting the poet in the ranks of those who had foresworn alcohol.

But if Mangan were not measurably affected by the abstinence activity on every side, he was decidedly touched by the overall change in the Irish climate of opinion about drinking. The highly visible Apostle of Temperance and his work had the general effect of taking drinking as such out of the realm of largely private behaviour and making it a public concern. Nothing is more obvious about Mangan than his need for personal privacy and freedom from restriction. When crossed in these, he could do foolish, self-destructive things. Now, this man who had found comfort drinking in the company of friends, sitting unobtrusively in a public house snug, sipping his glass of whiskey punch hour in and hour out, had his behaviour held up for criticism by a newly censorious public. Whether the response was pity or contempt, moral judgement was passed on him. A striking contrast exists between early accounts of the young Mangan enjoying time with Tighe and Bligh in cosy bar parlours or meeting with co-workers from the Ordnance Survey in the Phoenix Tavern, and later stories of his solitary "disappearances" when it was said he sought out the lowest haunts of the city for periodic drinking bouts. Although any strong implication of cause and effect would be unjustified, a change definitely occurred in the pattern of his drinking; after so much effort at controlling and restricting it, he began to lose the battle. But the culture itself was undergoing an alteration, too; a reform that culminated in "respectable" Victorianism was commencing, and Fr Mathew was in the vanguard.

The consumption of alcohol became, further, not only a community concern, but also a matter of national consideration. This was, in one sense, nothing new. The failure of the Uprising of 1798 had sometimes been blamed on the drunkenness of the Irish participants. But the new nationalism, led by O'Connell, only very cautiously embraced the new temperance movement. O'Connell and Fr Mathew were both such powerful personalities that it is scarcely surprising they had a hard time sharing the Irish stage. O'Connell was always wary of any force he could not control, and this now included Fr Mathew and his masses of followers. Conversely, the Liberator could certainly not oppose or write off the peasants and labourers who literally in their millions found a spiritual and also a temporal guide in the priest. Nor did he want to.

For the most part, his caution was shared by the Catholic clergy though it is more surprising to discover how lukewarm they were in supporting one of their own than to find O'Connell hedging his approval. But the clergy, with noteworthy exceptions, formed a conservative force in Ireland, by and large much more concerned with directing and comforting their flock in its adversity than in revolutionizing it by social change. While Fr Mathew urged teetotalers (an unusually silly word for a serious subject, derived from what the Oxford dictionary terms "reduplication of *total*" and dated only to about 1833) not to get involved in politics, O'Connell just as eagerly sought their co-operation. Duffy, it seems, found a middle way and in welcoming the priest to the North spoke eloquently about the need for teetotal societies to sponsor reading rooms, libraries, and education, so that the newly freed minds of the people could be enriched and prepared to handle new national responsibilities.

As events transpired, O'Connell emerged victorious, being "largely successful in capturing the teetotal crusade". In fact, only a few years later, in 1843, O'Connell's Monster Meetings which were held all over the country were literally made possible by the sobriety and good behaviour of the hundreds of thousands of "pledged" Irish who converged upon some designated rural or village spot to demonstrate for repeal of the Union. If there had been lingering doubts about the far-reaching effects of the crusade, they were eradicated at this time, as newspapers reported one gathering after another where feelings ran high, oratory was loud and moving, bands filled the air with stirring national tunes—and crowds were sober.

1 Silhouette of James Clarence Mangan, 1822. The silhouette and its verso (see ill. 4) are reproduced by courtesy of the Library of the RIA. Originally planned as a frontispiece for this volume, this illustration replaces the reproduction of Rocque's map listed as illustration 1.

2 No. 3 Fishamble Street, Dublin, where Mangan was born

3 No. 6 York Street, Dublin, where Mangan trained as a scrivener

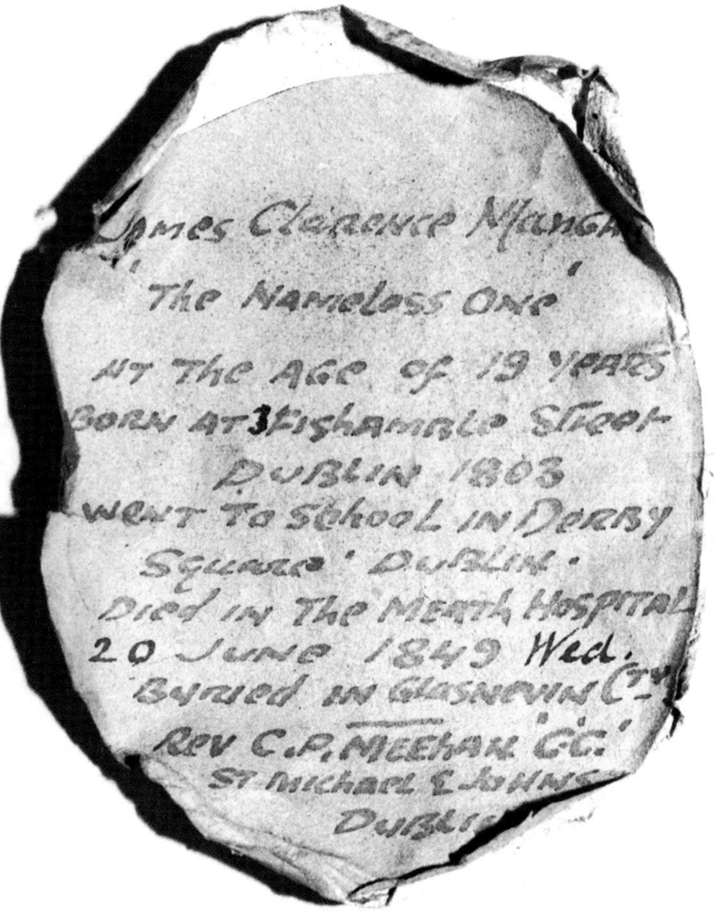

4 Reverse of the silhouette of Mangan; it reads: James Clarence Mangan "The Nameless One" at the age of 19 years. Born at 3 Fishamble Street, Dublin, 1803, went to school in Derby Square, DUBLIN. Died in the Meath Hospital 20 June 1849 Wed. Buried in Glasnevin Cty. Rev. C.P. Meehan "C.C." ST MICHAEL & JOHNS DUBLIN.

ames Tynan, Dublin.– 6. Mr. Terry M'Merry, (P. M'Dermott) of
lery dale, in the Manor of Mirth; to Miss Fanny M'Funny of Fro-
ome fort, in the Parish of Pleasure.– 7. Simon Frisby, Harris-
n, Co. Kilkenny.– 8. James Delany, Melitia.– 9. Mr Peter Puff.
nes Tighe.) – 10. John Byrne, Kilmichael, Gorey.– 11. Pat M'Der-
t, Kells.– 12. "Hermogenes" Moyne, Co. Galway.– 13. Miss Jo-
na Kehoe, near Rathvilly, Carlow.– 14. M. Fay, addressed to
s —— English.–
Address, Extraordinary, (2 pages,) by * * * * * * (James
ngan.)
ne 15 Rebuses, were by:– 1. James Tighe, Dublin.– 2. Michael
tty O'Reilly, Esq. Oldcastle (Jas Martin,) addressed to Wm.
an, Parsonstown.– 4. James Tynan, Dublin.– 5. James Delany,
itia.– 6. John Byrne, Kilmichael, near Gorey.– Pat M'Dermott,
ls.– 8. Bernard O'Farrell, Belanagare.– 9. Mr.— Drumcondra,
B. Perry.) – 10. Henry Proctor, Edenderry.– 11. S. T. Colclough.–
James Nowlan, Gorey.– 13. "Giles in the Country," addressed
Villiam Behan, Parsonstown.– 14. S. Topping, near Castle Blay-
.– 15. KLRKN. (Killerkin, near Carlow.)
he 18 Charades were by:– 1. James Mangan, Dublin.– 2. Mich-
Blatty O'Reilly, Esq. Oldcastle.– 3. James Tynan, Dublin.– 4.
L——.– 5. James Delany, Melitia.– 6. Miss Mary Swallic,
n Moyle,) Kilbarry.– 8. Mr. Peter Puff, (Jas Tighe.) – 9. Pat M'
mott, Kells.– 10. Henry Proctor, Edenderry.– 11. S. T. Colcl-
h.– 12. Miss Anne M'Gee, Brooklawn, near Durrow.– 13. Bryan
gan, Archerstown, (his first appearance in Grant.) – 14. Miss
anna Kehoe, near Rathvilly, addressed to Miss Eliza Ger-
in, Tobinstown Cottage, Co. Carlow.– 15. By C. K. D. Gurteen.–
Thomas Glynn, L. S, Gurtymadden, Loughrea, addressed to
liam Moyle, Kilbarry.– 17. Miss Sarah Sidney Ladymantle,
kfield.– 18. Owen Muldoon, Castlefield Lodge, Rathcool.

he Mathematical portion missing, but according to the Diary
he succeeding year, there were 14 Mathematical Questions, in
same Grant's Almanack for 1825.
Solutions to these Missing Questions of 1825. { See these Questions, page 303a
estions 1, and 2, } not being solved were reproposed in 1826.
–A Solution by the Proposer, Owen M'Namara, L. S. Carrick-on-
nnon, given in 1826.– Who in an Algebraical demonstration
gs out 6 may be taken at pleasure, so that 6^2 may exceed 63; if
8, then $y = 128$, and $x = 57344$; hence the sides are 576×256,
0×256, and 674×256; or 576, 350, and 674.
–A Solution by Maurice Doyle, Philomath, Leighlinbridge given
o in an Algebraical investigation, from "Saunderson's Algebra,"
gs out the value of $x = \frac{25}{24}$; hence the area of first is $\frac{x^4}{24}$, which
tiplied by x^2 the perimeter, $= \frac{x^6}{24} - \frac{5x^6}{144}$ (the product of the
es $= \frac{x^6}{144}$ = a square;) and so of the rest.

.– A Geometrical Solution by the Proposer, Patrick Finn, Philo-
th, given in 1826.– Tangent of half the difference of the angles
d B = 25° 30'; BC = 79½; sine angle C, = 22° 00°; the for-
r angle C found = 41° 55'; adding both, X will be found = 63° 55'
required course in the SE quarter.
.– A Solution by the Proposer John Cahill, Killane, Co. Carlow,
en.– From the words "Tangent of half," &c. the Solution of
Question.
.– A Geometrical Solution by the Proposer, William Gartlany,
.S. Riverstown, given.
.– A Geometrical Solution by John Delahunty, P. M. Higgin's-
n, Kilkenny, given.
. A Solution by the Proposer, John O'Brien, Doonane Coalmiles,
en's Co. given.– Who in an Algebraical investigation brings out
$\frac{md}{cr})^{\frac{1}{4}} = 1$; consequently $y = \frac{mr}{s}$, as required.
.– A Solution by the Proposer, Peter Connolly, Loughrea, given,
onstrating it, Geometrically, from a figure given in "Gibson's Sur-
ing."
.– A Solution by the Proposer, James Cherry, Dublin given.– From
sum of their squares = 1728; then x = 21,753: hence the sides
21753; 1814·5, and 26625; and perpendicular, 14718.
2.– Not Solved, therefore proposed in 1826.
3.– A Solution by Maurice Coffey, L. S. Cross Keys, County Meath
en.– Since the man on monument had his feet 30 feet above my
, and his head 36 feet above same, $(30 + 6 \times 30)^{\frac{1}{2}} = 32{\cdot}85$ feet
least distance of eye from monument; hence per 47. 1. Euclid, his
d is 48 feet 9 inches, and his feet 44 feet 6 inches from my eye;
per Trigonometry, his maximum angle is 5° 13', as required.
4.– A Solution from "the very excellent and ingenious Edward
Golding, Boot lane, Dublin," given in 1826.– By an Algebrai
process bringing out $y^2 = \frac{2}{72} = \frac{1}{36}$, ergo $y = \frac{1}{6}$ as required

MARK MORTON, Editor, 12 Great Ship street, Dublin.

Only the Revd John Edge has Grant's Almanack for 1826,
last published, which he has kindly placed at my disposal.
Was this individual copy that was used by the learned Ma
thew Collins, B.A. when he transcribed most of the Math
matical Question out of same, for "The Lady's Farmer's a
Mathematical Almanack, 1861."

GRANT's, With Enigmas, Rebuses, Mathematical Questio
the Fairs of Ireland, &c. &c.

1826.

The usual intimation to Correspondents.

ANSWERS to the ENIGMAS Proposed last year. (1825.
1. The end of the Enigma.– 2. Reform.– 3. A Bird confined in
Cage.– 4. A Burning Glass.– 5. A Suicide.– 6. Drollery.– 7. A Hea
8. Marriage.– 9. Memory.– 10. Poverty.– 11. Tomorrow.– 12. Bear
13. Peacock.– 14. Marigold.

(In consequence of William Jones's indisposition, there w
no Answerers' Names given this year, to the Enigmas, Rebuse
or Charades.)

NEW ENIGMAS for 1826.

1. Enigma, by James Tighe, Dublin, addressed to James Mang

Frae new come folk wha tarry near,
I aften for my Jamie spier,
As how he liked the bye gone year,
An' sic discourse;
An' if his-what d'ye call it?– fear
Is naething worse.

On fine strung nerves, that witch can
play
Sic dirgefu' notes by night an' day,
Till Fancy sees a dread array
O' clouds, an' gloom;
Arching a dark, a dismal way,
Down to the tomb.

Some canna' thole the mental pain,
That racks a nerve disordered brain,
Hence deadly dives an' draughts are ta'en
To smoor the way,
As some prefer the sharp wee skein
Like Castlereagh!

When pilot Reason quits the pow
Man! what a crazy thing art thou
Alas! around thy chartless brow,
An' shattered form;
The winter waves o' life do row
A rude wild storm.

Och! Jamie shake away the dole
That hath *too long* o'ercast thy so
I'll no commend the reekin' bow
Or Gill-house fun,
But just a morn' an' evenin' strol
An' loup an' run.

Farewel my friend, in whom I fin
Reflected bright loved Leonard's
mind–
Leonard, the modest, gentle, kir
Whose soul's embrace,
Enclosed within it's love refine
The human race!

2. Enigma, by M. E. (James Mangan.)

In the unbeginning first ere earth arose,
From chaos old,
Thy lonely empire, Spirit of Repose!
Thou didst uphold!
The splendid firmament is vast to view–
Can Fancy roam
That wilderness of silver and of blue!
It is thy home!
The untrodden solitude was thine– and is,
And the grey ruin,
Whereon Decay through buried centuries, his
Work hath been doing!
And the red desert, where her sand waves revel,
In the Simoom,
Or all as desolate, lie hushed and level,
Through glow and gloom;
Down to the chambers of the soundless deep,
Where life and light,
Exist not, but all things are clothed in sleep,
Thou goest by night!
Or where there is no breath to curl her billow,
And on her brow
The melancholy night beam finds a pillow–
There mournest thou!
Yea, in corruption and the charnel vault,
Darksome and lone,
For everlasting years, thou dost exalt
Thy dim, dim throne.
Spirit!– of universal essence, by
What single spell,
Thou harmonizest earth, sea, stars and sky,
May language tell!
Handmaid of Him who is the Invisible Word,
The Unseen, the All-seeing,

5 Page copied from *Grant's Almanack* by John McCall showing Mangan's poem later published as "Silence" and James Tighe's poem to his friend

6 Brooklawn House, Love Lane, Dublin, possibly where Mangan met the men who introduced him to his career.

THE

COMET.

"KNOWLEDGE IS POWER."

No. 58.—Vol. II. SUNDAY, JUNE 2, 1832.

Published this Day,

A BRIEF COMPILATION of the POPULAR TREATMENT of CHOLERA MORBUS, By Thomas Wilson, Member of the Royal College of Surgeons in Ireland.

TAIT'S EDINBURGH MAGAZINE, No. 3, for JUNE.

IMPORTANT TO ALL

MR. M'INTYRE

FASHIONABLE AND MERCANTILE PENMANSHIP.

TERMS MODERATE.

NO. 46, COLLEGE-GREEN.

THE HAMILTONIAN SYSTEM IMPROVED.

THE FRENCH LANGUAGE.

THE HOLY SCRIPTURES IN GREEK.

A CARD.

DR. BARRINGTON'S GALLERY AND MUSEUM.

LUKE DILLON

ROYAL HIBERNIAN ACADEMY.

TO BE LET,

TO WORKMEN AND GENTLEMEN.

NEW GROCERY ESTABLISHMENT.

TO OPEN on MONDAY NEXT

PATRICK O'LOUGHLIN, Proprietor.

LADIES' FASHIONS FOR JUNE.

MILLINERY AND DRESS WAREROOMS.

M. HAYDN

TUSCAN AND DUNSTABLE BONNETS.

THE DUBLIN FOREIGN LACE WAREHOUSE.

W. ATKINSON

TO DISTILLERS AND BREWERS.

THOMAS COFFEY

LIVERPOOL.

THE EMERALD

DR. JARDINE'S

THE

DUBLIN PENNY JOURNAL,

PUBLISHED EVERY SATURDAY.

No. I. Vol. I. J. S. FOLDS, 56, GREAT STRAND-STREET. June 30, 1832.

The Custom House and Harbour of Dublin.

HISTORICAL NOTICE OF THE CITY OF DUBLIN.

The period of the foundation of our City is involved in as much obscurity as the etymology of its name. It may easily be supposed that men would congregate at such a convenient spot for fishing and commerce as the ridge of land that rose above the last place where the Liffey was fordable, before it joined the sea; and therefore it is very probable that such a position, presenting means of safety and support, of offence and defence, was very early seized on. The geographer Ptolemy places (A. D. 140,) a town exactly in the parallel of Dublin, and calls it "*Civitas Eblana.*" Our city therefore has a just claim to an antiquity of *seventeen* centuries. But we are inclined to suppose that though the Greek cosmographer had good reason to lay down such a place as "*Civitas Eblana,*" yet it is to the Vikingar—pirates, or "Sea-Kings," of Scandinavia—that the settlement of Dublin, as a place of commerce, and as a fortified town, may be attributed.

These bold intelligent Ostmen, (as the Scandinavians were called by the Irish, because they came from a comparatively Eastern country,) saw that Dublin harbour was one of the best, and the river Liffey one of the most commodious, and the valley of Dublin one of the most fertile, in the island. They therefore selected this central position, and landed their troops, where, according to custom, they erected a fortified Rath; and on that ridge that hangs over the lowest ford of the Liffey, on the exact spot where the Cathedral of Christ's Church now stands, they excavated large vaults or crypts, in one of which St. Patrick, the apostle of Ireland, is said to have celebrated the sacred offices of his religion.* Here they deposited the produce of their commerce and their plunder, and used to retreat to them on occasion of any sudden invasion of their enemies.

But very probably, it is to the sea-king, Avellanus, that we owe the establishment of our city as a place of military and commercial importance. He, with his brethren, Siterick and Yvorus, having heard from their roving countrymen of the fertility and capabilities of the green western isle, landed a fresh swarm from the Baltic, and proceeded to win, by their swords or their policy, a settlement in Ireland. Yvorus, who was doubtless the more cautious of the three, and had a good military eye, pitched on Limerick; Siterick, struck with the great commercial advantages that the junction of the Nore, the Suir, and the Barrow, presented, sailed up that fine estuary, and landed at Waterford; but Avellanus, with the eye of a *king*, saw at once that neither the waters of the Shannon or the Suir would answer his purpose; and so he selected that spot where the Awn-Liffey ceased to be navigable, and on the rising ground that rose from its southern bank, he planted himself, convinced that if ever Ireland was to come under the sway of one monarch, it would become the seat of the metropolis of the island. Stanihurst, on the authority of Giraldus Cambrensis, asserts that the city owes its name to this Avellanus, and with the license of an etymologist deduces it in this way:—

Avellana—Eblana—Dublana.

But this surely cannot be the derivation; for Ptolemy, upwards of six hundred years before, called it Eblana Civitas. Probably the author of the life of St. Kevin gives the best derivation. Speaking about St. Garban, he says, "he lived near Ath Cliath, which is also called by the Irish, Dubh Linn, signifying the dark bath." Now any one who observes the Liffey may see good reason why the ford over this unusually dark flowing stream might be called the *black bathing place*.*

* Over one of these early Danish vaults or fornices, or crypts, sanctified, as tradition says, by the consecration of St. Patrick, Sietricus, son of Avellanus, king of the Ostmen of Dublin, built Christ's Church. There are still many of these under ground Danish depositories in Ireland, of which we may very probably give some account in our Journal. In the county Antrim we have seen them, where they are called Picts' holes. Within six miles of Dublin, and adjoining the beautiful village of Lucan, there is a fine and commanding Danish Rath, in the centre of which there is one of those artificial caves spoken of above. About twenty years ago, the author of this article was shown a very large and double circular cave in the side of the hill between Rathcoole and Naas, a few hundred yards from the ten-mile stone in that line of road.

* The other and more ancient name *Bally Ath Cliath*, the town of the ford of hurdles, arose from a common practice of the Irish ... to make muddy rivers, such as the Liffey was, near its junction with the sea, and near bogs and marshes, fordable by means of hurdles or kishes laid down where they desired to pass. It was a ... substitute for a bridge, and did more mischief than perhaps those who laid them down thought of—for the course of rivers was impeded ... formed, and swamps established.

PARSON'S HORN-BOOK.

PART II.

BY THE

COMET LITERARY AND PATRIOTIC CLUB.

Nos numerus sumus et fruges consumere nati.
HORACE.

Here's a jolly set of us,
Well fed PARSONS ! !
FREE TRANSLATION.

———— Quid non mortalia pectora cogis
Auri SACRA fames ?
VIRGIL.

Oh ! "SACRED famine" for accursed gold,
How hast thou cased in steel the human breast
Against the voice of Pity!

PARSON M'CLINTOCK's *version of the Æneid, published at* "NEWTOWNBARRY," *June* 18, 1831, *price* £2 10*s*. ! ! !

DUBLIN:
[PR]INTED AND SOLD BY BROWNE AND SHEEHAN,
AT THE COMET OFFICE,
NO. 10, D'OLIER-STREET.
1831.

DUBLIN
UNIVERSITY MAGAZINE.

No. XVIII. JUNE, 1834. VOL. III.

CONTENTS.

DUBLIN
WILLIAM CURRY, JUN. AND COMPANY,
SIMPKIN AND MARSHALL, LONDON.
SOLD BY ALL BOOKSELLERS IN THE UNITED KINGDOM.

My hAnDy young MAN.

I owed you no ode - no one ode! - no one ode you an ode - any one ode! - no one knowed that any one owed you any one ode - or if any one knowed that anyone owed you any one ode, I am not that one - <u>o-de</u>-ar, not I! - Hear me for my caws, as the rook said - I look on odes as ode-ious compositions - adulatory stuff - flattery of the flattest sort, worthy to be paid for, not in the glorious renown which all honest, honorable, high souled and high heeled men seek - but - out of the purse - one pound one a line - not a came... less! Now you know I spit upon this sort of thing - I never <u>take</u> money for what I write - it is always given me - ...

nothing to record, Spectators being tired looking on at nothing, and Vindicators finding nothing that <u>could</u> be Vindicated - in fine that Nature, Art, & the Universe were all about to give up the ghost - You laugh! Take care, my fine fellow, then, that the next time I dream such a dream I don't clap you into it! - how dare you put me into such a passion - <u>Mens tuus ego</u>" - i.e. Mind your eye!

The  in the 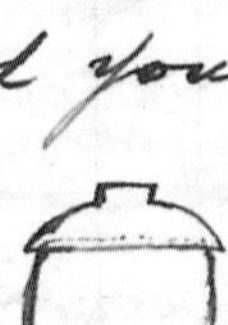

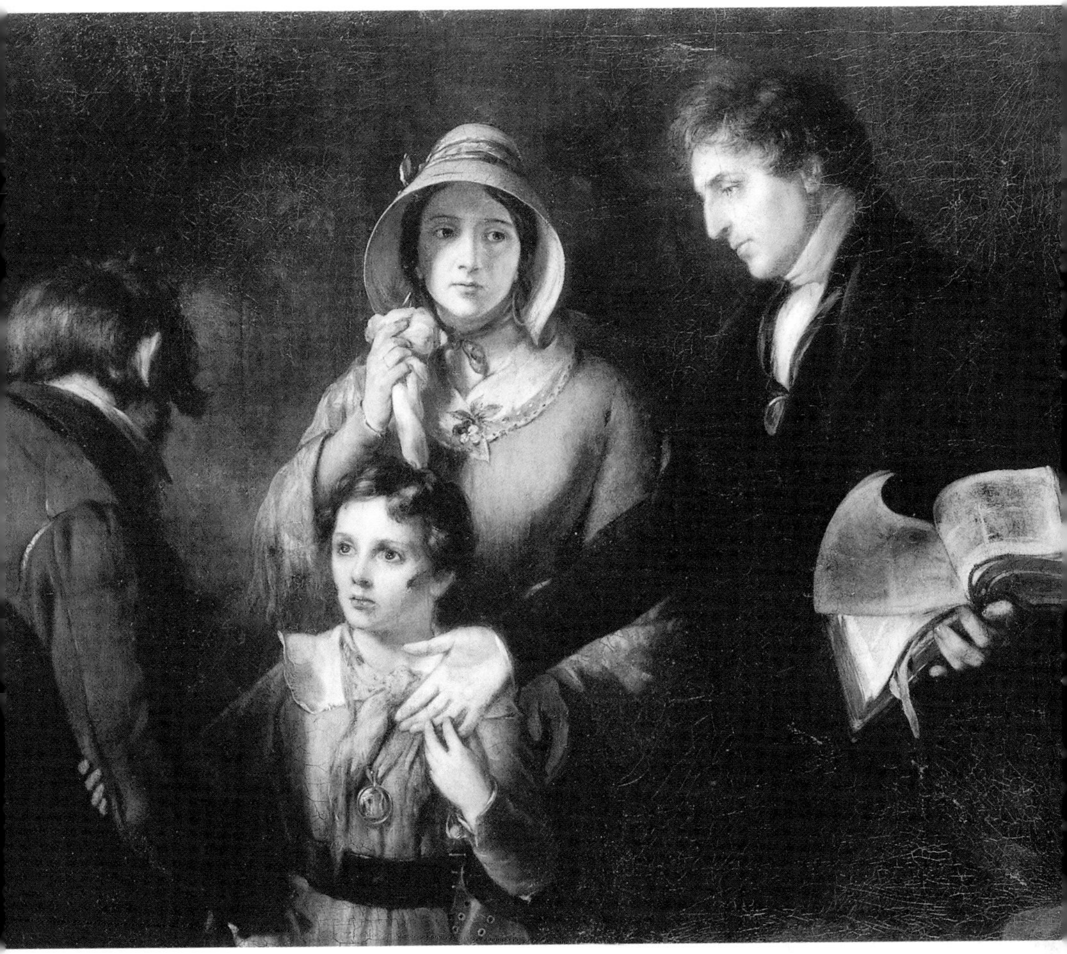

19 Opening and closing lines of Mangan's letter to Duffy, 1840

20 "Fr Mathew Receiving a Repentant Pledge-Breaker" by Joseph Haverty

21 Total Abstinence Pledge card

22 "James Clarence Mangan" by Charles Mills, for D.J. O'Donoghue's centenary edition of Mangan's poems, 1903

JAMES CLARENCE MANGAN

(From a Drawing by Charles Mills)

THE NATION.

VOL. I.—No 1. DUBLIN, SATURDAY, OCTOBER 15, 1842. PRICE 6d.

THE O'CONNELL COMPENSATION FUND

O'CONNELL TRIBUTE.

UNION OF SAINTS MARY, THOMAS, AND GEORGE.

CITY OF WATERFORD.

O'CONNELL TRIBUTE TESTIMONIAL.

THOMAS ARKINS.

CAUTION.

LOYAL NATIONAL REPEAL ASSOCIATION.

TO PRINTERS.

23 Front page of the *Nation*, vol. 1, no. 1, 15 October 1842

24 "Birth of the *Nation*", showing (left to right) Thomas Davis, Charles Gavan Duffy, and John Blake Dillon

25 "Reading the *Nation*" by Henry MacManus

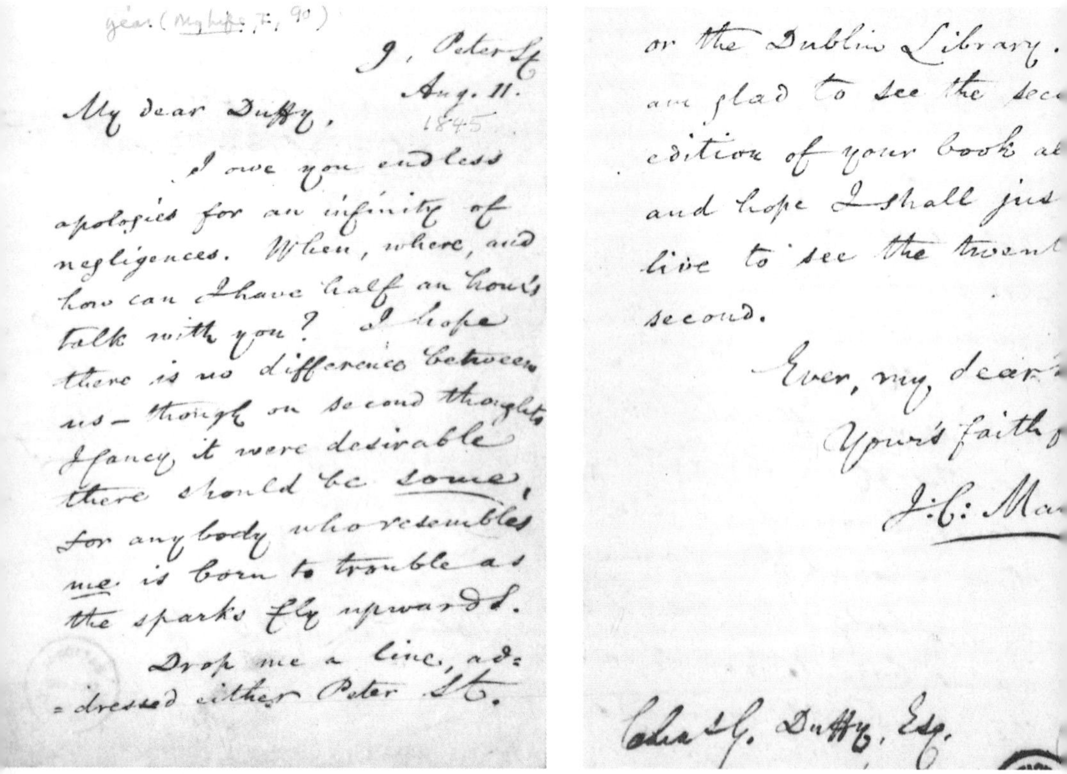
9, Peter St
Aug. 11.
1845

My dear Duffy,

I owe you endless apologies for an infinity of negligences. When, where, and how can I have half an hour's talk with you? I hope there is no difference between us – though on second thoughts I fancy, it were desirable there should be some, for anybody who resembles me is born to trouble as the sparks fly upwards.

Drop me a line, ad=dressed either Peter St.

or the Dublin Library.

am glad to see the sec edition of your book a and hope I shall jus live to see the twent second.

Ever, my dear

Your's faith

J.C. Man

Chas G. Duffy, Esq.

26 Mangan's letter to Duffy, 11 August 1845. The book mentioned is *The Ballad Poetry of Ireland*.

27 John Mitchel (1815–75)

Anthologia Germanica.

GERMAN ANTHOLOGY:

A SERIES OF

TRANSLATIONS

FROM THE MOST POPULAR OF THE GERMAN POETS.

BY

JAMES CLARENCE MANGAN.

IN TWO VOLUMES.

VOL. I.

DUBLIN:
WILLIAM CURRY, JUN. AND
LONGMANS, BROWN AND CO. LON
1845.

THE

POETS AND POETRY

OF

MUNSTER:

A SELECTION OF IRISH SONGS

BY THE POETS OF THE LAST CENTURY,

WITH POETICAL TRANSLATIONS

BY THE LATE

JAMES CLARENCE MANGAN,

NOW FOR THE FIRST TIME PUBLISHED.

With the Original Music,

AND

BIOGRAPHICAL SKETCHES OF THE AUTHORS.

BY JOHN O'DALY,

Editor of "Reliques of Irish Jacobite Poetry," "Kings of the Race of Eibhear;" Author of "Self-Instruction in Irish," and Assistant Secretary to the Celtic Society.

DUBLIN:
JOHN O'DALY, 7, BEDFORD ROW.
MDCCCXLIX.

28 Title page of *Anthologia Germanica* (6½" x 4"), 1845

29 Title page of *The Poets and Poetry of Munster*, (6½" x 4"), 1849

30 "The Leaders of the Irish Confederation in Council" by Edward Glew. Left to right, standing: John Blake Dillon, P.J. Smyth(?), William Smith O'Brien, John Mitchel, Thomas Devin Reilly, Thomas Francis Meagher(?), Thomas D'Arcy McGee(?), Richard O'Gorman(?); seated: John Martin (l), Charles Gavan Duffy (r)

31 "Daniel O'Connell" by George Mulvany

32 The smaller of two sketches of Mangan made by Sir Frederick Burton after the poet's death

33 The larger and better-known of two sketches. Signed: F.W. Burton ft. June 1849

34 Mangan's gravestone, Glasnevin Cemetery

[3]

> I send you six pages "Our Budget", "Pokeriana", "Pokerisms", "Flim-flams and Whim-whams" anything you like to call them-isms—"Scraps and Scrapings" "Attic Stories"—They are facetiae (at least I hope so) in the American fashion and might do for your fourth page,—pray Heaven you don't imagine they'd *do for* your paper altogether. . . .
>
> Mangan to Duffy, 5 May 1840

There was no hard and fast rule, but it had long been understood that a writer who contributed regularly to one periodical would not contribute much if anything to another. The *Dublin University Magazine* editors definitely subscribed to that standard and spoke proprietorially of "our correspondents". We would have to turn the pages of the calendar back to December 1835 to find anything by Mangan appearing anywhere but in the *DUM*, where he was now recognized and appreciated, though not by name, as the author of the "Anthologia Germanica". Then, in 1839, their *de facto* monopoly ended when five of his poems were reprinted in the Belfast *Vindicator*.

Duffy, hard at work in Belfast, was putting a stamp of quality on his newspaper's four twice-weekly pages. The format was the usual: main news on the first page, shorter news items on the second, advertisements on the third, and everything else on the fourth, where, in this case, the far left column was reserved for "Select Poetry". It was he himself, perhaps, who chose the poems by Mangan that were first reprinted here: "The Lover's Farewell", the second of the sonnets "To Caroline" now titled "A Despairing Sonnet", " A Fast Keeper", "Live" and "The Philosopher and the Child". When he asked his friend for something in 1840, however, it was not for poetry, but for "political articles". What he discovered, it may be to his disappointment, was that the poet had moved light years away from the punning political whimsy of the *Comet*. He responded, "Don't ask me for political articles just now—I have had no experience in that *genre decrire*, and I should infallibly blunder." This was not as sweeping a statement as the one he had sent James Tighe a year-and-a-half earlier, but it was the same sort of warning flag of trouble. He was sending something—"facetiae", as he called them—which filled some half-dozen pages, but then he reiterated: " . . . as to any formal political essay I fear I am not equal to it at all. We shall see by and by, however."

All in all, Duffy would have five prose articles from him, this first one, three in the generally non-political "Editor's Room" series, and a final personal essay. The selection of less than two dozen reprinted poems seems to have been random. The ones picked up from the *University Magazine* and the *Irish Penny Journal* closely followed publication in those periodicals. Those chosen from the *Comet*, as Chuto has pointed out, "appeared in the original chronological order, as if someone was going through his files". Only one poem had a first printing in the *Vindicator*, "Sighs of an Unloved One", a translation from Bürger.

Mangan's letter about his "flim-flams and whim-whams" began on a flamboyant note, before the tightening of the coil of anxiety from which, as usual, he was unable to free himself. The envelope was addressed in a wildly beautiful script and like a certain amount of the letter was showily whimsical: "Chas. (or Conrad) George (or Gaspar) Duffy. *Vin-di-ca-tor Office* BELFAST." One wonders how this struck others in the office who must have seen it. After discussing the slight items he was sending he came to the matter of payment, a business that always was distasteful to Mangan, though he found it relatively easier to accept money for prose than for the poetry. "As to payment, in case you approve—a most problematical point, I admit—" he wrote hesitantly, "We are both, I hope, inclined to be reasonable—36 of the pages I send you make a sheet of the University Mag. for which I get £8—the sixth would of course be £1.6.8, but if you think the quantum in question worth £1 or 15s, even, we shall agree right well." Which, again, reinforces the observation that it was awfully easy to "buy" Mangan at less than the going rate. Nothing, it seems, where prose was concerned, was writ in stone, a vastly different attitude than he took toward his poetry which was a matter for serious consideration right through to the setting of capital letters and typographical details. "If you dislike the Introductory part strike it out. . . ," he continued. "Make, in short, any alterations you please—I have left a blank for the heading." Here, he suggested the title that Duffy actually settled on: "Sprinklings from our Attic Saltbox".

But this did not end his worries. The letter apparently concluded, he returned to the content. "I am thinking, though, after all, that you will not consider these squibs as far enough north for you—that they are too Dublin—too local—the fault is an unavoidable one, as I know next to nothing of Ulster." And, again, the admonishment to "Do whatever seemeth good, in your eyes"; he closed with what all-too-soon would become a familiar note of desperation in his voice, "write to me as soon as you can,—*before Saturday if possible*." Evidently he feared his tone was something less than friendly and easy-going, for he signed himself, taking the bite out of it, "Ever your's growlingly" or, it may be, "groaningly", the script being so flowery as to be almost illegible, followed by a magnificently curlicued "J.C. *Mangan*".

His point about the Dublin character of the material was well taken. An anecdote about two men named Brady and Grady from near Ballybough Bridge obviously recalled Tighe and Bligh. One scene was set in (the

Dublin printer) Curry's back shop, with Anster, Carleton, Surgeon Jephson (possibly the same Jephson who had contributed satires to the *Parson's Horn-book* back in 1831), and "The Poker" present. "The Poker" figured prominently in Mangan's sketches, and although "The Editor" also appeared there, may be Duffy (or Mangan?) in another *persona*. Insider allusions, those popular bits that made readers feel part of the "glamorous" world of journalism and literature, were fairly numerous, too, among them a story related by The Poker about "a man . . . [who was] so completely worn away by whiskey-bibbing, that, according to the opinion of the most accurate inspectors, his shadow was a *leetle* more substantial than himself!" It was finished off by an entirely Manganesque observation that, "We'll be dreaming of ghosts tonight, after that."[21] There were no more "Sprinklings", so it may have been that Duffy, too, thought they were more appropriate for Dublin than for Belfast.

In July 1840, the first of three "Editor's Room" columns appeared, almost entirely prose, but sporting an occasional verse or verse epigram, sometimes of a political nature. Duffy confessed high hopes for this feature in an introduction explaining that when he lived in Dublin he had had "a round table of choice friends" including a successful novelist, a dramatist, an artist, a "storyist", a translator, and more, each of whom had agreed to contribute a chapter. No names were given, but a fair conjecture would be that the list alluded to individuals who were later named by Mangan in his columns—William Carleton and Duffy's friend Henry MacManus being quite possibly the novelist and artist of the group, while Mangan himself was of course the translator. Duffy did not necessarily mean to be taken literally when he called them his "choice friends", but he may have had John Anster and George Petrie in mind along with Charles Lever who would qualify as the "storyist".

Duffy knew various journalists, of course, including James Price who was editor of the *Evening Packet* and a sometime contributor to the *Vindicator*, and James Coffey, proprietor of the thrice-weekly *Monitor*. The latter he substituted in Mangan's "Colloquii Personae" for his "Second Conclave" by crossing out the poet's choice, "William Stackpoole", and writing in Coffey's name. Perhaps he suspected that Margaret's brother, now taking Orders in the Church of Ireland, would not appreciate being placed in such droll company. The fact that Mangan had used the name probably meant that he was still in touch with the Stackpooles, however. By this year, Mrs Stackpoole had moved to Kingstown and was keeping her "select school" in George's Place; William would not receive his Bachelor of Arts from Trinity until the spring of 1842 and probably remained in the city. To complete the persons of the "conclave" Mangan used a number of made-up names such as "Incog" "Non-Compos", and "Count Klapptrapp", and, for himself, invariably "The Man in the Cloak", which others sometimes shortened to "Cloaky".

Most of the dialogue occurred among Carleton, The Poker (described in "Sprinklings" as "a certain uncertain friend" always "poking his long nose into other peoples' platters and matters"), and himself. Often The Man in the Cloak was the chief speaker. For instance, "Shall I read you my last from the Far-away-down-in-the-south-Gazette—my safety valve when I am desirous of letting out my redundant poetical steam?" introduces a lengthy passage. "Read—read—read!" They respond. "If you don't read we'll forthwith break so many bottles of ginger beer against your wigged sconce that whithersoever you go in future for the next thirty years it shall be conjectured from the scent of your saturated cloak that you have but just bolted from a tee-totaller's shop." So he does, and then:

> Here the Man in the Cloak surceases and looks out from the eylet-holes [*sic*] of his garment for applause, when he discovers that the apartment has been vacated by the rest of the conclave. Marvelling much what such a general desertion may mean, he flings himself into an arm-chair, and in another minute is as fast as an anchor.[22]

In the third and last "Conclave" which appeared in the *Vindicator* on 8 August, The Poker quoted a line from Maginn which Mangan paraphrased at least twice in his writings: "Dinnerless, loafless, milkless, soupless, punchless"—luxuries so faded from his memory, he swore, that he was considering "writing an antiquarian treatise about them, and putting George Petrie's name on the title page." And here, too, was one of the rare verses from this series. Proposing a contest between himself and The Poker—"I'll bet my cloak, against the Poker and his poke"—to determine who can extemporize the better quatrain, he produced:

> As Larry Gough, the vintner, trying
>   To coax a license
> By hook or crook, was buttering
>   Justice Snooks,
> Quoth Carleton, with that wit
>   of which he has a nice sense,
>   "How like a fawning Publican he looks!"

"Larry Gough", explains Chuto, can be read as Mangan's punning on Rabelais' "*boire à tire-larigot*", translated as "to drink galore". But "Cloaky's" rhyme lost to the Poker's politicism:

> "When is the Hoose prorogued?" speared Jeffrey at
> O'Connell, in an accent richly brogued—
> "*Pro*-rogued?" said Dan; "I don't know about that,
> But, if I live, I'll have it soon *un*-rogued!"

There was no vintage Mangan in the *Vindicator*. He collected a few odd pounds from Duffy, but that was all. During 1840 the *University Magazine* had two anthologies from him in April and June—nothing more. But *The Irish Penny Journal*, under Petrie's direction, commenced publication in July, and though Mangan's contributions were certainly limited, it enjoyed the signal distinction of printing his first translations from the Irish language.

[4]

> . . . it was in that office Mangan penned his since famous ballad, "The Woman of Three Cows", and I verily believe the composition did not occupy him half an hour.
>
> W.F. Wakeman quoted in Stokes, *Life of Petrie*

For the past two years, George Petrie had been much engaged with the idea of starting another periodical along the lines of the *Dublin Penny Journal*. In 1838, Larcom had taunted him, "I yet believe you would never forgive yourself if you left [the Survey] to become a scribbler of articles for Irish Annuals or The Penny Pirate", belittling the whole notion of Irish journalism, and Petrie had stayed on with the Ordnance Survey.[23] However, it was becoming more and more evident that the Survey was winding down, or rather, was being wound down, and as the pressure to get as much as possible accomplished increased, his need for a "safety valve to let off redundant poetical steam" probably also grew. *The Irish Penny Journal's* first number was dated 4 July 1840. Its full title was an abstract of Petrie's hopes: *The Irish Penny Journal of Information for the People, forming a National Library of Useful Knowledge Connected with the History, Antiquities, and Scenery of Ireland: With Numerous Original Legends and Stories (written esp. for this work) by Mrs. S.C. Hall, William Carleton, Martin Doyle, George Petrie, etc.* Mrs Hall was a popular author of the time, Doyle was an agriculturalist and a poet with one well-known satire to his credit, and Carleton was of course widely appreciated as a story-teller. Mangan's name was conspicuous by its absence. It may be that Petrie was being circumspect in neither revealing the poet's participation to the *University Magazine* nor adding another Ordnance Survey worker to his list.

Volume I, Number One, contained a Mangan poem, "The World's Changes", based on a poem by Rückert. About this poem, and in fact about most of the poems from this period, including even those from the Irish, there is a quality of distance, almost as if the poet were remote from his subject, an observer. This had been apparent in "Twenty Golden Years Ago" in which the speaker was literally "above it all" surveying the street from his garret, and it is certainly evident in "The World's Changes" which tells the story of the prophet Elias, or Khidder, who, according to legend, returns to the earth every five hundred years to see how things have changed. The remoteness of the viewer from the viewed is the essence of the poem. Mangan followed Rückert fairly closely in this version, less closely in one he did a few years later. Both expand the time between visits to a thousand years: "Thus said or sung/Khidder, the ever-young:/Journeying, I passed an ancient town—", and so on, until, "But when a thousand years were come and gone,/Again I passed that way, and lo!/There was no city. . . ."

The Irish poems Mangan now translated, or rather transformed, into English poems, for Eugene O'Curry did the "scut work" of putting them into literal English, were only four in number, but they are still counted among his finest: "The Woman of Three Cows", "An Elegy on the Tironian and Tirconnellian Princes Buried at Rome", "The Lamentation of MacLiag for Kincora", and "Kathaleen Ny-Houlahan".[24] In each highly individualistic instance, he worked his own magic on the material, a process resulting in four almost flawless poems. Why, then, were there no more until 1845? Why didn't he continue with the work that was so well begun? In answering this question, one sees it was not only his Irish poetry that was the victim of his creative malaise and sense of remoteness from life that marked this time: it was all his work. He did (often enough) what he was requested to do, but very little more. Original inspiration would seem to have fled. If 1840, because of the prose pieces for the *Vindicator* and the *Irish Penny Journal*, looks productive, the fact remains that his output from that year through 1844 was relatively sparse. Conversely, and importantly, the *quality* did not decline; the power that organized and propelled his finest work may still be felt just below the surface.

Wakeman's succinct but evocative observation at the top of this section can be read as evidence of the casual attitude Mangan took toward the first of the Irish poems. Indeed, he must have approached the challenge a little like he did the wager to write an elegy for the butcher Johnny Kenchinow. In much the same spirit, he sometimes produced original poems, if James Price is to be trusted as a witness. It would appear that neither original composition nor writing from a literal prose rendering of a poem engaged his imagination (at least at this time) to the extent that "true" translating did. The fact that O'Curry's translations were so accurate (taking his word that they are) may have reduced the appeal of the process even further. Instead of confronting the mystery of another poet's thought hidden in the mystery of his language, it may have seemed to Mangan that he was confronted with the flat, literal expression of none-too-subtle and quite repetitive stories, which he had "only" to versify.

On 1 August, O'Curry wrote O'Donovan and commented in rather garbled English that still leaves his meaning reasonably clear: "Mr P[etrie] is working, on Mangan's back, for the life, on the P.J.", that is, the *Penny Journal*.[25] Without straining the imagination, one can envision Petrie nagging the poet, staying after him to write the poetry they all knew he was capable of. Mangan could be susceptible to this kind of cajolery. He did want very much to oblige his friends; on the other hand, he often protested (though perhaps obliquely) against "doing what he was told". He had, as far as we can ascertain, seventeen items in the *Irish Penny Journal* over the course of seven months, from July 1840 through January 1841. Like the *Vindicator*, for which he stopped writing at about this time, the *Penny Journal* continued publication for only a few months after he ceased to be a contributor. Of the seventeen pieces, five were prose, largely fables; four were from German sources, and one, "The Clown with the Grey Coat", was from Irish. Although it was attributed not to Mangan but to O'Curry in one bibliography, John O'Daly gave it to Mangan. Chuto has observed, "The truth of the matter probably is that, as was the case with the Irish *poems* translated for the *IPJ*, O'Curry provided Mangan with a literal translation." Of the dozen poems, four were from Irish, four were from German, two were original poems being reprinted, and one each came from French and Moldavian.

There is something a little eerie about the fact that he had seventeen items in the *Penny Journal* and seventeen poems reprinted in the *Vindicator*, and had just written "Twenty Golden Years Ago" which took him back to his seventeenth year. A few years later in 1848 when he wrote his autobiography, he emphasized the seventeen centuries that Pompeii lay buried, comparing them to the seventeen years of his "career", from 1831 until 1848. However, without anything further to go on, this is nothing but an intriguing happenstance which must be relegated to the "sheer coincidence" pigeon-hole and left there unless and until something more concrete can be discovered about Mangan and numerology.

The only way to overestimate the importance of these Irish poems is to view them as the beginning of an uninterrupted chain of Irish work building up to 1846, and the climax of Mangan's career. This they were not. They were, rather, a favour done for a friend; a minor literary miracle. The four have much in common. All are, for instance, rather impersonal and distanced. The poet himself, except in the case of MacLiag and his lament for Kincora, is not a participant, and MacLiag has been made remote by the losses he mourns. Although as poor as the people he writes about, the poet of "The Woman of Three Cows" places a goodly distance between the Woman and himself and also between himself and her neighbour. Although the speaker of the "Lament for the Princes . . ." is nearly in tears, the sixteenth stanza still begins "What do I say? Ah, woe is me!" which underscores the distance in space and time that separates himself and the heroes of the preceding ritualistic recitation. And "Kathaleen Ny-Houlahan's" narrator is "close" only in being Irish; even the personal pronouns are plural: "the nobles of our land", "our matchless Kathaleen", and "Let us pray to Him", for example. This neither detracts nor distracts from the poems, but it creates a different emotional tone than that of, let us say, "Dark Rosaleen", "The Dream of John MacDonnell", "O'Hussey's Ode to the Maguire", and "A Lamentation for the Death of Sir Maurice Fitzgerald", to mention only a few. The distancing in Mangan's work at this point calls attention to his state of mind as perhaps nothing else could.

Of the four, only "Kathaleen Ny-Houlahan" did not contain a lengthy central section consisting of a catalogue of Irish heroes and/or battles. Each important national memory portion was integrated with great finesse into each of the other poems, but it can also be excised without losing the sense, as Mangan himself was shown by Duffy when the *Vindicator* editor cut three of five such verses from "The Woman of Three Cows" and printed it just three days after it appeared in the *Penny Journal*. Mangan was upset, and on 15 September wrote saying, "I thank you for clapping 'The Three Cows' into pound in your paper. But why did you omit the three stanzas? Are you able to give me a reason? Not you, I *take* it. However, you can make me some amends shortly."[26] Probably Duffy left them out because they were very similar to the two he left in. The last of the five, which he did include, with the final stanza and the "Summing Up" (in which Mangan peeps through "the eyelet holes of his garment" at his readers, it seems) follow:

> The O'Carrolls, also, famed when Fame was only for the boldest,
> Rest in forgotten sepulchres with Erin's best and oldest;
> Yet who so great as they of yore in battle or carouse?
> Just think of that, and hide your head, good Woman of Three Cows!
>
> Your neighbour's poor, and you, it seems, are big with vain ideas.
> Because, *inagh*! you've got three cows—one more, I see, than *she* has.
> That tongue of yours wags more at times than Charity allows,
> But if you're strong, be merciful, great Woman of Three Cows!
>
> The Summing Up
>
> Now, there you go! You still, of course, keep up your scornful bearing,
> And I'm too poor to hinder you; but, by the cloak I'm wearing,
> If I had but *four* cows myself, even though you were my spouse,
> I'd thwack you well to cure your pride, my Woman of Three Cows!

Mangan would one day write laments and elegies that tear the heart because he, as poet, was so involved in the emotion of the poems and w his reader in with him. But this "Elegy" and "Lamentation", ıough very fine, are not of that ilk. Both poets, Hugh MacWard and cLiag (no christian name given) wrote stirringly, but MacWard was tant in space and MacLiag in time from the griefs they extolled. "O nan of the Piercing Wail,/Who mournest o'er yon mound of clay" nediately established the point of view in the "Elegy": the poet was an server. Nuala, sister of the two brothers, Rudh-raidhe and Cathbharr O'Donnell, and aunt of another young chieftain, all three of whom died in Rome in suspicious circumstances, is distinctly alone; the words are heard with the heart, not the ears. The poem is virtually all catalogue, a content justified by the poet's cry that if Nuala were "among the Gael" she would *not* be alone with her grief. Sean Lucy termed this elegy "one of our indispensable poems", and in vocabulary approaching the theological, "a vessel of continuous creation [whose] living language pours out, continually in need of refreshment to cope with the complexity of its statements, and continually finding it".[27]

Each of the eighteen stanzas is composed of twelve lines that actually divide into two stanzas, and the rhyme scheme is an entirely regular *abc abc*. More subtly, Mangan varied the iambic tetrameter by giving each third line only two accents. This had two excellent results. On the very practical level, it avoided the creation of a sing-song poem. And more artfully, it reproduced the cadence of quiet, weary weeping broken by regular sobs. This was an effective auditory device for a *caoine* and was apparently Mangan's contribution, not the original poet's. Mangan was pleased with the poem, and in the same letter to Duffy noted above wrote:

> In No. 15 [actually, it was No. 16] of Camerons [the *IPJ*], there will be a *transmagnificanbandancial* elegy of mine (a perversion from the Irish), on the O'Neills and O'Donnells of Ulster, which is admired by myself and some other *impartial* judges.[28]

The opening stanza follows:

O Woman of the Piercing Wail,
Who mournest o'er yon mound of clay
With sigh and groan,
Would God thou wert among the Gael!
Thou wouldst not then from day to day
Weep thus alone.
'Twere long before, around a grave
In green Tirconnell, one could find
This loneliness;
Near where Beann-Boirche's banners wave
Such grief as thine could ne'er have pined
Companionless.

In "The Lamentation of MacLiag for Kincora", the poet MacLiag, mourning the loss of his Master Brian Boru and the downfall of Kincora, the great "palace whose beauty is fled", proceeded similarly with an introduction of his own woe compounded by the catalogue of national disasters: "O where, Kincora! is Brian the Great?/ And where is the beauty that once was thine?" "And where . . . ?" "And where . . . ?" "And where . . . ?" Then, all too familiar, came the answer: "They are gone, those heroes of royal birth . . . Oh, my grief!" Terrible, isolating events have left MacLiag alone by the Lake with the ruins of the great hall, Kincora, near Killaloe on the River Shannon, for company—and memories, and Time for the cataloguing of the kings. Only in the last section of four stanzas, and especially in the final one, is there a truly personal presence; only at the end do we learn "I am Mac Liag, and my home is on the Lake." No distancing device could be more effective than the impersonality of his memorializing litany of heroes, gathering them all together as if on some vast Field of Honour, while he himself has lost the one hero and leader who connected him to them. Of all Mangan's poems structured on the somewhat predictable but always engaging contrast between glorious past and empty present, none is more poignant than this lament of the lonely survivor, a man as homeless as Mangan felt himself to be.

Poem after poem in Mangan's canon explores the themes of homelessness and wandering. Not for him the simple satisfactions of the abstract; he never underestimated the importance of the concrete and the physical, although this opinion might take cover under negation, as when he denied the necessity of food. His search was not only for a true home of the mind, but also for a real place of physical comfort and affection. From Kerner's "Where Is My Home?" to Salis's wistful exile's "Alas! I am a stranger everywhere"; from the Earth Mother who calls to her child, "Come home", to the mourning at the "vacant place beside the cheerless hearth" in the late "Owen Reilly: A Keen", this motif was never far from his thoughts. But one home, and one only, was sure for everybody, as the keening mother in "Owen Reilly" anticipated:

> But come ye to my grave when, in the days of May,
> The gladsome sun and skies grow warmer,
> And say, "Here sleeps Kathleen, where tempest cannot harm her,
> Soft be her narrow bed of clay!"
>
> And count your beads, and pray, "Rest her poor soul, O God!
> She wished no ill to breathing mortal—
> Grant her, then, Thou, a place within Heaven's blessèd portal,
> Now that her bones lie in the sod!"

Transition

By far the most intriguing piece of writing Mangan produced in all of 1841 was the personal essay "My Bugle and How I Blow It" which appeared in the *Vindicator* on 27 March. It was preceded by a poem of Kerner's which, in 1836, Mangan had translated as "Where is my Home?" His July anthology this year contained a second version, "Home-sickness", as he again worked the apparently inexhaustible vein of homelessness.

WHERE IS MY HOME?

A mystical bugle calls o'er
    The earth to me everywhere—
Peals it from forest halls or
    The crypts of the azure air?
From the snow-enrobed mountains yonder?
    From the flower-strewn vales below?
O! whithersoever I wander
    I hear it with sweetest woe!

Alone in the woods, or present
    Where mingle the song and dance,
That summoning sound incessant
    Is piercing my heart like a lance.
Till now hath my search been ceaseless,
    And its place I have nowhere found,
But my spirit must ever be peaceless
    Till that Bugle shall cease to sound!

"My Bugle and How I Blow It" was the last thing Mangan presented to Duffy's paper, the "Song for Punch-Drinkers" in December almost certainly being borrowed by Duffy himself from its earlier publication in the *Satirist*. As of the end of 1841, the poet's work would again appear exclusively for a few months in the *University Magazine.*

"My Bugle and How I Blow It" was signed "By the Man in the Cloak", and its main subject was the meaning and importance of that signature. His diction here defies the observation that Mangan didn't much care to use the first person singular pronoun; the essay is filled with "I". On the other hand, he emphasized his cloak *as his identity*, and clearly, it was a feature of dress which served a multiple purpose: it hid, it identified, and it mystified.

After a thoroughly eccentric start in which he declared himself to be the bugle-player of Kerner's poem, and fancied himself playing within the hearing of the German poet, Mangan explored his signature word by word. This early passage envisions the reader as enquiring after the identity of the poet:

> And who, you ask, is the poet? That will I tell you instanter. The original grubber-up of the gem that I have set in gold, silver, or pewter, as the metal may turn out to the touch-stone, is, be it known to you, Justinus Kerner, man of many accomplishments—poet, physician, metaphysician, hobgoblin-hunter, widower, and weeper. . . . Little did Kerner imagine the first evening the bugle smote his ears that the Man in the Cloak, whom he saw climbing the hill to the right, was his electrifier! Up went his dexter ogler along the rocks, and there encountered—a goat: him the poet did not for a moment suspect of practising on either of his own horns; and so down went his sinister peeper to the flood below, where, however, it was at once rebuked by a corpulent codfish, whose interrogative eye appeared fixed on "the first demonogolist in Europe", with a library of wandering questions in the pupil thereof. I, my cloak, and my bugle, meantime, had vanished for the night.

He got around to introducing himself a number of paragraphs later:

> Public, do you listen: you are elevated to the high honour of being my confidante. I am about to confer an incredible mark of my favour on you, Public. Know, then, the following things:— Firstly.—That I am not *a* Man in *a* Cloak, but *the* Man in *the* Cloak. My personal identity is here at stake, and I cannot consent to sacrifice it. Let me sacrifice it, and what becomes of me? "The earth hath bubbles as the water hath", and I am thenceforth one of them. I lose my cloak and my consciousness both in the twinkling of a pair of tongs; I become what the philosophy of Kant (in opposition to the Cant of Philosophy) denominates a *Nicht-ich*, a Not-I, a *Non-ego*.

More passages of a similar nature followed. In the process, Mangan rejected other apparel, defended the rights of people to dress as they please, and concluded that he would continue to wear his cloak whatever others did—the belligerence is inescapable, but is turned to amusing use:

> I quarrel with nobody for his taste or want of taste. I do not approach any mooncalf in the public street with an uplifted crowbar, poker, pike, pitchfork, or pickaxe in my grasp, because his toggery is of a different order from my own. I could not do so, independent of my intuitive benevolence of disposition, I have what Harriet Martineau would call "a powerful preventive check" in my sense of what is due to the *bienseances* of society. On the other hand, however, I yield not up a whit of my own liberty. . . . What did I buy my cloak for? Why did I pay fifteen shillings and sixpence, besides boot, for it to a Jew hawker of old rags, but that I might don it, and never doff it, I should be glad to know?

In considering such statements, the critic walks a tightrope, for there is a risk of taking them too seriously on one hand or of not taking them seriously enough on the other. Exactly how much of this did the poet "mean"? Mangan himself would have had no problem with the identification of the cloak as a "mannerism", a subject on which he had had something to say—ironically negative—in "An Extraordinary Adventure in the Shades". It was assuredly no secret to him that he was also playing the now-you-see-it-now-you-don't game with his pseudonyms and his doubtful ascriptions, though in the latter instance, it is possible that some were sheer accidents, the result of reading and retaining vast quantities of bits and pieces from numerous authors and sometimes getting them mixed up.

Undoubtedly Mangan suffered some genuine concern that beneath the disguises, he might have no really solid identity after all. The tendency to cynicism which strips away one cherished opinion or belief after another until none are left was part of his make-up. At the same time, he would have known that "that which is aware" was, itself, the very identity called into question, and so he could reject the possibility of the "Nicht-ich" or "Non-ego"—though he needed yet another protective disguise to do so. Conflating the author with the persona of such a piece as "My Bugle" is almost inevitable, so it is wise to remind oneself that Mangan wore what has been described as "a very little cloak", hardly "a cloak [of] a quarter of a hundred weight, with expansive wings at the sides, and a hood that hung down from the head, obscuring the light of my countenance . . ." as the speaker described so enthusiastically here.

Mangan's restlessness was very real. The last pose he struck in this essay was of the Wanderer, which he was spiritually, if not literally:

> I may not remain an abider within any town. Your surprise, Reader, is, doubtless, excited—ah! you know not what a vagabond I am! . . . It is an awful thing to behold me at each completion of my term scampering off like Van Woedenblok of the Magic Leg—galloping along roads—clearing ditches—dispersing the affrighted poultry in farmyards as effectually as a forty-eight pounder could. Other men sojourn for life in the country of their choice; there is a prospect of ultimate repose for most things. . . . But for me there is no hope; at home or abroad I tarry not. . . . A fearful voice, to all but me inaudible, for ever thunders in mine ear. "Pack up thy duds!—push along!—keep moving!"

* * * *

The Ordnance Survey was closing down in 1841. The long-anticipated blow fell at last, and funds were withdrawn. Petrie and his men spent the last half-year in a desperate effort to finish all they could and to put things in order, a job continued by the skeleton staff that remained in 1842. The question of who could be kept on an additional month, and who had to be let go at once, became a painful problem. A few of the letters and notes from Larcom to Petrie this year show the strain under which all were labouring.

21 June What in the world have the people [8 in number] . . . been about since October last—?

22 June How long will it take to complete the Kerry Inquisition? and how long in Cork?

6 August Mangin should do first the [illegible—perhaps Baronies] O'D. has not yet visited in Kerry and of Cork we already have [enough] done by Mr Fowler. I send it . . . but of course Mangin had better copy on square paper —I will send the list of names of Cork—that Mangin may not be doing them over again—

17 August [Have you] Mangin at work copying the descriptive remarks from the Cork townlands of that county? If not I find I can still employ Mr Fowler who has copied a part of the county already—and Mr Mangin can be employed in the Inquisitions to get them out of hand as soon as possible.

18 August By putting Mr Fowler to copying the [illegible] descriptive remarks I should save Mr Mangins time for other work—the most pressing is the copying of the inquis. for Cork—but from your note of yesterday I gather that it is not desirable to employ him on the Inquisitions because he has not sufficient knowledge of Latin—or do I misunderstand you? What else can he be made available for?[1]

On 25 November, Larcom again asked about Cork, enquiring "whether Mr Mangin and Mr Fowler between them have or have not copied the whole" and requesting a memorandum of the "present employment of each of the party in Charles Street". Petrie responded the same day with this information:

Mr O'Donovan is constructing an ancient map of the W. of Galway which is nearly finished.

Mr O'Conor is copy [*sic*] the Cork Inquisitions at the Tower.

Mr O'Keefe is similarly occupied.

Mr Eugene Curry is making researches in the MS libraries of Trinity College and the Royal Irish Academy for documents relative to the topography of the County of Cork.

Mr Anthony Curry is copying Irish documents for Cork in the college.

Mr O'Sullivan is similarly employed in the library of the R.I. Academy.

Mr Russell is copying all of the passages in Mr O'Donovan's translation of the Annals of the Four Masters relative to Cork County.

Mr Mangan is copying the passages in the Pacata Hi [bernia] for the same County.[2]

In a letter also sent this day late in November, Petrie told Larcom that he was communicating word to those who were subject to the reductions taking place, then:

> I do not know whether it would be possible to set Mangan on the Inquisitions or not; I fear not, but I shall enquire. He is today at the Down Survey office comparing Mr Fowlers copies with the originals, and I am inclined to think that all relative to Cork has not been copied, and if so, it might be well to employ Mangan there. It is a great pity that Mr Fowlers copies should have [been] made on two different sized papers—one half of which can never be bound—and both of them differing from Mangan's portion, which is on the usual quarto paper.[3]

A follow-up note confirmed that the Down Survey for Cork had indeed not been completely copied, some four Baronies remaining—"and Mangan found Mr Fowler at work on them". That Mangan was now an efficient, ready worker is apparent throughout these exchanges.

And on 26 November, as if still unable to face the total disbanding of the office, Larcom again declared to Petrie:

> We must now look reduction sternly in the face. On the 31st Dec. your copying will be so advanced that all but O'Donovan, Curry and perhaps one other hand may be dispensed with—think of this and make it known—I need not say how much rather I would maintain the whole force if I were permitted.[4]

Interestingly, this note contains the only criticism I have read from Larcom of Mangan's work, and it is almost illegible, saying in part, "I do not like Mangin's copy of this [illegible] could he not work at the. . . ." and the remainder of the sheet of paper has been pasted under.

The last letter from Larcom to Petrie about the full operation at No. 21 Great Charles Street was written on the 31st of December. In its entirety it read: "As this is the last day of your large force—you will have to make other arrangements tomorrow for finishing the Inquisitions—O'Donovan and the elder Curry being alone left to you."[5]

In his fashion, Petrie had struggled long and hard over the problem of keeping on the unreliable O'Keefe and eventually had had his way. But in August 1839 Larcom had written Petrie:

> I am not to be told I am keeping him [O'Keefe] there [in Carlow] cruelly as he now implies. I will then consider him on sick leave . . . and I am of opinion it will be desirable to discharge him at once—your milky heartedness will cry mercy—which like other such things is no mercy at all—but just the reverse—he will do very well for Todd—but not for us and it is a bad example to keep a man who is in this state of mind—[6]

Petrie's "milky hearted" kindness was proverbial, and his great wish at the close of 1841 was to place as many of his men as possible in other jobs. The reference to James Henthorn Todd, Trinity College librarian in charge of classifying and arranging Irish manuscripts, identifies the designated benefactor of the Ordnance Survey men whose nerves became too bad for strenuous employment. "He will do very well for Todd" may also have been the prevailing opinion of Clarence Mangan, and after he was discharged from the Ordnance Survey—his Latin not being good enough to justify keeping him on the severely reduced staff—he went to work as a cataloguer in Trinity College Library.

A very brief and slightly comic description of Mangan as he looked at this time appeared in an amusing article in the October issue of the *Dublin University Magazine*, already referred to in these pages, in which the Editor found his contributors in Germany. The poet was said to be "a pale and emaciated figure, whose face scarce offered surface for his moustachos"; if any question remained as to who was being described, he "had spouted Schiller till midnight".[7] Purportedly in the German inn were assembled Caesar Otway, Charles Lever, Isaac Butt, John Anster, William Carleton, and Mangan. The talk was loud and boisterous. Mangan sat at the end of the table and observed, "What a noise—what a confusion—better far to be on the sea-lashed cliffs of lofty Moher, with the white foam curling at our feet", the last words of his "soft silvery voice . . . lost in the din around".

13

For Sires and Mothers

[1]

Man! canst thou build upon aught in the pride of thy mind?
Wisdom will teach thee that nothing can tarry behind;
Though there be thousand bright actions embalmed and enshrined,
Myriads and millions of brighter are snow in the wind.

Mangan, "Gone in the Wind", (Rückert)

Bleakly beginning, January 1842 found the poet in a discomfiting transition between jobs. All he said, ever, about being a wanderer without a home on earth rings hollowly when sounded against the practical need he felt for comfort, continuity, and stability. At least occasionally, he must have been aware of this contradiction in himself, and felt appreciation for the steady job Petrie had made certain he kept, and even for the years his parents had stayed on at No. 9 Peter Street. Moreover, he surely knew that having what promised to be a reasonably congenial job to go to, courtesy of Dr Todd again by way of Dr Petrie, was objectively a very good thing. In spite of that, the change itself, and the alterations in his life that it would require, loomed ominously. He must have asked himself anxious questions as he approached his new work. Would the place be tolerable? Would the people he had to associate with at least be inoffensive? Would he measure up? The oath he took to have his name placed on the library's Readers Register was administered on 17 January.[1] A job description for his position was dated just four weeks later, and he probably took up his duties at that time, Monday 14 February.

The work Dr Todd had found for him was the cataloguing of Trinity College's library collection. This was an on-going task. Not many years previously, the whole excellent collection had been barely accessible because there was no catalogue to it, and with the addition of 20,000 or so volumes acquired toward the beginning of the century from the Chief Minister of Holland, Hendrik Fagle, it had become imperative to get about the job. Presumably, it could absorb about as many men as the College could afford to pay. Mangan's salary was figured quarterly at £15, just the amount he had been earning at the Ordnance Survey, and thus satisfactory. For the rest of 1842, all of 1843, and the first nine months of 1844, he worked full time. He was off for the last quarter of 1844 and the first quarter of 1845, and thereafter he had a half-time position until the end of 1846. His work was entirely routine. He collated books in the Fagle collection with "the same books in the Bodleian Catalogue", and entered titles into the Trinity Library Catalogue. He was referred to as a Library Clerk, a lowly position indeed.

These books were housed in what had come to be known as the Fagle Library, the east pavilion of the famed Long Room, itself a cavernous and insalubrious—if prestigious—repository.[2] The Fagle was relatively small, being only 54 feet long and about half as wide, with a 16-foot ceiling, while the Long Room was 200 feet long and 40 feet wide, with a proportionately high ceiling. Described in 1846 in the *Nation*, the Long Room sounded a forbidding spot, and one can almost see the chilled forms of readers bent over books, their breath hazing the air around their pinched faces. "In this enormous apartment", the paper's contributor wrote, "there is no warmth —the sun can scarcely pass the recessed windows,—and it is built without any fireplace, while its only ventilation is produced by the continual passage of visitors up and down behind the readers' chairs."[3] Mangan may conceivably have worked in some cosy cubbyhole, but it is extremely unlikely. Predictably, though, he made time to dip into some of the books. Before he ever met him, John Mitchel discovered the poet doing just that one day in 1845:

> Being in the college library, and having occasion for a book in that gloomy apartment of the institution called the "Fagle Library", which is the innermost recess of the stately building, an acquaintance pointed out to me a man perched on the top of a ladder, with the whispered information that the figure was Clarence Mangan. It was an unearthly and ghostly figure, in a brown garment; the same garment (to all appearance) which lasted till the day of his death. The blanched hair was totally unkempt, the corpse-like features still as marble; a large book was in his arms, and all his soul was in the book.[4]

One change in his life brought about by the closing down of the Survey may have been almost immediately damaging to his health. Whereas Great Charles Street lay north of the Liffey, Trinity College Library was south of it, almost within a stone's throw of the poet's haunts. The walking that he had necessarily done virtually came to an end now, as he was rarely required to leave his immediate demesne. Possibly he liked it that way. Be that as it may, it could not have been an improvement for it meant that, with the exercise itself, he had lost the social contacts that had been his as he walked along Dame Street, crossed Carlisle Bridge, and made his way up Sackville Street to Summerhill and Great Charles Street. His new routine allowed him, if he so chose, to see almost no one from the start of a day till its close. Alone going to work, alone at work—for there is not a hint that he had anything like a fellow worker—alone going home: his inclination to solitariness, which had always been present and for which he often seems to be apologizing a little bit, now slowly became an obsession.

Another great change between life at Great Charles Street and life in Trinity Library was the companionability of the one and the solitariness of the other. His poems for the first year after the change are awash with loneliness, including "The Ride Round the Parapet", "O, Maria, Regina Misericordiae", "Gone in the Wind", and some of the German poet Freiligrath's desolate and desert poems. Energetically, however, he announced that he was returning to his first love, German ballads and legends.

One of the finest of this or any year was "The Ride Round the Parapet" by Friedrich Rückert. Interestingly, for his very readable version, he altered the original name of the haughty Lady, rechristening her "Eleanora von Alleyne", thus not only recalling the name he had used for his own unfaithful "early love"—"Eleanor" of "My Transformation"—but also punning on the German *allein*, "alone". The story is well known. The Lady sends out the challenge that she will marry any knight who can ride a horse around the parapet of her castle. After the deaths of three dozen or so, the Margrave Gondibert succeeds—and rejects her, already being a married man. Another Mangan motif also appeared here, the changing of a human being into something stiff and unliving—"And, woe! her end was tragic; she was changed, at length, by magic,/To an ugly wooden image, they maintain. . . ." Her ill-conceived efforts to remedy her loneliness being unsuccessful, however, she does at least receive homage:

> And he that won't salute her must be fined in foaming pewter,
> If a boor—but, if a burgher, in champagne.

If there is a trace of humour in the case of the Lady Eleanora, the same cannot be said about the other poems of loneliness. The solitariness of the Knight whose story is told in "O, Maria, Regina Misericordiae", by Karl Simrock, is quite breathtaking. Although superficially he would seem to have been social enough, "draining Pleasure's poison-bowl" with the best—or the worst—of them, he was without any warmth of fellowship. His only true contact with another being was with the Virgin, to whom, through sin and sorrow, he prayed always, "O, Maria, Regina Misericordiae", "O, Mary, Queen of Mercy". Having at last grown weary and repentant, he entered "an humble cloister", but still his life lacked human contact and for this grave failure, and in place of choral singing and prayers, "He mortified his flesh to stone"—yet another instance of Mangan's use of this motif:

> And thus he lived, long, long; and, when
> God's angels called him, thus he died.
> Confession made he none to men,
> Yet when they anointed him with oil,
> He seemed already glorified.

According to Fr Meehan, who was with Mangan when he died, among the last words he uttered, also, were "O, Mary, Queen of Mercy".

"Gone in the Wind", of which four lines appear at the opening of this chapter, is different in that there is no central figure, but rather a central void. *Everything* is gone. Similar to Shelley's "Ozymandias" in theme, this poem, also by Rückert, is more bleak. At least in Shelley's poem, people speak to one another: "I met a traveller from an antique land/Who said . . ." and so on, describing the face and trunk of the huge statue toppled over and half buried in the sand of a great desert. By contrast, Mangan stripped away every sentient thing, including even Rückert's lilies, for even Solomon's "throne" and Babylon's "might" are "present" only in their absolute absence: "Solomon! where is thy throne? It is gone in the wind./Babylon! where is thy might? It is gone in the wind." At the very last, as if from a great distance across desert wastes, comes the sound of a human voice. It is the poet's, but the only voices audible to him are "voices from Hades like bells on the wind".

In Ferdinand Freiligrath's poems, the subject of the eighteenth German anthology in January 1843, Mangan found a new fascination, in part because the German wrote about such very unique things—a skating Negro, the Alexandrine metre, spectre caravans, the King of the Congo, tea made from Iceland moss, and many more—but largely because both men were enthusiasts and burned with an inner intensity that led to extravagant emotional states. "Iceland-Moss Tea", which Freiligrath wrote when he was only sixteen years old, perhaps reminded Mangan of his own youthful poetry. It presented a weird and awesome solitude:

Where clouds lie black on cinder-piles,
    And all night long the lone Seal moans,
    As, one by one, the mighty stones
Fall echoing down on far-off isles—

Where, in a word, hills vomit flame,
    And storms for ever lash the sea,
    There sprang this bitter moss for me,
Thence this astringent potion came.[5]

The Irish poet closely translated five of Freiligrath's half-dozen "sand-songs", probably because he wanted to keep to that number and still include a last one largely his own, a little poem ending:

The moonless heaven is dim once more,
The waves break on the shingly shore—
I listen to their mournful tone,
And pace the silent Sands alone.

In Freiligrath's description of an "enthusiastic young German poet . . . [who] literally burned out of life by the fire of his imagination", Mangan found a counterpart of himself. All the loneliness that he had known and that became such a haunting presence after 1842,was summed up in this last word on loneliness:

"Alone the Poet lives—alone he dies.
Cain-like, he bears the isolating brand
Upon his brow of sorrow. True, his hand
Is pure from blood-guilt,but in human eyes
His is a darker crime than that of Cain,—
Rebellion against Social Wrong and Law!"
Groaning, at length I slept, and in my dreams I saw
The ruins of a Temple on a desolate plain.[6]

[2]

Spiritualism: . . . The belief that the spirits of the dead can hold communication with the living, or make their presence known to them in some way, esp. through a "medium"; the system of doctrines or practices founded on this belief.

Oxford Universal Dictionary

At the top of the new year Mangan made his only published statement about his personal experience with ghosts. It was obliquely and only in parenthesis that he mentioned himself, but there is no question that the subject now absorbed a fair share of his attention. At the same time, in preparing the article "Chapters on Ghostcraft: Comprising some Account of the Life and Revelations of Madame Hauffe, the Celebrated Wirtemberg Ghost-Seeress",[7] he tapped into a major interest of many readers, for the Age of Spiritualism, as it might be called, was about to get under way.

This very peculiar piece of prose dealt with the unseen world, from ghosts to the Spiritual Inner Sun, as experienced by a rather remarkable woman. The first chapter began and ended tongue-in-cheek, but what lies between is, or at any rate seems to be, perfectly serious. I suspect he occasionally had difficulty himself knowing if he meant precisely all he said. He had a brilliant, rational and potentially highly critical mind, while at the same time his belief in the reality of the unseen world made him vulnerable to ideas that in retrospect seem fanciful in the extreme. Addressing his "Spectacled Reader" (who would know that "spectre" and "spectacle" both derive from *specere*), he reminded him, "Thou art already aware that the all-important question of Ghosts or No-ghosts is one which has been severely agitated in Germany but peradventure mayest not know that the Pro-ghostial party are to be considered as having already conquered." In the pages that follow, his manner and tone range from "informed" acceptance through contemptuous attacks on his readers' benighted intelligence. Only one thing is clear throughout: he was extremely interested in the subject.

The overall impression he aimed to create was that of scholarly consideration. Almost certainly he had read the ten books that he listed in a bibliography on the first page, works on ghosts, demoniacal possession, life after death, and "the Essential Connection subsisting between the Poetic Spirit and the faculty of Magnetic Lucid Vision", all written by purported medical men and academicians. In essence, his task was, first, to try to understand what Dr Justinus Kerner had written about Madame Hauffe, and then, to select and summarize the main findings, revelations, and teachings so his report would do justice, even in shortened form, to the Ghost-seeress.

Dr Kerner had worked with Madame Hauffe for many years. Plainly, she had been one of those individuals who fascinate their doctors while at the same time they frustrate all efforts at cure, or even diagnosis. Besides enduring many painful physical symptoms, she also had suffered intense and frequent psychic disturbances. Neurotic, usually physically ill, unstable yet stubbornly sane, and, like Swedenborg, often visionary, she managed during her altered states of consciousness to produce a rather intricate and generally coherent, if fantastic, body of description of what she saw, heard, and learned about the psyche.

Madame Hauffe certainly had been a "haunted" woman, but the question remains, "haunted by what?" About watching over her once while she lay in what he defined as a "half-waking" state, though her eyes were closed, and drew a picture of an intricate "Sun-ring" with circles inside circles, Dr Kerner wrote, "She appeared to me as a spidress at work upon a web, spinning and still spinning, without any visible instrument to assist her in getting through her task." This conceptual intricacy, so labyrinthine, no doubt appealed on quite a different level to the boy in Mangan who loved puzzles. The beauty of the seeress' concept of rings of spiritual light comprising the human being, the delicate sensuality of the relationship between Soul and Spirit, and the nobility of her overall vision appealed to the sensitive man and poet. In "To My Life-ring", she articulated her faith and described the wondrous fulfillment awaiting one at death. The poem ends:

> And all forgotten words and thoughts, and things,
>   And feelings Language here so ill defines,
> Shall shine out meaningful from darkest Rings,
>   And give me back the Past in Cypher-signs.

Mangan might call his reader "a Sumph of the muddiest water" but on the whole he did not poke fun at Madame Hauffe herself. On only one subject was he not quite able to restrain a subversive impulse to mock at what were clearly the notions of a rather naive intellect. Madame Hauffe observed that as far as she had been able to tell, ghosts do not cast shadows, and the poet, with what seems a perfectly straight face, mused, "It is probably that the ghost, with a view to avoid perplexing the ghost-seer, leaves his shadow at home; for it requires a long-practised ghostial eye to discern the difference between a ghost and the mere shadow of a ghost." The matter of shadowlessness caused Mangan to digress slightly, and it is here we learn what he found so irresistible about that notion. Not only do ghosts not cast shadows, but ghost-seers and ghost-raisers "are for the most part shadowless persons". Madame Hauffe seems to have been the soul of innocence herself, but her gift put her in the unhallowed company of those who dabble in the Black Arts. One of their skills is, it is said, shadow-shifting. Mangan referred specifically to Simon Magus who "caused his shadow to go before him"; and he dwelt for a paragraph on one of his personal favourites, *The Lay of the Last Minstrel*, by Scott "(whom few things escaped)", and his anecdote about the students of magic who, at one point in their training, must dash through a subterranean hall "where the devil literally catches the hindmost" while the fastest lose only their shadows to Lucifer. "In the latter case the person of the sage never after throws any shade; and those who have thus *lost their shadows* always prove the best magicians."

Mangan, perhaps intentionally, held back details about the seeress' actual ghost-seeing until the last four pages of his seventeen page article, but once having waded through the material on the soul, spirit, inner life, and so on, he took on the subject with zest. It was here, surely, that he (or Madame Hauffe) offended the anti-Catholic sentiments of the *Dublin University Magazine*, and he seems to have been aware that he ran that risk. Although Madame Hauffe, he took pains to point out, was "a Lutheran, and of the Augsburg Confession of Faith" she explained the existence of her ghosts in a Purgatorial Realm by stating what is for Protestants an unacceptable conviction: "But, alas! It is only too certain a truth, that a man who has lived for seventy years in sin and ignorance cannot all at once enter upon a state of purity and enlightenment after death." Hence, Purgatory.

Her other "revelations" about ghosts were generally unexceptional: only some ghosts can see people, just as only some people can see ghosts; ghosts "resemble thin but untransparent clouds" and are almost all grey; ghosts can pass through solid matter sometimes, but not always; to speak with ghosts was no pleasure and drained the strength; ghosts ask for prayers, being unable to help themselves out of their plight. She also believed that to see ghosts a man (or a woman) must live in the "heart-pit" and not be "brain-ridden", since anyone who "lives in his brain" will only see a ghost imperfectly "for the brain at once chases it away". On this the poet begged to differ slightly:

> (He [the brain-ridden man] will never, we think, be a visionist by daylight. But even a brain-ridden man can see ghosts in the normal half-waking state, whenever his eyes happen to open while as yet his soul continues lingering about the sphere of the Dream-ring. This we can bear witness to from our own personal experience.)

Thus in parenthesis he made his sole statement about his own encounters with ghosts, encounters more in the nature of hallucination or hypnagogic image than of incorporeal beings.

[3]

> "To create and foster public opinion, and make it racy of the soil."
> The motto of the *Nation*

Though he must have been, at first, extremely pleased to have Gavan Duffy move back to Dublin that autumn, the poet soon discovered that a gulf of class and condition had now opened between them. Mangan was in his fortieth year and in the (continuing) midst of a serious personal and creative crisis. Duffy was still in his twenties, a successful editor, and recently married to a Belfast woman, Emily McLoughlin. In Dublin, the couple took up residence on Homeville (or Holmeville) in Rathmines, which was fast becoming a popular suburb. Having prospered on the *Vindicator*, Duffy was no longer a penniless country journalist, full of aspirations but empty of experience. Moreover, he would soon complete his law terms and could expect to be called to the Bar. Perhaps most significantly, considering the course his life now took, he had already earned his first stripes as a fighting political journalist. During his final months at the *Vindicator*, he and the paper had been prosecuted by the Government for printing a fervent defense of the rights of Catholics to be tried by their peers. "Dragged" to Dublin to stand trial, Duffy was found guilty and was awaiting sentencing, set for November. He pled for leniency. Being put away in a dungeon would be a virtual death sentence, he declared, due to his ill health.[8] But he had not backed away from his convictions or apologized for his inflammatory rhetoric.

He moved back to the capital specifically to help start the *Nation* newspaper, a course he and his friends, Thomas Davis and John Blake Dillon, determined on in discussions in the spring, or as some reports have it, in July. This action was to have implications almost as far-reaching for Mangan as for Duffy himself. The moment when the idea for the new national paper originated is preserved, it is said, in a familiar picture, "The Birth of the *Nation*", the name for the newspaper suggested by Davis after Duffy opted for the *National*. The artist has portrayed the three seated on a bench "under a noble elm" not far from the Wellington Memorial in the Phoenix Park. Duffy is the central figure, for the original idea came from him. With paper spread out on his knee and pencil in hand, he has the rapt attention of Davis on his right and Dillon on his left, as if symbolizing their importance in the endeavour. The level of excitement is suggested by Davis's hat and cane, tossed hastily aside along with a newspaper, a critical comment, perhaps, on the quality of newspapers in the city at that time. All three men are nattily dressed in black cut-aways, narrow trousers, waistcoats, cravats, and top-hats.

From the start, there was little question of who would do what on the *Nation*. Duffy, as the most experienced journalist, became proprietor and editor, but he happily acknowledged that "Davis was our true leader" because he was more inspiring and "loved labour better". Dillon played a solid middle role, as contributor and consultant. Both he and Duffy were Catholics, while Davis was a Protestant. He and Davis were Trinity College graduates and attorneys, while Duffy's training was all in the practical realm, a trial by fire that they had experienced only briefly the previous year as they tried to breathe fervour back into the old *Morning Register*.

The scope of the paper they aspired to publish would exceed that of any other journal in the city. It was to be a weekly, appearing every Saturday. Sixteen pages long and four columns wide, it would cost sixpence, a high price for a country so poor and so used to penny journals. Time was of the essence, for they wanted to launch the venture the first week in October when everyone returned to Dublin from assorted summer activities. As it was, they ran only one week late, and Volume I, Number 1, was dated 15 October 1842.[9]

Their first task in the summer had been to muster contributors with well-known names so that a good Prospectus could be issued. This may not have been easy, for the list seems a little thin and strained for effect. John O'Connell's name headed it, in large black type, a sort of imprimatur. But besides that endorsement from the Liberator's son, and those of the three editors, there were only five other names: O'Neill Daunt, who would never play a very important part on the paper but was active in Repeal causes generally; J.F. O'Callaghan, author of the popular *Green Book*; scholar-priest Joseph Fitzgerald; Terence McMahon Hughes, Duffy's cousin and eventually his brother-in-law, one-time editor of the *London*

Magazine and Charivari; and "Clarence Mangan, Esq., Author of *Anthologia Germanica* and *Litterae* [*sic*] *Orientales*". On 14 October 1992, the *Irish Times* carried an article commemorating the 150th anniversary of the founding of the *Nation* and headlined it: "*Nation* created vision of a pluralist Ireland". And so it did. It continued publication for fifty years. After a hiatus during the period of the Uprising of 1848, it resumed publication in 1850. Then, growing more conservative as time went by, it nonetheless supported Parnell and finally became another victim of that scandal in 1891.

Mangan's biographers, with the important exception of O'Donoghue, have treated his years of association with the *Nation*, 1842 until 1848, as a single unit, though accurately placing emphasis on 1846–7. While not entirely wrong, this was more advantageous to the formation of the myth of Mangan than for the presentation of the man's life as he actually lived it. It was true that he began enthusiastically with "Our First Number", in all probability because Duffy had embraced him as a friend and fellow nationalist and asked him for a rousing ode. Because two years earlier he had turned down Duffy's request for something along political lines, it is especially significant that he made this major effort to oblige his friend. Nothing seems more shallow than occasional verse, especially political verse, after the occasion is over, but in its day, this poem was lavishly praised and often reprinted. It began:

> 'Tis a great day and glorious, O Public! for you—
> This October Fifteenth, Eighteen Forty and Two!
> For on this day of days, lo! THE NATION came forth,
> To commence its career of Wit, Wisdom, and Worth—
> To give genius its due—to do battle with wrong—
> And achieve things undreamed of as yet, save in song.
> Then arise! fling aside your dark mantle of slumber,
> And welcome in chorus THE NATION'S FIRST NUMBER.

During the two weeks that followed, he contributed five witty, epigrammatic verses, the sort of thing he continued to believe in his heart that Duffy really liked to get from him. To an extent, he was probably right, too. The editor sometimes took note of such items while letting a poem like "Dark Rosaleen" appear without a word of comment. These five were signed "Vacuus", "Hi-Hum", "Mark Anthony", and, the first and last, "Terrae Filius". But "James Clarence Mangan" was nowhere to be seen. Nor did he sign his name or initials to the brief review of his friend Tighe's satirical temperance poem "Sal Swig" early in December.

After these three months, his first period with the *Nation* came to an abrupt end, and his work dropped out of its pages. Early in 1843 Duffy reprinted a handful of his friend's amusing lines from the *Vindicator*, as if pleading with him to reestablish the now broken contact, but without results. Then even that trickle dried up. It has been customary to explain Mangan's unexpected disappearance from the *Nation*, if it is mentioned at all, as having been caused mostly by Duffy's and Davis's sudden emergence as poets in their own right, an interpretation reinforced by the fact that, after Davis's death in 1845, Mangan returned to the paper. Duffy himself seems to have looked upon the intimidating effect of the energetic young men of the *Nation* on Mangan's aging and somewhat weary spirit as accounting for the poet's retreat. But these possible causes were only peripheral; Mangan was actually quite confident where his poetry was concerned and had long associated with men as robust as any on the *Nation* staff.

Rather, two specific occurrences in his life seem more probable explanations, the first of his withdrawal from the entire journalistic and literary scene for 1843 and a fair portion of 1844, the second of his absence from the *Nation* for the greater part of three years. Since neither of these was known about until recently, biographers cannot be faulted for not taking them into account. Now that they have come to light, however, their importance must be carefully weighed. The first chronologically, though not in importance, was an almost certain run-in with Duffy, a contretemps with both personal and professional verberations, that occurred in October 1842. The second was the death of Mangan's father on 26 September 1843.

On 29 October 1842, the *Nation* carried its first genuinely nationalistic poem, "Faugh a Ballagh" (Clear the Road). It opened:

"Hope no more for fatherland,
    All its ranks are thinned or broken;"
Long a base and coward band
    Recreant words like these have spoken;
    But WE preach a land awoken;
Fatherland is true and tried
    As your fears are false and hollow;
Slaves and dastards, stand aside—
    Knaves and traitors, *Faugh a Ballagh!*[10]

This poem, or song, as it is often called, became the Charter Song of the *Nation* and has always been attributed to Charles Gavan Duffy although, interestingly enough, he never specifically claimed it as his own. However, if the poem is examined closely, and if other evidence is considered as well, the conclusion almost has to be that the chief poet was not Gavan Duffy, but James Clarence Mangan. "Faugh a Ballagh" has so many characteristics of a Mangan poem and so few of those we can identify in Duffy's verses, that it is hard to imagine Duffy had much part in the composition. This is not the place for detail, but we can mention the many feminine rhymes, a relatively subtle rhyme scheme—*ababbcdcd*—and effective use of alliteration and repetition as being among the most obvious. Not one of Duffy's poems is comparable, not even his best-known "The Muster of the North" or "The Irish Rapparees". He was a very new hand at poetry in the autumn of 1842, and he never put himself forward as a poet in any case, recognizing that Davis, among the three editors, was much more skillful. Characteristically, Duffy wrote hearty, thumping, serviceable stanzas—"Faugh a Ballagh" is a good cut above that level.

The poem first appeared with the "vulgarly spelt" title ("Fag an Bealach" being more correct) at the top and centre of the important ninth page of the *Nation*. Although it was described as "A national hymn, chaunted in full chorus at the last symposiac of the editors and contributors", no author's name was given. Anonymous work was common, of course, but the implication was that it came either from one of the editors or from Mangan, the paper's official poet, so to speak. And that might well have been all that was heard from it. However, in its next edition, that of 2 November, the Galway *Vindicator*, a Repeal paper along the lines of the Belfast *Vindicator*, enthusiastically reprinted the poem and this confident note of attribution:

> We take the following glorious stanzas headed *Faugh a Ballagh*, from the last number of *The Nation*. This is, indeed, the speaking voice of a national heart— . . . there is but ONE man in Ireland could have penned these magnificent lines—that man is the Korner of our revived literature—even our friend, Clarence Mangan, to whose name be honor!

The notice was unsigned, and again, the story might have stopped there, with few people outside Galway being the wiser. But the *Nation* itself picked up this friendly paper's item and reprinted the attribution in its entirety in the "Answers to Correspondents" column of the next issue, 5 November. It scarcely needs to be pointed out that this in effect confirmed the fact of Mangan's authorship.

At first it might be assumed that Duffy by doing this was merely setting the record straight. Mangan would be complimented on his song and that would be that; nothing more would need to be said about it. But the situation was less simple and straight-forward than it appeared. Though beyond this point we can only conjecture about motives, always a risky activity, the effects that we see argue convincingly to certain causes. Not for the first time in his life, Mangan now found himself close to a humming political hive. Duffy was less than two weeks away from the date on which he was to be sentenced, and he had already pled for mercy. For him to be thought the author of a song like "Faugh a Ballagh", which was apparently the case after the singing at the symposium, would do his cause no good.

Most especially was this true given the decision he had arrived at, perhaps unbeknownst to his friends, to recant his earlier bold words and beg for a pardon from the Attorney General. His biographer, Cyril Pearl, found that decision more pragmatic than contemptible. Had Duffy been imprisoned at this time, the *Nation* almost surely would have gone under. With his whole heart and most of his capital invested in the paper, he could ill afford to see it fail. What Pearl found harder to excuse was that Duffy conveniently "forgot" all about this episode in writing his memoirs. We have seen other examples of his tendency toward revisionism. At best, it may be that the old man's memory really did fail him; at worst, he preferred to sacrifice the facts for the sake of his image in the eyes of posterity.

As for Mangan, Duffy must have determined that his friend ran less risk as the author of an inflammatory song than he did himself, and could safely be identified in print as the composer. Everyone knew that the authorities at Trinity College were arch-conservatives, and that there was a certain danger in an employee's getting on their wrong side, but to their credit it must be said that for the most part their interference was minimal. Neither now nor at any later date do they seem to have cared about the politics of their clerk, a generous disinterest for which Dr Todd may have been largely responsible. Nevertheless, in violating the poet's anonymity on the newspaper by printing the attribution, Duffy betrayed a trust and put him in harm's way. At the least, Mangan now should have received credit for the poem, but that did not follow. As events developed, the editor was given a full pardon. Within a year, he, along with two other editors and Daniel O'Connell himself, would be in trouble (again) with the Government, and this time he would wind up in prison, but for crucial months his name was cleared.

Mangan's withdrawal from the *Nation* may conceivably have been prompted in part by some anxiety about Dr Todd's or others' concerns about his nationalist associations, but it is far more probable that he was both hurt and offended at the use to which he had been put. Thus while Duffy won his appeal to the Attorney General and continued to garner praise for "Faugh a Ballagh", Mangan came up a loser on all counts. Typically, he would have said nothing in protest but would have done exactly what he seems to have done: withdrawn in offended silence.

The second occurrence that profoundly influenced the amount of writing the poet did during these years was his father's death on 26 September 1843. That the old man was failing in health and perhaps seriously ill for weeks or months before his demise seems likely. He was now seventy-eight years old. If his son had not been spending much time at the Peter Street residence before, he probably had to do so now to help his mother who was also elderly and perhaps not in robust health. A grim and distressing scene may well have been played out from the spring of 1843 until the day James Mangan senior breathed his last.

Falling upon the poet's thin (and now getting stooped) shoulders would have been the burden of taking care of practical household matters. William was almost certainly no help. As for Catherine Mangan, although she had once had enough business sense to prompt her aunt to leave her the grocery shop property, it had been years since she had exercised it. Apparently, she was unable even to keep track of the one elderly servant, a housekeeper, whom they had; Mangan's cousin, a Mrs Coffee, when asked about the family told John McCall that an "old woman, a confidential servant" had, "after Mangan Senior's death and when Mrs Mangan became stricken in years . . . robbed her right and left". Incredibly, she even "time after time, made away with most of the furniture", a somewhat garbled way of saying that she removed the furniture a piece at a time from the premises.[11] Where James and William were while this was going on, we have no way of knowing. But as one of the poet's letters reveals, he had only a small amount of furniture left to sell when he broke up the family home once and for all in 1847.

The death of a beloved relative is a terrible grief to bear, but it is simple and straight-forward, and the sympathy of friends and other family members is sustaining and then healing. The death of a person as close as a father who has been both loved and hated is emotionally much more complex. On the one hand, the poet must have felt the relief of a huge and eternal-seeming burden lifted at last, but it would have been a relief darkened by remorse, guilt, and the sad realization that all hope was lost of ever making things better between himself and his father. The man from whom he had often escaped by "running into a mousehole" had escaped *him* by running into the greatest "mousehole" of them all. But the peace that he may have anticipated was not to be. His father's body was laid to rest in Glasnevin Cemetery, beside that of John Mangan, but his restless spirit disturbed his son, and, perhaps, his widow for years. Or so, at any rate, Mangan declared. So preoccupied with ghosts was he, so immersed in the atmosphere of death at this time, that it would have been remarkable if he had not had such a spectral visitor.

How he responded to his loss we do not know. He may have sought solitude, or he may have sequestered himself with his mother. He may—just conceivably—have gone his normal way and shown no sign of inner turmoil. What he did not do was write or translate poetry or, for that matter, anything, for many months, a silence which itself was probably his response. The *Dublin University Magazine* received two chapters of on-going anthologies from him, a short "Stray Leaflets from the German

Oak—Fifth Drift" in February 1844, and a full-length "Literae Orientales" article, also the fifth, in May, but this was his total new output for publication from January 1843 until November 1844.

Of what he did write, an unusually large proportion was original. "Selber", who had not been heard from since June 1840, put in two appearances in the February 1844 anthology. "Schnapps" was sheer fun—a drinking poem such as had not been seen from Mangan in years:

> I've but one pocket for quids and coppers,
> Which last moreover are mostly raps,
> Yet, 'midst my ha'pence and pipes and stoppers
> I still find room for a flask of Schnapps.

By contrast, "The Coming Event" was an apocalyptic warning, its message being the exhortatory, Stop drinking and carousing and prepare yourselves for the great Change that is nearing. That Mangan was thinking eschatologically now became increasingly apparent. In addition to his personal situation was the fact that many fundamentalist Christian biblical scholars had settled on 1844 as the year of the Last Judgement. Mangan tended to be respectful of prophecy, and prophecies in the Old Testament's Book of Daniel as well as in the New Testament's Apocalypse or Book of Revelations could be interpreted as identifying this year as the Endtime. Thus his poem anticipated some dreadful if unspecified occurrence:

> Darken the lamp, then, and bury the bowl,
> Ye Faithfullest-hearted!
> And, as your swift years hasten on to the goal
> Whither worlds have departed,
> Spend strength, sinew, soul, on your toil to atone
> For past idlesse and errors;
> So best shall ye bear to encounter alone
> THE EVENT and its terrors.

In the "Literae Orientales" six of the ten poems have been determined by Jacques Chuto to be "almost certainly" or "probably" Mangan's own compositions. The poet himself left several unidentified. Among them were two major works from his "Eastern period": "The Caramanian Exile" and "The Wail and Warning of the Three Khalenders".[12] Mangan used the phrase "doleful jocularity" to describe the tone of the latter, and indeed, it also could apply to other poems here as well. He seems to have been in a curiously mixed mood. Although "The Caramanian Exile" preserved a consistent gloom, the others did not share it. Commencing, "I see thee ever in my dreams,/Karaman!/Thy hundred hills, thy thousand streams,/Karaman! O Karaman!", it was a straightforward song of longing and remorse:

My boyhood's feelings, newly born,
Karaman!
Withered, like young flowers uptorn,
Karaman! O, Karaman!
And in their stead sprang weed and thorn;
What once I loved now moves my scorn;
My burning eyes are dried to horn,
Karaman!
I hate the blessed light of Morn,
Karaman![13]

Mangan viewed "The Wail and Warning of the Three Khalenders" as a light-weight ballad by comparison with the foregoing. He observed, "One is not often electrified by such bursts of passion and feeling in Ottoman poetry. The chief characteristics of that poetry consist rather of deep religious fervour and a certain tone of tender melancholy—", then, in a rather surprising and perhaps revealing conclusion, "—the result of opium-eating and coffee-drinking. . . ." According to Mangan, "Khalenders" were Eastern troubadours, "half minstrels, half mendicants, whose wild and wandering habits must have excited to the highest pitch of activity both their animal spirits and intellectual faculties". The opening verse of this ballad follows:

La'laha il-Allah!
Here we meet, we three, at length,
Amrah, Osman, Perizad,
Shorn of all our grace and strength;
Poor, and old, and very sad!
We have lived, but live no more,
Life has lost its gloss for us,
Since the days we spent of yore
Boating down the Bosphorus. . . .

Although these poems represent a large amount of original composition in a very short time for a poet whose total original output was relatively small, they did not signal a return to a normal level of contribution to the periodicals. Another seven months would elapse before that happened, and even then he would continue to "boycott" the *Nation*.

Mangan was now forty years old. If he had stopped writing altogether or if he had died at this point, he would be remembered as a very interesting, quirky, minor poet and translator of considerable promise and international tastes in literature. But so far he had not met the criteria of the major poet: he had produced a fair-sized body of work, true, but it would have been hard to identify thirty or forty outstanding poems; and he had not produced even a handful of poems so superior that they would readily be acknowledged as "his glory and his crown". However, he did not stop writing, and he did not die. Instead, as a middle-aged man, he went on to achieve an intensive run of fine work including his greatest poems—an unprecedented accomplishment in the history of Romantic poetry.

[4]

> "One dark chill November evening", as Joseph Hudson told the story, he and a friend went to a "free-and-easy" close by Camden Street and found Mangan there. "In the midst of this jolly assembly might be seen one silent, solitary individual, generally seated near the fire—so near as to make one suppose that the faded colour of his brown coat was scorched from its heat. Speak to him—his reply is short and civil, his voice soft and musical, and hushed almost to a whisper. . . . Mangan declined to sing, but repeated with great delicacy of feeling the words of an old German song, "All my Riches are my Songs"; then, pointing to his glass, said in sad tones, "You found me poor and have kept me so."
>
> O'Donoghue, *Life and Writings of James Clarence Mangan*

While 1843 was something of an *annus horribilis* for Mangan, much of great moment was going on in Ireland. Daniel O'Connell designated this "the great Repeal Year", and his legions were awake and eager, though for exactly what was not so clear. Repeal rent, that penny-a-month per head that the population contributed to the Repeal Association, now amounted to thousands of pounds annually. It was spent on publicity, travel, stipends, propaganda—everything except weapons which O'Connell eschewed and which were in any case prohibited and extremely difficult to acquire.

Spring saw the first of the great public gatherings that soon came to be called, justifiably, Monster Meetings. These rallies or demonstrations were held in support of the cause of Repeal of the Union and were occasions for music-making and enjoyment as well as for speeches of encouragement and political agitation. The first took place at Trim in March, and thereafter, one occurred every week or sometimes twice a week all over the island. Attendance soared as time went on. The perhaps exaggerated figures reached almost a million for the meeting at Tara. The most astounding quality, to Irishmen and foreigners alike, was that sobriety and good discipline prevailed. For that, Fr Mathew's temperance crusade deserved much of the credit. Three years earlier, on the last day of 1840, O'Connell himself had "announced his conversion to teetotalism at a crowded meeting held at the Rotunda in Dublin".[14] Rather revealingly, he urged his audience to "avoid all those rascally bowel cordials", calling attention to one of the loopholes in the priest's original pledge.

Duffy and the *Nation* encouraged the cause of Repeal with supportive editorials and column after column reporting the attendance and the speeches at the meetings, often with a detailed eye-witness account. Besides the size, the rhetoric, too, escalated, becoming increasingly warlike in tone and vocabulary as time passed, in spite of the fact that the Liberator passionately urged non-violence. Under the circumstances, it would have been irresponsible for the English not to have taken the threats seriously, except for one thing: the Irish had virtually no arms or weapons of any kind. By contrast, the English garrisons were well equipped, and the supply of guns was increased until by the autumn of 1843 their weaponry stood at battle-ready.

The greatest of the Monster Meetings so far was to be held in Dublin, in Clontarf, on 7 October, a Saturday. A million men and women were expected to attend. The roads to the city, it is said, were crowded several days in advance of the date as people made their way in from the countryside. Then, only the day before, when all was in readiness, the rumour, first, and then its confirmation spread throughout Dublin—the Government were prohibiting the gathering:

> The proclamation was pasted on the walls of the city at three o'clock. At five the sun would set and it would not be read by any wayfarer until dawn. In those hours O'Connell had to decide between obedience and resistance. In Conciliation Hall he met his followers and made his decision. He called off the meeting . . . .
>
> The Government struck again. With six others O'Connell was charged with conspiracy and incitement to sedition, and called for trial.[15]

Among the six others was Duffy. A guilty verdict was never in doubt because the jury was packed. In May 1844, the sentence was handed down, and within a couple of months the men were sent to prison. Confinement was not arduous. Mitchel reported that "Duffy might have been seen on a rustic bench, surrounded by certain young poets, his pale face illuminated with a glow that looked very like the light of enthusiasm, and almost genius. . . ."[16] But it took an emotional toll. As for Monster Meetings, they continued to be held and were reported faithfully in the Nation. Never again, however, was the same high emotional pitch reached as for the interdicted rally at Clontarf.

In 1844, Mangan was without a single old friend to whom he could comfortably turn. It was undoubtedly off-putting that both James Tighe and James Price had become teetotalers while he himself had declined to make any such commitment. O'Donovan was busy with his family, and Duffy was in prison. He had had one other friend, however, about whom we know something: Owen Connellan, whose acquaintance, it may be recalled, dated back to at least 1834. He had probably seen little of Connellan after the somewhat uncharitable treatment Connellan received from Petrie as a result of their having been on opposite sides of the antiquarian argument, but this friendship was now revived. Connellan lived at No. 30 Lower Mecklenburgh Street, a densely populated old thoroughfare that ran between Lower Marlborough Street and Lower Buckingham Street north of the River Liffey. His neighbours were, many of them, dishearteningly poor. A cook, tallow chandler, printer, coach painter, sculptor, nailer, vintner, and dressmaker shared the street with numerous provision dealers, tenements, and the Female Penitents' Retreat.

Connellan's occupation is not listed in the *Dublin Directory*, but he now was pursuing a most unlikely calling; he was making another translation of *The Annals of the Kingdom of Ireland by the Four Masters*. The only possible reason for him to do so was to steal a march on rival John O'Donovan, whose struggle to get his translation published had been going on for at least five years. Technical problems with the wide variety of type-faces and unfamiliar characters had combined to cause serious cost overruns, as they would be termed nowadays, and to drag out the process. That Connellan would please his patron, Sir William Betham, by getting his work into print first was self-evident. In fact, his efforts, clumsy and inaccurate though they were, brought him a reward denied O'Donovan; when the new Queen's College, Cork, opened, he was appointed to a Professorship in Irish.

Connellan was under no illusion about the quality of his English and he called upon Mangan to go over his manuscript and make corrections, and, one assumes, small improvements. Thus Mangan had a hand, and it may have been an important one, in the production of both nineteenth-century translations of the work of The Four Masters. Because Connellan was hurrying to get it into print, he brought it out a section at a time, "Price 1 shilling", from Bryan Geraghty's bookshop at No. 8 Anglesea Street. Of the three men involved in this endeavour, Connellan, Mangan, and Geraghty, only Connellan benefited appreciably. Mangan needed the small fee he no doubt was paid, being out of work for six months of the 1844–5 winter; and the companionship of Connellan and Geraghty would have been valued by him. But poor Geraghty as publisher bankrupted himself and died not many years later, his worldly possessions being sold at auction on 29 February 1848. Among the Irish materials were manuscripts purchased by McGlashan, John O'Daly, and Dr Stokes.[17]

The importance of Connellan's English translation of the *Annals*, as

Dr Patricia Boyne has pointed out, is that it was the first such work to reach print. A previous translation into Latin prompted O'Donovan to think that Latin would be a better choice for *his* work too, though Hardiman and other friends urged him to stick with the "rougher" English, which he did. But except for that, not much credit is due Connellan. O'Donovan's friend, J.W. Hanna, coming across it at Geraghty's sale, wrote to him, "Surely, surely it is not the same thing [as yours] at all, not even the text, for even there, I find entries omitted altogether and in others the meaning altogether distorted, while through the whole book the footnotes have no reference to the text itself." [18]

O'Donovan was furious at Connellan and also understandably jealous. In response to reading the "Foray of Con O'Donnell" by the young poet Denis Florence MacCarthy, who was also an acquaintance if not a close friend of Mangan's, he declared that while he hoped MacCarthy would not be annoyed, he still had to tell him the poem should be "recast" because it was "all wrong". MacCarthy unhappily had been "misled by that vulgar translation of The Annals of the Four Masters made by Owen Connellan, a peasant from Tireragh [Tyrone], *who has as much brains as a hatching goose*" and by Philip MacDermot, "an apothecary from Cavan . . ." who made the annotations. He concluded, "Behold the first results of a false translation of these Annals in your excellent poem! Poisoned it is from beginning to end with false assumptions!" [19] Mercifully, he seems to have held Mangan free from blame.

Another friend to whom Mangan might have turned during this period was the poet Edward Walsh, the translator of *Reliques of Irish Jacobite Poetry* which was published this year. He, too, was acquainted with Geraghty and Connellan. Walsh is an interesting figure, but his role in Mangan's life, while perhaps quite important, is little understood. Mangan used the *Reliques* and also Walsh's later *Irish Popular Songs* to a certain extent in preparing some of his own translations from the Irish, but that is virtually all that is known about their mutual lives. It has been suggested that the initials "E.W." purportedly signed to the impersonal autobiography were meant to stand for Edward Walsh, although the persona of that piece of writing identified himself as "a medical man". In any case, there is no reason to believe they referred to the poet Walsh who in 1849 was teaching school in the Cork Union Workhouse.

Born in 1805 in the city then called Londonderry, though of County Cork parents, Edward Walsh was a sensitive, serious, intelligent schoolmaster and Irish scholar. He was tall and slightly stooped. His hair was "black as night and straight as a Delaware Indian's" and, falling over his coat collar, it "swept with one deep wave" over his high, intellectual forehead. His black eyes were shadowed by "remarkably long lashes".

Sometime around 1840, he married Bridgid Sullivan, seventeen years his junior, and by 1848 they were the parents of four children. It was said his love for his family was "almost morbidly intense". While not a Young Irelander himself, he nevertheless felt intense sympathy for the group's position. When John Mitchel was deported in June 1848, Walsh was teaching the "small convicts" of Spike Island and made a secret trip to the *Shearwater* to see him. Mitchel, in *Jail Journal*, described him as "a tall, gentleman-like person, in black but rather over-worn clothes" who "came up to me and grasped both my hands with every demonstration of reverence. . . . He stooped down and kissed my hands. 'Ah!' he said, 'you are now the man in all Ireland most *to be envied*.' "[20]

Walsh's early work had been published in the *Dublin Penny Journal*, but as he was teaching at that time in a National school in County Waterford, it seems unlikely that he met Mangan or indeed any Dublin people. In 1843, however, he began contributing to the *Nation*, and Duffy, he claimed, soon urged him to move to Dublin and even promised to find him a good position there. Unfortunately, by the time Walsh got to the city early in 1844, Duffy was embroiled in the legal dispute following Clontarf and had little time to spend doing anything on his behalf. Walsh wrote his publisher, John O'Daly, still in Kilkenny, that Duffy really did intend to keep his promise and find "a respectable situation [for me] after the trials . . . Duffy is a true man". Still, the country poet was regretting ever "coming up here".[21]

Duffy eventually did find a job for him on the *Monitor*—Duffy's friend James Coffee was editor, it may be remembered—as a sub-editor (according to his memoirist, the poet Charles Kickham) or a reporter (according to Walsh himself). His health, however, was so completely broken that he was unable to cover the State trials and had to be let go. When he was up and around again, he went to the Corn Exchange Rooms and got a job "where I am engaged in a purely literary capacity, and am treated with respect".[22]

All but the earliest of Walsh's letters from this time were addressed from No. 5 Richmond Cottages, between Summer Hill Parade/Richmond Street and Richmond Parade. Mangan, a few years earlier, had used No. 5 Richmond Street as an address, and this may have been the same house. The warren of ancient lanes, ways, rows, and streets was so confused in this vicinity that the possibility Mangan merely used the wrong designation is worth considering. The *Dublin Almanac and General Register* listed "Patrick Smith, carpenter" at No. 5 Richmond Cottages; the fact that Mangan's uncle Patrick Smith cannot be located with his brothers Michael and John in No. 3 Fishamble Street and Copper Alley, and even that the poet's brother William was a cabinet-maker, lend some weight to this speculation. Mangan himself was now staying at Peter Street, almost certainly, but a room at his uncle's would have been a good, inexpensive lodging for the impoverished Walsh, and Duffy—or Mangan, if he had met Walsh by this time—may have suggested it.

The two poets surely were acquainted at least by mid-March 1844, for on St Patrick's Day, Walsh wrote to O'Daly, "I assure you that a certain friend of mine who is a deep Phrenologist says upon examination of my scull that I have 'Benevolence' and 'Attachment' uncommonly developed."[23] We cannot be absolutely certain that this character was James Clarence Mangan, but the description fits so well the actions he took when he first met someone, as we know from Fr Meehan's amusing account, that it is altogether likely to have been he. Besides, Walsh probably had not so quickly made two friends who were "deep phrenologists".

To conclude, then, about Edward Walsh: He was touchy and he could be caustic. His standards for poetry were high, and he lacked tolerance for anything second-rate. In this aspect of his temperament, he was quite different from Mangan who, as far as we can see, bore with weaknesses and even tolerated fools, if not gladly, then at least patiently. To O'Daly, Walsh wrote in February, "In Poetry, Mr Daly, there can be no such thing as middling—Poetry must be at all times good and carry its distinguishing marks about it—otherwise it is trash. . . ." In August, he seems to have been deeply troubled about the mechanics of printing his *Reliques of Ancient Jacobite Poetry*. "Why did you not get someone at least to count the feet in each line . . ." he asked O'Daly, about the way the poems had been set on the pages, "so that his [the original poet's] lines may preserve some rude semblance to the tune of the Irish song? God may forgive your worse than vandalism. I cannot."

We know only a very little about what Mangan thought of Walsh or Walsh of Mangan, and that little bit is professional, not personal. About Walsh, Mangan observed that he was "a gentleman to whose literary exertions Ireland is indebted almost beyond the power of repayment".[24] About Mangan, Walsh said less, and even that was negative and merely by inference, when he declared that the "peasant poet" John Keegan "had more *natural* talent than all 'Young Ireland. . . .'" Oddly enough, we do know that neither man had a very high opinion of Thomas Davis. Mangan we only infer was less than enthusiastic about Davis, who in fact worked actively to get the poet's *Anthologia Germanica* published in book form, from the rhyme in which he mentioned Davis—his one and only allusion to the man whom so many saw as the finest individual of his time. The relevant lines in "Counsel to the Worldly-Wise" are scarcely what one would call a tribute: "*Dare to live*, though sneering groups/Dub you *rara avis*—/. . . And whene'er your spirit droops, /Think of Thomas Davis!"[25]

Walsh's feeling against Davis was more intense and more negative. He was resentful and jealous of Davis for removing a few of his, Walsh's, poems from the *Spirit of the Nation*, to make room as he believed for more of Davis's own. "I have no objection that my untaught strains should give way to any of the numerous songs of Mr Davis that adorn the collection, or to that of any other person who may be honoured in a niche in your national temple", he vowed unconvincingly to Duffy in July 1844. However, he did protest that a very good poem of his, one of which he was properly proud, was to be printed without his name in the second part of the *Spirit of the Nation*, while an inferior poem in the first part carried his signature. In fact, although Duffy asked Walsh for some "songs", the poet does seem to have been shorted. While Davis was represented by eight pieces, Walsh had only one.[26]

Walsh had scarcely settled in Dublin before John O'Daly was talking about moving to the city and asking him to find a suitable place for him to live. Walsh, in spite of being so sick, obliged. On 15 February he wrote to describe a very good set of rooms. He had gone to a street

> between Dame Street and the Quay and found a place that I thought wd. exactly suit you. It is a shop in Anglesea Street, opposite Duffy's [this was James Duffy, bookseller and printer, No. 25], with a Parlour off the shop and either a back or front drawing room. The rent on this is £30 a year. Anglesea Street is well established and 30 I should suppose low.[27]

By 1849, O'Daly may have moved again, the *Poets and Poetry of Munster* giving No. 7, Bedford Row, a continuation of Anglesea Street, as his address, but he is always recalled as a bookseller from Anglesea Street. Among his fellow bookmen were Michael William Rooney, the lucky finder of an early edition of *Hamlet*, from whom Mangan often borrowed books; and Patrick Kennedy who, O'Donoghue notes, was "a literary man of no mean order". O'Daly moved to Dublin no later than the autumn of 1845. The earliest the poet mentioned him in print was October 1846, however, when he said of the poem "Sarsfield", "For the original of the following poem I am indebted to my friend Mr Daly." Of one thing we can be sure: Whenever O'Daly moved to Anglesea Street, Mangan made his acquaintance not long thereafter.

In John Keegan's words, O'Daly had "the most magnificent Munster brogue on his tongue that I ever had the luck to hear." Also in the words of the blunt Keegan, O'Daly was "low-sized, a merry countenance, fine black eyes, vulgar in appearance and manner. . . ." A card from one of the patent "weighing machines" of the day recorded that on 23 August 1852, he stood 5 ft 5 in tall (probably with his shoes on) and weighed 11 stone 12 pounds, that is, 166 pounds. In other words, he was short and stocky.[28]

In his home, he and Mangan must have worked many hours on Irish translations throughout the remaining years of the poet's life as they prepared *Poets and Poetry of Munster* and *The Tribes of Ireland*. O'Daly told Douglas Hyde about their "informal joint *modus operandi*", and Hyde repeated the story thus: "Mangan did not know Irish, and . . . it was his custom to stretch his body halfway across the counter, while John would translate the Irish song to him and [he] would versify it, half-sitting and half-lying on the counter."[29]

O'Daly's career had not been without blemish. A Catholic, he had converted to Protestantism in the mid-1820s and remained "tossed on the broad unsettled principles" of that faith, to quote his own words, for close to twenty years.[30] He was more than a simple "souper", that is, a hungry Catholic who abandoned some of his religion's practices, or even converted to Protestantism, for a Friday meal of a bowl of meat soup. Thanks to his mastery of Irish, he became Inspector of Schools for the infamous Irish Society which used the teaching of the native language as a ruse to inculcate Protestant doctrine. Keegan met O'Daly when the latter was, in Keegan's phrase, "teaching Irish to the Wesleyans". But it was more than the Wesleyans, early-day Methodists, who were instructed. By 1840, the Society had placed some seven hundred Irish teachers in schools throughout Ireland, and the majority of their students were Catholic.

To give him his due, O'Daly might himself originally have been duped into believing that these teachers were particularly interested in children's learning the Irish language. Although by 1843 he had taken the initiative in exposing the operation as "a humbug", articles and accusations continued to fly back and forth in the *Kilkenny Journal* for years, and the stubborn refusal of the issue to go away may have played some part in his decision to move to Dublin. D.J. O'Donoghue discreetly glossed over this period in O'Daly's life, only repeating an amusing story about his "coquetting with the 'soupers' ": When the little boys in Kilkenny began to run after him, calling "souper", he thought it time to give up his new friends, and used to mollify the urchins by saying, "Aisy, boys, amn't I goin' to lave them?" John O'Donovan, himself a Kilkenny man, was highly incensed at this perversion of Irish instruction and hesitated even to have his Irish grammar brought out under the aegis of the Church of Ireland's College of St Columba at Rathfarnham, Dublin, for fear of being suspected of some similar scheme. He only gave in and allowed the connection when no other means of publishing the work could be found.

O'Daly was not taken entirely seriously as a scholar, in part because he was such a blatherskite, but also because he was too often somewhat slap-dash in his work. Walsh recognized this quality in him and faulted him severely for it as noted in his comments about poetry. O'Donoghue restrainedly observed that "O'Daly was chiefly known as a publisher and editor of Gaelic books, but he [also] brought out other works of a creditable character." Mangan probably did not pass judgement on him. O'Daly, after all, was very generous-hearted and open-handed. He may not have had the wherewithal to pay the poet the going magazine rate for the work he did for *Duffy's Irish Catholic Magazine* which O'Daly had a hand in publishing in 1847 and 1848, however. A receipt Mangan gave O'Daly for the poem "Upon the Expulsion of the Franciscans from Multifarnham" printed as "On the Suppression of the Monasteries" noted: "Recd from John Daly Esq. 10s. . . ."[31] Yet the poem was 126 lines long which should have earned him £1.5s at magazine rate, and this was in February 1848 when his need was desperate for every penny he could possibly earn from his writing. Joseph Brenan or Bernard Fulham described O'Daly's kindness to Mangan in the Press Notice for later editions of *Poets and Poetry of Munster*:

> [John O'Daly], poor fellow, little richer than [Mangan himself] in this world's goods, did give, with a kind hand, such as well becomes the true Celt's generous nature, the little he could afford . . . a seat at his humble hearth—half the poor meal that an occasional profitable speculation in some old book enabled him to purchase, a few pens, an ink bottle, a candle . . . .[32]

[5]

> After a week of irksome labour, mental and physical, almost my only pleasure is when, long after midnight, in my lonely room, I read *The Nation*, and, forgetting the men I have to herd with, feel myself once more, in heart, thought, and feeling, an Irishman.
>
> Mangan, *Nation*, 23 November 1844

The 2 November 1844 issue of the *Nation* reprinted "My Bugle and How I Blow It" with a curiously coy note in which Duffy explained that the "pleasant extravaganza" had been given him "some years earlier . . . for a publication of a literary character" (disguising the identity of the *Vindicator* for reasons now unknown), by a "popular writer" who "may not choose to be identified with the particular politics of the *Nation*". The implication, possibly, was that Mangan had been making himself scarce because he did not hold with the *Nation's* political position; or it may conceivably have alluded to his unwillingness to have his name put on "Faugh a Ballagh".

An article in the 16 November number, again probably from Duffy's pen, remarked on the progress being made by Germany towards the formation of a ballad history, a fact familiar, the author noted, to readers of "Mr Mangan's translations". Then it continued:

> How we wish the author of "The Barmecides" would lend his help to an Irish ballad history! His power of making his verses racy of the soil [a key phrase in the *Nation's* motto] cannot be doubted by any one who read his "Paraphrase of Kathaleen ny Houlahan" and "Elegy on the Princes" in the *Dublin Penny Magazine*.

Thus he asked readers to recall things printed four years previously, though the titles are inaccurate and he should have written the "*Irish Penny Journal*", not the "*Dublin Penny Magazine*".

Another week passed and other notes were exchanged. A conversation took place between Duffy and Mangan in which Mangan suggested that his friend was free to use those much admired poems in his ballad history if he wanted to, but corrected the name of the publication in which they had appeared. The editor responded: "We have read the ballads of"—and here a small printer's hand pointed across page 104 of the *Nation* towards a new poem of Mangan's which graced page 105—"with pleasure, and we will be glad to have his help in the projected Ballad History; but we cannot insert poems which have already been published, no matter in how obscure a vehicle." This policy was to be revised. When *The Ballad Poetry of Ireland* was published in 1845, Mangan was represented by four poems, three of them reprints from the *Irish Penny Journal*.

The poem to which the little hand pointed was "A Lane for Freedom", the first in a projected new series from Mangan to be called "Echoes of Foreign Song". To it he hoped to contribute some "specimens of the modern poetry of European nations" that would "reflect the public mind of each country, which is always to be gathered in some shape from its popular poetry." Remarkably, "A Lane for Freedom" was almost another "Faugh a Ballagh". Translated from the "Young German" poet George Herwegh, it replicated the Irish poem in form, content, and even the arrangement of its subject matter. By thus sending it to Duffy, Mangan would seem to be saying, "This time, put my name on it when you print it." So it was that "A Lane for Freedom" became the first of his *Nation* poems to carry the signature "J.C.M." The opening stanzas of "Faugh a Ballagh" and "A Lane for Freedom" follow:

FAUGH A BALLAGH (Fag an Bealach)

"Hope no more for fatherland,
    All its ranks are thinned or broken;"
Long a base and coward band
    Recreant words like these have spoken;
    But WE preach a land awoken;
Fatherland is true and tried
    As your fears are false and hollow;
Slaves and dastards, stand aside—
    Knaves and traitors, *Fag an Bealach*!

A LANE FOR FREEDOM

"My suffering country shall be freed,
And shine with tenfold glory!"
So spake the gallant Winkelried,
Renowned in German story.
"No tyrant, even of kingly grade,
Shall cross or darken *my* way!"
Out flashed his blade, and so he made
For Freedom's course a highway![33]

On 14 December, Mangan wrote a letter to Duffy, that is unique as the sole surviving piece of correspondence in which he spoke directly of his mother and his obligation to care for her. It is also important in confirming the extent of his nationalistic feelings and his belief in the value and necessity of aggressive action. Because it has never appeared in print, the letter is given here in full.

14th December [Saturday] 1844

My dear Duffy,

I am seriously uneasy that I have not been able to see you this evening, to explain to you that it will unfortunately, be impossible for me to have the pleasure of meeting you to-morrow. My poor mother lies dangerously ill—and I cannot leave her. I enclose you a song from the German. Before the end of the week (say on Friday, at 3 o'clock) I will call at the *Nation* office; and, if you should be there, it will not take 10 minutes (entre *nous*) to arrange the plan, or system, upon which my poor contributions to the *Nation* shall be—I will not say *received*, but—*proffered*. I will write for you, from the beginning of next year, either in prose or verse, as you please.

I would express to you, my dear friend, my sincere regret, that you are compelled to devote such a large proportion of your journal to "frothy speeches" (I quote the words of your own paper.) Believe me, that until you remedy this defect, the great mass of *earnest* readers will peruse even *The Nation* with some degree of apathy and indifference. We at present want men who can *act*: the speeches of *some* Men, are, I admit, *Acts*, properly speaking; but we have not had of late any specimen of this kind of practical oratory before the Public. I fear to say anything more, lest I might possibly offend or shock you. Commend me to our friends!

Ever your's, my dear Duffy, J.C. Mangan[34]

P.S. I write this in the Dublin Library, and shall leave it to be sealed in the Nation Office [which was across the street].

Quite possibly, the editor and the poet did get together to firm up an arrangement for Mangan's contributions, although the evidence is not to be found in the ensuing months. "Our Fatherland", the second in the "Echoes of Foreign Song" series, appeared a fortnight later, but thereafter the all-too-familiar silence set in again. Except for the "ditty" titled "The Blackwater" on 22 March 1845 in the "Answers to Correspondents" column (almost an insult to a poet of Mangan's repute), he vanished from the pages of the *Nation* until late summer, when the eighth poem in the "Echoes" series was published. Other poets' work had accounted for the intervening numbers; as Mangan felt a strong proprietorial interest in the title and the endeavour, he may have taken umbrage at having been replaced. Whatever the cause, he was seen no more in the *Nation* for almost a year, until spring, 1846, when his richest period of composition and contribution began.

14

Days of Darkness

[1]

Ay! where's my money? That's a puzzling query.
 It vanishes. Yet neither in my purse
Nor pocket are there any holes. 'Tis very
 Incomprehensible. I don't disburse
For superfluities. I wear plain clothes.
 I seldom buy jam tarts, preserves, or honey;
And no one overlooks what debts he owes
 More steadily than I. Where *is* my money?
Mangan, "Where's My Money?", (Gaudy)

The poet fell upon hard times financially during the last quarter of 1844 and the first quarter of 1845, or, more accurately, hard times fell upon *him*. It was the first time he had been completely unemployed, not briefly or by choice between jobs, for close to twenty years. Whether or not he was merely in that anomalous state of being temporarily laid off is not clear from the Trinity College records. In any case, he received no further pay until June 1845, when he got £5, suggesting that he had done no more than a month's work in that quarter of the year. Thereafter, he returned to regular but only half-time employment in the College library for another year-and-a-half, until the end of 1846. A notation in the library minutes of 27 October 1845, stated "ominously enough", as Jacques Chuto observed:

> Mr. Mangan has been engaged for four hours every day. Under his superintendence the arrangement of the slips of the Large Library in alphabetical order has been commenced. A first rough arrangement, by the two first letters only, has been completed; but it is feared that no effectual progress can be made, until a competent person can be engaged to superintend the work.[1]

This state of affairs in the cold, dark winter months must have subjected the three individuals who now comprised the Peter Street household, Mangan, his mother, and his brother, to very real hardship, or at least to the threat of it. Still, he did not try to publish any more than usual. In addition to the scanty items in the *Nation*, there was only one German anthology and one "Stray Leaflets" in the *University Magazine* from May 1844 through March 1845. It may testify to his troubled finances that these appeared one after the other in January and February 1845, but they would have earned him only a meagre £12. Unless William went to work, the family would have been hard pressed to meet their bills, and the best guess as to how they managed is that again Catherine's brothers came to their rescue.

Some good poems are to be found in the deep-winter group, one or two of them real stars in the poet's crown. "And Then No More" was long a favourite. Misused by those who have taken it to be autobiographical—although "I saw her once, one little while, and then no more:/'Twas Eden's light on Earth a while, and then no more" can hardly be said to be relevant to any romance Mangan is known to have had—it remains a fine, sensitive translation of Rückert's "Und dann nicht mehr". "Eighteen Hundred Fifty" is much more likely to have been personal. Not only did he sign it "Selber", but he filled it with short, wistful hints about his own predicament. It began:

> I am I,—mineself, and none beside:
> That's a fact, in spite of Herr Jacobi. [Friedrich H. Jacobi, philosopher, 1743–1819]
> Would it were not! for I cannot hide
> From my heart my growing autophoby.
> Were metempsychosian figments true,
> I'd bequeath, good world, an ugly gift t'ye—
> My sad soul to wit, which waits the new
> State of things in Eighteen Hundred Fifty![2]

One cannot help believing that the refrain with its variations came from his heart: "And, alas! I dwell alone!", "And, alas! I live alone!", "I mope alone!", "I drink alone!", "I stand alone!", then, finally, "And, alas! I want A LOAN!"

He had more to say here about "Selber". He was, Mangan wrote, a hard man to pin down or to critique. He was not a Young Germanist, "though, from certain passages in his works, he might pass for one—nay for one of the reddest-hot revolutionists". He could most aptly be described as "a compound of supernaturalist, republican, moral philosopher, and utilitarian—the supernaturalist predominating. . . ." He had Selber quote Herr Jacobi, who "could doubt his own identity and that of every man!", pronouncing him "a happy fellow", much happier than Selber himself because "Ich bin ich, und leider bin kein Andrer[*sic*]!" Ironically, his "growing autophoby" was the price he paid for an increasing, and we would probably say a healthier, sense of his own identity.

It was almost certainly the realization that he was in something like dire financial straits that prompted Mangan's friends to initiate an effort at this time to get a collection of his poems published. He had now produced nineteen German anthologies, and he enjoyed a solid reputation as a stimulating, unorthodox, translator—"nameless" because his work was unsigned and he remained an unknown quantity to the majority of readers. The situation is different in the world of publication today, but this state of affairs was not at all unusual in the 1840s. Such a reputation did not make it easy, however, to convince any book publisher to bring out a "collected works".

Duffy was behind the move to have a selection of the German translations published for his friend's benefit. Mangan's admirers, he wrote, "wished to procure for him [Mangan] a wider recognition and more adequate income". Thomas Davis agreed with Duffy in this and approached his friend, Daniel Owen Madden, "to negotiate with an English publisher for the production of Mangan's poems in London, where money might be had which no publisher in Ireland would spend upon German translations." After briefing Madden on the poet—"He has some small salary in the College Library, and has to support himself and his mother. His health is wretched."—Davis asked him to see if the publisher Newby would do the job, "giving Mangan £50 for the edition". The generous effort came to nothing, although it is obvious that Davis was filled with sympathy for the poet who, he said, "poor fellow, is so nervous that it is hard to get him to do anything businesslike, but he is too good and too able to be allowed to go wrong."[3]

Mangan may have suffered from poverty, but poverty seems not to have tamed his pride, which was fierce and, I suspect, could be irritating. He did not appreciate philanthropy which he may have felt underscored his inadequacies and the need to market his work, a necessity for which he had great contempt. Davis's well-meant sympathy may have seemed condescending. At the same time, he possessed a grateful heart and recognized kind intentions.

After Davis's efforts failed, the next move was up to Duffy himself. Reasonably enough, he approached Mangan's publisher on the *University Magazine*, James McGlashan. The Scotsman had not become a financial success, and the managing director of William Curry and Company, by catering to the needs of impecunious poets.[4] He agreed to go along with the scheme only if Duffy would put up £50 to fund it. This Duffy agreed to do. The publisher believed, rightly as it turned out, that there was not a big market for German poetry (two volumes were planned) and that consequently the price would have to be high, cutting down the number of potential buyers even further. The £50 would be divided between the publication costs and Mangan. For his investment, Duffy would receive one hundred copies of the book, "many of which I felt persuaded my friends would purchase". And so in the spring of 1845, the plan was launched and by midsummer the volumes of the *Anthologia Germanica* were published. It was the only book of Mangan's poetry to be published during his lifetime. He evidently received £25 for it. It is very doubtful if he ever realized another penny on the sales.

He must have given a fair amount of time to picking out the poems he wanted to include; there were 130 in all, from thirty-eight authentic German poets—no "Selber" or "Drechsler" here. In a letter to Duffy written in February or March, he had a word to say on the subject, humorously and yet pointedly referring to the whole matter as a particularly humble business transaction:

> My dear Duffy,
>
> I have just received your exceedingly kind note. You are the soul of goodness and generosity. Will you be at leisure on Saturday, Sunday, or Monday evening? If you can I will be most happy to call out (and out) on you. I say out-and-out, as I conceive that as yet I have made you only a series of half (*and* half—that's paying you back, eh?) drop-in Paul Pryish visits, or visitations. [Paul Pry was a character in an 1825 comedy of that name, an unemployed, meddling man, with no occupation, who was always sticking his nose into other people's business.] I have made out an inventory for the sale (excluding, as you advised, pots and pans) and put it into the hands of M'Glashan.[5]

Volume I opened with Schiller and contained several selections from such Mangan favourites as Uhland, Tieck, Kerner and Bürger. The second volume began with Goethe, but also devoted twenty pages to Rückert and forty to the poet's fairly recent favourite, Freiligrath. There were single selections from many more. The collection spanned the poet's whole career at the *University Magazine*, from the earliest Schiller, "To My Friends", to "The Deserted Mill" by August Schnezler which had just appeared in February's "Stray Leaflets". In short, it gave a representative sample of the poet's own preferences and provided a showcase for his range of skills.

An interesting question is whether or not McGlashan intended to include a short biographical memoir of Mangan as a sort of introduction to this publication. Chances are that he did, the poet's name and history being so unfamiliar. Several autobiographical letters written by Mangan in 1845, some already noted here, were apparently abandoned as the source of a sketch for these volumes, and were later lent by McGlashan to James Price. They were, if Price's selected passages from them are in any way representative, not really suitable for what McGlashan would have had in mind. In them, Mangan first propounded the "six-year age error" stating that he was thirty-six (he was actually forty-two) at the time of writing, "but twice the number in soul". In general, the information he gave, and his interpretation of his early years, were much the same as in the *Autobiography*, although that short memoir was composed some three or three-and-a-half years later. This in itself is important to know for when he wrote it he had not yet experienced the horrors of the Famine, or the deprivations of 1847 and 1848 to which his dark vision of his life has sometimes been attributed. What is clear is that the misery, the anxiety, and the "natural tendency to loneliness, poetry, and self-analysis", were all fully formed by 1845.

That he could be perfectly professional when the situation required it, the four-hundred word, serious, straight-forward piece of writing that appeared as the Preface to the volumes attests. It is the only thing of any length he ever wrote in which he spoke directly to his readers without benefit of disguise or jest. It is, thus, interesting in and of itself, but somewhat dry compared to what readers were used to hearing from him. The first paragraph explained where the translations had first appeared, and obliquely thanked his friends, "admirers, like myself, of German literature", for their efforts on his behalf. In the second, he noted that most of the poems were selected from "poets who have flourished within the current century", and he explained why the earlier authors and their work were rarely represented. In the third, he stated merely that he was furnishing "select samples of some particular kinds" of poetry, rather than "miscellaneous samples of all kinds". And finally, he acknowledged that he intended his translations to be "faithful to the spirit, if not always to the letter, of their originals", and he somewhat lengthily commented on how favourable had been the reception critics had generously accorded him —"I am exceedingly anxious to express,and I do here once for all express, my most grateful acknowledgement of the very favorable reception they have experienced. . . ."[6] The Preface appears in its entirety in Appendix E.

The *German Anthology* was well-received, but at an expensive twelve shillings, it sold slowly, just as McGlashan had predicted. Reviews were fairly numerous, some twelve in all, but were, for the most part, very brief, mere notices of publication rather than comprehensive appraisals. The *Foreign Quarterly* panned it. The *Cork Examiner's* reviewer did not even take time to know what he was looking at, and wrote that all the poems were by Simrock (whose poems composed the twentieth "Anthologia" in July), taking a paltry three lines to do that meagre favour, while giving twenty lines of enthusiastic praise to the first volume in Duffy's Library of Ireland, *Irish Volunteers*, by Thomas MacNevin.[7] The best British notice was in the *Quarterly Review*: "As a whole, these translations not only display a practised ear and much felicitous versification, but, beyond this, that sympathy with deep poetic feeling without which translations from the German, however grammatically faithful, must always be worthess."[8] Somewhat surprisingly, there was a review in the not very reputable *World*. Yet another appeared in *Tait's Edinburgh Magazine* as part of an article on "The Lyric Poetry of Germany" which may have been the work of

Thomas De Quincey.[9] Notable by their absence were commentaries in *Blackwoods*, *Fraser's*, and, closer home, the *Dublin University Magazine*.

Predictably, the *Nation* and the *Dublin Review* were highly laudatory. The *Review* gave the publication twenty pages with generous examples to illustrate the range and quality of the translations. Its most perceptive and often-quoted lines may be those in which the reviewer declared, "[Mangan's] pen seems to take its colour from the food it feeds upon—it is pious and didactic with Hölty or Klopstock—humourous and burlesque with Dunkel—it plunges into the depths of mysticism with de la Motte Fouqué—and laughs at the world with Kotzebue or Bürger." One epithet often attached to Mangan may have been used here first: "The writer is a complete literary Proteus."[10]

Either Duffy or Davis wrote the *Nation's* commentary. After asserting that Mangan had the most essential quality for a translator, "he is a high poet", the reviewer declared him to be "an absolute master of the language into which he interprets". In fact this review attempted to do more than merely assess the quality of the poetry in the *German Anthology*. The writer tried to define something of the unique quality of Mangan's style and to explain why his popularity with the ordinary reader was (and would probably remain) limited:

> The hot bronze of his genius runs into the most delicate and sinuous tracery with the same freedom and finish it would into a lumpish mould. Indeed, the slowness of his popularity is greatly owing to this. He rarely uses the common English metres. He uses whatever form the original or the first budding of the translation suggest.
>
> These metres are hard to be read at first—their harmony is not sing-song; many a person throws down a translation of MANGAN'S, saying this is mysterious prose; when, if he had read on, he'd have called it glorious music.[11]

It was also during the "spring and glorious summer" of 1845 that Duffy's hopes for a book of Irish ballad poetry were realized in the publication of the second number in his "Library of Ireland" series. Financially, it could not have meant anything to Mangan, but Duffy's unstinting praise must have been welcome. "Among the recent native poets, whose ballads enrich our collection", he wrote, "the first place indisputably belongs to Clarence Mangan." At the same time, he acknowledged that not many people could be aware of this. That name "will sound strange to many ears", he confessed, because Mangan had "comparatively seldom chosen to illustrate our native literature". Even that might be considered an overstatement. Of the hundreds of poems by Mangan that had been printed up to this time, literally only a handful were from the Irish.

The Ballad Poetry of Ireland, or *Bolg an Dana*, reprinted four Mangan poems as previously mentioned, three from the *Irish Penny Journal* and one from the *Dublin University Magazine*.[12] The latter may well have been a publication mistake, however, for this translation of Goethe's "Irish Lamentation" would not logically have been used instead of the fourth *Penny Journal* poem, "Lamentation of MacLiag for Kincora", which was inexplicably omitted. In the same collection appeared ten poems by Samuel Ferguson, six each by Edward Walsh, J.J. Callanan, and Thomas Davis, and four each by John Banim and Gerald Griffin, as well as several by other poets, anonymous ballads, and street songs. The review in the *Nation*, written by Davis, lauded Mangan's "perfect mastery of versification" and spoke of his "flexibility of passion from the loneliest grief to the maddest humour". But it added that next to his, Callanan's and Ferguson's poems stood up best and were also "simpler and more Irish in idiom". The book was immensely popular and continued to be reprinted for decades.

Mangan's friends were also publishing significant work during the first half of this year. Owen Connellan's *Annals* continued to appear piece by piece, but "the peasant from Tireragh", may not have enjoyed much of an immediate reward from his efforts, a shilling an installment being a rather high price for the not very well done translations. This year, too, John O'Donovan produced a *Grammar of the Irish Language* and it was well received, although he himself had grave doubts about the wisdom, or decency, of allowing it to be brought out under the auspices of the College of St Columba, a body of the Church of Ireland, as previously noted here. "I was told", he had written to Hardiman in 1844, "that no one reads Irish now but those bloody Swaddlers. It is a disgrace to read it."[13] But as no other sponsor came forward, and as Dr Todd encouraged him to go ahead with the project, O'Donovan let the *Grammar* appear. George Petrie, someone upon whom Mangan could count for encouragement if not close association, also was publishing. Still resident at No. 21 Great Charles Street, for it had been his home before it was the office of the Ordnance Survey's topographical department, he at last saw in print his important work, *Essay on the Round Towers of Ireland.*

Connellan, O'Donovan, and Petrie, with their diverse standards and their occasional bouts of internecine warfare (although it was always Connellan *versus* the other two in any serious dispute), were looking back to, and endeavouring to recapture the Irish past. All three appreciated that the beat of the heart of Ireland's history was heard most strongly in the cabins of rural Ireland. The urban regions,and especially the Pale, often seemed as remote as foreign territory from Kerry, Connemara and Donegal. Even though the Gaelic language was interdicted, there still existed a coherence between the olden days and the nineteenth century that was preserved by an oral tradition of great richness and variety. What no one could foresee, mercifully, in June and July of the unusually warm summer of 1845, was that this living continuity was about to be destroyed, not in part and not for a while, but almost completely, and forever.

[2]

> ". . . disappointment has been my lot in life; but praise to God! I am resigned. . . . if I possess any [ability] it has been the cause of my undoing. My juniors in the ministry have been preferred to me, in every instance, and I am convinced that a *less enlightened* set of men than those who have rapidly risen above me, can no where be found in the Irish Church."
>
> The Rev. C.P. Meehan to James Hardiman, 1848

Mangan's introduction to the Rev. Mr Charles Patrick Meehan came about as a result of the publication of the *German Anthology*. The priest had been a curate at SS Michael and John's for ten years, and he had frequently seen the poet "standing before the book-stalls at the Four Courts [then on the same side of the Liffey as the church building], the College wall, and elsewhere", but he had never met him. Perhaps significantly, he evidently had not seen "the strange individual" at Mass, either. But just "a few days after the appearance of the *German Anthology*", he wrote, "a gentleman employed on the *Nation* brought him to my attic [in the Presbytery] and formally introduced me to the author of the exquisite translations of which I had spoken rapturously." This introduction has already been mentioned in relation to Mangan's belief in phrenology, for the poet immediately "ran his hand through my hair *phrenologically*", much to Fr Meehan's amused surprise, after which the visit progressed in a more usual social fashion. This meeting was to have immense importance to the poet; the priest would be a faithful friend to him for the rest of Mangan's life.

From this point onward, Mangan was made welcome in the Presbytery, a large, tall, brick and granite-built structure with double, but narrow, Gothic style windows adjacent to the Church. In it was Fr Meehan's residence, his "attic", the comfortable quarters in the upper storey where they gathered. He invited to table whomever he pleased, and his friends were numerous, including the popular priest Fr James Healy and many of the young men who were active in Young Ireland or on the *Nation*. Mangan had stayed away from the *Nation* staff's social evenings, Duffy explained, because the high spirits of the young men intimidated the shy, melancholy poet, but at Fr Meehan's he read and recited to everybody's enjoyment, according to the priest. There is also the possibility that he avoided the newspaper men's get-togethers for the simple reason that he might have been expected to stand everyone a round of punch, and that he obviously could not do. Here he was a guest. The group in the Presbytery was sometimes as large as eight or ten, and it included a number of individuals Mangan also would have seen at the evening suppers had he attended them, men such as Thomas Meagher, R.D. Williams, Denis Florence MacCarthy, and Thomas D'Arcy McGee among them. The congenial society pleased him and was the first such friendly association he had had on a regular basis since the break-up of the Ordnance Survey.

Fr Meehan was thirty-three years old at this time and very well educated, particularly in languages, literature, and history. In fact, he confided in James Hardiman that a "purely literary life would be congenial to my tastes", and when the new colleges began to be discussed and then founded in the 1840s, he determined to try to get an appointment to one of them. He believed that he would be able to "profess French, Latin, Italian, and Greek", and that "in the department of German and English I would not be found deficient. . . ."[14] This, of course, sounds very much like Mangan himself speaking. The confidence such a scholar had in his ability to teach and translate may raise questions in the minds of readers who probably feel good about their achievement if they are fluent in a couple of languages and can read another one or two, but educational expectations and standards have changed drastically. In any event, a year later his hopes had faded. As matters turned out, he remained at SS Michael and John's for fifty-five years, always as a curate denied the least advancement, almost certainly because he was an intellectual, a vocal nationalist, and a dyspeptic, often ill-tempered, opinionated man who spoke his mind far more freely than the clerical hierarchy could tolerate.[15] He wrote, and he devoted much time to the care of the poor in his parish; but after 1848, he turned his back on politics.

Mangan almost certainly returned to a more active practice of his faith through the influence of Fr Meehan. There can be little doubt that his confidence in the clergy and its ability to help him when he asked for guidance had been sorely damaged by the reactions he had elicited from his spiritual advisors back in the 1820s. John Sheehan's assessment of the poet's interest in any church as "undemonstrative", or lukewarm, was almost certainly accurate. While he had no intention of becoming other than Roman Catholic, he had dipped often, if not especially deeply, into Eastern and esoteric religions. But Mangan liked to please his friends when he could, and the burden of showing up for Mass in SS Michael and John's would not have been onerous. However, the priest, in writing to Hardiman in July 1849, seemed to heave a sigh of relief when he told him, "I am glad to be able to inform you that Mangan received the sacraments and died like a Christian."[16] It is just as well we have this contemporary comment, because as an old man the priest was to write that Mangan had prayed and "heard Mass almost every day"; that he "occasionally" received communion and "knelt at the altar rail"; and that in "intervals of self-denial", when he was not drinking, "frequented the sacraments, and scrupulously kept faith with those who had secured his literary services."[17]

About Fr Meehan's influence on Mangan's drinking, not much is known. He certainly tried to discourage his overindulgence, and urged him to take Fr Mathew's pledge which, it has been said, he eventually took and broke several times over. A devoted temperance worker himself, Fr Meehan wrote that what the poet saw of the "marvellous revolution wrought by Fr Mathew impressed him beneficially" so that for months at a time he would give up alcohol altogether, and that during those intervals they had particularly enjoyable gatherings in the "attic".

In later years, Fr Meehan would insist that Mangan had had little or no tolerance for alcohol; writing to D'Arcy McGee in 1887, he observed that even "a spoonful" of an alcoholic beverage, whether whiskey or wine, seriously "upset [the poet's] nervous system". He also maintained that Mangan was " a *pure* man . . . *never* lowering himself to ordinary debaucheries or sensuality of any sort." As noted earlier here, he was to assert to friends that the poet had felt more fondness for opium than he ever had for drink. Fr Meehan, like Gavan Duffy, was not necessarily averse to revising the past, one suspects. Still, he left a valuable description of the poet in which one does not hear the amused if affectionate contempt that marred Wakeman's description, the self-righteous criticism of James Price, or the sensationalizing of John Mitchel. It follows in full.

> He was about five feet six or seven in height, slightly stooped, and attenuated as one of Memling's monks. His head was large, beautifully shaped, his eyes blue, his features exceedingly fine and "sicklied o'er" with that diaphanous pallour which is said to distinguish those in whom the fire of genius has burnt too rapidly even from childhood. And the dress of this spectral-looking man was singularly remarkable, taken down at haphazard from some peg in an old clothes shop—a baggy pantaloon that was never intended for him, a short coat closely buttoned, a blue cloth cloak still shorter, and tucked so tightly to his person that no one could see there even the faintest shadow of those lines called by painters and sculptors drapery. The hat was in keeping with the habiliment, broad-leafed [broad-brimmed] and steeple-shaped, the model of which he must have found in some picture of Hudibras. Occasionally he substituted for this headgear, a soldier's fatigue cap, and never appeared abroad in sunshine or storm without a large malformed umbrella, which, when partly covered by the cloak, might easily be mistaken for a Scotch bagpipe.[18]

Mangan wrote in his fourth biographical memoir for the *Irishman* that "Mr Meehan's distinguishing trait in all things is his earnestness", though he did not want to imply "anything morose or Puritanical. . . . Precisely the opposite". The priest had, as indeed had many of Mangan's associates and his father as well, a Milesian temperament, which meant that his nature was "lively, quick and bordering on choleric" and that he could be "carried away by impulse". Mangan was, on the whole, more generally positive in what he had to say about Fr Meehan than in his comments about O'Donovan, Petrie, Anster, or Todd, perhaps because he had been an employee of theirs, even of O'Donovan's in a sense, and thus subservient in his relationship with them. His friend Mr Meehan, he wrote, "is a genuine human being; not a mere make believe, a bundle of old clothes with a mophead at the top of them". He had not, at the end, quite finished his comments. Alone among his nine subjects, the priest, he declared, was the "one who will bear to be written of, over and over".[19]

[3]

'Tis true, that wrestling with the throng,
Ev'n in his inborn weakness strong,
He never lay defeated long:
The griefs that left him never gay,
Seem'd all in song to roll away; . . .
John de Jean Frazer, "The Doom of the Dreamer"

The lovely summer continued to spin out its long, lazy days. In Dublin, Mangan produced seven pages of "Stray Leaflets" for the *University Magazine* in August, along with the four-page "Khidder", another version of Rückert's "Chidher". This, and "The Wayfaring Tree" from the anthology, are among his most interesting compositions. Not major poems, perhaps, and not characteristic of his work as a whole because so easy-going and undemanding, they are comparable to "Twenty Golden Years Ago" in their illustration of how well Mangan could write with "the common touch" when he chose.

"Khidder's" modernity startles one at first sight. Instead of Rückert's simple ballad stanza, Mangan used an almost *vers libre* form which allowed for developments and variations totally lacking in the original poem. The story is that of the prophet Elias, called Khidder, who returns to visit the earth—every five hundred years in Rückert's poem, every thousand in Mangan's—to see if "mankind have filled up the measure of their sins, or whether the judgment of the world can yet be postponed a little longer." Where Rückert's poem consists of five stanzas of nine lines each, Mangan's is made up of ten stanzas of varied lengths for a total of 210 lines. Khidder/Elias passes the same spot each time he returns, and each time finds it dramatically altered. The ancient town, after a thousand years, has disappeared, for instance, and has given way to a pasture in a wilderness, leaving not even a memory of its existence with the shepherd. Mangan's final section was almost entirely his own. Here he described the city he himself knew, its noisy vitality and its excitement. *Sounds* predominate as again Mangan proves that his most powerful imagery is auditory. Perhaps because it is such a maverick, the poem has never been re-printed. A fair-sized sample of the last main division is given here:

How rose the strife
Of sounds! the ceaseless beat
Of feet!
The noise of carts, of whips—the roll
Of chariots, coaches, cabs, *gigs*—all
Who keep the last-named vehicle we call
Respectable—horse-trampings, and the toll
Of bells; the whirl, the clash, the hubbub-mingling
Of voices, deep and shrill; the clattering, jingling,
The indescribable, indefinable roar;
The grating, creaking, booming, clanking, thumping,
And bumping;
The stumping
Of folks with wooden legs; the gabbling,
And babbling,
And many more
Quite nameless helpings
To the general effect; dog-yelpings,
Laughter, and shout, and cry; all sounds of gladness,
Of sadness,
And madness—
For there were people marrying,
And others carrying
The dead they would have died for, to the grave—
(Sadly the church bell tolled
When the young were burying the old,
More sadly spake that bodeful tongue
When the old were burying the young.)
Thus did the tumult rave
Through that fair city—nor were wanting there
Or dancing dogs or bear,
Or needy knife-
Grinder, or man with dismal wife,

* * * * *

Or other doleful men, that blew
The melancholiest tunes—the which they only knew—
On flutes, and other instruments of wind;
Or small dark imp, with hurdy-
Gurdy,
And marmoset, that grinned
For nuts, and might have been his brother,
They were so like each other;
Or man,
That danced like the god Pan,
Twitching
A spasmy face
From side to side with a grace
Bewitching,
The while he whistled
In sorted pipes, all at his chin that bristled;
Or fiddler, fiddling much
For little profit, and a many such
Street musics most forlorn,
In that too pitiless rout quite overborne.[20]

It still sounds a lot like Grafton Street on a Saturday afternoon. It also sounds a bit like those other city poems of Mangan's, "The Howl Clew Man" and the "Lament for Johnny Kenchinow", both many years in the past.

If Mangan were looking over the world in a sort of time-travel fashion in "Khidder", he was surveying his own life in "The Way-faring Tree". He signed it "Selber" in his last use of that pen-name, perhaps a foreshadowing of the fact that he would before long abandon pseudonyms altogether. It is as if he now took "Selber's" statement as his own, which, of course, it was: *I am I and unfortunately I can be no other!* Here, too, the tone was one of museful, slightly sad, but generally resigned acceptance of things as they were. The very name "wayfaring tree" is so inherently paradoxical that it may have attracted the poet to build a poem around the image. The real plant is a large bush or shrub that flourishes along roadsides, providing shade for wayfarers. It is also sometimes called the snowball bush because of the appearance of its flowers. Whether Mangan ever really rested beneath a favourite "Wayfaring Tree" we have no way of knowing, but this pleasant imagery can be set over against that of the "Great Tree of my Existence" which in the *Autobiography* he described as "blasted", unable to put forth fruit or blossom. As with "Khidder", so with "The Way-faring Tree": the poem has never been anthologized, so the sample printed here is longer than it would otherwise be:

Old bachelor bards, having none to mind us,
Are seized at seasons with such a heart-aking
That, leaving home and its wants behind us,
We hie elsewhither, the spirit's car taking
Us east and west, and aloft and nether,
And thus I, also, both night and day faring
From Hartz to Hellas, pass weeks together
(In vision) under mine old Wayfaring
Tree,
My childhood's dearly beloved Wayfaring
Tree!

Free
Of pinion, then, like the lonely pewet,
I watch through Autumn its golden leaves dropping,
And list the sighs of the winds that woo it—
A somewhat silly but sinless eavesdropping!—
And sadly ponder those rosy dream-hours
When Boyhood's fancies went first a-May-Fairing . . .
Ah! we may smile, but the joys that *seem* ours
Soon leave us mourners beneath our Wayfaring
Tree!
Insolvent mourners beneath our Wayfaring
Tree!

Me
No Muse amuses or flatters longer,
No couplet cozens, no trashy trope troubles,
Yet, though my judgment grows daily stronger,
I love this blowing of psychic soap bubbles.
The soul tends always in one direction,
Its course is *homeward*; and, like a fay faring
Through airy space, even each deflection
But brings it nearer its destined Wayfaring
Tree.
Its way is short to its final Wayfaring
Tree.[21]

This summer, too, although probably more towards the end than the beginning, he arranged to contribute to the new *Irish Monthly Magazine.* Perhaps he knew the editor, Theobald Purcell; otherwise, it seems more than a little extraordinary that he should just now have begun a connection with such a rabidly unionist publication, although it at least had been re-named from its previous title of *Irish Union Magazine*. The first of his series, "Loose Leaves from an Odd Volume", appeared in October. His second contribution was a November short story, his final piece of fiction,

"The Threefold Prediction. A Psychological Narrative". It was nineteen pages long. In the same issue, another chapter of "Loose Leaves from an Odd Volume" appeared, although it and the last in January were very short. In the first were eighteen short pieces from Rückert. "Yes! true Poetry is wizard power . . ./But the Poet, what is he? Enchanted/Or Enchanter?. . ./Haunts he the World soul Tower?/ Or is he himself the world soul haunted?" Mangan asked with Rückert in "The Poet also an Artist". But the most memorable lines were undoubtedly in the lyric "The Night Is Falling":

> The night is falling in chill December,
> The frost is mantling the silent stream, . . .
> My soul is weary: I now
> Remember
> The days of roses but as a dream.

"The Threefold Prediction" was definitely what the poet would have called of a very strange order. Essentially its plot was that of "Appointment in Samarra", or Mangan's own short poem "The Angel of Death", an anecdote from the *Koran*. The gist of each is that Death cannot be escaped, but will meet one where Destiny has determined, no matter who or what interferes. More a summary of a plot than a developed plot and subtitled "A Psychological Narrative", it has more of the supernatural than the psychological about it, although where the poet himself was concerned, the line between the two might be very ill-defined.

Numerous instances of favourite Mangan motifs and subjects appear fleetingly throughout the text: references to numerology and especially to the number 17, Maugraby the magician, a whimsical hope that "you do not wear a wig", the reading of *Manfred*, Doppelgängers, the man without a shadow (Peter Schlemihl), the death of a student on the all-important date 4 March, and on and on. Most noteworthy of all is the romantic heroine's name—Frances—the name Mangan used for his first fickle love in "To xxxxxxx xxxxxxx". As usual, too, the poet could not pass up the chance to use comical names. The narrator is a physician, Dr Grosstrotter. There is also a "Herr Schmallwitz" and a couple of men named "Mohl" and "Groller" which let him observe that "Mohl is droll but Groller is droller".

The doctor, a resident of Vienna, is visited by his old friend Baron Kammerwill who seeks help for Frances, his wife, who is "committing the blunder of dying without any apparent wound", that is, of a psychical disorder. In due course, the doctor, who is very skeptical of the power of the invisible world's influence, confesses to the Baron that once even he, the doctor, has been "carried out of himself . . . by an emotion of divine enthusiasm", losing control when the woman he had courted (fourteen years previously) turned down his proposal of marriage. In a rage he had berated her, "Hope not to escape me!. . . For I am your Destiny!" What he does not tell the Baron, but what the reader has already surmised, is that the woman is Frances, the Baron's wife.

There is no doubt that the Baronness is really dying, although she is considered an hysterical hypochondriac and a victim of monomania or *idée fixe*. She has had disturbing predictions of her death. One came from a gypsy who warned her of the numbers 30 and 31—the date is 28 June 1824, and she is thirty-one years old, when the story opens. Another came from an apparition that appeared after her emotional reading of *Paul and Virginia* and pointed at a coffin engraved with her name and death date: "Frances, Baroness von Kammerwill . . . the 30th of June, 1824."

The climax of the narrative arrives two days later during a dinner party at the Baron's. The scheme is to distract the Baronness and ease her gently by the crucial hour of midnight. To this end, the doctor at her request patiently rereads *Paul and Virginia* to her and then gives her what he thinks is a "composing draught" that will "still the tumult" of her nerves without recourse to laudanum—he has declared himself against narcotics because "their operation is so various according to the constitution of the patient." Most unfortunately, the "droller" Groller has been up to mischief, and for a practical joke has switched medications—"the mad young man had wantonly transposed the places and labels of my medicines!" as the doctor expresses it in despair. Frances dies. Instead of a soothing syrup, the Baronness "had swallowed two ounces of quintessential laudanum. Yes! *I had been her destiny!*" The story thus illustrated not only the power of Destiny, in which Mangan claimed not to put much store, but also the power of the desire for revenge, about which he had written, the "revenge of personal wrongs is a mean passion". Mean, perhaps, but very strong. In a most extraordinary fashion, "The Threefold Prediction" was a continuation of "My Transformation. A Wonderful Tale". We find Mangan in his medical man persona most "innocently" taking revenge on his "Frances", known in "My Transformation" as "Eleanor Campion", who had jilted him in the context of that "Tale" just fourteen years earlier, the period also identified by "Dr Grosstrotter" as the time that had elapsed since *his* misadventure in love.

In the prose sections of the "Loose Leaves" he expressed opinions on a variety of topics somewhat in the manner of "A Sixty-Drop Dose of Laudanum". Here, he commented on Swedenborg, Schiller, the Ghost Seeress of Prevorst, and more ancient individuals such as Pythagoras, Zeno, Plotinus, "and many others of the old philosophers [who] recognize the existence of an all-creative Sun", the concept he had found and responded to in Dr Kerner's writings about Madame Hauffe. The seven short untitled prose items in the third and final "Loose Leaves" were Mangan on Mangan: "It is a senseless charge to bring against any eccentric gentleman who prefers health to fashion and comfort to custom, that he sets at defiance the opinions of society." And, declaring that Society as he knew it had no opinions, but only "usages": "The eccentric gentleman is clearly the monopolist of such opinions as are at all to be got at. It is society that sets *his* opinions at defiance." And further: ". . . there is little malevolence now in the world. We are simply afraid to tolerate anything unlicensed. . . . Civilization, like conscience, makes cowards of us all."

Evidently "The Threefold Prediction" was well received, for by the first of the year Mangan was writing another tale for the *Irish Monthly Magazine* and having trouble finishing it by the deadline, 10 January. On 8 January he wrote to editor Purcell asking for an extension because of the amount of time the translating for the *University Magazine* had taken (his last "Literae Orientales" chapter, fourteen pages long, appeared this month), and because he had been ill. Pleading for "editorial mercy", he promised, "Henceforward I shall rather be before than behind with you . . . ."[22] He finished this second story, but it did not appear in the March number which, as it turned out, was the magazine's last issue. On 25 April or slightly earlier he wrote about it to Duffy. "Martin Keene" was the publisher:

> I told you that I had written a tale for Martin Keene's Mag. It was Irish, and of a very strange order. I fear he *imagines* (I think he cannot conscientiously believe) that I owe him £1 sterling, and therefore keeps the MS from me. It would have made about 2 sheets for the Mag. Without at all resorting to the "spinning process", I am certain I could extend it to the proportions of a shilling volume. But more of this hereafter.[23]

Unfortunately, there was no "more of this hereafter". Mangan's story disappeared. The hints about its content certainly arouse curiosity, but not only has the story never been found, but neither has any other mention of it ever been identified. So it is that a thirty-two page story on an Irish subject, and of a "very strange order", by a most renowned Irish poet may come to light someday and give literary treasure-seekers a rare and glorious moment of discovery.

All things being equal, Mangan should have been fairly well off financially by September or October of this year, but he was no money manager, and as usual the pounds and pence probably slipped through his fingers before he had a chance to make their acquaintance. He had at last once again produced a full year's work, however, an indication that his health and his spirits were both improved. He had begun a new series in the *University Magazine*, "Spanish Romances and Songs", which never developed beyond this beginning, but which at least indicated renewed interest. Altogether he was represented by sixty-five pages of translations and commentary in the *University Magazine*, the material already noted in the *Irish Monthly Magazine*, and two poems in the *Nation*. With the publication of his two-volume *German Anthology* in the summer, things were looking up for him, and he undoubtedly was aware of it. But the good times had not long to continue.

[4]

For our dead no bell is ringing,
Round their forms no shroud is clinging,
Save the rank grass newly springing,
Kyrie Eleison
Whereso'er our steps are led,
They can track us by our dead,
Lying on their cold earth bed.
Kyrie Eleison

[Lady Jane Elgee Wilde], "A Supplication",
Nation, 18 December 1847

It was a bitter coincidence that the first appearance of the lethal potato blight in Ireland and the death of Thomas Davis both occurred in mid-September of the same year. The shattering effects of the latter on the hopes and dreams of the men of Young Ireland were immediately apparent. By contrast, the blight was for months, perhaps even a year or two, thought to be just another instance of a recurrent problem in the long list of problems besetting a society almost totally dependent for sustenance on one vulnerable food crop. Famines of lesser intensity had struck various segments of the rural population twenty-four times from the first quarter of the eighteenth century until 1851. As the population increased, the one-crop evil became all too apparent. "In 1821 and 1822 the potato failed completely in Munster and Connaught; distress, "horrible beyond description", was reported in and near Skibbereen"; and in Donegal, Galway, Ulster and elsewhere throughout Ireland, crops failed in 1830, 1831, 1832, 1833, 1834, 1835, 1836, 1837, 1839, 1841, and 1844. In short, potato crop failures had become so common that they were an ordinary part of economic life. Moreover two million people, around a quarter of the population of Ireland, were "in a state of semi-starvation every year, whether the potato failed or not".[24]

In spite of the widespread indifference to the poverty of rural people, there was concern about this particular potato blight almost from the moment it appeared. It had first showed up in England, Holland, and France, and it was clear from the beginning that the destruction it caused was complete. With devastating accuracy, Dr John Lindley, the first professor of botany in the University of London and the man behind the founding of Kew Gardens, wrote in late August 1845 that "a fearful malady" had descended upon the potato fields. In September when the blight was first reported in Ireland, he wrote in the leading British horticultural newspaper, "We stop the Press with very much regret to announce that the potato Murrain has unequivocally declared itself in Ireland. The crops about Dublin are suddenly perishing . . . where will Ireland be in the event of a universal potato rot?"[25]

The pleasant dry weather changed abruptly in July when "one continued gloom" settled over Ireland, with low temperatures, chilling rain, and scattered fog, but this did not much discourage potato growers, and the *Freeman's Journal* and *Nation* still predicted an abundant crop. Whether or not the weather had anything to do with the severity of the blight is uncertain. Heavy rains fell in September and damaged the crop, blighted or not. But it was not until October when most potatoes were dug that the more disturbing stories began to appear. Even then, Dublin was insulated by being able to draw its market supplies from areas that were unaffected. Rural areas themselves were shielded from immediately experiencing the worst effects of the destruction by two factors: they had—some of them—a few left-overs from the previous year's crop as well as other food supplies on which they could manage to survive for another half-year or so; and many areas were isolated enough to imagine that only local crops had been destroyed, as in the limited famines of years past, so their anxiety, while great, was not yet overwhelming. From the first, however, the Government in Dublin and London realized that "it was necessary to be prepared for famine in Ireland", and that it was going to be extremely difficult to find a food substitute for the potato.

Duffy, who almost never took a rest, had agreed to a holiday in July and August. Leaving his pregnant and not very healthy wife at home, and Thomas Davis in charge at the *Nation*, he set out on a typically energetic nineteenth-century walking tour. With him went his friends and fellow-nationalists John O'Hagan, who wrote poetry as "Sliabh Cuillinn" in the *Nation*, John Mitchel, a young solicitor who lived quietly with his wife in Banbridge and devoted a good deal of his professional time to defending accused Catholics, and John Martin, Mitchel's friend, eventually to be editor of the *Irish Felon*. The foursome planned a route that would take them through Ulster, but it was soon cut short. Within days, Duffy was called back to Dublin by his wife's serious illness. As soon as she had improved somewhat, he went into Wicklow to complete his holiday, but he did not remain long at peace there, either: Davis fell ill in early September.

At first, he assured Duffy it was only "English Cholera" with "perhaps a touch of scarlatina". The distinction between choleras was an important one, for the European or English variety was a relatively mild infection with recovery coming about in five days or less. By contrast, Oriental or spasmodic cholera was a deadly infection. A few days later, Davis was not much better. In an almost illegible scrawl he told Duffy that the illness was "a bad case of scarlatina", but he still expected to recover soon. His pathetic little note was filled with hopes and plans. Duffy took him at his word and answered light-heartedly, obviously confident that he would soon be seeing his friend in health again. It was not to be. Davis improved enough to go out briefly, evidently to visit Annie Hutton, the young woman to whom he had become engaged only the past July, but his condition worsened rapidly after he returned home, and he died before morning on Tuesday, 16 September.

The death of Davis, the golden child of Young Ireland, had incalculable repercussions. In him had been harmonized the discordant ideals and ideas of Celtic and Anglo cultures. Men such as Daniel O'Connell, who did not always concur in Davis's hopes and beliefs, agreed that his plans might be feasible if only everyone were as rational and honourable as Davis himself. That he was an urban Protestant, with a Trinity College education, and yet held a vision of a whole and healed Ireland in which such individual qualities would not set Irishmen at each other's throats made him unique in the political scene. His personal qualities of integrity and charm, in the best sense of that abused word, secured him a sympathetic audience where other men had failed to do more than antagonize their listeners. Although he had not yet acquired a countrywide following, he probably would have in time. But of time there was no more.

His loss inflicted such wounds upon his friends, who tended to be more devoted than merely fond, that it is doubtful if some, including Duffy, ever recovered from the shock of the sudden grief. Certainly, the hopeful alternative which he offered to divisiveness and hatred was, much of it, buried with him in the grave in Mt Jerome Cemetery. Duffy described the funeral in *Young Ireland*:

> . . . it was no cold funeral pageantry that accompanied him to the grave. In all the years of my life, before and since, I have not seen so many grown men weep bitter tears as on that September day. The members of the Eighty-two Club, the Corporation of Dublin and the Committee of the Repeal Association took their place in the procession as a matter of course, but it would have soothed the spirit of Davis to see mixed with the green uniforms and scarlet gowns, men of culture and intellect without distinction of party, and outside of all political parties. . . . The names best known in Irish literature and art might be read next day in the long list of mourners.[26]

All, it could be added, except that of James Clarence Mangan.

Other griefs besides the loss of Davis afflicted Gavan Duffy this autumn. His young wife, who had had such a difficult pregnancy, died only days after Davis, in giving birth to their second child. Or rather, she died of tuberculosis—"consumption"—whose effects were intensified by the pregnancy. This child, John, later went to Australia with his father and step-mother and would become a Cabinet Minister there.[27] Then, within a short time, another compatriot fell away when John Dillon, a co-founder of the *Nation*, was ordered by his physician to move to a warmer climate if he wanted to survive the consumption from which *he* was suffering. Additionally, the brilliant and personable young Thomas MacNevin, whose work in history had been honoured by being the first volume in the Library of Ireland series, and who could always produce a prompt, well-written article upon request, was stricken with "the most painful affliction that can befall a man of intellect". Only a few years later he would die in an English insane asylum of the mental disorder which now overtook him. Before long, John O'Hagan and John Pigot had to move to London to complete their legal training.

Duffy, emotionally desolated by so many losses in such a short time, and deprived of almost every friend and supporter from both the newspaper and his personal life, had to take some action, soon, to shore up not just the enterprise, but himself. "When I add that McCarthy and [Michael Joseph] Barry wrote only verses or occasional critical papers", he explained in his memoirs, "and Mangan and Williams verses exclusively, and Doheny's strength did not lie in journalism, it will be understood at what disadvantage the paper and the party were about to be placed". Enter, the stage direction might read, John Mitchel.

While the two branches of the Repeal Association, Old Ireland and Young Ireland, had not yet split *de jure*, they had in many senses already suffered a *de facto* division. Davis had been skilled at blending the two ideals in print; without completely alienating Old Ireland, he had been diplomatic enough to express convincingly the position of Young Ireland. That particular ability was not to be found in John Mitchel. Mitchel had already been made a member of the Eighty-two Club, the select social-cum-military group of Young Irelanders who dressed in green-and-gold uniforms for their meetings. Duffy liked Mitchel with whom he had spent part of his abbreviated holiday. He was impressed with "the vigour and liberality of his opinions, as well as by his culture and suavity". Mitchel was Trinity-educated, and it must have seemed to Duffy, a fellow-northerner, that he was able to choose quite independently the way he wanted to live. From youth, Mitchel had taken chances in situations where Duffy would have played it safe.

John O'Donovan, commenting on Mitchel, revealed that Mitchel's hatred for the British Empire had originated from two youthful imprisonments: the first had come about while he was attending school in Liverpool and got into trouble for "some daring act of boyish folly"; while the second resulted from his eloping with "a ward in Chancery, for which he was imprisoned for three months".[28] Meagher likewise admired Mitchel but may have stood in some awe of him, describing him as "quiet, stern, and fearless", a real Milesian.

Duffy's observations on Mitchel's appearance are interesting. Just "above the middle size", he was "well-made and with a face which was thoughtful and comely, though pensive blue eyes and masses of soft brown hair, a stray ringlet of which he had the habit of twining round his finger while he spoke, gave it, perhaps, too feminine a cast." He tended to be solitary, "silent and retiring". Although he spoke slowly, it was in "a form which would be abrupt and dogmatic if it were not relieved by a pleasant smile".

One feels it would have been unwise to rely too much on that "pleasant smile" to mitigate the harshness of what the man was saying, for he could be dangerous when forced, as it were, into the open. Although he had chosen to "live much alone", circumstances had now abrogated this choice by placing before him a challenge which it was not in his nature to reject. Thomas Flanagan, editor of a recent edition of Mitchel's *Jail Journal*, called the young barrister "a conservative anarchist", who waged war against the nineteenth century on behalf of the past. His thinking, even held in check by the limitations of the *Journal* and a keen irony, was often "apocalyptic". His language, while "splendid and various in its resources of rage, irony and invective", tended to fall short when he tried, or believed that he wanted to try, to affirm rather than to denounce.

Mitchel would be of great importance among the several men friends who touched the poet's life. In all cases, from James Tighe to the final name on the list, the youthful Joseph Brenan, they were gentlemen with great driving energy and excellent personal qualities: idealism, intelligence, imagination, and sensitivity. This was obviously no accident; Mangan's sights were set high—he aspired to excellence himself, reaching for the best or the truest, and perhaps paying an inevitable price in failure for his unrealistic aspirations. Most of these friends were also considerably younger than he, though more worldly-wise. His first affection for each was intense, and it moderated over time, as do most intense loves; but it was enduring. The men themselves were fond of the poet and had sufficient depth of character to be able to bear with his weaknesses and his sometimes irritating eccentricities. Of well-defined, often ambitious, character, several possessed the "Milesian" temperament, though others, such as Tighe and Duffy, seem to have been more sanguine than fiery. Interestingly, and perhaps inevitably, the poet first became acquainted with each of these friends at a moment of heightened emotion in his life. This autumn his own unusual personal well-being contrasted starkly with the stricken lives of those with whom he was in closest association. When Mitchel entered upon the scene, vigorous, fresh-minded, and brimming with righteous anger against Ireland's oppressors, he must have been irresistibly appealing to the grief-stunned *Nation* company, Mangan among them.

Mitchel was employed as writer-manager of the *Nation* and moved to Dublin in, it appears, either October or November 1845. He was to meet Mangan in the office of that newspaper, "a feat not easily accomplished; for Mangan had a morbid reluctance to meet new people", but he had seen him sometime earlier, as already noted in these pages, perched on the top of a ladder in the Fagel Library. The next passage comes as a surprise until it is remembered that the vast majority of the poet's contributions to periodicals had been unsigned:

> I had never heard of Clarence Mangan before, and knew not for what he was celebrated; whether as a magician, a poet, or a murderer; yet took a volume and spread it on a table, not to read, but with pretence of reading to gaze on the spectral creature upon the ladder."[29]

The selection of "a magician, a poet, or a murderer" is eye-catching, to say the least. Mitchel did not know how long Mangan worked in the Fagel Library, but he did not hesitate to assert that the poet carried "the proceeds in money to his mother's poor home, storing in his memory the proceeds which were not in money, but in another kind of ore, which might feed the imagination. . . . All this time he was the bond-slave of opium." As noted earlier in this memoir, Mitchel sometimes exaggerated or got his facts wrong, but it is hard to see how he could have been mistaken about this matter. He was, after all, referring to the specific period during which he met and became well acquainted with the poet.

As also noted earlier, Mitchel hated the whole British Empire, and he took the greatest pleasure in pointing out that, like himself, Mangan was opposed to things culturally British. After observing that Americans did not know Mangan's poetry because "British criticism gives the law throughout the literary domain of that semi-barbarous tongue in which I have now the honour to indite", he exalted:

> Mangan was not only an Irishman,—not only an Irish papist,—not only an Irish papist rebel;—but throughout his whole literary life of twenty years, he never deigned to attorn to English criticism, never published a line in any English periodical, or through any English bookseller, never seemed to be

> aware that there was a British public to please. He was a rebel politically, and a rebel intellectually and spiritually,—a rebel with his whole heart and soul against the whole British spirit of the age.[30]

To Mitchel, the "British spirit of the age" was barbarous commercialism and ruthless *laissez faire*. A spirit that placed an inordinate value on the activities of buying and selling, it was more and worse than that: cold, legalistic, self-righteous, pompous, and certain of English superiority. It did not so much devalue human beings as it ignored the existence of any claim they might make to consideration. He and Mangan, he believed, recognized each other as fellow creatures leagued against the forces of depersonalization. And a few months later, the poet would indeed write, "I hate thee, Djaun Bool", that is, "John Bull", a sentiment he cannot be imagined expressing before John Mitchel entered his life.

In November and December, the *Nation* reported that plenty of potatoes were for sale cheap in Dublin markets, but only because they were being rushed there "lest the rot spread and [the farmer's] whole stock become a mass of putrescence". The blight was surrounded by an aura of evil, and the words used to describe conditions—filth, corruption, putrescence, rot—added to the horror. The editors believed, optimistically as it turned out, that about half the potato crop would be lost, a frightening enough prospect, certainly, and exclaimed, "Alas! . . . for the unhappy country that has no power within it to take a step for its own salvation." Thus from the first, the situation had a political dimension. It was already clear to some in the Government that exporting enormous quantities of grain and other foodstuffs to England while Ireland faced starvation was not only an inhuman act but a stupid application of *laissez faire*. Nevertheless, that policy won out, and it would continue to be applied in spite of protests and frantic arguments against it. For that reason alone, it is accurate to say that British economic policy, not potato blight, was the actual cause of the death of over a million Irish, and the emigration of over a million more, during the five years of the Famine.

15

A Soul Redeemed

[1]

Thou wert a voice of God on earth—of those
prophetic souls
Who hear the fearful thunder in the Future's
womb that rolls,
And the warnings of the angels, as the
midnight hurried past,
Rushed in upon thy spirit, like a ghost-o'er-
laden blast.
Richard D'Alton Williams, "Lament for Clarence Mangan"

By the close of 1845 Duffy was striving to reconstruct a Young Ireland party, and he recruited a group of new men, or rather, he drew toward the centre several who had previously been on the periphery, writing for the *Nation* in some cases, but not closely involved. Of these, he was to declare, "Their opinions and policy were the same as those of their predecessors", and they were equally determined "that the National cause must not be sacrificed to any intrigue".[1] With hindsight, we know that although their "opinions and policy" might have been the same, their ideas on how to achieve their goals were different in quite important ways.

To preserve and consolidate whatever he could from the old cadre, Duffy first turned to the *Nation's* poets, or at least he named them first in his memoirs. Here were Denis Florence MacCarthy, Michael Joseph Barry, and James Clarence Mangan, men who, Duffy asserted, though erstwhile strictly verse writers, now "contributed critical papers of great interest". Unless some prose of Mangan's remains to be discovered, this was an overstatement in his case. And for some reason, the editor neglected to include the name of one of his most faithful poets and a friend of Mangan's, Richard D'Alton Williams who as "Shamrock" had written for the paper almost from the beginning.

Two individuals of whom Duffy hoped more than he received were Thomas Wallis and John Fisher Murray. The former had been Davis's tutor at Trinity College and was deeply, "perhaps inordinately", admired by Davis, the only criticism which I think Duffy ever made of his beloved friend. For his part, Wallis had returned Davis's affection and respect, and, Duffy complained, "sometimes suggested the audacious hypothesis that it was he who made Davis a Nationalist". One can read a chilly judgement of Mangan in Duffy's observation that Wallis lived "as secluded and unwholesome a life as Mangan"; but perhaps in that similarity is to be found also an explanation for Davis's tolerance of the poet's ways. Not only had Davis admired Wallis, but the latter's experience with journalism as editor of the *Citizen* might have been expected to make him particularly useful. As it turned out, he was a great disappointment and accomplished "next to nothing" in Duffy's opinion. However, at this same time, Wallis brought to fruition his hopes to publish some of Davis's works, only a one-volume selection but still more than Duffy managed, and this may have been a sore point with the editor. As for John Fisher Murray, he contributed an introductory elegy to Wallis's edition of Davis. A vigorous and able man, he exhibited habits as eccentric as Jonathan Swift's, in the eyes of the increasingly conservative Duffy. Still, he had encouraged Duffy in his work on the Belfast *Vindicator* and was induced to write pieces that were "racy and original" for the *Nation*, "a new feature in Irish journalism", Duffy averred. But he lived in London, and consequently he could not take any part in the day to day action in Ireland.

Six of Duffy's new men were particularly interesting as far as Mangan's story is concerned. Many of them were years younger than Duffy, who was himself only twenty-nine at this time, and were thus virtually a whole generation younger than Mangan. Once again, the poet's associates were his juniors. This raises the question not so much of why he was attracted to individuals younger than himself, since, given the situation, he had not much choice, but what he did if anything, to "adjust" to the discrepancy. It has been suggested that the "six year age error" was possibly a deliberate misstatement made because he feared being, or, it may be, seeming, middle-aged. While that seems too simplistic as a solution, it is likely that, at forty-two, he did feel like an old man with the twenty-year-olds of this group, and he can be envisioned explaining that he was not as old as he looked.

These young men are usually thought of as comprising Young Ireland's leadership: Thomas Francis Meagher, Thomas D'Arcy McGee, Richard O'Gorman, Thomas Devin Reilly, John O'Hagan who had been with Duffy, along with John Mitchel and Mitchel's friend John Martin, on the ill-fated tramp of the preceding summer—and, of course, most fatefully, John Mitchel himself. Pointedly, Duffy omitted from his list the name of Fr Charles Meehan who maintained such a close personal friendship with Mangan and others of the group, and who strongly advocated the cause of Young Ireland. The movement enjoyed little approval from the Catholic Church, partly because of the Protestant presence in it of men like Davis and partly because of the growing antipathy between Young Ireland and Daniel O'Connell. For this reason, in part, priests were few in its ranks, none besides Fr Meehan taking a very open or active part in Dublin, while somewhat farther afield Fr Kenyon lent his voice and support (and offered Mangan a home in Templederry when his darkest days were upon him).

It is not easy to trace Mangan's friendships in this group. Not a letter to any but Duffy has survived, nor, perhaps, did he have occasion to write to the others. He did not attend the *Nation's* weekly social gatherings and thus would have met some of the men only incidentally in the paper's office. Others besides Mitchel and Duffy may have invited him to their homes, but he would probably have declined those invitations just as he declined Mitchel's. He spoke of calling on Duffy at his home, but this may well have been a very rare occasion.

People's homes in general seem to have been intimidating arenas for him. Fr Meehan's was another matter, however. The "attic" Mangan visited at least frequently, if not regularly, and there he proved himself a genial companion, "ever ready to make or enjoy a joke". Whether his use of alcohol had become a matter of serious concern by this year is highly problematical. Duffy said his friend did not outwardly show the effects of heavy drinking until 1847, and there is no reason (beyond Duffy's record of considerable inaccuracy) to doubt his word. However, Fr Meehan may well have been seeing more of the poet at this time than did the extremely busy and increasingly political Duffy, and his tone certainly implies the worst. Emphasizing the intervals when the poet was "freed from that influence", he gave this example of Mangan's comradely presence among them:

> One evening in my attic when Meagher in the presence of D.F. MacCarthy, R.D. Williams, and half a dozen more, was reciting Antony's oration, over Caesar's corpse, and came to the "lend me your ears"—Mangan stood up gravely and said, "That's a wrong reading." "No," replied the reciter, "it's so in the book." "No matter, sir," rejoined Mangan, "the correct reading is, 'lend me your *cars*,' for Julius was killed near a car-stand, and Antony wanted to get up a decent funeral. What could be more absurd than to ask the loan of their ears?" [2]

Of the several men who were now the poet's companions, Richard D'Alton Williams stands out as noteworthy, and friendship with this young medical student may have honed Mangan's already strong interest in bodily health and "the vocation of medical man". Like Mangan, Williams was shy, diffident, and hesitant to attend the weekly get-togethers. But he had—also like Mangan—a keen sense of humour and a warm heart. Williams was a student at St Vincent's Hospital in St Stephen's Green when Mangan was admitted there in May 1848. Not much more than a year later he would write "Lament for Clarence Mangan", mourning his death and lauding the "mystic songs, faint, sad, and solemn" which flowed from his pen "Like light that left the distant stars ten thousand years ago". Some sense of Mangan's reputation as a seer, a concept that may be among the most difficult to appreciate today, is gained from Williams's verse, a portion of which appears as the headnote for this section.

Meagher and MacCarthy were the others named specifically by Fr Meehan in the intimate assembly in the Presbytery. Meagher made his political reputation as "Meagher of the Sword" on the strength of one fiery speech he delivered; from Duffy's point of view he was very limited, being primarily an orator. He was only twenty-two years old at this time, but the editor defended him against charges of looking like a dandified youngster with a "languid air", and called him rather "a great gentleman". MacCarthy was a favourite of Fr Meehan's, but Duffy believed that he loved his "Young Ireland colleagues more than he shared their political views", and "never developed revolutionary tendencies". Like Mangan, he had written for the *Satirist*, so they may have met as much as a decade before, although MacCarthy had been only seventeen when his first poem was printed there. He admired and respected O'Connell, joined the prestigious '82 Club, and would become a member of the Irish Confederation. More a literary man than an activist, however, MacCarthy followed a course that did not lead to the confrontation, trial, exile, or early death in a foreign land, one or more of which would prove the fate of Williams, Meagher, McGee, Reilly, Smith O'Brien, Duffy, and Mitchel.

Thomas D'Arcy McGee was the youngest of the men, but perhaps the most experienced. Life had not been easy for him, though it had not been dull, either. Before the age of twenty, he had worked in a newspaper office in New England, been employed as London correspondent for the *Freeman's Journal*, and learned some harsh lessons in survival. He was, I believe, the only one of the men ever to recant, and he came to speak condescendingly of the group's work and ideals. By the 1860s, he was praising Britain, denouncing Fenians, and underrating the influence of the Irish in the United States. He achieved a high position in government in Canada, but was "executed" by the Fenians before his forty-third birthday. Be that as it may, in the mid-1840s no fiercer Irish patriot was to be found than he, and Samuel Ferguson, at least, admired his poetry unstintingly, calling him the best of the Young Ireland poets. Duffy, who has himself been called "horse-faced", found McGee's physical appearance somewhat off-putting. It was not because he had "an unaccountable Negro cast of features" (which sometimes led to his being jokingly called "Darky" instead of "D'Arcy"), but because he looked "odd", even "ugly". That he had an "expressive" face and an agreeable manner was the best compliment Duffy could pay him on this score.

It must have been in 1847 or 1848 that McGee wrote a newspaper article that was half-memoir and half-critique of Mangan and his verse. It did not appear until 1852, in the *Nation*, where it was doctored to make it seem to have been written after the poet's death. For the most part, he simply repeated what others had said, including, "he is German with the Germans, a Mussulman among Turks, and a very *Senachie* among the Celts. . . ."; and, "his inspiration, like that of the Dervishes he is so familiar with, comes from opium eating." However, his description of the poet was vivid. He looked, McGee said, "like an anatomy new risen from the dead, with grizzled white hair bristling on his colourless and once handsome face; his cold big blue eyes staring vacantly, and his thin hand clutching a walking stick."[3] We tend to forget that Mangan wore a moustache during these years; like many men, he doubtless tried to shave—or be shaved—once a week, but having "white hair bristling on his . . . face" was probably the way he usually looked. That the poet had "cold blue" eyes is an original touch of McGee's, though many commented on the intensity of their blue colour and their large size.

Richard O'Gorman was another one of this group who looked like "a young dandy", and he had, further, the superficial reputation of being a playboy. Denny Lane, a *Nation* poet in Cork, half-seriously advised Duffy to be more like O'Gorman:

> Your amusements are too intellectual; you ought to ride, play billiards, hunt, shoot, and kick up shindies. Cultivate the society of O'Gorman: he has what you want—the intense enjoyment of physical existence. He would want, as I told him, to be put upon Tennyson and soda-water for half a year, while on the other hand your regimen ought to be beefsteaks and porter, fox-hunting and a main of cocks. Make yourself more of a brute without delay. Acquire low tastes and gratify them. . . .[4]

Duffy had known Thomas Devin Reilly for years, both having come from Monaghan where they had been friends, although Reilly was seven years the younger. In 1846 he was still "a big, clumsy, careless, explosive boy" in Duffy's phrase, but vigorous and able. Perhaps because Reilly eventually became a disciple of John Mitchel and left the *Nation's* ranks when Mitchel did, Duffy was obliquely critical of him. He observed, somewhat gratuitously, that Reilly's nervous headaches "disturbed his judgment, and even distorted his affections", though perhaps he meant only to explain Reilly's "disloyalty" in this way. Mitchel, for his part, praised Reilly as "the boldest of all Irish rebels", whose "master passion was love of Ireland, [and whose] religion was hatred of England". Obviously a man after Mitchel's own heart.

John Mitchel shouldered some of the editorial duties as early as December 1845, but responsibility for what appeared in the paper remained Gavan

Duffy's. He thus found himself in the unenviable position of having full accountability without full control. In spite of his emotional exhaustion and physical weakness he must surely have been knowledgeable about most of what was going into the *Nation*, but before the old year was out he was in trouble with the Government because of something Mitchel had written. In a lengthy article in the 10 January 1846 number, he explained the paper's official editorial position on what Mangan termed "the railway matter". The gist of the dispute was that Mitchel had blazed away at England, declaring that it was unacceptable and threatening for "anyone" to menace Ireland with the use of the railways against the interests of the country, an offence which he believed English authorities had committed. If such a threat were carried out, he warned, retaliation would be swift and effective. Duffy stood up for him and for this position, asking, "Does any slave think that these atrocities should be threatened against Ireland by an insolent enemy and receive no answer. . . ?" These were fighting words. The authorities were not pleased. In the 24 January issue, readers learned that Duffy had been indicted for "seditious libel" and that John Mitchel would be the attorney for the defence in the trial that was to take place in the summer.

Duffy meanwhile was still in very poor health and undoubtedly suffering from depression. It did not improve his shaky condition that internal disruptions were increasing in the Repeal Association. In fact, from about this juncture, the differences between O'Connell's so-called "Old Ireland" and the men of "Young Ireland" were progressively well-defined in terms of their radically divergent attitudes towards the use of force to achieve their goals. In this, O'Connell may appear to have been on the side of the angels, for he was a pacifist who vehemently rejected physical (though certainly not verbal) confrontation. By contrast, many Young Irelanders embraced the notion of combat. It has sometimes been speculated that O'Connell's conviction was strictly practical, that, seeing no possible way of getting weapons, he pragmatically rejected the use of weapons; but it was also a principled position. Certainly the other side in the debate could have gained by an infusion of practicality. Somehow, they seemed to believe pikes and staves and a few old firearms would suffice in the hands of men with a just cause—an idealistic fantasy for which John Mitchel must bear much of the responsibility. Eventually, Duffy, among others, would turn away from the possibility of using force against the English and opt instead for a political campaign based on education and argumentation. But that time was not yet, and 1846 opened on a miserably contentious note, without any sign of harmony on any hand, and the worst months of the first year of the Famine still ahead.

[2]

9 January 1846

My dear Duffy,
I am truly grieved by what you tell me. Let us, however, hope for the best. I have myself "that within which passeth show", but I never despair—though I confess that I do look forward to death as a relief. Will you say Thursday in lieu of Tuesday? I shall, at all events, call on you on the evening of that day (the 15th) and if I cannot see you I will call again on Friday evening. . . .
Yours through aeons of aeons,

J.C. Mangan

How often Mangan stopped by the *Nation* office during the disturbed autumn of 1845 is simply unknown, but because of his anxiety about his mother and the upheaval among the newspaper's staff after Davis's death, one imagines that it probably was not very frequently. From August onward, everything he wrote went for a while to the *Irish Monthly Magazine*. In December, for the January number, he sent it what would be his last "Loose Leaves from an Odd Volume". Also this month what turned out to be his final installment of the "Literae Orientales" was printed in the *Dublin University Magazine*. Although the last paragraph of this chapter told readers that another would appear and would deal with a complicated business, "the extraordinary metres, peculiar to Oriental poetry" and the rules that guided their poets, it was not to be. The assignment, though certainly not simple, normally would have been a pleasant challenge for Mangan, but the circumstances of this period were anything but normal.

The "Loose Leaves" revealed the subject on which his attention was now to be increasingly focused: God, and man's spiritual nature. Over the remaining years of his life, the poet would be much given to declarations about God and faith. Here, he quoted with approval Shelley's dictum that "Every religious man is a poet." But in the midst of familiar "spiritual" subjects such as Madame Hauffe, Swedenborg, and the Inner Sun, readers found themselves confronted with the rather startling piece of theology that "When a man [has] attained the highest degree of religiousness [he] should find that he had no religion at all."[5] While it would not be accurate to say that Mangan himself reached such a state, it is true (as noted already in these pages) that Fr Meehan seems to have heaved a sigh of relief when he was able to declare that Mangan had "died a Christian".

The poet never seems to have questioned the existence of God or the "large tenets" of his faith, but his inquiring mind led him to read widely about all sorts of religions, and, as we will see, not all the things he found himself believing were orthodox. Very surprising to encounter is this, for instance:

> In the religious man, hate must precede love. Such a man must first hate the spirit of the world. He must hate with immitigable hatred all that the world loves—Pleasure—Glory—Riches, "yea, and his own life also." When his hatred is perfect, his love is born from it as its legitimate antithesis. This is Holy Love, commencing for the Highest Being, and terminating for the lowest, but not at all including the lover himself.[6]

Nothing like this had been heard from Mangan before this time. He had so often written tenderly about love, forgiveness, and loss, reserving his dark emotions for a more or less attractive melancholy or grotesqueries like "The Four Idiot Brothers", that it is difficult to associate him with the violent expression of an emotion such as hatred. The last phrase—"not at all including the lover himself"—was, in and of itself, and without further qualification, almost a heresy.

February 1846 saw Mangan's first nationalist poem published in the *Nation*; "The Warning Voice's" route into print was not an easy one. Apparently, he wrote the verses sometime in January and turned them over to the newspaper. D.J. O'Donoghue relates this story that had been told to him by the Dublin physician Dr Nedley about this transaction:

> A certain distinguished Dublin physician informs me that he saw him one bitterly cold night, insufficiently clad, steal into the *Nation* office, and hand into Mr Fullam [or Fulham], the manager, a few pages of manuscript, begging at the same time that some money should be given to him on account. The manager told him that he was prohibited from doing so; he had received peremptory orders not to advance money to any contributor. Mangan implored so earnestly that at last he was given a small sum, and my informant tells me that one would have imagined from his manner in receiving it that he had just been reprieved from a sentence of immediate death. The sequel is pathetic. The manuscript handed in was the "Warning Voice", which appeared in the next issue of the paper.[7]

In a few days he received the proofs and took them to Trinity College Library with him, because on 9 February he had to write Duffy:

> My dear friend, I have mislaid the proof somewhere among the College papers, amid which, a century hence, somebody
>
> "In digging the foundation of some closet
> May turn it up as an antique deposit."
>
> Will you have another pulled for me? I'll take care to divide and number [the stanzas], as you suggest, an will, an't please Apollo, make the whole tell well. Excuse my levity—it is merely in my ink stand, not in my nature—and may appear ill-timed just now, when, as I believe, we are on the verge of the most tremendous calamity of ancient times or modern.[8]

Although preoccupied with the problem which he had carelessly created, he still found time for speculating on religion, via one of Ralph Waldo

Emerson's essays: "I happen to be scribbling this on an open page of Waldo Emerson", he wrote, and had just encountered the words, "Paul, who calls the human corpse a seed". This was, he fumed, "Balderdash! Paul was a man of common sense. His words are, 'It is sown a natural body—it is raised a spiritual body.'. . . *The sowing is the giving of existence to man as a natural being in a natural world.*" He went on, "The resurrection—the (anastasis) (standing up) of St Paul, takes place in the spiritual world . . . the standing up of the true spiritual man in the spiritual world *is* the resurrection . . ." which is an interesting if not entirely orthodox conclusion.

By 18 February, he had received another copy of the proofs and had made some corrections. He sent it back to the newspaper with the following:

> My dear Duffy,
>
> An accident will deprive me of the pleasure of seeing you until next week [this was written on Wednesday. What the "accident" had been he did not say.] Name any day then you please, I hope to have another poem ready. I think the title of the present one might be altered with advantage. Suppose what I have suggested, or "A Second Voice as of one crying in the Wilderness"—if not too profane.
>
> I hope you will have the capitals looked to—they were all in the MS. . . . The words, "*and foam of the Popular Ocean*" form but one line.[9]

The biblical allusion probably seemed inappropriate or far-fetched to Duffy. The designation "one crying in the wilderness" is from Isaiah, but generally is taken to refer to John the Baptiser; it is followed by "Prepare ye the way of the Lord", with John's warning to repent and live purely to prepare for the advent of the Christ. Mangan's "warning", on the other hand, was more like that given by God to Moses at the end of the forty-years of wandering in the wilderness: "This is the land which I sware unto Abraham. . . . I have caused thee to see it with thine eyes, but thou shalt not go over thither."[10] Speaking to "the True and the Faithful", the poet warned that, although "an era/Of Knowledge and Truth,/ And Peace—the *true* glory!" was not a "chimera", nevertheless:

> On *you* its beams glow not—
> For *you* its flowers blow not,
> *You* cannot rejoice in its light,
> But in darkness and suffering instead,
> You go down to the place of the Dead!
> To *this* generation
> The sore tribulation,
> The stormy commotion,
> And foam of the Popular Ocean,

The struggle of class against class;
The Dearth and the Sadness,
The Sword and the War-vest;
To the *next*, the Repose and the Gladness,
"The Sea of clear glass,"
And the rich Golden Harvest.[11]

"The Warning Voice" appeared in the 21 February number of the *Nation* and was received with enthusiasm. It remained a favourite with nationalists for years and apparently far out-shone, in their eyes, the much finer "Dark Rosaleen". It was probably Duffy who called it "the most impressive poem, perhaps, we ever published". This was no small praise, since it set the work above Davis's, Ferguson's, Walsh's, and all those others whose poems had been applauded in the *Nation* for the past three-and-a-half years.

What made it so impressive to readers of the last century? Even O'Donoghue towards the close of the 1800s wrote that it soared "high beyond the sometimes petty plaints of the poets of the day". To begin with, then, a "call to arms" in such a prophetic voice had great appeal for those caught up in the prevailing apocalyptic atmosphere, and this meant most readers of the *Nation*. Moreover, "The Warning Voice" was made to be read aloud, which it often was; even today, when read with conviction to an interested audience, it generates considerable feeling. And, finally, it was of course all too timely. Although he used many abstractions, the poet grounded the poem in the concrete horror all around. Thus, after the opening—"A day is at hand/Of trial and trouble,/And woe in the land"—the second stanza drew the reader, line by line, straight into his newspaper's bleakest assessment of the disaster that threatened them. Surely, Mangan's refusal to make a blithely optimistic forecast rang true to people who in all honesty could not see a solution ahead for their plight, including its most appalling aspect:

And the Powers abroad
Will be Panic and Blight,
And phrenetic Sorrow—
Black Pest all the night,
And Death on the morrow!

This spring the *Nation* became a journal of Famine news. It was now clear that not "just" half, but almost the entire potato crop had been lost, as the potatoes which had been stored when they looked healthy were found, when taken out into the open again, to have rotted and turned into a "putrescent mass". A 14 February 1846 editorial anticipated disaster when all the healthy crop had been used:

> Nearer, nearer, wears the day that will see fell Hunger . . . Plague in its train, [stalking] over this devoted land. From almost every county in Ireland come reports of more and more urgent alarm and terror as the earthed-up potatoes are uncovered and found masses of loathsome rottenness.

In March the editor sorrowed, "It is a ghastly inspiration that Famine kindles, cypress and yew, and nightly-shrieking mandrake, furnish the dismal coronals that our poets are gathering these days." To a certain extent, the poets romanticized the tragedy, as the choice of words in the above sentence makes obvious, but this may have been the only way in which they could express the inexpressible. In fact, when Christopher Morash selected poems for *The Hungry Voice: The Poetry of the Irish Famine*, it became apparent that not much poetry of quality was produced on the subject until a couple of years into the disaster. Mangan, in short, was one of the few, if not the only, poet of merit to address the Famine in its early months.

The role of the *Nation* as a national newspaper was defined by its editorials on measures taken and not taken to counteract the effects of the Famine. Already, debate raged as to what these measures should be, and it was becoming obvious that all too often talk was to be substituted for effective action. O'Hagan wrote to Duffy in words that give the unfortunate impression that the Famine would be a good topic for political journalism. That was certainly not what he intended, but it shows that the equivalent of today's "photo-op" threatened even then to degrade journalism to the level of a mere commercial enterprise:

> Do you remember me speaking to you when you were here about keeping perpetually hammering at the famine, and the remedies which ought to have been and were not applied? I think there was an opportunity for you of putting the *Nation* at the head of public opinion in Ireland on that question. Gird yourself to the work and come out with one or two of your most forcible articles.[12]

Mangan, who had such a singular attitude towards food and eating, was perhaps more sensitive than most to what could be called the psychological import of famine. His rather specious contention that genius did not require much in the way of "animal diet" may have been a development of his last troubled months on this earth, and it may have been largely factitious; but there are enough allusions to eating in his work to suggest that he had come to that dangerous conclusion partly from making a virtue of necessity. Still, there is no indication that he suffered real hunger before the last two years of his life. He might not have had much to eat sometimes, but he had had something, and when he did not, the dearth most often had been caused by his own choice to spend his money on something else.

His situation thus involved one crucial element missing for the famine victims: the opportunity to *choose*. They had no control over what happened to them; their powerlessness was absolute. To regain a semblance of authority over their own lives some of the dying chose suicide, some parents chose to end their children's lives before they starved to death, some starving souls chose to start walking toward a mirage of hope, and still others chose to wrap themselves in a fragment of blanket and sleep life away on their cabin floor. Such impotence deeply moved the poet. His greatest sympathy was always for those who had lost every vestige of control over their lives; a great motivation in his own life was to hold on to what limited control he had over it.

Without doubt, had there been no Famine, Mangan would not so passionately have turned his best attention to Irish poetry. "Political" commitment alone would not have wrought the change. As Robert Welch explained in his consideration of Mangan's life, he "had the misfortune to live through one of the most chilling periods of Irish history", but he was not submerged in its tragedy without a struggle: "What is extraordinary is that he tried, for a few months, to measure up to it, and in doing so became something of a spokesman for the afflicted and starving. Unlike most of the other *Nation* poets he became national, even nationalistic, without failing to be a poet as well."[13] In fact, Mangan sustained this role not just for "a few months", but for three years; his last poem published during his lifetime was "The Famine" which appeared in the 9 June 1849 issue of the *Irishman* less than a fortnight before his death.

* * * *

The measure of Duffy's exhaustion was that in spite of knowing the sort of thing Mitchel was likely to write, he still left him in charge of the *Nation* and went into the countryside for the quiet and solitude he could not find in Dublin. He hoped also to spend some time working on the next volume for the Library of Ireland series. Dumdrum, the site of his retreat, was a pleasant health resort much favoured by city invalids who went there "to drink mountain goats' milk". Peace did not drop like balm upon him, however, and, "When the need arose I rushed into town and when it was over I rushed back again."[14] Meanwhile, he read the *Nation* very much like any subscriber and depended on his friends to keep him abreast of how matters were going in the office. He must have been away at least a month when, in early April, John O'Hagan wrote to warn him of dissatisfaction with Mitchel. The acting editor, O'Hagan protested, was dealing with too many "incongruous matters" and was ranging much too far afield in his articles, particularly in a late one about India. Mitchel had indeed been lambasting the British Empire, "that monstrous commercial firm", for its actions against the Sikhs, and he had suggested that "the blow which is to destroy the English Empire in the East is likely to be struck 'nearer home'." About this comment, O'Hagan almost despaired. "Heaven and earth", he exclaimed, "what is the meaning of this?"[15] Mangan had perhaps read this article about India in advance of its publication, for in the same number of the newspaper appeared a whimsical eight lines by him entitled "To the Pens of the Nation", ending "Sing a song of SIKHS, Pens."

There was also a brighter part in O'Hagan's letter. "You are doing remarkably well in poetry", he assured Duffy, adding the curious praise, "Mangan is sticking to you like a brick." Two Mangan poems to which O'Hagan specifically referred were "The Domiciliary Visit" and "The Song of Hatred". The former was a rhymed dramatic sketch, brief and entertaining, which wittily made the bitter point that in Ireland a man's home was scarcely his own, much less his castle. The latter, "The Song of Hatred", had much greater significance; it was the first in the Irish poet's short but shocking series of what can best be described as "hate poems". Viewed together, they are an aberration in his canon, their violent, angry tone making them very different from anything else he had written or would write. The first was a translation from the German poet Georg Herwegh, and it minced no words:

> No more oiled speech! it is time the drove
>   Of despots should hear their fate read—
> We have all had quite enough of love—
>   Be our watchword henceforth hatred!

Like the passage on the hatred of the world that must be felt before Holy Love can ensue, "The Song of Hatred" comes as a complete surprise to the reader. One suspects it may have surprised Mangan, too, to find himself uttering such sentiments. But Mitchel's vigorous and outspoken antipathy had introduced an alternative to the firm but polite utterances characteristic of the *Nation* men. Mangan and Mitchel were very dissimilar in temperament, but they shared at least one quality: a long and deep resentment—in the one, buried, in the other, perfectly open—of power exercised over them when they themselves had no force with which to counter it. Thus Mitchel opened a door through which Mangan gratefully bounded.

On 4 April appeared the second of the "hate poems", "Freedom and Right", with the challenge, "Yes! tremble, ye Despots! The hour will have birth/When, as vampires and bats, by the arrows of Light,/Your nature, your names, will be blasted from Earth!" And on 11 April there was another, "Fire and Light", from Herwegh: "Beware, the Fire, the Light we kindle!/If, of the two great rival Powers/Now Arming, one be doomed to dwindle,/'Tis you and yours, not we and ours!"

Probably no later than mid-April Duffy gave up on his holiday and returned to Dublin. It was also at this time that Mangan's final two hate poems, both original, appeared in print: the knife-sharp "To the Ingleeze Khafir Calling Himself Djaun Bool Djenkinzun", that is, "To the English Infidel Calling Himself John Bull Jenkinson"; and the inimitable "Siberia". The latter has always been recognized as one of his finest poems, while the former, although much less has been said about it, is an outstanding example of the poet's sarcastic wit at play, a masterpiece of its kind.

These two poems make a wonderfully contrasting pair, as if Mangan had written them to show the extremes of hatred—hot and cold—and perhaps he did just that. Although light-hearted, "To the Ingleeze Khafir" is venomous, and as hot as "Siberia" is cold. The settings first establish the contrast, the opposite climates of Persia and Siberia speaking volumes about the subject matter. The word "hate" itself leaps out at the reader from the first line of "To the Ingleeze Khafir"; in the chill of "Siberia's silence" it does not appear at all. The *soi disant* "old fogy" Moslem who is the narrator of the former poem is literally spitting mad as he talks to the despised Englishman:

I hate thee, Djaun Bool, . . .
I hate thee like sin,
    For thy mop-head of hair
Thy snub nose and bald chin,
    And thy turkey-cock air; . . .

I spit on thy clothing,
    That garb for baboons,
I eye with deep loathing
    Thy tight pantaloons![16]

An articulate curser and name-caller, he has utter contempt for "John Bull", for his appearance, his behaviour, and, interestingly enough and most of all, for his lack of respect for his "mufty", the Pope. By contrast, the omniscient but uninvolved narrator of "Siberia" speaks through teeth clenched—against the cold. "Siberia", as paralyzed and frigid as "To the Ingleeze Khafir" is busy and torrid, depicts a frozen world where the numbing of the feelings is absolute. No life flourishes; the only inhabitants are "exiles" whom Mangan depersonalizes by using the singular noun, not even capitalizing it, though the reader hears it as THE EXILE, a representative figure like The Wanderer or The Outcast. "Blight and death alone" exist "in Siberia's wastes". Even Pain, though "acute", is "dead", and salty tears "freeze within the brain". We learn of hatred here only by oblique suggestion in references to paralysis so complete the exile cannot even "curse the Czar" who has sent him into this outer darkness. Indeed, hate itself is immobilizing. Not the cloven tongue, but "the sands and the snows" in the hearts of all those sent to this remote place have rendered them speechless. Hopelessness is their lot. The exile, when he finally dies, will be "scarce more a corpse than ere/ His last breath was drawn."

> In Siberia's wastes
> Are sands and rocks.
> Nothing blooms of green or soft,
> But the snow-peaks rise aloft
> And the gaunt ice-blocks.
>
> And the exile there
> Is one with those;
> They are part, and he is part,
> For the sands are in his heart,
> And the killing snows.[17]

Mangan produced a highly original poem in writing "Siberia", but it had a fair assortment of precedents. One poet of his own time to take up such extraordinary subjects on a regular basis was the German Ferdinand Freiligrath who, in "Iceland Moss Tea" and "The Skating Negro", both translated by the Irish poet, dealt with material that, like Mangan's "Siberia", was far beyond the experience of his readers. But his more important indebtedness was to Dante. The "wounding Ice-wind", "blackened blood", tears frozen within the brain, sands in the heart, killing snows, and a place where "man lives, and doth not live/Doth not live—nor die" come straight from the frozen Lake of Cocytus in the bottom-most pit of Hell in *The Divine Comedy*. This region of ultimate sin, evil, and despair, Dante had reserved for traitors (which no doubt exiles in Siberia may be assumed, after the custom of the country, to have been). It was to this lowest pit that he relegated the thirteenth century Count Ugolino who, with his sons, was treacherously walled up in a tower and left to starve to death. This grisly story was said to be one of Mangan's favourites. According to Fr Meehan, the poet enjoyed hearing it recited by a young priest friend of theirs, a member of the group that assembled in the "attic" for social evenings. According to others, Mangan himself liked to recite the passages. Suffice it to say that it contained several motifs which had grim applications for him including a father and his sons wrapped in a death-agony, and depressing betrayal from an ill-defined, never overtly identified, origin.

The critic Welch read in "Siberia" a profound metaphor for the condition of Ireland in 1846 and also for the condition of the poet himself: frozen, as one with the dead. The "cloven tongue" image—"Each man's tongue is cloven by/The North Blast, that heweth nigh/With sharp scymitar"—he took to be a symbol of "the psychological difficulty Mangan had expressing himself in his own voice"; and also of the suppression of the Gaelic language and the imposition of English. Wisely, he opined that the use of this metaphor was "almost certainly unconscious" on Mangan's part. Like most writers would, perhaps, he found it a powerful image for blocked or inhibited expression, and he called attention to its use by such modern authors as Thomas Kinsella, John Montague, and Sean O'Riordan for whom he believed it represented "a mutilation performed by the Saxon" amounting to "a kind of cultural emasculation".[18]

Mangan followed these poems on 2 May with another original work for the *Nation*, "The Peal of Another Trumpet", which put aside the theme of hatred, as such, and sounded "another trumpet" for his readers' ears. He included a call to arms in a headnote said to be from "a celebrated French Pythoness"—"*Irlande, Irlande, rejouis toi! Pour toi l'heure de vengeance est sonné*"—and also challenged readers: "Are you dastards? Are you dolts?/Irishmen! shall *you* be seen/ With white lips and faltering mien. . . ?" Whereas the fourth and fifth stanzas praised Irishmen for possessing "gentler gifts" which would not permit them to ignore what they saw and heard on every side, he did not conclude on this note:

—the wail of Want,
The despairing cry of Weakness,
    Rings throughout a stricken land,
And blood-blackening Plague and gaunt
    Famine roam it hand-in-hand!

And the final stanza rallied his audience:

But for more, far more, than this,
    Youths of Ireland, stand prepared!
Revolution's red abyss
    Burns beneath us, all but bared—
And on high the fire-charged Cloud
    Blackens in the firmament,
And afar we list the loud
    Sea-voice of the unknown Event.
    Youths of Ireland, stand prepared![19]

Although he must have been under great emotional stress by this time, he held himself together during the days and nights of caring for his mother and through the weeks of worsening famine news and political contention. Indeed, the poem that general acclaim designates his greatest,

"Dark Rosaleen", would be published in the *Nation* before the end of May.

[3]

O my Dark Rosaleen,
    Do not sigh, do not weep!
The priests are on the ocean green,
    They march along the Deep.
There's wine . . . from the royal Pope
    Upon the ocean green;
And Spanish ale shall give you hope,
    My Dark Rosaleen!
    My own Rosaleen!
Shall give you heart, shall give you hope,
Shall give you health, and help, and hope,
    My Dark Rosaleen.

Mangan, "Dark Rosaleen"

Not much past the middle of April 1846, Mangan wrote Duffy an undated letter that is of crucial importance for its precise statement of just how far the poet now felt ready to go in committing himself to the national cause. Mangan always used words with much care, so his exact phrasing is worth noting. He gave Duffy credit for the change: "I know your generosity. It amazes me: by my soul it does!" he wrote, and it probably did, for he would grow increasingly sure that he did not deserve the kindnesses shown him. Then he continued with this critical sentence: "If you can derive any satisfaction from knowing that it has given new impetus to my determination to devote myself almost exclusively to the interests of my country in future I shall feel the less remorse for having so monstrously trespassed on you."[20] With the words "to devote myself almost exclusively to the interests of my country" he made it clear not only that he was taking another cautious step along the road to full dedication, but also that he was still leaving himself a way back, or out—yet another instance of the "mousehole" he still had to have available. Nevertheless, with this said, he moved just that much closer to full commitment than he had ever dared move before.

It could not have been easy for him to decide to dilute the identity of "German poet" and internationalist which he had cultivated for over ten years. Moreover, the poet never underestimated the importance of any step of his journey; indeed, by the usual standards, he probably overestimated the importance of such things as every New Year, every new acquaintance, and every shift in routine. Predictably, then, before he could turn to Irish poetry, he had to bring his long-running "Anthologia Germanica" to a close, which he did with the twenty-second chapter in the June number of the *Dublin University Magazine*. Hereafter, he would translate some from German and other European and Eastern poets, but the focus of his concentrated attention was forever altered. His bond with the *University Magazine* had lasted for eleven years; essentially it had been for four sheets annually of mostly German poetry. What his "almost exclusive devotion" and, not much later, his complete dedication, to his country's interest entailed for him was giving up this role, and the security of his most reliable income. In addition, it was even possible the editors would jettison him from their conservative unionist pages altogether, no small concern for a man in his position. In short, to become an "Irish poet" required authentic risk and sacrifice.

He closed sadly: "Circumstances, my dear friend, prevent me from going out in the evening. But I will only work the harder for my self-imposed imprisonment." That he was sole nurse for his mother seems fairly certain; finances and the perfidy of the old woman servant who stole the furniture had probably seen to that. But no matter how sad or serious the import of a letter to Duffy might be, the poet invariably tried to end on a light note, and the postscript's puns on lines from *Julius Caesar* probably gave his friend a chuckle. Abbreviated, it went thus: Mark Antony had "a cask of brandy-and-water marked N.V.S. (Not Very Strong)". His maidservant drank it up and refilled the cask with sea water, which caused it to burst, leading to the mighty line: "Sea-water rent the N.V.S. cask—eh (or ah!), maid?" That is, of course, "See what a rent the envious Casca made."

True to his word, he sent his first Irish poem to the *Nation* just a month after writing this letter: an eighty-line rhymed version of "The Dream of John McDonnell." Fourteen years earlier, "The Dream" had appeared in the *Dublin Penny Journal* in an anonymous blank verse version that has often since been attributed to Mangan, although almost certainly the work of John O'Donovan. He left with Mangan an attractive literal translation of "The Dream", probably hoping it would inspire him to the versification of the poem. Mangan almost certainly worked either from this manuscript, which is still a part of a Mangan manuscript collection in the National Library of Ireland, or from the *Penny Journal* poem.[21] In effect, his choice of this poem to start his Irish translations told O'Donovan and perhaps Petrie that he was ready at last to take up the challenge of Gaelic verse. The four fine Irish poems he had done for Petrie in 1840 had been exactly that—done for Petrie— and as we know, he had not chosen to follow them up. Now, as if he had just laid his pen aside momentarily, he began in earnest where he had left off six years before.

"The Dream of John McDonnell" was a competent translation of a type of poem known as an *aisling*, or dream poem, with the traditional elements of the dreamer, a fair young woman who appears to him and then disappears, a journey in search of her, the final discovery of her identity, and the dreamer's awakening. More interesting than the poem itself was what it heralded. Over the next six months, *Nation* readers would encounter "Dark Rosaleen" (30 May), "The Captivity of the Gaels" (13 June), "Cean Salla" (4 July), "A Vision of Connaught in the Thirteenth Century" (11 July), "The Lovely Land" (18 July), "Lament over the Ruins of the Abbey of Teach Molaga" (8 August), "A Lamentation for the Death of Sir Maurice Fitzgerald, Knight of Kerry" (29 August), "Sarsfield" (24 October), "A Cry for Ireland" (31 October), "Far, Far, Still So Far", (28 November), and "The Sorrows of Innisfail" (5 December), to name the most outstanding.

Also to be considered as the product of this burst of inspired energy were three translations which Mangan may have intended for either the *Nation* or the *Dublin University Magazine*, but which for reasons unknown appeared instead in a little volume edited by Henry R. Montgomery and titled *Specimens of the Early Native Poetry of Ireland*. All three poems are noteworthy: "Prince Aldfrid's Itinerary Through Ireland", "To the Ruins of Donegal Castle", and "O'Hussey's Ode to the Maguire."[22]

With "Dark Rosaleen", Mangan struck pure gold, or rather, he achieved a sort of literary magic, transforming his pleasant source poem, the Gaelic "Roisin Dubh", into something rich and rare. It has been thought in the past that he worked from English translations found in Hardiman's *Irish Minstrelsy* and in Samuel Ferguson's review of that anthology. However, it is just as possible that he also had in front of him another English version made by John O'Daly whom he would soon begin to call "My friend Mr Daly" in thanking him for the originals of such poems.[23] Be that as it may, Mangan's poem was not much like any of these. Generations of Irish school children have memorized Mangan's "Dark Rosaleen", whose opening lines stand at the head of this section, scarcely knowing the others existed.

Musical, powerful, sensual—whether it is thought of as a love poem or a patriotic poem in which "Rosaleen" represents Ireland—and it has been considered both—"Dark Rosaleen" seems to many readers and critics to be without peer in the intensity of its emotional expression. From first stanza to last, the passion which gripped the speaker demanded increasingly compelling imagery. In fact, one significant change Mangan made in the original was in its tone, which he pitched considerably higher emotionally than any version from which he might have worked. Images, words, phrases—all contribute to the effect. Even the little pause he introduces with an ellipsis into the fifth line of each stanza (except the last) makes it sound as if the speaker needs to catch his breath before he can go on.

The most noteworthy alterations made by the nineteenth-century poet in his seventeenth-century material, however, were in the characters of the speaker and of Dark Rosaleen, both of whom he placed *in extremis*. In the first stanza the reader is told that Dark Rosaleen herself is in need of virtually everything—"health, and help, and hope", the poet summarizes, alliterating the triad. And before the poem's conclusion, the speaker vows to perform impossible feats "To heal your many ills!" Just as pressing were his own "ills", and indeed, more stanzas deal with these than touch on Rosaleen's. He suffers a "wasted soul", a "fainting heart", "woe and pain, pain and woe", and requires the ultimate in aid: "A second life, a soul anew". By the next-to-last stanza, Rosaleen and her hero both seem fragile creatures of pure, sheer hope and refined sensibility which ill-suit them for this world. They can exist, it may be, only amidst the gold and emerald sheen of an enchanted bower: he, the eternal Knight, she, his Lady, who with "one beamy smile" can give him strength to perform miraculous feats on her behalf, were she but strong enough to smile.

So it seems, that is, until the last stanza. There, with a sudden rush of energy and a huge reversal, the poet shatters altogether the mood he has so beautifully created. As if the foregoing were a fantasy he can no longer indulge, he abandons it for violent, bloody action: chaos must reign above and slaughter below—indeed, the Apocalypse must arrive—before he will allow his Dark Rosaleen to die:

O! the Erne shall run red
    With redundance of blood,
The earth shall rock beneath our tread,
    And flames wrap hill and wood,
And gun-peal, and slogan cry,
    Wake many a glen serene,
Ere you shall fade, ere you shall die,
    My Dark Rosaleen!
    My own Rosaleen!
The Judgment Hour must first be nigh,
Ere you can fade, ere you can die,
    My Dark Rosaleen![24]

Mangan took other liberties with his source poem besides raising the emotional pitch and changing the nature of the speaker and his Dark Rosaleen. *The Poets and Poetry of Munster* (1849) contained two more translations by Mangan of separate versions of the Gaelic poem, both different from the above. In regard to them, the editor John O'Daly observed that, "The allegorical allusions to Ireland under the name of *Roisin*, have long been forgotten, and it is now known by the peasants merely as a love song."[25] The times being what they were, O'Daly may well have thought it prudent to exaggerate the extent to which the Irish peasantry had "forgotten" all about the allegorical significance of "Dark Rosaleen". What is certain is that Mangan had not, and did not. Characteristically, he removed references which were too physical to suit him, such as those to "round white breasts" and "doing a trick behind the ring fort". The effect was as he desired: to elevate "love" out of any physical particularity and into the spiritualized realm of the universal. This made easier the restoration, in readers' minds, of the national allegorical significance of "Dark Rosaleen".

Another change Mangan made would appear to be very particular to himself. No religious element as such is to be found in the old Gaelic poem. Priest, Mass, and so on are mentioned, but without any importance beyond their mere presence in the story of thwarted but hopeful love. By contrast, Mangan's poem is a devotional hymn, a prayer. In fact, by the time the last stanza is reached, the reader may well be wondering whether the speaker is addressing a woman or the Virgin Mary, for the *mise en scene* is a Renaissance heaven where he will kneel in breathless adoration before a golden throne set in "an emerald bower" where "my Queen,/My life of life, my saint of saints" reigns "and reigns alone" in her glory. With her "holy delicate white hands" she will girdle her champion with steel, and when he goes forth to "heal her many ills" she will pray ceaselessly for him. An air of adoration envelopes the entire poem, as if the gestures and the phrases were part of some rite of sacrifice or sanctification. Again, it is worth emphasizing that absolutely nothing of this existed in the poet's source poem, and it may be that he was already approaching that mood in which he could vow, "GOD is the idea of my mind".

Whenever any poet creates such an emotional outpouring as "Dark Rosaleen" readers invariably question the motivation, the state of mind, of the poet at the time. Certainly Mangan was in a very emotional, highly charged state in the spring and summer of 1846. In particular, he had his mother very much on his mind and in his heart this spring, and it would have been strange indeed if this feeling had not made its way into his verse. His mother was very dear to him. Fail him she might, and understand him she might not, but she had never abandoned him. And now she was dying, beyond any power of his to "heal her many ills". The past of which the poet was a victim, and in which he was both trapped and sheltered, was irretrievably, perhaps frighteningly, coming to an end. Considered as an expression of this extraordinary moment in his life, "Dark Rosaleen" gains a further dimension: to its romantic, nationalist, and spiritual facets can be added the personal.

What does an editor, whom it behooves to be cautious as his trial date approaches, do about publishing such a poem? First, he prints it; then, he maintains a discreet silence about it. So it was that "Dark Rosaleen" appeared in the *Nation* without a word of comment from Duffy. Directly beneath it was the notification of his trial date; it was to be the next Saturday, 6 June. When that Saturday arrived, the *Nation* carried a Mangan poem, but only in the "Answers to Correspondents" column. His ferocious "The Impending Time"—"Up, then! And here be this our vow—/We'll strive till streams of blood dye/ Our virgin swords! We conquer now/ Or—DIE AS HEROES SHOULD DIE!"—was defanged by the careful Editor's note: "Here is a hot war-song (too hot for this weather), by a most sanguinary German Professor." Moreover, Mangan himself seems to have under-estimated the power of "Dark Rosaleen", for he, too, played down the importance of the poem. It was, he said, only "an impassioned little song [that] . . . purports to be an allegorical address from Hugh [O'Donnell] to Ireland on the subject of his love and struggles for her. . . ." As noted earlier in this chapter, "The Warning Voice" was always more popular with the *Nation* group than was "Dark Rosaleen".

Much has been written over the years about "Dark Rosaleen", most of it enthusiastic. If one poem of Mangan's is to be anthologized, it will almost certainly be this one. It is more accessible than "O'Hussey's Ode to the Maguire", which is the favourite of many critics, and it is more representative than the charming "The Woman of Three Cows". D.J. O'Donoghue, in his biography of the poet, posed the question which, he said, "was then and is now asked: 'Is it translation . . . or is it original?' " and called the poem "a national apotheosis".[26] William Butler Yeats referred to it as "quite wonderful with the passionate self-abandonment of its latter stanzas".[27] James Joyce, a little more cautious, pointed out that when the music of Mangan's verse "shakes off its languor and is full of the ecstasy of combat", then it "is tremulous with all the changing harmonies of Shelley's verse".[28] Among major literary men who have touched on the subject, only Padraic Colum took exception to the poem's being almost faultless, and he insisted that it lacked structural consistency: " 'Dark Rosaleen' for all its exaltation and prophetic fervour is not a masterly poem", he declared. But he was not satisfied to leave it at that. Mangan, he concluded had changed "patriotic feeling" into "devotional ecstasy" in the poem and had transmuted "Roisin Dubh", the "secret name", "into an esoteric, into a sacred name in the wonderful litany that is 'Dark Rosaleen'."[29] One wonders why he bothered to cavil at all. Rudolf Patrick Holzapfel wrote succinctly that creating a poem such as "Dark

Rosaleen" "would have made any man immortal".[30] Peter MacMahon, the only scholar to have done a full-length study of "Dark Rosaleen", spoke without exaggeration in saying, "The poem takes the reader by storm, awakening a restless, then ecstatic mood . . . [with its] incantatory cadences."[31]

[4]

Oh, wanderer! the hour that brings thee back
  Is of all meet hours the meetest.
Thou now, in sooth, art on the track,
  Art nigher to Home than thou weetest. . . .
Mangan, "The Saw-Mill"

Overshadowed by "Dark Rosaleen" though they are, three original poems of Mangan's that appeared in one issue after the other of the *Nation* in July do more than *suggest* a reader might relate them to the poet's life at this juncture: they *require* it. The first of these was the least memorable. Signed "A Yankee", "An Invitation" which appeared in the 4 July number probably was written in honour of the American Independence Day, and vividly enumerated the Old World's decline, country by country. Its stanzas urged emigration, a somewhat surprising tack for an Irish nationalist to take, it would seem; but Mangan had his reasons:

Cross with me the Atlantic's foam,
  And your genuine goal is won.
    Purely Freedom's breezes blow,
Merrily Freedom's children roam
  By the doedal Amazon,
    And the glorious Ohio![32]

A new land, free from all the old problems, was an "invitation" that John O'Donovan, for one, almost ached to accept. But he did not—nor, of course, did Mangan.

The second poem, "A Vision of Connaught in the Thirteenth Century", was introduced with the headnote, "*Et moi, j'ai ete aussi en Arcadie.*—And I, I too have been a dreamer. —Inscription on a painting by Poussin." (He was almost right; the inscription is actually "*Et moi, aussi je viens en Arcadie*".) Metaphorically, Arcadia has long stood for that perfect place where there are no ills, where the sun shines and the people are happy from one blissful day to the next. But in another pastoral painting, Poussin included a heavy marble tomb engraved "*Et in Arcadia Ego*" to make the dark statement that even in such a perfect-seeming place, there is death. This was the theme of Mangan's vision poem. Besides revealing a desolated past, "A Vision of Connaught in the Thirteenth

Century" suggested the bitter irony of life in the nineteenth century: in beautiful, fruitful Ireland, people were starving to death. "An Invitation" shows a daydreaming poet; this poem's persona is a real dreamer, under a spell:

> I walked entranced
> Through a land of Morn;
> The sun, with wondrous excess of light,
> Shone down and glanced
> Over seas of corn
> And lustrous gardens aleft and right.
> Even in the clime
> Of resplendent Spain,
> Beams no such sun upon such a land;
> But it was the time,
> 'Twas in the reign,
> Of Cáhal Mór of the Wine-red Hand.

Finding by his side "a man/Of princely aspect and port sublime", he enquires of him what "golden time" this is, and in what clime. Upon being told that the land is Erin and the time is that of Cáhal Mór, he has, as it were, his first vision:

> Then saw I thrones,
> And circling fires,
> And a Dome rose near me, as by a spell,
> Whence flowed the tones
> Of silver lyres,
> And many voices in wreathèd swell . . .

He then seeks out the hall and enters, and finds therein that a different mood prevails. Instead of lightness and happiness, all is gloom. "King, nobles, all,/Looked aghast and strange. . . ." The people seem not to know that they are in the days of Cáhal Mór, but are beset instead by a "dread amaze", a terror, though of what they know not.

The exterior world, too, has in the meantime undergone a fearsome change, and the poem ends:

> I again walked forth;
> But lo! the sky
> Showed fleckt with blood, and an alien sun
> Glared from the north,
> And there stood on high,
> Amid his shorn beams, a skeleton!
> It was by the stream
> Of the castled Maine,
> One Autumn eve, in the Teuton's land,

That I dreamed this dream
Of the time and reign
Of Cáhal Mór of the Wine-red Hand![33]

Not until this ending does the reader learn that the whole experience has been a dream, dreamed by the poet while "in the Teuton's land" and thus far away from his own country. Looking at his native land from a distant perspective, he saw a splendid long-ago vision of a happiness which had been overwhelmed by misery and death. "A Vision of Connaught in the Thirteenth Century" is the story of a dreamer's waking to a sad, shocking realization: Like old Europe's of "An Invitation", the glory of his home has fled.

By contrast, the third poem of the series, "The Lovely Land", developed the theme from the reverse angle, depicting a speaker awakened to awareness of the authentic present, which, though not previously apprehended, is close at hand. Standing before a beautiful noontime scene purportedly executed by the Irish artist Daniel Maclise, a painting entitled "The Lovely Land", the poet-viewer muses that the trees and rocks look exactly like scenery by Veronese, and that even Poussin could not have pictured a lovelier sun and river. Surely, he says to himself, this must be a painting of "Some lone land of genii days,/Storyful and golden!" Once that thought has occurred to him, he lets his imagination go, wishing that with some "magic power" he might "wander/One bright year through such a land!" Then, as if he has actually been able to enter the picture, he stops short, arrested by what he sees there:

But what spy I? . . . O, by noonlight!
 'Tis the same!—the pillar-tower
 I have oft passed thrice an hour,
Twilight, sunlight, moonlight!

The light of noon reveals the world most clearly, without pockets of shadow or shadings. In that light—which pervades the picture—the speaker at last sees something that is very familiar to him and recognizes the scene as a view of his homeland. He is stricken with remorse. Caught up in the fascination of places far away in space or time, he had failed to recognize "the lovely land"—his home. He ended this truly landmark poem:

Shame to me, my own, my sire-land,
 Not to know thy soil and skies!
 Shame, that through Maclise's eyes
I first see thee, Ireland!

No! no land doth rank above thee
 Or for loveliness or worth!

So shall I, from this day forth,
Ever sing and love thee![34]

And so he would. It is impossible to say if this poem were inspired by some visit Mangan had paid to an exhibition in Dublin, but it is thought-provoking to discover that no painting by Maclise sounds as if it could be the one described here. The epiphany which Mangan shared with his readers may well have been an inner one of the spirit.

* * * *

The private home life of a nineteenth-century man, whether happy or sad, was not usually deemed appropriate subject matter for correspondence, and so we find Mangan rarely (almost never, in fact) saying anything about his family to Duffy or, probably, anyone else. Undoubtedly, much misery resulted from such reticence, for Mangan and other men and women who, like himself, generally preserved a proper secretiveness save for a few stunted sentences uttered in the study or the sewing room. Three letters that the poet wrote Duffy during the spring and summer of 1846 survive, however: one from April, one from June, and one from July. They may be assumed to allude to his mother and her illness and the strain he was under as a consequence.

Writing in the third week of April, he declared in the letter quoted at some length in the third section of this chapter that he was "in a peculiarly critical position" which required him to make a certain (but unspecified) request of his friend. Probably it was for a loan.[35] In the second letter written 16 June he recounted a dream which revealed immense anxiety and preoccupation with death:

> I had a singular dream a few nights back. There was a light and a throng—not the "livid light and trampling throng" of Coleridge, yet quite as impressive. In other words, a monster moon shone in the firmament, and a crowd of people were beneath, with whom I held, as I suppose, a long conference. I say, "as I suppose," for all that I distinctly remember was that, turning away from them, I found myself on the verge of a precipice, with these words of St John in my mouth—"and none of you asketh me, Whither goest thou?"[36]

The words may be "of St John", but in the fifth verse of Chapter 16 of that Gospel they are spoken by Jesus, and the "throng" around him is made up of his disciples. He admonishes them not to be fearful, and he warns them of what will await them after his crucifixion. After saying that he "is going to the one who sent me", he then reproves them, or so it sounds: "Not one of you has asked, 'Where are you going?' Yet you are sad at heart. . . ." For Mangan to dream of himself speaking Jesus's words is extraordinary, it must be said, and one wonders about Duffy's reaction. Mangan, it has already been noted, often identified himself with suffering

"Man", and he doubtless thought of himself as a "suffering servant". Although he spoke of himself as "one whom some have called a seer", he surely would have been appalled if it had been suggested that he was comparing himself in any way to Jesus.

By 10 July, when the third of these letters was written, the poet had been reduced to a really pathetic condition, and we read the earliest, or one of the earliest, instances of those terrible begging letters which he was to write to his friends and which biographers have found such painful reading ever since. After beseeching Duffy to get £5 for him from the publisher James Duffy "on account of the work you spoke of (which I am ready to commence)", he swore, "*I will never again thus annoy you*—no!—as God is my judge, even if I live to repay the immense debt I owe you,—morally no less than physically." Then, as if this were not enough to move his friend, "Could you see my condition at this moment—could you look into my heart and read my anxiety, my anguish—and above all could you understand the causes of these, you would indeed pity me." [37]

Breaking with the Past

July 1846 was an intensely political month. Duffy's trial for seditious libel finally came up, and much to his own and everyone else's surprise, he was acquitted. Victory was a fluke, the result of an irresistibly appealing speech delivered by Robert Holmes, the counsel for the defense. To interpret Duffy's being released as an indication that the Government's position was softening would have been a foolish mistake.

The 18 July issue of the *Nation* carried a lengthy editorial by Duffy that was to have more far-reaching consequences than he perhaps anticipated. "Moral Force" summarised the progress of the nationalist cause since 1843 and pointedly called attention to the different approach taken in the newspaper since that time. There had been, he wrote, a new emphasis on the need to preach and teach a slow and deliberate mode of action, "to create a new moral force in the country. Education and Conciliation were their means." On the strength of what he said here, Duffy was accused by the leadership of the Repeal Association of having tried in 1843 "secretly and occultly" to raise a revolution in Ireland.[1]

In the Association meeting which started on 27 July, contention between the two factions came to a boil. A Peace Resolution introduced by O'Connell's men totally renounced the use of force; it was rejected by the Young Irelanders. On the first day, debate was long and heated, and eventually the meeting was adjourned to be reconvened on Tuesday. Tempers, however, did not cool much overnight.

The next day, 28 July, Thomas Meagher delivered the stirring speech that made him famous and earned him the sobriquet "Meagher of the Sword". Ironically, Meagher was not much of a republican, assuredly not one of Mitchel's stamp, but rather a patriot who approved of the Irish being, as they were sometimes described, "one of the most aristocratic people in the world".[2] The "brilliant boy", as Duffy called him, put it to the assembly: "Abhor the sword and stigmatise the sword? No, my lord . . . ," and followed with a recitation of examples of splendid swords down through the years. As Duffy's biographer Cyril Pearl quipped, "How many more historic swords Meagher might have unsheathed it is impossible to say" because John O'Connell rudely brought the speech to a halt. In response to the perceived insult, many Young Irelanders walked out. William Smith O'Brien led the way, followed by Meagher, Mitchel, Fr Meehan, and others. Thus it was that the break which all parties had been trying for months to avoid finally came about.

Not too far distant, another scene altogether was being played out in the Dublin Library. Mangan had retreated there, perhaps to escape from his home for a few hours, definitely to make use of the free writing materials that were supplied, and he had already filled several pages to Duffy. It is obvious from this letter that he still thought his poems were going to make up, or at least be included in, one of the volumes in the Library of Ireland. After commenting on two poems that "you know I owe you on the score of the last advance", he suggested meeting with Duffy the next Friday, the last day of the month:

> I have a proposal to make to you which I trust you will not consider objectionable. . . . I fear that J.D. [James Duffy, the printer] is off with me as to the 'Echoes': at least I don't see any announcement of the volume in *his* advertisements. If my surmise be correct strike out the line connected with my ill-omened name in *yours*. I am really heart-broken: I have made promises, and thought to be able to fulfill them in October; but an adverse destiny perpetually fights against me. Yet all my solicitudes have ever been for others —very few indeed for myself—. . . .

As was so characteristic, he closed his letter with a little joke for Duffy: "May Gog and Magog watch over thee, my dear friend, and the great Pan [in Greek letters] (whom this weather must have turned into a frying pan), extend thee his protection!"

It may have been just when he was ready to fold up the sheets and go across the street to drop them off in the *Nation* office, that news about the walk-out came from Conciliation Hall. He added a fourth page, prominently marked "PRIVATE":

> I have just glanced at O'Connell's letter. *Read* it I could not. My disgust overpowered me. "Pity the sorrows of a poor old man"—"whose trembling" soul "has driven him to" retract his own sentiments and accuse his country's—this is the motto, this the burden of it. Oh! the shuffling sneaker! But I am much mistaken if this last act of treachery on his part will not be found to have alienated three fourths of the clergy and people of Ireland from him. All Ireland *must* resound with Paeans to Smith O'Brien. For mine own poor part I merely await the announcement of a more decided policy by your paper, and your gracious permission withal, to place this question respecting moral and physical force in its genuine and proper light.[3]

Thus again, Mangan took Duffy mildly to task for being too conciliatory, the first such scolding having been administered back in 1844 when the two of them failed to come to terms about the poet's contributions to the paper. Mangan, of course, could afford to fling down bold challenges. Duffy couldn't. And so on this fevered note, the unusually hot July drew to a close.

The months that followed would see played out a rather curious political game. The Repeal Association, for all its bravado, was in tatters, but Young Ireland itself was anything but firmly put together. A writing branch called the Phalanx was organized by Smith O'Brien, with members assigned space in the *Nation* to discuss pertinent issues. Throughout the country, "remonstrances" bearing the signatures of hundreds of Repeal Association members protested the course pursued by the O'Connell leadership. Everyone was more or less unhappy with the new state of affairs, but not unhappy enough to agree to the compromise that was required to get the factions back together. Both took the high moral ground, and when that is the case, only a miracle can effect reconciliation. In the event, no miracle occurred.

Against their wishes, several of Mangan's friends were ousted from the Repeal Association. Mitchel swore, "I think I have a right to an explicit statement of the reason of my expulsion", but he was denied the courtesy of any response beyond a brusque refusal to "enter into any correspondence with you on the subject".[4] So it went also with Fr John Kenyon of Templederry and with Fr Meehan, who received a sharp rebuke as well as an expulsion notice. Even the philanthropist James Haughton found himself forced to withdraw from the Association because he believed that the "war-like errors" of Young Ireland should be handled within the membership.[5]

Once again, the lack of a solid political centre such as Thomas Davis might have provided became a critical factor in Irish history. Charles Gavan Duffy and John Mitchel, each in his own fashion, wished to, or wished that he could, provide that leadership, but neither was of sufficient stature to do so. Daniel O'Connell was elderly and failing fast, and not one of his sons had the capacity to succeed him. Only co-operation could have saved the cause that, in their hearts, they all loved; but co-operation was beyond them.

William Smith O'Brien is usually credited with initiating, this autumn, the formation of a new group that came to be called the Irish Confederation. Its membership was drawn in large part from the men who had been expelled or had resigned from the Repeal Association, and in effect it functioned as an alternate to that now truncated organization. Much evidence, however, points to Duffy as the actual founder. According to D'Arcy McGee, "Duffy projected the Confederation. . . . He not only founded but *made* the Confederation."[6] Richard Davis in *The Young Ireland Movement* recently noted the two men's relative positions, observing that Duffy, the real founder, "insisted on O'Brien's being the 'official leader' ". In October, Duffy wrote O'Brien an important letter that still survives in the Royal Irish Academy Library. In it, he discussed a plan "to develop and give a *direction* to the sound opinion of the country" and named twenty-five men in whom he had confidence and who, he assured

O'Brien, could be relied on to do "occasional papers" on national subjects for the *Nation*. This he held to be essential, "certainly the first step . . . preliminary to organisation or action".[7] Almost all the names are familiar ones—Dillon, McGee, Meagher, MacCarthy, Meehan, Mitchel, and so on. O'Brien's name stood at the top of the list. At the foot were those of "R.D. Williams, Clarence Mangan (A greater poet than Davis) and C.G. Duffy". The complete list will be found in Appendix F.

* * * *

On Thursday, 6 August, Catherine Smith Mangan died. She had been the only woman in her son James's life who had not abandoned him in one way or another, and her loss was devastating for him. She was buried in the family plot in Glasnevin Cemetery beside her husband and her son John. The brothers would remain at the No. 9 Peter Street residence for close to a year, probably surrendering it reluctantly at the last because it cost too much to keep. Obviously, the poet's uncles would no longer help out financially; William rarely if ever had work; and James would lose his job in Trinity College Library at the end of the year. Much has been said of Mangan's penchant for roaming about and for having no settled address; it was undoubtedly true that he often felt like a wanderer in this world, and that it became a pose he struck and a "mannerism" he affected. But the fact was that he valued "home" too much not to have wanted one. He did not intentionally allow his and his brother's living arrangements to deteriorate to the sad state they reached in the next two years, when they had only one poor room to share, or none at all.

No letter, no poem, by Mangan about his mother exists to testify to what her loss meant to him. Indeed, he may not have written any such thing. Nevertheless, four laments, three of them translations and one an original poem, almost certainly commemorated her and allowed the poet to grieve, if not openly, at least with audible words from his secret heart. The earliest of these was "A Lamentation for the Death of Sir Maurice Fitzgerald, Knight of Kerry" which appeared in the 29 August edition of the *Nation*. The fine opening stanza:

There was lifted up one voice of woe,
    One lament of more than mortal grief,
Through the wide South to and fro,
    For a fallen Chief.
In the dead of night that cry thrilled through me,
    I looked out upon the midnight air!
Mine own soul was all as gloomy,
    And I knelt in prayer.

Even more poignant was "A Cry for Ireland" which began:

O my land! O my love!
What a woe, and how deep,
Is thy death to my long mourning soul!
God alone, God above,
Can awake thee from sleep,
Can release thee from bondage and dole!
Alas, alas, and alas!
For the once proud people of Banba!

The third poem in this group was the original "Far, Far, Still so Far" that was published on 28 November; it is one of the most melancholy poems Mangan ever wrote. The poet—it is not quite fair to say "Mangan"—is completely worn out with waiting for "the longed-for morrow" of hopes and visions fulfilled:

Oh! darkly it looms, this time of sorrow,
When, when shall dawn the longed-for morrow
Now far, far, still so far?
The hopes our souls at morn have shrined,
The sinking sun sees banned and banished!
We only dream to wake and find
The vision once again has vanished,
So far, far, still so far!

* * * *

Our spirits are worn, and lorn, and pining,
The star of all our hopes keeps shining
So far, far, still so far!
The darkest hour, one often hears,
Is when the Night first nears the Morning,
But still the Bell of our Night's years
Knolls, tolls alway the one sad warning—
"Tis far, far, still so far!"

Finally, on 5 December, came "The Sorrows of Innisfail" in which Ireland is addressed as "mother of light and Song" and the poet cries, "Through the long drear night I lie awake, for the sorrows of Innisfail./ My bleeding heart is ready to break; I cannot but weep and wail":

How long, O mother of light and Song, how long will they
fail to see
That men must be bold, no less than strong, if they truly
will be free?

* * * *

The letter he wrote to Duffy in June of this year brought to light a curious fact: so far, Mangan had not been paid anything for what he had written for the *Nation*. He evidently had wanted to preserve the fiction that he was *giving* Duffy poems. That Duffy was loaning him money was part of his self-deceptive gentleman's agreement. "Base is the slave", he observed, "[who] talks of rates of payment." Yet there was no escaping the need: "My rate, then, is simply magazine rate, i.e., 10s for every 50 lines. If you agree to this I have liquidated 10£ of my debt. . . ."[8] What, one wonders, was the grand total. It would take all the poems going back to "The Warning Voice", approximately a thousand lines of verse, to erase the £10. It was this sort of deal, this *quid pro quo*, that Mangan had been avoiding since 1844 when he had assured Duffy (prematurely but agreeably) that he was ready to arrange with him some "plan or system" by which his "poor contributions" would be sent to the newspaper. Little had come of it; in the months following, the poet wrote almost nothing for the *Nation*. There can be little question but that Duffy insisted upon some orderly arrangement, now that Mangan was regularly appearing in the poetry column, while Mangan in his heart still wanted no such thing.

It is important to note how adamantly the poet defended his pride, how resolutely he fought not to become a "hack". And yet he found himself increasingly in the position of paid poet. His new dedication may have made payment even more disagreeable. As he produced something for the *Nation* every two or three weeks, however, there was no disguising the fact that he (quite rightly) was paid for his work. In the best of circumstances, there was not much to be earned by the pen. The old servant woman who declared, "Lord, forgive you, Mr Mangan, you might be rolling in your coach if you'd only keep from liquor, and make *ballads* for Mr Nugent in Cooke-street" only committed a common fallacy; Cook Street ballad-makers were, if anything, worse off than other writers.[9] Thomas Moore may have been the only Irish poet of the day who went "rolling in a coach", and he was not doing it in Ireland, nor could he have done it at all without the generosity of his English friends.

Several poems were named in the preceding chapter along with "Dark Rosaleen" as being of the highest quality of this or any other year. Of these, "Lament over the Ruins of the Abbey of Teach Molaga" and "O'Hussey's Ode to the Maguire" were outstanding. Although previous translators had laboured honestly to produce literal versions, and Ferguson, at least, a readable one, of "Lament over the Ruins of the Abbey of Teach Molaga", Mangan was "lifted as upon eagles' wings" of inspiration. Specifically this poem was improved under his hand in one minor and one major way. In general, Ferguson and other translators were more "true" to the original, which meant including in the final stanza a very awkward analogy between the speaker's heart and a nut. In the original was to be read: "There is wo on my face;/My heart is as the kernal of a nut . . . " and in Ferguson: "Wo is written on my visage,/In a nut my heart would lie—." Mangan, by contrast, scrapped the difficult comparison altogether and used his final stanza to complete the major change he made in the poem. Instead of having his speaker simply wandering by the sea and coming upon the ruins of the abbey, he had set him "wandering forth at night alone,/Along the dreary, shingly, billow-beaten shore". And, when his musings upon the ruin were finished, he did not merely leave him on the shore as in the other versions but, rather, returned him homeward:

> I turned away, as toward my grave,
> And, all my dark way homeward by the Atlantic's verge,
> Resounded in mine ears like to a dirge
> The roaring of the wave.[10]

It is a much more effective and dramatic conclusion than that of the original poem or its other translations; and yet another illustration of the importance to the poet of the theme of home-going.

The poem went to Duffy along with the note which contained the reference to "Clarence" that has often been taken as Mangan's explanation of his choice of pen-name: "Clarence is come—false, fleeting, perjured Clarence, who stabbed me in my grave near (Timoleague)", he wrote, "Timoleague" being "Teach Molaga". He continued, "I trust, my dear Duffy, that poor Shane O'Colain [the author of the poem] will not thus greet me on my entrance into Hades. . . . 'My soul is heavy, and I fain would sleep!' [Another line from *Richard III*] . . . In truth, I feel as if I should never laugh again."[11]

The second of these two fine poems, "O'Hussey's Ode to the Maguire", has garnered almost as much praise as "Dark Rosaleen". It was Mangan's task here not to weaken the original, a powerful and moving poem even in literal translations, but to shape it into a finished work of art in English. Achieving this, he created one of those rare poems in which there is no discrepancy at all between the content and the poet's manner of treatment. Where "Dark Rosaleen" radiated a supremely feminine energy, "O'Hussey's Ode" was powerfully masculine. Where he freely altered the stanzaic form in "Dark Rosaleen", he faithfully followed the antique Gaelic structure of "O'Hussey's Ode". The first, fourth, and fifth stanzas of fifteen are given below:

> Where is my Chief, my Master, this bleak night, *mavrone*!
> O, cold, cold, miserably cold is this bleak night for Hugh,
> It's [*sic*] showery, arrowy, speary sleet pierceth one through and through,
> Pierceth one to the very bone!
>
> Though he were even a wolf ranging the round green woods,
> Though he were even a pleasant salmon in the unchainable sea,

Though he were a wild mountain eagle, he could scarce bear, he,
This sharp, sore sleet, these howling floods.

O, mournful is my soul this night for Hugh Maguire!
Darkly, as in a dream, he strays! Before him and behind
Triumphs the tyrannous anger of the wounding wind,
The wounding wind, that burns as fire! [12]

The poet terminated his "Literae Orientales" anthology in January, and his "Anthologia Germanica" in June of this year. A further anthology, not yet planned, as far as we know, but a natural development given his new commitment, would be titled "Anthologia Hibernica" and would consist of three installments, in February, May, and July of 1847. At the close of 1846, it became clear to him that his "Echoes of Foreign Song" was not going to become a Library of Ireland publication; the decision had been made that it was not the best choice for such a disturbed time. How many hopes the poet had pinned on this volume cannot even be guessed, but he had plainly been working on the collection. It may be that some of the quite randomly selected poems in his "Lays of Many Lands" in the *University Magazine* from September 1847 until January 1849 had been destined for the "Echoes".

In the December number of the *Dublin University Magazine*, Mangan illustrated his theory of translation using only three poems to do so. "Leonora" was another translation of the popular poem by Bürger, and Mangan presented it as an example of the translations he did that were highly faithful to their originals. The second poem, "Prince Kazink and the Vaivodes. A Narrative Poem from the Servian", served to exemplify what he termed "adaptation", perhaps his most effective, yet most critcized, method of re-working his sources. The third, the poet wrote, "is—as will, doubtless, be apparent from its defects—altogether my own, though I confess that I am indebted for the idea that it embodies to a certain anecdote by an Oriental writer." "The Angel of Death. A Persian Legend" recounted the familiar tale of attempted flight from Death—only to find Death is already there, awaiting you where you have fled.

By October 1846 it was apparent that the potato blight had recurred, and that Ireland faced yet another year of famine. The *Nation's* columns were filled with accounts of desperate efforts to meet this second year of catastrophe. Weekly reports of starvation in Kells, Tipperary, and Sligo revealed that the spread of the infection was tragically wide. An especially harrowing story from Lisadell in County Sligo showed the terrible dimension that human greed could add to the natural disaster:

> . . . landlords have distrained crops and cattle for the May rent; and, as the potatoes are entirely destroyed, the consequence is that their unfortunate

> tenants are reduced to complete destitution. . . . Could not Sir Robert [Peel] have waited till spring, when the parties would have had an opportunity of emigrating to America? It is said that the land they occupied is almost valueless, owing to the constant drifting of the sand from the sea; but this is the very reason why the poor people should not have been expelled at this period of the year, on the eve of winter, when they cannot find a shelter in the country, nor procure the means of getting it. [13]

Still, life in Dublin imitated normalcy. Publishing continued, and the *Nation* carried reviews of three books with which Mangan's name is associated. Owen Connellan's *Annals of the Four Masters* finally appeared in a single volume, and in Rudolf Holzapfel's opinion, it was probably Mangan who reviewed it fairly generously on November 7. *Specimens of the Early Native Poetry of Ireland* was published by McGlashan and was reviewed along with D.F. MacCarthy's *Book of Irish Ballads* on 10 October. As noted, there were three new Mangan poems in Montgomery's *Specimens*—"Prince Aldfrid's Itinerary through Ireland", "To the Ruins of Donegal Castle", and the aforenoted "O'Hussey's Ode to the Maguire"—as well as three reprinted poems. MacCarthy included five previously published poems by Mangan, including "Dark Rosaleen" and "A Vision of Connaught in the Thirteenth Century". The *Nation* reviewer observed that "two poets eminently bear the bell, both in poetry and national tone—Ferguson and Mangan. Whether in translation or original, they seem almost alone in the art of reproducing for us the inner heart and outward vesture of the bygone ages of Ireland. . . ."

* * * *

An October letter from Mangan to Duffy showed the poet was greatly distressed. The handwriting was unusually poor, and his comments about William show he must have been almost at the end of his patience with his feckless brother. Although undated, it appears to have been sent about the middle of the month. The first two paragraphs are included here. The closing two discussed an article about William Maginn that he planned to write (and which probably did appear in the *Irishman* in 1849) and had more to say about the Irish poems.

> My dear Duffy,
>
> I have been for the last hour translating and transcribing (at the same moment) a poem from the Irish . . . but my hand no longer follows my mind with the same speed as it did some years back. I have but half of it done—I will however finish it in your office or in the Dub. Lib. I am exceedingly anxious that it should appear to-morrow—for Daly of Anglesea Street who gave it to me thinks I am trifling with him as I have promised any time these 3 weeks that it should appear in the NATION. It will occupy about a column. ["A Farewell to Patrick Sarsfield, Earl of Lucan" was sixteen four-line stanzas

long. It would have earned Mangan something over twelve shillings.]

[He and his brother had compared notes—"not bank notes"—and had found they had only two or three shillings left.] On my own account I despise those matters, but I cannot bear to see a brother in suffering. I have often very, very bitterly thought that there was much truth in the heartless and hard sentiment of Goethe—"Happy are they who have no relatives, for the entire business of one's life consists in getting rid of them." [14]

Another letter, this one written 10 November, disclosed a man under severe stress, but holding himself together. Toward the conclusion, his handwriting became increasingly chaotic and very uneven:

My dear Duffy, 10 November 1846

I have been uneasy all the evening from the apprehension that I may possibly have made a mistake as to the place of our appointment, and that, consequently, I may have kept you waiting, either at your own house, or at the Office. Believe me, my dear friend, that I really thought you told me you would call on me, and that I felt very deep pain and humiliation at the moment in thinking that you would not or could not allow me the favour of waiting on you instead. This matter, however, is past remedying

You have most generously offered to advance £10 to me, and have negotiated with McGlashan for another advance of the same amount. I cannot consent to accept such a sum at present. If by Friday you could oblige me with £5 it would meet all my difficulties for some time—and the rest you could oblige me with as you saw that I deserved it.

The wisdom of his reluctance to accept an advance—or "loan" or "gift" —of the large sum of £20 is self-evident; that was virtually a third of the income he could live on for a year. Whether Duffy heeded his wish or not we do not know. The letter continued:

I have received two books, Histories of Ireland—yesterday. The stupid servant-woman told me that they were sent me "from the Post Office". I rather imagine, however, that they came from another office, nearer to Carlisle Bridge. [By which he meant the *Nation* office.] I shall be glad if my conjecture is correct, because I think they will furnish abundance of materials for the construction of the Irish Historical Romances anent which we have both so often conferred.

P.S. I shall call on you at the office on Friday. J.C.M.[15]

So much for Mangan's letters as 1846 drew to a close. His friend John O'Donovan, that indefatigable letter-writer, was also busy with pen and ink. Back in August he had observed to Hardiman that 1,050 pages of his *Annals of the Four Masters* had been "printed off", little guessing how long it would be before the whole massive work was completed. In the same letter he had declared with refreshing frankness, "I am one who thinks that we—Young Ireland—will be a great people after old King Dan has been buried, and gone to his obscure ancestors", but he took no part in politics. By December, he was chortling over an in-house argument between "the Archeologists and the Celtics": "They (that is [Matthew] Kelly and [W.E.] Hudson) think that Curry *charges too much* for transcribing *Irish* and so they have petitioned the Council of the R.I. Academy to allow a Mr Daly of Anglesea Street, a bookbinder, and an amateur Irish scholar to copy from their Mss." The petition was turned down. "This, in my opinion", O'Donovan went on, "will create dissentions, which will set the Archeologists and the Celtics to fight. This will be great fun! But the Celtics will be beat."

O'Donovan certainly knew that Mangan lost his position in the library of Trinity College at the end of the year. In the spring, he would write contemptuously of "Dr Wall, who would not allow him to attend at the Library, because he wears a *moustache*, has sent me a pound for 'poor *Mangan*' through Dr Todd. . . ."[16] This throws a new and different light on why Mangan was let go and may or may not be factual. O'Donovan was always quick to repeat stories, whether or not he had checked them out, a habit completely at odds with the way he worked professionally. A startling example of this weakness shows up in a letter he wrote to Hardiman on the last day of December. After a lot of amusing nonsense and just before wishing him "many happy returns of the season", he crowded in this single line: "The poor poet, Mangan, is just dead! Ah, poor human genius!"[17] He was wrong, of course. James Clarence Mangan still had two-and-a-half years of life remaining.

16

Signs of the Final Wrath

January The gloomy, chilly Friday that opened the New Year of 1847 found Mangan, at the age of forty-three, without employment or the prospect of any. With his job gone, his mother dead, and his longtime home almost certain to slip away from him for want of money to keep it, he stood in dire need of shoring up. Yet Duffy, Mitchel, and other *Nation* associates were hardly at a point to be able to take care of more concerns than their own.

The first meeting of the new Irish Confederation was held on the thirteenth of the month. Their policy was to be conciliatory: "Substantially the policy of the Repeal Association, honestly and vigorously worked out". Scarcely a month would pass without an effort being made to get Old Ireland and Young Ireland back together, but nothing came of it. Mitchel described the almost giddy excitement that infused their meetings and wrote that they were flushed with their own daring and "met weekly at the house of one or the other; and there were nights and suppers of the gods, when the reckless gaiety of the Irish temperament bore fullest sway."[1] Doubtless Mangan kept away from these "nights and suppers of the gods" just as he had avoided Comet Club suppers and *Nation* Saturday evenings gatherings.

Ten days later, it was announced in the *Nation* that the Council of the Irish Confederation had decided that all members of the Repeal Association who were "Seceders", that is, who had left the Association willingly or otherwise, or who had signed what was called the Dublin Remonstrance the previous December, would automatically be Confederation members, unless of course they chose not to be. Mangan, as far as we know, had not been a member of the Association or signed the Remonstrance; the "James Mangan" on its list was not the poet. So, in effect, the new organization acquired members rather speedily, and Confederate Clubs were formed all around the country. The Council itself was the inner circle, and again, membership was not difficult to achieve. It was comprised of thirty-nine men, in theory, but in practice it was a good bit larger than that, sometimes including "all the leading Young Irelanders". There was even room in its ranks for Denis Florence MacCarthy who "had recently disclaimed all political interest". Nevertheless, "some of the male poets like Mangan and [John de Jean] Frazer were, however, left out."[2] In both cases, exclusion was probably the result of "disreputable" appearance and eccentric habits.

Not only was Mangan left out of the Council, he was kept out of the Confederation altogether, most surprisingly by his friend Gavan Duffy. Late in January or early in February, very much in keeping with his devotion to their cause, he applied to Duffy for admission to membership, but Duffy flatly turned him down. In his 1908 memoir in the *Dublin Review*, Duffy explained:

> The poet felt all the passion he uttered; he came to me after a time and asked to be proposed a member of the Irish Confederation, that he might share its labours and dangers. I combated the proposal warmly; he could not be of the slightest use to the Confederation; he had none of the qualities that make a man at home in a political assembly; he was shy, timid, and eccentric, always clothed in a manner which excited curiosity and perhaps ridicule, and though he could not be of service to the public cause he might and must bring disastrous consequences on himself.[3]

This was self-deluding nonsense. In the earlier *My Life in Two Hemispheres*, Duffy had not struck this pose but had declared frankly, "His fantastic dress and eccentric habits made him unfit to mix with the crowd." For his decision, Duffy ultimately paid a heavy price in remorse. He knew in his heart that he had wronged his friend for the sake of the supposed "respectability" of the Confederation. In further explanation he claimed he was afraid that if Mangan joined the Confederation he would lose his library position. In actuality, he must have been aware that Mangan had already lost it. He also claimed to be anxious about how *Dublin University Magazine* editors might react to the poet's being a member of a nationalist group. Yet he must have known how slight their interest was in contributors' politics, and he certainly knew how valuable Mangan was to the magazine.

He was probably correct in his judgement that the poet could not be of much use to "the public cause" through membership, however, and it is true that he urged him to make his patriotic contribution where he best could, in his poetry. But in actuality, the wound he dealt his friend by rejecting him seriously affected the poet's "usefulness" to the *Nation*, where his contributions ceased altogether for a number of months, reaching only six for the entire year. Instead, he turned his attention to his old standby, the *University Magazine*, and to a newcomer on the periodical scene, [James] *Duffy's Irish Catholic Magazine*.

In retrospect, it is hard to see any point to Duffy's behaviour; it would have been very easy to slip Mangan's name onto the membership list in any of several ways. It was customary, for instance, for prospective members' names to be submitted in batches, with little attention given to an individual candidate. In addition, though Duffy deplored the practice, many men insisted on keeping their identity secret by using a pseudonym.

Thus the Subscription Book has numerous identifications such as "A Protestant Repealer", "A Contrite Whig", and "An Ulster Orangeman".[4] Moreover, nothing could have been simpler than to admit the poet anonymously and request that he keep his lips sealed about being a member. And so on. In fact, the rather suspicious sounding "I.D. Gooch Mangan, Esq., Paris" noted on the May list and in the "Accounts of the National Defense Fund" as having sent a pound in June "per C.G. Duffy", may disguise the poet; but if his wish were granted in this way, it was a secret both he and Duffy carried to their graves. Probably no such thing occurred, and it must have been galling for him to read the name of his cousin, Michael Smith, displayed among the Council members.

The Famine was now becoming a nightmarishly repetitive story. A regular *Nation* feature, "The State of the Country", carried famine news picked up from local newspapers, and it was always heartrending. By contrast, little or nothing about the Famine's effects in Dublin was reported. Mitchel spoke of the theatres, concert rooms, and streets that still were filled with "brilliant throngs", and likened their behaviour to that of the Florentines when the Black Death ravaged their city in 1348.

O'Donovan's experience was different, perhaps in part because he did not socialize as much as Mitchel did and lived near a major route into the city, whereas Mitchel's residence was in Rathmines. "The number of beggars, that rap at this door, is awful", O'Donovan wrote to Hardiman in Galway early in the month. Like most pathetic spectacles, this riled him to what looks like anger until one realizes it is frustrated, helpless pity. In addition, the situation was frightening. "I fear an attack on the house every night", he exclaimed. "They attempted to force open the back door a few nights [ago?], but failed to open it."[5] O'Donovan might well fear for his young household on another score, also. He and Marianne were now the parents of three young sons, John, Edmund (named for their first child who had died at the age of two), and William; Richard would be born the following year. The *Annals of the Four Masters* was still being printed, which meant constant reading and correcting of proofs, and work on the *Book of Rights* was in progress. But none of this brought in much money; O'Donovan was always hard pressed to earn enough to support his family. When he wanted to help Mangan and said he had to go out and "beg" for the poet, he may have meant it literally.

February This month *Duffy's Irish Catholic Magazine* began publication. It was the product of the printer James Duffy's ambition to bring into existence a Catholic periodical that would be as excellent as the Protestant *Dublin University Magazine*, and to a certain extent he succeeded. Its appearance was scholarly and its content was of a high quality. It was also the product of Fr Meehan, an editor, and John O'Donovan was not alone in fearing that Daniel O'Connell would "paw [it] . . . with his lion talons" if he found out the truth about the Young Ireland involvement. Partly for that reason, no names appeared on the masthead during the first year. More practically, O'Donovan doubted if it could survive a year, given the state of the country and Irish magazine publication in general. Yet, he noted, "Duffy is determined to sustain the periodical at least for two years even at a loss." He was right in that prediction, the magazine lasting through the December 1848 issue, when a small note at the top of the front page told readers that "the depressed state of trade in Ireland" made it impractical to continue publishing. O'Donovan was without many illusions. "We have only one [magazine] in Dublin . . . struggling these years for existence", he wrote to Hardiman, "and even this one is fed by the little bits of Protestant bigotry which ornament it from time to time. . . . Were it not for the spirit and Scottish cleverness of MacGlashen the Dublin University Magazine would have gone '*to the wall*' long since."[6]

The sad truth was that the *Irish Catholic Magazine*, for all its high-minded aspirations, was dry reading. From its inception, by contrast, the *University Magazine* had struck sparks, sometimes with bias and venom, but always with fine touches of humour throughout its pages. James Duffy evidently failed to appreciate how necessary that facet of a publication was to the Irish reader. In the first sentence of the first number, he explained: "The very highest aspiration we can make for our infant Periodical is, that it may be the forerunner of a Catholic literature in Ireland." Such literature he deemed "the essential want" in the country. If his magazine was, as a consequence, too stuffy, too laden with accounts of ancient history, learned essays on quaint customs, and stories about obscure Catholic heroes, he at least could afford to print what his conscience and taste dictated. A native, like Gavan Duffy, of County Monaghan, by the time he was twenty-one years old he had begun his own publishing business. His "Sixpenny Library" of "books of devotional and national interest" was successful, and by the age of thirty-eight he had made a considerable fortune. No. 10 Wellington Quay, the site of his business, had a rental valuation of £90. He usually employed around 120 workers, but the figure is sometimes given as 300 or 400. Reputedly, he "never took a regular holiday nor allowed one to his staff, although otherwise [he was an] . . . excellent employer."[7] Eventually, he would offer Mangan a home, but as we will see, the poet declined with thanks.

Mangan was associated with the *Catholic Magazine* from the start, having altogether thirteen poems in it over the course of the next year-and-a-half. Taking the editor's suggestions about what to translate, he contributed seven new poems to the first volume and one reprint, "Pompeii", which now made its last appearance during his lifetime. Of the seven, half-a-dozen were on religious themes and one was nationalistic or, more accurately, historical. Although he was obviously amenable to Fr Meehan's recommendations, when he urged him to translate the apostrophe to the Virgin from Canto 33 of Dante's *Paradiso*, "he excused himself, saying, he 'was unequal to such a performance—you might as well ask me to paint a sound'."[8] One can only speculate as to what extent his heart was in writing his religious poems. Comments by John Keegan suggest he was only carrying out an assignment, but Keegan may have been too biased to be objective. Mangan was undoubtedly now moving in what might be called a devotional direction. It is interesting, I think, that he declined to translate the Dante for artistic reasons, whereas the reason R.D. Williams gave for not translating the "Stabat Mater Dolorosa" was his own lack of "holiness".

Mangan's first poem in the magazine was the hymn "Te Deum Laudamus", from the Latin. Like most of his *Catholic Magazine* poems, it was signed "J.C.M." In fact, he was now to give up using pseudonyms altogether, a highly significant change in what had been his custom for the past twenty-five years. In short, he stopped posing and he dropped the mannerism of disguise. Some pieces might still be unsigned, and Duffy would slip a "Terrae Filius" onto an epigram in the 1 January 1848 *Nation*, but in 1847, Mangan's days as the elusive, disguised, "nameless one" came to an end. Increasingly, he would sign his work with his full name, "James Clarence Mangan". In the last year-and-a-half of his life, there would be only two unsigned pieces, neither one of any length or consequence, while every other piece of his writing was identified with his full name or the three distinguishing initials "J.C.M.". The obvious conclusion is surely justified: at last he had an authentic identity and was proud to assert it.

The poet acted with alacrity on Duffy's suggestion that he should make himself useful to the cause through the medium of his poetry. Not many months had passed since he had declared he was ready to spend "almost all" his energy working for his country. Now, that partial commitment gave way to total dedication, and a formal declaration to that effect appeared in the first chapter of the "Anthologia Hibernica" in the February *Dublin University Magazine*.[9] Addressing his "Courteous Reader", he vowed, "Slender as our talents are, we have become exceedingly desirous to dedicate them henceforth exclusively to the service of our country." His statement seems surprisingly nationalistic, given the venue of its publication, for he went on to suggest that a new era was approaching "when Ireland shall have re-assumed her place among the nations"; and, he believed, "it surely cannot fail to be a peace-offering both to thy manes and ours, that we, both of us in our day, in some sort contributed towards the glorious event of her regeneration." One wonders how his conservative Unionist readers took this.

The first chapter of the new Irish anthology offered half-a-dozen assorted poems from four eighteenth-century poets, two of them well known, John O'Tuomy and Andrew Magrath, and two anonymous. The O'Tuomy poem, "Pulse of the Bards", was an impassioned anti-English "Jacobite relic", with lines such as "Mother of the Saints! . . . oh, help us in this hour—/Strike our tyrants down . . . and bless our cause anew!/ Give us back our Bards . . . and elevate the True/Old Church to its once proud power!" The Magrath poem was the neutral "Neither One Thing nor T'other", a very amusing rhyme in Mangan's hands, less so in Walsh's. The poet narrator bewails his condition: once a Catholic, he has converted to Protestantism only to find himself berated by both priest and parson. He is "on the shughraun . . . day and night", a term Mangan explained as "a phrase of a nature peculiar to the Irish language. . . . A man who is on the *seachran* is rather shabby than positively poor". Further, "He sneaks through by-lanes in an elbowless coat, and breakfasts at an uncertain hour and place in the afternoon, on a pennyworth of bread, a red herring, and a tumbler of porter." Was it himself Mangan described? As we will see, John Keegan declared this June that Mangan "didn't have a spark of religion" about him. Although he never switched to Swedenborgianism, and assuredly not to Protestantism, or any other "ism", he seems to have remained away from the active practice of Catholicism for sometime even after meeting Fr Meehan.

Mangan eventually would have some two dozen poems from the Irish in the *University Magazine*, but none was lovelier than a poem he included in this first Irish anthology. "Love Song" is a traditional ballad sometimes titled "The Unquiet Grave". He probably made use of Walsh's translation in *Irish Popular Songs*, but Mangan's delicate poem captured the sorrow of the bereaved as that poet's stanzas failed to do. Moreover, the moving first stanza, which set the tone and prepared the story, was entirely his own; neither Walsh's nor more recent translations such as Frank O'Connor's has anything comparable to this:

Lonely from my home I come,
To cast myself upon your tomb,
And to weep.
Lonely from my lonesome home,
My lonesome house of grief and gloom,
Where I keep
Vigil often all night long,
For your dear, dear sake,
Praying many a prayer so wrong
That my heart would break![10]

March On the 27th of the month, the *Nation* carried this unusual account of "Distress in the City":

> Daily scenes of misery make even the humane callow. So many and various are the forms in which wretchedness presents itself in Dublin, that charity is almost palsied in the midst of perplexing calls for food. Many, obviously unskilled in the hard lessons of mendicancy, creep out of alleys and lanes, in the grey of the evening, and make mute signs to the passengers in the streets, stretching out their hands with an indecision which plainly shows the struggle going on within. But the most doleful of all sights and sounds to us, is to hear and see starving women and children attempting to sing for alms. On every side of us despairing and broken tones are chanting "Where is the Land Like the Land of the West", "Home, sweet Home", and "Erin is my Home." [11]

The constant, searing misery on every side could not but torment the sympathies of someone like Mangan. On the other hand, for the first time in his life, it may be, he found more to pity outside himself than inside. He consequently ceased to be the primary object of his own commiseration. His plaints were sparse and to the point this month and indeed, until he was overwhelmed by illness, poverty, and drink, he forebore moaning altogether. As Holzapfel has said, Mangan was not "an old groaner".

On 2 March, W.E. Hudson wrote to O'Donovan a letter that revealed a good bit about the poet:

> Your description of poor Mangan is awful . . . and but for that I should have waited till I may next meet you. Here is more of my besotted ignorance; I have never even *seen* (to know him) James Clarence Mangan! He was well known to poor Davis—so it is strange I never came across his path. I have heard of his oddness . . . but that would not repel me . . . but I confess I have some horror of the opium-eating as of any other besetting besotment—or perhaps a [dram?] more: I dare say that may have prevented my actively seeking him out—
>
> What you say is enough:—you will not mention my name nor even let it be guessed whence the pittance I enclose (£2) comes—but he must not be left to starve—I have a great opinion of his powers. As to "schemer" [which O'Donovan had told him O'Curry considered Mangan to be]—thats [*sic*] nonsense. [12]

A general understanding seems to have prevailed among the friends and acquaintances of the poet, with the exception of Gavan Duffy, that he used opium at this time. Whether they were right or not is another matter, but it does not seem probable that so many should have been entirely mistaken. As for Mangan, who did not want another "sin" upon his head, he may have allowed himself to reason that the "one occasion" he acknowledged using laudanum had been the "occasion" of *illness*, however long and drawn-out.

On 6 March, Mangan gave O'Donovan a note that tells its own story: "I owe John O'Donovan, Esq., Barrister-at-Law, Twenty Shillings sterling, which sum I promise to pay him (D.v.) before the end of the current month."[13] This little note is written on a much-folded third of a sheet of paper, and the fact that it is still with O'Donovan's things among the "James Graves Papers" suggests that the debt was not repaid. O'Donovan related the story of this visit to Hudson when he wrote back to his friend:

> He is nearly in a state of idiocy,* and it is very wrong for *Curry* (who thinks him a schemer) or any one else to look upon him in the light of a schemer, or humbugger. [The * was to these lines that followed the signature:] He described to me with the most graphic details his visit to the next world, and his interview with his deceased father there, and his conversation with several spirits, and I was obliged to listen to him with the most sober patience. He called to me to borrow 20 shillings—He has not a clean shirt nor a bed to lie on, and all this is owing to the bad advisers [he] has had latterly.

To Hudson O'Donovan also wrote on 13 March the letter in which he fumed that Dr Wall had dismissed Mangan because the poet wore a moustache, and continued:

> Your contribution towards keeping poor Mangan from utter want, will I hope, be appreciated in another world—I found him out by great exertion through Anster, who is a good and kind friend of his, and who has been advising and assisting him for years unknown to the world.
>
> Now I do not know what to do *quo ad illum*. He is as proud as Lucifer, and to tell him that I am giving him money from the friends of literature for charity will not do, for he would rather starve than receive one fraction in that light. He insists upon the fact that he visits the other world regularly, and converses with spirits there, who were once here enclosed in an earthly shell called '*the Body*'. But this is a bad sign.[14]

Mangan's troubles multiplied. On 24 March he wrote a letter to O'Donovan in which he masked his worst anxiety in a sort of glib bravado. O'Donovan evidently knew his friend had misplaced a poem and may have inquired about the printer's reaction:

> Dear O'Donovan,
>
> Mr. MacDonnell has acted in the kindest and most generous spirit towards me. He has indeed the true soul of a gentleman. He almost condoled with me on the loss of the poem—as if I, and not he, were the suffering party. I need not tell you that he at once gave me the pound note. God for ever bless him!
>
> And now I have one slight favour to ask of you. Mr. MacDonnell has *not* the original—nor has he any copy. He obtained the translation from Mr. [Eugene] Curry. What Mr. Curry, however, has given him once he can give him again—and I will tell you what I propose should be done. The length of the poem (according to my rendering) would be 320 lines—somewhere about

£3 worth. Now, if Mr. Curry will be good enough to make a second transcript Mr. McDonnell [*sic*] will place the £3 in *his* hands, and he (Mr. Curry) will pay me just 30s. out of this. I ask no more, and I think you will allow that this is a fair proposal. So, the favour I have to ask of you amounts merely to this, that you would make the proposition to Mr. Curry.

O'Curry's anger at being asked to produce another transcript of this long poem can be assumed, but no doubt he swallowed it, inasmuch as he was being offered 30 shillings for the work. O'Curry's rates for copying had been criticized as too high, but ten shillings per hundred lines could scarcely have been his ordinary fee. Because he thought Mangan a "schemer", he may have accepted this "offer" and taken the extra amount as a fair enough reimbursement for the extra trouble. He had not much patience, and nothing indicates he bore with the poet the way O'Donovan did. The lost poem was almost certainly "On the Inauguration of the O'Brien" which appeared in the third "Anthologia Hibernica" in July. Mangan closed:

I have been in such trouble for the last week or so that I have not had time to thank you individually for what you have done for you [*sic*]—perhaps even—how can I tell?—at some sacrifice to yourself. But believe me that I am not forgetful. [The money O'Donovan had been collecting had evidently reached him.] Believe further, that I will shortly repay you all. And believe, yet further still, that, as the Living God exists, I will exhibit at no distant period something of that "force of character" of which you spoke to me yestereven.[15]

To John Anster, Mangan also wrote of having had a very bad week. On 26 March he thanked him for his generosity—presumably both O'Donovan and Anster had produced certain sums of money to help the poet—and explained his predicament. Although a rather long letter, it is so typical, and so revealing, that it is given in full:

My dear Dr. Anster,

I do not know for which I ought to be more grateful to you—your delicacy or your generosity. God bless you! You needed not, however, have selected anybody as the medium of your bounties. From a purse-proud aristocrat I should certainly have resented anything of the kind as an insult—to you I have only to offer my humblest thanks. I hope to be able to wait on you soon, and make my acknowledgements in person. Meantime, allow me to assure you that I am at present placed beyond the necessity of trespassing farther on your kindness. I am still struggling, it is true, and struggling most strenuously, but I hope to be able to hold my head [up] in society yet. As far, at least, as penitence for the past and exertion for the future can retrieve me, I will, and with the help of the Living God, before many days, emancipate myself.

O'Donovan was right about Mangan's pride. Reading between the lines of this opening paragraph we can hear it speaking. Anster had apparently tried to defuse the poet's gentlemanly resistence to "charity", but had inevitably—any move he could have made would have been "wrong"—offended him. Somewhat huffily Mangan assured him he was now "placed beyond the necessity of trespassing farther on your kindness"; but there was no truth in it, as the rest of the letter made all too clear:

> I fear I write very incoherently—for I have been in a very feverish state for the last week or so. I owe £5 to my landlord, and his forbearance towards me in not casting me into prison half maddens me. I see him almost once a day, and as I sneak by him, I feel as if I had lost a year of my existence. I have long wished to leave this neighbourhood for a healthier locality, but alas! in reference to him I am compelled to say, as Priuli remarks to Jaffier [in *Venice Observed*, a note tells us] "*Rent* is our bond".—And of course I must respect this.
>
> You perceive that, after all, I could not conclude without a very indifferent effort at a joke.[16]

His words confirm the supposition that the Mangans let the first floor at No. 9 Peter Street, and that John and Thomas Stewart, presumably the owners, for their names appeared in the *Dublin Almanac and General Register* listing, occupied the ground floor. Thus every time he went in or out of the house the poet may indeed have passed under the eye of his landlord. His comment about wanting to move to a "healthier locality" may have been inspired by the fact that this section of Peter Street was in decline, the properties around it already being of considerably less value than No. 9. From his early experience with the "hovel" in Chancery Lane, the poet had acquired a horror of such places. Unhappily, worse lay ahead.

April Little could be earned from single poems, but that was all Mangan had published in March and April. His earnings during these two months could not much have exceeded £4. Even if the *Catholic Magazine* paid magazine rate, which it may not have done, the forty-two line "David Lamenteth Saul and Jonathan" would have brought less that half a pound; "Stabat Mater Dolorosa", just over five shillings; "Lamentation of Jeremias over Jerusalem", about £2; and "Pompeii" ten shillings. He re-entered the ranks of the *Nation* this month with the blood-thirsty "The Glaive Song" which was over one hundred lines and should have earned him at least £1. But that was the total, while the minimum required for subsistence must have been no less than £10.

He obviously could not go on long at this rate and avoid the workhouse, although he would never voluntarily have resorted to that final expedient of the impoverished. In the spring of 1848, he would be in the fever sheds of the South Dublin Union workhouse, but whether he spent any other time there is not known. Life in the South Dublin Union was not easy. Its budget calculated, in the pre-Famine economy, that the cost to maintain a pauper was two shillings and four pence weekly.[17] This purchased two meals a day of the "house dietary", seven ounces of oatmeal and a cup of milk made into stirabout for breakfast, and three or four pounds of potatoes, probably the mealy "lumpers", and another cup of milk made into soup for dinner. There was no supper for adults. At that, it was a feast compared to what many people had to survive on by 1847 and probably more than the poet himself customarily ate.

O'Donovan, who had erroneously reported Mangan's death to Hardiman back in December, had forgotten that he had done so by the time he answered some letters from Hardiman on 8 April:

> Poor Mangan, whose death I see you mentioned in one of your letters to me is still at this side of the grave, but barely moving. He is a perfect demonstration of a ghost, and visits the next world every night, and carries on long conversations with the spirits who have shaken off their bodies. . . . The poor creature called on me here a few days since, and I had to go *beg* for him; but I trust he will not die of starvation. His death will be a mere dream!!![18]

During this early spring, the poet grew increasingly wraithlike as he ate less and drank more. His appearance has been compared to that of his favourite fictional character, "the man without a shadow", and his movements to those of one in a dream, as he "glided" through Dublin streets. O'Donovan seems to have stood now in something rather like awe of his friend, so much of the ghostly and other-worldly hung about him. As Joseph Brenan would say, Mangan looked as if "the sword is eating through the sheath".

Of the *Catholic Magazine* poems, "Stabat Mater Dolorosa", from the Latin, was at least as moving and as fine as most versions of this famous hymn. Still, it did not come up to the standard required by the Sisters of Charity of St Vincent's Hospital in St Stephen's Green who were compiling a new book of hymns and prayers at this time. R.D. Williams was asked by the Sisters for a new translation, but he declined, observing, "Clarence Mangan tried it the other day, and utterly failed. . . . And besides, one should be very holy to do *that*."[19] Interestingly, when he finally did try his hand at it, he placed the initial emphasis in the poem on the Man of Sorrows, while Mangan, like more modern translators, stressed the Mourning Mother.

May Mangan's first original poem since the previous November was a macabre companion piece to the news of the day. The ghoulish "A Tale of a Coffin" was probably based on some eastern yarn; its appeal for the poet obviously lay in its supernatural elements and in its characters, two brothers and a dreadful spectre. Narrated by one Muslim to another as they prepare to enter a mosque, it is the story of how the mosque came to be built. Two brothers lived in the town, the narrator began. When the "sodden sot" of the two died, the townspeople forbade his burial, and only his brother was left to stand watch over his coffin as "The sad winds went sighing/Through the long, dim death room drearily." As discussed earlier here, the poem featured what was, for Mangan, the nightmarish image of "A large copper mask, whereon was graven/These words: 'Rivetted for ETERNITY'."

Whatever horror Mangan might imagine in a poem fell short of the reality all around him. On 8 May, the *Nation* carried an appalling account of famine and fever that spoke of Cork as "a city of the plague—the unburied corpses trip men in the streets." The writer, perhaps Mitchel, did not hesitate to place blame: "These deaths are as clearly chargeable on the English Government as Abel's death upon Cain. . . ." The 15 May newspaper reported famine riots in the counties of Limerick, Kerry, Tipperary, and Clare, and the blood-chilling news that Famine fever had also reached Dublin. "The scourge which has swept the provinces has now entered the capital", the story began. Two dozen or more men and women stricken with the fever were refused admission to hospital every day because of overcrowding. The Fever Hospital in Cork Street in which Mangan had spent some days over twenty-five years earlier was still the main facility to house fever victims. It had been enlarged to accommodate some 250–300 patients, but sheds and tents now held hundreds more. Still, its twenty-five hundred beds were inadequate to meet the demand. Dr Stokes, who worked through this epidemic, wrote that these figures really gave no idea of the actual number of the sick, because so many of the poor never thought of entering hospital. The epidemic would peak in June, but no decline in numbers of the sick or dying occurred until the next February; that is, the *peak* rate of infection continued for some ten months.

The situation seems not only terrible but surrealistic when one reads, one after the other, accounts of famine or fever deaths and the food market reports. Thus the *Nation's* front page of 15 May carried the advertisement of Mangan's cousin Michael Smith's Copper Alley establishment. Here, it informed readers, were offered for sale both "family" beef and "prime mess" beef, "prime mess pork in barrells, 200 lbs each", sugar-cured ham, cheese, flour, Indian meal and "White Boiling Beans, (best substitute for potatoes. . . ." All were proffered "on advantageous terms".

Soup kitchens had by this time been opened all over the country. In Dublin, one was placed at the Royal Barracks in Parkgate Street, just north of the Liffey. This "model soup kitchen" was a wooden building thirty feet wide and forty feet long, with long tables running its length, and a door at each end. In the centre stood a 300 gallon soup boiler. The hungry gathered outside, and at the sound of a bell, one hundred were admitted by one door. They filed past the boiler, each receiving a spoon attached by a chain to a metal bowl into which the soup was ladled. When they finished eating, they turned in the bowl and spoon, received a portion of bread, and left by the other door. In theory, the eating utensils were rinsed before being passed out to the next hundred. In practice, the haste with which everything had to be done probably increased the carelessness that always prevails at mass feedings. And there was haste. The kitchen was designed to distribute a maximum of 5,000 bowls of soup daily, that is, fifty seatings were deemed possible. How even this could have been managed is baffling enough. How the 9,000 who came could have been fed is beyond understanding.[20]

Various recipes were used for the soup that was supposed to save lives. Opinion varied on whether it did that or merely lengthened suffering, for a liquid diet increased the starving person's diarrhea and resultant weakness. French chef Alexis Soyer had concocted a recipe that cost just three farthings per quart to make, and it already had been distributed to the London poor. Now, this was tried in Ireland. It was, Cecil Woodham-Smith observed, an "alarmingly economical" recipe. Yet for a bowl of this broth, thousands waited hours daily, and hundreds had to be turned away, the supply exhausted. Soyer's receipt was simple in the extreme, but perhaps "not untasty", as he declared "people of standing" whom he had asked to sample it had assured him. To two gallons of water were added a quarter pound of beef, two ounces each of dripping and vegetables (often onions), a half-pound each of flour and pearl barley, three ounces of salt and a half ounce of brown sugar. Pretty clearly, every ingredient except the water, flour, and barley was merely flavouring. When each supplicant was ladeled out two cups of this soup, a generous estimate, he or she had received, in effect, the day's food ration: two tablespoons of flour and one tablespoon of barley.

Mangan wrote briefly to McGlashan this month:

> My Dear Sir,—
>
> I thank you from my heart for your kindness. I enclose you additional stanzas of "the Death Chant" [of King Regner Lodbrok]. The difficulty of varying the forms of expression in such a peculiar poem increases on me of course as I proceed.
>
> Would you want a Midsummer Anthology for June? or a Polyglot for the opening volume in July? or a very striking story, the scene of which should be laid in our college?[21]

McGlashan's "kindness" may have been something as ordinary as paying Mangan for his second chapter of the "Anthologia Hibernica" that appeared this month in the *University Magazine*. Like the first, it was a third short of a full sheet, and a generous guess would be that he was paid £5 for it. This chapter presented his translations of another seven poems; a number of the "originals", or, more accurately, translations he had found in Walsh's *Irish Popular Songs* and John O'Daly's manuscripts, and he had reworked or versified them to please himself. The most readable, today, of this group is the charming "Ellen Bawn", styled by Mangan a "miniature poetical gem". It is little short of amazing to find him, at this juncture, able to use a lighter, livelier touch than at almost any other time in his life. This poem of five stanzas opened:

> Ellen Bawn, O Ellen Bawn, you darling, darling dear, you,
> Sit awhile beside me here, I'll die unless I'm near you!
> 'Tis for you I'd swim the Suir and breast the Shannon's waters;
> For, Ellen dear, you've not your peer in Galway's blooming daughters!

As to the rest of Mangan's short letter, the poem of which he spoke and to which he continued to make additions, "The Death Chant of King Regner Lodbrok", appeared in August. He did not do a "Midsummer Anthology" for McGlashan nor was there a "Polyglot Anthology" in July, although "Lays of Many Lands" in September may have been what he had in mind. The "story" was almost certainly the same one he had mentioned before that had not been returned to him by the editor of the *Irish Monthly Magazine* when it ceased publication. Now, apparently, it was back in his possession; it would be interesting to know how it was disposed of at his death, for it was never printed.

On the page just before the Irish anthology, the *University Magazine* carried a poem titled "To Clarence Mangan" by the Right Rev. William Fitzgerald. It neatly set forth some of the complexities of Mangan's position: he was a bard confronted by "the true Irish metre" which was "full of tricks and rogueries" that slip "from your fingers at unawares", and he handled it expertly:

> Various and curious are thy strains, O, Clarence Mangan!
> Rhyming and chiming in a very odd way:
> Rhyming and chiming—the like of them no man can
> Easily find in a long summer's day!

Towards the close, he turned political:

> I do not care a button for Young Ireland, or Old Ireland;
> But, as between the two, I rather like old Dan,
> And I wish the Nation would let the agitation
> Die a humbug as it first began![22]

Late in the month, the city sustained a shock about "old Dan" for which no amount of anticipation had prepared it. Daniel O'Connell, who, unwell and greatly aged, had left for Italy earlier in the spring, died in Genoa on 15 May. The news took over a week to get back to Ireland, but on 29 May the *Nation*, heavily bordered in black, carried a lengthy and laudatory obituary of "the illustrious and venerable leader of the Irish people". The shock of the loss was enormous. As soon became apparent, only the presence of the beloved and powerful figure of the Liberator had kept the politics of the island from erupting into a chaotic contest for power. Even in the machinations around the funeral, there was ugly rivalry between Young Ireland and Old Ireland.

Unhappily, an unexpected streak of meanness of spirit showed up on this occasion in some of the Young Irelanders. Fr Kenyon was one. When Mitchel refused to publish the priest's snide and insulting protest against mourning, Duffy, perhaps unwisely, over-rode, his co-editor in the interest of freedom of speech and elicited a flock of angry reactions from readers. That Fr Meehan held views similar to Fr Kenyon's but was keeping them to himself was leaked to the *Pilot* and the *Weekly Register*, O'Connell's papers, and they heatedly protested. Making matters worse was Devin Reilly's "fulsome piece of 'stilt[ed] exaggeration' in praise of O'Connell" which the *Nation* also rather foolishly printed. Mitchel, from whom one might have anticipated something opinionated and fiery, evidently held his peace; he observed two years later, according to Henry Boylan's *Dictionary of Irish Biography*: "Poor old Dan! Wonderful, mighty, jovial and mean old man! . . . What a royal yet vulgar soul! . . . Pray . . . that the good God who knew how to create so wondrous a creature may have mercy on his soul."

A notice in the "Answers to Correspondents" column in the same number of the *Nation* that carried O'Connell's obituary was almost certainly addressed to Mangan, a possibility strengthened by the fact that his name does not appear in the list of poets that is given: "M.—a series of papers on our latter poets—Callanan, Griffin, Maginn, Davis, Moore —would be a fine exercise for your poetical taste and an acceptable service to the country."[23] Here, perhaps, is the origin of the idea for the late series of prose papers he did for the *Irishman*.

June On the first day of the month, Mangan sent a critically important and entirely professional letter to Charles Gavan Duffy, addressing him as an editor rather than as a friend. A great deal of thought must have gone into this piece of writing. The long letter and its accompanying document have been quoted piecemeal so often, with bits misleadingly reproduced out of context or with paragraphs to which they have no relationship, that they are both given in full here.[24]

My dear Duffy,

The document that I enclose you I would wish to send as a sort of circular among some of my literary friends. There would, of course, be some slight variations in the phraseology—particularly in that of the concluding sentence—but the purport of the entire would be mainly the same.

Believe me that if I did not feel within myself energies that lie smothering and dormant, and capabilitites that have never yet seen the daylight, I should consider any appeal to you or others a very presumptuous impertinent proceeding on my part. It is simply because I *know* that I can yet repay you twenty-fold that I dare to address you at all. Let me be tested henceforth by my acts. Whatever man can achieve for himself or others, that, so help me Heaven! I will try, strive—or, as the Greek of the N.T. has it—agonise to accomplish. But more upon this subject as soon as I shall be settled—[He was thinking of leaving Peter Street, it appears.]

Meantime I shall see you according to your wish, at 2 o'c. to-day.

You must throw me two columns of the NATION open for the Elegy on O'Connell—(i.e. if you chuse to accept my contribution) and I will try to make it worthy of the occasion—but you must also permit me to do the thing in the form of an address to yourself.

The "document" was the poet's declaration of intent:

I, James Clarence Mangan, promise, with all the sincerity that can attach to the declaration of a human being, to dedicate the portion of my life that may yet remain to me to penitence and exertion.

I promise, in the solemn presence of Almighty God, and, as I trust, with His assistance, to live soberly, abstemiously and regularly in all respects.

I promise in the same Presence that I will not spare myself, that I will endeavour to do all the good within my power to others, that I will constantly advocate the cause of temperance, the interests of knowledge and the duties of patriotism, and finally, that I will do all these things irrespective of any concern personal to myself, and whether my exertions be productive of profit and fame to me, or, as may happen in the troublous times that I believe are at hand, eventuate in sinking me further into poverty and (undeserved) ignominy.

Lastly, I promise, in a special manner—and my friend Duffy may, if he will, make the promise public—that I will begin in earnest to labour for my country henceforward, and that, come weal or woe, life or death, glory or shame, the triumphal chariot or the gallows, I will adhere to the fortunes of my fellow-patriots. And I invoke the vengeance of hell upon me if I ever prove false to this promise.

Again, Duffy chose not to make public the poet's dedication to the nationalist cause, and also, in this case, his desire to take a temperance pledge. He never gave any reason for refusing Mangan's request. If he thought the wording was too florid, if he assumed the promise to stop drinking would soon be broken, if he did not want the responsibility for the poet's future on his shoulders—whatever may have occasioned his second rejection of his friend, it was, again, an action which he regretted in his heart and would find himself covering up in his memoirs.

In the next week, the two men met and talked. Mangan evidently accepted Duffy's negative decision without protest, and it was at least sweetened with a generous offer. On 8 June, he wrote another long letter asking for help, and the editor was perhaps instrumental in getting "The Death Chant" printed in August and the Irish anthology the next month:

> "Private" 8th June—9 Peter St
>
> My dear Duffy,
>
> May God for ever bless you! I know you too well to suppose that you are one to "keep the word of promise to the ear and break it to the hope."
>
> You spoke of getting up as much for me as might pay for half a year's board. I dare say that would be at least £15—though I consume, God knows, very little food indeed. Suppose you were to say a quarter's, instead of a half year's, and allow me the difference in hand to enable me to dispose of my poor half broken-hearted brother, and settle with my landlord withal. If you can do this you will rescue me from the depths of despair. Or, if you cannot do this I will tell you what you *can* do for me without in the least inconveniencing yourself. McGlashan has an Anthology (an Irish one) of mine in his hands—and he also has a Scandinavian poem—"The Death Song of Regner Lodbrok"—of which I have made half a sheet. He has had them a long time in his hands, and he owes me about £2 on them. But as they have not yet appeared (though the Anthology is in type) I have an utter repugnance to ask him for any more money. I paid *him* the £7.10 which he granted me at the same time with your equally liberal loan. Would to God that I had worked as zealously since for you, my best, my truest, my noblest-hearted friend! But I will yet retrieve the Past in this respect, or may my name be blotted out for ever from the page of the Book of Life! To the point, however, I have, in my despair, begun a Polyglot Anthology which I calculate on finishing within a week— for I translate at the rate of about 80 lines a [day].[25]

Unfortunately, the last line has long been missing, but Duffy himself completed it "day", no doubt correctly. Nothing more was heard of the "subscription"; whether the plan came to fruition or died a-borning is not known.

The letters the poet wrote to McGlashan have been lost, probably many years ago, with the papers of James Price who printed portions of them in his *Evening Packet* articles about Mangan. The paragraphs that follow were undated and somewhat misarranged by Price but would seem to have been written by Mangan one after the other in a letter or letters from this period. They definitely followed closely on the above:

> Henceforward, I will labour with redoubled sedulousness. I enclose you a Polyglot Anthology, comprising translations from the Irish, German, Danish,

> Swiss dialect, French, Spanish, Welsh, and Persian. They are all *bona fide* ones; and I purpose, if you please, to send you also poems from the Servian, Romaic, and Turkish; but perhaps you might think these would lengthen the article too much. But in truth, I *must* rise early and work hard, as I feel that I shall almost go mad if I have not constant employment both for my head and my hands.

And another passage:

> I have always, my dear sir, found you very kind and offhand in your pecuniary transactions; indeed, in this respect, I know nobody like you. I make you now a fresh proposal, and I pledge myself to work for you with all the powers of my mind and intellect. I pledge myself to rise early, to labour hard, not to spare myself, to endeavour to cultivate my intellectual powers to their highest point, and, in fine, to redeem the last and past years of my life as far as may be possible. In fact, I pledge myself to become a new man in soul, body, mind, character, and conduct. But my fate now, I say it solemnly, [is] in your hands. You have been hitherto the kindest of friends to me, and I trust in Heaven you will not now, in the darkest hour of my life, abandon me.

McGlashan was anything but "kind and offhand" in his financial dealings, which Mangan knew very well, yet he had to cajole and flatter—anything to gain the assistance necessary. And just as he had sworn self-renewal to Duffy, so he swore it to McGlashan. A little later, there was another cry for help; with a surprising twist:

> In the name of Heaven, advance me something with the generosity which has always characterised your dealings with me. If you will not, let me know the worst. I have been offered the situation of French and German correspondent in a Commercial House in Liverpool, (Wilmington and Pratts,) and though I know the hours will kill me, I am almost determined to accept the offer. . . . My circumstances have rendered me quite reckless.[26]

It seems unlikely that any business firm could have offered him employment, and no "Wilmington and Pratts" has been found in a Liverpool directory. Still, it would be ill-advised to assume he made it up, for Mangan had more connections than we know about. A few days later, in a calmer mood, he retracted his request for an advance. He had evidently promised himself (as well as others) that he wouldn't resort to that expediency, not even, as he said here, "for the sake of others", as it meant submitting "to the forfeiture of self-respect".

John Keegan was in the city this spring and wrote back to his friend Margaret Campion in the country, as noted previously. Some of his news was literary gossip about the *Irish Catholic Magazine*—Edward Walsh, it appeared, had been "discarded from its pages" because he had disagreed in the *Register* with Denis Florence MacCarthy, one of Fr Meehan's favourites. It was also in this letter that he gave the most unpleasant description of Mangan that has come down to us: "pale face, little cat-like eyes, sleepy in his appearance, and slovenly, sottish, and clownish in exterior". On 25 June, he again was in Dublin and again wrote Miss Campion, this time with a less derogatory comment about the poet:

> I got an invitation to hold a *tete-a-tete* with Clarence Mangan some day next week, and I think I will accept of it. I will be happy to know that highly gifted man. He is a most extraordinary fellow, living in strict seclusion, and seldom appearing abroad except in tap rooms and low public-houses. He might earn £20 a week by his pen, but he cares nothing if he can get enough of wine and whiskey, fuel and plain clothes. He is about my age, slovenly in his person, and cares nothing for what the world may say or think of him or his talents.[27]

Although Keegan may have been exaggerating, it is certain that Mangan was now in a sad condition, desperately trying to cling to his home and his dignity, and to earn enough to support himself and his brother. That he was caught in the drinker's dilemma in which one more drink requires one more drink seems certain. Nevertheless, it was sheer nonsense for Keegan to suggest that Mangan could "earn £20 a week by his pen", as if he had but to concentrate on his writing to be a rich man. To have earned that amount, at the best rate he had ever been paid, he would have had to produce almost three hundred lines a day.

At about this time, he wrote O'Daly:

> My dear Daly Monday morning
>
> If you can really obtain me 10s.—say by Thursday—you will save me from a doom that I dread to contemplate. I shall be obliged to leave my lodgings and perhaps will die in the streets. If you *can* so far serve me in this matter, *I can promise you that you and all my friends will see me henceforth a new man. . . .* Oh! No one but myself knows what longings I have after a purer and better life. The only thing in my favor is, that amid disease and misery I still work hard. But to how much more purpose would I work under improved circumstances! If you can get me those ten shillings they will prove my salvation.

He would have preferred to remain in the family home, of that there can be no question. Nor can there be much doubt that he knew he simply was not going to be able to manage it. And to be homeless was the "doom I dread to contemplate", as well it might be. It raises the possibility that it had always been the dread of homelessness that had prompted him to write so often on the subject. He went on:

> Perhaps it was Providence that raised you up to me as a friend, and led you to call on me yesterday. My brother has taken what little money I had, and my landlord threatens to turn me out of doors, and seize on what little furniture is still left me.
>
> Serve me in this matter and I will regularly translate for the "Atheneum" or the "Nation" as many poems from the Leabhar na g-Ceart [The Book of

> Rights that O'Donovan was working on] as you like, besides making the copyright (formally, if you wish) over to you. But if you fail me I am lost—I know not what to do.[28]

The following tragic letter Duffy included with the document Mangan had sent him and also in the context of the publication of the *Anthologia Germanica* (1845), but it surely belongs to the period we have now reached:

> My dear Duffy,
>
> I am utterly prostrated. I am in a state of absolute desolation of spirit.
>
> For the pity of God, come to me. I have ten words to say to you. I implore you to come. Do not suffer me to believe that I am abandoned by Heaven and man.
>
> I cannot stir out—cannot look any one in the face. Regard this as my last request, and comply with it as if you supposed me dying.
>
> I am hardly able to hold the pen, but I will not, and dare not, take any stimulants to enable me to do so. Too long and fatally already have I been playing that game with my shattered nerves. Enough. God ever bless you. Oh, come!—Ever yours, J.C. Mangan[29]

In the 25 June number of the *Nation* appeared a poem that asked a pertinent question and that called attention to something regular readers must already have noticed: the newspaper had become almost entirely a political publication, to the exclusion of literature. "Where have all the poets gone?" the writer asked:

> Where, above all, art thou oh! Clarence Mangan?
> And here you will allow me just to state,
> Although I am no bruiser, like Jack Langan,
> And not in any sense a man of weight,
> Yet I would walk from Rathlin to Rathangan
> That man to fight, call out, or lick, or slate,
> And spoil his taste for vision and for victual,
> Who would attempt to wrong thee in a tittle.

July Where was Clarence Mangan indeed? Rents were due quarterly. He did not have the wherewithal to pay his, and, as he had written to O'Daly, his long-suffering landlord had already threatened to turn him out of doors. That this was exactly what happened seems all too probable. Mangan thus began the final woeful two years of his life as an uprooted wanderer.

Acquaintances sometimes offered him a place to stay, but he turned down almost all these invitations, perhaps because William was not included. Occasionally he went to Fr Meehan's Presbytery and perhaps spent some time there. He dropped a note to Duffy about one such visit telling him, "My room is on the second floor—it is the back room."[30] Fr Kenyon also would have made him welcome in Templederry, but for the poet to leave Dublin for an unfamiliar locale would have been almost unthinkable. James Duffy "made him a generous offer of bed and board, and a fair allowance of money in his house on Wellington Quay", but there were strings attached. According to Fr Meehan, he refused both Fr Kenyon and James Duffy because he dreaded "what he regarded as a surrender of liberty"—and especially the requirement that he abstain from drink. Nothing in the poet's nature equipped him to adapt to living with others. Restlessness, almost certainly irritability when his needs or wants were challenged, and an incorrigible willfulness would have made him a difficult guest. O'Donoghue described him as "extremely docile in all things except his course of life".[31]

He did accept one invitation. Early in July, he spent some time with the family of the Dublin alderman and merchant William C. MacDermott in Glasnevin, and while there wrote an extra stanza for a poem by the poet Robert Bloomfield that MacDermott's composer brother, Thomas Harris MacDermott, was setting to music:

All around me liveth still,
    All, as in my childhood's hours;
Still flows on the tinkling rill,
    And still the dell is rich with flowers.
Here again my heart lives o'er
    Its early golden dreams of joy,
And now, amid these groves once more,
    I feel myself almost a boy.[32]

He also seems to have presented a serious challenge to their sister Mary, a passionate temperance advocate. She failed to reform him and "never forgave Mangan for baffling her efforts". He was soon away from this retreat and back in Dublin in cheap rooms and serious trouble.

About the middle of the month when he and William had secured one of their "miserable lodgings", the two quarreled and, according to Mangan, his brother drove him out "with buffetings and blows which, thank God, I did not return". For several days and nights he stayed in the streets. Eventually writing to Duffy, he tried to describe his mental state. He had felt, he wrote, that he had lost any possibility of appeal to those men who had assisted him before. "I knew nobody to whom I could apply", he wrote. Then, sensing the glaring contradiction between that and his past history, corrected himself: "Perhaps I should say to whom I *would* apply—for my spirit seemed to rise in inverse proportion to the depth of my destitution." Was he, as some have observed, actually revelling in at last really going under? Had he, in a clinical sense, temporarily lost his mind? His words almost sound as if this were the case: "I had a melancholy consolation in thinking that I should be found dead of hunger somewhere about the suburbs of the city", he confessed. He was very tired of the battle. There must have been a certain amount of relief in thinking that he was finally being overwhelmed by odds plainly too great to overcome. But that did not happen.

It would appear that he actually had not dragged himself very far from his home turf, for he was eventually found by a stranger who took him to his cousin Michael Smyth, as it was sometimes spelled, in Copper Alley. Smyth did not humour him. Rather, he gave him a bed ("a rug upon straw") in a barrel-loft of the warehouse for two or three nights "and sent me up a cup of tea at intervals. God bless him!" The poet must have been in deplorable shape, unwashed, unkempt, and much the worse for drink, to explain Smyth's not having him in his house. Mangan implied as much himself. After a few days on cups of tea, "I then waited on my cousin myself". This was the same cousin who belonged to the Council of the Irish Confederation and, the poet said bluntly, "owned the house that ought to be mine". Mustering his dignity, he "just said, 'Michael, I am going down to your father's—your family have often solicited me to pay them a visit—I will now test their sincerity.' He coldly told me that I would be welcome—and I set off."

On 21 July, a week or so after his arrival at his mother's family home near Kiltale in County Meath, he wrote lengthily to Duffy, telling him all of the above and tracing the course of his "cure":

> [I] paid my last maravedi for a seat in the Caravan. And so, here I am—with the fresh breezes of Heaven blowing about me—with rivers of the purest spring water to drink—but with nothing, positively nothing to eat, excepting eggs, which I direct to be boiled very hard, to compensate for the absence of bread—though if you consider that the bread itself here (mill-stone griddle bread) is a thousand times harder than the eggs can be made, you may regard my assertion as more paradoxical than beseemeth.
>
> My health is, after all, improving—but my mind is destroying me. What with the clear spring water and fresh air on one hand—and the absence of all stimulants on the other—I find myself in a hybrid state which I shall not attempt to describe. I left my poor brother without a shilling for himself—and I retained but two or three shillings in my own pocket.[33]

He was stranded. The "lonely farm house in the heart of a wilderness" had no neighbour for two miles and the nearest post-town was five miles away. Evidently there was no source of temptation in the house, and it is interesting to consider how very abstemious the Smith (or Smyth) family seems to have been. He must have been made reasonably welcome, as he remained with them for about six weeks, not returning to Dublin until the end of August or the first of September.

Meanwhile, his third "Anthologia Hibernica" appeared. With it, he had begun work on Irish historical poems. There were only two in the chapter, but they made up a selection fourteen pages long. The literal translations had been supplied by "the celebrated Irish scholar, Mr. Eugene Curry". Each was in its own way nationalistic. The last words of "On the Inauguration of the O'Brien, AD 1469" were "We are not FREE", while "The Panegyric of Thomas Butler" was a catalogue of the murders and pillagings committed by the Elizabethan conqueror of Ireland. Although Mangan expressed the intent and wish to do more Irish anthologies, this would be his last. I suspect that the editors sensed an ulterior motive behind such bombastic entries as these two and decided he had crossed the line between national poems and nationalist propaganda.

The *Nation's* query, "Where have all the poets gone?" drew a smattering of answers, and a notice in the issue of 17 July claimed it had produced so fine a selection that "we will not only publish an armful of them, but cashier the old corps in favor of the young competitors . . . there is a good time coming, when parliamentary politics will be scarce and poetics plenty." But it was not yet. The "armful" consisted mostly of fairly clever parodies of the work of such contributors as Duffy, Williams, and Mangan. One of the neatest was "A Vision of Ireland in the Nineteenth Century", a parody of Mangan's "A Vision of Connaught in the Thirteenth Century". It has been suggested that Mangan wrote it himself, but as Williams was such a good parodist, the palm should probably go to him. The opening stanza:

I walked aghast
Where the land was filled
With famine and death from morn to night;
The Spring had passed
Over fields untilled,
And broken up high ways aleft and right.
Even in the clime
Where the wild wolf strays,
There is no such land as that land of woes;
For it was the time
We were in the days
Of R[andolp]h R[out]h of the wine-red nose.[34]

Routh, as Commissary General, had a reputation for enjoying parties, but he was not by any means Ireland's worst overseer during these awful years.

August After long delays, Daniel O'Connell was laid to rest in Glasnevin Cemetery on 5 August. Political bickering among the nationalists had been unseemly and ill-tempered, with blame for every ill from Ireland's plight to O'Connell's death flung indiscriminately by both Old and Young

Ireland. In the event, Young Ireland as represented by the Confederation played no part at all in the funeral. The *Nation*, however, carried a long account including the order of march, but no long commemorative poem by Mangan or anyone else. In the country, Clarence Mangan missed the whole affair, writing poetry in pencil as he leaned back against a haystack "after a fast (like St Leon's in the Dungeon of Bethlem Gabor) of thirty-six hours". Once again, he was considering the non-essential nature of eating: "I am clearly convinced that there may be worse intemperance in eating than even in drinking", he mused.

Like every such respite, his country "idyll" had to come to an end eventually, and he was unceremoniously received back into the city without any more income than he had had when he left and without any place to stay. Presumably, his prospect of being fit for regular writing was much improved, however. Penniless, he had to take whatever sort of lodging he could get, and he may well have returned to the territory around Fishamble Street. Fr Meehan left an account of Mangan probably dating from this time:

> One fine summer evening, after more than a fortnight's absence, an old crone who might have personated one of Macbeth's witches, brought [Mangan] to the door of the old trysting-place [the Presbytery], and stated that she had turned him out, because she could get no good of him. On inquiry, it transpired that she had given him lodging in her hay-loft in [Copper Alley]; and that he quarrelled with her because she wouldn't allow him a candle in the night time. "Sure sir," she said, "you might as well think of bringin' a burnin' sod of turf into a powder magazine, and I'll have no more to do with him, let him pay me, and he can have his tar water, and the papers that he was writin'." [35]

September For a while, the poet's letters are pleasantly different from those he had been writing during the first half of the year. He had taken action, successfully, to "retrieve the Past" and to "become a new man". He was clear headed and capable of working hard. Promptly, he returned to McGlashan the proofs of another month's "Lays of Many Lands", a total of 484 lines, for which he should have received almost £5. The editor and the poet may have reached a new understanding, if Mangan's reference to his "monthly contribution" is taken literally:

> I fancy I have discovered the true key to my health, and please the Fates! hope to unlock with that same key the portal that bars from me the free and uncontrolled exercise of my intellect. You shall have the remainder of my monthly contribution by Monday. There will be some striking and fiery ballads therein. It will conclude, unless you object, the "Stray Leaflets". [November's was the last.] I am rather anxious to be done with the German, and to enter upon some new track. How glad I should be to get that Danish

volume of Ewald's *Poems* which I bespoke of [to] you. The Irish Anthologies, however, are those to which I mean now chiefly to devote my attention.[36]

He was able to sustain the monthly pace only through January 1848, when, with his fourth "Lays", the series stopped appearing for six months. Each installment was just about long enough to bring him £5, which would have been just about enough for him to live on. Of the Irish anthologies, however, no more materialized.

With the above letter he returned the proofs of Lamartine's "Napoleon" (*DUM*, October 1847) which, he declared, he thought the finest thing he had ever done. About payment for his manuscript, which happened to be the one written leaning against a haystack, he wrote:

> My dear Sir
>
> With what you so kindly and off-handedly gave me on Tuesday I was enabled to procure several articles of dress (shirts, stockings, etc.). I was, in truth, very much in need of them. If you will say £2 for the enclosed contribution I shall be quite satisfied. ["Napoleon" was 180 lines long, so this was fair.] This will enable me not only to settle with my worthy hostess, and, I am sorry to say, unworthy laundress, but, my dear sir, it will provide me with the means of procuring some books of Danish and Swedish poetry.[37]

That would give him the greatest pleasure, he added, because "I would prefer the possession of one book purchased with my own earnings to that of a hundred presented to me by others."

Also at about this time he sent McGlashan the manuscript of "The Marvellous Bell", which appeared in October, saying:

> I now propose, as far as possible, to retrieve the past, and I hope I shall be sustained by your kind offices. I enclose you a legendary ballad from the Bohemian, the literature of which language I have now been studying for several months. Could you favour me with the usual price for it? It is with great pain that I bring myself to make this request, as, when I consider the multitude of my past obligations to you . . . I am overwhelmed. But please God! I will yet achieve more for my reputation than I have yet accomplished. That I might not be tempted to relapse into my old habits, I have renewed my vow of abstinence.[38]

This was one of his most candid assertions about his drinking. The next letter which James Price included, as well as a few others from approximately this date, were also unusually frank on the subject. In this context, only "stimulants", Mangan confessed, had made it possible for him to concentrate or even to hold a pen, and he hinted at his deviousness in asking his friends for money: "I have now no longer the same motive for requesting money . . . I am now and henceforth a water drinker. . . ." But most poignant was this passage:

> I have but one request to make of you, that is, that you will not judge me by what you have known of me. I have really only begun to exist within the last month. You perhaps remember that Godwin describes St Leon, after the latter has been imprisoned bodily for twelve years, as "the mere shell and shadow of a man—of no more worth and power than that which a magic lanthorn inscribes on a wall." Imagine, then, what my condition must have been, shut up within the cell of my own chafed and miserable spirit for fifteen years![39]

Without equivocation, Mangan thus pinpointed the year, 1832, when he began not only his "career" but also the habit that had proved so destructive and that he desired with his whole heart to put behind him. He gave it his best try. If he did not succeed, it was because nothing in his life that had caused him to turn to drink for both solace and strength had altered. If anything, times were worse, and he was certainly older and more world-weary.

October It now became obvious that for the third consecutive year there was to be no potato crop. The reason was, if possible, doubly tragic: although the blight itself was not much in evidence, the people had had no seed potatoes to plant in the spring and hence nothing to harvest in the fall. The *Nation* carried stories of evictions from all over the island. In County Clare, eight hundred families were newly destitute. In County Galway, one hundred people were dispossessed in a single week. In County Kerry, thousands were dependent on public employment "of which there is none, or public charity", of which there was very little.[40]

O'Donovan's letters show the progress of the disaster. In June, he had described for Hardiman his efforts to get food in Dublin, almost humorously complaining that he had had to "lay out a great deal of my hard-earned money (treasured up for old age!!) for *peas*, bread, and American beef, which *I* could hardly chew!!"[41] Now, to a relative, Francis Daniel McCarthy, in Paris he declared more sombrely, "The state of the country is truly frightful. . . . Ireland will be converted into one vast poor house."[42] There was much pity along with the usual anger. He had, he wrote, "visited and examined ten thousand Irish cabins", and he understood all too well: the country was "just now *ruined*". In fact, the antiquarian community, better perhaps than any other body of observers, knew that an entire way of life was dying.

Meanwhile, the Irish Confederation in its Council worried over the question of what could be done to alleviate the worst of the suffering. Their resolutions have a hollow ring because, good intentions notwithstanding, they had absolutely no power of enforcement. Mitchel, for instance, proposed, Devin Reilly seconded, and the assembled members passed a motion acknowledging that it was their "duty" to make sure no one starved to death during the next year. Obviously, they did not have the authority, or the funds, to see that their "duty" was done.

As day followed terrible day, the differences between Duffy and Mitchel grew more divisive, and finally on 19 October, Mitchel proffered his resignation to the Council. It was refused, and he was begged not to withdraw, but the die was cast. Over the course of the year, he had come increasingly under the influence of James Fintan Lalor, a radical thinker who linked the Irish land problem with national independence and, like Mitchel, believed that the English had deliberately adopted a policy to exterminate the peasantry and "turn the country into a stock farm".[43] The *Nation* tried to air Duffy's and Mitchel's views evenhandedly, so the scope of their division was evident to anyone who read the newspapers. They split on several main issues, from the old debate over the legitimacy of the use of force, to class division and the Coercion Bill. In broad strokes, it was apparent that Duffy was the more conservative and conciliatory, bent on slow progress through education and deliberation; Mitchel was virtually his antithesis, supporting action, challenge, and if it seemed as if nothing else would work, as much force as they could muster. Mangan was caught between his old friend and the radical whose fire-breathing philosophy appealed strongly to him. He did not yet have to choose between them, but the time was growing closer when he would decide to do so.

The most singular poem of Mangan's this month and perhaps for many months was "Moreen: A Love Lament", notable for two stanzas at about mid-poem which have been taken out of context and widely anthologized as "Shapes and Signs". Although according to Mangan a translation from the Irish poet Charles Boy MacQuillan, the poem has not been found among his known works and offers so much that seems personal to Mangan that it has been almost impossible not to read it as being of his composition. In fact, no less a scholar than Jacques Chuto believes that the poem was probably original to Mangan.

The persona is a man doomed by—one knows, although the word does not appear—an uncontrollable craving for drink. The first thing about it which strikes one as being not at all like Mangan, however, is that he is quite fascinated by himself and his horrible condition, which he revels in describing. Moreover, the dramatic monologue is addressed so particularly to a specific woman, Moreen Mulhall, and the story is so specific to their relationship, that to imagine Mangan writing, not translating, the poem is almost impossible. By 1847, the invention of a love story was the farthest thing from his mind. In MacQuillan's poem, "Moreen" has returned and begged for a reconciliation with the speaker, but he refuses her request, first, because he now "exults alone in one wild hour", that hour when "the red cup drowns/The horrors it anon renews"; and also because "Memory's ever-festering barb" tells him "that of all my foes/ The falsest was Moreen Mulhall,/The traitress under Friendship's garb!". The end has already been defined:

The Gone is gone! Man cannot track
Afresh his course of blasted years,
Or bid flower bloom where fires have been!
Our goals,—for you, Contrition,
For me, Despair,—are set.
My path lies onwards to Perdition:
Your tears may save you yet!

Mangan, or someone, rewrote the poem, and it was printed as "Groans of Despair" in the *Nation* for 6 October 1849, almost four months after his death. The name "Moreen Mulhall" was dropped, and the poem was addressed to "my friend", in imitation of "The Dying Enthusiast to His Friend". About half the stanzas were eliminated, and necessary changes were made in several others. Only three were left almost identical with those of the poem in its first incarnation, and of these, two are often anthologized as "Shapes and Signs", a title taken from "The Nameless One" and first used in the 1900 publication of Stopford A. Brooke's and T.W. Rolleston's *A Treasury of Irish Poetry in the English Tongue*. They were not then treated as an autonomous poem. However, they were so sensational that they invited reprinting, and as Chuto has written, "It is a pity that later anthologists should have . . . printed 'Shapes and Signs' as if it were a complete poem." [44]

The existence of such passages in a writer's work proves nothing about the writer, although the temptation, as Augustine Martin has pointed out, is to believe that Mangan's life itself is "guarantee enough that these are confessional lyrics witnessing to a spiritual condition in his own experience".[45] It is better to read them for what they genuinely are, however, the evocation of "a mental landscape of terror and desolation remarkable even in the post-Romantic convention to which they adhere". To that end, the stanzas appear below:

I see black dragons mount the sky;
I see Earth yawn aneath my feet;
I feel within the Asp, the Worm,
That will not sleep and cannot die,
Fair though may show my winding-sheet!
I hear all night, as through a storm,
Hoarse voices calling, calling
My name upon the wind,
All omens monstrous and appalling
Afright my guilty mind!

I exult alone in one wild hour,
    That hour wherein the red cup drowns
        The horrors it anon renews
In ghastlier guise, in fiercer power;—
    Then Glory brings me golden crowns,
        And visions of all brilliant hues
            Lap my lost soul in gladness,
                Until I awake again,
            And the dark lava fires of madness
                Once more sweep through my brain.[46]

November/December Mangan mentioned in an earlier letter that he was working on the *Leabhar na g-Ceart* or *Book of Rights* which was also now occupying John O'Donovan. The 13 November *Nation* carried his translation of "The Testament of Cathaeir Mor" which is found in the *Book*. To McGlashan he had written: "It strikes me that a very telling thing might be made out of 'The Will of Cathaeir Mor', in O'Donovan's Leabhar na g-Ceart. I would cast the translation in the same irregular metre as the original, only occasionally doubling the rhymes in a single line, which has a very good effect on an English ear." McGlashan had not taken any action on the poet's further observation, that "It would, if attractively rendered, appear as one of the most characteristic and extraordinary of our archeological literary relics." But Duffy was interested. It is instructive to listen to Mangan planning the shape of a poem; his ear and his taste were (as a rule) excellent, and in this case he did exactly what he had told McGlashan he thought would work best. As a result, "The Testament of Cathaeir Mor" is a very impressive poem and a sort of oddity as well, a strange combination of homely domestic information and legal arrangement. Mangan also dramatized the material, so it is much more entertaining to read than one might expect.

It was printed the next year in a special edition as a presentation copy celebrating the first anniversary of the founding of the Celtic Society.[47] Some changes were made, which O'Donovan oversaw. On 9 December he wrote, again, to Hudson to tell him how they were proceeding, a letter which made it clear that Mangan, although he might know little Irish, certainly had his own ideas about the little he did know. Speaking before a Mangan centenary celebration gathering in 1903, the musician and historian W.H. Grattan Flood maintained that he "had got indisputable evidence that he [Mangan] was not only a tolerable Irish scholar, but that he knew a great deal more than some of the academic scholars of today. . . ." O'Donovan, however, might not have agreed.

From the last paragraph of O'Donovan's letter, it would appear that the good effects of the poet's summer cure had worn off and that he had begun drinking again. O'Donovan was no advocate of abstinence, but it is still a little surprising to hear him speak so lightly about Mangan's fondness for whiskey:

> I think our true poet [Mangan—often the epithet by which they identified him] is wrong in praying *for the soul* of Cathaeir Mor, and I have suggested a change which will set his imagination on the wing. You must allow him his *lion* for *lian*, but I do not like his *Berve* for *Bervha*. If you would allow him the Anglicized form "*Barrow*" then would he have his choice of some grand rhymes.
>
> I do not know the present whereabouts of the true poet, you will have to make him out through the Duffys [that is, Gavan or James] or Magee. Father Meehan says that he has taken again to that divine intoxicator of the soul, "Raw Whiskey" which was always his '*opium*'." [48]

And so from O'Donovan we have yet another negative voice added to the debate over whether or not Mangan used opium.

"The Testament of Cathaeir Mor" is a difficult poem to excerpt to any good effect, but a sample at least needs to be read, if only because the poem has rarely (if ever) appeared in an anthology. The scene is the distribution by the king to his heirs of all his treasures and land. His first bequest is to Ross Faly, "son of my best affection". There follow suitable gifts to six more sons until he reaches his youngest, Fiacha. Gone is everything, from swords and shields to chessmen and chessboard. What can he leave this boy?

> Now Fiacha—youngest son was he,
> Stood up by the bed . . . of his father, who said,
> The while, caressing
> Him tenderly:—
> "My son! I have only for thee my blessing,
> And naught beside—
> Hadst best abide
> With thy brothers a time, as thy years are green."
>
> Then Fiacha wept, with a sorrowful mien:
> So Cathaeir spake, to encourage him, gaily,
> With cheerful speech—
> "Abide one month with thy brethren each,
> And seven years long with my son, Ross Faly;
> Do this, and thy sire in sincerity,
> Prophesies unto thee fame and prosperity."
>
> And further he spake, as one inspired:—
> "A Chieftain flourishing, feared, and admired
> Shall Fiacha prove!
> The gifted man from the boiling Berve,
> Him shall his brothers' clansmen serve."

And so on, for another seventeen lines, as his young son's glowing future is foretold. The prophecy is concluded:

"And many a country thou yet shalt bring
To own thy rule as *Ceann* and King.
    The blessing I give thee shall rest
        On thee and thy seed
            While Time shall endure,
    Thou grandson of Fiacha the Blest!
        It is barely thy meed,
            For thy soul is childlike and pure!"[49]

Change was in the air as the old year drew to a close. Many familiar configurations—people in offices they had held for years, long-standing arrangements—were to be altered as 1848 began. O'Donovan continued to think seriously about emigrating to America. Fr Meehan sought to give up his curacy by being appointed a professor of languages at one of the new Queen's, or provincial, colleges. To Hardiman, he confided that "a purely literary life would be congenial to my tastes. . . ."[50] At the *Dublin University Magazine*, McGlashan's imprint was dropped from the page where it had appeared since the spring of 1846. And most significantly for the poet, John Mitchel left the *Nation*. Duffy told John McCall, it appears, early in the new year, and McCall jotted down Duffy's statement in the back of one of his notebooks: "For the last five weeks one of my closest friends and most valued contributors John Mitchel has ceased to be connected with the Nation."[51]

With the cluster of poems which Mangan sent to the *University Magazine* for January's "Lays of Many Lands" he included a note for McGlashan:

> The year draws to a close. It has furnished me with grave and serious matter for reflection, and, as I should hope, sees me a better and a wiser man than at its commencement. Henceforth, and with the beginning of the new year especially, I lead a new life. I may be unhappy, but I shall no longer be imprudent or criminal.[52]

He was using "criminal" in a metaphorical sense, but to him, his "imprudence" must sometimes have seemed to reach that proportion. This resolve, another New Year's hopeful promise, is reminiscent of "My Adieu to the Muse" written ten years earlier in which he declared that he had not given in to the evil pressures of this world. And so, he struggled on.

Want, and Sickness, and Houseless Nights

[1]

And he fell far through that pit abysmal,
The gulf and grave of Maginn and Burns,
And pawned his soul for the devil's dismal
Stock of returns.
Mangan, "The Nameless One"

No one took care of James Clarence Mangan when he most needed it. No one could. His pride, independence, and shy aloofness erected a barrier too high. From time to time he could be rescued and restored to a modicum of health in a brief period of recovery, but never much more than that. At the end of the day, he also probably believed that there was no one he could put much trust in; and he may have been right. His friends were virtually overwhelmed by problems of their own.

A few general observations about the poet during the last year and a half of his life may be useful. The tone of these difficult months was set as early as January 1848. He now viewed the past, his past, as done and over with. He might analyze it and try to understand what had led him to the place he had reached, but there is no longer any sense of urgency in his agonizing about his delinquency nor does he keep promising to "reform myself" or "redeem the past". From his correspondence as well as from the various comments made by his friends and others with whom he came into contact, it would appear that either he had quit drinking and was suffering only (only!) from illness and malnutrition, or he had accepted himself as he was, weaknesses and all, and was simply getting on with life as best he could. Poverty now exacted its full toll. In addition, he still laboured under the queer belief that genius and half-way decent health did not require much food. His nervous condition, not surprisingly, deteriorated. And finally, as if anything needed to be added to this litany of woe, one of Fr Meehan's memoirists referred to Mangan's "consumptive nature".

The significance of the fact that at this time he ceased to use any form of pen-name or pseudonym on his published work, and instead signed his name or initials to both prose and poetry, hardly needs to be stressed. Now it was with him truly "*Ich bin ich, und leider bin kein Andrer*." The assumption of full responsibility for what he wrote was something altogether new for Mangan. It well may be, as he said, "for God alone to scrutinize causes", but it is tempting to ask the "why" of this changed state. Perhaps it was because, as he now stood alone, parentless, he could at last risk being himself. Perhaps it was that death, which may have seemed quite near, would bring that moment when the last mask could be dropped and the true face revealed.

Another generalization, this one about the poetry more than the man, is that his best work was now behind him, but that what he produced during the final eighteen months of his life would be, nevertheless, rich in range and tone, and include some very interesting prose as well as poetry. Most noteworthy among the poems from 1848 were "The Two Envoys", "My Three Plagues", and "A Voice of Encouragement" in January; "A Vision of A.D. 1848", "St Patrick's Hymn Before Tarah", and "Hush-a-By Baby. A Lullaby" in February; "The Devil and the Wind" and "The Parricide" in July; and "Mother and Son" in November. This does not exhaust the list, but suggests the variety this year alone included.

At this time, also, the poet became more involved in the nationalist movement than had been hitherto the case, and there is no question but that he meant to be at the centre of the action. He was, younger or older, well or ill, an enthusiast; the emotions which moved him could be brief but were always intense. The last full year of Mangan's life, 1848, was the decisive year for Irish hopes, whether that meant Repeal of the Union or independence. Duffy and Mitchel parted company, the Government took restrictive measures against them, an abortive rebellion was staged in Ballingarry in County Tipperary, and by autumn all the leaders of Young Ireland were in prison, in exile, or in hiding.

* * * *

Duffy and Mitchel had split openly by the beginning of the year and the latter's plans for an alternative paper, the *United Irishman*, had taken shape. Mitchel told Duffy, "I am quite certain I could not have worked in subordination to *any other man* near so long as I have done with you", and the two remained friends for a while longer.[1] But John Martin wrote to William Smith O'Brien, "I do not see how Mitchel can remain in Dublin", nor did he see how Mitchel was to proceed as he envisioned:

> He will not dream of starting a paper in opposition to Duffy—that is, a weekly paper. There is talk of getting a daily paper established as a share-holding concern with him for editor, and that he should be entirely uncontrolled save by the interference of a committee at the end of each year, to dismiss him if thought advisable. But he won't conduct any paper except one which shall be his own property. . . . I wish he were fairly started in this new undertaking. It may give new life to the National cause. . . . Mitchel and Duffy are still the most cordial friends.[2]

The time found Mangan homeless again and with almost no income; in desperation he wrote to the aforenamed philanthropist and Young Ireland sympathizer, James Haughton. This letter suggested, at least by omitting any reference to the contrary, that Mangan was not drinking, and indeed, it may well have been so, since the New Year always gave him a new surge of good intentions. However, there was also quite pointedly no promise to abstain from alcohol, although Haughton was a temperance advocate; and only the assurance that a past promise was *kept in mind*:

> Perhaps I may venture to hope that you have not altogether forgotten me. I, on my part, have never ceased to remember my promise to you. That promise has, if I may so speak, burned itself into my brain and memory. It is written on my heart, and chronicled on the tablets of my spirit. It forms my last thought before I lie down at night—my first when I rise in the morning.

Mangan sought aid and suggested to Haughton that it would help him keep that promise. The last long paragraph is of the greatest interest:

> I write to you, dear sir, from a fireless and furnitureless room, with a sick brother near me, whom I have supported for years. My heart sinks within me as I contemplate the desolation around me. I myself have abstained from animal food for a long period; yet I regretted that I was unable to buy him more than an egg on Christmas Day. But this matter of diet is a trifle. Healthy persons require little nourishment, they can subsist on bread and water. It was the apothecary's bill which, on Christmas Eve, left us without a shilling, and has obliged me even to resort since then to the pawnbroker.[3]

Mangan took the letter to Haughton's home at No. 35 Eccles Street himself, though he feared, "perhaps, you may not have leisure to see me". Whether he gained anything from his efforts, we do not know.

The hope of a new beginning always inspired a new effort, and even this grim New Year was no exception. "A Voice of Encouragement—A New Year's Lay" for the *Nation* was his response, but that it would have "encouraged" anyone seems highly doubtful. The second stanza summed up the time in which he wrote:

> Friends! the gloom in our land, in our once bright land, grows deeper.
> Suffering, even to death, in its horriblest forms, aboundeth;
> Thro' our black harvestless fields, the peasants' faint wail resoundeth.
> Hark to it, even now! . . . The nightmare oppressèd sleeper
> Gasping and struggling for life, beneath his hideous bestrider,
> Seeth not, dreeth not, sight or terror more fearful or ghastly
> Than that poor paralysed slave! Want, Houselessness, Famine, and lastly
> Death in a thousand-corpsed grave, that momently waxeth wider.

After the poet urged hope and effort—"Follow your destiny up! Work! Write! Preach to arouse and/Warn, and watch, and encourage!"—the final stanza closed on an ominously macabre figure:

Omen full, arched with gloom and laden with many a presage,
Many a portent of woe, looms the Impending Era
Not as of old, by comet—sword, Gorgon, or ghastly Chimera,
Scarcely by lightning and thunder, Heaven to-day sends its message.
Into the silent heart—down thro' the caves of the spirit,
Pierces the silent shaft—sinks the invisible token—
Cloaked in the Hall, the Envoy stands, his mission unspoken,
While the pale, banquetless guests await in trembling to hear it.[4]

The "Envoy", who may seem a mysterious figure today, was not particularly so to Mangan's readers, the capital letter telling them that this eerie visitor was Death or Death's Messenger. It would not be overreaching to suggest that the messenger, a "Man in a Cloak", may also represent Mangan himself, and the "banquetless guests" the starving people of Ireland. In Mangan's poem "The Two Envoys" which also appeared this month, one envoy on the way to deliver an unspecified message meets a second Envoy, who eventually leaves him lying dead in a frozen waste. The silence, the cold, and the presence of none save the lonely human messenger and his ghostly companion—"I come," said the Stranger, "from Silentland,/. . . And this is my name: From-God-His-Hand!"—remind one of "Siberia", another poem about a place under siege by Death.

On a completely different note, Mangan also translated the Irish poem "My Three Plagues" for this same number of the *Dublin University Magazine*. For the original, he observed, "I am indebted to the kindness of the distinguished Irish scholar, Eugene Curry, Esq., of the Royal Irish Academy." Light-hearted, ironic, and amusing, "My Three Plagues" is still a charming piece of verse. The "plagues" are, we learn, "My Sons, the Worms, and the great old Devil", and they are all out to get the speaker. Two stanzas follow:

Three there be who are eager to revel
 On me and my havings when I depart—
 I wish they were hanged with all my heart,
My Sons, the Worms, and the great old Devil.

For my cash and my chattels my sons flock round me,
 The worms are eager to gnaw my flesh;
 And the net of Old Nick has many a mesh
For that gudgeon, my soul, when Death shall have bound me.[5]

Mangan, as we saw in "The Four Idiot Brothers" and certain other poems and prose over the years, sometimes flaunted a gargoylesque humour, and he exercised it neatly here especially in the stanza dealing with the worms' ambition—"All *they* want is just to dine off my clay,/And get drunk off my bones on white marrow-toddy."

In January, the *Nation* boldly printed Mitchel's articles urging that all patriotic and able-bodied men should immediately be given "sound instruction upon military affairs", especially guerilla warfare. His words did not pass uncriticized among his fellow Young Irelanders, however. O'Brien protested against Mitchel's continued presence on the Council of the Confederation, and he soon withdrew, this time completing the move that he had tried to make earlier. Meagher, too, opposed his urging open warfare. McGee went further and proclaimed that he disliked both Mitchel's principles and his policy, "not because they are bold, but because they are mad, not because they are seditious, but because they are insane".[6]

The 22 January saw published on the first page of the *Nation* a notice of the new newspaper, Mitchel's *United Irishman*, which was to begin appearing on 12 February, with editors Mitchel, Devin Reilly, and John Martin. For motto, Wolfe Tone's words were chosen: "Our independence must be had at all hazards. If the men of property will not support us, they must fall; we can support ourselves by the aid of that numerous and respectable class of the community *the men of no property*."

Mangan at this point made an emotional choice to cast in his lot with Mitchel and the *United Irishman*. In spirit, he had already been a follower of Mitchel's for some two years. In the friendship between himself and Duffy, as already detailed here, a rift had developed. By 1848, beneath the fondness that was visible on the surface of the relationship, Mangan may have cradled a degree of contempt for Duffy who was too political and pragmatic to suit the poet. Likewise Duffy harboured an almost-voiced contempt for the poet in his "disreputableness". The two rejections that Duffy had dealt his friend, first refusing to admit him to membership in the Confederation and then refusing to print his "Declaration", may have been forgiven by Mangan, but they surely were not forgotten. When Mangan left the *Nation*, he left boldly with a deliberate "goodbye" poem: "Farewell to My Country", translated from the French nationalist politician and poet, Alphonse de Lamartine. It appeared a fortnight before he entered the ranks of the *United Irishman* contributors. Two of the sixteen stanzas show why he chose this particular poem to speak for him:

But oh! the soul hath instincts of her own,
    Like those bold birds whose pinions waft them far
O'er leagues of wave and waste, from zone to zone,
    She seeks a happier bourne—a brighter star—. . .

Therefore in solitude of soul I go
    To appeal for weal or woe to another zone.
What need to heed where Winter-storms o'er throw
    The scathèd tree whose leaves and blooms are flown?

My bones may bleach in Syria's far-off sands—
God knoweth! Him in silence I adore.
My life, my death, my doom are in His hands,
His will be done! I ask no more.[7]

The *United Irishman* did not long survive the intensifying attention of the Government, but even that short time, one might have thought, would have produced more than three poems from Mangan. Yet that was his total. The first was "A Vision, A.D. 1848", which appeared 26 February; it derived its title from "A Vision of Connaught in the Thirteenth Century", and like that poem, had a dream as its narrative framework. The tone was apocalyptic, and the mood gloomily prophetic. Like many of his finest efforts, it had a four-part division, and the sections were actually titled: "The Anointing 1839–1842", "The Muster 1842–1845", "The Famine 1845–1848", and "The End 1848–185*". The general prophecy was of coming conflict, all the rest having been preparation. Following a vision of earthquake and looming, lurid cloud, the dream and the poem ended:

What next might befal?
And how ended all?
This, too, friends, I know not—
For here were my cords
Of Sleep suddenly broken,
The bell booming Three;
But there seemed in mine ears,
As I started up, woken,
A noise like fierce cheers,
Blent with clashings of swords,
And the roar of the sea!

The second poem was a translation of "The Marseillaise", a set of verses representative of their time but not especially distinctive in any way. The third and last was by title the most ambitious of all Mangan's nationalist poems, for he wrote it to be the "Irish National Hymn". It was also the last of his stirring original poems of Irish nationalism, the slightly later "Tribune's Hymn for Pentecost" being more prayer to "the alway-faithful God" than a challenge to Ireland. The "National Hymn" opened:

O Ireland! Ancient Ireland!
Ancient! yet for ever young!
Thou our mother, home and sire-land—
Thou at length hast found a tongue—
Proudly thou, at length,
Resistest in triumphant strength.

And closed:

Within itself must grow, must glow—
    Within the depth of its own bosom,
    Must flower in loving might, must broadly blossom,
The hopes that shall be born ere Freedom's Tree can blow. . . .
The Time, the Hour, the Power are near—
    Be sure thou soon shalt form the vanguard
    Of that illustrious band, whom Heaven and man guard:
And these words come from one whom some have called a Seer.[8]

Mangan still continued to be represented in a couple of the other publications with which his name is associated. One of his finest and most unusual poems, a father's lullaby titled simply "Hush-a-By Baby. A Lullaby", appeared this spring in the *Dublin University Magazine*. Edward Walsh's version was published in his *Reliques of Irish Jacobite Poetry* which our poet probably used as a source. Mangan's emphasis was as usual on the communication of feeling rather than on the strict reproduction of word or line patterns. A little of this poem follows:

O, hush-a-by Baby! why weepest thou?
The diadem yet shall adorn thy brow—
And the jewels thy sires had long agone
In the regal ages of Eoghan and Conn
        Shall all be thine!
        O, hush-a-by, hush-a-by, child of mine!
        My sorrow, my woe, to see thy tears
        Pierce into my heart like spears![9]

In the *Irish Catholic Magazine* appeared "St Patrick's Hymn Before Tarah". No version has surpassed Mangan's in its sense of the dramatic, and his is unique in the use of the phrase "At Tarah Today . . . " rather than the more familiar "I arise today. . . ." It may or may not be judged an effective change, but it had the advantage of several times invoking the image of an Irish holy place. The best-known part of the hymn is that lengthy stanza beginning with a summoning of powers to place between oneself and evil. Mangan rendered this invocation in part:

        Christ, as a light,
        Illumine and guide me!
Christ, as a shield, o'ershadow and cover me!
Christ be under me! Christ be over me
        Christ be beside me
        On left-hand and right!
Christ be before me, behind me, about me!
Christ this day be within and without me![10]

Although he was now gone from the *Nation*, Mangan's presence was still a potent shadow in its pages. In the same issue of the paper that carried his "goodbye poem", the "Answers to Correspondents" column printed a letter from "Peregrine Patchwork" in which the pseudonymous author described his vision of a big bookcase which kept expanding before his eyes to accommodate a growing number of Irish books "first among them being *Bolg-an-Dana, a Budget of Irish Verse* by Clarence Mangan".

[2]

But yet redeemed it in days of darkness
And shapes and signs of the final wrath,
When death, in hideous and ghastly starkness,
Stood on his path.
Mangan, "The Nameless One"

So it was that Gavan Duffy with one group, and John Mitchel with another, were pressing towards their separate solutions to the political impasse when something occurred in France that took the initiative from their hands. The so-called February Revolution, a working-class revolt, almost bloodlessly overturned the monarchy of Louis Phillippe and established a republican form of government in the nation. The event would prove to be a most powerful catalyst in nineteenth-century Irish history. A meeting of the Irish Confederation was in progress when news of the French revolt arrived, and a furore ensued with cheering and speech-making beyond most celebrations heard previously in the hall. Significantly, it was not the more conservative Duffy, although he spoke movingly, who inspired the most applause, but the fire-brand Mitchel. Over the next several days, Duffy, who quickly assessed the situation and realized that the tide was flowing in the direction of the use of force, now restructured the editorial position of the *Nation* so that it was soon almost as strident in its tone and recommendations as Mitchel's paper.

The months of March and April were crammed with talk, action (of a sort), controversy, and efforts to reconcile not just Mitchel and Duffy but also Old and Young Ireland. The newspaper accounts make sad reading, not only because one knows how extremely long it took for any of the great hopes to be realized, but also because in the shorter term it is evident that in spite of good intentions, the differences that divided the parties were simply not going to be put aside. If the *Nation* and the *United Irishman* vied for honours in flaming editorializing, both calling for a national guard and directions on how to conduct guerilla warfare, the award for wishful thinking must go to the *Nation* where this fantasy appeared on March 11:

> *Second Week of the Irish Revolution* Dublin, First Week of Liberty—
>
> Tranquility is entirely restored. . . .The large mansions in Stephen's Green last occupied by the English Chancellor and English Archbishop have been opened as hospitals for the wounded. . . . We are rejoiced to hear that Dr Petrie has accepted the office of guardian of our national antiquities. . . . no expense will be spared to preserve the monuments that still remain to us. The government place them under the guardianship of the Irish people. . . .
>
> The commission sitting at the Mountjoy Barracks are preparing a report on the manuscripts illustrating Irish history entitled to immediate publication. Capt. Larcom, who has elected to remain in Ireland, John O'Donovan, Samuel Ferguson, Eugene Curry and the secretaries of the Arch. Society, and the Celtic Athenaeum form the commission. . . .[11]

Thus, many of Mangan's old friends and associates were, in a manner of speaking, present and accounted for, including John O'Daly who was active in the Celtic Athenaeum. Interestingly, artist Daniel Maclise and poet Thomas Moore, both of whom had gone to England to seek and secure their fame, were excluded from this band of brothers. The "resident artist" was to be Frederick Burton, but no "resident poet" was identified; Ferguson may have been the candidate the author had in mind. Sadly, and, I think, strangely, Mangan was missing from this projection of hopes, but it was perhaps because he was too debilitated to be thought of in a positive way; and perhaps, also, because he had taken himself off the *Nation*. Probably both.

An uprising seemed certain to take place. Mitchel declared, "We await attack. We shall not provoke the shedding of blood; but if blood is shed, we will see the end of it." But who, it has to be asked, did Mitchel think would lead the armed response, and with what? Primarily, it seems, he anticipated a "spontaneous peasant uprising" which would presumably spread like wildfire throughout the island. To that end, as much weaponry as possible, including guns and pikes, had been amassed; but the grand total was pathetically small. However, it was also expected that, although no direct help from France was to be hoped for, an "inevitable war between England and revolutionary France would enable Ireland to make her own terms" with England. In the event, as we know, there was no such "inevitable war". At the same time, O'Brien "called for peace between the Repeal factions", believing that if the sides could get together a leader would be sure to come forward. This, too, was a chimera. So many "conditionals" were included in the aspirations of the nationalists that it is hard to see how they could have built so many dreams upon such a shaky foundation. But they did.

A great demonstration which took place on 21 March, delayed from St Patrick's Day in order "to persuade Old Irelanders to take part", saw a gathering of somewhere between 10,000 and 20,000 at the North Wall. There was much speech-making. Duffy, Mitchel, O'Brien, and others predicted, exhorted, and proclaimed; but at the end of the day no action was taken. The Government, however, again paid nationalist activity the compliment of taking it seriously, and shortly thereafter, Mitchel, O'Brien, and Meagher were arrested and charged with sedition. "The *Nation* declared that war had begun", as Richard Davis in *The Young Ireland Movement* expressed it, and, "the momentum was now too rapid for realistic reflection. . . . The intoxicating effects of Meagher's spellbinding rhetoric and Mitchel's crackling prose turned real setbacks into apparent successes. A type of revolution by analogy appeared to have already taken place in Ireland."[12]

And what of James Clarence Mangan while this excitement was going on in the streets of the city? Mitchel gave this description of him:

> About this time he often visited the office of the *United Irishman*, in Trinity Street; and if his present biographer chanced to be found alone, the visitor would sometimes remain in conversation, or more properly in discourse of his own, for an hour; for though extremely silent, shy, and reserved habitually, yet with those in whom he confided, he was much given to strange and desultory talk, which seemed like the soliloquy of a somnambulist. His blue eyes would then dilate, and light up strangely the sepulchral pallor of his face. His manner and voice were always extremely gentle; and I never heard him blame anybody but himself.[13]

Mitchel it was, also, who bluntly spoke about "two Mangans . . . one well known to the Muses, the other to the police". D.J. O'Donoghue scolded Mitchel for this, saying it was "decidedly exaggerated" because it implied that the poet "was a brawler". This is not quite true, and Mitchel almost certainly did not mean to suggest such a thing. He also said of the two Mangans that "one soared through the empyrean and sought the stars—the other lay too often in gutters of Peter Street and Bride Street", from which the police, who may well have been familiar with him and his ways, quite possibly rescued him. Mitchel is likewise the only one of Mangan's early memoirists to take on the possibility of the poet's near-madness, and his conclusion is worth noting:

> By some tie or other he did assuredly hold on to his anchorage upon the firm ground of reason, and did not drift into unknown seas. "Every man holds, chained up within him, a madman:" so it is written; and nothing is more fearful than to watch in some men how perilously their maniac inmates tug at the chain, and to think, If a link should break now?—

He went on, creating yet a further analogy by referring to Homer's seamen, sailing swiftly through the night:

> . . . inside, you have still a cabin-lamp burning, and air to breathe and human companionship; without, the infinite black waste of the roaring, ravening sea, and between these, trembling and creaking, a half-inch plank. . . . Poor Mangan's lamp, though often sadly dimmed by thick vapours of sickness, and horror, and shame, yet burned still (somewhat blue), and lighted his pathway to the grave.[14]

This would have been an obvious moment for Mangan to return to the pages of the *Nation* with some striking poem, but he did not do so. The rupture between himself and Duffy was, evidently, permanent. So, too, was that between Duffy and Mitchel. These two may be characterized by their differing attitudes towards the poet. Mitchel clearly saw the dark and despairing side of Mangan and was not judgemental about it. Duffy, by contrast, could not accept that the poet might not be the glowing soul he so appreciated, and he contradicted Mitchel by saying that he himself had never seen Mangan behave other than as a gentleman. At the same time, however, he rejected him for his appearance and eccentric behaviour. Gavan Duffy came to describe Mitchel as "dogmatic and arrogant", as a man who "used to be a modest and courteous gentleman, [but who] now demeaned himself as if the French Revolution and the new opportunities it furnished were his personal achievements." For his part, John Mitchel spoke of Duffy as "a bitter personal enemy to me: the only enemy I have, worth mentioning". James Clarence Mangan was caught between the two.

Mangan now wrote a letter to Mitchel which the editor inserted in the 25 March *United Irishman*; this paralleled the Declaration he had sent Duffy that Duffy had refused to publish. After Mitchel published the letter Duffy angrily and inaccurately blamed him for causing all Mangan's troubles including losing his job at Trinity College Library, although actually they had beset him months or years earlier.

Mangan's statement read:

> My dear M.—There is a rumour in circulation, that the government intend to commence a prosecution against you. Insignificant an individual as I am, and unimportant to society as my political opinions may be, I, nevertheless, owe it, not merely to the kindness you have shown me, but to the cause of my country, to assure you that I thoroughly sympathize with your sentiments, that I identify my views of public affairs with yours, and that I am prepared to go all lengths with you and your intrepid friend, Devin Reilly, for the achievement of our national independence.
>
> I mean to write you, in a few days, a long letter, explanatory of the course which I think it becomes the duty of every Irish patriot to pursue, at the present eventful epoch. Meanwhile you are at liberty to make what use you please of this preliminary communication.
>
> Yours, in life and death, James Clarence Mangan[15]

There can be no question but that Mangan did genuinely identify his view of public affairs with Mitchel's. For years he had been admonishing Duffy to get tougher. Ill-equipped as he plainly was to take any action himself, he was capable of choosing among the options which presented themselves. Mitchel appreciated that and did not scoff at him. Duffy, on the other hand, wrote with a sort of scornful pity, "Self-sacrifice is natural and proper in a revolutionary movement, but one could scarcely think pushing a woman or a child into the fire was a permissible sacrifice." Mangan did not think of himself as a woman or a child; nor did Mitchel think of him in such terms. The editor explained his willingness to publish the statement by saying, "This letter was the only expression (in prose) of the writer's political sentiments which I have ever seen or heard of." The long letter Mangan said he was going to write never reached Mitchel who suggested that it may have taken the form of the "Irish National Hymn" which was published on 13 May. He added, "The desolate writer was by this time too much enfeebled in mind and body to think or act persistently in any matter whatever. But to the last he could sing."

Short-lived rebel newspapers sprang up—and perished—in some profusion that spring. Among them was the *Young Irishman* which was, in a sense, typical. Not badly written, it presented a few pages of fervently patriotic exhortation and middling-poor poetry meant to raise the spirits and hopes of nationalists. This particular paper lasted about a month and was evidently put out by young men, perhaps those of The Irish Polytechnic Institute or The Students' Club (of which Mangan's friend D'Alton Williams was a member). None of the signatures—"C", "Jewmas", "J.S.", and so on—have been identified. As might be expected from a student publication, it was full of bloodthirsty rhetoric: "The proclamation [of Irish Independence is] to be read even in the confusion of smoke and ball, by the cannon's flash in the noontide, or by the barricade at night—to be read, when the gore-gilt pavement will out-dye the crimson of a wintry sun. . . . " It addressed its readers as "Fellow Sufferers—Brothers in Bondage", and it swore, "You have said you would be free, and free you shall be." Although an echo, to a large extent, of the *Nation* and the *United Irishman*, the *Young Irishman* and other such publications had the effect of reinforcing from below, as it were, what was said at the upper levels of journalism, and probably increased to some extent the nervousness of the Government.

* * * *

In looking at the poet's life at this point, and indeed, from now until the end, balance and perspective are required. He was certainly a figure to pity: wasted, homeless, hungry, sometimes seriously affected by drink, often ill. At the same time, and in a rather curious fashion, he now came into his own at last: he knew himself and he claimed his cause. Wretched as it was, his life achieved a certain nobility, or, if that word jars, a courage that perhaps had not been evident before.

April was a yet more desperate month for him than March. On the 28th of the month—and it may be many other times as well—he turned to John Anster and asked for help, but this time not for himself, but for his brother who was evidently still with him. The sad little exchange was reported by O'Donoghue. The poet wrote from No. 61 New Street:

> My Dear Sir,
>
> My brother will convey this note to you. He is, like myself, in a very wretched and deplorable state. He is of opinion that you might, perhaps, be able to recommend him to some person who would give him employment. His trade is cabinet-making. If you could but grant him what he petitions for you would confer a great and lasting favour on him and me.

He signed the letter, "Ever yours faithfully and gratefully, John Anster."[16] O'Donoghue, who had the letter in his possession, observed that "the genial recipient" Anster had written on it, "This strange note is from Mangan; on being examined as to what the meaning of putting my name to it was, his brother replied, that he supposed it was nervousness." Whether or not anything came of this plea, O'Donoghue did not say; probably he did not know. Anster surely gave William something, but he may have had no employment to suggest. The trade of cabinet-making had declined over the years, more work coming from English manufactories than ever before, and William would not have been the only such craftsman to find himself deprived of any way to earn a living.

Fr Meehan described one of Mangan's accommodations at this time as being a "dismal two-pair back room" and at greater length spoke of finding "him and his brother in a miserable back room destitute of every comfort, a porter bottle doing duty for a candlestick, and a blanketless pallet for a bed and writing table." Early in May, at the priest's recommendation, the poet was admitted to St Vincent's Hospital in St Stephen's Green. New at the time, this charity hospital had been founded by Mary Aikenhead, also Foundress of the Sisters of Charity who ran it. It was the first such establishment in Ireland to be operated by nuns, and nothing testifies more to Mangan's extreme need and debilitation than his admission here. He was described by Sarah Atkinson in her life of Aikenhead:

> One day there came another poet [besides R.D. Williams who was a medical student there] to St. Vincent's, not indeed, to pay his respects to Mrs. Aikenhead, but to seek rest and healing in her hospital with the poor and the ungifted. A pale, ghost-like creature, with snow-white hair tossed over his lordly forehead, and falling lankly on either side of a face handsome in outline,

bloodless and wrinkled, though not with age, James Clarence Mangan was carried up to St. Patrick's Ward, and laid on a nice fresh bed. His weird blue eyes, distraught with the opium-eater's dreams, closed beneath their heavy lids, and his head fell back in sleep just as it is pictured fallen back in death by Frederick William Burton's magical pencil. The change from poor Mangan's wretched garret to the comforts of the hospital ward, was fully appreciated by the sufferer, who, however did not pour forth his gratitude in tide of song. "Oh! the luxury of clean sheets!" he exclaimed.

The sisters, being fond of the poet Williams, were unusually interested in their new patient. He did not quite disappoint them, but he fulfilled their expectation in a different fashion than they may have hoped:

All they could discover of the poetic organisation in this strange, sad man, was the acutely sensitive and painfully restless temperament supposed to be a characteristic of genius. The author of the German and Irish anthologies was, in truth, a rather troublesome patient. One of the sisters, willing to excuse his peculiarity, simply remarked: "These poets have nerves at every pore."[17]

While he was hospitalized, Mangan wrote to both John McGlashan and John O'Daly. The letter to O'Daly was dated 1 May, that to McGlashan 18 May, according to O'Donoghue, but one of these dates is probably an error. All things considered, the later may be the more likely possibility; in any case, the letters seem to have been written at about the same time. To O'Daly, Mangan wrote:

My dear Daly,

It is here that I am at last. I will take it as a great favour if you can pay me a visit at your leisure, and bring with you any poems you may wish to have versified. The usual days of admission are Sundays and Thursdays—from 12 to 1, but directions have been given to the attendants to admit all friends of mine on any day—only, however, before 3 o'clock. You will forgive me for not having written sooner, but I have been dreadfully upset of late.

Don't be afraid to come—there is no fever in *this* hospital.[18]

Mangan and O'Daly had been working together at Irish translations over the past several months, and it is sadly ironic that as Mangan lay in the hospital, a cheery notice of their projected book, *The Poets and Poetry of Munster*, appeared in the *Nation*:

Mr John O'Daly, of Bedford-row [a continuation of Anglesea Street], has issued a specimen of a new publication, "Selections from the bardic Remains of Munster, with Translation by James Clarence Mangan. . . ." We wish Mr O'Daly 50,000 subscribers, and the subscribers the enjoyment of his selections of the loving, sorrowful, warlike songs of the Muse of Munster.[19]

The specimen consisted of a seven-page sample of "Dark-Haired Little

Rose" which would become "Little Black-Haired Rose" in the publication. O'Daly assured readers that the edition "will be put to press as soon as one hundred and fifty names shall be received".

Mangan wrote to McGlashan in much the same vein:

> Here I am at last—here, where I shall have ample time for repentance, for I cannot leave for some months, and during all that time I shall be rigorously denied everything in the shape of stimulants. My intellect is becoming clearer. As I shall have so much leisure on my hands, possibly you might wish for some contribution after my former manner. My general health is better than it has been for years, but my lower limbs are in a dreadful state. I write to you from bed, from which I have not risen since I came hither.[20]

While the poet remained in hospital being decently looked after, events in the world at large moved with great rapidity. On 6 May, Duffy flung down the gauntlet by printing his defiant "Creed of the Nation". In it, he acknowledged that war frightened many people more than repression did, but he asserted his belief that "Democracy . . . is the destiny of the world. Probably we are contemporary with the last race of kings." Meanwhile, Mitchel and Reilly withdrew from the Confederation. Mitchel succeeded in getting his trial postponed on a technicality, but his ploy so "enraged the Government" that on 13 May he was arrested and charged to answer an indictment for treason-felony. This was at least a degree less serious than treason, carrying the penalty of exile for the convicted, but not execution. At the time of his arrest, the *United Irishman* had the largest circulation of any newspaper in Ireland. It was immediately suppressed.

According to one John Kevin Reilly in his notebook which traces the life of the Irish poet, Mangan at this point "was ready if necessary to take up the journal [the *United Irishman*] and its responsibilities . . . but the seizure and confiscation of 'The United Irishman' . . . left it unnecessary that Mangan's proposal should be brought into practice."[21] Whether or not Reilly had any firm facts at hand we do not know, but the notion of Mangan's editing a paper at this time does not commend itself to common sense. Nor did he need to. Two small replacement papers quickly sprang into existence. The registered proprietors of the *Irish Tribune* were D'Alton Williams and Kevin Izod Doherty, both founders of the aforementioned Students' Club. Mitchel had just been arrested when the *Tribune* was announced; it was suppressed after five issues. Mangan had one poem in its pages, "The Tribune's Hymn for Pentecost". Although not one of his best poems, it can be appreciated at least for its fervour and for the intricacy he could manage even on his sickbed. A portion of the final stanza read:

Descend, then, Spirit of the Eternal King!
To thee, to Him, to His avenging Son,
The Divine God, in boundless trust we cling;
His help once ours, our nationhood is won.

He was not represented at all in the second of these papers, the *Irish Felon*. It was edited by John Martin, Devin Reilly, and James Finton Lalor, but also writing for it were "Eva of the Nation", John Savage, and John de Jean Frazer. It, too, lasted for just five issues.

We do not know how long Mangan stayed in hospital, certainly not the "months" he mentioned. But he was probably still there when John Mitchel was so expeditiously removed from the country. On 20 May, the *Nation* carried a protest against the expected jury-packing, but it did no good. The jury was packed, and Mitchel was convicted. Talk of trying to rescue him was quashed, although he himself thought the effort should be made in spite of the certainty that he would be killed in the attempt. It was, he felt, cowardly to submit to injustice without a struggle. Cooler heads, as they say, prevailed, one of them being Gavan Duffy's, and much discredit was cast on him for his role in restraining others from taking action. Mitchel was removed to the *Shearwater*, or, as he began his *Jail Journal*: "May 27, 1848 On this day, about four o'clock in the afternoon, I, John Mitchel, was kidnapped, and carried off from Dublin, in chains, as a convicted 'Felon'."[22]

As usual, John O'Donovan has left some of the keenest observations on all that was going on. At first unsettled in his opinions about the chance of any sort of revolution, he finally concluded in May, "The Irish are in earnest about Repeal at last, and will surely make an effort with the pikes!" He did not think much of Mitchel to begin with, either, but on 2 June wrote:

> I never believed him honest till the last day of his trial, but then saw clearly that he was a second Emmet. His mother, wife, and children are left in a deplorable condition. . . . I give Mitchel no credit for his rashness; he had no party in this kingdom able to dethrone a cat,—and it was folly for him to hurl defiance at King Victoria [*sic*] and her house of Brunswick.[23]

The young man who would be Mangan's last best-loved friend, his "brother and yet more than brother", Joseph Brenan, also worked on the *Felon*. When the two met is not known, but it could have been any time after March of this year, for it was about that month the young editor moved from Cork to Dublin. After seeing John Mitchel in Cork in January, he had come to admire him more than any other nationalist. Although only nineteen years old, Brenan was already a seasoned journalist, for he had been an editor of the *Cork Magazine* along with Frazer, Martin MacDermott, and Ellen Mary Downing, "Mary of the *Nation*", with whom he was in love. In the words of Michael Cavanagh who wanted to be his biographer, Brenan "was possessed of a vivid and creative imagination [and] an extraordinary spirit of fun". In fact, he had a number of qualities which would seem almost designed to endear him to Mangan. Cavanagh described him thus:

> This strange, delicate, big-eyed boy grew up a local prodigy. His bright intellect developed its young powers with absolutely painful rapidity. He was a boy wonder. . . . [Physically] there was nothing girlish in his appearance, except his beauty of features. He was a well built young fellow . . . of fair complexion, light brown hair, and clear blue eyes—eyes which were verily "windows of the soul", as in their liquid depths those who gazed on him in his varying moods might trace the thoughts and passions that filled his mind at the time. A loving friend, a bitter enemy; a boy in his playful humour, a girl in his passionate tenderness; his broad white forehead betokened the possession of that extraordinary genius for which he was distinguished among his youthful compeers . . .[24]

Brenan did not marry this "Mary", who entered a convent, but another Mary, John Savage's sister. He would die in New York before the age of thirty. For these men's thoughts on Mangan's failure to marry, see Appendix G.

Mangan must have taken himself out of the hospital no later than the end of June for Savage to have observed him thus:

> A crooked little street, called Trinity, off one of the greatest thoroughfares of the city. The principal propellors of the excitement which moves the city and country have their being in this crooked little street, famous in Irish history, in the shape of the two journals, the *Irish Tribune* and *Irish Felon*, both preaching the same creed and rivals only in their devotion to it. Out of either of these offices—they are side by side, like brothers in a fight—we perceive a strange-looking individual has glided, even as a shadow on a wall.
>
> That shy, abstracted-looking man has held not the least powerful talisman by which a nation is moved. We must look at him more minutely. He is about the middle size, and glides more than walks, yet at that is but infirm. He stoops, and is abstracted. A threadbare dark coat—is it brown or black?—buttoned up to the throat, sheathes his attenuated body. His eye is lustrously mild and beautifully blue, and his silver-white locks surround, like a tender halo, the once beautiful, and now pale and intellectual, face of the prematurely-aged man before us.[25]

Fr Meehan gave this account of Mangan's premature departure from St Vincent's and his further misadventure:

> The doctors refused the stimulants, but he, "infirm of purpose" as usual, must have them, and he consequently went out into the broadway of temptation, and relapsed into the old slough. A few mornings after that exodus he was a patient in the Richmond Surgical Hospital, bruised and disfigured by a fall

> of nearly fifteen feet, into the foundation of a house, then recently sunk. This occurred in the night time, when he was utterly unconscious of his whereabouts; and his escape from mortal accident seemed almost miraculous.[26]

Richmond Surgical hospital was for "the destitute and friendless". Although its wards were described as being inconvenient and "low and small", the author of *An Historical Guide to the City of Dublin* maintained that this condition was mitigated "by the strictest attention to cleanliness and ventilation".

Again, Mangan probably stayed the minimal amount of time to recover. The priest wrote that a few days after the poet left the hospital, "he got a lodging near the house in which he was born, and on revisiting *the* attic agreed to write the *Autobiography*. . . ." Fr Meehan seems to have compressed the time somewhat, for that little book was almost certainly not penned until autumn, but the poet did apparently return to his haunts of the past as soon as he was able.

He now lived almost literally from poem to poem, and it is not possible, if, in fact, it ever was, to judge anything about his condition or the time of writing by the order or dates of publication. The "Lays of Many Lands" chapters, which appeared in the *Dublin University Magazine* without any commentary, may have been turned over to McGlashan one poem at a time or in batches, and then grouped by the editor for publication. As for the *Irish Catholic Magazine*, he would have only four more poems in that periodical, the final one in July, although it continued to be published until the end of the year. James Duffy thus achieved his goal of keeping it alive for two years, and with that success, he gave up the struggle.

By then, the composition of the staff had changed. Fr Meehan had quit as editor late in 1847, explaining with some hauteur to Hardiman, "I have nothing more to do with the Catholic Magazine, which, I fear, will not succeed. I had to write three-fourths of it up to December, got tired of the drudgery, and left it, I trust, to abler hands."[27] The priest was an irascible character, but he was probably not exaggerating too much here. It may be recalled that Fr Meehan's name had not appeared on the magazine, nor, indeed, had the names of other regular contributors. But in March 1848, the Rev. Matthew Kelly of Maynooth who replaced him added a list of "permanent contributors" to the masthead. There were only seven. The first four names were those of priests, three from Maynooth and one from Limerick. The three remaining names were William Bernard MacCabe, author of *A Catholic History of England*, the Young Irelander and ecclesiastical architect James Joseph McCarthy, and James Clarence Mangan.

In June, the conservative side of the Confederation, represented by Gavan Duffy and John Dillon, joined with the more radical group headed by John Martin, Devin Reilly, and Fr Kenyon to plot a revolution, or, in somewhat more modest terms, an insurrection. In July the pot boiled over. Richard Davis has pointed up the varying attitudes of the rebels, the secrecy of the "conspiracy", and the wide departure taken from "Mitchel's open, spontaneous and leaderless revolution".[28] But the government—again—took the maneuvers seriously, and on 9 July, Duffy, John Martin, Kevin O'Doherty, and D'Alton Williams were arrested, and the *Tribune* and the *Felon* were closed down. Thus the cause was left, at last, without a single newspaper to sustain enthusiasm or rally support.

This is not the place to go into the details of the Rising at Ballingarry. Suffice it to say that nothing was planned to happen in the way of rebellion in Dublin, and the poet undoubtedly learned of the affair much as everyone else did, after it was over. William Smith O'Brien with a force that seems to have varied in size from several thousand to a few hundred or less scouted the southern countryside for days looking for some sign that the time was at long last right for an uprising. Nothing much happened to encourage them. In fact, support began to drop away. Even the few staunch confederate priests such as Fr Kenyon backed down when faced with their Bishops' disapproval. The spark that was necessary to set off a real "national conflagration" was never struck. As everyone who has read a little Irish history knows, a skirmish of minor proportions took place between O'Brien's men and forty or so police who barricaded themselves into the Widow McCormack's house at Boulah near Ballingarry in County Tipperary. O'Brien was a gentleman and "an extremely reluctant revolutionary" and would not burn them out, thus allowing time for police reinforcements to arrive. With some justification, the action has been called both a "cabbagepatch war" and a "literary rebellion", but the effects were nonetheless devastating for Mangan. Even Brenan, who was not arrested at this time and stayed active in the countryside, was taken prisoner after attacking, with a few others, a police barracks in Cappoquin in the autumn.

Newgate Prison housed the state prisoners, as the political rebels were called. It was an old prison and was intended for debtors and prisoners awaiting trial; it had not been modernized and it had a grim reputation. Duffy described its "dark, airless, unheated cells" and the "filth, foul air, darkness and horror" of the place. "It was built on the burying-ground of an ancient monastery", he observed, "and reeked with odours of an unknown origin". Still, state prisoners got the best accommodations the place afforded and were allowed to eat together in Duffy's room and have food sent in from a nearby hotel and served to them by another prisoner. Meagher and O'Brien, among the many the government arrested this year, were later tried and exiled to Van Dieman's Land. Escaping in disguise to

America would be Reilly, Dillon, Michael Doheny, and Thomas D'Arcy McGee. O'Gorman would make it to France. In short, there would soon not be a single one of Mangan's old compeers, friends from Fr Meehan's "attic" or the newspaper offices, left to buoy his spirits or offer a bit of assistance although, as we will see, the state prisoners, perhaps led by Joseph Brenan, did what little they could.

[3]

And tell how now, amid wreck and sorrow,
And want, and sickness, and houseless nights,
He bides in calmness the silent morrow,
That no ray lights.
Mangan, "The Nameless One"

Three noteworthy and unique pieces of writing are all that can be said with certainty to have come from the poet's pen in the autumn of 1848, and indeed for many months. All three were autobiographical: the poem "Gasparó Bandollo", the prose fragment known as the *Autobiography*, and the poem "The Nameless One". The first of these was his final poem in the *University Magazine*. The others were not published during his lifetime, and it is reasonably certain that he did not intend for them to be.

A comment by Mangan himself in the second chapter of his autobiography placed the composition of the original poem "Gasparó Bandollo" this autumn, perhaps in October and certainly no later than November: "See Dublin University Magazine for December 1848. No. cxcii" read his note to this description he had just given of his father: "His temper was not merely quick and irascible, but it also embodied much of that calm concentrated spirit of Milesian fierceness, a picture of which I have endeavoured to paint in my Italian story of 'Gasparó Bandollo'." (p. 13) To "Gasparó Bandollo", which finally appeared in the *University Magazine* in May 1849, one turns for the poet's last words on this man who had been such a terror to him. The story of a father and son who destroy each other came from Prosper Mérimée, as handled by Chamisso, and delineated "crime" and "punishment" of a unique sort. The setting was Italy and the characters were peasant rebels against a tyrannical government, very much the same situation as in Ireland. The poem can be read as a muted political comment by Mangan, but I am more inclined to see it as the expression of his personal situation, always bearing in mind that the role of authority, especially harsh and repressive authority, and his response to it, was a primary theme in his writing.

Left alone in the family house, Giambattista, young son of the peasant patriot Gasparó Bandollo, betrays to Government soldiers the hiding place of a rebel who has come seeking shelter. The rebel is captured. Arriving home, the boy's father learns the truth, and in Mangan's source story, kills his son for the betrayal. In Mangan's version, however, as the father prepares to shoot the boy, the child dies in an apotheosis of terror and remorse, thus in a sense eluding punishment. The hiding place into which he slips to avoid his father's wrath is *death*, a dramatic instance of the "mousehole" into which the poet and his brothers and sister had fled to escape *their* father.

Mangan condemned neither Bandollo nor his son, but saw them as mutual victims, and with rare explicitness acknowledged a sympathetic understanding of his own father under the figure of Giambattista's father. He found it almost impossible to voice the blame which he felt belonged to the old man, so the lines in the *Autobiography* in which he finally dared to speak the "forbidden words" of criticism are of the greatest importance. More often, and more consistently, even as the boy in this poem, he took the guilt mostly upon himself. Here he at least let the child speak: "O, father! I—this dreary room—/. . . I watch here so lonely/All day, and feel, oh! so bereaven,/With not a sight or sound to cheer me!" The poet's feelings of abandonment, vengefulness, isolation, and betrayal always struggled for expression. This autumn's writings were their last articulation in verse.

The final section of Mangan's poem contains the greatest sympathy and understanding for the parent:

> The child is dead of old Bandollo,
> And he, the sire, hath scarce to follow
> His offspring to the last dark barrow,
> So much hath Grief's long-rankling arrow
> Forestalled for him that doom of Death
> Which takes from Suffering nought save breath—
> A grief that speaks, albeit untold,
> And lives, where all seems dead and cold,
> And finds no refuge in the Past,
> And sees the Future overcast
> With broader gloom than even the Present.[29]

Mangan's own father had lived long, and, it may be, dragged out an unhappy existence after the money was spent and the parties had ended. But one senses that in his lines on grief, Mangan has become his own subject, too, identifying at least in that with his father.

In the poet's experience, no one was entirely guilty; no one was wholly innocent. But the guilty were rarely named, the innocent were never exonerated. A companion poem of "Gasparó Bandollo" was this November's "Mother and Son". In this eerie ballad, a variant of the familiar

"Edward, Edward", the mother and son talk obliquely about a murder the son may have (or must have) committed, although that always remains an obscure point. His sister is mysteriously missing, and his father and brother are known—at least by him—to be dead. The fascinating mystery resides for readers, as it must have for Mangan, in the strongly hinted guilt of the son who, along with his mother, has survived. Though the poet avoided the blood-dripping blade of "Edward, Edward", the guilt of his speaker is implicit in his secret knowledge of where the bodies of his brother and father lie, and in his suspicion about the fate of his sister, who has disappeared and "bides" somewhere. To his mother's pressing question, "When shall I again behold them?" the son answers:

> —"To thy bosom shalt thou fold them,
> Golden mother grey!
> Thou shalt once again behold them
> When the blighted tree shall blossom,
> Golden mother grey!"[30]

This can come about only at the end of time, giving the poem that apocalyptic touch which had become so prevalent in his verse: "When the Judgment Peal gives warning—/When the Dead shall every one rise,/ Golden mother grey!"

The *Autobiography* and the poem "The Nameless One" also were parallel compositions. In the prose, he dealt as closely as he could with what he called "the hidden springs of human frailty"—his own frailty, he meant—and attempted to represent the "simple and undecorated truth with regard to all that has so long appeared worst in my character and conduct". This was a harsh assignment, and he scarcely made a start on it, the narrative breaking off at 1831 when his "career" and real downfall, as he understood it, were just ready to begin. But he did identify the elements in his childhood and youth which were formative, as we have seen, and he courageously described the abuse that he had suffered and that had damaged him and his brothers and sister. This experience also was recorded in the poetry of "The Nameless One", which in addition continued his story until the last year of his life.

The first line of "The Nameless One" is "Roll forth, my song, like the rushing river", and so it was no coincidence that his "song", his life story told in the *Autobiography*, was recorded in a small, oblong music book, the text written between the staves. The 6" x 14" book has a cover of mottled blue and buff with gold touches, and the corners are bound in red leather.[31] Almost certainly, Mangan selected it for this specific purpose. It is not possible to know if he had first written his account on other paper and then recopied it here, in final form, but he went back even over this text, making improvements, deleting a few passages, and altering a few words.

It definitely was not written all at one time, or all in one place. At least four different colours of ink are identifiable: brown ink for the first thirteen pages, blue ink for the next eight, then back to brown, then almost black, and at the end, again a brown, only more faded looking. The handwriting, too, is inconsistent, from broken and erratic at the start, to severely angular, to beautifully flowing, to simple and legible, to exquisitely delicate. None of the variations, either of ink or handwriting, occur by content, sentence, or chapter, but only by page. The fact that the story breaks off at the foot of the last page also suggests that the text was recopied from an earlier draft.

It is plain that the poet took great care to produce this little book. Consequently, he must have been very hurt by the response of Fr Meehan, who had, in a manner of speaking, commissioned the piece of writing, when that curmudgeon snappishly criticized it as "the merest Reve d'une Vie, with here and there some filaments of reality in its texture." Unresistingly, Mangan agreed that he "dreamed it" and offered to destroy the manuscript. Although the priest would not let him do that, agreeing to keep it as "a souvenir", chances are good that the poet either burned or threw away the continuation of the account which had not yet been copied into a permanent book.

There has been too much doubt, I believe, that this continuation ever existed. Fr Meehan virtually revealed that it had by writing, inside the cover of the music book: "This fragment was written at my instance by poor Mangan. While composing it he lodged in Fishamble Street. The remnant of the biography never came into my possession, and I fear the author either lost or destroyed it." Which, considering his reaction to the first part, as Fr Meehan must have understood, the poet almost surely would have done. Finally, over thirty years later, the priest somewhat reluctantly allowed the fragment to be published, and it appeared in the *Irish Monthly* in 1882.[32] Even then, there were protestations that it was fabrication and exaggeration, and a complaint by the elderly John McCall at what Mangan had said about the behaviour of a member of the vintner trade. Others, invoking Victorian clichés about family and the *paterfamilias*, could not believe that a father could have behaved so badly to a son, nor did they think the son should have written in such terms about his father even if he had. The booklet did not appear until 1968, edited by James Kilroy and published by The Dolmen Press.[33]

No manuscript of "The Nameless One" has survived, as far as we know, although it may be recalled that Eva O'Neill, the New Orleans "Irish Princess", claimed to have been given one as a child in Dublin. Perhaps in some archive in Louisiana is a copy—"an antique deposit"—still waiting to be discovered. The poem first appeared in print in the 27 October 1849

Irishman where close to a dozen previously unpublished poems of Mangan's had been printed between July and October. In its lines, as in his autobiography, it is apparent that God was, indeed, foremost in his thoughts by this time: "God will inspire me" and "God had mated his soul with song", he wrote. This poetic autobiography traces the pathway of his life; the fourteen quatrains take him from boyhood—"one drear night-hour"—through a period of aspiration and ambition and into disastrous decline:

> And tell how trampled, derided, hated,
> And worn by weakness, disease, and wrong,
> He fled for shelter to God, who mated
> His soul with song—

There is a stanza for work when he is "condemned for years long/To herd with demons from hell beneath", and a stanza for false affections:

> Go on to tell how, with genius wasted,
> Betrayed in friendship, befooled in love,
> With spirit shipwrecked, and young hopes blasted,
> He still, still strove.

At last resigned, biding "in calmness the silent morrow", as the twelfth stanza, the epigraph to this section, has it, he sought for himself—the last appearance of his theme of homelessness—a final home in the hearts of mankind:

> Him grant a grave to, ye pitying noble,
> Deep in your bosoms! There let him dwell!
> He, too, had tears for all souls in trouble,
> Here and in hell.[34]

* * * *

Mangan managed to remain in the Fishamble Street room for several months. By early December, however, he was to be found at No. 151 Abbey Street, and he was being threatened with the loss of those lodgings if he did not come up with the rent immediately. For assistance, he now approached James Hardiman, perhaps for the first time. An acquaintance, the Joe Hamilton he names, had known Hardiman for twenty years and spoken warmly of his generosity, so Mangan wrote:

4 December 1848

Dear and Worthy Sir,

A series of unfortunate circumstances have reduced me to the lowest ebb of destitution. Money I have literally none; and I am threatened with expulsion from my lodging.

No fault of mine has brought about this unhappy state of things. How it has occurred I will explain when I have next the pleasure of seeing you. . . . It is

> a positive fact that there is not, at this juncture in my affairs, a single soul in Dublin to whom I could make a similar application. Our poor friend Joe Hamilton, an uphill-struggler against destiny, like myself, met me recently, and suggested to me this appeal to your kindness.

Mangan asked for only £1. Hamilton, it seems, had once approached Hardiman with the request that he write a letter of recommendation to the "Literary fund" on his behalf. Evidently it offered "pecuniary assistance" to worthy writers but only when backed by a reference from a nobleman, prelate, head of a college, or man of affairs; beseeching aid from the public treasury was in any case something Mangan obdurately refused to do. With poignant dignity his letter went on:

> Within about a month from hence I shall be able to earn as much by my literary labours as will fetch me £3 or £4—but I can obtain nothing earlier. Meantime I endeavour to keep something like a "shabby-genteel" coat on my back, but I am guiltless of wearing a shirt; and stockings are luxuries that I can only contemplate through the vista of memory.[35]

Hardiman responded promptly, and Mangan thanked him wholeheartedly in a letter of 7 December. He also added a note on the times; after saying they "are indeed dreadful", he continued:

> I myself have been for some time living, or rather half-living, upon two pence a day, or thereabouts. But it appears to me that something more awful than poverty and bankruptcy is impending. A new strange storm seems to be gathering in the heavens. All the political changes that have convulsed Europe of late would appear to be the precursors of some tremendous moral earthquake of which men entertain at present only a vague and dim presentiment. The pulpits of this city have rung with warnings to the people on this subject. May God arm and prepare us all for it, whatever may be its nature!

Several more sentences in this apocalyptic vein followed, after which he concluded, "We shall see strange things, if we live, in 1849 and 1850. Meantime, let us pray, work, and humble ourselves before God. He is our only trust and stay."[36]

Either he was not able to raise enough to pay his landlady, Mrs Kavanagh, or he misspent what he received, for he was put out of his rooms. John McCall may have witnessed this, for he "used to relate how on one occasion he saw poor Mangan ejected from his lodgings in Abbey Street". Perhaps the month was not unusually cold, but in his little brown coat and tight cloak, and without shirt or stockings, the poet must have severely felt the freezing weather of the week of 19 December. Finally, on 23 December, he was reduced to walking as far as John O'Donovan's and literally begging for help. O'Donovan gave Hardiman this account of the visit:

> The poet Mangan called here last night without a shirt to his back having slept in a hall the night before! I never saw any man in such a state of destitution. He told me that he had not the price of his lodging nor even one penny to buy a sheet of paper whereon to write a short poem for which he had been promised payment (that is the sum of six pence sterling). This beats Dermody and Dr Syntax hollow! His present condition is a scandal to Ireland starving as it is, and a disgrace to literature and to human nature. I gave him a few shillings to keep him alive for a few days, but I see clearly that he will be found dead in a few days, and perhaps buried without being recognized as the *author of Anthologia Germania* [*sic*]. He writes in public houses where he gets a pen and ink for nothing and sleeps in halls and garrets. I have written to the poet Anster to see if he could get him anything to warm his body not his imagination.[37]

Christmas Eve was, then, a grim occasion for the poet, now apparently alone in Dublin, William no longer figuring in any of his requests, as far as can be seen, nor accompanying him from one poor hallway or garret to another. The weather warmed a little on Christmas Day, but it was overcast and very dark.[38] By night, there were at least "a few dim stars in the zenith", and the temperature had moderated to a relatively mild 45 degrees. Fog, hoarfrost, drizzling rain, gloom, and flat masses of cloud prevailed until the New Year.

Lives He Still, Then?

[1]

Nightly must I make my choice
Between ill dreams and restless pillows,
But once in sleep I heard a voice,
Commingling with the roll of billows;
And in accents deep, it gave
Utterance to this mystic line—
March Forth, Eighteen Forty-nine!
Then sank silent as the grave—
March Fourth, Eighteen Forty-nine!
Mangan, "March Forth, Eighteen Forty-Nine"

As the new year opened, the *Irishman* took over where the *Nation* had left off in reporting nationalist and Famine news. In fact, during its last year, the *Nation* had been so caught up in politics that the Famine, now become all too plainly an everyday horror, had dropped from prominence. From the official Government position of at least wanting, and to some extent trying, to stem the tide of the disaster, the breathtakingly ruthless change to a non-interventionist, *laissez faire* policy had been made. Espoused by Charles Trevelyan and Charles Wood, this policy argued for "the application of natural causes system" which allowed the authorities to do nothing and feel good about it.

Yet 1848 had been, if possible, a worse year than 1847. Homeless beggars had continued to flock into the cities, and the jails, which were thought to give better food than the workhouses, were as over-crowded as the shelters and soup kitchens. In the words of Cecil Woodham-Smith, "The spring of 1848 was cold in Ireland; throughout February there were falls of snow, and the country people believed that snow would prevent the reappearance of blight" which in any case had all but disappeared in 1847. Although there were few potatoes to plant in 1847, those that were planted had done well and provided a small but excellent crop of seed potatoes. To obtain these in 1848, "Severe sacrifices were made . . . Clothes, bedsteads, tables and chairs were sold. . . ." But it was not to be. "The failure of the potato crop in 1848 was as complete as in 1846, and coming as it did upon a people already impoverished and enfeebled by distress, the results must be even more disastrous." In the first few months of 1849, Woodham-Smith continued, there was "as much, if not more, suffering than at any time since the potato failed." The effects had been cumulative. The expert the English had called upon rather early in the Famine, Count Strezelecki, was a compassionate, clear-sighted aristocrat and explorer. His observations carried weight, but he had no very salutarious effect on officialdom. The people were "skinned down to the bone" he now told whoever would listen. "A 'singular and melancholy-state of depression' . . . brooded over the western unions, and the people declared 'the land is cursed'."[1] Nothing more was done; nature was left to take its course.

The *Irishman* began publication in January, and was probably what Mangan had meant when he said he had a source of renewed income available to him in a few months. Bernard Fulham, previously of the *Nation*, was the proprietor before the release from prison of Joseph Brenan, who would then take over. Like the *Nation*, it was a sixteen-page paper and cost sixpence. The quality of the writing and editing was impressively good. Of Mangan's thirty-six contributions, twenty-four appeared while he lived, another twelve after his death. There is a strong possibility that he turned them over to Fulham, and then to Brenan, in bunches which the editor then spread out over several issues. He may just as well have written one whenever he needed another four or five shillings to live on. Whichever the case, the impression given is of consistency and control. Most of the poems were between forty and sixty lines in length, and the stanzas were neatly numbered with roman numerals, probably the editor's addition. Almost every second issue had a Mangan poem or prose sketch. Of these latter, there were nine, already noted here in some detail, but also worth considering as a group. Six appeared during his lifetime, three after his death. John McCall was of the opinion that Mangan intended to do a tenth sketch about Dr Robert James Graves, a physician co-worker with Mangan's doctor, William Stokes, at the Meath Hospital, which seems entirely possible, although Graves' role in the poet's life is not known.[2] As it happened, a sketch of Mangan's life was published as the tenth in the series, the so-called "impersonal autobiography".

In many ways, these nine articles were tributes to individuals who had profoundly touched the poet's life, and in that sense, they add greatly to what we know about James Clarence Mangan. The sketches appeared between 24 March and 28 July, a "Hail and Farewell" to the eight men and a woman whom he wanted to remember and commemorate. Charles Maturin influenced the poet's choice of material, slanting him toward Gothic story-telling and providing the archetype of Melmoth, as well as representing in his own person the brilliant, eccentric, lonely genius. George Petrie saw to it that Mangan had a comfortable berth at the Ordnance Survey and stood by him during the extended illness he suffered in 1838 and 1839. John Anster inspired him to translation and assisted him in later life when he needed help. The Rev. C.P. Meehan was his friend and curate at his Parish church, never condemning him, but always helping and challenging him to live up to the best in himself. Maria Edgeworth inspired his choice of the name "Clarence". Gerald Griffin exemplified for him the true Munster Man, but what, if anything else he meant to Mangan, we do not know. The Rev. Dr James Henthorn Todd was an administrator for Trinity College Library and gave Mangan a job there when the Ordnance Survey closed. John O'Donovan was an early friend and fellow-worker who helped the poet when he could, and probably always showed his fondness despite his sometimes rough disapproval. William Maginn gave Mangan enjoyment with a highly imitable (in the right hands) comic prose which some critics have felt played havoc with Mangan's own style.

One of the poet's last attempts to rally his readers to new patriotic effort was his first piece of writing in the *Irishman*, the poem "Look Forward!". In fact, there was very little positive to "look forward" to, and he returned to familiar religious rhetoric to ask "Have our lamps, then, been quenched/For the sins of our sires?" But he would not settle for a verdict of predestined doom, at least not altogether, and asserted, perhaps with too many exclamation points to carry conviction:

> We are true men, not traitors!
> We are stern malcontents!
> But, schooled by ripe Reason,
> We bide a sure season.
> The genuine creators
> Of Will are—Events![3]

However, he could not sustain the enthusiasm and closed on the old doubt, that their failure might lie in their not having sufficiently turned to God for help.

Not much has been said in these pages about the *Pilot*, the O'Connell newspaper, but it had not been closed down, sometimes pulling its punches, and depending on rhetoric that was ambiguous enough not to disturb anyone too much. Early this year a letter on Mangan's behalf appeared therein; it was quite long, somewhat stilted, and exceedingly polite in its phraseology. Although signed "Honestus", it has been suspected that Mangan himself sent it. That, however, seems unlikely to me, although he may have collaborated with a friend who wanted to help him with such an appeal. "Honestus" first explained his acquaintance with the poet:

> I have had the pleasure of knowing him for many years, even indeed from his childhood; and never was I more shocked than at meeting him a week ago in

> Great Britain-street, and perceiving the change that had taken place in him. Humble a man as I am in society, still he thought to shun me, but I prevailed on him to accompany me home, and there he disclosed to me a tale of suffering and destitution which you would hardly believe if I were to detail it.

Mangan did, in fact, live at one time in Great Britain Street, or nearby, information we have from no less a personage than Lady Mary Ferguson, the wife of Sir Samuel, who wrote:

> Poor Clarence Mangan sometimes lived in a garret in Johnson's Lane, off Britain Street and from time to time my dear husband and others among Mangan's well-wishers tried to save him from the misery which his habits brought on himself. . . . He would send a messenger from some den to say he was a prisoner, or very ill, or starving, and Sir Samuel would go and see him and give him money and advice, and do what he could to rouse him to exertion and give him a fresh start. . . .

"How to assist Mangan" was apparently a subject that came up fairly often these days when her husband and Dr Stokes got together.[4] Another Great Britain Street resident was his old friend James Tighe who was a bookseller there. Quite possibly, Mangan visited him from time to time; indeed, it is almost certain that he would have, and Tighe remained very fond of him until the end. Honestus's last passage:

> Am I too bold in venturing upon an appeal to you in his behalf? I am but an humble mechanic, but my uncle lodged in the house of Mr Mangan's father, in Fishamble-street, and I feel the deepest grief at seeing the happy and wild-spirited boy, whom I knew so many years back, transformed into the melancholy and broken-hearted man. I do not presume to suggest to you what might be done for him; but I think that a subscription from his friends generally would save him, and enable him to resume his literary labours— for, as he himself has told me, he believes that he has "as yet achieved nothing in comparison with what [improved] circumstances would enable him to accomplish."—I am, Sir, your obedient servant, HONESTUS [5]

The proprietor of the *Pilot*, Richard Barrett, may well have inscribed this reaction which was printed by way of introduction to the letter:

> We cannot express the sorrow we felt at the receipt of the following letter. The sad cases of Otway and Chatterton, we had hoped, were impossible of recurrence in this age; but we have no doubt that it was ignorance of his condition which caused an Irish public to allow for a moment one of the most gifted men that Ireland ever produced—James Clarence Mangan—to consort with beggary. How sure are we that when through our humble means, the truth is known, thousands will fly to the rescue.

Although there were no thousands "flying to the rescue", the *Freeman's Journal* for Monday, 8 January, carried a response from which we can conclude that Mangan must have been completely out of touch with his old friends who were now prisoners of the State. He probably felt beneath the notice of the respectable political prisoners now waiting out their time in Newgate, which held Duffy among others, or Kilmainham, where Brenan was incarcerated. It was no doubt Brenan who addressed the editor:

> The state prisoners at present confined in the gaol of Kilmainham have read with real regret a short account of the sufferings and destitution of their gifted countryman, James Clarence Mangan, which appeared in the pages of your contemporary the *Pilot*.
>
> They believe Mr. Mangan to be a man of the highest and purest genius, and they are ashamed to see the tragedy of *Robert Burns* re-enacted in this country. They have, therefore, subscribed the enclosed sum of £3 10s.—a small one, it is true, but as much as they (thanks to their paternal government) can afford—more in hope of inducing others to follow their example, than of alleviating, to any material extent, the sufferings of this fine-souled man.[6]

This was followed by:

> FUND FOR RELIEF OF JAMES CLARENCE MANGAN.
> We have received from the State Prisoners in Kilmainham gaol, for the use of Mr. Mangan, the above sum of £3 10s.

To some friend, probably J.W. Hanna, O'Donovan, in his acute fashion, penned this description of the poet as he now saw him:

> He cannot give up drinking, and, therefore, cannot attend to any description of business. Now and again he writes a short poem, which he composes as he moves like a shadow along the streets, and writes in low public-houses, in which he gets pens and ink *gratis*. One short poem of his exhibits *seven different* inks and seven different varieties of hands, good or bad, according to the number of glasses of whiskey he had taken at the time of making the copy.

It would seem that the "low public-houses" are owed a debt of gratitude for providing help that no one else was volunteering at the time. O'Donovan went on, not very generously:

> He never *inverts his style*, but transfers from the excited sensorium to the dirty piece of paper amid the din of drinkers. I feel ashamed of him, but still I think he should be prevented from dying of cold in the street. He seems to have no friends but the State prisoners, who seem to sympathize with the divine intoxication of his soul, but their subscription will not keep him in whiskey for one fortnight. He broke the pledge four or five times.

To which Hanna humanely responded on 26 January, "It is really a sad misfortune that Clarence Mangan so degrades himself and that he is in such a miserable condition. His vice of intemperance has spoiled a true genius in him. An asylum where he could get board[,] clothing and lodging would be the only remedy, for an annuity he would assign over before three months—."[7]

Such words come back to haunt the reader who encounters the fine poems which Mangan composed in such dire conditions: "The Time ere the Roses were Blowing", "The Everlasting Jew", and "The Irish Language" in January; "The Tragedy of Ruaghri and Dearbhorgilla" and "Duhallow" in February; "March Forth, Eighteen Forty-nine!", "Keen for Owen Roe O'Neill", and "The Funerals" in March; "For Soul and Country" in April; "A Word in Reply to Joseph Brenan" and "The Famine" in June, to name only the most memorable, and only those which appeared while he was still living. Hanna and O'Donovan were only grudgingly appreciative, and one has to ask, What more did they want from Mangan's "true genius" than they had already received? Of the few virtues Mangan claimed for himself was that, in spite of everything, he still worked hard. It was not a vain claim. By this time, the number of poems he had seen published neared one thousand.

[2]

> [John O'Daly] poor fellow, little richer than [Mangan] in this world's goods, did give, with a kind hand, such as well becomes the true Celt's generous nature, the little he could afford. What was that little?—a seat at his humble hearth—half the poor meal that an occasional profitable speculation in some old book enabled him to purchase, a few pens, an inkbottle, candle, and a literal prose version of those old songs. . . .
>
> "Press Notice" of *Poets and Poetry of Munster* in the *Irishman*, 3 November 1849

It seems fairly certain that a part of that "little" was also whiskey punch, O'Daly not being known for a teetotaler. He and Mangan worked often together during the last two years of the poet's life, as noted earlier in these pages, and the volumes they produced, *The Poets and Poetry of Munster* and *The Tribes of Ireland*, are remarkable testimony to Mangan's ability to keep going even when life was at its lowest ebb. Ironically, *The Poets and Poetry of Munster* would go to the printers the very day the poet died. *The Tribes* appeared in 1852, having been held up by O'Donovan's time-demanding note-making on the text and also by some worry about its highly controversial nature.

The quality of the translation in *Poets and Poetry of Munster* has too often been criticized, largely, I suspect, because the poems were thought to have been done rapidly—a misperception, as we have already seen—

and because they possess a clarity and rough-edged spontaneity not always appreciated in the last century. O'Donoghue, for instance, observed that Mangan "did a considerable amount of work for O'Daly of a more or less crude kind. . . . Many of [the poems in *Poets and Poetry of Munster*] are decidedly inferior to the previous versions by Edward Walsh, Ferguson, and Callanan."[8]

Far more to the point are the collection's merits. Each of Mangan's translations is accompanied not only by the Gaelic original, but also by the air to which it was set. In fact, each of the more than fifty English translations can be sung to its Gaelic melody, and thirty-nine different tunes are provided. Thus Mangan had produced not only poems, but also singable lyrics. Recently, Sean Dunne, author and compiler of a new *Poets of Munster*, has been inspired to pay homage to this work:

> *The Poets and Poetry of Munster* was a landmark on the road to the great revival of interest in Gaelic literature which began in the 1850s. Compared to the work of the Munster poets writing in English at the time of its appearance, it contains a depth of sincerity, an authenticity, which leave them far behind.

Echoing Anthony Cronin, he has referred to Mangan as "the first Irish poet to strike a chord that sounds true to the modern ear", a chord heard over and over again in *The Poets and Poetry of Munster*.[9]

The selection of poems is quite varied, although the form known as the *aisling* or vision poem predominates. By contrast, few drinking songs are included although this sort is represented by "John O'Tuomy's Drinking Song" and "Andrew Magrath's Reply". A fair number of love poems, traditional ballads, and patriotic songs complete the assortment. O'Daly took credit for the individual introductions to the poems and the poets, another feature which distinguishes this publication, but Mangan himself almost certainly wrote these, using information from the editor. A long portion of Mangan's own introduction was suppressed, no doubt by O'Daly because it seemed inappropriate to him. The manuscript is now lodged in the Pearse Street Library while O'Daly's manuscript of the literal translations from which Mangan worked is part of the collection of the Royal Irish Academy Library.[10] Perhaps because the former reveals Mangan's continuing reservations in regard to Gaelic poetry, O'Daly chose to omit all but a few remarks about "our translator" and a paragraph on Ulster, Leinster, and Connaught. It is for the first time that this material is printed, in Appendix H.

The Poets and Poetry of Munster went into several editions and is today virtually the only collection of Mangan's work that can be said to be in any way accessible, and that only in second hand and rare bookshops. Because of their undeserved reputation for mediocrity, the poems in the book have not been anthologized, and for obvious reasons only a tiny sample can be given here, two stanzas from one of the loveliest of vision poems, "Gile ne Gile", that is, "The Brightest of the Bright", and, at the other extreme, a couple of verses from John O'Tuomy's "Drinking Song" and Andrew Magrath's "Reply".

GILE NE GILE

The Brightest of the Bright met me on my path so lonely;
    The Crystal of all Crystals was her flashing dark-blue eye;
Melodious more than music was her spoken language only;
    And glorious were her cheeks, of a brilliant crimson dye.

* * * *

Oh, my misery, my woe, my sorrow and my anguish,
    My bitter source of dolor is evermore that she,
The Loveliest of the Lovely should thus be left to languish
    Amid a ruffian horde till the Heroes cross the sea.[11]

DRINKING SONG

I sell the best brandy and sherry,
To make my good customers merry;
    But, at times their finances
    Run short, as it chances,
And then I feel very sad, very!

Here's brandy! Come, fill up your tumbler,
Or ale, if your liking be humbler,
    And, while you've a shilling,
    Keep filling and swilling,
A fig for the growls of the grumbler![12]

REPLY

O'Tuomy! you boast yourself handy
At selling good ale and bright brandy,
    But the fact is your liquor
    Makes every one sicker,
I tell you that, I, your friend Andy.

You bow to the floor's very level,
When customers enter to revel,
    But if one in shy raiment
    Takes drink without payment,
You score it against the poor devil.[13]

At the same time he was working with O'Daly finishing this collection, Mangan was also working with him on a verse translation of *The Tribes of Ireland*, a late sixteenth or early seventeenth-century poetic satire consisting of over 100 quatrains by Aenghus O'Daly. A product of the time in history when poets had enormous powers to damage chiefs and clans, these verses, said John O'Donovan who eventually edited the whole work, were written by the original poet (on assignment) to lampoon and insult "the chiefs of the principal ancient Irish families, and such of the descendants of the Anglo-Normans as had adopted their customs and formed alliances with them". The bard Aenghus O'Daly, or the Red Bard—*the Bard Ruadh*, as O'Donovan usually referred to him—possessed a ferociously destructive gift of satire, and in this instance he put it to work in the service of the enemies of Ireland, Lord Mountjoy and Sir George Carew. According to O'Donovan, he got what was coming to him: "He received . . . that kind of reward which he did not anticipate, but which all recreant betrayers of their race, richly deserve. . . . he was stabbed through the heart by the order or command of O'Meagher, chief of Ikerrin."

The manuscript of this work includes the Irish original, O'Daly's literal English translation with copious notes by O'Donovan, and—in O'Daly's handwriting—Mangan's versified stanzas.[14] It would seem to have been written in only two sessions, although the possibility that so much reading and rhyming could have been done so swiftly boggles the mind. The first versified portion contains stanzas of six lines each, while the second portion consists of quatrains. O'Daly's handwriting, never the best, grows increasingly large, angular, and uneven as he goes along, and becomes especially wild and full of black slashes toward the middle of the manuscript. There the two men appear to have taken a break. It is clearer when the work resumes and the stanzas become quatrains; then it falls apart once more towards the end. It is not likely that they worked without refreshment, and if this were whiskey punch or porter, it would account for the extraordinary variation in the handwriting.

Mangan, I expect, enjoyed these hours with O'Daly more than most things he did this cold, wet spring. Evidently, O'Daly would tell the poet what the literal meaning of the Gaelic stanza was and then Mangan, in an on-the-spot versification, would dictate a rhymed version to O'Daly who would write it down. When the poet could not come up with something, O'Daly placed a brief prose interpretation in brackets and moved on to the next verse. Occasionally, Mangan declined to versify, it seems. One scatological stanza, for example, was passed over, with the two lines of the literal translation crossed out and "Stars here" written in as a direction for the printer. The two lines do not seem so awful when, with a little effort, they are made out, and they appear also in Latin in the unexpurgated *Tribes* in the National Library of Ireland collection: "The badger's fingers are getting the 'Quick'/From scratching his stinking arse." On the manuscript, O'Donovan wrote "See Rabelais' Life of Gargantua" and "They have infinitely more brutal verses than this still living. . . ."[15]

Everyone involved took some liberty with the Red Bard's work. Mangan as usual added little touches when he wanted to, something personal, or some "improvement" to the text. O'Daly, as all his notes here and elsewhere show, constantly had to choose among differing meanings for the Irish. O'Donovan rearranged the stanzas to make them orderly with those relating to Connaught coming first followed by those for Leinster, Ulster, and Munster. Someone, either O'Daly or O'Donovan in all likelihood, wrote additional lines, one couplet to connect Mangan's Connaught and Leinster portions, and others here and there for other purposes. Occasionally, Mangan's text was altered drastically.

The published version, which was reissued in a facsimile edition by Tower Books, Cork, in 1976, contained an introduction by O'Donovan, a dual-language Irish and English section with notes and text by O'Daly as corrected and greatly amplified by O'Donovan, and Mangan's versification with notes at the back. O'Donovan began editing the book in 1850. Over a year later, in August 1851, he wrote to Dr Graves: "I have been working at Aenghus's satire for Mr. John O'Daly. . . . If he publishes what I have written (Heaven what a mass of scandals) he will sell his pamphlet; but by Jove! let him remember the fate of Aengus!!"[16] When the book finally appeared the next year, the most insulting and obscene portions had been removed.

One example of the material found in *Tribes of Ireland* will serve several purposes here, exemplifying O'Daly's process, Mangan's style, and O'Donovan's editing. The Gaelic, in O'Daly's handwriting, appears first:

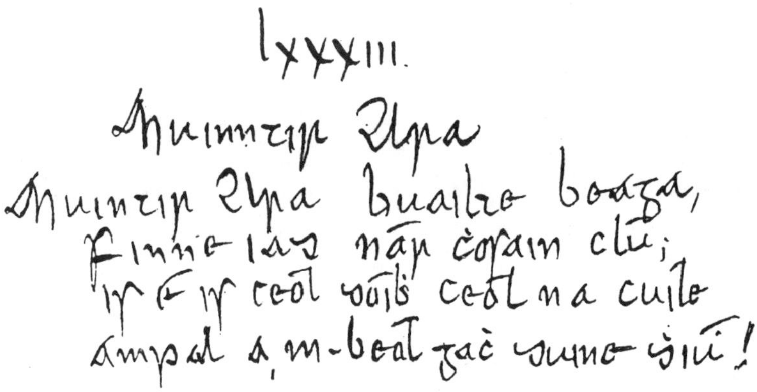
lxxiii.
Muintir Ara
Muintir Ara buailte boga,
Finne las nár ċosain clú;
Is é is ceol doiḃ ceol na cuile
Ampal a m-beal gaċ duine ḋíoḃ!

From O'Daly's oral literal translation, Mangan created this verse; as do all of his versions in the manuscript (but not in the book), it carried a title:

The Good People (not the Fairies) of Ara

The good people of Ara are four feet in height;
They are heroes, and really stand stoutly in fight;
But they don't sacrifice overmuch to the Graces,
And Hunger stares forth from their fly-bitten faces.

In his preface to the *Poets and Poetry of Munster*, O'Daly mentioned the *Tribes* and observed that the original "had lost none of its beauty in poor Mangan's hands". Although "beauty" may not be a very apt description for this satire, O'Daly was pleased with Mangan's work. He included the above stanza, making only one change, a substitution of "soldiers" for "heroes". When O'Donovan got hold of it, however, it underwent a metamorphosis, emerging as:

The families of O'Hara, of small Booleys, [dairies]
A tribe that never earned fame;
Their music is the humming of the fly,
And the grumbling of penury at each man's mouth.

Finally, either O'Donovan or O'Daly recast Mangan's quatrain to suit the corrected translation, and it was this version which appeared in the printed volume:

The tribe of O'Hara are men of some height,
But they've never been known to stand stoutly in fight;
They have no other music but the hum of the flies,
And hunger stares forth from their deep-sunken eyes!

More typical was this six-line verse which grew from O'Daly's four lines, Mangan, as the note shows, being allowed his own variation:

The literal:

Shrove-tide bread and flesh,
I would not eat but against my will;
Yet it is necessary to lay to it,
As it cannot be avoided.

Mangan's manuscript: *How they dined on Shrove Tuesday*

I called on them once on Shrove Tuesday at night
But the devil a pancake,
Flour, oatmeal, or brancake,
In parlour or kitchen saluted my sight.
I walked off. I'd have starved ere I'd pray to
One thief of the gang for a single potato!

Published *Tribes*: Seven lines reduced to five, "thief" changed to "imp", and, for some reason, an "e" put on the end of "potato".

To this it was probably O'Donovan who added the note: "Single potatoe. There is no mention of potatoes in the original. In Shakespeare's time potatoes were a luxury. The poet Mangan, who had a horror of potatoes, is not very happy in his translation here." *The Tribes of Ireland*, although not to everyone's fancy, amply illustrates the flexibility of Mangan's genius to the very end.

[3]

Evil angels tempt us in all places.
What but sands or snows hath earth to give?
Dream not, friend, of deserts and oases;
But look inwards and begin to live!
Mangan, "Advice Against Travel"

March offered some encouragement to Mangan and to the Irish cause, although as can be seen in the stanza at the start of this chapter, the poet was able to manage only the merriment of a favourite pun "march forth". The suppression of *habeas corpus* expired, and the legal rights of citizens were once more affirmed, at least to some extent. Joseph Brenan, along with a number of other State prisoners, was released, and thus he was free to assume control of the *Irishman*, leaving Fulham to continue as manager. Young as he was, Brenan appreciated Mangan and seems to have been genuinely fond of him, also. For Mangan, Brenan was another fine young friend—sensitive, witty, tender-hearted, and intelligent.

Brenan would write what would be, as strange as it seems, the only full-length obituary of the poet to appear in any Dublin paper or magazine. Therein he described his friend as he saw him during these last few months of his life:

> If you have passed through the streets of Dublin anytime these four years; if you were abroad when the twilight began to vanish, and the shadows grew blacker on the walls, you might have noticed a middle-sized man, infirm-looking and stooped, moving on slowly and with noiseless steps. His hair was white as new-fallen snow, which gave him the appearance of age before he was old. . . . His face is calm, though marked with thunder-scars. His eye is inexpressibly deep and beautiful, and centred therein there is a union of quiet love and daring thought. The mouth has lost the charm which it once had; but the forehead is unwrinkled and white as ever. His figure is wasted away—the sword is eating through the sheath. . . . If he speaks you cannot choose but listen to his low, touching voice. . . . The spell is upon you, and you remain docile and obedient.[17]

James Price also described Mangan as he appeared at this time, although briefly, as "crawling through our streets, grotesque in figure, mean in attire, bread, a comb, pens, and MS. sticking from his pockets, his hair long and unkempt, and with the dreamy enthusiasm of the opium eater flickering at times across his sallow features. . . ."[18] Both may have fit the poet. The difference lay in the feeling that each man had for him.

Gavan Duffy, having been released in April from Richmond Prison where he had been moved from Newgate, evidently paid no attention to his old friend, excusing himself in his memoirs by claiming that he, Duffy, had been "in prison the last year of Mangan's life". When the *Nation* was revived in the autumn, he promptly printed what passed for an obituary memoir, a piece of writing that O'Donoghue termed "perhaps unnecessarily crude", attributing the harshness to the fact that Mangan had had a "close connection with the chief rivals of the *Nation* during his last year or so, and especially to the *Irishman*. . . ." Part of Duffy's commentary ran, "It is a terrible but most certain truth that him, who will not save himself, all mankind banded together cannot save", and he referred to all the negatives he could muster in a brief space: "the curse of the fall", the will that lay "prostrate and impotent", and "the feet of tyrannic habit".[19] He said nothing at all personal.

Another friend, one who had perhaps not been as close to him as previously after scoffing at the *Autobiography* as "mere dream", was Fr Meehan. If there had been some falling away there, the breach now seems to have been closed. The priest wrote:

> Soon after the outbreak of Cholera in April 1849, he now and again came to the old quarters and there held forth on the origin and symptoms of the pestilence, maintaining, like Don Ferrante in the *Promessi Sposi*, that there was no such thing *in rerum natura* as contagion, and consequently that precautions of all sorts were unnecessary and delusive. Withal, from what I remember of these monologues I have no difficulty in stating that he had a presentiment that he was doomed to fall a victim to the terrible epidemic; for his mental vigour began to fail perceptibly, and he seldom lost an opportunity of alluding to his opening grave. . . .[20]

In fact, Mangan had long had a "premonition" of death, and it has to be said that one more or less may not mean much. Moreover, he fell ill of cholera, but he did not die of it. What is more accurate is that his "mental vigour" was failing. He lived nowhere. He earned little. He ate almost nothing. What else would one expect but a decline in both physical and mental health?

After having as an address No. 151 Upper Abbey Street, Mangan had moved out, that is, had been evicted, and from December 1848 his trail is lost for a while. It may well have been at this time that he had a room at

No. 126–7 Upper Abbey Street. An old photograph shows this building to have been a red brick, three-storey edifice with a bow window.[21] Many rooms, little more than closets, were being let in buildings of all sorts during these years, for again, as when Mangan's father was plotting to get rich by remodelling old houses into tenements, masses of poverty-stricken and starving people were pouring into Dublin and looking for cheap accommodations.

April was a bitterly cold month. On the 17th, heavy snow showers fell and the temperature dropped to 28°F. Although it had risen to above freezing by the next day, a thin layer of snow still covered the ground. By this point, Mangan had yet another address in Upper Abbey Street, No. 11, and on 22 April wrote to Dr. Anster:

> Dear Dr. Anster,
> The enclosed appeared in Saturday's *Irishman*. Perhaps you may have seen it, but I rather think that you have not. I know that I shall not see you this evening, but perhaps I may be able to gain a sight of you towards the end of the week.
> Ever yours faithfully, James C. Mangan.[22]

"The enclosed" was a copy of his "Sketch" of Anster which had just appeared as the third of the "Sketches and Reminiscences of Irish Writers". This little note is so normal that it is misleading, but Mangan was courageous to the end, putting as good a face as he could on his condition and situation. He was obviously proud of what he had written and evidently was in a fairly respectable lodging, for he added a reassuring "P.S.":

> If you do me the favour of a visit, pray turn into the doorway at the left side of the hall, and enquire for "Miss Atkins". The house itself you will recognise at once: there are pillars in front of it. *Kennst du das Haus? Auf saulen ruht die Dach!*"

That is, "Know you the house? On pillars rests the roof!" the opening lines from one of the poet's earliest translations, "Mignon's Song". Why Mangan had lived for these several months on Abbey Street is not known, but sometime in May or early June, he once more returned to the streets of his childhood.

In retrospect, there can be little question but that the poet was now convinced he had not long to live; that he was sure this spring would be his last. Although he had been so ill and so malnourished for so long that one stretch of misery may have seemed much the same as another to him, poem after poem acknowledged that he believed death was drawing very close. At the same time, this anguish had a commensurate cause in the fiasco of Young Ireland and the tragedy of four appalling years of famine, so his ability still to rally the troops, as it were, in "For Soul and Country" urging "Arise! my slumbering soul, arise!/And learn what yet remains for thee/To dree or do!" is all the more remarkable:

My countrymen! my words are weak,
  My health is gone, my soul is dark,
    My heart is chill—
Yet would I fain and fondly seek
  To see you borne in Freedom's bark
    O'er ocean still.
Beseech your God, and bide your hour—
  He cannot, will not, long be dumb.
    Even now His tread
Is heard o'er earth with coming power—
  And, coming, trust me, it will come,
    Else were HE dead![23]

The 12 and 19 May numbers of the paper carried two poems that are of rare significance in revealing the view of life which he had by now worked out, a view which gave him comfort and the strength to carry on. It was a philosophy of the reconciliation of opposites: the product of a lifetime of struggling with a duality which was one aspect, the physical-spiritual perhaps, of the polarization that was the ordering principle of his life. The resolution, when he reached it, was voiced in two poems, "Bear Up!"[24] and "Ghazel", and was alluded to in still others. "Ghazel" appears here almost in full. To sum it up, inadequately but perhaps usefully: he now resigned the struggle *against*—against "Nature", man's dark side, pain, suffering, Death—and affirmed that *all* is necessary to the perfection and wholeness of the great design. Only when Evil was seen as a part of, not apart from, the Universal, could he bear the awfulness of it and affirm "GOD is *the* idea of my mind."

GHAZEL

All that hath existence is eternal;
Therefore Bliss and Glory are eternal.
All that hath existence must remain;
Therefore Pain and Darkness are eternal.
All that hath existence must be twofold;
Wouldst thou have this proved? Behold the proof old
As the days of Abel and of Cain,
As the day when Abel perished, slain
By his murderous anti-brother Cain.
Love, and *therefore* Hate,—Good, *therefore* Evil,—
GOD, and *therefore* Man,—Man, *therefore* Devil.
Life, with all its well-known ways, and *therefore*
Death, with all its mysteries. "But wherefore

Doth not GOD abolish Hell and Pain?"
Friend! He cannot. He can *not*. The twain
Have their being in a source eternal.
Action and Reaction. Here behold
The One Law by none to be controlled!
Leaven *with* Lump, or *neither* Lump *nor* Leaven—
Heaven *and* Hell, or *neither* Hell *nor* Heaven—
Such is Nature, seen through Truth eternal.

* * * *

So, we part:—yet, take these words from me:
Blame not any. Love. Believe. And see
That thou keep thy conscience pure from stain.
Conscience also hath a life eternal.[25]

A poem titled "Have Hope!" published posthumously addressed "To A suffering Patriot Friend" defended "Hope" on this same ground, as expressed most poignantly in the fourth and fifth stanzas:

I, too, have borne, unseen, alone
    Mine own deep griefs, griefs writ on sand,
Until my heart grew like to stone—
    I struck it, and it hurt my hand.*   [*Shakespeare]
My bitter bread was steeped in tears,
    Another Cain's mark marred my brow—
I wept for long my wasted years—
    Alas! too oft I weep them now!

Yet I despair not! Ill bodes Good—
    And dark Time bright Eternity:
For aye the gay and mournful mood
    Turn on the spirit's axle-tree.
First Grief, then Joy,—first Earth, then Heaven—
    This is the eternal all-wise Law—
Such Law, by GOD the Almighty given,
    Let all revere with holiest awe![26]

The dualism that he found in himself, Mangan also found in the nature of his fellow Celts. In 1846, "The Peal of Another Trumpet" had warmly praised the "gentler gifts" he recognized in his countrymen and concluded "And 'tis well you thus can blend/ Softest moods of mind with sternest—", but he was under no illusion about the difficulty this characteristic could cause. In "Still a Nation", another poem to appear in the autumn after his death, he wrote:

Yes! we stand a Nation still;
    Yes! we scorn the Saxon's threat;

Yes! the Celt hath yet a will—
    Hath a power and purpose yet.
The dark, stern resolve of soul,
    And the tenderness that melts
Earth, Heaven, Nature, in one whole—
    These are all the Celt's!

* * * *

And, albeit I hasten home,—
    I, a nameless child of thine,
To the last, the lampless dome—
    Though I die, and make no sign,
My last thoughts shall be of thee—
    My rejoicings, my regret;
And even now I prophesy
    THY GRAND TRIUMPH YET![27]

It was also in the month of May that he, or someone who was working with him, penned the impersonal autobiography, to which much reference has already been made in these pages. Published posthumously more than a year after his death, it possesses internal evidence attesting that some person other than the poet had the major hand in putting it together: errors of fact which Mangan himself would surely not have made, accidental repetitions (very unlike him), and, simplest of all, the attribution of the piece to another person. Although this latter feature had not been unusual in earlier work, it was decidedly uncharacteristic of the poet during the final year or two of his life. On the other hand, the editor of the *Irishman*, perhaps again Bernard Fulham, for Brenan had been in America for almost a year, introduced it with:

> The following sketch of Mangan was written by himself about six weeks before his death. He had previously contributed nine "Sketches of Modern Irish Writers" to the *Irishman*; and in an eccentric mood, under a fictitious signature, thus described himself. The *Sketch* is, in our opinion, rather over-drawn, but few will fail to recognise its truthfulness in many parts. . . .[28]

The author of the Sketch began it:

> The somewhat impolite intrusion of this sketch into the society of the other sketches of eminent Irishmen which have appeared in this Journal, will, perhaps, be pardoned, when I state that I happen to be intimately acquainted with Mr Mangan, and that I have his entire sanction for giving it to the public.

The piece is divided into two sections, each a full column in length. It is the second part which is marred by repetition, and the suspicion grows that the editor, or someone, was padding the writing to make the piece stretch that far. The authentic contributions that this article makes to our knowledge about James Clarence Mangan have already been covered sufficiently—specifically, the "walk in the rain", the suspicion and denial of opium use, and a few more details about a love affair.

What Mangan or his amanuensis chose to put in, leave out, and repeat, would be an interesting study in itself but cannot concern us here at much length. A summary will best serve the purpose of his—now closing—life story. The first column summed up his early years, including his unhappy childhood and his association with the *University Magazine*. It noted that he "has been said" to translate from fourteen languages, but "really understands only eight". It ended with the assertion that "Mangan is *not* an opium-eater" and that Carleton was responsible for spreading that "report". Clearly, this had remained a painful accusation. The second part, in the same number of the newspaper, opened with the purported author's assessment:

> My professional avocations as a medical man have made me acquainted with many singular neuralgic cases, but I have never met anybody of such a strongly-marked nervous temperament as Mangan. He is in this respect quite a phenomenon: he is literally all nerves and no muscles. In accordance with such a temperament Providence has endowed him with marvellous tenacity of life. He has survived casualties that would have killed thousands—casualties of all kinds— . . . and he ascribes them all to his power of writing, facetiously deriving *calamity* from *calamus*, a quill.

There followed a lengthy repetition about how many languages he knew and a similarly long passage about German humour, illustrated with a shortened version of the story of *The Man Without a Shadow*. These sections accounted for three-fourths of the column. A rather too brief paragraph commenced, as we have already seen, "From habits of prayer and fasting, and the study of the Lives of the Saints, Mangan was at one period of his mysterious life drawn away, and enticed into the snare of Love. . . ." By then the bottom of the page had almost been reached, and it was time to conclude. That paragraph follows in full:

> I have said that Mangan is neglected and forsaken; but I had forgotten. There is one friend of his, who has known him only in adversity, but who occasionally visits him, and of late has been exerting himself for the relief of the poet's exigencies, though hitherto, I believe, without success; I mean Mr. Mooney, the portrait painter, and himself a poet also of no mean order.

No such portrait painter has been discovered. The only poet named Mooney who was writing more or less during this period was one Robert Gerald Mooney, and nothing except his fleeting allusion to "the fair picture he had drawn for himself" connects him with painting in any way. No connection has been made between this man and the poet.

The author ended the sketch:

> If it be not too late, possibly Mangan may yet be rescued and restored to society; but when a fly is rapidly sinking in a glass of water, and not a soul in the house besides himself, it is difficult for him to forbear conjecturing that he must go [to] the bottom.

It would be impossible to get much more Manganesque than that; the slightly macabre whimsy, the gentle irony, even the theme of drowning which we have seen Mangan use in one form or another over and over again—these are almost enough to convince one that he wrote the piece single-handedly.

[4]

> Thou art the Prospero, of resistless wand—
> King by the "right divine" of mystic lore,
> Dreamer of dreams, now gloomy as La Morgue,
> Through which, as through "glass darkly" loom the Dead,
> Now like the Angel-trance of Swedenborg,
> When heavenly portals opened o'er his head . . .
> Joseph Brenan, "To Clarence Mangan"

So Joseph Brenan addressed Mangan in the poem that was printed in the 26 May number of the *Irishman*. "Brother and friend" he called the poet—and gently pled with him:

> Herr Mangan, listen:—Live with Cathal More,
> Sojourning in the wondrous "land of morn";
> Or, an' thou will'st, with Koerner, bow before
> The air-borne music of the "marvellous horn;"
> Laugh the quaint laugh, or weep the bitter tear,
> Be gay or sad—be humorous or sublime;
> One thing remains—but one—Herr Mangan, hear!
> *To live thy poetry—to act thy rhyme!*

Perhaps one brighter note can be heard through these lines—at least Brenan did not think Mangan was beyond saving. When the poet responded in the next issue of the newspaper, a mischievous "Printer's Devil" set these words at the top of the poem, making it clear that not everyone was moved by the pathos of Mangan's life or Brenan's affectionate sympathy: "Note,—The Poets have fallen in love with each other—they like themselves much better than their readers like them." Three stanzas of "A Word in Reply to Joseph Brenan" are given below:

I

Friend and brother, and yet more than brother,
 Thou endowed with all of Shelley's soul!
Thou whose heart so burneth for thy mother, [Ireland]
That, like *his*, it may defy all other
 Flames, while time shall roll!

V

Dream and Waking life have now been blended
 Longtime in the caverns of my soul—
Oft in daylight have my steps descended
Down to that dusk realm where all is ended,
 Save remeadless dole!

X

Fare thee well! we now know each the other,
 Each has struck the other's inmost chords—
Fare thee well, my friend and more than brother,
And may scorn pursue me if I smother
 In my soul thy words![29]

Like others from this period, it was really a poem of leave-taking. The poet, significantly, promised nothing, except not to "smother in his soul" the admonitions of the young editor, a statement which meant nothing beyond promising not to forget what he had said.

Mangan's last poems to be published in the *Irishman* while he lived were, "Let Not the Gael Despair", a translation, and "The Famine", an original poem. The former is a vision poem, of sorts, in which a dreamer has a rather curious auditory hallucination, for want of a better phrase. Here, "As I lay last night on my couch alone,/ There arose a sound as of thunder—" which grew into "the Martial tread/Of a myriad warlike legions". Upon the vision's passing, the poet asks, grief-stricken, "Why are our lives but disasters?" Why do the Gael "Crouch thus at the feet of their masters?" And the poem ends:

My prayer of fire to my death will be thus:—
 "May my friends ever aid each the other!"
If *we* help ourselves, then our GOD will help *us*—
 Our GOD and His ever Blessed Mother![30]

If ever a man refused to give up in the face of overwhelming odds, it was surely Mangan. "The Famine" begins pleasantly in a land that is really "the lovely land" of his poem of that title. Then all changes: "God struck on every heart, and men grew pale—/ Their bliss was metamorphosed into bale", and despair overtakes them:

Despair? Yes! For a blight fell on the land—
The soil, heaven-blasted, yielded food no more—
The Irish serf became a Being banned—
Life-exiled as none ever was before.
The old man died beside his hovel's hearth,
The young man stretched himself along the earth,
And perished, stricken to the core!

O, GOD! Great GOD! Thou knowest, seest, Thou!
All-blessed be Thy name! This work is Thine—
To Thy decrees, Thy law, Thy will, we bow—
We are but worms, and Thou art THE DIVINE!
But thou wilt yet in Thine own day redeem
Thy Faithful; and this land's bright sun shall beam
To Earth a Pharos and a Sign! [31]

Another wave of cholera swept Ireland this spring, and Mangan contracted the disease late in May. His condition worsened, and early in June he was admitted to the cholera sheds in Kilmainham. According to Fr Meehan, he "remained there some days", then, "thinking that he had well nigh recovered", he left the makeshift hospital and "took refuge in a miserable garret in Bride-street".[32] The sheds were little more than a "pest-house for the dying", but had he stayed there, he would have received food, at least, and had a bed to rest in while he regained some strength. But he did not, or could not be restrained for so long, and he undoubtedly left as soon as he was able to totter out the door. Among the worst possible treatments for people recovering from cholera is alcohol, and opium is little less dangerous, yet in all probability, he sought out the former and maybe the latter drug as well, as soon as he was free of medical control.

By mid-June, he had grown weaker, not stronger. The story told by James Price is probably accurate enough: "He had been discovered, we believe, by Dr. Wilde [Oscar Wilde's father] during one of his antiquarian researches among our poorest districts—discovered in a state of indescribable misery and squalor, occupying a wretched hovel where he had retired to die. . . ."[33] Fr Meehan wrote that, "Growing weaker and weaker, he was removed to the Meath Hospital by the advice of the late Dr Stokes, who pronounced his case hopeless."[34] John O'Daly, who had been working so closely with Mangan earlier in the spring, told a slightly different story: "On his recovery we found him in an obscure house in Bride Street, and, at his own request, procured admission for him to the Meath Hospital on the 13th of June . . . ."[35]

A large, bulky, granite edifice, the Meath Hospital still stands on Long Lane not very far from Camden Street. Completed on Christmas Eve,

1822, the new building with what the *Lancet's* editor called its "pompous pile of steps" soon became the main hospital in the area. The wards were heated by fires around which the men patients sometimes gathered in the evening, and it may be recalled that the Meath had been innovative in allowing only one patient to a bed. Two physicians and six surgeons were attached to the Hospital (a grim indication of what usually required that a person be admitted to a hospital!). One of its most outstanding physicians had been Dr Whitley Stokes, the father of the Dr William Stokes who had long attended Mangan. Hospital staff still recount the story of Mangan's death there and remind the listener that Brendan Behan, too, died in the Meath—in 1964.

Mangan is said to have taken "a well-worn volume of German poetry" to the hospital with him and to have pored over it "frequently while consciousness remained". Price affirmed that "it was found after death with him in bed!", but a tale such as this may be more fiction than fact. Hercules Ellis, editor of *Romances and Ballads of Ireland* which contained a very fair proportion of works by our poet, confirmed that Mangan was translating while in hospital and kept his German book in his pocket and his notes in his hat, but Ellis was not there to observe, so could only have been relaying a story he had heard.

For the first three or four days after he was admitted, he was expected to recover. He no longer was ill with cholera—that was over—but because of his shocking state of malnutrition and his weakness he would have been unable to eat much, if anything. Dr Stokes may or may not have been the physician who admitted him, but according to his daughter Margaret, he "watched over him for three days, till he died. One morning [the poet] turned on his pillow and said to him, 'You are the first man who has spoken a kind word to me for years'." Unfortunately, severe suffering has little or no memory of better times. Price wrote that while in hospital Mangan received "every care and comfort" and the "cleanliness and restoratives brought him back for a very brief space to look upon dear life again with natural longing", but that he only "survived his admission seven days". Some of this was Price romanticizing; I doubt that the poet now "longed" for anything but death.

Joseph Brenan may have seen him in hospital, for he recorded that "at their last meeting, the mind of the poet reverted to his dismal experience in the attorney's office." But there were few of his friends to call, few who even knew where he was. John Mitchel was 10,000 miles away, but wrote knowledgeably, presumably on the basis of what his friends told him, that Mangan was "assiduously waited on by a few friends, and Mr Meehan, a good priest—who had always appreciated him as a poet, loved him as a man, and yearned over him as a soul in the jaws of perdition—anxiously and affectionately sought to console him in his last hours." Fr Meehan himself half-apologetically wrote that it wasn't until Mangan had been several days in hospital that Dr Stokes "conveyed to the writer poor Mangan's earnest desire to see him", and that only then did he hasten to the hospital. Gavan Duffy was out of prison, resting up, and preparing to tour the south and west of Ireland with Thomas Carlyle, an expedition that commenced in July. He did not see his old friend.

During his hospitalization, Mangan was looked after by several men: a Dr Gilbert, Dr Stokes, perhaps Dr Wilde, and also, Price wrote, by the resident apothecary, Mr Parr. Price hazarded, "His last words contained an expression of fervent gratitude to Mr. Parr for his kindness." John McCall, more modestly than Price, attributed his own knowledge of the poet's last days to "a literary friend", leaving his source anonymous but suggesting William Hayes, to whom he applied that epithet in his the *Life of Mangan*. In his anecdote we have the only record of the fate of Mangan's final writings. Upon being admitted to hospital, the poet was "entrusted to the care" of a Dr Gilbert of York Street "who knew him well and intimately, and who did all in his power to alleviate the poor poet's bodily afflictions," wrote McCall. Seeing that Mangan was using "whatever strange scraps of paper . . . happened to be in his reach" to write on, and feeling certain that these would be precious to someone after the poet's death, the physician arranged for him to be supplied surreptitiously with better bits:

> . . . without having the sufferer's suspicions aroused, ostensibly as wrappers around medicine bottles, powders, etc., he had a quantity of paper transmitted to him from time to time, likewise giving peremptory orders to the nurse on no account to disturb her patient, but leave him as much as possible to himself. . . .

So it was that his privacy and his pride were both preserved. As it turned out, Mangan died at night, and the next morning the following scene unfolded:

> . . . when the kind-hearted doctor entered the ward and found the curtain drawn over the deceased's secluded couch . . . his first inquiry naturally was to ascertain if all of the old papers under the patient's pillow, and which he had amused himself scribbling on in his lucid intervals, were preserved intact? To his great amazement, the fussy attendant informed him that, not wishing to have any useless old papers scattered about the ward, as such negligence on her part had got her into a previous scrape, she had just consigned the whole collection to the fire-grate.[36]

So disappeared up the chimney Mangan's last "disjointed fragments", whatever they may have been.

As he grew weaker, the poet requested that one of the penitential psalms be read to him, and the one chosen was perhaps Number 129, the "De Profundis", which begins with the cry Mangan had declared he uttered while young and wandering, miserable and abused, in the fields around Dublin:

> Out of the depths have I cried unto thee, O LORD:
> LORD, hear my voice!
> Oh, let thine ears consider well
> the voice of my supplication.
> If thou, O LORD, shalt mark iniquities:
> LORD, who shall abide it?
> For with thee there is propitiation:
> and because of thy law I have waited for thee, O LORD.
> My soul hath waited on his word:
> my soul hath hoped in the LORD.

Soon Fr Meehan arrived and took a chair beside Mangan's bed: ". . . the poor fellow playfully said, 'I feel that I am going. I know that I must go *unhousel'd* and *unanneal'd* but you must not let me go *unshriven* and *unanointed*.' The priest in attendance being called, heard his confession, and administered the Last Unction."[37] So, to the end, he was very much himself, quoting from *Hamlet*, that most familiar story of a son haunted by the ghost of his father, and punning on "unhouseled" and "unannealed"—that is, "unannalled"—by which he meant homeless and without his story told.

Wednesday, 20 June, was a mild day, not one of the soft June days that had always so beguiled Mangan, but a day with early temperatures around 55°F and a morning sky filled with fleecy clouds. By evening, they had lowered and become a heavy, flat mass with scud, the misty, vapoury clouds that are driven before a wind. Fr Meehan stayed by his friend that night. The poet lay quite still with his arms crossed on his breast. By ten o'clock, death was at hand. He "manifested sentiments of edifying piety", wrote the priest, in the pompous but somehow touching idiom of his day. "And then, with a smile on his lips faintly ejaculating, 'O, Mary, Queen of Mercy!' . . . his soul was summoned to the Judgment Seat of God."

Epilogue

The body of James Clarence Mangan was removed to the morgue of the Meath Hospital shortly after his death, but his burial had to wait upon the times. Fr Meehan felt this indignity sorely: "Although the burial rite should have followed fast on the decease, his remains were not interred till Friday, 23rd June [actually this date was Saturday], because of the difficulty of procuring either coffin or hearse, owing to the awful mortality then desolating the city."

The only immediate obituary notice appeared on 22 June in *Saunders' News-Letter:*

> Clarence Mangan is no more. A few days ago he was found by one of the few friends that remained to him in a most wretched lodging, from whence he was removed to the Meath Hospital, where, under the kind care of Dr. Stokes, he appeared to make a slight rally. About ten o'clock on Wednesday night he had just expressed his gratitude to one of the officers in the institution for the kindness which he received, when he turned round in his bed and expired, apparently without a struggle.

On the day of the funeral, Brenan's longer tribute appeared in the *Irishman*: "He is dead, all that was earthly of him has returned to the worms, the immortal Spirit revels in that universal knowledge whose mysteries he almost penetrated in life. . . ." Brenan continued:

> His genius was a Midas-gift, which came saddled with a curse. Whoso has heard his name has heard his history. . . .
>
> It is enough to say that he was the greatest of our modern Irish poets; that he was unrivalled as a translator; that his mastery over metre and words was almost superhuman; that a truer bard, in nature, as in genius, never lived than our poor friend Mangan. . . .

Brenan knew him well, but only during the final year or so of his life, and his observations have an immediacy that Price's, let us say, for all his decorative passages, lacks. Brenan went on:

> He was a sincere friend, and never forgot a kind action. It is a curious fact, and worth noting for his biographer, that, although he passed the greater portion of his life in the regions of the Ideal, he was not at all unacquainted with the Real . . . he was naturally a practical man. . . . This was the source of his humour, quaint and rich, the very flowering of common sense; for humour was as much a characteristic of his, as fancy. . . .

Brenan also paid homage to his friend's love of Ireland, calling him "an enthusiastic patriot", albeit "little of a politician", and concluding, "His great hope was that he might do something for his country—that he might leave good deeds as a legacy."

The delay in the funeral allowed two other men to see Mangan after his death, men who would not otherwise have played any part in the poet's story—Hercules Ellis, a barrister, poet, and editor, and Sir Frederick Burton, the painter. Ellis wrote movingly in the introduction to his *Romances and Ballads of Ireland*:

> I had not been acquainted with Mangan, except through the medium of his writings. I had never even seen him, when, in the month of June, 1849, I was startled by a newspaper announcement that the poet, who had so long afforded me instruction and delight, had just died in the Meath Hospital. I hastened to the hospital to ascertain if this report were correct. There, for the first time, I beheld James Clarence Mangan. Wrapped in a winding sheet, and stretched upon the table of the dead-house in the Meath Hospital, lay [th]e poet, whose works had so long formed the theme of universal admiration, an attenuated corpse, wasted to a skeleton, by want, and sickness, and misery, and despair.

Of yet greater interest is the visit made by Burton. Like Ellis, he had not known the poet, although he recalled being introduced to him once. His friend Dr Stokes dropped by his house at breakfast time on Thursday, 21 June, and told him that Mangan had just died and lay in the hospital morgue, suggesting that he "should make use of the opportunity to preserve some record of the poet's appearance". He went on:

> There was no time to be lost. The day was a sultry one in summer or early autumn [he did not quite recall], and interment could not be long deferred. I went at once to the hospital, and made the drawing which, at a later period, and at the request of Mr. Henry Doyle, I presented to the National Gallery of Ireland.
>
> The sight of poor Mangan, as he lay in the mortuary, with head unsupported, and the long, partially grey hair fallen back from the fine and delicately shaped forehead, was intensely interesting and pathetic.
>
> I recollected that when I had seen him living some years before, his forehead was completely hidden by an unkempt-looking mass of hair like a glibb so that its beautiful structure was a surprise to me when I finally saw it. . . .

Some slight mystery attends this picture. In fact, there are two such pictures, although obviously only one of them was actually made by Burton that warm June day in 1849. As he said, in 1872 he presented one to the National Gallery: the larger of the two, and the more finished, with shadings of white along with red and black conté, which he had signed "FW Burton ft June 1849". The second picture, also in the National Gallery, is considerably smaller and lacks finishing touches. Burton apparently made it for Dr Stokes, who in turn left it to his daughter Margaret, whose estate presented it to the Gallery in 1900. It is not signed, but carries the identification "Clarence Mangan" in the space where Burton's signature appears on the other. Usually, the drawing signed by Burton is identified as the one made first, but, it is curious that D.J. O'Donoghue, who was in close touch with Burton and heard the story directly from him, chose to include, not the large drawing, but the small one, to illustrate his 1897 *Life of Mangan*. The question is discussed more fully in Appendix J.

It would surely have brought a wry smile to the poet's face if he could have known how much attention he was going to be paid, stretched so unresponsively on the slab in the Meath Hospital's dead-house. Another person to visit him there was his doctor who went to make a plaster cast for a death-mask of the poet's face. If it was made in the usual fashion, oil was put on the face, strips of cheesecloth were carefully laid on, and plaster of Paris was spread evenly over all. The plaster hardens quickly, the lubricant inside the mask allows it to be easily lifted from the face, and it serves as a mold from which a form is cast. This relic, after disappearing for a while, was rediscovered toward the end of the last century by C.P. Curran in an old bookshop in Dublin and is now in the Civic Museum.

The funeral for the poet was pathetically small. Joseph Brenan wrote that five people were present, but Fr Meehan claimed that there were only three, whom he named as the poet's uncle Michael Smith, "one who had been many years connected with the *Nation*" (probably Bernard Fulham—certainly not Duffy), and himself. The figure five seems more likely, for Brenan and John O'Daly also were most probably in attendance. If the mourners included the poet's brother William, no one made mention of him; although O'Daly said William survived his brother but died not much later, no record of his death or burial place has been found. Whichever number is correct, both are too small for it to make much difference.

Today, matching grey tombstones mark the Mangan-Plunkett burial plot, JB 34, in Glasnevin Cemetery, a cousin of the poet's having married a Plunkett. Until recently, the inscription on Mangan's stone read only "IHS Erected to the Memory of James Clarence Mangan Who Died 21st June, 1849, Aged 46 Years. Requiescat in Pace." The date, it will be noted, is wrong. Fr Meehan was supposed to prepare the inscription for the blank space left on the front of the stone, but chose not to have any further engraving added because he was angry with the nation and fumed that the mere name of the poet was all it deserved. As this biography was being prepared for the press, however, a yellowed sheet of paper bearing a draft of the priest's planned inscription, as well as Mangan's personally selected epitaph, came to light—a rare find indeed. Fr Meehan, failing in memory, but as loving of Mangan and as cantankerous as ever, had written:

In your charity
Pray for the soul of
James Clarence Mangan,
Who Departed this Life the ____ of June 185__
A Man of Intellectual Powers of Rare Excellence
Gifted with poetic Genius,
of a hyper order unfortunately
He Made Literature and the exercise
of His Poetic Talents, the sole Pursuit
In a country that had Dwindled
Into a colony, in which
All Intellectual Pursuits are
necessarily unproductive,
And where the Depressing Influence
of Disappointment, Neglect, and Recurrent
Embarrassment Lead to Unfortunate
Results By No Means unusual Attendants
of Unrequited Literary Labor.

It may be that he realized how unsuitable it was and gave up the effort. On the reverse he had set down, perhaps as an alternative choice, this observation along with own epitaph quoted from *Romeo and Juliet*:

Long Before the Death of
James Clarence Mangan
With the feelings of a Man doomed
Irretrievably to Misery
He adopted these words for his Epitaph
"Affliction is enamoured of thy purity
And thou art wedded to Calamity."

And so matters long stood. In 1909, a memorial to the poet was erected in St Stephen's Green by the National Literary Society. Mounted on a limestone pedestal is a bronze bust of the poet, the work of the sculptor Oliver Sheppard, and below it is a marble medallion of the head of "Roishin Dubh", Dark Rosaleen, the last work by the patriot artist William Pearse. Finally, in 1981, at the request of my husband Richard Mangan and myself, the Dublin Cemeteries Committee permitted these further lines to be added to the Glasnevin Cemetery stone : "Ireland's National Poet" followed by "O my Dark Rosaleen, Do not sigh, do not weep!" But perhaps Mangan himself really had penned in "My Adieu to the Muse" his own best epitaph in the form of a wish, or a prayer, for how he might be remembered:

—Let Truth but give to Fame
My virtues with my failings; if this be,
Not all may weep, but none will blush for me:

And whatsoever chronicle of good,
Attempted or achieved, may stand to speak
For what I was, when kindred souls shall seek
To unveil a life but darkly understood—
Men will not, cannot, write it on my grave
That I, like myriads, was a mindless clod,
And trod, with fettered will, the course they trod,
Crouched to a world whose habitudes deprave
And sink the loftiest nature to a slave—
Slunk from my standard and renounced my God.

Appendices

[A]

TO JAMES MANGAN
By James Tighe

Frae new-come folk what tarry near
I aften for my Jamie spier,
As how he liked the bygone year,
    And sic discourse;
And if his—what d'ye call it?—fear
    Is naething worse.

On fine-strung nerves that witch can play
Such dirgefu' notes by night and day,
Till Fancy sees a dread array
    'O clouds and gloom
Arching a dark, a dismal way
    Down to the tomb.

Some canna' thole the mental pain
That racks a nerve-disordered brain,
Hence deadly dives an' draughts are ta'en
    To smooth the way,
An' some prefer the sharp, wee skein,
    Like Castlereagh.

When pilot Reason quits the prow,
Man! what a crazy thing art thou?
Alas! around thy chartless brow,
    An' shattered form
The Winter waves of life do row
    A rude, wild storm.

(The final two stanzas appear in Chapter 4.)

[B]

Mangan's possible *Morning Register* poems

EVENING
[unsigned]

There is an hour when leaves are still and winds sleep on the wave;
When far beneath the closing clouds the day hath found a grave;
And stars, that, at the note of dawn, begin their circling flight,
Return, like sun-tired birds, to seek the sable boughs of night.

The curtains of the mind are closed, and slumber is most sweet,
And visions to the hearts of men direct their fairy feet;
The wearied wing hath gained a tree, pain sighs itself to rest,
And beauty's bridegroom lies upon the pillow of her breast.

There is a feeling in the hour which tumult ne'er hath known,
Which nature seems to dedicate to silent things alone;
The spirit of the lonely wakes as rising from the dead,
And finds its shroud adorned with flowers, its night-lamp newly fed.

The mournful moon her rainbow hath, and mid the blight of all
That garlands life some blossoms live, like lilies on a pall;
Thus while to lone Affliction's couch some stranger-joy may come,
The bee that hoardeth sweets all day hath sadness in its hum.

Yet some there are whose fire of years leaves no remembered spark
Whose summer-time itself is bleak, whose very day break's dark.
The stem, though naked, still may live, the leaf, though perished, cling,
But if at first the root be cleft, it lies a branchless thing.

And oh, to such—long hallowed nights their patient music send:
The hours like drooping angels walk, more graceful as they bend;
And stars emit a hope-like ray, that melts as it comes nigh,
And nothing in that calm hath life that does not wish to die.

2 August 1828

POETICAL PORTRAIT
[unsigned]

Being of beauty and of grief:
Thy portraiture should be
Written in burning words and brief—
Tears, tears for thee!

A rose that by a lonely tomb
Hangs whitening in the sun,
The phantom of its former bloom
Yet lingering on;

A rill once by a mountain side,
Companion blythe and boon,
Till scorching suns its sweet depths dried,
And quenched its tone:—

A violet that no sheltering leaf
Hides from the strong rain's swell;
Being of beauty and of grief,
These thy fate tell!

Desolate in each place of trust,
Thy bright soul dimmed with care,
To the land where is found no trace of dust,
Oh! look thou there!

28 February 1829

THE SUN DIAL
[unsigned]

The sunbeam laughs upon the stone
That tells its march of light;
But, oh! 'tis by a shade alone
We trace its glowing flight.

'Tis thus in life—a gloom is cast
On present thoughts alone;
While on the future and the past,
A dreamy smile is thrown.

Ay! memory lights the parted hours
That wondered by in gloom;
And Hope is crushed amidst her flowers—
The shade is on their bloom!

28 September 1829

BEAUTY VANISHED
[unsigned]

A creature beautiful as dew-dipp'd roses,
Symmetric as the goddess sprung in marble
From out the sculptor's mind, deeply reposes
In a rich sleep of thought; and the clear warble
Of birds that greet Aurora in blue skies
Hath not a sound so holy as the sighs
That part her fruit-like lips. Is she not dreaming
A poesy inspired of panting love,
Divine as that with which the heavens are streaming
When the intense eye of the west is wove
With the aurient sun-set? She is gone! I weep—
For so all beauty passeth from the vision;
And clouds of darkness o'er the spirit creep,
Making of all her light obscure elision.

9 June 1830

SONG
[unsigned]

When palest stars are keeping
Vigils through night-hours;
When languid winds are sweeping
Dewy, slumb'ring flow'rs;
When meekest moon-light streameth
Through lorn, ghostly tow'rs;
When ev'ry lover dreameth
Of his dear one's bow'rs:
Then, with thy lyric voice, oh breathe
Unto mine ear
Some feeling lay, which I should
All but die to hear.

Some old, impassion'd measure,
Which, from lips like thine,
Were, in each word, a treasure;
In each tone—divine!
Sing of the fond *Forsaken*,
Of warm love's decline;
And that sad song shall waken,
Saddest thoughts of mine;
Until each mournful note, each
Solemn, sighing tone—
Each sob from thy wrung breast be
Echo'd by mine own.

28 September 1830

[C]

Kay Redfield Jamison, *Touched With Fire: Manic-Depressive Illness and the Artistic Temperament* (The Free Press, a division of Macmillan, Inc.: New York, 1993), pp. 61–2, 72.

To study the occurrence of mood disorders and suicide in a consecutive sample of poets born within a hundred-year period, I examined autobiographical, biographical, and medical records (where available) for all major British and Irish poets born between 1705 and 1805. There was within this group, as might be expected, a wide range of biographical, medical, and family history information available. For some, such as Lord Byron, both the quantity and quality of the material were excellent; for others—such as Robert Fergusson, John Bampfylde, and William Collins—the information, especially of a psychiatric nature, was far less complete. . . . A strong emphasis was placed upon both the severity and the recurrence of symptoms; in all cases it was the *patterning* of mood, cognitive, energy, sleep, and behavioral symptoms that formed the focus of study. The family histories of the poets, although more difficult to ascertain, were similarly analyzed. . . .

It can be seen that a strikingly high rate of mood disorders, suicides, and institutionalization occurred within this group of poets and their families. Six (William Collins, Christopher Smart, William Cowper, Robert Fergusson, John Codrington Bampfylde, and John Clare) were committed to lunatic asylums or madhouses, a rate easily twenty times that of the general population living during the same time period. Two others (Thomas Chatterton and Thomas Lovell Beddoes) committed suicide. More than one-half of the poets showed strong evidence of mood disorders. Thirteen, or more than one out of three of the poets, seem likely to have suffered from manic-depressive illness (Christopher Smart, William Cowper, George Darley, Robert Fergusson, Thomas Chatterton, William Blake, Samuel Taylor Coleridge, George Gordon, Lord Byron, Percy Bysshe Shelley, John Clare, Hartley Coleridge, Thomas Lovell Beddoes, and James Clarence Mangan). . . . The genetic nature of mood disorders is underscored by the family histories in many of the poets of depression, mania, suicide, violence, or insanity (for example, in the families of Byron, Gray, Cowper, Chatterton, Bampfylde, the Coleridges, and Campbell; and, suggestively, in the families of Johnson, Crabbe, Blake, Clare, Beddoes, and Mangan).

[D]

PHRENOLOGICAL DESCRIPTION OF MANGAN'S HEAD

This is the head of one capable of warm attachment, and of having his mind enthusiastically wrought up to the consideration of any subject or the accomplishment of any purpose. He would be apt to live much more in the world of romance than in that of reality, and with respect to the other sex, he would be inclined to cherish fanciful notions of their dispositions and characters. He has a bright imagination and possesses the spirit of poetry in a very high degree, but he would be subject to great alternation of feeling, and would be susceptible of great extremes, both of joy and grief. His mind is of an inquiring order, and he possesses ability for philosophy, but in general, and for a continuance, a literature of a lighter and more imaginative kind would suit him best. He appears to have but little combativeness, destructiveness, acquisitiveness, or self-esteem, which, with large cautiousness and no great degree of firmness, would render him very likely to be much influenced by the spirit of his associates: on the other hand having but little veneration, he would not be disposed to yield much submission to authority. He has a tender and compassionate heart for others, but especially for the young and innocent. He has also a strong desire to acquire the good will of others, and more particularly of those who are themselves great or amiable. He would not be of a domineering, insolent, or quarrelsome disposition; he would rather err in the contrary extreme and regard the crimes and follies of others with too lenient an eye. In religion, he would be more speculative than devotional.In politics, he would prefer the people to the Crown. In all the affairs of life generally, he would be more imaginative than prudent. He has but little secretiveness, and would then be inclined to express his sentiments without disguise on all occasions, perhaps often indiscreetly. Constructiveness is hardly developed at all, on which account he would not have a genius for mechanism or inventions generally, but he would possess the power of magnifying, embellishing and beautifying in the highest degree. A tendency to exaggerate and amplify would pervade whatever he undertook. He has great Form and Language, and would have an exquisite perception of the beauty of figure from the first, and a remarkable memory for words from the latter. His memory for places would be also great. In argument he would be quick-thoughted, but singular and prone to dissent from commonly received opinions. In action he would be rather irresolute, unless operated upon by some strong motive, on which occasions he would be rather impetuous. In conclusion, this is the head of one who is susceptible of strong impressions, great joy or great sorrow, but who would live much more in the past and future than in the present, and would be reckoned somewhat eccentric by the world. The principal ingredients of the character it indicates are taste, wit, extravagance, vividness of fancy, generosity, and proneness to yield to the solicitations of others.

J. Wilson, 11 February 1835

[E]

Preface

The translations comprised in these volumes have (with a single exception) been selected from a series which have appeared at irregular intervals within the last ten years in the pages of *The Dublin University Magazine*. They are now published in their present form at the instance of some valued friends of mine, admirers, like myself, of German literature, and, as I am happy to believe, even more solicitous than I am to extend the knowledge of that literature throughout these kingdoms.

It will be seen that the great majority of the writers from whom they are taken are poets who have flourished within the current century. In confining myself generally to these I have acted less from choice than from necessity. Little or none of that description of material which a translator can mould to his purposes is to be found in the lyrical or ballad compositions of the earlier eras of the German muse; and the elaborate didactical poems of the seventeenth and eighteenth centuries would not, I apprehend, be likely to suit the highly-cultivated tastes of readers of the present day. My design, I need scarcely remark, has been to furnish, not miscellaneous samples of all kinds of German poetry, but select samples of some particular kinds; and if I have succeeded in this design I have achieved all that I proposed to accomplish, and, I may venture to add, all that my readers would, under any circumstances, have thanked me for accomplishing.

Of the translations themselves it is not for me to say more than that they are, as I would humbly hope, faithful to the spirit, if not always to the letter, of their originals. As a mere matter of duty, however, I am exceedingly anxious to express, and I do here once for all express, my most grateful acknowledgment of the very favorable reception they have experienced from the various periodical publications of the day, and more especially from the newspaper press. Though I may at times be induced to think that the language of my reviewers has been too flattering, I nevertheless gladly accept it as evidence of a generous good-will on their part towards me, which, while it does them honor, should excite me to such endeavours as might in some degree qualify me to deserve it.

J.C. Mangan, Dublin, June 1845

[F]

LIST OF NAMES PROPOSED BY DUFFY

1 W.S. O'Brien
2 John B. Dillon
3 John O'Hagan
4 T.D. McGee
5 T.F. Meagher

6 John E. Pigot
7 Mr J. Barry
8 R. O'Gorman
9 T.D. O'Reilly—a writer of wonderful vigour
10 D.F. McCarthy
11 T. Brandon [?] The Celtic Atheneum
12 Denny Lane—Cork
13 J.T. Varian [?]—Cork
14 M. Doheny
15 Rev. Mr Meehan
16 Rev. Mr Kenyon
17 Dr Cane—Kilkenny
18 Dr Griffin—Limerick
19 John Martin—Newry
20 John Mitchel—*Nation*
21 E.F. Murray—London
23 R.D. Williams
24 Clarence Mangan (A greater poet than Davis)
25 C.G. Duffy

[G]

The question of why Mangan did not marry finds something of an answer in a story related by Michael Cavanagh in a letter to O'Donoghue, January 1897. Cavanagh, along with Mangan's friend Brenan and John Savage, often met and read Mangan's poems. One evening they were reading his "The Rye Mill" and after Brenan recited the third stanza's "In its neighbourhood, we all know how slips/The long day away with a boy while at play,/With a girl while gathering cowslips", Cavanagh winked at John Savage and asked, "Joe, did Mangan intend that comma should follow the word *play*, or was it a typographical error?"—"Of course Mangan intended it", he replied, "Why do you ask?" "Only because to my idea, the simile would be vastly improved by its omission." Joe read it over slowly again and then his eyes flashing with laughter, he exclaimed: "You're right, my boy, you have improved on Mangan's poetry." Maybe it is owing to my having a more natural conception of the situation that he had?

[H]

SUPPRESSED MANGAN "PREFACE"

And now, having brought our introductory labours to a conclusion, we might here conscientiously lay down our pen and take farewell of our readers, were we not desirous of offering a few observations on the character and structure of the Irish [stories] in general.

The first peculiarity likely to strike an English reader is the remarkable sameness that prevails in the pieces that assume a narrative form. The poet usually wanders forth of a summer evening over moor and mountain, mournfully meditating on the wrongs and sufferings of his native land, until at length, sad and weary, he lies down to repose in some flowery vale, or on the slope of some green and lonely hill-side. He sleeps, and, in a dream, beholds a young female of more than mortal beauty, who approaches and accosts him. She is always represented as appearing in naked loveliness,—a fancy evidently borrowed from ancient Greece, for the Irish, renowned though they have always been for their inventive faculties, do not seem, at least until of late years, to have exhibited themselves any original genius for the arts of sculpture or painting. . . . The enraptured poet enquires whether she be one of the heroines of ancient story, Semiramis, Helen or Medea—or, if his mind be more familiar with the illustrious women of his own country,—Deirdre, Blahmuid, or Cearnuit—or some Banshee, like Aoibhill, Chria, or Aine;—and the answer he receives is that she is none of those eminent personages, but *Eire*, once a queen, and now a slave,—of old in the enjoyment of all honour and dignity, but today in thrall to the foe and the stranger. Yet, wretched as her condition is, she does not despair, and encourages her afflicted child to hope, prophecying that speedy relief will shortly reach him from some quarter or other—France, perhaps, or Spain—a melancholy illustration, by the way, of the fact that the oppressed Irish never appear to have had sufficient moral strength to rely on themselves. The song then concludes, though in some instances the poet appends a few consolatory reflections of his own, by way of winding up his poetical clock gracefully.

Another characteristic of the Irish song is the frequent, indeed almost the continual introduction into it, of the heroes and heroines, the gods and goddesses, of the Heathen Mythology. But the Englishman [Mangan first wrote "he". Why he seems here and in the first sentence of the paragraph just above to be addressing English readers is not obvious.] who has ever, in the course of his travels, chanced to come into proximity with an Irish "Hedge-school", will be at no loss to conjecture the origin of these allusions. They are to be traced, we may say, exclusively to that intimate acquaintance with the Classics which the Munster peasant never failed to acquire from the instructions of the road-side pedagogue. . . . Alas! that the acuteness of intellect, and extensive capacity for the reception of instruction, for which the Irish peasant is remarkable, should not have afforded a hint to our rulers amid their many and fruitless attempts at what they call conciliation! Would it not have been a policy equally worthy of their judgment, and deserving of praise in itself, to establish schools for the Irish in which they might be taught at least the elementary principles of education through the medium of their native tongue?

A third, and the last, peculiarity that we shall notice, is one of a rather singular order. It is the frequent and almost perpetual employment by the Irish poet of the word **gan**, *without*. With him it is always **gan**—, without pleasure, **gan**—, without hope, **gan solas**, without light, **gan**—, without friends. We are the more struck by this peculiarity, because our translator, a German scholar, has informed us that the favorite Saxon phrase is—in contra-distinction to the Irish—mit, *with*, as when they write, *mit* Gott, *with* (the help of) God, *mit* Muth, *with* courage, *mit* unseren guten Schwesten,—*with* our own good swords. [These are telling examples against the Irish character in view of his comment about the lack of "sufficient moral strength to rely on themselves". No wonder O'Daly chose to put these pages away in a drawer!] But as the contrast between the Celtic and the Saxon character in this respect, might, if we pursued this topic further, be brought out into a relief too humiliating to our countrymen to contemplate, we forbear from any metaphysical speculation with respect either to the origin of the anomaly, or of the causes that may have contributed to its growth and progress.

[He concluded with "one word with reference to our translator", who had "peculiar skill in versification", and with an adjuration to "the east, west, and north of Ireland" to be inspired by the poetic work from Munster to "a spirit of emulation and rivalry that might at least urge them to literary endeavours equalling, if not surpassing, those of the south."]

[I]

BEAR UP!

I

Time rolleth on, and, with our years,
    Our sorrows grow and multiply—
        Our visions fade;
With late remorse and withering fears
    We look for Light to days gone by,
        But all is Shade.
Our dear fond friends have long been gone;
    No moon is out in Heaven above;
        The chill winds blow;
The dolorous Night of Age comes on;
    The current of our Life and Love
        Moves low and slow.

II

The Earth hath still a twofold dower:
    On desert sands the palm-trees rise
        In greenest bloom;
The dawn breaks at the darkest hour;
    Stars brightliest shine when Midnight skies
        Are palled in gloom;
The Deep hath treasures unrevealed
    Of gold and gems and argosies,

And gallant ships;
The sword strikes hurtless on the shield,
And from the once plague-laden breeze
Health greets thy lips!

IV

Bear up! even though thou be, like me,
Stretched on a couch of torturing pain
This weary day,
Though Heaven and Earth seem dark to thee,
And thine eyes glance around in Vain
For one hope-ray!
Though overborne by Wrong and Ill—
Though thou ha[st] drained, even to its lees,
Life's bitter cup—
Though Death and Hell be round thee, still
Place faith in GOD ! He hears! He sees!
Bear up! Bear up!

[J]

In "The Face of Mangan", *Hermathena*, Autumn 1967, Dr Michael Wynne of the National Gallery of Ireland argues that the larger of the two drawings of Mangan made by Sir Frederick Burton is the one done in the morgue:

> The poet's unsupported head is placed identically in both drawings. The manner of treatment in black conté—with some highlights in red—reveals the same hand. The scale, however, is different and—more important—the larger drawing reveals a directness and vitality which is somewhat lacking in the smaller work.

Dr Wynne, with whom I spoke shortly before this biography was due to go to press, confirmed his earlier judgement and emphasised the "vitality" of the larger work as contrasted with the smaller. As an expert on such matters, he is probably correct, but I have to add that to my less trained and experienced eye, the smaller drawing seems to be the more likely candidate. When I put this to Dr Wynne, he accounted for the impression by explaining that Burton would have drawn hastily in the morgue, but finished the drawing carefully when he was at home.

Evidently Burton kept the drawing himself and presented it to the National Gallery upon the personal request of the Director, Henry Doyle. The sole remaining puzzle is the writing on the back of the matt upon which the smaller drawing is centred: "Drawn in the Meath Hospital immediately after death. By Sir Frederick W. Burton".

Notes

CHAPTER ONE

1 Dr Thomas Wall Archives, Irish Institute of Pastoral Liturgy, Carlow.
2 National Library of Ireland microfilm no. 133, "SS Michael and John Marriages", no. P7358 Births.
3 Patrick Madden, Kiltale, interview, 1980. The families were united by the 1893 marriage of Mary Jane Smith (b. 1871), a daughter of John Smith, and Laurence Madden. Marriage Register T153/17.
4 John T. Gilbert, *History of the City of Dublin*, 3 vols. (Shannon, Ireland: Irish University Press, 1972. First published 1854–1859), I, p. 94.
5 NLI microfilm no. 133, "SS Michael and John Marriages"; no. P7358 Births. Here, too, were recorded their children's births. See also David Lloyd, *Nationalism and Minor Literature: James Clarence Mangan and the Emergence of Irish Cultural Nationalism* (Berkeley, California: University of California Press, 1987).
6 James Clarence Mangan, *The Autobiography of James Clarence Mangan*, James Kilroy, ed. (Dublin: The Dolmen Press, 1968. First published 1882). In subsequent references page numbers follow citations.
7 ["E.W."] (James Clarence Mangan), "Sketches of Modern Irish Writers. James Clarence Mangan", *Irishman*, 17 August 1850, pp. 27–8.
8 James C. Prichard, *A Treatise on Insanity and Other Disorders Affecting the Mind* (Philadelphia: Harwell, Barrington and Hanna, 1837) p. 20. I am indebted to Patricia R. Casey, MRC, Professor of Psychiatry, U.C.D., for this reference.
9 Seamus O'Casaide, "James Clarence Mangan and His County Meath Relatives. New Light on the Poet's Circumstances", *Father Mathew Record*, June 1941, pp. 4–5.
10 NLI ms. 7959, "John McCall Manuscript Collection for his *Life of Mangan*". Reprinted by McCall in *The Life of James Clarence Mangan* (Blackrock: Carraig Books Reprint, 1975. First published 1882), p. 4.
11 James Joyce toyed with the mystery of "Mangan's sister" in "Araby" in *Dubliners* where the sister of the boy-narrator's playmate, surnamed "Mangan", is never named but inspires the boy's desire to go to "Araby", the bazaar, and buy her something there, thus repeating the formula of Mangan's own story of "the walk in the rain". Also of interest is the record in the Archives of the Church of Jesus Christ of Latter Day Saints, Salt Lake City, Utah (Microfiche E0021, "British Isles and Ireland", Batch M. 70095–1, p. 21), of the marriage of a Catherine Mangan and Patrick Flinn, 1 October 1832, at the Church of St Michael the Archangel, located in a Dublin area not too distant from the Mangans, although nothing more is known about this couple. On the other hand, Joyce's "The Sisters", the opening story in *Dubliners*, concerns a priest named James Flynn and his two sisters, Nan and Eliza. His odd character includes many traits associated with James Clarence Mangan, and the imagination plays with the possibility that in him Joyce created a nephew for the poet.

12 McCall, *Life of Mangan*, pp. 4–5.
13 NLI ms. 7959, "McCall Manuscript Collection for *Life of Mangan*".
14 F. Carroll, "Clarence Mangan's Age Complex" in "Notes and Queries", *Irish Book Lover*, September 1957, pp. 133–4, was the first to call attention to the consistency of the six-year age error Mangan made in the *Autobiography* when he referred to the age he was at such-and-such a time. Even William Hayes's and James Price's memory of, and reference to, him as very young, "juvenile", and "a student" suggest that as early as 1828–32 he believed himself to be considerably younger than his actual age.
15 Marie-Louise Von Franz, *Puer Aeternus* (Zurich: Spring Publications, 1970), p. 3; and Carl Gustav Jung, *Psychology of the Unconscious* (New York: Dodd, Mead and Co., 1965. First published 1916), p. 125.
16 Charles P. Meehan, "Introduction", *Anthologia Germanica, Or a Garland from the German Poets, and Miscellaneous Poems*, 2 vols., 2nd ed. (Dublin: James Duffy, 1884. First published 1845), I, p. xvii.
17 George A. Little, *Fr Thomas Betagh, S.J.* (Dublin: Irish Messenger, 1960), pp. 2–3.
18 John Mitchel, ed., "James Clarence Mangan: His Life, Poetry and Death", *Poems by James Clarence Mangan* (New York: D. and J. Sadleir and Co., 1866. First published 1859), p. 9.
19 Gilbert, *History of Dublin*, I, pp. 44–6.
20 McCall, *Life of Mangan*, p. 4.
21 O'Casaide, "Mangan and His County Meath Relatives", pp. 4–5.

CHAPTER TWO

1 James Joyce, "James Clarence Mangan", *James Joyce Review*, I (1957), p. 33. Reprinted from *St Stephen's*, vol. I, no. 6, May 1902, pp. 116–18.
2 Trinity College Dublin ms. S.2.11 (2063) (Phillips ms. 17093) 692 Mason, "Parish Records: A Collection of Records, Notices, etc. 1669–1822".
3 Daniel Corkery, *The Hidden Ireland* (Dublin: Gill and Macmillan, 1977. First published 1924), p. 157.
4 Dr Thomas Wall Archives, Irish Institute of Pastoral Liturgy, Carlow. Also see John J. O'Shea, *The Two Kenricks* (Philadelphia: J.J. McVey, 1904), p. 267, *passim*.
5 National Library of Ireland ms. 13848 (in re. *Irish Catholic*, 21 March 1896), "John McCall Papers, Cuttings and Notes on Historical Subjects . . . mainly towards his work on almanacks and his *Life of Mangan*".
6 James Price, "Gallery of Contemporary Writers, No. 2: James Clarence Mangan", *Evening Packet*, 22 September 1849, [p. 3].
7 [D.C.] "Clarence Mangan", *Nation* (New Series) 13 October 1849, p. 106.
8 William Dillon, *Life of John Mitchel*, 2 vols. (London: Kegan Paul, Trench and Co., 1888), I, p. 21.
9 John McCall, *The Life of James Clarence Mangan* (Blackrock: Carraig Books Reprint, 1975. First published 1882), p. 7.
10 John Power, *List of Irish Periodical Publications (Chiefly Literary) from 1729 to the Present Time* [Written in 1868] (London: Printed for private distribution only, n.d.), pp. 9–10.

11 The National Library of Ireland possesses one copy of this extraordinarily rare publication. See also Edward Evans, *Historical and Bibliographical Account of Almanacks, Directories, etc. Published in Ireland from the Sixteenth Century* (Blackrock: Carraig Books, 1976. First published 1897), p. 1, *et passim*.

12 The Royal Irish Academy Library has one copy of the equally rare 1823 *Grant's*. As far as can be known, no copies of the *New Ladies'* are extant.

13 NLI ms. 138, "James Clarence Mangan Manuscript Letters and Poems", nos. 1–1b.

14 Weston St John Joyce, *The Neighbourhood of Dublin* (Dublin: M.H. Gill and Son, Ltd., 1913), p. 244.

15 G.N. Wright, *An Historical Guide to the City of Dublin* (Dublin: Four Courts Press, Ltd., and Irish Academic Press, Ltd., 1980. First published 1825), pp. 216–24.

16 J. Warburton, J. Whitelaw and Robert Walsh, *History of the City of Dublin from Earliest Accounts to the Present Time* (London: Cadell and Davies, 1818), p. 706.

17 *Oxford English Dictionary*, referring to Good's *Study of Medicine*, 1822.

18 Gerard Chrzanowski, "Neurasthenia and Hypochondriasis", in *American Handbook of Psychiatry*, 2 vols, Silvano Arieti, ed. (New York: Basic Books Inc., 1959), I, pp. 259–60.

19 Otto Fenichel, *Psychoanalytic Theory of Neurosis* (New York: W.W. Norton and Co., 1945), p. 263.

20 See especially Susan Sontag, *Illness as Metaphor* (New York: Vintage Books, 1979), p. 8.

21 Sarah Atkinson, *Mary Aikenhead: Her Life, Her Work, and Her Friends* (Dublin: M.H. Gill and Son Ltd., 1879), pp. 117–18; and in the 1882 edition, pp. 130–1.

CHAPTER THREE

1 Thomas Wall, "Introduction", in Edward Evans, *Historical and Bibliographical Account of Almanacks, Directories, etc. Published in Ireland from the Sixteenth Century* (Blackrock: Carraig Books, 1976. First published 1897), p. viii.

2 Royal Irish Academy ms. SR/24 F/20, "Silhouette of James Clarence Mangan".

3 D.J. O'Donoghue, "The Unknown Mangan", *Irish Independent*, 16 March 1903. Also found in National Library of Ireland ms. 4172, "D.J. O'Donoghue's *Life and Writings of James Clarence Mangan*, with many manuscript corrections and additions. Copy of a revised edition prepared for printers", p. 16.

4 John McCall, "Clarence Mangan's Contributions to 'Jones's Diaries', 1821 to 1826, under the name of James Tynan." Dr Thomas Wall Archives, Irish Institute of Pastoral Liturgy, Carlow. Also NLI ms. 13848, "Cuttings and Notes on Historical Subjects . . . mainly towards . . . his *Life of Mangan*", f.8.

5 John McCall, "James Clarence Mangan, His Early Life and First Poetical Attempts", *Nation*, 24 October 1874, p. 10.

6 *Grant's Almanack*, 1820.
7 NLI ms. 138, "James Clarence Mangan Manuscript Letters and Poems", no. 5.
8 Rudolf Holzapfel has suggested that "James Tynan" may have been a portmanteau name which Mangan and Tighe concocted to identify poems they wrote together. Jacques Chuto has conjectured that a real "James Tynan" let Mangan use his name to "steal" extra space.
9 *New Ladies' Almanack*, 1826. Now to be found in NLI ms. 7953, "John McCall's History of Irish Almanacs", pp. 233–4.
10 NLI ms. 7953, "McCall's Irish Almanacs", p. 214.
11 Rebus 5, *New Ladies' Almanack*, 1823. Now to be found in NLI ms. 7954, "John McCall's History of Irish Almanacs", p. 667.
12 Weston St John Joyce, *The Neighbourhood of Dublin* (Dublin: M.H. Gill and Son Ltd., 1913), p. 244.
13 RIA ms. 12/P/18, "Autobiography of James Clarence Mangan". Mangan had first written these words on p. 25 of this little music book, then changed his mind and crossed them out.
14 John Mitchel, ed., "James Clarence Mangan: His Life, Poetry, and Death", *Poems by James Clarence Mangan* (New York: D. and J. Sadlier and Co., 1866. First published 1859), *vide* p. 13 for Mitchel's description of Mangan's intense concentration while reading.
15 Charles P. Meehan, "Introduction", *Anthologia Germanica, Or a Garland from the German Poets, and Miscellaneous Poems*, 2 vols, 2nd ed. (Dublin: James Duffy and Sons, 1884), I, p. xiv.
16 *A Catalogue of the Books in the Lending Department of the Dublin Library Society, D'Olier Street, to the First of August, 1823* (Dublin: Kelly and Son, n.d.), pp. 1–60.
17 Roger de Wendover, *Flowers of History*, J.A. Giles, trans.. 2 vols., (London: Henry G. Bohn, 1849. First published 14th century).
18 George K. Anderson, *The Legend of the Wandering Jew* (Providence, R.I.: Brown University Press, 1965), p. 45.
19 W.H. Grattan Flood, "Mangan and the Melodies in *The Poets and Poetry of Munster*", in "Clarence Mangan Centenary Celebration", *Herald*, 2 May 1903.
20 NLI ms. 7954, "McCall's Irish Almanacks", p. 669.
21 Rudolf Patrick Holzapfel, annotation of the author's "James Clarence Mangan . . . in the Context of His Time", University College Dublin dissertation, 1989.
22 NLI ms. 138, "Mangan Manuscript", nos. 1–1b. It is also found in the almanac on pp. 6–7.
23 "To My Native Land", *Comet*, 15 July 1832, p. 94.
24 Richard Dowling, "Some More Old Letters", *Irish Book Lover*, December 1919, p. 40.

CHAPTER FOUR

1 James Price, "Gallery of Contemporary Writers, No. 2: James Clarence Mangan", *Evening Packet*, 22 September 1849, [p. 3]. Quoting Mangan to James McGlashan.

2 John McCall, *The Life of James Clarence Mangan* (Blackrock: Carraig Books Reprint, 1975. First published 1882), p. 17.
3 Ibid., p. 13.
4 Price, "Gallery No. 6", *Evening Packet*, 3 November 1849, [p. 3].
5 Royal Irish Academy ms. 3/B/52, "Journal of Charles Lever, 1828–1829". Also, W.J. Fitzpatrick, *The Life of Charles Lever*, 2 vols. (London: Chapman and Hall, 1879).
6 National Library of Ireland ms. 14271 "John McCall Papers, Extracts", 27 February 1883.
7 NLI microfilm, *Morning Register*.
8 ["Pastorini"], Charles Walmesley, *The General History of the Christian Church* (Dublin: n.p., 1790), p. 472. Gearoid O'Tuathaigh in *Ireland Before the Famine, 1798–1848* identified Christmas Day 1824 as the expected "day of fulfilment".
9 ["Pastor Fido"], *Pastorini Proves to be a Bad Prophet and a Worse Divine in an Address to the Roman Catholics of Ireland* (Dublin: M. Goodwin, 1823), p. 20.
10 Robert Kee, *The Most Distressful Country*, Vol. I of *The Green Flag* (London: Quartet Books, 1981), pp. 182–6.

CHAPTER FIVE

1 R.O.V. Lloyd, Dublin, established the eighteenth-century origin of the house and names of various owners.
2 James Price, "Gallery of Contemporary Writers, No. 6: James Clarence Mangan", *Evening Packet*, 3 November 1849, [p. 3].
3 John McCall, "Mangan's Love Episode. Notes on Mr Lecky's New Version", *Irish Emerald*, 7 July 1894, p. 711.
4 John McCall, "Clarence Mangan and The Comet Club", Dr Thomas Wall Archives, Irish Institute of Pastoral Liturgy, Carlow; also a photocopy in author's collection.
5 Manuscript, Dr Thomas Wall Archives, 22 November 1887.
6 Like Mangan's, Griffin's poetry abounds in verses addressed "To" someone or something. I find it extremely interesting, then, that this poem was called "To ****" while the others identify the addressee; all Mangan's original poems substituting "x" or asterisks for a name—only a few—also refer to someone he actually knew. The relevant stanza in Griffin's "To ****" is:

    And say while ye pause o'er each sweet recollection,
    "Let love like mine own on his spirit attend—
    For to me his heart turned with a poet's affection,
    Just less than a lover and more than a friend.["]

7 John McCall, *The Life of James Clarence Mangan* (Blackrock: Carraig Books, Reprint 1975. First published 1882), p. 15.
8 National Library of Ireland ms. 138, "James Clarence Mangan Manuscript Letters and Poems", nos. 3 and 3b.
9 Price, "Gallery No. 2", 22 September 1849, [p. 3].
10 George O'Neill, "Some Unpublished Mangan Manuscripts", *Studies*, Vol. IX, March 1920, no. 2, p. 118.
11 J. Cashel Hoey, ["Mangan Memoir"]. *Universal News* (London), 1 February

1868. As reported in private manuscript of John McCall. Holzapfel notes in *James Clarence Mangan: A Check-List of Printed and other Sources* that the article is signed "Clinton Hoey".

12 Nathaniel Burton, *Letters from Harold's Cross* (Dublin: John F. Fowler, 1850), p. 7.

13 *The Friend*, 26 January 1830, pp. 141–2. The poet changed little more than the opening line when he republished this poem as "The Two Sorts of Human Greatness" in the *Dublin University Magazine* for April 1835.

14 Between them, Rudolf Patrick Holzapfel and Jacques Chuto located Mangan in this periodical, Holzapfel discovering the poems there and Chuto linking the dates of their publication with those of the notices to "I.X.M." as follows:

22 December and 29 December 1829 as noted.

29 December: "Our friend I.X.M. will find that we have appreciated his favours. It will give us pleasure to hear from him again."

5 January 1830: "Our friend I.X.M. shall have an early place."

12 January: "The Desolation of Pompeii" published.

19 January: "Our esteemed correspondent I.X.M. is requested to accept thanks for his continued favours."

26 January: "The Two Sorts of Human Glory" (Blumauer) published.

2 February: "To our valuable correspondent I.X.M. we again offer our acknowledgement." In this same number appeared "The New-Year's Night of an Unhappy Man".

This was the final number of the *Friend*.

15 Generally speaking, these interpretations represent Chuto's, Holzapfel's and my own ideas respectively.

16 "Answers to Correspondents", *Comet*, 4 December 1831, p. 252.

17 Charles P. Meehan, "Introduction", *Anthologia Germanica, Or a Garland from the German Poets, and Miscellaneous Poems*, 2 vols., 2nd ed., (Dublin: James Duffy and Sons, 1884), p. xi.

18 D.J. O'Donoghue, *The Life and Writings of James Clarence Mangan* (Dublin: M.H. Gill and Son and T.G. O'Donoghue, 1897), p. 35.

19 Maria Edgeworth, *Belinda*, 2 vols. (Dublin: H. Colbert, and J. Stockdale, 1801), I, pp. 12–13.

20 Ibid., p. 11. There are other resemblances Mangan may have viewed sympathetically, too, including Clarence Hervey's fondness for sprinkling his conversation with French phrases and even Edgeworth's observation toward the end of the novel that "All the Herveys were odd. . . ." (II, p. 309).

21 D.J. O'Donoghue, ed., *Poems of James Clarence Mangan* (Dublin: O'Donoghue and Co., M.H. Gill and Son, 1903), pp. 130–1.

22 Price, "Gallery No. 6", 3 November 1849, [p. 3].

23 ["E.W."] (James Clarence Mangan), "Sketches of Modern Irish Writers. James Clarence Mangan", *Irishman*, 17 August 1850, p. 28.

24 William Butler Yeats, "Clarence Mangan (1803–1849)", *Uncollected Prose by W.B. Yeats*, John Frayne, ed., 2 vols., (New York: Columbia University Press, 1970), I, pp. 114–19. First published *Irish Fireside*, 12 March 1887, pp. 169–70.

25 John Mitchel, "James Clarence Mangan: His Life, Poetry, and Death", *Poems by James Clarence Mangan*, John Mitchel, ed. (New York: P.M. Haverty, 1859), p. 11.

26 Charles Gavan Duffy, "Personal Memories of James C. Mangan", *Dublin Review*, April 1908, pp. 286–7.
27 Price, "Gallery No. 6", 3 November 1849, [p. 3].
28 Gerard Kennedy, Director, Clare Heritage Centre, Corofin. In a letter to the author, October 1986, citing "Stackpoole Family Records". Also helpful were "Stackpoole Baptismal Records", fiche 3, St Helen's Church, Ipswich, Suffolk, England; and particularly Hugh Weir, *Houses of Clare*, in conversation with the author, summer 1986.
29 Price, "Gallery No. 6", 3 November 1849, [p. 3].
30 Ibid.
31 John McCall, "James Price . . . Memoir of Another Forgotten Irish Writer", *Irish Emerald*, 17 June 1893, pp. 1495–6.
32 "My Transformation. A Wonderful Tale", *Dublin Satirist*, 19 October 1833, p. 141.

CHAPTER SIX

1 James Price, "Gallery of Contemporary Writers, No. 2: James Clarence Mangan", *Evening Packet*, 22 September 1849, [p. 3].
2 *Morning Register*, 1 and 4 January 1831, [pp. 1 and 3].
3 E.J. Hobsbawm, *The Age of Revolution 1789–1848* (London: Sphere Books Ltd., Abacus edition. First published 1965), p. 140.
4 [The Knight of Innishowen] (John Sheehan), "Dublin Political Satire and Satirists Forty Years Ago", *Gentleman's Magazine*, December 1874, p. 688.
5 John McCall, *The Life of James Clarence Mangan* (Blackrock: Carraig Books Reprint, 1975. First published 1882), p. 18.
6 W.H. Grattan Flood, "Mangan and the Melodies in *The Poets and Poetry of Munster*" in "Clarence Mangan Centenary Celebration", *Herald*, 2 May 1903. A glaring objection to Flood's theory is that in the *Autobiography* Mangan's young man declared himself to be "a Catholic Christian" while Lever—and Lover—were Protestants.
7 D.J. O'Donoghue, *The Life and Writings of James Clarence Mangan* (Dublin: M.H. Gill and Son and T.G. O'Donoghue, 1897), p. 28, note *.
8 *The Parson's Horn-Book* (Dublin: Browne and Sheehan, 1831).
9 *The Parson's Horn-Book, Part II* (Dublin: Browne and Sheehan, 1831).
10 *Comet*, 1 May 1831, [p. 1]. This was almost surely written by John Sheehan.
11 National Library of Ireland ms. 13848, "John McCall Papers, Cuttings and Notes on Historical Subjects . . . mainly towards his work on almanacks and his *Life of Mangan*", f.8.
12 The possibility also exists, as noted, that the introduction came via Charles Lever and Samuel Lover, although neither was a Roman Catholic.
13 University College Dublin Archives, LA 15, "O'Donoghue Papers", no. 457, Ian Dowling, Terenure, to D.J. O'Donoghue, 18 September 1891.
14 Nigel Oxley, Queen's University, Belfast, working under the supervision of Professor Jacques Chuto who passed Oxley's finding on to the writer in October 1985.
15 R.O.V. Lloyd, photograph. Dating by Canon John Crawford, St Catherine and St James, Donore Avenue [previously Love Lane], Dublin.

16 PRO County of Dublin 1828–32. Books 103 and 104, "Barony of Donore", p. 256.

17 "An Extraordinary Adventure in the Shades", *Comet*, 27 January 1833, p. 319.

18 "Annals of Dublin: 1832", *Dublin Almanac and General Register of Ireland, 1843* (Dublin: Pettigrew and Oulton, n.d.), n.p.

19 Royal Irish Academy ms. 12/N/10, "A Collection of Letters from John O'Donovan to James Hardiman in part relating to Irish literature and history, 1828–1855".

20 Price, "Gallery No. 2", 22 September, 1849, [p. 3].

21 Ibid.

22 It is tempting to think, given the unexplained significance Mangan seemed to attach to March 4, that a short poem in the *Comet* on that date may have been his. However, the signature "J.C." later appeared on items that could scarcely have been written by him; nor is "A Fragment. The Exile" characteristic of his style. This is the first of three stanzas:

He loved thee, Erin—wished thee free—
He fought—he struggled, but in vain—
He would not bow to tyranny—
He scorned to wear a tyrant's chain,
And thither had he fled.

23 "The Dying Enthusiast to His Friend", *Comet*, 5 August 1832, p. 118. Also see Price's *Evening Packet* articles on Mangan in reference to this and other moments of composition.

24 "Answers to Correspondents", *Comet*, 11 September 1832, p. 156.

25 Three sonnets translated by Mangan from Filicaja appeared in the *DPJ* on 10 November and 1 December 1832, and on 2 March 1833. The first and second were signed "C., Clarence Street, Liverpool"; and the third was signed "C". However, it seems likely Mangan had submitted them together as from "C., Clarence Street, Liverpool".

26 NLI ms. 138, "James Clarence Mangan Manuscript Letters and Poems", pp. 5–6b *passim*.

27 Brian Inglis, *The Freedom of the Press in Ireland, 1784–1841* (London: Faber and Faber, Studies in Irish History Series, vol. VI, 1954), p. 198.

28 NLI ms. 7524, "Larcom Papers: Correspondence on Ordnance Survey . . . 1839–1869", 10 [or 16?] August 1828, no. 5. The first little note from O'Donovan, Larcom carefully preserved among his multitudinous papers.

29 NLI, ms. 792, "Six volumes containing . . . Letters . . . from and to George Petrie, 1824–66", vol. IV, nos. 395–6.

30 RIA ms. 12/N/11, "Miscellaneous Correspondence of John O'Donovan largely relating to Irish history and literature, 1830–1835", 10 September 1832. O'Donovan told his friend Myles O'Reilly that he had given his own, that is O'Donovan's, translation "with some notes and observations to the editor of the Dublin Penny Journal", where it appeared with his critique of "Timid Love" the next Saturday.

31 The first person to attribute this "Dream" to Mangan was F. Carroll, *Irish Book Lover*, 1957. However, there is very slight evidence for this attribution, and a good bit to link the poem with O'Donovan, especially the literal but powerful translation in what appears to be O'Donovan's handwriting in NLI

ms. 138, from which the more polished blank verse poem was almost certainly made.

32 *Letters Relating to Londonderry*, Michael O'Flanagan, ed. (Bray: typescript, 1927), 26 August 1834, p. 53. Specifically, he wrote about his efforts at blank verse-making: "If my friend Clarence should ever see it, he will send me a warrant from the court of Apollo and the Muses, ordering [them] to have me confined in Mount Parnassus. . . ." Also see 8 September 1834, p. 81, for a sample of O'Donovan's efforts.

33 John O'Donovan, "Irish Literature", *Dublin Penny Journal*, 15 September 1832, p. 93.

34 "The Dublin Penny Journal", *Dublin University Magazine*, January 1840, p. 114.

35 *Comet*, 13 January 1833.

36 He could be vicious, although he seems to have been unaware of the effects such remarks might have on his friends, and when he fell seriously ill in 1840 and no one called on him, he was terribly hurt and offended. Perhaps the meanest I have ever read of his jibes was his sneering comment about Dr Petrie's "volcanic headache which attacks him regularly once a month" (RIA ms. 12/N/10, no. 27, p. 90) with its implied comparison to a woman's monthly cycle.

37 *Letters Relating to Galway*, Michael O'Flanagan, ed. (Bray: typescript, 1927), I, 19 September 1838, p. 67.

38 NLI ms. 792, "Letters . . . to . . . Petrie", no. 402, 7 July 1838.

39 Seamus Fenton, "A Great Kilkennyman. John O'Donovan", a lecture delivered 19 April 1940, p. 18.

40 NLI ms. 132, "John O'Donovan Correspondence 1846–1861", pp. 92/103; also F. Carroll, "Clarence Mangan's Age Complex", in "Notes and Queries", *Irish Book Lover*, September 1957, p. 134.

41 "Sketches and Reminiscences of Modern Irish Writers . . . no. VIII. John O'Donovan, M.R.I.A.", *Irishman*, 14 July 1849, p. 443.

42 "Sketches of Modern Irish Writers . . . no. II. Dr Petrie", *Irishman*, 7 April 1849, p. 218.

CHAPTER SEVEN

1 There are almost two dozen names in the poem, including the Archbishop of Dublin ("Shovel-hat Whately"), the still famous Francis Moore of *Old Moore's Almanac* fame, and the dashing O'Gorman Mahon—"The O'Gorman". "Lord Brougham" was Henry Peter Brougham, first Baron of Brougham and Vaux, an arrogant eccentric who supported the Reform Bill (1832) but had no sympathy for the poor; and "Eldon" was John Scott, first Earl of Eldon, who opposed the same Bill. Except for a very few, such as "Bassegio", a famous Dublin perfumer and hairdresser, all are easily identified.

2 The identities of "Clanricarde", "Ulna", and "Peregrine" have been lost, but "Tim Rooney" may well have been the gentleman's true name. Custom in the Comet Club seems to have dictated single pseudonyms; thus we read of Sheehan's "Philander"; "Figaro" for Dominic Ronayne after his star-quality success with "Figaro in Dublin" in the *Horn-Book*; "O'More" for Thomas

Kennedy; "Perdu" for Sterling Coyne; "Foudriangle" for Thomas Browne; "Nebula" for George Dunbar; "Carolan" for John Cornelius O'Callaghan; "Bertor" for Robert Knox; "Beppo" for John Boulger; "Brasspen" for L'Estrange—but "J.P." for Price!—and on and on.

3 It is also an interesting coincidence that two Stackpoole sisters were named "Eliza" and "Anna", but they were only fourteen and fifteen years old respectively; moreover, nothing suggests that Stackpooles ever lived on Summerhill.

4 "Bessie Bell and Mary Gray" is a poignant ballad by Allan Ramsey about two seventeenth-century women and a young man in love with both. After they retire to Mary Gray's country home to escape the Plague of 1666, he takes them provisions, and all three die of the disease.

5 James Price, "Mr McMahon's Ball", *Comet*, 19 May 1833, p. 448.

6 *Der Freischütz* (1821) by Von Weber was a Gothic opera that contained elements of spectacular magic and supernatural effects especially as wrought by "Zamiel", The Black Huntsman, or Devil. Mangan would have encountered specifically the fragments translated by Charles Lever for the *Dublin Literary Gazette*. The Incantation Scene, in the 26 June 1830 number, contained a few lines of a "Frightful Chorus", but as they do not include (or inspire) a "Haw! haw! haw!" he must have read other sections of the opera as well.

7 John McCall, "Clarence Mangan and the Comet Club", Dr Thomas Wall Archives, Irish Institute of Pastoral Liturgy, Carlow; also a photocopy in author's collection.

8 *Comet*, 4 August 1833, p. 532 . To "sky the copper" was to play at pitch-and-toss, or pitch-penny, and a "cropper" was a half-glass of whiskey.

9 John McCall wrote out a summary history of these newspapers in the *Comet* file now in a private collection:

In December 1831, the great split took place in the Comet Club, when John C. O'Callaghan, and most of the great folk quitted its fold for ever, and formed themselves into a Society called "The Irish Brigade". Browne still continued on the staff, but he too finally dissevered himself from the old Club . . . and started a rival newspaper of his own. . . .

The newly formed Irish Brigade with O'Callaghan at their head soon commenced to make a stir in the political and literary world. It was they that projected and started "The Irish Monthly Magazine" which had a long run, the first number of which appeared in May 1832. They also brought out a newspaper published bi-weekly, "The Repealer and Tradesman's Journal", the first number appeared in May 1832; it, however, had not a prosperous career, and after the first six months or so, it commenced to decline.

The pompous Browne started in opposition [to the *Comet*] his famous "Buckthorn's Comet", it too had but a short existence; and on 9 March of 1833 it was merged into O'Callaghan's paper, "The Repealer". It was announced with a great flourish, that the combined newspaper for the future would be conducted by the famous Buckthorn himself, with Figaro, Perdu, Bertor, Beppo, etc. but all this combined talent could not long keep afloat "The Repealer-Buckthorne", and when this two-faced Janus passed away, in three months or so, "The Dublin Satirist" was started on the ruins of both, 22 June, 1833.

On March 3, 1833, another new venture entitled "The True Comet", unstamped, price 1½d. was issued; I believe Tim Rooney, another of the old "Comet" staff, was chief Editor and Proprietor. It had even a more limited career, as only five or six numbers were published, till it too gave up the ghost.

The original "Paddy Kelly's Budget", an unstamped penny publication, was also projected and carried on by young Alfred Howard (son of Henry Howard, Vintner) as "Paddy Kelly", a leading contributor both in prose and verse to John Sheehan's favorite paper. The first number appeared on Wednesday, November 14, 1832, and was published at "The Comet" office, 2 Church Lane.

CHAPTER EIGHT

1 Rudolf Patrick Holzapfel, "Mangan's Poetry in *The Dublin University Magazine*: A Bibliography", *Hermathena*, no. CV, Autumn 1967, p. 42.

2 John Dryden, "Dedication of the Aeneis", *Essays*, W.P. Kerr, ed. (Oxford: Clarendon Press, 1900), vol. II, p. 228; and "Anthologia Germanica. No. V. Faust, and the Minor Poems of Goethe", *Dublin University Magazine*, March 1836, p. 279.

3 "The Death-Chant of King Regner Lodbrok", *Dublin University Magazine*, August 1847, p. 214.

4 Percy Bysshe Shelley, "A Defence of Poetry", *Shelley's Prose: The Trumpet of a Prophecy*. D.L. Clark, ed. (Albuquerque: New Mexico University Press, 1954), p. 280.

5 John Millington Synge, *The Aran Islands* (Dublin: Maunsel and Co. Ltd., 1911), p. 190. For an excellent discussion of these citations and others of equal importance on the subject of Mangan as translator, see Jacques Chuto, "James Clarence Mangan, Poète-Traducteur", 2 vols. (Dissertation, Université de Paris 3—Sorbonne Nouvelle 1987), I, pp. 63–9ff.

6 *Alumni Dublinensis: A Register of the Students, Graduates, Professors and Provosts of Trinity College in the University of Dublin (1593–1860)*. George Burtchall and Thomas Sadleir, eds. New edition. (Dublin: Alex Thom and Co., 1935). See also Peter Denman, "Ferguson and *Blackwood's*: The Formative Years", *Irish University Review*, Autumn 1986, p. 148 and 148n.

7 Michael Sadleir, "*Dublin University Magazine*: Its History, Contents and Bibliography", a paper read before the Bibliographical Society of Ireland, April 1937 (Dublin: n.p., 1938), p. 68.

8 [C.R. Maturin] (James Wills). *The Universe: A Poem* (London: Henry Colburn and Co., 1821).

9 "A Word to our Friends", *Dublin University Magazine*, December 1833, p. 7.

10 But Mangan, although often assumed to be almost by definition a Romantic, did not see poets as "romantic" figures for the most part. He would perhaps have agreed with the assessment that they are by and large a cold and calculating lot, converting the warmest emotions into poetry even as they feel them.

11 National Library of Ireland ms. 14270, "John McCall, History of the *Comet*, 'Political Tract Society', started early 1831"; also excerpt of *Salmagundi*, 15 February 1834.

12 *Saturday (Evening) Herald*, 2 May 1903, p. 3. No "Mary" from Tipperary or anywhere else figures in other accounts of Mangan's romances; nor is there an "Isabel". However, Frances, Anna and Leonora (in poem, if not—we could say—in story) are familiar names. We would not expect "Catherine" to be here, as she was scarcely a part of his *Comet/Satirist* world. And if this were written around 1833, it was too early to include "Margaret". However, "Eleanor" and "Caroline" are notably absent.

13 Stackpoole Family Records, Clare Heritage Centre, Corofin, County Clare. Also see *Burke's Irish Family Records* (London: Burke's Peerage Ltd., MCMLXXVI).

14 Royal Irish Academy ms. 24/O/39, "James Graves Papers", Bundle 7, 23 March 1834.

15 John McCall, "James Price . . . with Selections from His Writings in Prose and Verse", *Irish Emerald*, April–18 July 1893. Pagination not inclusive. According to McCall, Price was a veritable Don Juan. Many of Price's "Recollections" recounted amusing incidents from his assorted (and purported) love affairs. This particular quotation is from "My Own Adventure—The Veil" in which he revealed a flair for description just bordering on the objectionable as he traced a girl's development after the age of fourteen. He swore he would never marry, but he did, and had three "little J.P.'s". He died at the age of forty in 1853.

16 Chuto, "James Clarence Mangan", I, p. 76.

17 See Hervey Allen, *Israfel: The Life and Times of Edgar Allan Poe* (New York: Farrar and Rinehart, Inc., 1934), a good, if highly dramatised, biography.

18 John Petrie O'Byrne, "Romantic Career of an Irish Princess—A Clue to Clarence Mangan's 'Nameless One' ", *Weekly Freeman*, 23 December 1893, p. 10.

19 Bernard Burke, *Vicissitudes of Irish Families, and Other Essays* (London: Longman, Green, Longman, and Roberts, 1859), pp. 149–61.

20 That is, quarterly installments of fifteen pages each. A "sheet", which formed sixteen pages in the *Magazine*, was the basic unit. With titles, spacing, and so on, Mangan was contracted, then, for four sheets per year—£32 worth.

21 *Weekly Dublin Satirist*, 7 February 1835, p. 267.

22 "Review of *A Memoir of the Life and Philosophy of Spurzheim*", *Dublin University Magazine*, May 1833, p. 593.

23 *Weekly Dublin Satirist*, 21 February 1835, p. 283.

24 *Catalogue of Sale* [James Hardiman Collection] 26 March 1856.

25 RIA ms. 12/N/11, "Miscellaneous Correspondence of John O'Donovan largely relating to Irish history and literature, 1830–1835", 13 January 1833 and 24 October 1834.

26 University College Dublin Archives, LA 15, "O'Donoghue Papers", no. 587.

27 RIA ms. 24/O/39, "James Graves Papers", Bundle 5.

28 "Anthologia Germanica—No. IV. The Poems of Matthison and Salis", *Dublin University Magazine*, October 1835, p. 403.

29 "Sonnet", *Dublin University Magazine*, June 1835, p. 724; and "Stanzas", p. 723.

30 "Sonnets", *Dublin University Magazine*, September 1835, p. 296.

31 "Anthologia Germanica—No. IV", *DUM*, October 1835, pp. 418–19.

32 From "Elegiac Verses on the Early Death of a Beloved Friend", *Comet*, 10

February 1833, p. 334; and in "A Polyglott Anthology . . .", *DUM*, April 1839, pp. 492–4.

Enough:—I go to join the hollow crowd—
Mirth rings among us, and the laugh is loud,
For here society exacts her task,
And each assumes his own peculiar mask.

33 Coyne did not last long in his editorial position on the radical English humour magazine; accusations of plagiarism led to his resignation.

CHAPTER NINE

1 T.F. O'Sullivan, *The Young Irelanders*, Davis Centenary ed. (Tralee: The Kerryman Ltd., 1945), pp. 13–14.

2 Cyril Pearl, *The Three Lives of Gavan Duffy* (Kensington N.S.W., Australia: New South Wales University Press Ltd., 1979), p. 7.

3 León O'Broin, *Charles Gavan Duffy, Patriot and Statesman* (Dublin: James Duffy and Co. Ltd., 1967), p. 4.

4 Charles Gavan Duffy, "Personal Memories of James C. Mangan", *Dublin Review*, April 1908, pp. 278–82.

5 "Anthologia Germanica—No. VII. Kerner's Lyrical Poems", *Dublin University Magazine*, August 1836, p. 151.

6 "Stray Leaflets from the German Oak", *Dublin University Magazine*, August 1836, p. 163. This "Stray Leaflets" is merely a continuation of the "Anthology". Why it was given a separate title is unclear.

7 "Anthologia Germanica—No. VII", pp. 154–5.

8 Duffy, "Personal Memories", p. 286.

9 John Mitchel, ed., "James Clarence Mangan: His Life, Poetry and Death", *Poems by James Clarence Mangan*, John Mitchel, ed. (New York: D. and J. Sadlier, 1866. First published 1859), p. 11.

10 There is a possibility, of course, that Mangan made up the story, but his only reason for doing so would have been to add romance to a mundane rejection by Margaret and to save his feelings—or to prevent Duffy from courting her. But such dog-in-the-manger behaviour is not consonant with what we know of the poet's character. Moreover, it would also have been risky—Duffy might mention it to William Stackpoole, for instance, and learn it was not true. And finally, it would have entailed a full-blown lie to a young, admiring friend. Mangan may have been evasive, and he may have exaggerated, but outright lying was a different matter.

11 *A Catalogue of Graduates Who Have Proceeded to Degrees in the University of Dublin* (Dublin: Hodges, Smith, and Foster, 1869), p. 534.

12 "Anthologia Germanica—No. X. Tieck and the Other Song-Singers of Germany", *Dublin University Magazine*, March 1837, p. 273.

13 Ibid., p. 288.

14 "Literae Orientales. Persian and Turkish Poetry—First Article", *Dublin University Magazine*, September 1837, p. 278. That, it could be said, was indeed a very misleading statement. He continued, however, with references to orientalists including Augustus Schlegel, Sir William Jones, D'Herbelot, and, many times, Joseph von Hammer-Purgstall in whose four-volume

Geschichte der osmanischen Dichtkunst (1836–38) Chuto found "a good many pieces in this series" in their German translations.

15 Ibid., p. 283.

16 D.J. O'Donoghue, *The Life and Writings of James Clarence Mangan* (Dublin: M.H. Gill and Son and T.G. O'Donoghue, 1897), p. 94.

17 "Literae Orientales, First Article", p. 275.

18 Ibid., pp. 291–2.

19 "Annals of Dublin: 1837", *Dublin Almanac and General Register of Ireland, 1843* (Dublin: Pettigrew and Oulton, n.d.), n.p.

CHAPTER TEN

1 Royal Irish Academy ms. 24/O/39, "James Graves Papers", Bundle 5. It is only from Mangan's letters that we learn of his work as the next pages of this chapter reveal.

2 Ibid., Bundle 3, O'Donovan to W.E. Hudson, 2 February 1847.

3 In the letter of 20 January, the first, Mangan requested his pay—"Six pounds sterling"—for "the three books you left me are finished. . . ."

4 Most of his other letters deal with money owed him; these are virtually the only "personal" letters of Mangan's extant.

5 *Ordnance Survey Meteorological Observations Taken During the Years 1829–1852*. Capt Cameron, R.E., ed. (Dublin: Alexander Thom and Sons, 1856). Also "Annals of Ireland", *Dublin Almanac and General Register of Ireland, 1843* (Dublin: Pettigrew and Oulton, n.d.) n.p.

6 "Cross-writing", that is, writing across the page at a right angle to the already written text, when it goes across the text itself, can make a nineteenth-century letter virtually illegible.

7 "Mangan's Recipe to Make Tar-Water", *Essays in Prose and Verse*, C.P. Meehan, ed. (Dublin: James Duffy and Co., Ltd., 2nd ed. 1906), p. xv.

8 Trinity College Dublin ms. 4629, "Autograph note by James Clarence Mangan, and other materials from Seamus O'Sullivan Collection". Part of a note signed J.R.H.: "The tar-water story was exploded by Dr Petrie and W.F. Wakeman, who surreptitiously examined the bottle when Mangan was working. . . ."

9 National Library of Ireland ms. 7565, "Larcom Papers. Larcom to Petrie, 1838–1844", 10 February 1838.

10 J.H. Andrews, *A Paper Landscape* (Oxford: The Clarendon Press, 1975), is an excellent study of the O.S. A contemporary booklet, *Heads of Inquiry*, 1832, NLI ms. 7550 "Larcom Papers", briefly describes the four main divisions of the study: Geographical, Topographical ("artificial state"), People, Divisions and Townlands. The formidable comprehensiveness envisioned is apparent in the discussion under "People", especially, for it embraces everything from habits and house styles, to food, families, customs, recreations, tales, music, and funeral cries.

11 See Patricia Boyne, *John O'Donovan (1806–1861): A Biography* (Kilkenny: Boethius, 1987).

12 NLI ms. 7564, "Larcom Papers, Larcom to Petrie 1837+", 30 December 1837.

13 *John O'Donovan Sale Catalog*, 7 November 1867, p. 28. The exact references are to nos. 1073 and 1074, "Translation of the same [*The Annals*], by O'Donovan, with notes in three parcels, (two in the writing of James Clarence Mangan)".

14 *The Catalogue of the Extensive and Valuable Library of the Late Dr R.R. Madden etc.*, 6 December 1886, noted as no. 429, and *Catalogue of the Sale of Books of Richard Caulfield*, 27 January 1882, no. 525. A single page from this catalogue is pasted inside the front cover of NLI ms. 132 "John O'Donovan Correspondence 1846–1861". It contains the information about the transfer to San Francisco. The unhappy conclusion comes from my own research.

15 NLI ms. 7565, "Larcom Papers. Larcom to Petrie, 1838–1844".

16 "Letters Relating to Galway", Michael O'Flanagan, ed. (Bray: typescript, 1927), I, p. 40, 8 September 1838. Also RIA ms. 12/N/5, "Petrie Papers", 9 September 1838.

17 "Letters Relating to Galway", I, p. 58, 14 September 1838.

18 ["E.W."] (James Clarence Mangan). "Sketches of Modern Irish Writers, James Clarence Mangan." [The Impersonal Autobiography], *Irishman*, 17 August 1850, p. 28.

19 "Literae Orientales. Turkish Poetry—Second Article", *Dublin University Magazine*, March 1838, p. 312.

20 Ibid.

21 Ibid., p. 294.

22 León O'Broin, *Charles Gavan Duffy, Patriot and Statesman* (Dublin: James Duffy and Co. Ltd., 1967), p. 5; and RIA ms. 12/P/16, "Gavan Duffy's Curios", no. 17, "Foundation of an Irish Press Association at Dublin, in 1838". Noted as "Missing since 1944".

23 "Anthologia Germanica—No. XIII. M. Klauer Klattowski's Publications" [*Popular Songs of the Germans, 1836; Select Lyrical Poems of the Germans,* 1837; *Ballads and Romances, Poetical Tales, Legends and Idylls of the Germans,* 1837; all published London: Simpkin and Marshall, as Mangan explained in a note]. *Dublin University Magazine*, August 1838, pp. 168–9, 170–1, 176–7, and 179.

24 "Literae Orientales. Turkish Poetry—Third Article", *Dublin University Magazine*, September 1838, p. 331.

25 Ibid., p. 342.

26 Ibid., pp. 341, 344, and 345–6.

27 NLI ms. 7524 "Larcom Papers. Correspondence on the Ordnance Survey and Census of 1857 . . . including letters from John O'Donovan and Eugene Curry, 1839–1869".

28 D.J. O'Donoghue, *The Life and Writings of James Clarence Mangan* (Dublin: M.H. Gill and Son and T.G. O'Donoghue, 1897), p. 91.

29 NLI ms. 7565, "Larcom Papers. Larcom to Petrie, 1838–1844", 29 September 1838.

30 Ibid., 3 November 1838 and 1 November 1838.

31 NLI ms. 4172, "D.J. O'Donoghue's revision of *The Life and Writings of James Clarence Mangan*". The letter was to be placed at the close of chapter VII, p. 83.

32 O'Donoghue, *Life and Writings*, p. 92, pp. 125–6.

33 William Stokes, *Life and Labours in Art and Archeology of George Petrie* (London: Longmans, Green and Co., 1868), pp. 96–7.

34 W.F. Wakeman, "Old Dublin, no. XVIII—no. 3, Lord Edward Street, Birthplace of the Poet Mangan", *Evening Telegraph*, New Series, 7 May 1887, [p. 2]; also, "Clarence Mangan's Birthplace", *Evening Telegraph Reprints* (Dublin: *The Freeman's Journal*, n.d.), p. 36.

35 Diarmud O'Giollain, "The Leprechaun and Fairies, Dwarfs and the Household Familiar: A Comparative Study", *Bealoideas*, vol. 52, 1984, pp. 98ff. The story of King Brian Boru, the druid dwarf Fernal, and the woodnymph Oona was told by William J. Murray, U.S.A., in a letter to me in 1985. He heard it from his grandmother who heard it from *her* grandmother of Ballina, County Mayo. None of the accounts refers to *flasks*, perhaps Mangan's own touch.

CHAPTER ELEVEN

1 "Anthologia Germanica, No. XV—Wetzel's Remains—Second Article", *Dublin University Magazine*, December 1839, p. 697.

2 "Anthologia Germanica—No. XIV. Gellert's Tales and Fables", *Dublin University Magazine*, January 1839, p. 53.

3 Ibid., p. 59.

4 "Annals of Dublin: 1839", *Dublin Almanac and General Register of Ireland, 1843* (Dublin: Pettigrew and Oulton, n.d.), n.p.

5 Harry Gersh, *The Sacred Books of the Jews* (New York: Stein and Day, 1968), p. 131.

6 "The Funerals", *Irishman*, 31 March 1849, p. 203.

7 *Dictionary of Psychology*, revised edition, J.P. Chaplin, ed. (New York: Dell Publishing Co., 1983), "Complex". Also Carl Gustav Jung, *Psychology of the Unconscious* (New York: Dodd, Mead and Co., 1965. First published 1916), *passim*. Also David Miller, *Ghosts! Holy and Not So Holy*, a lecture delivered and taped 28 October 1983, Portland, Oregon.

8 William Stokes, *Life and Labours in Art and Archeology of George Petrie* (London: Longmans, Green and Co., 1868), pp. 96–7.

9 Miller, *Ghosts!*.

10 D.J. O'Donoghue, *The Life and Writings of James Clarence Mangan* (Dublin: M.H. Gill and Son and T.G. O'Donoghue, 1897), p. 144, perhaps quoting Thomas D'Arcy McGee. Also, McGee, "Reminiscences of an Exiled Confederate. Clarence Mangan", *Nation*, 25 September 1852, p. 58.

11 National Library of Ireland ms. 3038, "A Volume of Miscellaneous Autograph Letters, 1838–92", 13 March 1847.

12 "Letters Relating to Galway", Michael O'Flanagan, ed. (Bray: typescript, 1927), vol. III, p. 136, 3 August 1839.

13 McGee, "Reminiscences of . . . Clarence Mangan".

14 *Minutes of the Sixteenth General Conference of the Ministers and Other Members of THE NEW CHURCH, signified by the New Jerusalem* (London: Thomas Goyder, 1823–67, pp. 44–5 and 71.

15 Stephen Larsen, "Introduction", *Emanuel Swedenborg, The Universal Human and Soul-Body Interaction*, George F. Dole, ed. (New York: Paulist Press, 1984), p. 10.

16 William Butler Yeats, "Swedenborg, Mediums, and the Desolate Places", *Uncollected Prose by W.B. Yeats*, John P. Frayne, ed., 2 vols., (New York: Columbia University Press, 1970), II, p. 39.

17 Emanuel Swedenborg, *The Universal Human*, p. 210.

18 "A Tale of a Coffin", *Nation*, 8 May 1847, p. 491.

19 O'Donoghue, *Life and Writings*, p. 112.

20 "A Polyglott Anthology. Developed in the form of a dialogue", *Dublin University Magazine*, April 1839, p. 485.

21 *The Poems of Richard D'Alton Williams, "Shamrock" of "The Nation"*, P.A. Sillard, ed. (Dublin: James Duffy and Co., 1894), p. 183.

22 "Anthologia Germanica, No. XV—Wetzel's Poems—First Notice", *Dublin University Magazine*, July 1839, p. 73.

23 Michael Sadleir, "The Dublin University Magazine: Its History, Contents and Bibliography". A paper read before the Bibliographical Society of Ireland, April 1937 (Dublin: n.p., 1938), pp. 61–81. See also "Introduction", *The Wellesley Index to Victorian Periodicals, 1824–1900*, Walter E. Houghton, ed., 4 vols. (Toronto: University of Toronto Press, Routledge and Kegan Paul, 1987), IV, p. 198.

24 Charles Gavan Duffy, "Personal Memories of James C. Mangan", *Dublin Review*, April 1908, p. 287.

25 "Anthologia Germanica, No. XV—Wetzel's Remains—Second Article". *Dublin University Magazine*, December 1839, p. 697.

26 F.P. Carey, *Father Charles P. Meehan* (Dublin: Catholic Truth Society, n.d.), p. 28. About 1885, Carey wrote, Fr Meehan "proved to a certain circle in Dublin" that Mangan was "enslaved to a narcotic" more than to alcohol. Laudanum, a tincture of opium, was doubtless the "narcotic" Meehan meant.

27 Louise Imogen Guiney, "James Clarence Mangan: A Study", *James Clarence Mangan, his Selected Poems*, Louise Imogen Guiney, ed. (Boston and New York: Lamson, Wolffe and Co., 1897), pp. 19–23. See also Guiney-O'Donoghue exchange of letters in UCD Library Archives, LA 15, "O'Donoghue Papers".

28 University College Dublin Archives, LA15, "O'Donoghue Papers", no. 312, 20 May 1896.

29 "Literae Orientales, no. IV. Arabian, Persian and Turkish Poetry", *Dublin University Magazine*, April 1840, p. 378.

30 "The Kiosk of Moostanzar-Billah", p. 381.

31 "The Howling Song of Al-Mohara", p. 383.

32 "Stammering or Tipsy Ghazzel by Foozooli, of Stambool", p. 385.

CHAPTER TWELVE

1 National Library of Ireland ms. 5757, "Charles Gavan Duffy Letters", pp. 35–9.

2 Patricia Boyne, *John O'Donovan (1806–1861): A Biography* (Kilkenny: Boethius, 1987), p. 118.

3 Royal Irish Academy ms. 12/N/10. "A Collection of Letters from John O'Donovan to James Hardiman in part relating to Irish literature and history,

1828–1855", 25 February 1840, p. 37. Also NLI ms. 792, "Six Volumes [with] Letters . . . from and to George Petrie", 25 March 1840.

4 RIA ms. 24/O/30 "James Graves Papers", Bundle 5, 22 October 1840.

5 D.J. O.Donoghue, *The Life and Writings of James Clarence Mangan* (Dublin: M.H. Gill and Son and T.G. O'Donoghue, 1897), pp. 120–21. Also see Maynooth ms. C 63 "Eugene O'Curry Gaelic Poems and Translations" in which O'Curry asks Mangan to "put some skin of poetry" on the "Raw-meish" of David O'Brudar.

6 NLI ms. 1426 "Letter of John O'Donovan to J.T. Gilbert giving a Biographical Sketch of Eugene O'Curry", 2 December 1853".

7 NLI ms. 7567, "Larcom Papers. Correspondence on matters pertaining to the Ordnance Survey Memoir 1833–1861", 18 March 1840.

8 "Stray Leaflets from the German Oak—Seventh Drift", *Dublin University Magazine*, August 1845, p. 151.

9 RIA ms. 23/G/33 "Letters from Thomas Crofton Croker, and from Owen Connellan to Sir William Betham", Connellan to Betham, 1 December 1840, "g".

10 William Stokes, *Life and Labours in Art and Archeology of George Petrie* (London: Longmans, Green and Co., 1868), p. 143.

11 NLI ms. 3038, "Miscellaneous Autograph Letters, 1838–1892, [John O'Donovan]", p. 149.

12 University College Dublin Archives, LA 15, "O'Donoghue Papers", no. 1267, 6 September 1896.

13 Gavan Duffy, *My Life in Two Hemispheres*, 2 vols. (London: T. Fisher, Unwin, 1898), I, p. 203.

14 O'Donoghue, *Life and Writings*, p. 191.

15 Elizabeth Malcolm, "*Ireland Sober, Ireland Free", Drink and Temperance in Nineteenth-Century Ireland*, Irish Studies Series (New York: Syracuse University Press, 1986), pp. 144–5.

16 John Mitchel, "James Clarence Mangan: His Life, Poetry and Death", *Poems by James Clarence Mangan*, John Mitchel, ed. (New York: D. and J. Sadlier, 1866. First published 1859), p. 14.

17 "Letters Relating to Clare", Michael O'Flanagan, ed. (Bray: typescript, 1927), I, pp. 83–92, 4 December 1839.

18 "Father Mathew" in "Our Portrait Gallery—No. LIV", *Dublin University Magazine*, June 1849, pp. 694–706.

19 Charles P. Meehan, "Preface", *The Poets and Poetry of Munster: A Selection of Irish Songs by Poets of the Last Century*. 3rd ed. (Dublin: James Duffy and Sons, 1883. First published 1849), p. xvi.

20 Malcolm, "*Ireland Sober, Ireland Free*", p. 137.

21 NLI ms. 5756, "Charles Gavan Duffy Letters"; also (Belfast) *Vindicator*, 9 May 1840, [p. 4].

22 RIA ms. 3/C/6 "Letter to John O'Daly from James Clarence Mangan" in "Letters to and from W.E. Hudson". On the reverse: "Ms of a contribution of Clarence Mangan to *Belfast Vindicator*". This was "The Editor's Room—Second Conclave", (Belfast) *Vindicator*, 25 July 1840, [p. 4].

23 NLI ms. 7565 "Larcom Papers. Larcom to Petrie, 1838–1844".

24 In the *Irish Penny Journal*: 29 August 1840, pp. 68–9, "The Woman of Three Cows"; 17 October 1840, pp. 123–5, "An Elegy on the Tironian and

Tirconnellian Princes Buried at Rome"; 9 January 1841, pp. 220–1, "Lamentation of MacLiag for Kincora"; 16 January 1841, pp. 228–9, "Kathleen Ny-Houlahan".

25 RIA ms. 24/O/39. "James Graves Papers". Information from Dr Nigel Oxley in a letter to Professor Jacques Chuto, 3 February 1987.

26 O'Donoghue, *Life and Writings*, p. 120.

27 Sean Lucy, *Irish Poets in English.* Thomas Davis Lectures on Anglo-Irish Poetry (Cork and Dublin: Mercier Press, 1973), p. 212.

28 O'Donoghue, *Life and Writings*, p. 120.

TRANSITION [Chapter 12 to Chapter 13]

1 National Library of Ireland ms. 7567, "Larcom Papers. Correspondence on matters pertaining to the Ordnance Survey Memoir, 1833–1861", 1841.

2 NLI ms. 7524, "Larcom Papers. Correspondence on the Ordnance Survey and census of 1857 . . . including letters from O'Donovan and Curry, 1839–1869".

3 Ibid.

4 NLI ms. 7567, "Larcom Papers", 1841.

5 Ibid.

6 NLI ms. 7566, "Larcom Papers. Correspondence on matters pertaining to the Ordnance Survey Memoir, 1833–1861", 1 August 1839.

7 "Our Contributors at the Brunnens", *Dublin University Magazine*, October 1841, p. 501.

CHAPTER THIRTEEN

1 Jacques Chuto, "Mangan's 'Antique Deposit' in the TCD Library", *Long Room*, no. 2, Autumn-Winter 1970, pp. 38–9. See also: Chuto, "A Further Glance at Mangan and the Library", *Long Room*, no. 5, Spring 1972, pp. 8–10.

2 Peter Fox, ed., *Treasures of the Library: Trinity College Dublin* (Dublin: Royal Irish Academy, 1986), pp. 158 ff.

3 "Public Libraries of Dublin", *Nation*, 20 June 1846, p. 570.

4 John Mitchel, "James Clarence Mangan: His Life, Poetry, and Death", *Poems by James Clarence Mangan*, John Mitchel, ed. (New York: P.M. Haverty, 1859), p. 13.

5 "Anthologia Germanica—No. XVIII. Freiligrath's Poems", *Dublin University Magazine*, January 1843, p. 31.

6 Ibid., "Grabbe", p. 40.

7 "Chapters on Ghostcraft: Comprising some account of the Life and Revelations of Madame Hauffe, the celebrated Wirtemberg Ghost-Seeress. In two Parts: Part I", *Dublin University Magazine*, January 1842, pp. 1–17.

8 Cyril Pearl, *The Three Lives of Gavan Duffy* (Kensington, N.S.W., Australia: New South Wales University Press Limited, 1979), p. 14.

9 Charles Gavan Duffy, *Young Ireland: A Fragment of Irish History, 1840–1845*, 2 vols. (Dublin: M.H.Gill and Son, 1884), I, pp. 17–18.

10 "Faugh a Ballagh", *Nation*, 29 October 1842, p. 41.

11 National Library of Ireland ms. 7959, "John McCall's Manuscript Collection for his *Life of Mangan Mangan*", p. 271.

12 "Literae Orientales. Ottoman Poetry. Fifth Article", *Dublin University Magazine*, May 1844, pp. 536–40.

13 Henry J. Donaghy, *James Clarence Mangan*, English Authors Series (New York: Twayne Publishers, Inc., 1974), p. 33, points out an interesting similarity between this poem and James Ryder Randall's "Maryland, My Maryland" and relates that Randall was trying to find an eloquent mode of expression for a poem about his home state of Maryland then (1861) deeply engaged in the American Civil War. The "haunting refrains" he found in "The Karamanian Exile" in "his volume of Mangan [that] had been lying on his desk" kept running through his mind, and "after a sleepless night, he settled on the meter of Mangan's poem. . . ." Donaghy cites Francis J. Thompson, "Mangan in America: 1850–1860", *Dublin Magazine*, XXVII (1952), p. 39; and Louise Imogen Guiney, *James Clarence Mangan: His Selected Poems* (Boston: Lamson, Wolffe and Co., 1897), pp. 359–60. Joseph Brenan supposedly gave Randall a copy of Mangan's verse, and Guiney opined this must have been John Mitchel's 1859 edition; but as Brenan died in 1857, this particular romanticized connection must be apocryphal. This is not to say that Randall could not have seen Mangan's poetry, some of which was certainly in circulation among Irish ex-patriates at that time. In any case, "Maryland, My Maryland" is one of only a handful of memorable, singable state songs.

14 Pearl, *Gavan Duffy*, p. 23.

15 Sean O'Faolain, *King of the Beggars. A Life of Daniel O'Connell* (Dublin: Poolbeg Press Ltd. 1980), pp. 290ff. See also Michael Doheny, *The Felon's Track* (1849), and Pearl, *Gavan Duffy*, pp. 28–31.

16 John Mitchel, *The Last Conquest of Ireland (perhaps)* (Dublin: *The Irishman* Office, 1861), p. 76.

17 Royal Irish Academy ms. 12/W/30 *Bryan Geraghty Sale Catalogue*, 29 February 1848.

18 RIA ms. 24/O/39 "James Graves Papers", Bundle 6.

19 NLI ms. P 2407, no. 1, "Denis Florence McCarthy Mss".

20 John Mitchel, *Jail Journal*, Thomas Flanagan, ed. (Dublin: University Press of Ireland, 1982. First published 1854), p. 11.

21 NLI ms. 2261, "Walsh's Letters [to John O'Daly]", 1844.

22 Charles Kickham, "Edward Walsh", *The Celt*, 5 December 1857, p. 306.

23 NLI ms. 2261, "Walsh's Letters", 17 March 1844.

24 D.J. O'Donoghue, *The Life and Writings of James Clarence Mangan* (Dublin: M.H. Gill and Son and T.G. O'Donoghue, 1897), p. 176.

25 "Counsel to the Worldly-Wise", *Nation*, 3 October 1846, p. 811.

26 RIA ms. 12/P/19–20, "Letters and Papers of Gavan Duffy, including diaries and the brief for the defence at his trial, 1848."

27 NLI ms. 2261, "Walsh's Letters", 15 February 1844.

28 NLI ms. 5454, "The Volume of Critical Notices evidently bound for John O'Daly with his MS notes", p. 6.

29 Peter MacMahon, "James Clarence Mangan; The Irish Language, and the Strange Case of *The Tribes of Ireland*". *Irish University Review*, vol. VIII, Autumn 1978, no. 2, p. 220.

30 NLI ms. 5454 "Quarto Volume of Critical Notices . . . for John O'Daly".
31 O'Donoghue, *Life and Writings*, pp. 166 and 168 and plate facing p. 206.
32 "Press Notice of *Poets and Poetry of Munster*", *Irishman*, 3 November 1849, in *The Poets and Poetry of Munster*, 3rd ed. (Dublin: James Duffy and Sons, 1883) pp. lvii–lx.
33 "Echoes of Foreign Song. A Lane for Freedom", *Nation*, 23 November 1844, p. 105.
34 Mangan to Duffy, 14 December 1844. In the author's collection.

CHAPTER FOURTEEN

1 Jacques Chuto, "Mangan's 'Antique Deposit' in the TCD Library", *Long Room*, no. 2, Autumn-Winter 1970, pp. 38–9.
2 "Eighteen Hundred Fifty", "Anthologia Germanica—No. XIX—Miscellaneous Poems", *Dublin University Magazine*, January 1845, p. 104.
3 D.J. O'Donoghue, *The Life and Writings of James Clarence Mangan* (Dublin: M.H. Gill and Son and T.G. O'Donoghue, 1897), p. 140.
4 Thomas Wall, *The Sign of Dr Hay's Head* (Dublin: M.H. Gill and Son, Ltd., 1958), pp. 124–5.
5 O'Donoghue, *Life and Writings*, p. 141.
6 Please see Appendix E for the text of the Preface.
7 "Review of *German Anthology*", *Cork Examiner*, 23 July 1845, [p. 2].
8 "Review of *German Anthology*", *British Quarterly Review*, November 1845, pp. 582–3.
9 Grevel Lindop, *The Opium Eater. A Life of Thomas De Quincey* (Oxford: Oxford University Press, 1985), pp. 304–72. De Quincey stayed with *Tait's* until 1851.
10 "Review of *German Anthology*", *Dublin Review*, December 1845, p. 313.
11 "Review of *German Anthology*", *Nation*, 9 August 1845, p. 715.
12 "The Woman of Three Cows", "Kathleen Ny-Houlahan", and "A Lament for theTironian and Tirconnellian Princes, buried at Rome" were the *IPJ* poems.
13 Royal Irish Academy ms. 12/N/10, "A Collection of Letters from John O'Donovan to James Hardiman in part relating to Irish literature and history, 1828–1855".
14 RIA ms. 12/N/20, "Letters to Hardiman", no. 147, 4 October 1847.
15 *Memories of Father Healy of Little Bray* (London: Richard Bentley and Son, 1898), pp. 162–83.
16 RIA ms. 12/N/20, "Letters to Hardiman", no. 153, July 1849.
17 Charles P. Meehan, "Preface", *The Poets and Poetry of Munster*, 3rd ed. (Dublin: James Duffy and Sons, 1883. First published 1849), pp. xvi–xvii.
18 Ibid., p. xv.
19 "Sketches and Reminiscences of Irish Writers—No. IV. The Rev. C.P. Meehan", *Irishman*, 12 May 1849, p. 299.
20 "Khidder", *Dublin University Magazine*, August 1845, pp. 238–9.
21 "The Wayfaring Tree", "Stray Leaflets from the German Oak—Seventh Drift", *Dublin University Magazine*, August 1845, pp. 151–2.
22 "Mangan and the *Monthly Magazine*", *Irish Book Lover*, April 1915, p. 137.

23 National Library of Ireland ms. 138, "James Clarence Mangan Manuscript Letters and Poems", no. 20.
24 Cecil Woodham-Smith, *The Great Hunger. Ireland 1845–9* (London: New English Library, 1977), p. 57.
25 Ibid., p. 35.
26 Charles Gavan Duffy, *Young Ireland: A Fragment of Irish History, 1840–1850* (New York: Da Capo Press, 1973. First published 1881), p. 761.
27 León O Broin, *Charles Gavan Duffy, Patriot and Statesman* (Dublin: James Duffy and Co., Ltd., 1967), p. 27.
28 NLI ms. 132, "John O'Donovan's Correspondence, 1846–1861", to Francis Daniel McCarthy, 8 May 1848.
29 John Mitchell, "James Clarence Mangan: His Life, Poetry, and Death", *Poems by James Clarence Mangan*, John Mitchel, ed. (New York: P.M. Haverty, 1859), p. 13.
30 Ibid., p. 8.

CHAPTER FIFTEEN

1 Charles Gavan Duffy, *My Life in Two Hemispheres*, 2 vols. (London: T. Fisher, Unwin, 1898), I, p. 126.
2 Charles P. Meehan, "Preface", *The Poets and Poetry of Munster*, 3rd ed. (Dublin: James Duffy and Sons, 1883. First published 1849), p. *x*, note.
3 [Thomas D'Arcy McGee] "Reminiscences of an Exiled Confederate. Clarence Mangan", *Nation*, 25 September 1852, p. 58.
4 Duffy, *My Life*, I, p. 153.
5 See the prose sections of the two "Loose Leaves from an Odd Volume", II (November 1845), pp. 232–4; and III (January 1846), pp. 393–4.
6 That is not to say Mangan's poetry is not filled with violent expressions—it is. From war-making to natural occurrences, he revelled in imagery strong enough to set even the tamest reader's blood coursing, but *hatred* was never before an explicit factor.
7 D.J. O'Donoghue, *The Life and Writings of James Clarence Mangan* (Dublin: M.H. Gill and Son and T. G. O'Donoghue, 1897), pp. 164–5.
8 National Library of Ireland ms. 138, "James Clarence Mangan Manuscript Letters and Poems", no. 15.
9 Ibid., no. 14.
10 Deuteronomy 34:4.
11 "The Warning Voice", *Nation*, 21 February 1846, p. 297.
12 Duffy, *My Life*, I, p. 137.
13 Robert Welch, *Irish Poetry from Moore to Yeats*, Irish Literary Studies 5 (Gerrards Cross, Bucks.: Colin Smythe, 1980), p. 105.
14 Duffy, *My Life*, I, p. 136.
15 Ibid., p. 137.
16 "To the Ingleezee Khafir, Calling Himself Djaun Bool Djenkinzun", *Nation*, 18 April 1846, p. 427.
17 "Siberia", *Nation*, 18 April 1846, p. 425.
18 Welch, *Irish Poetry*, p. 108.
19 "The Peal of Another Trumpet", *Nation*, 2 May 1846, p. 457.

20 NLI ms. 138, "Mangan Manuscript", no. 20.
21 Ibid., nos., 22–3 and "The Dream of MacDonnell *Claragh*", *Dublin Penny Journal*, 22 December 1832, p. 202.
22 Henry R. Montgomery, ed. *Specimens of the Early Native Poetry of Ireland* (Dublin: James McGlashan, 1846).
23 Royal Irish Academy ms. 12/Q/12, "John O'Daly's Manuscript of *Poets and Poetry of Munster*".
24 "Dark Rosaleen", *Nation*, 30 May 1846, p. 521.
25 O'Daly's information is contained in a note to the second of these poems, "Little Black-haired Rose", pp. 260–1.
26 O'Donoghue, *Life and Writings*, p. 179.
27 William Butler Yeats, "Clarence Mangan (1803–1849)", *Uncollected Prose*, John P. Frayne, ed., 2 vols., (New York: Columbia University Press, 1970), I, p. 118. Reprinted from "Irish Authors and Poets", *Irish Fireside*, 12 March 1887, pp. 169–70.
28 James Joyce, "James Clarence Mangan", *St. Stephen's*, May 1902, p. 117. Also cited in Ellsworth Mason and Richard Ellman, eds., *Critical Writings of James Joyce* (London: Faber and Faber, 1959).
29 Padraic Colum, "James Clarence Mangan", *Dublin Magazine*, April–June 1933, p. 38.
30 Rudolf Patrick Holzapfel, "Dangerous Hero", *Hibernia,* 32, 1 November 1968, no. 12, Autumn Book Supplement, n.p.
31 Peter MacMahon, "An Exegesis of James Clarence Mangan's 'Dark Rosaleen' " (Dissertation, New University of Ulster, 1983), p. 197.
32 "An Invitation", *Nation*, 4 July 1846, p. 601.
33 "A Vision of Connaught in the Thirteenth Century", *Nation*, 11 July 1846, p. 619.
34 "The Lovely Land", *Nation*, 18 July 1846, p. 633.
35 NLI ms. 138, "Mangan's Manuscript", no. 20. Some of his "desperate and disorderly" jokes from the postscript were printed as "Hints from the Antique" in the *Nation's* "Answers to Correspondents" column, 25 April 1846, p. 440.
36 Ibid., no. 8, 16 June 1846.
37 Ibid., no. 18, 10 July 1846.

BREAKING WITH THE PAST [Chapter 15 to Chapter 16]

1 "Report of the Repeal Association Meeting", *Nation*, 25 July 1846, p. 649.
2 Royal Irish Academy ms. 12/P/9, "Manuscript Book of Materials for an Autobiography of T.F. Meagher, in his own MS".
3 National Library of Ireland ms. 4184, "Fr Lee" Manuscripts, Mangan to Duffy, 28 July 1846.
4 *Nation*, 29 August 1846, p. 732, an exchange of letters.
5 *Nation*, 19 September 1846, p. 780, an exchange of letters.
6 Cyril Pearl, *The Three Lives of Gavan Duffy* (Kensington, N.S.W., Australia: New South Wales University Press, Ltd., 1979), p. 67.
7 NLI ms. 441, "Correspondence of William Smith O'Brien including letters (many undated) from C. Gavan Duffy, etc. Mainly concerning the Young Ireland Movement, 1847–48", Item 2229 [or 229].

8 NLI ms. 138, "James Clarence Mangan Manuscript Letters and Poems", no. 8, 16 June 1846.
9 Charles P. Meehan, "Preface", *The Poets and Poetry of Munster*, 3rd ed. (Dublin: James Duffy and Sons, 1883. First published 1849), p. xviii.
10 "Lament Over the Ruins of the Abbey of Teach Molaga", *Nation*, 8 August 1846, p. 681.
11 D.J. O'Donoghue, *The Life and Writings of James Clarence Mangan* (Dublin: M.H. Gill and Son and T.G. O'Donoghue, 1897), p. 182.
12 "O'Hussey's Ode to the Maguire", *Specimens of the Early Native Poetry of Ireland*, Henry R. Montgomery, ed. (Dublin: James McGlashan, 1846), pp. 137–8. The entire poem extends to p. 141 in this small volume. Montgomery signed his "Advertisement", i.e., his Preface, from Belfast. Although it may be unlikely Mangan was acquainted with him, Montgomery gave special notice to the poet, observing (p. iv), "It is but just to state that the only poetical versions original to this volume are those by Mr Mangan."
13 "Famine Report", *Nation*, 3 October 1846, p. 805.
14 NLI ms. 138, "Mangan Manuscript", no. 13, headed only "Friday".
15 Ibid., no. 9, 10 November 1846.
16 NLI ms. 3038, "Miscellaneous Autograph Letters", 1838–1892, [John O'Donovan], O'Donovan to Unnamed Friend, 13 March 1847, p. 149.
17 RIA ms. 12/N/10, "A Collection of Letters from John O'Donovan to James Hardiman in part relating to Irish literature and history, 1828–1855", 31 December 1846, p. 145.

CHAPTER SIXTEEN

1 John Mitchel, *The Last Conquest of Ireland (perhaps)*, (Dublin: *The Irishman Office*, 1861), pp. 215–16.
2 Richard Davis, *The Young Ireland Movement* (Dublin: Gill and MacMillan, 1987), pp. 119–20.
3 Charles Gavan Duffy, "Personal Memories of James C. Mangan", *Dublin Review*, April 1908, p. 293.
4 Royal Irish Academy ms. 23/H/62, "Subscription Book [of Irish Confederation], 1848".
5 RIA ms. 12/N/10, "A Collection of Letters from John O'Donovan to James Hardiman relating in part to Irish literature and history, 1828–1855".
6 Ibid., 7 January 1847.
7 Henry Boylan, *A Dictionary of Irish Biography* (Dublin: Gill and MacMillan, 1879), "James Duffy".
8 Charles P. Meehan, "Introduction", *Anthologia Germanica, Or a Garland from the German Poets*, 2 vols. (Dublin: James Duffy and Sons, 1884. First published 1845), I, p. xxiv.
9 "Anthologia Hibernica—No. I.", *Dublin University Magazine*, February 1847, pp. 239–50.
10 Ibid., p. 248.
11 "Distress in the City", *Nation*, 27 March 1847, p. 392.
12 RIA ms. 24/O/39, "James Graves Papers", Bundle 8, W.E. Hudson to John O'Donovan. Also O'Donovan's report of Mangan's visit, 2 March 1847.

13 Ibid., 6 March 1847.
14 National Library of Ireland ms. 3038, "Miscellaneous Autograph Letters, 1838–1892, [John O'Donovan]", p. 149.
15 NLI ms. 138, "James Clarence Mangan Manuscript, Letters and Poems", no. 10, 24 March 1847.
16 D.J. O'Donoghue, *The Life and Writings of James Clarence Mangan* (Dublin: M.H. Gill and Son and T.G. O'Donoghue, 1897), p. 194.
17 *Abstracts of the Accounts of the South Dublin Union for the Half-Year Ended 29th September 1840* (Dublin: Alexander Thom, 1841), pp. 7–8.
18 RIA ms. 12/N/10 "O'Donovan to Hardiman", 8 April 1847, p. 205.
19 Sarah Atkinson, *Mary Aikenhead: Her Life, Her Work, and her Friends* (Dublin: M.H. Gill and Son, 1882), p. 288.
20 Cecil Woodham-Smith, *The Great Hunger. Ireland 1845–9* (London: New English Library, 1977), pp. 173–4.
21 O'Donoghue, *Life and Writings*, p. 151.
22 [William Fitzgerald] "To Clarence Mangan", *Dublin University Magazine*, May 1847, p. 623.
23 "Answers to Correspondents", *Nation*, 29 May 1847, p. 536.
24 NLI ms. 5757, "Charles Gavan Duffy Letters", pp. 35–9.
25 NLI ms. 138, "Mangan Manuscript", no. 19, 8 June 1847.
26 James Price, "Gallery of Contemporary Writers, No. 6: James Clarence Mangan", *Evening Packet*, 3 November 1849, [p. 3].
27 O'Donoghue, *Life and Writings*, pp. 177–8.
28 RIA ms. 3/C/6, "Letter to John O'Daly from James Clarence Mangan" in "Letters to and from W.E. Hudson and others concerning contributions to the *Nation*", undated.
29 O'Donoghue, *Life and Writings*, pp. 204–5.
30 Trinity College Dublin ms. 4629, "Autograph note of James Clarence Mangan and other materials from Seamus O'Sullivan Collection".
31 O'Donoghue, *Life and Writings*, p. 124.
32 Ibid., p. 193. The poet Robert Bloomfield (1766–1823) had also been the subject of the young Mangan's charade "My first is with the wildest flower . . ." in *Grant's Almanack*, 1823. He had compared him with Goldsmith, Burns and Dermody.
33 NLI ms. 138, "Mangan Manuscript", no. 11, 21 July 1847.
34 "A Vision of Ireland in the Nineteenth Century", *Nation*, 17 July 1847, pp. 650–1.
35 Charles P. Meehan, "Preface", *The Poets and Poetry of Munster*, 3rd ed. (Dublin: James Duffy and Sons, 1883. First published 1849), p. xix.
36 O'Donoghue, *Life and Writings*, p. 151.
37 Ibid., p. 165.
38 Price, "Gallery, No. 2", 22 September 1849, [p. 3].
39 Ibid.
40 "Evictions", *Nation*, 9 October 1847, p. 839, and 23 October 1847, p. 871.
41 RIA ms. 12/N/10, "O'Donovan to Hardiman", 21 June 1847, p. 193.
42 NLI ms. 132, "John O'Donovan Correspondence 1846–1861", no. 8, 13 October 1847, p. 15.
43 "Report of the Irish Confederation", *Nation*, 23 October 1847, p. 867; also

Richard Davis, *The Young Ireland Movement* (Dublin: Gill and Macmillan, 1987), p. 140.

44 Jacques Chuto, "James Clarence Mangan, Poète-Traducteur", 2 vols. (Dissertation, Université de Paris 3—Sorbonne Nouvelle, 1987), II, p. 461.

45 Augustine Martin, "Anglo-Irish Poetry: Moore to Ferguson", *Talamhan Eisc: Canadian and Irish Essays*, Cyril J. Byrne and Margaret Harry, eds. (Halifax, Canada: Nimbus Publishing, Ltd., 1984), p. 97.

46 "Moreen: A Love-Lament", "Lays of Many Lands—No. II", *Dublin University Magazine*, October 1847, p. 409.

47 *The Testament of Cathaeir Mor* (Dublin: Celtic Society, February 1848). A rare pamphlet. One in a private collection is inscribed by John Daly: "Please circulate this as extensively as you can, for the more members are got, the more books the council [of the Celtic Society] can give to each for his Annual Subscription." See also W.H. Grattan Flood, "Mangan and the Melodies in *The Poets and Poetry of Munster*" in "Mangan Centenary Celebration", *Herald*, 2 May 1903.

48 RIA ms. 24/O/39, "James Graves Papers", Bundle 5, 9 December 1847.

49 "The Testament of Cathaeir Mor", *Nation*, 13 November 1847, p. 921.

50 RIA ms. 12/N/20, "Letters to Hardiman", no. 147, 4 October 1847.

51 NLI ms. 7959, "John McCall's Manuscript Collection for his *Life of Mangan*", vol. V, 8 January 1848.

52 O'Donoghue, *Life and Writings*, p. 195.

CHAPTER SEVENTEEN

1 Charles Gavan Duffy, *My Life in Two Hemispheres*, 2 vols. (London: T. Fisher, Unwin, 1898), I, p. 245.

2 Ibid, p. 244 note.

3 D.J. O'Donoghue, *The Life and Writings of James Clarence Mangan* (Dublin: M.H. Gill and Son and T.G. O'Donoghue, 1897), p. 204.

4 "A Voice of Encouragement—A New Year's Lay", *Nation*, 1 January 1848, p. 9.

5 "My Three Plagues", "Lays of Many Lands—No. IV", *Dublin University Magazine*, January 1848, p. 52.

6 "Meeting of The Irish Confederation", *Nation*, 5 February 1848, p. 93.

7 "Farewell to My Country", *Nation*, 12 February 1848, p. 105.

8 "A Vision. A.D. 1848", "The Marseillaise", and "Irish National Hymn", appeared 26 February (p. 43), 18 March (p. 89), and 13 May (p. 211), *United Irishman*, 1848.

9 "Hush-A-By Baby. A Lullaby", *Dublin University Magazine*, February 1848, p. 247.

10 "St Patrick's Hymn Before Tarah", *Duffy's Irish Catholic Magazine*, February 1848, p. 7.

11 "Second Week of the Irish Revolution", *Nation*, 11 March 1848, p. 169.

12 Richard Davis, *The Young Ireland Movement* (Dublin: Gill and Macmillan, 1987), pp. 150–1.

13 John Mitchel, "James Clarence Mangan: His Life, Poetry, and Death", *Poems by James Clarence Mangan*, John Mitchel, ed. (New York: P.M. Haverty, 1859), p. 16.

14 Ibid., pp. 16–17.
15 "Correspondence. Mr Mangan to the Editor of the UNITED IRISHMAN", *United Irishman*, 25 March 1848, p. 106.
16 O'Donoghue, *Life and Writings*, p. 203.
17 Sarah Atkinson, *Mary Aikenhead: Her Life, Her Work, and Her Friends* (Dublin: M.H. Gill and Son, 1882), pp. 286–7.
18 O'Donoghue, *Life and Writings*, p. 206. O'Donoghue actually says this letter was written on 18 May, but it is dated 1 May.
19 "Answers to Correspondents", *Nation*, 13 May 1848, p. 312.
20 Ibid., pp. 205–6.
21 National Library of Ireland ms. 19783, "John Kevin Reilly, notebook".
22 John Mitchel, *Jail Journal* (Dublin: The University Press of Ireland, 1982. First published 1854), p. 1.
23 NLI ms. 132, "John O'Donovan Correspondence, 1846–1861", no. 2, 2 June 1848.
24 NLI ms. 3225, "Hickey Collection. Young Ireland, Michael Cavanagh, typescript, 'Joseph Brenan' ".
25 O'Donoghue, *Life and Writings*, pp. 201–2.
26 Charles P. Meehan, "Preface", *The Poets and Poetry of Munster*, 3rd ed. (Dublin: James Duffy, 1883. First published 1849), p. xxiv.
27 Royal Irish Academy ms. 12/N/20, "Letters to Hardiman", no. 148, 22 January 1848.
28 Davis, *Young Ireland*, pp. 158–9.
29 "Gasparó Bandollo", *Dublin University Magazine*, May 1849, PP. 650–2.
30 "Mother and Son", "Lays of Many Lands—No. VI", *Dublin University Magazine*, November 1848, p. 542.
31 RIA ms. 12/P/18, "Autobiography of James Clarence Mangan".
32 "Fragment of an Unpublished Autobiography", *Irish Monthly*, November 1882, pp. 675–89.
33 *The Autobiography of James Clarence Mangan*, James Kilroy, ed. (Dublin: The Dolmen Press, 1968).
34 "The Nameless One", *Irishman*, 27 October 1849, p. 683.
35 RIA ms. 12/N/20, "Letters to Hardiman", no. 138, 4 December 1848.
36 Ibid., no. 139, 7 December 1848.
37 RIA ms. 12/N/10, "A Collection of Letters from John O'Donovan to James Hardiman in part relating to Irish literature and history, 1828–1855", 24 December 1848, p. 211.
38 *Ordnance Survey Meteorological Observations Taken During the Years 1829–1852*, Capt. Cameron, R.E., ed. (Dublin: Alexander Thom and Sons, 1856), December 1848.

CHAPTER EIGHTEEN

1 Cecil Woodham-Smith, *The Great Hunger. Ireland 1845–9* (London: New English Library, 1977), pp. 360–75.
2 "James Clarence Mangan, and Fulham's Irishman Newspaper, 1849", Dr Thomas Wall Archives, Irish Institute of Pastoral Liturgy, Carlow.
3 "Look Forward!", *Irishman*, 13 January 1849, p. 25.
4 Lady Mary Ferguson, *Sir Samuel Ferguson in the Ireland of His Day*, 2 vols.

(London: William Blackwood and Sons, MDCCCXCVI), I, pp. 60–1. See also vol. II, pp. 109, 239–40.

5 "Neglected Genius", *Pilot*, 5 January 1849, [p. 2].

6 "James Clarence Mangan", *Freeman's Journal*, 8 January 1849, [p. 2].

7 Royal Irish Academy ms. 24/O/39, "James Graves Papers", Bundle 10, John O'Donovan probably to J.W. Hanna, 26 January 1849.

8 D.J. O'Donoghue, *The Life and Writings of James Clarence Mangan* (Dublin: M.H. Gill and Son and T.G. O'Donoghue, 1897), p. 167.

9 Sean Dunne, "Introduction", *Poets of Munster*, Sean Dunne, ed. (Dingle, Co. Kerry: Brandon Book Publishers, Ltd., 1985), pp. 17 and 15.

10 Dublin Public Libraries ms. 90, "Gilbert Collection. J.C. Mangan manuscript"; RIA ms. 12/Q/12, "John O'Daly's Manuscript of *Poets and Poetry of Munster*".

11 "Gile ne Gile", *Poets and Poetry of Munster* (Dublin: John O'Daly, 1849), pp. 30–1.

12 Ibid., pp. 79 and 81.

13 Ibid., pp. 81 and 85.

14 RIA ms. 24/M/13, "Tribes of Ireland" in "John O'Daly Collection".

15 Ibid., O'Donovan's annotation.

16 RIA ms. 24/O/39, "James Graves Papers", Bundle 1, 22 April 1850, note from C.B. Gibson; and O'Donovan to Graves, August 1851.

17 [Joseph Brenan], "James Clarence Mangan", *Irishman*, 23 June 1849, p. 393.

18 James Price, "Gallery of Contemporary Writers, No. 2: James Clarence Mangan", *Evening Packet*, 22 September 1849, [p. 2].

19 [Charles Gavan Duffy], "Clarence Mangan", *Nation*, 20 October 1849, pp. 114–15.

20 Charles P. Meehan, "Preface", *The Poets and Poetry of Munster*, 3rd ed. (Dublin: James Duffy, 1883. First published 1849), p. xxv.

21 Dr Thomas Wall Archives, Irish Institute of Pastoral Liturgy, Carlow.

22 O'Donoghue, *Life and Writings*, p. 215.

23 "For Soul and Country", *Irishman*, 28 April 1849, p. 267.

24 "Bear Up!", *Irishman*, 12 May 1849, p. 299. See Appendix I.

25 "Ghazel", *Irishman*, 19 May 1849, p. 315.

26 "Have Hope!", *Irishman*, 10 November 1849, p. 715.

27 "Still a Nation", *Irishman*, 8 September 1849, p. 571.

28 ["E.W."] (James Clarence Mangan). "Sketches of Modern Irish Writers. James Clarence Mangan" [The Impersonal Autobiography], *Irishman*, 17 August 1850, pp. 27–8.

29 "A Word in Reply to Joseph Brenan", *Irishman*, 2 June 1849, p. 347.

30 "Let Not the Gael Despair", *Irishman*, 9 June 1849, p. 363.

31 "The Famine", *Irishman*, 9 June 1849, p. 363.

32 Meehan, "Preface", *Poets and Poetry of Munster*, p. xxvi.

33 Price, "Gallery No. 2", *Evening Packet*, 22 September 1849, [p. 2].

34 Meehan, "Preface", *Poets and Poetry of Munster*, p. xxvi.

35 John O'Daly, "James Clarence Mangan", *The Poets and Poetry of Munster*, (Dublin: John O'Daly, 1849), p. xiv.

36 John McCall, *The Life of James Clarence Mangan* (Blackrock: Carraig Books, 1975. First published 1882), pp. 29–30.

37 Meehan, "Preface", *Poets and Poetry of Munster*, p. xxvi.

Select Bibliography

GENERAL: BOOKS, PERIODICALS, NEWSPAPERS, PERSONAL CONTACTS

Abstracts of the Accounts of the South Dublin Union for the Half-Year ended 29th September 1840 (Dublin: Alexander Thom, 1841).

Allen, Hervey, *Israfel: The Life and Times of Edgar Allan Poe* (New York: Farrar and Rinehart, 1934).

Alumni Dublinensis: A Register of the Students, Graduates, Professors and Provosts of Trinity College in the University of Dublin (1593–1860), George Burtchall and Thomas Sadlier, eds., New edition (Dublin: Alex. Thom and Co., 1935).

Anderson, George K., *The Legend of the Wandering Jew* (Providence, R.I.: Brown University Press, 1965).

Andrews, J.H., *A Paper Landscape: The Ordnance Survey in 19th Century Ireland* (Oxford: The Clarendon Press, 1975).

"Annals of Dublin", *Dublin Almanac and General Register of Ireland, 1843* (Dublin: Pettigrew and Oulton, n.d.).

Atkinson, Sarah, *Mary Aikenhead: Her Life, Her Work, and Her Friends* (Dublin: M.H. Gill and Son, 1879).

Bowen, B.P., "The Comet Newspaper (1831–1833)", *Irish Book Lover*, vol. XXVII, May 1942, no. 5–6, pp. 120–7.

— "A Scribe of the Liberties: John McCall", *Historical Record*, vol. V, March-May 1943, no. 3, pp. 81–91.

Boylan, Henry, *A Dictionary of Irish Biography (Dublin: Gill and Macmillan,* 1979).

Boyne, Patricia, *John O'Donovan (1806–1861): A Biography* (Kilkenny: Boethius, 1987).

[Brenan, Joseph], "A Word to James Clarence Mangan", *Irishman*, 26 May 1849, p. 331.

[Brenan, Joseph], "James Clarence Mangan", *Irishman*, 23 June 1849, p. 393.

Brown, Malcolm, *The Politics of Irish Literature. From Thomas Davis to W.B. Yeats* (Seattle: University of Washington Press, 1972).

Burke, Bernard, *Vicissitudes of Families and Other Essays* (London: Longman, Green, Longman, and Roberts, 1859).

Burke's Irish Family Records (London: Burke's Peerage, MCMLXXVI).

Burton, Nathaniel, *Letters from Harold's Cross* (Dublin: John F. Fowler, 1850).

Carey, F.P., *Father Charles P. Meehan* (Dublin: Catholic Truth Society, n.d.).

Carroll, F., "Clarence Mangan's Age Complex"; in "Notes and Queries", *Irish Book Lover*, vol. XXXII, September 1957, no. 6, pp. 133–4.

—"The Dream of Mac Donnell *Claragh*"; in "Notes and Queries", *Irish Book Lover*, vol. XXXII, September 1957, no. 6, pp. 134–6.

Catalogue of the Books in the Lending Department of the Dublin Library Society, D'Olier Street, to the First of August, 1823 (Dublin: Kelly and Son, n.d.).

Catalogue of Graduates who have Proceeded to Degrees in the University of Dublin (Dublin: Hodges, Smith and Foster, 1869).

Catalogue of the Extensive and Valuable Library of the late Dr R.R. Madden, etc., 6 December 1886.

Catalogue of the [Bryan] *Geraghty Manuscripts Sold* [29 February] *1848*.

Catalogue of the Sale of Books of Richard Caulfield, 27 January 1888.

Catalogue of Sale [James Hardiman Collection], 26 March 1856.

Catalogue of Sale [John O'Donovan Collection], 7 November 1867.

Chamisso, Adelbert von, *Peter Schemihl*, Leopold von Loewenstein Wertheim, trans. (London: Calder and Boyars, 1970).

Chrzanowski, Gerard, "Neurasthenia and Hypochondriasis", in *American Handbook of Psychiatry*, 2 vols., Silvano Arieti, ed. (New York: Basic Books, Inc., 1959).

Chuto, Jacques, "A Further Glance at Mangan and the Library", *Long Room*, no. 5, Spring 1972, pp. 8–10.

— "James Clarence Mangan, Poète-Traducteur", 2 vols., Dissertation, l'Université de Paris 3—Sorbonne Nouvelle, 1987.

— "Mangan, Petrie, O'Donovan, and a Few Others: The Poet and the Scholars", *Irish University Review*, vol. VI, Autumn 1976, no. 2, pp. 169–87.

— "Mangan's 'Antique Deposit' in the TCD Library", *Long Room*, no. 2, Autumn-Winter 1970, pp. 38–9.

— "The Sources of James Clarence Mangan's Oriental Writings", *Notes and Queries*, New Series, vol. 29, June 1982, no. 3 pp. 224–8.

Colum, Padraic, "James Clarence Mangan", *Dublin Magazine*, vol. VIII, April-June 1933, no. 2, pp. 32–40.

Co[o]mbe, George, *A System of Phrenology*, 2nd ed. (London: Longman, 1825).

Connellan, Owen, ed. and trans., *The Annals of the Kingdom of Ireland, translated from the Original Irish of the Four Masters* (Dublin: Bryan Geraghty, 1846).

Corkery, Daniel, *The Hidden Ireland* (Dublin: Gill and Macmillan, 1977, first published 1924).

Crone, John S., *A Concise Dictionary of Irish Biography* (Dublin: The Talbot Press, 1928).

Cronin, Anthony, "Foreword", *Selected Poems of James Clarence Mangan*, Michael Smith, ed. (Dublin: Gallery Press, 1973).

— "James Clarence Mangan—A Reconsideration", *Hibernia*, vol. XXXVI, 12 May 1972, no. 10, p. 14.

[D.C.], "Clarence Mangan", *Nation* (New Series), 13 October 1849, p. 106.

Davis, Richard, *The Young Ireland Movement* (Dublin: Gill and Macmillan, 1987).

Deane, Seamus, *A Short History of Irish Literature* (London: Hutchinson, 1986).

Denman, Peter, "Ferguson and *Blackwood's*: The Formative Years", *Irish University Review*, vol. 16, Autumn 1986, no. 2, pp. 141–58.

De Quincey, Thomas, *Confessions of an English Opium Eater*, Vol. I in *Works of De Quincey*, 2nd ed. (Edinburgh: Black, 1862).

Dillon, William, *Life of John Mitchel*, 2 vols. (London: Kegan Paul, Trench, 1888).

Donaghy, Henry J., *James Clarence Mangan* (New York: Twayne Publishers, English Authors Series no. 171, 1974).

Donnelly, M. (Nicholas), *A Short History of Some Dublin Parishes*, vol. VIII (Blackrock: Carraig Books reprint, n.d.).

Dowling, Richard, "Some More Old Letters", *Irish Book Lover*, vol. XI, December 1919, no. 5, p. 40.

Dublin Almanac and General Register of Ireland, 1832–1837 and *1841–1846* (Dublin: Pettigrew and Oulton, 1831–45).

"Dublin Penny Journal", *Dublin University Magazine*, vol. XV, January 1840, no. 85, pp. 112–19f.

Duffy, Charles Gavan, *Four Years of Irish History 1845–1849: A Sequel to Young Ireland* (London: Cassell, Petter, Galpin, 1883).

— *My Life in Two Hemispheres*, 2 vols. (London: T. Fisher, Unwin, 1898).

— "Personal Memories of James C. Mangan", *Dublin Review*, CXLII, April 1908, no. 285, pp. 278–94.

— *Young Ireland: A Fragment of Irish History, 1840–1850* (New York: Da Capo Press, 1973. First published 1881).

Dunne, Sean, "Introduction", *Poets of Munster*, Sean Dunne, ed. (Dingle, Co Kerry: Brandon Book Publishers, 1985).

Edgeworth, Maria, *Belinda*, 2 vols. (Dublin: H. Colbert and J. Stockdale, 1801).

Ellis, Hercules, ed., *Romances and Ballads of Ireland* (Dublin: James Duffy, 1850).

Evans, Edward, *Historical and Bibliographical Account of Almanacks, Directories, etc., Published in Ireland from the Sixteenth Century* (Blackrock: Carraig Books, 1976. First published 1897).

["E.W."] (James Clarence Mangan), "Sketches of Modern Irish Writers. James Clarence Mangan" [the Impersonal Autobiography], *Irishman*, 17 August 1850, pp. 27–8.

"Fag an Bealach", *Spirit of the Nation*, 59th ed. (Dublin: James Duffy, 1934. First published 1843).

Fenichel, Otto, *Psychoanalytic Theory of Neurosis* (New York: W.W. Norton, 1945).

Fenton, Seamus, "A Great Kilkennyman, John O' Donovan", a lecture delivered in the Kilkenny Town Hall (Kilkenny, 19 April 1940).

Ferguson, [Lady] Mary, *Sir Samuel Ferguson in the Ireland of His Day*, 2 vols. (London: William Blackwood and Sons, MDCCCXCVI).

Ferguson, Samuel, "Hardiman's Irish Minstrelsy, No. III", *Dublin University Magazine*, vol. IV, October 1834, no. 22; "Hardiman's Irish Minstrelsy, No. IV", *Dublin University Magazine*, vol. IV, November 1834, no. 23.

Fitzgerald, William, "To Clarence Mangan", *Dublin University Magazine*, vol. XXIX, May 1847, no. 173, p. 623.

Fitzpatrick, W.J., *The Life of Charles Lever*, 2 vols. (London: Chapman and Hall, 1879).

Flanagan, Thomas, "Critical Introduction" to John Mitchel, *Jail Journal*, Thomas Flanagan, ed. (Dublin: University Press of Ireland, 1982).

Flood, W.H. Grattan, "Mangan and the Melodies in the *Poets and Poetry of Munster*", an address delivered before the Mangan Centenary Celebration, *Herald*, 2 May 1903.

Franz, Marie-Louise von, *Puer Aeternus*, 2nd ed. (Santa Monica, Cal.: Sigo Press, 1981).

Gerard, Francis, *Pictureseque Dublin, Old and New* (London: Hutchinson, 1898).

Gerwig, Henrietta, *University Handbook for Readers and Writers*, Apollo ed. (New York: Thomas Y. Crowell, 1965).

Gilbert, John T., *History of the City of Dublin*, 3 vols. (Shannon, Ireland: Irish University Press, 1972; reprint of James McGlashan 1854 edition).

— *On the Life and Labours of John O'Donovan, LL.D.* (London: Thomas Richardson and Son, MDCCCLXII.)

Godwin, William, *St Leon: A Tale of the Sixteenth Century*, 2 vols. (Dublin: Patrick Wogan, 1800).

Grant's Almanack 1803, National Library of Ireland, Dublin, Ireland.

Grant's Almanack 1823, Royal Irish Academy Library, Dublin, Ireland.

Guiney, Louise Imogen, "James Clarence Mangan: A Study", *James Clarence Mangan, his Selected Poems*, Louise Imogen Guiney, ed. (Boston and New York: Lamson, Wolffe and Co., 1897).

— "James Clarence Mangan", *Atlantic Monthly*, vol. LXVIII, November 1891, pp. 641–59.

Hayley, Barbara, "Irish Periodicals from the Union to the *Nation", Anglo-Irish Studies, II*, 1976, pp. 83–108.

Hayter, Alethea, *Opium and the Romantic Imagination* (Berkeley: University of California Press, 1970).

Hobsbawm, E.J., *The Age of Revolution 1789–1848* (London: Sphere Books Ltd., Abacus edition. First published 1965).

Holzapfel, Rudolf Patrick, "Dangerous Hero", *Hibernia*, vol. XXXII, 1–14 November 1968, no. 12, p. 11.

— *James Clarence Mangan: A Check List of Printed and Other Sources* (Dublin: Scepter Publishers Ltd., 1969).

— "Mangan's Poetry in the *Dublin University Magazine:* A Bibliography", *Hermathena*, no. CV, Autumn 1967, pp. 40–54.

[Honestus], "Neglected Genius" *Pilot*, 5 January 1849, [p. 2].

Inglis, Brian, *The Freedom of the Press in Ireland, 1784–1841* (London: Faber and Faber, Studies in Irish History Series, vol. VI, 1954).

Irish Poetic Gems from Mangan, Moore and Griffin (Dublin: M.H. Gill and Son, 1887).

Jeffares, A. Norman, *Anglo-Irish Literature* (Dublin: Gill and Macmillan, 1982).

Joyce, James, *Dubliners* (New York: Viking, Compass Books, 1958. First published 1916).

— "James Clarence Mangan" *James Joyce Review* (1957) pp. 31–8.

— "James Clarence Mangan", *St Stephen's*, vol. I, May 1902, no. 6, pp. 116–18. Also in *Critical Writings of James Joyce*, Ellsworth Mason and Richard Ellman, eds. (London: Faber and Faber, 1959).

Joyce, Weston St. John, *The Neighbourhood of Dublin* (Dublin: M.H. Gill and Son, 1913).

Jung, Carl Gustav, *Psychology of the Unconscious* (New York: Dodd, Mead, 1965. First published 1916).

Kee, Robert, *The Most Distressful Country*, vol. I of *The Green Flag* (London: Quartet Books, 1981).

Kickham, Charles, "Edward Walsh", *Celt*, 5 December 1857, p. 306.

Lecky, Walter, *Green Graves in Ireland* (Baltimore: John Murphy and Co., 1894).

Lindop, Grevel, *The Opium Eater: A Life of Thomas De Quincey* (Oxford: Oxford University Press, 1985).

Little, George A., *Fr Thomas Betagh, SJ* (Dublin: Irish Messenger, 1960).

Lloyd, David, *Nationalism and Minor Literature: James Clarence Mangan and the Emergence of Irish Cultural Nationalism* (Berkeley: University of California Press, 1987).

Lloyd, R.O.V., Personal letters to the writer, 10 September 1983 and 6 May 1986, with photograph of Brooklawn House.

Lucy, Sean, ed., *Irish Poets in English*, Thomas Davis Lectures on Anglo-Irish Poetry (Cork and Dublin: The Mercier Press, 1973).

MacLysaght, Edward, *Surnames of Ireland* (Dublin: Irish Academic Press, 1978).

MacMahon, Peter, *An Exegesis of James Clarence Mangan's "Dark Rosaleen"* Dissertation, New University of Ulster, 1983.

— "James Clarence Mangan: The Irish Language and the Strange Case of *The Tribes of Ireland*", *Irish University Review*, vol. VIII, Autumn 1978, no. 2, pp. 209–22.

Malcolm, Elizabeth, *'Ireland Sober, Ireland Free', Drink and Temperance in Nineteenth-Century Ireland*, Irish Studies Series (New York: Syracuse University Press, 1986).

Mangan, James Clarence, *Anthologia Germanica. German Anthology* (Dublin: William Curry, June 1845).

Mangan, Michael and Phyllis, Cahirlestrane, County Galway.

Mangan, Sr Petra, Sion Hill Convent, Blackrock, County Dublin.

"Mangan and the *Monthly Magazine*", *Irish Book Lover*, vol. VI, April 1915, no. 9, pp. 137–9.

Mannin, Ethel, *Two Studies in Integrity, Gerald Griffin and the Rev. Francis Mahony ('Father Prout')*, (New York: G.P. Putnam's Sons, 1954).

Martin, Augustine, "Anglo-Irish Poetry: Moore to Ferguson"; in *Talamh an Eisc: Canadian and Irish Essays*, Cyril J. Byrne and Margaret Harry, eds. (Halifax, Canada: Nimbus Publishing, 1984).

— "Apocalypse Then. Pastorini, Ferguson, Mangan, Yeats", *Gaeliana 8* (Caen: Centre de Publications de l'Université de Caen, 1988, pp. 55–62.

Maturin, Charles Robert, *Melmoth the Wanderer*, (Lincoln, Nebraska: University of Nebraska Press, 1961. First published 1820).

McCall, John, "Clarence Mangan and the Comet Club", "Clarence Mangan's Contributions to 'Jones Diaries', 1821–1826, under the name of James Tynan", and "James Clarence Mangan, and Fulham's Irishman Newspaper, 1849", Dr Thomas Wall Archives, Irish Institute of Pastoral Liturgy, Carlow.

— "James Clarence Mangan, his Early Life and first Poetical Attempts", *Nation*, vol. XXXII, 24 October, p. 10; 21 November, p. 10; 28 November, p. 10; 5 December, p. 10; 1874.

— "James Price: . . . Memoir of Another Forgotten Irish Writer, with Selections from His Writings in Prose and Verse", *Irish Emerald*, 1, 8, 15, 22, 29 April; 6, 13, 20, 27 May; 3, 10, 17, 24 June; 11, 18 July 1893; pagination commencing 1319, concluding 1570, not inclusive.

— *The Life of James Clarence Mangan* (Blackrock: Carraig Books, 1975. First published 1882).

— "Mangan's Love Episode. Notes on Mr Lecky's New Version", *Irish Emerald*, vol. III, 7 July, pp. 711–12; and 14 July, pp. 727–8; 1894.

McCall, P.J., *In the Shadow of St Patrick's: A Paper Read before the Irish National Literary Society, 27 April 1893* (Blackrock: Carraig Books, 1975. First published 1894).

[McGee, Thomas D'Arcy], "Reminiscences of an Exiled Confederate, Clarence Mangan", *Nation*, 25 September 1852, p. 58.

McGregor, John James, *New Pictures of Dublin, Comprehending a History of the City, an Accurate Account of its Various Establishments and Institutions, and a*

Correct Description of all the Public Edifices Connected with Them (Dublin: Johnston and Deas, 1821).

Meehan, Charles P., ed., *Essays in Prose and Verse by J. Clarence Mangan* (Dublin: James Duffy and Sons, 1884).

Memories of Father Healy of Little Bray (London: Richard Bentley and Son, 1898).

Mitchel, John, ed., *Poems by James Clarence Mangan* (New York, P.M. Haverty, 1859).

Mitchel, John, *Jail Journal*, Thomas Flanagan, ed. (Dublin: University Press of Ireland, 1982. First published 1854).

— *The Last Conquest of Ireland (perhaps)* (Dublin: *Irishman* Office, 1861).

Morning Register, Michael Staunton, ed. (Dublin, 1824–31).

"Obituary: James Clarence Mangan", *Saunders Newsletter*, 22 June 1849.

O'Broin, León, *Charles Gavan Duffy, Patriot and Statesman* (Dublin: James Duffy, 1967).

O'Byrne, John Petrie, "Romantic Career of an Irish Princess—A Clue to Clarence Mangan's 'Nameless One' ", *Weekly Freeman*, 23 December 1893, p. 10.

O'Casaide, Seamus, "James Clarence Mangan and his County Meath Relatives. New Light on the Poet's Circumstances", *Father Mathew Record*, vol. XXXV, June 1941, no. 6., pp. 4–5.

O'Daly, John, ed., in *The Poets and Poetry of Munster* (Dublin: John O'Daly, 1849).

O'Donoghue, D.J., ed., *The Poems of James Clarence Mangan*. Centenary Edition (Dublin: O'Donoghue, and M.H. Gill and Son, 1903. Also, New York: Johnson Reprint Corp., 1972).

— *The Life and Writings of James Clarence Mangan* (Dublin: M.H. Gill and Son, and T.G. O'Donoghue, 1897. Also, New York: Johnson Reprint Corp., 1972).

— *The Poets of Ireland. A Biographical and Bibliographical Dictionary of Irish Writers of English Verse* (New York: Johnson Reprint Corp., 1970. First published 1893).

— ed., *The Prose Writings of James Clarence Mangan. Centenary Edition* (Dublin: O'Donoghue and Co., and M.H. Gill and Son, 1904. Also New York: Johnson Reprint Corp., 1972).

— "The Unknown Mangan", *Irish Independent*, 16 March 1903.

O'Donovan, John, ed. and trans., *Annals of the Kingdom of Ireland by the Four Masters*, 7 vols. (Dublin: Hodges and Smith, 1848–56).

— *Letters Relating to County Clare, County Derry, County Donegal, County Down, County Galway and County Mayo*, reproduced under the direction of the Rev. Michael O'Flanagan (Bray: typescript, 1927).

— *The Tribes of Ireland: A Satire* (Dublin: John O'Daly, 1852).

O'Duffy, Richard J., *Historic Graves in Glasnevin Cemetery* (Dublin: James Duffy, 1915).

O'Faolain, Sean, *King of the Beggars. A Life of Daniel O'Connell* (Dublin: Poolbeg Press, 1980).

O'Farachain, Roibeard [Robert Farren], "James Clarence Mangan", *Thomas Davis and Young Ireland*, M.J. MacManus, ed. (Dublin: Stationery Office, 1945).

O'Giollain, Diarmud, "The Leipreachan and Fairies, Dwarfs and the Household Familiar. A Comparative Study", *Bealoideas*, vol. 52, 1984, pp. 75–150.

O'Hegarty, P.S. "A Bibliography of James Clarence Mangan", *Dublin Magazine*, vol. XVI, January-March 1941, no. 1, pp. 56–61.

O'Neill, George, "Some Unpublished Mangan MSS", *Studies*, vol. IX, March 1920, no. 2, pp. 118–28.

O'Neill, T.P., *Social Life in Ireland 1800–45*, R.B. McDowell, ed. (Cork: Mercier Press 1976, Cultural Relations Committee of Ireland edition).

O'Shea, John J., *The Two Kenricks* (Philadelphia: J.J. McVey, 1904).

O'Sullivan, T.F., *The Young Irelanders*, Davis Centenary ed. (Tralee: The Kerryman, 1945).

O'Tuathaigh, Gearóid, *Ireland before the Famine 1798–1848* (Dublin: Gill and Macmillan, 1972).

Ordnance Survey Meteorological Observations Taken During the Years 1829–1852, Capt. Cameron, R.E., ed. (Dublin: Alexander Thom and Sons, 1856).

Parsons Horn-Book Parts I and II (Dublin: Brown and Sheehan, 1831).

[Pastor Fido], *Pastorini Proves to be a Bad Prophet and a Worse Divine in an Address to the Roman Catholics of Ireland* (Dublin: M. Goodwin, 1823).

["Pastorini"] (Charles Walmesley), *The General History of the Christian Church* (Dublin: n.p., 1790).

Pearl, Cyril, *The Three Lives of Gavan Duffy*, (Kensington, N.S.W. Australia: New South Wales University Press, 1979).

"Phrenological Description of Mangan's Head [by J. Wilson]", Essays in Prose and Verse by J. Clarence Mangan, C.P. Meehan, ed. (Dublin: James Duffy and Sons, 1884).

"Phrenology and Its Opponents.—No. I", *Dublin University Magazine*, vol. III, May 1834, no. 17, pp. 570–4ff.

Phrenology and the Moral Influence of Phrenology (London: Akerman, n.d. [ca. 1835].

Power, John, *List of Irish Periodicals (chiefly Literary) from 1729 to the Present Time* (London: Printed for private distribution only, n.d.); [written in 1868].

Price, James, "Adolphus Softbotham" in "Notebook Sketches", *Weekly Dublin Satirist*, 21 March 1835, p. 314.

— "Gallery of Contemporary Writers: James Clarence Mangan", *Evening Packet*, no. 2, 22 September 1849, [pp. 2–3]; no. 5, 11 October 1849, [p. 3]; no. 6, 3 November 1849, [p. 3].

Prichard, James C., *A Treatise on Insanity and Other Disorders Affecting the Mind* (Philadelphia: Harwell, Barrington and Hanna, 1837).

"Review of *A Memoir of the Life and Philosophy of Spurzheim*", *Dublin University Magazine*, vol. I, May 1833, no. 5, pp. 582–95.

"Review of *German Anthology*":

— *British Quarterly Review*, vol. II, November 1845, pp. 582–3.

— *Cork Examiner*, 23 July 1845, [p. 2].

— *Dublin Review*, vol. XIX, December 1845, no. 38, pp. 312–31.

— *Evening Packet*, 26 July 1845, [p. 3].

— *Foreign Quarterly Review*, vol. XXXVI, October 1845, pp. 238–40.

— *Freeman's Journal*, 18 July 1845, p. 3.

— *Nation*, 9 August 1845, p. 715.

— *Tait's Edinburgh Magazine*, in "The Lyric Poetry of Germany", vol. XIII, May 1846, pp. 94–103.

Sadleir, Michael, "*The Dublin University Magazine*. Its History, Contents and

Bibliography" (Dublin: The Bibliographical Society of Ireland, vol. 5, no. 4, 1938, pp. 61–81).

"Second Week of the Irish Revolution", *Nation*, 11 March 1848, p. 169.

Sheehan, John (the Knight of Innishowen), "Dublin Political Satire and Satirists Forty Years Ago", *Gentleman's Magazine*, vol. XIII, December 1874, no. LXXIV, pp. 685–701.

Sheridan, John Desmond, *James Clarence Mangan* (Dublin: Talbot Press, 1937).

Somerville-Large, Peter, *Irish Eccentrics: A Selection* (New York: Harper and Row, 1975).

Sontag, Susan, *Illness as Metaphor* (New York: Vintage Books, 1979).

Specimens of the Early Native Poetry of Ireland, Henry R. Montgomery, ed. (Dublin: James McGlashan, 1846).

Spirit of the Nation, 59th ed. (Dublin: James Duffy, 1934. First published 1843).

Stokes, William, *The Life and Labours in Art and Archeology of George Petrie, LL.D., MRIA* (London: Longmans, Green, 1868).

Swedenborg, Emanuel, *The Universal Human and Soul-Body Interaction*, George F. Dale, ed. (New York: Paulist Press, 1984).

Synge, John Millington, *The Aran Islands* (Dublin: Maunsel, 1911).

Thompson, Francis J., "Mangan in America, 1850–1860: Mitchel, Maryland and Melville", *Dublin Magazine*, vol. XXVII, July-September 1952, no. 3, pp. 30–41.

Tracey, Alice, "John O'Donovan's Work on the Ordnance Survey", *Carloviana* I, December 1964, pp. 22–4; 42–4.

Treasures of the Library: Trinity College Dublin, Peter Fox, ed. (Dublin: Royal Irish Academy, 1986).

Valentine Post-Bag Containing Letters to Public Characters (Dublin: Browne and Sheehan, 1831).

"Vision of Ireland in the Nineteenth Century", *Nation*, 17 July 1847, pp. 650–1.

Wakeman, W.F., "Old Dublin, No. XVIII.—No. 3, Lord Edward Street, Birthplace of the Poet Mangan", *Evening Telegraph*, New Series, 7 May 1887, [p. 2].

Wall, Thomas, "Introduction"; in Edward Evans, *Historical and Bibliographical Account of Almanacks, Directories, etc., Published in Ireland from the Sixteenth Century* (Blackrock: Carraig Books, 1976. First published 1897).

— *The Sign of Dr Hay's Head* (Dublin: M.H. Gill and Son Ltd., 1958).

Walsh, Edward, *Reliques of Irish Jacobite Poetry* (Dublin: Samuel J. Machen, 1844).

[Walsh, John Edward], *Ireland Ninety Years Ago*; a new revision of *Ireland Sixty Years Ago* (Dublin: M.H. Gill and Son, 1885).

Warburton, J., J. Whitelaw and Robert Walsh, *History of the City of Dublin from Earliest Accounts to the Present Time* (London: Cadell and Davies, 1818).

Welch, Robert, "In wreathèd swell: James Clarence Mangan, Translator from the Irish", *Eire-Ireland*, vol. XI, Summer 1976, no. 2, pp. 36–55.

— *Irish Poetry from Moore to Yeats*, Irish Literary Studies 5, (Gerrards Cross, Bucks.: Colin Smythe, 1980).

Wellesley Index to Victorian Periodicals, 1824–1900, 4 vols, Walter E. Houghton, ed. (Toronto: University of Toronto Press, Routledge, and Kegan Paul, 1987).

Wiley, Lulu Rumsey, *The Sources and Influence of the Novels of Charles Brockden Brown* (New York: Vantage Press, Inc., 1950).

Williams, R.D., *The Poems of Richard D'Alton Williams, "Shamrock" of "The Nation"* (Dublin: James Duffy, 1894).

Woodham-Smith, Cecil, *The Great Hunger. Ireland 1845–9* (London: New English Library, 1977).

Wright, G.N., *An Historical Guide to the City of Dublin* (Dublin: Four Courts Press, and Irish Academic Press, 1980. First published 1825).

Wynne, Michael, "The Face of Mangan", *Hermathena*, no. CV, Autumn 1967, pp. 55–9.

Yeats, William Butler, "Clarence Mangan (1803–1849)", *Irish Fireside*, 12 March 1887, pp. 169–70.

— "Clarence Mangan's Love Affair", *United Ireland*, 22 August 1891, pp. 5–6.

— *Uncollected Prose by W.B. Yeats*, 2 vols., John P. Frayne, ed. (New York: Columbia University Press, 1970).

MANUSCRIPTS

National Library of Ireland

MS 132	"John O'Donovan Correspondence 1846–1861".
MS 138	"James Clarence Mangan Manuscript Letters and Poems".
MS 2261	"Walsh's Letters [to John O'Daly]".
MS P2407	"Manuscripts of D.F. McCarthy".
MS 3038	"Miscellaneous Autograph Letters, 1838–1892", [John O'Donovan].
MS 3225	"Hickey Collection. Young Ireland, Michael Cavanagh, typescript, 'Joseph Brenan' ".
MS 4172	"D.J. O'Donoghue's Revision of *Life and Writings of James Clarence Mangan*, with many manuscript corrections and additions".
MS 4184	"Fr Lee Manuscripts".
MS 5443	"Letters from John O'Donovan to the Rev. J.H. Todd 1836–1858".
MS 5454	"Quarto Volume of Critical Notices evidently bound for John O'Daly with his MS notes".
MSS 5756, 5757	"Charles Gavan Duffy Letters".
MS 7524	"Larcom Papers: Correspondence on the Ordnance Survey and census of 1857 . . . including letters from John O'Donovan and Eugene Curry, 1839–1869".
MS 7550	"Larcom Papers: Booklet entitled Heads of Inquiry".
MSS 7563–67	"Larcom Papers: Correspondence on matters pertaining to the Ordnance Survey Memoir, 1833–1861".
MSS 7953, 7954	"John McCall's History of Irish Almanacs".
MSS 7955–59	"John McCall's Material in five volumes for his *Life of James Clarence Mangan*".
MS 13848	"John McCall Papers, Cuttings and Notes on Historical Subjects mainly towards his work on almanacks and his *Life of Mangan*".
MS 14269	"John McCall Clippings and Notes for his *Life of Mangan*".
MS 14270	"John McCall, History of the *Comet* 'Political Tract Society' started early 1831".

MS 14271	"John McCall Papers. Extracts from the *Nation* and other periodicals . . . 1880–1889".
MS 19783	"John Kevin O'Reilly, notebook".
Microfilm no. 133	"SS Michael and John Marriages (No. P7358 Births)".

Royal Irish Academy Library

MS 3/B/52	"Journal of Charles Lever, 1828–29".
MS 3/C/6	"Letter to John O'Daly from James Clarence Mangan".
MS 12/N/10	"A Collection of Letters from John O'Donovan to James Hardiman in part relating to Irish literature and history, 1828–1855".
MS 12/N/11	"Miscellaneous Correspondence of John O'Donovan largely relating to Irish history and literature 1830–1835".
MS 12/N/20	"Letters to [James] Hardiman".
MS 12/P/9	"Manuscript Book of Materials for an Autobiography of T.F. Meagher, in his own MS".
MS 12/P/16	"Gavan Duffy's Curios".
MS 12/P/18	"Autobiography of James Clarence Mangan".
MS 12/Q/12	"John O'Daly's Manuscript of *Poets and Poetry of Munster*".
MS 23/G/33	"Letters from Thomas Crofton Croker and Owen Connellan to Sir William Betham".
MS 23/H/40	"Minutes of The Irish Confederation".
MS 23/H/44	"(Private) Proceedings of Council of Irish Confederation".
MS 23/H/62	"Subscription Book [of Irish Confederation]".
MS 24/F/20	"Silhouette of James Clarence Mangan".
MS 24/O/39	"James Graves Papers".

Trinity College Dublin Library

MS S.2.11(2063) (Phillips MS 17093) 692 Mason	"Parish Records: A Collection of Records, Notices, etc. 1669–1822".
MS 4629	"Autograph note of James Clarence Mangan and other materials from Seamus O'Sullivan Collection."

Other

Dublin Public Libraries MS 90, Gilbert Collection, "J.C. Mangan MS".
Irish Institute of Pastoral Liturgy, Carlow, "Dr Thomas Wall Archives".
Maynooth MS C 63, "Eugene O'Curry Gaelic Poems and Translations".
PRO County of Dublin 1828–1832, Books 103 and 104, "Barony of Donore".
University College Dublin Library Archives, LA 15, "O'Donoghue Papers".

Index